¡Así se dice!

SPANISH 2

Conrad J. Schmitt

Mc Graw Hill Education

Bothell, WA • Chicago, IL • Columbus, OH • New York, NY

Information on featured companies, organizations, and their products and services is included for educational purposes only and does not present or imply endorsement of the ¡**Así se dice!** program. Permission to use all business logos has been granted by the businesses represented in this text.

mheducation.com/prek-12

Copyright © 2016 McGraw-Hill Education

Send all inquiries to:
McGraw-Hill Education
8787 Orion Place
Columbus, OH 43240-4027

ISBN: 978-0-02-141264-8
MHID: 0-02-141264-2

Printed in the United States of America.
11 12 13 14 15 16 17 18 LWI 27 26 25 24 23 22 21 20

About the Author

Conrad J. Schmitt

Conrad J. Schmitt received his B.A. degree magna cum laude from Montclair State University, Upper Montclair, New Jersey. He received his M.A. from Middlebury College, Middlebury, Vermont, and did additional graduate work at New York University. He also studied at the Far Eastern Institute at Seton Hall University, Newark, New Jersey.

Mr. Schmitt has taught Spanish and French at all academic levels—from elementary school to graduate courses. He served as Coordinator of Foreign Languages for the Hackensack, New Jersey, public schools. He also taught courses in Foreign Language Education as a visiting professor at the Graduate School of Education at Rutgers University, New Brunswick, New Jersey.

Mr. Schmitt has authored or co-authored more than one hundred books, all published by The McGraw-Hill Companies. He was also editor-in-chief of foreign languages, ESL, and bilingual education for The McGraw-Hill Companies.

Mr. Schmitt has traveled extensively throughout Spain and all of Latin America. He has addressed teacher groups in all fifty states and has given seminars in many countries including Japan, the People's Republic of China, Taiwan, Egypt, Germany, Spain, Portugal, Mexico, Panama, Colombia, Brazil, Jamaica, and Haiti.

Contributing Writers

Louise M. Belnay
Teacher of World Languages
Adams County School District 50
Westminster, Colorado

Reina Martínez
Coordinator/Teacher of Foreign Languages
North Rockland Central School District
Thiells, New York

Student Handbook

Why Learn Spanish? SH1

Reading and Succeeding SH2

Tour of the Student Edition SH8

Dinah Zike's Foldables® SH20

El alfabeto español SH34

El mundo hispanohablante SH35

El mundo SH36

España SH38

La América del Sur SH39

México, la América Central y el Caribe SH40

Estados Unidos SH41

Andrew Payti

Student Handbook

GeoVistas
Explorando el mundo hispanohablante

Explorando el mundo hispanohablante . . SH42

España SH44

México SH46

Guatemala, Honduras SH48

El Salvador, Nicaragua SH50

Costa Rica, Panamá SH52

Colombia, Venezuela SH54

Ecuador, Perú, Bolivia SH56

Chile, Argentina SH58

Paraguay, Uruguay SH60

Cuba, República Dominicana, Puerto Rico SH62

Estados Unidos SH64

Repaso

A Amigos, alumnos y parientes.............. R1

B En casa y en la escuela R10

C Personalidad y salud...................... R20

D Los deportes R28

E De compras R36

F De vacaciones R46

Capítulo 1　En avión

Objetivos

You will:
- talk about packing for a trip and getting to the airport
- tell what you do at the airport
- talk about being on an airplane
- discuss air travel in South America

You will use:
- verbs that have **g** in the **yo** form of the present tense
- the present progressive tense

Introducción al tema
En avión 2

Vocabulario 🎧
Vocabulario 1 4
Vocabulario 2 8

Gramática
Presente de **hacer, poner, traer, salir** 12
El presente progresivo 15

Pronunciación 🎧
La consonante **r** 19

Conversación 🎧 🔄
En el aeropuerto 20

Lecturas culturales 🎧 🔄
El avión en la América del Sur 22
Un viaje interesante 24

Prepárate para el examen
Self-check for achievement 26
Practice for oral proficiency 28
Practice for written proficiency 29

Repaso del Capítulo 1
Gramática 30
Vocabulario 31

Repaso cumulativo 🔄 32

David H. Brennan

Capítulo 2 ¡Una rutina diferente!

Objetivos

You will:
- identify more parts of the body
- talk about your daily routine
- talk about backpacking and camping

You will use:
- reflexive verbs
- commands with **favor de**

Introducción al tema
¡Una rutina diferente!. 36

Vocabulario
Vocabulario 1 38
Vocabulario 2 42

Gramática
Verbos reflexivos 46
Verbos reflexivos de cambio radical 50
Mandatos con **favor de** 52

Pronunciación
La **h**, la **y** y la **ll** 53

Conversación
De camping. 54

Lecturas culturales
Los mochileros 56
El camping 58

Prepárate para el examen
Self-check for achievement 60
Practice for oral proficiency. 62
Practice for written proficiency. 63

Repaso del Capítulo 2
Gramática 64
Vocabulario 65

Repaso cumulativo 66

Index Stock Imagery, Inc.

Capítulo 3 En tren

Objetivos

You will:
- use vocabulary related to train travel
- discuss interesting train trips in Peru and Mexico

You will use:
- the preterite of irregular verbs
- the verb **decir**
- prepositional pronouns

Introducción al tema
En tren 70

Vocabulario
Vocabulario 1 72
Vocabulario 2 76

Gramática
Pretérito de los verbos irregulares 80
El verbo **decir** 83
Pronombres después de una preposición . . . 85

Conversación
En la ventanilla 86

Lecturas culturales
Viajes ferroviarios fabulosos 88
De Panamá a Colón en tren 92

Prepárate para el examen
Self-check for achievement 94
Practice for oral proficiency 96
Practice for written proficiency 97

Repaso del Capítulo 3
Gramática 98
Vocabulario 99

Repaso cumulativo 100

Literatura 1
El Quijote 358
Miguel de Cervantes Saavedra

Language Arts Practice 1
El arte 384

Capítulo 4 En el restaurante

Objetivos

You will:
- order and pay for a meal at a restaurant
- identify more foods
- identify eating utensils and dishes
- discuss restaurants in Spain and Latin America

You will use:
- stem-changing verbs in the present and preterite
- adjectives of nationality
- the passive voice with **se**

Introducción al tema

En el restaurante 104

Vocabulario 🎧 .106

Gramática

Presente de los verbos de cambio
   radical **e → i** 110

Pretérito de los verbos de cambio
   radical **e → i, o → u** 112

Adjetivos de nacionalidad 114

La voz pasiva con **se** 116

Conversación 🎧 ↺

Una comida muy buena. 118

Lecturas culturales 🎧 ↺

Restaurantes de España y
   Latinoamérica 120

Sé lo que pedí. 124

Prepárate para el examen

Self-check for achievement 126

Practice for oral proficiency. 128

Practice for written proficiency. 129

Repaso del Capítulo 4

Gramática 130

Vocabulario 131

Repaso cumulativo ↺ 132

(l)Westend61/age fotostock, (r)David H Brennan

Capítulo 5 ¿Qué se celebra?

Objetivos

You will:
- talk about several Hispanic holidays
- compare holidays that you celebrate with those in some Spanish-speaking countries

You will use:
- regular and irregular forms of the imperfect tense

Introducción al tema

¿Qué se celebra? 136

Vocabulario 🎧

Vocabulario 1 138
Vocabulario 2 142

Gramática

Imperfecto de los verbos en **-ar** 146
Imperfecto de los verbos en **-er, -ir** 148
Imperfecto de los verbos irregulares. 150
Usos del imperfecto 151

Conversación 🎧 ↺

El Día de San Juan. 152

Lecturas culturales 🎧 ↺

Unas fiestas hispanas 154
La Nochevieja en España. 158

Prepárate para el examen

Self-check for achievement 160
Practice for oral proficiency. 162
Practice for written proficiency. 163

Repaso del Capítulo 5

Gramática 164
Vocabulario 165

Repaso cumulativo ↺ 166

terry harris just greece photo library/Alamy

Capítulo 6 Tecnomundo

Objetivos

You will:
- talk about computers, the Internet, and e-mail
- talk about a digital camera and an MP3 player
- make and receive phone calls
- discuss technology in Hispanic countries

You will use:
- the preterite and imperfect tenses

Introducción al tema
Tecnomundo 170

Vocabulario 🎧
Vocabulario 1 172
Vocabulario 2 176

Gramática
Verbos como **querer, creer**
   en el pasado 180
El pretérito y el imperfecto 181
Dos acciones pasadas en la
   misma frase 184

Conversación 🎧 ↻
Se cortó la línea. 186

Lecturas culturales 🎧 ↻
En un mundo tecnológico 188
La tecnología de hoy y ayer 190

Prepárate para el examen
Self-check for achievement 192
Practice for oral proficiency 194
Practice for written proficiency 195

Repaso del Capítulo 6
Gramática 196
Vocabulario 197

Repaso cumulativo ↻ 198

Literatura 2 📖
Versos sencillos 364
   José Martí

Language Arts Practice 2 🔤
La ecología 388

Yellow Dog Productions/Getty Images

Capítulo 7 En el hotel

Objetivos

You will:
- check into a hotel or hostel
- ask for things you may need while at a hotel or hostel
- discuss hotel stays in Latin America and Spain

You will use:
- the present perfect tense
- double object pronouns

Introducción al tema
En el hotel 202

Vocabulario 🎧 .204

Gramática
El presente perfecto 208

Participios irregulares. 210

Dos complementos **me lo, te lo, nos lo** 211

Dos complementos con **se** 213

Conversación 🎧↻
En la recepción. 214

Lecturas culturales 🎧↻
Un hostal y un parador 216

El Camino de Santiago. 218

Prepárate para el examen
Self-check for achievement 220

Practice for oral proficiency. 222

Practice for written proficiency. 223

Repaso del Capítulo 7
Gramática 224

Vocabulario 225

Repaso cumulativo ↻ 226

Andrew Payti

Capítulo 8 Ciudad y campo

Objetivos

You will:
- describe life in the city
- describe life in the country
- discuss the differences between the city and the country in Latin America

You will use:
- the future tense
- object pronouns with infinitives and gerunds

Introducción al tema
Ciudad y campo 230

Vocabulario 🎧
Vocabulario 1 232
Vocabulario 2 236

Gramática
Futuro de los verbos regulares 240
Futuro de los verbos irregulares. 242
Los pronombres con el infinitivo y
    el gerundio 244

Conversación 🎧 ↻
Un verano en el campo 246

Lecturas culturales 🎧 ↻
La ciudad y el campo 248
Una ciudad interesante 252

Prepárate para el examen
Self-check for achievement 254
Practice for oral proficiency. 256
Practice for written proficiency. 257

Repaso del Capítulo 8
Gramática 258
Vocabulario 259

Repaso cumulativo ↻ 260

(l)Glowimages/age fotostock, (r)Richard Brommer

Capítulo 9 ¿Vas en carro?

Objetivos

You will:
- talk about cars and driving
- give directions
- discuss the Pan American Highway

You will use:
- **tú** affirmative commands
- the conditional

Introducción al tema
¿Vas en carro? 264

Vocabulario 🎧
Vocabulario 1 266
Vocabulario 2 270

Gramática
Imperativo familiar—formas regulares . . . 274
Imperativo familiar—formas irregulares 276
El condicional 277

Conversación 🎧 ↻
Un sitio para aparcar 280

Lecturas culturales 🎧 ↻
La Panamericana 282
Tráfico y más tráfico 286

Prepárate para el examen
Self-check for achievement 288
Practice for oral proficiency 290
Practice for written proficiency 291

Repaso del Capítulo 9
Gramática 292
Vocabulario 293

Repaso cumulativo ↻ 294

Literatura 3 📖
Marianela 368
   Benito Pérez Galdós

Language Arts Practice 3 🔤
César Chávez 390

Capítulo 10 Cocina hispana

Objetivos

You will:
- talk about foods and food preparation
- talk about a Hispanic recipe

You will use:
- the subjunctive
- formal commands
- negative informal commands

Introducción al tema
Cocina hispana. 298

Vocabulario 300

Gramática
El subjuntivo. 304
El imperativo formal. 307
El imperativo familiar—formas
    negativas. 309

Conversación
¿Yo? ¿En la cocina? 310

Lecturas culturales
Una receta hispana 312
Una receta para «la ropa vieja» 314

Prepárate para el examen
Self-check for achievement 316
Practice for oral proficiency. 318
Practice for written proficiency. 319

Repaso del Capítulo 10
Gramática 320
Vocabulario 321

Repaso cumulativo 322

Andrew Payti

Capítulo 11 ¡Cuídate bien!

Objetivos

You will:
- identify more parts of the body
- talk about exercise
- talk about having a little accident and a trip to the emergency room
- discuss physical fitness

You will use:
- the subjunctive with impersonal expressions
- **ojalá, quizás, tal vez**
- the subjunctive of stem-changing verbs
- the comparison of like things

Introducción al tema
¡Cuídate bien!........................326

Vocabulario 🎧
Vocabulario 1 328
Vocabulario 2 332

Gramática
El subjuntivo con expresiones impersonales 336
¡Ojalá! ¡Quizás! ¡Tal vez! 338
El subjuntivo de los verbos de cambio radical 339
Comparación de igualdad 340

Conversación 🎧 ↺
Un accidente..........................342

Lecturas culturales 🎧 ↺
Vida activa y buena salud 344
Médicos Sin Fronteras 346

Prepárate para el examen
Self-check for achievement 348
Practice for oral proficiency.............350
Practice for written proficiency..........351

Repaso del Capítulo 11
Gramática 352
Vocabulario 353

Repaso cumulativo ↺ 354

Photodisc Collection/Getty Images

Literary Reader

Literatura 1
El Quijote 358
Miguel de Cervantes Saavedra

Literatura 2
Versos sencillos 364
José Martí

Literatura 3
Marianela 368
Benito Pérez Galdós

LA PRACTICE Language Arts Practice

Language Arts Practice 1
El arte 384

Language Arts Practice 2
La ecología 388

Language Arts Practice 3
César Chávez 392

Student Resources

InfoGap SR2

Grammar Review SR14

Verb Charts SR28

Spanish-English Dictionary SR34

English-Spanish Dictionary SR60

Culture Index SR82

Grammar Index SR86

Guide to Symbols

Throughout **¡Así se dice!** you will see these symbols, or icons. They will tell you how to best use the particular part of the chapter or activity they accompany. Following is a key to help you understand these symbols.

Audio link This icon indicates material in the chapter that is recorded.

Recycling This icon indicates sections that review previously introduced material.

Paired activity This icon indicates activities that you can practice orally with a partner.

Group activity This icon indicates activities that you can practice together in groups.

Critical thinking This icon indicates activities that require critical thinking.

InfoGap This icon refers to additional paired activities at the end of the book.

¡Bravo! This icon indicates the end of new material in each chapter. All remaining material is recombination and review.

Literary Reader This icon lets you know that you are prepared to read the indicated literature selection.

Language Arts Practice This icon refers to additional practice at the end of the book that will help you practice Language Arts skills while using your Spanish.

¡Viva el español!

Spanish is currently the fourth-most-spoken language in the world. Studying Spanish will help you explore other cultures, communicate with Spanish speakers, and increase your career possibilities.

It's fascinating!

Culture Hispanic culture is full of diverse expressions of music, art, and literature. From dancing the tango or salsa to admiring a modern painting by Salvador Dalí, your studies will introduce you to an array of what the culture has to offer. You'll learn about the various customs, traditions, and values in Latin America and Spain. From food and family to school and sports, you'll learn all about life in the Hispanic world.

It's all around us!

Communication The United States is home to more than fifty million Hispanics or Latinos. Whether on the radio, in your community or school, or in your own home, the Spanish language is probably part of your life in some way. Understanding Spanish allows you to sing along with Latin music on the radio or chat with Spanish speakers in your school, community, or family. No matter who you are, Spanish can enrich your life in some way.

If you plan to travel outside the United States, remember that Spanish is the official language of many countries. Experiencing another country is more fun and meaningful when you can understand restaurant menus, read newspapers, follow street signs, watch TV, and better yet converse with the locals.

CULTURA
Dancers of the tango on the streets of Argentina

Andrew Payti

A Spanish-speaking dentist

It's a lifelong skill!

Career Do you know what career you plan to pursue? Medicine, business, social work, teaching? What will you do if you have a Spanish-speaking patient, client, or student? Speak Spanish, of course! Whatever your career, you will be able to reach more people if you are able to converse in Spanish. After all, it's spoken by more than 16 percent of the U.S. population. You will also be open to many more career opportunities if you know Spanish. Businesses, government agencies, and educational institutions are always looking for people with the ability to speak and read more than one language.

It's an adventure!

Challenge When you study a language, you not only learn about the language and its speakers but also about yourself. Studying a language requires that you challenge yourself and more fully develop your skills. When you know about the customs and values of another culture, you are better able to reflect upon your own. Language is a means of self-discovery. Enjoy!

Reading in a New Language

Following are skills and strategies that can help you understand what you read in a language you have just begun to learn. *Reading and Succeeding* will help you build skills and strategies that will make it easier to understand what you are reading in your exciting new language.

The strategies you use frequently depend on the purpose of your reading. You do not read a textbook or standardized testing questions the same way you read a novel or a magazine article. You read a textbook for information. You read a novel or magazine article for fun.

In the early stages of second-language learning, your vocabulary is, of course, very limited in comparison to the vast number of words you already know in English. The material presented to you to read in the early stages must accommodate this reality. Your limited knowledge of the language does not have to deter you from enjoying what you are reading. Most of what you read, however, will come from your textbook, since original novels and magazine articles are not written for people who have limited exposure to the language.

As you develop your reading ability in Spanish, you will encounter basically two types of readings.

Intensive Readings

These readings are short. They are very controlled, using only language you have already learned. You should find these readings easy and enjoyable. If you find them difficult, it means you have not sufficiently learned the material presented in the chapter of the textbook.

The vast majority of these informative readings will introduce you to the fascinating cultures of the Spanish-speaking world.

A very important aspect of reading in Spanish is to give you things to "talk about" in the language. The more you read, speak, and use the language, the more proficient you will become. Whenever you finish reading one of the intensive reading selections, you should be able to talk about it; that is, you should be able to retell it in your own words.

Extensive Readings

Since it is unrealistic to assume that you will never encounter new words as you branch out and read material in Spanish, you will also be presented with extensive readings. The goal of these extensive readings is to help you develop the tools and skills you need in order to read at some future date an original novel or magazine article. They do indeed contain some words and structures that are unfamiliar to you. In this *Reading and Succeeding* section, you will learn to develop many skills that will enable you to read such material with relative ease.

BananaStock/Jupiter Images

Use *Reading and Succeeding* to help you:

- adjust the way you read to fit the type of material you are reading
- identify new words and build your vocabulary
- use specific reading strategies to better understand what you read
- improve your ability to speak by developing strategies that enable you to retell orally what you have read
- use critical thinking strategies to think more deeply about what you read

Identifying New Words and Building Vocabulary

What do you do when you come across a word you do not know as you read? Do you skip the word and keep reading? You might if you are reading for fun. If it hinders your ability to understand, however, you might miss something important. When you come to a word you don't know, try the following strategies to figure out what the word means.

Reading Aloud

In the early stages of learning a second language, a good strategy is to sit by yourself and read the selection aloud. This can help you understand the reading because you once again hear words that you have already practiced orally in class. Hearing them as you read them can help reinforce meaning.

Identifying Cognates

As you read you will come across many cognates. Cognates are words that look alike in both English and Spanish. Not only do they look alike but they mean the same thing. Recognizing cognates is a great reading strategy. Examples of cognates are:

cómico	**nacionalidad**	**entra**
popular	**secundaria**	**clase**
cubano	**matemática**	**prepara**
video	**blusa**	**televisión**

Identifying Roots and Base Words

The main part of a word is called its root. From a root, many new words can be formed. When you see a new word, identify its root. It can help you pronounce the word and figure out its meaning.

For example, if you know the word **importante,** there is no problem determining the meaning of **importancia.** The verb **importar** becomes a bit more problematic, but with some intelligent guessing you can get its meaning. You know it has something to do with importance so it means *it is important,* and by extension it can even carry the meaning *it matters.*

Identifying Prefixes

A prefix is a word part added to the beginning of a root or base word. Spanish as well as English has prefixes. Prefixes can change, or even reverse, the meaning of a word. For example, the prefixes **in-, im-,** and **des-** mean *not.*

**estable/inestable   posible/imposible
honesto/deshonesto**

Using Syntax

Like all languages, Spanish has rules for the way words are arranged in sentences. The way a sentence is organized is called its syntax. Spanish syntax, however, is a bit more flexible than English. In a simple English sentence someone or something (its subject) does something (the predicate or verb) to or with another person or thing (the object). This word order can vary in Spanish and does not always follow the subject/verb/object order.

Because Spanish and English syntax vary, you should think in Spanish and not try to translate what you are reading into English. Reading in Spanish will then have a natural flow and follow exactly the way you learned it. Trying to translate it into English confuses the matter and serves no purpose.

Example

English always states: *John speaks to me.*
Spanish can state: *John to me speaks.* or
To me speaks John.

The latter leaves the subject to the end of the sentence and emphasizes that it is John who speaks to me.

Using Context Clues

This is a very important reading strategy in a second language. You can often figure out the meaning of an unfamiliar word by looking at it in context (the words and sentences that surround it). Let's look at the example below.

Example

The glump ate it all up and flew away.

You have no idea what a *glump* is. Right? But from the rest of the sentence you can figure out that it's a bird. Why? Because it flew away and you know that birds fly. In this way you guessed the meaning of an unknown word using context. Although you know it is a bird, you cannot determine the specific meaning such as a robin, a wren, or a sparrow. In many cases it does not matter because that degree of specificity is not necessary for comprehension.

Let's look at another example:
The glump ate it all up and phlumped.

In this case you do not know the meaning of two key words in the same sentence—*glump* and *phlumped.* This makes it impossible to guess the meaning and this is what can happen when you try to read something in a second language that is beyond your proficiency level. This makes reading a frustrating experience. For this reason all the readings in your textbook control the language to keep it within your reach. Remember, if you have studied the vocabulary in your book, this will not happen.

Understanding What You Read

Try using some of the following strategies before, during, and after reading to understand and remember what you read.

Previewing

When you preview a piece of writing, you are looking for a general idea of what to expect from it. Before you read, try the following.

- Look at the title and any illustrations that are included.
- Read the headings, subheadings, and anything in bold letters.
- Skim over the passage to see how it is organized. Is it divided into many parts? Is it a long poem or short story?
- Look at the graphics—pictures, maps, or diagrams.
- Set a purpose for your reading. Are you reading to learn something new? Are you reading to find specific information?

Using What You Know

Believe it or not, you already know quite a bit about what you are going to read. Your own knowledge and personal experience can help you create meaning in what you read. There is, however, a big difference in reading the information in your Spanish textbook. You already have some knowledge about what you are reading from a United States-oriented base. What you will be reading about takes place in a Spanish-speaking environment and thus you will be adding an exciting new dimension to what you already know. Comparing and contrasting are important critical skills to put to use when reading material about a culture other than your own. This skill will be discussed later.

Visualizing

Creating pictures in your mind about what you are reading—called visualizing—will help you understand and remember what you read. With the assistance of the many accompanying photos, try to visualize the people, streets, cities, homes, etc., you are reading about.

Identifying Sequence

When you discover the logical order of events or ideas, you are identifying sequence. Look for clues and signal words that will help you find how information is organized. Some signal words are **primero, al principio, antes, después, luego, entonces, más tarde, por fin, finalmente.**

Determining the Main Idea

When you look for the main idea of a selection, you look for the most important idea. The examples, reasons, and details that further explain the main idea are called supporting details.

Reviewing

When you review in school, you go over what you learned the day before so that the information is clear in your mind. Reviewing when you read does the same thing. Take time now and then to pause and review what you have read. Think about the main ideas and organize them for yourself so you can recall them later. Filling in study aids such as graphic organizers can help you review.

Monitoring Your Comprehension

As you read, check your understanding by summarizing. Pause from time to time and state the main ideas of what you have just read. Answer the questions: **¿Quién?** *(Who?)* **¿Qué?** *(What?)* **¿Dónde?** *(Where?)* **¿Cuándo?** *(When?)* **¿Cómo?** *(How?)* **¿Por qué?** *(Why?)*. Summarizing tests your comprehension because you state key points in your own words. Remember something you read earlier: reading in Spanish empowers your ability to speak by developing strategies that enable you to retell orally what you have read.

BananaStock/PictureQuest

Thinking About Your Reading

Sometimes it is important to think more deeply about what you read so you can get the most out of what the author says. These critical thinking skills will help you go beyond what the words say and understand the meaning of your reading.

Compare and Contrast

To compare and contrast shows the similarities and differences among people, things, and ideas. Your reading experience in Spanish will show you many things that are similar and many others that are different depending upon the culture groups and social mores.

As you go over these culturally oriented readings, try to visualize what you are reading. Then think about the information. Think about what you know about the topic and then determine if the information you are reading is similar, somewhat different, or very different from what you know.

Continue to think about it. In this case you may have to think about it in English. Determine if you find the similarities or the differences interesting. Would you like to experience what you are reading about? Analyzing the information in this way will most certainly help you remember what you have read.

- Signal words and phrases that indicate similarity are **similar, semejante, parecido, igual.**
- Signal words and phrases that indicate differences are **diferente, distinto, al contrario, contrariamente, sin embargo.**

Cause and Effect

Just about everything that happens in life is the cause or the effect of some other event or action. Writers use cause-and-effect structure to explore the reasons for something happening and to examine the results of previous events. This structure helps answer the question that everybody is always asking: Why? Cause-and-effect structure is about explaining things.

- Signal words and phrases are **así, porque, por consiguiente, resulta que.**

Using Reference Materials

In the early stages of second-language learning, you will not be able to use certain types of reference materials that are helpful to you in English. For example, you could not look up a word in a Spanish dictionary as you would not be able to understand many of the words used in the definition.

You can, however, make use of the glossary that appears at the end of your textbook. A glossary includes only words that are included in the textbook. Rather than give you a Spanish definition, the glossary gives you the English equivalent of the word. If you have to use the glossary very frequently, it indicates to you that you have not studied the vocabulary sufficiently in each chapter. A strategy to use before beginning a reading selection in any given chapter is to quickly skim the vocabulary in the **Vocabulario 1** and **Vocabulario 2** sections of the chapter.

Expand your view of the Spanish-speaking world.

¡Así se dice! will show you the many places where you will be able to use your Spanish.

Cultural and geographic information is at your fingertips with **GeoVistas**, your virtual field trip to the Spanish-speaking countries.

Start your journey into language and culture.

Opening photo provides a cultural backdrop for the chapter.

Aquí y Allí introduces you to the chapter theme and invites you to make connections between your culture and the cultures of Spanish-speaking countries.

Objectives let you know what you will be able to do by the end of the chapter.

Use your online resources to enhance learning.

Get acquainted with the chapter theme.

Explore each chapter's theme with vivid cultural photos and informative captions.

See how the theme relates to different countries in the Spanish-speaking world.

Talk about the chapter theme with your new vocabulary.

Vocabulary is introduced and practiced in two manageable sections.

Recorded presentation ensures proper pronunciation.

Watch video clips to experience the diversity of the Spanish-speaking world while reinforcing the language you have learned and improving your listening and viewing skills.

Photos and illustrations aid comprehension and vocabulary acquisition.

New words are used in a meaningful context.

Practice and master new vocabulary.

Look for this symbol to find additional information to help you meet the ACTFL World-Readiness Standards for Learning Languages.

Practice authentic communication with InfoGap activities.

Practice and master your new vocabulary with your Workbook.

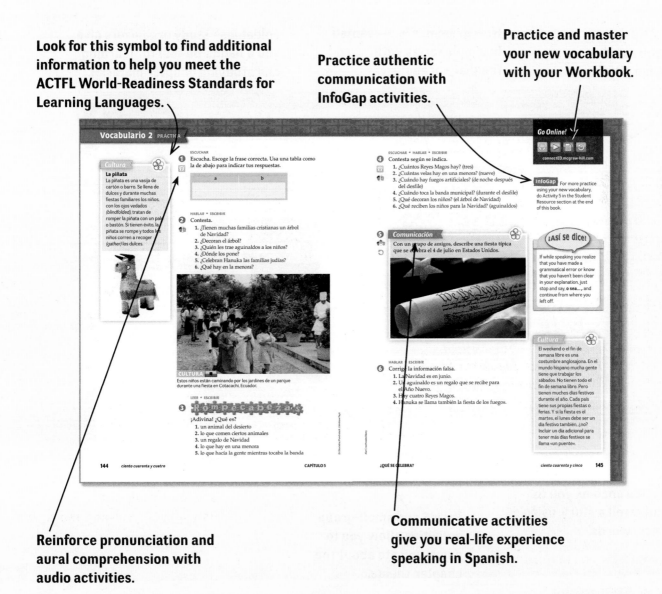

Reinforce pronunciation and aural comprehension with audio activities.

Communicative activities give you real-life experience speaking in Spanish.

Learn grammar within the context of the chapter theme.

Useful tips help you avoid language pitfalls.

New grammar is presented in simple terms with familiar vocabulary.

Foldables® study organizers give you a hands-on tool for learning and studying chapter material.

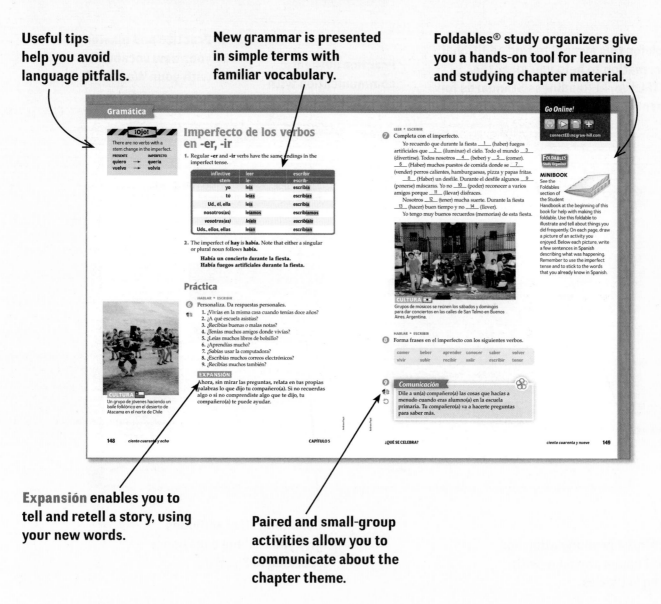

Expansión enables you to tell and retell a story, using your new words.

Paired and small-group activities allow you to communicate about the chapter theme.

Build on what you already know.

You will build confidence as you complete activities that progress from easy to more challenging.

Cultural photos are explained by captions that use grammar and vocabulary that you can understand.

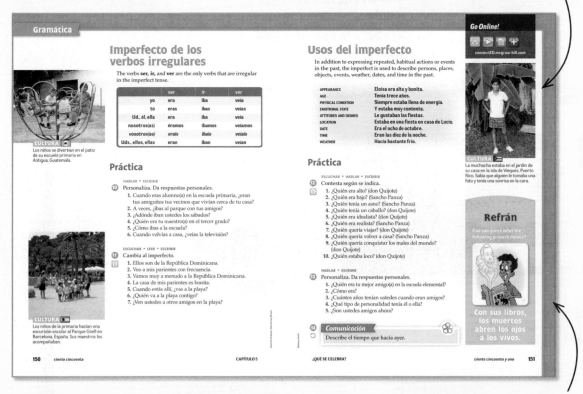

Gramática

Imperfecto de los verbos irregulares

The verbs **ser**, **ir**, and **ver** are the only verbs that are irregular in the imperfect tense.

	ser	ir	ver
yo	era	iba	veía
tú	eras	ibas	veías
Ud., él, ella	era	iba	veía
nosotros(as)	éramos	íbamos	veíamos
vosotros(as)	erais	ibais	veíais
Uds., ellos, ellas	eran	iban	veían

CULTURA
Los niños se divertían en el patio de su escuela primaria en Antigua, Guatemala.

Práctica

HABLAR • ESCRIBIR
10 Personaliza. Da respuestas personales.
1. Cuando eras alumno(a) en la escuela primaria, ¿eran tus amiguitos tus vecinos que vivían cerca de tu casa?
2. A veces, ¿ibas al parque con tus amigos?
3. ¿Adónde iban ustedes los sábados?
4. ¿Quién era tu maestro(a) en el tercer grado?
5. ¿Cómo ibas a la escuela?
6. Cuando volvías a casa, ¿veías la televisión?

ESCUCHAR • LEER • ESCRIBIR
11 Cambia al imperfecto.
1. Ellos son de la República Dominicana.
2. Veo a mis parientes con frecuencia.
3. Vamos muy a menudo a la República Dominicana.
4. La casa de mis parientes es bonita.
5. Cuando estás allí, ¿vas a la playa?
6. ¿Quién va a la playa contigo?
7. ¿Ven ustedes a otros amigos en la playa?

CULTURA
Los niños de la primaria hacían una excursión escolar al Parque Güell en Barcelona, España. Sus maestros los acompañaban.

150 ciento cincuenta

CAPÍTULO 5

Usos del imperfecto

In addition to expressing repeated, habitual actions or events in the past, the imperfect is used to describe persons, places, objects, events, weather, dates, and time in the past.

APPEARANCE	Eloísa era alta y bonita.
AGE	Tenía trece años.
PHYSICAL CONDITION	Siempre estaba llena de energía.
EMOTIONAL STATE	Y estaba muy contenta.
ATTITUDES AND DESIRES	Le gustaban las fiestas.
LOCATION	Estaba en una fiesta en casa de Lucio.
DATE	Era el ocho de octubre.
TIME	Eran las diez de la noche.
WEATHER	Hacía bastante frío.

Práctica

ESCUCHAR • HABLAR • ESCRIBIR
12 Contesta según se indica.
1. ¿Quién era alto? (don Quijote)
2. ¿Quién era bajo? (Sancho Panza)
3. ¿Quién tenía un asno? (Sancho Panza)
4. ¿Quién tenía un caballo? (don Quijote)
5. ¿Quién era idealista? (don Quijote)
6. ¿Quién era realista? (Sancho Panza)
7. ¿Quién quería viajar? (don Quijote)
8. ¿Quién quería volver a casa? (Sancho Panza)
9. ¿Quién quería conquistar los males del mundo? (don Quijote)
10. ¿Quién estaba loco? (don Quijote)

HABLAR • ESCRIBIR
13 Personaliza. Da respuestas personales.
1. ¿Quién era tu mejor amigo(a) en la escuela elemental?
2. ¿Cómo era?
3. ¿Cuántos años tenían ustedes cuando eran amigos?
4. ¿Qué tipo de personalidad tenía él o ella?
5. ¿Son ustedes amigos ahora?

14 **Comunicación**
Describe el tiempo que hacía ayer.

Go Online!
connectED.mcgraw-hill.com

CULTURA
La muchacha estaba en el jardín de su casa en la isla de Vieques, Puerto Rico. Sabía que alguien le tomaba una foto y tenía una sonrisa en la cara.

Refrán

Can you guess what the following proverb means?

Con sus libros, los muertos abren los ojos a los vivos.

¿QUÉ SE CELEBRA?

ciento cincuenta y uno **151**

Have fun using your Spanish to figure out the meaning of Spanish proverbs.

Engage classmates in real conversation.

You will have a sense of accomplishment when you are able to comprehend the conversation.

Conversación

El Día de San Juan

Patricia   José, eres de Puerto Rico, ¿no?
José   Sí, ¿por qué?
Patricia   Pues, ¿me puedes decir lo que es una fiesta patronal?
José   ¡Cómo no! Es una fiesta en honor del santo patrón de un lugar. El santo patrón de Puerto Rico, por ejemplo, es San Juan Bautista.
Patricia   ¿Hay una fiesta en su honor?
José   Sí, el 24 de junio. Durante toda una semana hay fiestas.
Patricia   ¿Qué hacen para celebrar la fiesta?
José   Pues, hay una tradición interesante. El Día de San Juan todos vamos a la playa y a la medianoche entramos en el mar.
Patricia   ¿Siempre nadan el Día de San Juan?
José   No dije que nadamos. Dije que entramos en el mar. ¿Sabes cómo? Caminamos hacia atrás hasta llegar al mar.
Patricia   Y, ¿por qué andan hacia atrás?
José   Entrar en el mar así nos trae buena suerte durante el año.

152 *ciento cincuenta y dos*   CAPÍTULO 5

Go Online!
connectED.mcgraw-hill.com

¿Comprendes?

A Completa según la información en la conversación.
1. José es de _____.
2. Una fiesta patronal rinde honor a _____.
3. El santo patrón de Puerto Rico es _____.
4. Su fiesta patronal es _____.
5. Todo el mundo va _____.
6. _____ para entrar en el mar.
7. Si entran en el mar así, van a tener _____.

B **Resumiendo** Cuenta la información en la conversación en tus propias palabras.

CULTURA
Maite preparaba a su amigo del continente para las celebraciones del Día de San Juan. Le enseñaba como andar hacia atrás.

C **Analizando** Los sanjuaneros tienen una costumbre interesante. ¿Qué hacen? ¿Por qué lo hacen?

¿QUÉ SE CELEBRA?   *ciento cincuenta y tres* **153**

The lightbulb icon indicates a critical thinking activity.

Heighten your cultural awareness.

Cultural reading uses learned language to reinforce chapter theme.

Recorded reading online provides options for addressing various skills and learning styles.

Step-by-step reading strategies help to develop your reading skills.

Verify your comprehension throughout the selection with Reading Checks.

Un poco más reading reinforces the chapter theme and expands your understanding of the Spanish-speaking world.

Questions follow the reading to check comprehension and to give you practice with standardized testing format.

An additional reading in each chapter reinforces learned language and chapter theme.

Show what you know!

Review what you have learned and prepare for your chapter test.

Reference notes direct you to the correct section for review.

Apply what you have learned!

Use your new skills to communicate orally in meaningful, open-ended activities.

Practice what you have learned while improving your written Spanish.

Writing Strategy gives you the tools you need to develop better writing skills.

Graphic organizers make practice clear and easy.

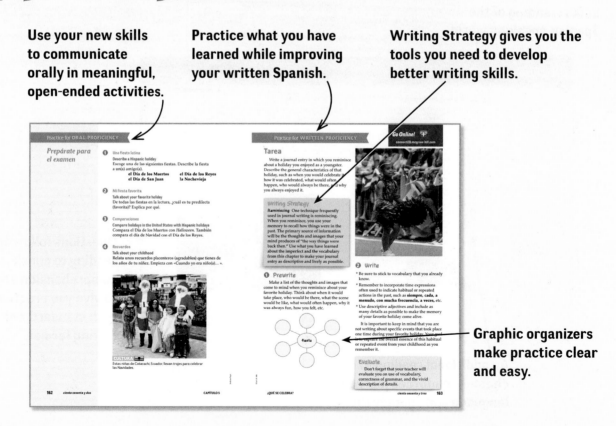

Review grammar and vocabulary at a glance.

Succinct grammar notes help you efficiently review chapter material.

Use this vocabulary list to review the vocabulary you have learned in this chapter.

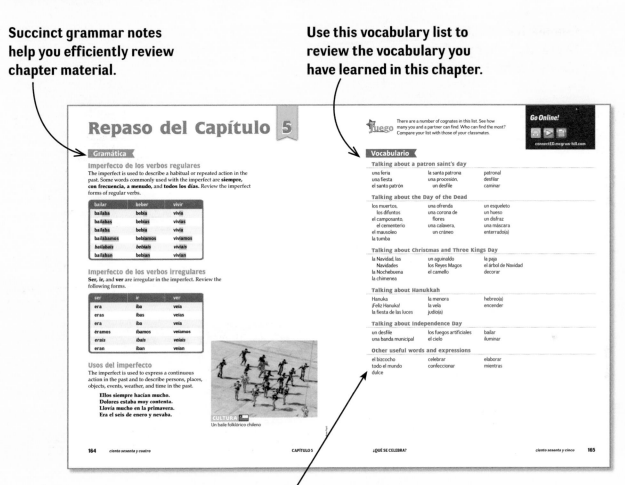

Repaso del Capítulo 5

Gramática

Imperfecto de los verbos regulares

The imperfect is used to describe a habitual or repeated action in the past. Some words commonly used with the imperfect are **siempre, con frecuencia, a menudo,** and **todos los días.** Review the imperfect forms of regular verbs.

bailar	beber	vivir
bailaba	bebía	vivía
bailabas	bebías	vivías
bailaba	bebía	vivía
bailábamos	bebíamos	vivíamos
bailabais	bebíais	vivíais
bailaban	bebían	vivían

Imperfecto de los verbos irregulares

Ser, ir, and **ver** are irregular in the imperfect. Review the following forms.

ser	ir	ver
era	iba	veía
eras	ibas	veías
era	iba	veía
éramos	íbamos	veíamos
erais	ibais	veíais
eran	iban	veían

Usos del imperfecto

The imperfect is used to express a continuous action in the past and to describe persons, places, objects, events, weather, and time in the past.

Ellos siempre hacían mucho.
Dolores estaba muy contenta.
Llovía mucho en la primavera.
Era el seis de enero y nevaba.

CULTURA
Un baile folklórico chileno

Vocabulario

There are a number of cognates in this list. See how many you and a partner can find. Who can find the most? Compare your list with those of your classmates.

Go Online!
connectED.mcgraw-hill.com

Talking about a patron saint's day

una feria	la santa patrona	patronal
una fiesta	una procesión,	desfilar
el santo patrón	un desfile	caminar

Talking about the Day of the Dead

los muertos,	una ofrenda	un esqueleto
los difuntos	una corona de	un hueso
el camposanto,	flores	un disfraz
el cementerio	una calavera,	una máscara
el mausoleo	un cráneo	enterrado(a)
la tumba		

Talking about Christmas and Three Kings Day

la Navidad, las	un aguinaldo	la paja
Navidades	los Reyes Magos	el árbol de Navidad
la Nochebuena	el camello	decorar
la chimenea		

Talking about Hanukkah

Hanuka	la menora	hebreo(a)
¡Feliz Hanuka!	la vela	encender
la fiesta de las luces	judío(a)	

Talking about Independence Day

| un desfile | los fuegos artificiales | bailar |
| una banda municipal | el cielo | iluminar |

Other useful words and expressions

el bizcocho	celebrar	elaborar
todo el mundo	confeccionar	mientras
dulce		

164 *ciento sesenta y cuatro*   CAPÍTULO 5   ¿QUÉ SE CELEBRA?   *ciento sesenta y cinco* 165

Vocabulary is categorized to help recall.

Practice what you have learned so far in Spanish.

Cumulative activities allow you to practice what you have learned so far in Spanish class.

Illustrations recombine material to remind you what you have already learned in Spanish. Use the illustration as a prompt to demonstrate how much you can say or write.

Enhance your appreciation of literature and culture.

Literary Reader gives you another opportunity to apply your reading skills in Spanish.

Literary selections present another view of Hispanic culture.

Level-appropriate literature selections make reading fun.

Practice your Language Arts skills.

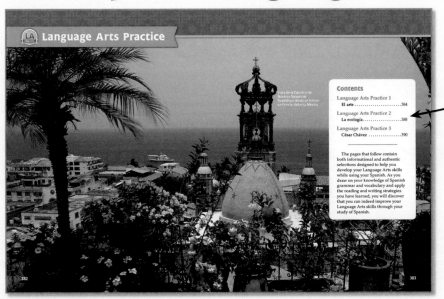

Informational and authentic texts will provide you with the opportunity to improve your Language Arts skills while using your Spanish.

Dear Student,

Foldables are interactive study organizers that you can make yourself. They are a wonderful resource to help you organize and retain information. Foldables have many purposes. You can use them to remember vocabulary words or to organize more in-depth information on any given topic, such as keeping track of what you know about a particular country.

You can write general information, such as titles, vocabulary words, concepts, questions, main ideas, and dates, on the front tabs of your Foldables. You view this general information every time you look at a Foldable. This helps you focus on and remember key points without the distraction of additional text. You can write specific information—supporting ideas, thoughts, answers to questions, research information, empirical data, class notes, observations, and definitions—under the tabs. Think of different ways in which Foldables can be used. Soon you will find that you can make your own Foldables for study guides and projects. Foldables with flaps or tabs create study guides that you can use to check what you know about the general information on the front of tabs. Use Foldables without tabs for projects that require information to be presented for others to view quickly. The more you make and use graphic organizers, the faster you will become able to produce them.

To store your Foldables, turn one-gallon freezer bags into student portfolios which can be collected and stored in the classroom. You can also carry your portfolios in your notebooks if you place strips of two-inch clear tape along one side and punch three holes through the taped edge. Write your name along the top of the plastic portfolio with a permanent marker and cover the writing with two-inch clear tape to keep it from wearing off. Cut the bottom corners off the bag so it won't hold air and will stack and store easily. The following figures illustrate the basic folds that are referred to throughout this book.

Good luck!

Dinah Zike

Dinah Zike
www.dinah.com

Category Book

Los números Use this *category book* organizer as you learn dates and numbers.

Step 1 **Fold** a sheet of paper (8½" x 11") in half like a *hot dog*.

Step 2 On one side, **cut** every third line. This usually results in ten tabs. Do this with three sheets of paper to make three books.

Step 3 **Write** one Arabic number on the outside of each of the tabs. On the inside write out the respective number. As you learn more numbers, use *category books* to categorize numbers in this way.

Other Suggestions for a *Category Book* Foldable

A *category book* foldable may be used to practice conjugating Spanish verbs. On the top tab, write the infinitive form of a verb. On the following tabs, write the subject pronouns: **yo, tú, él, ella, Ud., nosotros(as), ellos, ellas, Uds.** Then open each tab and write the corresponding form of the verb.

Forward-Backward Book

Las estaciones Use this *forward-backward book* to compare and contrast two seasons of your choice.

Step 1 **Stack** three sheets of paper. On the top sheet, trace a large circle.

Step 2 With the papers still stacked, **cut out** the circles.

Step 3 **Staple** the paper circles together along the left-hand side to create a circular booklet.

Step 4 **Write** the name of a season on the cover. On the page that opens to the right list the months of the year in that particular season. On the following page draw a picture to illustrate the season.

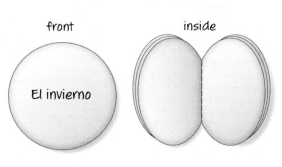

front   inside

El invierno

Step 5 **Turn the book upside down** and write the name of a season on the cover. On the page that opens to the right list the months of the year in that particular season. On the following page draw a picture to illustrate the season.

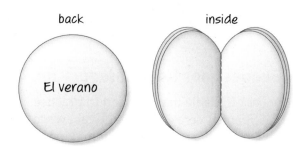

back   inside

El verano

Other Suggestions for a *Forward-Backward Book* Foldable

You may wish to use a *forward-backward book* foldable to organize vocabulary pertaining to the city and the country. On the front cover write **la ciudad.** Open your book. On the right-hand page list words you have learned that pertain to the city. On the next right-hand page, draw a picture illustrating the words on your list. Close your book and flip it over. On the back cover write **el campo** and do the same.

It may be helpful to use a *forward-backward book* foldable to organize the food groups. You could use the name of a food group in Spanish (meat, vegetable, fruit, etc.) as the title. On the inside, list as many foods in this food group as you can on the right-hand page and illustrate these foods on the opposite page. Give the same information for a second food group by reversing the book.

Pocket Book

La geografía Use this *pocket book* organizer in your ongoing study
of all the countries in the Spanish-speaking world.

Step 1 **Fold** a sheet of paper (8½" x 11")
in half like a *hamburger.*

Step 2 **Open** the folded paper and fold one of the long sides up two
inches to form a pocket. Refold the *hamburger* fold so that the newly
formed pockets are on the inside.

Step 3 **Glue** the outer edges of the two-inch fold with a small
amount of glue.

Step 4 **Make a multipaged booklet** by
gluing six pockets side-by-side. Glue a cover
around the multipaged *pocket book.*

Step 5 **Label** five pockets with the following geographical areas: **Europa, la América del Norte, la América del
Sur, la América Central,** and **Islas del Caribe.** Use index cards inside the pockets to record information each time
you learn something new about a specific country. Be sure to include the name of the country (in Spanish, of
course) and its capital.

Other Suggestions for a *Pocket Book* Foldable

You may wish to use a *pocket book* foldable
to organize masculine and feminine nouns or
singular and plural forms. You can make an
index card to put in the correct pocket each
time you learn a new word.

A *pocket book* foldable may be used to
organize information about several subjects.
For example, to organize information about
airplane travel, label pockets with topics such
as *preparing for a trip, getting to the airport, at
the airport,* and *on the airplane* in Spanish.

Make cards for all the words and phrases you
know that go with each topic.

If you wish to organize what you are learning
about important people, works of art, festivals,
and other cultural information in countries that
speak Spanish, a *pocket book* foldable may be
helpful. You can make a card for each person,
work of art, or event that you study, and you
can add cards and even add categories as you
continue to learn about cultures that speak
Spanish.

Vocabulary Book

Sinónimos y antónimos Use this *vocabulary book* to practice your vocabulary through the use of synonyms and antonyms.

Step 1 **Fold** a sheet of notebook paper in half like a *hot dog*.

Step 2 On one side, **cut** every third line. This usually results in ten tabs. Do this with two sheets of paper to make two books.

Step 3 **Label** the tops of the *vocabulary books* with the word **Sinónimos** on one and **Antónimos** on the other. As you learn new vocabulary in each unit, try to categorize words in this manner. Remember also to think of words you have previously learned to fill in your books.

Other Suggestions for a *Vocabulary Book* Foldable

You may wish to use a *vocabulary book* foldable to help you practice your informal commands. On the front of each flap, write the infinitive form of a verb. Then open each flap and write the informal **(tú)** command of the verb.

You can use a *vocabulary book* foldable to help remember any verb conjugation in Spanish. Write the infinitive at the top. If you know several tenses of a verb, you should also write what tense or tenses are being practiced. On the outside of the foldable, write the pronouns and, on the inside, write the corresponding verb form. You can use this as a quick study and review tool for any verb. At a more advanced level, you may wish to write many verbs on the outside and entire conjugations on the inside.

You may wish to use a *vocabulary book* foldable to help organize different kinds of clothing. Come up with categories in Spanish to list on the outside, such as *school, casual, men's, women's, summer, winter,* etc. On the inside, list as many articles of clothing fitting the category as you can in Spanish.

You can use *vocabulary book* foldables to practice adjective forms. Create two *vocabulary book* foldables, one for singular forms and the other for plural forms. On the singular book, write either masculine or feminine singular adjective forms on the outside and the other forms on the inside. To make this more challenging, write a mix of masculine and feminine forms on the outside, with the corresponding form on the inside. Repeat this process on the second book for the plural forms.

Tab Book

Preguntas Use this *tab book* to practice asking and answering questions.

Step 1 Fold a sheet of paper (8½" x 11") like a *hot dog* but fold it so that one side is one inch longer than the other.

Step 2 On the shorter side only, **cut** five equal tabs. On the front of each tab, **write** a question word you have learned. For example, you may wish to write the following.

Step 3 On the bottom edge, **write** any sentence you would like.

Step 4 Under each tab, **write** the word from your sentence that answers the question on the front of the tab.

Other Suggestions for a *Tab Book* Foldable

You may also use a *tab book* foldable to practice verb conjugations. You would need to make six tabs instead of five. Write a verb and a tense on the bottom edge and write the pronouns on the front of each tab. Under each tab, write the corresponding verb form.

You may wish to use a *tab book* foldable to practice new vocabulary words. Leave extra space on the bottom edge. Choose five or six vocabulary words and write each one on a tab.

You may also use a *tab book* to practice the subjunctive. On the top of each tab, write an expression that requires the subjunctive, for example **Es imposible que...** . Then open each tab and write a sentence using that expression with the subjunctive.

Miniature Matchbook

Descripciones Use this *miniature matchbook* to help communicate in an interesting and more descriptive way.

Step 1 **Fold** a sheet of paper (8½" x 11") in half like a *hot dog*.

Step 2 **Cut** the sheet in half along the fold line.

Step 3 **Fold** the two long strips in half like *hot dogs*, leaving one side ½" shorter than the other side.

Step 4 **Fold** the ½" tab over the shorter side on each strip.

Step 5 **Cut** each of the two strips in half forming four halves. Then cut each half into thirds, making twelve *miniature matchbooks*.

Step 6 **Glue** the twelve small *matchbooks* inside a *hamburger* fold (three rows of four each).

Step 7 On the front of each *matchbook*, **write** a subject you are going to tell or write about, for example, **la escuela.** Open up the tab and list any words you think you could use to make your discussion more interesting. You can add topics and words as you continue with your study of Spanish. If you glue several sections together, this foldable will "grow."

Other Suggestions for a *Miniature Matchbook* Foldable

You may use a *miniature matchbook* foldable to test each other on your knowledge of the vocabulary. Work in pairs with each partner making a blank *miniature matchbook* foldable. Each partner writes a topic related to the subjects you have just studied on the front of each *matchbook*. You may use categories of vocabulary, verbs you have recently learned to conjugate, or the subject of a reading. Your partner then writes as much as he or she can about that topic under the flap. This can alert you if you need to go back and review a topic.

A *miniature matchbook* foldable may help you organize and remember information you have read. After doing a cultural or literary reading, write down a concept presented in the reading on the front of each *matchbook*. Open up each tab and write down supporting details that support the idea.

Single Picture Frame

Dibujar y escribir Use this *single picture frame* to help you illustrate the stories you write.

Step 1 **Fold** a sheet of paper (8½" x 11") in half like a *hamburger*.

Step 2 **Open** the *hamburger* and gently roll one side of the *hamburger* toward the valley. Try not to crease the roll.

Step 3 **Cut** a rectangle out of the middle of the rolled side of paper, leaving a ½" border and forming a frame.

Step 4 **Fold** another sheet of paper (8½" x 11") in half like a *hamburger*.

Step 5 **Apply** glue to the picture frame and place it inside the *hamburger* fold.

Variation:
- Place a picture behind the frame and glue the edges of the frame to the other side of the *hamburger* fold. This locks the picture in place.
- Cut out only three sides of the rolled rectangle. This forms a window with a cover that opens and closes.

Other Suggestions for a *Single Picture Frame* Foldable

You may wish to write about a shopping trip using a *single picture frame* foldable. Before you begin, organize what you will say by drawing your path through the shops at the market, through the supermarket, or through the mall. You can then write about the shopping trip using your drawings as a guide.

Work in small groups. Each student should create a *single picture frame* foldable with a picture glued into it. You may either cut out a magazine picture or draw your own, although it should be fairly complex. Then give your foldable to another member of the group who will write sentences about what is in the picture and what people in the picture are doing. That student will pass it on to a third student who will write sentences about what is not in the picture and what people in the picture are not doing. The foldables can be passed to additional students to see if they can add more sentences.

Minibook

Mi autobiografía Use this *minibook* organizer to write and illustrate your autobiography. Before you begin to write, think about the many things concerning yourself that you have the ability to write about in Spanish. On the left pages, draw the events of your life in chronological order. On the right, write about your drawings.

Step 1 **Fold** a sheet of paper (8½" x 11") in half like a *hot dog*.

Step 2 **Fold** it in half again like a *hamburger.*

Step 3 Then **fold** in half again, forming eight sections.

Step 4 **Open** the fold and **cut** the eight sections apart.

Step 5 **Place** all eight sections in a stack and fold in half like a *hamburger.*

Step 6 **Staple** along the center fold line. **Glue** the front and back sheets into a construction paper cover.

Other Suggestions for a *Minibook* Foldable

Work in pairs to practice new verbs and verb forms using a *minibook* foldable. Illustrate different verbs on the left pages. If it is not clear what pronoun is required, you should write the pronoun under the drawing, for instance to differentiate between *we* and *they*. Then trade *minibooks* and write sentences to go with each picture on the right pages, using the new verb and the pronoun illustrated or indicated.

A *minibook* foldable can be used to help practice the imperfect tense. On each page, draw a picture of an activity that you enjoyed doing frequently. Below each picture, write a sentence describing what was happening. Remember to use the imperfect and to stick to the words you already know in Spanish.

Paper File Folder

Las emociones Use this *paper file folder* organizer to keep track of happenings or events that cause you to feel a certain way.

Step 1 **Fold** four sheets of paper (8½" x 11") in half like a *hamburger*. Leave one side one inch longer than the other side.

Step 2 On each sheet, **fold** the one-inch tab over the short side, forming an envelopelike fold.

Step 3 **Place** the four sheets side-by-side, then move each fold so that the tabs are exposed.

Step 4 Moving left to right, **cut** staggered tabs in each fold, 2⅛" wide. Fold the tabs upward.

Step 5 **Glue** the ends of the folders together. On each tab, write an emotion you sometimes feel. Pay attention to when it is that you feel happy, sad, nervous, etc. Describe the situation in Spanish and file it in the correct pocket.

Other Suggestions for a *Paper File Folder* Foldable

You may use a *paper file folder* organizer to keep track of verbs and verb forms. You should make a folder for each type of regular verb and for each type of irregular verb. Write the conjugations for some important verbs in each category and file them in the *paper file folder* organizer. Add new tenses to the existing cards and new verbs as you learn them.

A *paper file folder* organizer can be useful for keeping notes on the cultural information that you will learn. You may wish to make categories for different types of cultural information and add index cards to them as you learn new facts and concepts about the target cultures.

Envelope Fold

Un viaje especial Use this *envelope fold* to make a hidden picture or to write secret clues about a city in the Spanish-speaking world you would like to visit.

Step 1 **Fold** a sheet of paper into a *taco* to form a square. Cut off the leftover piece.

Step 2 **Open** the folded *taco* and refold it the opposite way, forming another *taco* and an X-fold pattern.

Step 3 **Open** the *taco fold* and fold the corners toward the center point of the X, forming a small square.

Step 4 **Trace** this square onto another sheet of paper. Cut and glue it to the inside of the envelope. Pictures can be drawn under the tabs.

Step 5 Use this foldable to **draw** a picture of the city you would like to visit. Or if you prefer, **write** clues about the city and have your classmates raise one tab at a time until they can guess what city the picture represents. Number the tabs in the order in which they are to be opened.

Other Suggestions for an *Envelope Fold* Foldable

An *envelope fold* can be useful for practicing vocabulary related to airports, trains, technology, or driving. Draw a scene that depicts many of the vocabulary words. Then write on each of the four flaps the new words that are represented under that flap. You could also give the picture to a partner and have the partner fill in the words.

You may want to use an *envelope fold* to review a selection you have read. Depict a scene from the selection on the paper covered by the tabs. Number the tabs in the order they are to be opened and have a partner open the tabs one at a time to guess what scene is illustrated. The partner should then write a description of the scenes.

Large Sentence Strips

El presente y el pasado Use these *large sentence strips* to help you compare and contrast activities in the past and in the present.

Step 1 Take two sheets of paper (8½" x 11") and **fold** into *hamburgers*. Cut along the fold lines, making four half sheets. (Use as many half sheets as necessary for additional pages in your book.)

Step 2 **Fold** each half sheet in half like a *hot dog*.

Step 3 Place the folds side-by-side and **staple** them together on the left side.

Step 4 About one inch from the stapled edge, **cut** the front page of each folded section up to the top. These cuts form flaps that can be raised and lowered.

Step 5 To make a half-cover, use a sheet of construction paper one inch longer than the book. **Glue** the back of the last sheet to the construction paper strip, leaving one inch on the left side to fold over and cover the original staples. Staple this half-cover in place.

Step 6 With a friend, **write** sentences on the front of the flap, either in the present tense or in the past tense. Then switch your books of sentence strips and write the opposite tense inside under the flaps.

Other Suggestions for a *Large Sentence Strips* Foldable

You may work in pairs to use *large sentence strips* to practice using direct and/or indirect object pronouns. On the front of each flap, write full sentences that have direct or indirect objects or both. Then trade sentence strips. You and your partner will each write sentences under the flaps replacing the direct or indirect objects with object pronouns.

Large sentence strips can help you contrast summer and winter activities. On the front of each flap, write sentences about activities that you do in either summer or winter. Under each flap, you should write that in the other season you do not do that activity, and you should tell what you do instead. This may be done as an individual or a partner activity.

You may use *large sentence strips* to practice using verbs that can be used reflexively and nonreflexively. Write a sentence using a reflexive verb on the outside of each flap. Under the flap, write a sentence using the same verb nonreflexively.

Project Board With Tabs

Diversiones favoritas Use this *project board with tabs* to display a visual about your favorite movie or event. Be sure to make it as attractive as possible to help convince others to see it.

Step 1 **Draw** a large illustration, a series of small illustrations, or write on the front of a sheet of paper.

Step 2 **Pinch** and slightly fold the sheet of paper at the point where a tab is desired on the illustrated piece of paper. Cut into the paper on the fold. Cut straight in, then cut up to form an L. When the paper is unfolded, it will form a tab with the illustration on the front.

Step 3 After all tabs have been cut, **glue** this front sheet onto a second sheet of paper. Place glue around all four edges and in the middle, away from tabs.

Step 4 **Write** or draw under the tabs. If the project is made as a bulletin board using butcher paper, tape or glue smaller sheets of paper under the tabs.

Think of favorite scenes from a movie or cultural event that you enjoyed and draw them on the front of the tabs. Underneath the tabs write a description of the scene or tell why you liked it. It might be fun to not put a title on the project board and just hang it up and let classmates guess the name of the movie or event you are describing.

Other Suggestions for a *Project Board With Tabs* Foldable

You may wish to use a *project board with tabs* to practice your formal commands. Think of the food words you know in Spanish and use them to create a recipe of your own. Draw a small picture of each ingredient in the order you will use it in your recipe. Next, lift each tab and write instructions about how to prepare each ingredient for your recipe using formal commands. For a more complex recipe, combine two or more *project boards with tabs*.

You may also use a *project board with tabs* to illustrate a party, museum, sport, or concert. Draw one aspect of it on the outside of the tab and write a description of your drawing under the tab.

You may work in pairs to practice the comparative and superlative. Each of you will make a *project board with tabs*. On the outside of each tab, draw a different comparison or superlative. Then trade with your partner and under each tab write a sentence describing the other's illustrations.

You may also wish to use a *project board with tabs* to practice the use of object pronouns. Draw a series of scenes involving two or more people on the outside of the tabs. Write sentences using object pronouns describing the people's conversations.

Sentence Strip Holder

Para practicar más Use this *sentence strip holder* to practice your vocabulary, your verbs, or anything else you might feel you need extra help with.

Step 1 Fold a sheet of paper (8½" x 11") in half like a *hamburger*.

Step 2 Open the *hamburger* and fold the two outer edges toward the valley. This forms a shutter fold.

Step 3 Fold one of the inside edges of the shutter back to the outside fold. This fold forms a floppy L.

Step 4 Glue the floppy L tab down to the base so that it forms a strong straight L tab.

Step 5 Glue the other shutter side to the front of this L tab. This forms a tent that is the backboard for the flashcards or student work to be displayed.

Step 6 Fold the edge of the L up ¼" to ½" to form a lip that will keep the sentence strips from slipping off the holder.

Vocabulary and verbs can be stored inside the "tent" formed by this fold.

Other Suggestions for a *Sentence Strip Holder* Foldable

You may wish to practice new or irregular verbs using a *sentence strip holder*. Work in pairs. Make flash cards showing the infinitives of the verbs to practice in Spanish. You should each take half of the cards and take turns setting one verb on the *sentence strip holder*. One partner will then say as many sentences as possible using different forms of that verb, and the other will write down the subject and conjugated verb form (or just the verb form) for each sentence. Partners should check to make sure each verb form is spelled correctly. You can repeat this activity for each verb.

You may practice food vocabulary working in small groups and using a *sentence strip holder*. Groups may make flash cards containing the names of local restaurants that everyone will be familiar with, making sure to include different types of restaurants. Put the cards up on the *sentence strip holder* one at a time. Students will spend several minutes writing about what they like to eat at that restaurant. After writing about each restaurant on the list, share your favorite foods with the group.

El alfabeto español

a <u>a</u>vión

b <u>b</u>ebé

c <u>c</u>esta

d <u>d</u>edo

e <u>e</u>lefante

f <u>f</u>oto

g <u>g</u>emelas

h <u>h</u>amaca

i <u>i</u>glesia

j <u>j</u>abón

k <u>k</u>ilo

l <u>l</u>ago

m <u>m</u>ono

n <u>n</u>ariz

ñ <u>ñ</u>ame

o <u>o</u>so

p <u>p</u>elo

q <u>q</u>ueso

r <u>r</u>ana

s <u>s</u>ala

t <u>t</u>é

u <u>u</u>va

v <u>v</u>aca

w Washington, D.C.

x e<u>x</u>amen

y <u>y</u>eso

z <u>z</u>apato

ch chicle

ll lluvia

rr guitarra

Ch, *ll*, and **rr** are not letters of the Spanish alphabet. However, it is important for you to learn the sounds they represent.

Spanish is the language of almost 400 million people around the world. Spanish had its origin in Spain. It is sometimes fondly called the "language of Cervantes," the author of the famous novel *El Quijote*. The Spanish **conquistadores** and **exploradores** brought their language to the Americas in the fifteenth and sixteenth centuries. Spanish is the official language of almost all the countries of Central and South America. It is the official language of Mexico and several of the larger islands in the Caribbean. Spanish is also the heritage language of more than fifty million people in the United States.

CULTURA
México

CULTURA
Perú

CULTURA
Puerto Rico

CULTURA
España

OCÉANO ÁRTICO

Mar de Beaufort

Bahía de Baffin

GR

Mar de Bering

Golfo de Alaska

CANADÁ

Bahía de Hudson

Mar del Labrador

AMÉRICA DEL NORTE

ESTADOS UNIDOS

OCÉANO ATLÁNTICO

MÉXICO

Golfo de México

MAR CARIBE

OCÉANO PACÍFICO

VENEZUELA

GUYANA
SURINAM
GUAYANA FRANCESA

COLOMBIA

ECUADOR

AMÉRICA DEL SUR

PERÚ

BRASIL

SAMOA

POLINESIA FRANCESA

BOLIVIA

PARAGUAY

TONGA

URUGUAY

CHILE   ARGENTINA

GOLFO DE MÉXICO

BAHAMAS

TURCAS Y CAICOS (R.U.)

OCÉANO ATLÁNTICO

CUBA

MÉXICO

PUERTO RICO (EE.UU.)

ISLAS VÍRGENES (EE.UU. y R.U.)

HAITÍ

REPÚBLICA DOMINICANA

ANTIGUA Y BARBUDA

BELICE

JAMAICA

SAN CRISTÓBAL-NEVIS

GUADALUPE (FR.)

GUATEMALA

DOMINICA

HONDURAS

MAR CARIBE

MARTINICA (FR.)

SANTA LUCÍA

EL SALVADOR

ARUBA

SAN VICENTE Y GRENADINES

BARBADOS

NICARAGUA

GRANADA

TRINIDAD Y TOBAGO

COSTA RICA

PANAMÁ

OCÉANO PACÍFICO

VENEZUELA

GUYANA

COLOMBIA

SURINAM

OCÉANO ÁRTICO

Mar de Groenlandia
ISLANDIA
Mar de Noruega
Mar de Barents
Mar de Kara
Mar de Láptiev

RUSIA

ASIA

Mar de Ojotsk

Mar del Norte

EUROPA

KAZAJSTÁN

MONGOLIA

Mar Negro
GEORGIA
ARMENIA
UZBEKISTÁN
KIRGUIZTÁN

CHINA

COREA DEL NORTE
Mar del Japón
JAPÓN

MELILLA
TURQUÍA
TURKMENISTÁN
TAYIKISTÁN

COREA DEL SUR

CEUTA
LÍBANO
SIRIA
AZERBAIJAN
AFGANISTÁN

OCÉANO PACÍFICO

MARRUECOS
ISRAEL
IRAK
IRÁN
PAKISTÁN

TÚNEZ
JORDANIA

NEPAL
BHUTÁN
Mar de la China oriental

ARGELIA
LIBIA
EGIPTO
KUWAIT
BAHREIN

HARA ENTAL

QATAR
EMIRATOS ÁRABES UNIDOS
INDIA
BANGLADESH
MYANMAR
TAIWÁN

MAURITANIA
MALÍ
NÍGER
CHAD
SUDÁN
ARABIA SAUDITA
OMÁN

LAOS

GAL

ÁFRICA
ERITREA
YEMEN
DJIBOUTI
Golfo de Bengala
TAILANDIA
Mar de la China meridional
FILIPINAS
MARSHALL

GUINEA
BURKINA FASO
NIGERIA
ETIOPÍA
VIETNAM
MICRONESIA

GHANA
BENIN
REPÚBLICA CENTROAFRICANA
SRI LANKA
CAMBOYA
BRUNEI
PALAU
KIRIBATI

MARFIL
LIBERIA
TOGO
CAMERÚN
MALAYSIA

SAN TOMÉ E PRÍNCIPE
UGANDA
KENYA
MALDIVAS
SINGAPUR
NAURÚ

GUINEA ECUATORIAL
GABÓN
REP. DEL CONGO
RUANDA
REP. DEM. DEL CONGO
BURUNDI
SEYCHELLES
OCÉANO ÍNDICO
INDONESIA
PAPÚA-NUEVA GUINEA
SALOMÓN

TANZANIA
ISLAS COMORES
Mar del Coral
TUVALU
WALLIS Y FUTUNA
VANUATU

ANGOLA
MALAWI
ZAMBIA
MOZAMBIQUE
MADAGASCAR
MAURICIO
ISLAS FIJI

OCÉANO ATLÁNTICO
ZIMBABWE
NAMIBIA
BOTSWANA
REUNIÓN
AUSTRALIA
NUEVA CALEDONIA

SUDÁFRICA
SWAZILANDIA
LESOTHO
Mar de Tasmania

NUEVA ZELANDIA

ANTÁRTIDA

NORUEGA
FINLANDIA
SUECIA

IRLANDA
REINO UNIDO
DINAMARCA
ESTONIA
LETONIA
LITUANIA
RUSIA

PAÍSES BAJOS
BÉLGICA
ALEMANIA
POLONIA
BELARÚS

OCÉANO ATLÁNTICO
LUXEMBURGO
REPÚBLICA CHECA
UCRANIA

FRANCIA
SUIZA
ESLOVAQUIA
MOLDOVA

AUSTRIA
HUNGRÍA

ANDORRA
ESLOVENIA
CROACIA
RUMANIA

PORTUGAL
MÓNACO
BOSNIA-HERZEGOVINA
YUGOSLAVIA (Fed. Rep.)
Mar Negro
GEORGIA

ESPAÑA
ITALIA
BULGARIA

MELILLA
ALBANIA
MACEDONIA
TURQUÍA

CEUTA
Mar Mediterráneo
GRECIA
SIRIA

ÁFRICA
MALTA
CHIPRE
LÍBANO

EL MUNDO HISPANOHABLANTE

OCÉANO ATLÁNTICO

FRANCIA

MAR CANTÁBRICO

Golfo de Vizcaya

La Coruña
Santiago de Compostela
Oviedo
Santander
San Sebastián
Roncesvalles
ANDORRA
Asturias
Cantabria
Bilbao
Galicia
CORDILLERA CANTÁBRICA
País Vasco
LOS PIRINEOS
León
Burgos
Pamplona
Navarra
Rioja
Río Ebro
Cataluña
Castilla y León
Zaragoza
Barcelona
Valladolid
Río Duero
Aragón
Salamanca
Segovia
Ávila
SIERRA DE GUADARRAMA
Río Tajo
PORTUGAL
Madrid
Madrid
Comunidad Valenciana
ESPAÑA
Menorca
Islas baleares
Palma
Castilla-la Mancha
Valencia
Mallorca
Río Guadiana
Ibiza
Extremadura
Formentera
Lisboa
MAR MEDITERRÁNEO
Alicante
Río Guadalquivir
Murcia
Córdoba
Murcia
Sevilla
Cartagena
Granada
Andalucía
SIERRA NEVADA
Jerez de la Frontera
Málaga
COSTA DEL SOL
Cádiz
Marbella
Estepona
Estrecho de Gibraltar
Gibraltar (R.U.)
Ceuta (Esp.)
Tánger
Melilla (Esp.)
OCÉANO ATLÁNTICO
ARGELIA

MARRUECOS

Islas Canarias
La Palma
Santa Cruz de Tenerife
Lanzarote
Gomera
Las Palmas
Fuerteventura
Tenerife
MARRUECOS
Hierro
Gran Canaria
ÁFRICA
OCÉANO ATLÁNTICO
SAHARA OCCIDENTAL

MAR CARIBE

OCÉANO ATLÁNTICO

Barranquilla
Cartagena
Maracaibo
Lago de Maracaibo
Caracas
Río Orinoco
VENEZUELA
GUYANA
SURINAM
GUAYANA FRANCESA
Medellín
Santafé de Bogotá
COLOMBIA
Cali
Río Magdalena
Ecuador
Otavalo
Quito
ECUADOR
Guayaquil
Cuenca
Islas Galápagos (Ecuador)
Río Amazonas

PERÚ
BRASIL
El Callao
Lima
Cuzco
CORDILLERA DE LOS ANDES
Lago Titicaca
BOLIVIA
La Paz
Cochabamba
Santa Cruz
Sucre
Brasília

Trópico de Capricornio
PARAGUAY
Asunción
CHILE
Río Paraná
Vicuña
Córdoba
OCÉANO PACÍFICO
Valparaíso
Santiago
Rosario
Buenos Aires
La Plata
URUGUAY
Montevideo
Río de la Plata
ARGENTINA
Mar del Plata
OCÉANO ATLÁNTICO
Puerto Montt
PATAGONIA
Estrecho de Magallanes
Islas Malvinas (R.U.)
Tierra del Fuego
Punta Arenas
Cabo de Hornos

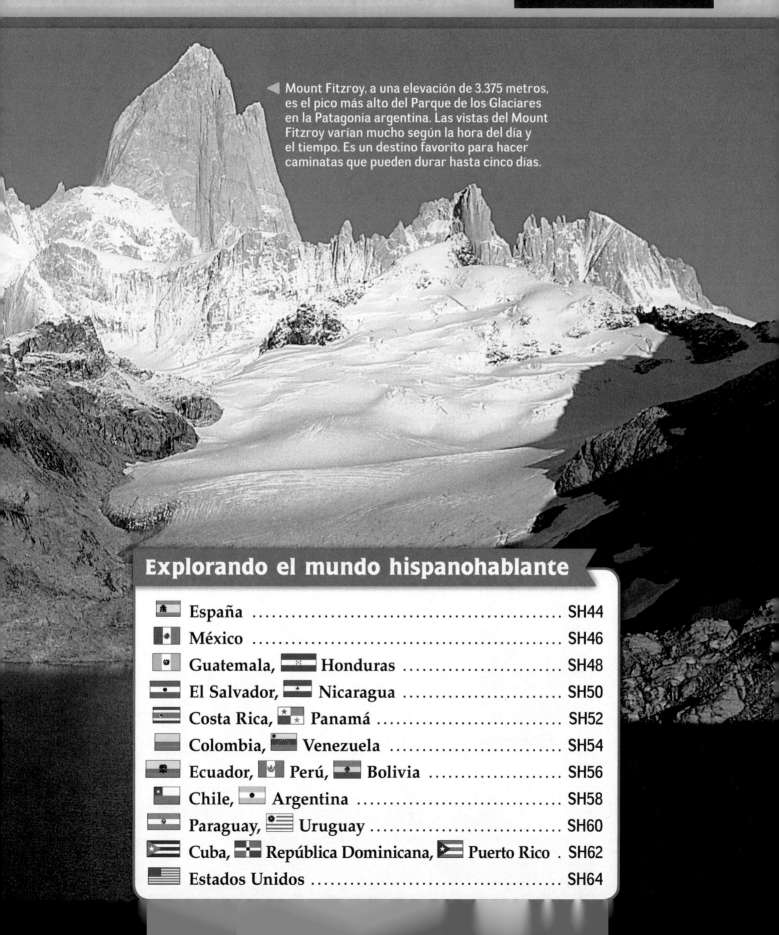

Mount Fitzroy, a una elevación de 3.375 metros, es el pico más alto del Parque de los Glaciares en la Patagonia argentina. Las vistas del Mount Fitzroy varían mucho según la hora del día y el tiempo. Es un destino favorito para hacer caminatas que pueden durar hasta cinco días.

Explorando el mundo hispanohablante

España	SH44
México	SH46
Guatemala, Honduras	SH48
El Salvador, Nicaragua	SH50
Costa Rica, Panamá	SH52
Colombia, Venezuela	SH54
Ecuador, Perú, Bolivia	SH56
Chile, Argentina	SH58
Paraguay, Uruguay	SH60
Cuba, República Dominicana, Puerto Rico	SH62
Estados Unidos	SH64

GeoVista

España

Mezquita de Córdoba

España

Palacio de Comunicaciones en la Plaza de Cibeles en Madrid, la capital de España

España

Una pescadería en Gijón, Asturias

(tl)Fernando Fernández/age fotostock, (others)Andrew Payti

España

Bailarinas de flamenco en Estepona, España

España

Casares, un pueblo típico en las montañas de Andalucía en el sur de España

España 🏴

Molinos de viento en La Mancha, una región en el centro de España

España 🏴

Naranjas de Valencia

España 🏴

Un retrato del famoso hidalgo don Quijote de la Mancha

España 🏴

Un erizo. En España viven dos especies, el erizo europeo y el erizo moruno.

Golfo de Vizcaya

Mar Cantábrico

FRANCIA

La Coruña

San Sebastián

Bilbao

Santiago de Compostela

Pamplona

LOS PIRINEOS

Río Ebro

Río Duero

Salamanca   Segovia   Zaragoza   Barcelona

SIERRA DE GUADARRAMA

Madrid

Islas Baleares

ESPAÑA

PORTUGAL   Mérida   *Río Tajo*   Valencia

Río Guadiana

Mar Mediterráneo

Córdoba

Río Guadalquivir   **SIERRA NEVADA**

Sevilla   Granada

Cádiz   Marbella

Estepona

Estrecho de Gibraltar   Ceuta

Islas Canarias

Melilla   **SH45**

MARRUECOS

GeoVista

 México

México

Una vista de la catedral en Tepoztlán en Morelos, México

México

Edificios modernos en la Ciudad de México

México

La mariposa monarca es famosa por su migración anual desde el norte de Estados Unidos hasta el sur de California y los estados de México y Michoacán.

México

Una máscara típica para el Día de los Muertos

México

El balneario de Cancún en la península de Yucatán en la costa del Caribe

ESTADOS UNIDOS

Golfo de México

Golfo de California

OCÉANO PACÍFICO

DESIERTO DE SONORA

DESIERTO DE CHIHUAHUA

SIERRA MADRE OCCIDENTAL

SIERRA MADRE ORIENTAL

SIERRA MADRE DEL SUR

Mar Caribe

MÉXICO

BELICE

GUATEMALA

Tijuana
Mexicali
Ciudad Juárez
Chihuahua
Río Grande
Río Bravo
Nuevo Laredo
La Paz
Monterrey
Matamoros
Río Grande de Santiago
San Luis Potosí
Guanajuato
Puerto Vallarta
San Miguel de Allende
Guadalajara
Río Lerma
Lago Chapala
México, D.F.
Puebla
Veracruz
Volcán Pico de Orizaba
Oaxaca
Acapulco
Campeche
Cancún

México 🇲🇽

El monumento de la Independencia en el famoso Paseo de la Reforma en la Ciudad de México, la capital

México 🇲🇽

Una tienda de artesanía en isla Mujeres cerca de la costa de la península de Yucatán en México

México 🇲🇽

Ruinas famosas de varias civilizaciones indígenas de México en Monte Albán en el estado de Oaxaca en el sur de México

México 🇲🇽

Un mercado en Mérida, México

GeoVista

 Guatemala **Honduras**

Guatemala

El lago Atitlán y el volcán San Pedro en Guatemala

Guatemala

Una calle de la ciudad colonial de Antigua, Guatemala

Honduras

Un puesto de artesanía en una playa de Honduras

Es un coatí. Los coatíes pasan la mayor parte de su tiempo encima de los árboles pero están cómodos también en el suelo.

Honduras

Una cancha de pelota y una estela en Copán, Honduras

(tr b)Richard Brommer, (t)l©Glow Images/SuperStock, (others)Lori Ernfridsson

MÉXICO

Mar Caribe

Islas del Cisne

BELICE

Tikal

Flores

Islas de la Bahía

Golfo de Honduras

Río Dulce

Puerto Barrios

Puerto Cortés

GUATEMALA

SIERRA DE LOS CUCHUMATANES

Cobán

San Pedro Sula

La Ceiba

SIERRAS DE MERENDÓN

El Progreso

Río Ulúa

Lago de Izabal

Huehuetenango

Río Motagua

SIERRA MADRE

Volcán Tajumulco

Quetzaltenango

Lago de Yojoa

HONDURAS

SIERRA DE AGALTA

Río Patuca

Puerto Lempira

Coatepeque

CORDILLERA DE OPALACA

Copán

Juticalpa

Río Coco

Mazatenango

Lago Atitlán

Guatemala

Cerro Las Minas

Escuintla

Tegucigalpa

Danlí

Puerto Quetzal

EL SALVADOR

Choluteca

Golfo de Fonseca

NICARAGUA

Guatemala

Un quetzal—el pájaro nacional de Guatemala

Guatemala

Se aprecian los tejidos guatemaltecos en el mundo entero. Estos tejidos se venden en un mercado de Santiago de Atitlán.

Guatemala

Dos muchachas llevando una típica falda tejida en Chichicastenango

Honduras

La Plaza Morazán y la Catedral de San Miguel en Tegucigalpa, la capital de Honduras

GeoVista

Nicaragua

Una vista de Managua,
la capital de Nicaragua

Nicaragua

La Catedral de Granada

Nicaragua

El Palacio Nacional de Cultura en Managua
que sirve hoy día de Museo Nacional

El Salvador

El mono araña sigue habitando
unas regiones de El Salvador.

El Salvador

El volcán Izalco, a unos
45 kilómetros de la capital,
San Salvador

El Salvador

La Catedral Metropolitana domina la Plaza Barrios en San Salvador.

Nicaragua

Bueyes en un camino rural del Viejo León

Nicaragua

Un joven pescador en el lago Nicaragua

GUATEMALA

HONDURAS

Lago Güija

Cerro El Pital

CORDILLERA DE TILARAN

Río Coco

Santa Ana

Embalse Cerrón Grande

El Mozote

Puerto Cabezas

Volcán Santa Ana

Sensuntepeque

San Salvador

Lago Ilopango

Pico Mogotón

CORDILLERA ISABELIA

Acajulta

La Libertad

Río Lempa

San Miguel

Volcán de San Miguel

Mar Caribe

Puerto El Triunfo

EL SALVADOR

Río Grande de San Miguel

Golfo de Fonseca

Estelí

Matagalpa

Río Grande de Matagalpa

Chinandega

León

NICARAGUA

Corinto

Lago Managua

Río Escondido

Islas del Maíz

Managua

Granada

Bluefields

OCÉANO PACÍFICO

Lago Nicaragua

Rivas

Isla de Ometepe

San Carlos

Río San Juan

COSTA RICA

Nicaragua

Cerámicas de mujeres nicaragüenses

GeoVista

 Costa Rica ★ **Panamá**

Panamá ★

Una vista de los rascacielos modernos de la Ciudad de Panamá

Costa Rica

Un grupo de turistas visitando uno de los muchos lugares de turismo ecológico en Costa Rica

Costa Rica

Un papagayo en una selva costarricense

Panamá ★

Una vista del canal de Panamá →

Panamá ★

La Iglesia de San Francisco de Asís en el barrio histórico de la Ciudad de Panamá

SH52

NICARAGUA

Mar Caribe

Lago Nicaragua

CORDILLERA DE GUANACASTE

Río San Juan

Liberia

Lago Arenal

COSTA RICA

Nicoya

CORDILLERA CENTRAL

Puerto Limón

Alajuela

Puntarenas

Caldera

San José

Volcán de Irazú

CORDILLERA DE TALAMANCA

Puerto Quepos

San Isidro

Bocas del Toro

Volcán Barú

Golfito

CORDILLERA CENTRAL

David

PANAMÁ

Río San Pablo

Santiago

Isla de Coiba

El Porvenir

Canal de Panamá

Río Chagres

Colón

Ciudad de Panamá

Lago Gatún

Balboa

Vacamonte

Río Chepo

Penonomé

SERRANÍA DE SAN BLAS

Archipiélago de San Blas

SERRANÍA DEL DARIÉN

Lago Bayano

Isla del Rey

Archipiélago de las Perlas

La Palma

Río Tuira

Yaviza

Golfo de Panamá

COLOMBIA

OCÉANO PACÍFICO

Panamá

Jóvenes del grupo indígena emberá de la selva tropical cerca de la Ciudad de Panamá

Panamá

El monumento de Vasco Núñez de Balboa en la Ciudad de Panamá

Costa Rica

El Parque Nacional del volcán Poás se considera uno de los lugares más impresionantes de Costa Rica.

GeoVista

Colombia   Venezuela

Colombia

Aquí vemos un cafeto, la planta que produce el café— un producto importantísimo de Colombia.

Venezuela

El Salto Angel en el Parque Nacional Canaima

Sancocho, un plato tradicional venezolano, tiene variaciones en Colombia también. Aquí hay un sancocho de carne.

Venezuela

Uno de los miles de flamencos que se ven en las lagunas o en vuelo en un parque nacional en Venezuela

(tl)Kelli Drummer-Avendaño, (tr)Digital Vision/age fotostock, (c)Nico Tondini/Alamy, (b)©MedioImages/SuperStock

Isla de Providencia

Isla de San Andrés

Mar Caribe

Archipiélago Los Roques

Isla de Margarita

OCÉANO ATLÁNTICO

Santa Marta
Pico Cristóbal Colón
Golfo de Venezuela
Coro
Caracas

Barranquilla
Puerto Bolívar
Cartagena
Maracaibo
Lago Maracaibo
Valencia
Maracay
Lago Valencia

SIERRA NEVADA DE SANTA MARTA

Río Magdalena

PANAMÁ

Pico Bolívar
Mérida
Río Apure
Río Orinoco
Ciudad Guayana

Cúcuta
San Cristóbal
San Fernando de Apure
VENEZUELA

Ciudad Bolívar

Bucaramanga

Río Caroní

GUYANA

Medellín

Canaima

Puerto Ayacucho

Río Meta

Bogotá
Río Guaviare

Ibagué
COLOMBIA

Buenaventura

Cali

LOS ANDES

Pasto

Río Caquetá

Río Putumayo

Río Amazonas

ECUADOR

BRASIL

PERÚ

Venezuela

Una vista de Caracas,
la capital de Venezuela

Venezuela

Un excursionista
andino en Venezuela

Colombia

Una típica callejuela en la zona
colonial de Cartagena, Colombia

Venezuela

Un teleférico en las montañas de Mérida

Colombia

La Catedral Primada de Bogotá y su Capilla
del Sagrario en la Plaza de Bolívar en Bogotá

GeoVista

Ecuador · **Perú** · **Bolivia**

Perú

Una vista parcial de las ruinas de la ciudad imperial de los incas, Machu Picchu

Perú

Una vista de la catedral y la Plaza de Armas en Cuzco

Ecuador

La Iglesia de San Francisco en el centro del barrio colonial de Quito

Perú

Una señora vendiendo tejidos en las orillas del lago Titicaca

Ecuador

Una playa en la ciudad portuaria de Manta

(cr b)Andrew Payti, (others)Richard Brommer

Ecuador

Unos indígenas en un mercado de Otavalo. Los otavaleños tienen fama mundial por sus tejidos.

Bolivia

Un señor en su balsa en el lago Titicaca

Bolivia

La salina más grande del mundo se encuentra en el Salar de Uyuni ubicado a más de 3.800 metros sobre el nivel del mar.

SH57

Argentina

Una pareja joven bailando el tango en San Telmo, un barrio de Buenos Aires, la capital de Argentina

Argentina

Ushuaia, Argentina, está ubicada a orillas del canal Beagle en el extremo sur de Tierra del Fuego. En los meses de verano, de noviembre a febrero, salen de su puerto barcos con destino a la Antártida.

Argentina

La Casa Rosada en la Plaza de Mayo en Buenos Aires

Chile

Una pescadería en Puerto Montt

Chile

Arica, la ciudad más norteña de Chile, con una vista del desierto de Atacama

Andrew Payti

Chile

Caballos en el Parque
Nacional Torres del Paine
en la Patagonia chilena

Chile

Una vista del valle del Elqui en el norte de Chile

Argentina

Los lobos marinos están tomando el sol en las rocas de
Punta Loma cerca de Puerto Madryn. Aquí hay una
gran colonia de lobos marinos durante todo el año.

Argentina

Casas típicas del
pintoresco barrio
La Boca en
Buenos Aires

SH59

GeoVista

Uruguay 🏳️

Una vista de la Plaza de la Independencia con el monumento al héroe uruguayo José Gervasio Artigas en el centro de Montevideo, la capital de Uruguay

Uruguay 🏳️

Un guitarrista tocando en una calle de Colonia

Paraguay 🇵🇾

Un joven de ascendencia guaraní

Uruguay 🏳️

Una vista de Pocitos, un bonito barrio playero de Montevideo

(t)Glow Images, (tr)Richard Bromer, (c)Brian Atkinson/Alamy, (b)Andrew Payti

OLIVIA

Capitán Pablo
Lagerenza

Fuerte Olimpo

PARAGUAY

GRAN CHACO

Río Pilcomayo

Río Paraguay

Río Paraná

Pozo
Colorado

Pedro Juan
Caballero

Concepción

BRASIL

Asunción

Villarrica

Ciudad del Este

Formosa

San Juan
Bautista

Encarnación

Río Paraná

ARGENTINA

Río Uruguay

Artigas

Rivera

Salto

URUGUAY

Lago Artificial de
Rincón del Bonete

Río Negro

Lago Artificial de
Paso del Palmar

Melo

Paysandú

Mercedes

CUCHILLA
GRANDE

Treinta
y Tres

Laguna
Merín

Nueva Palmira

Minas

▲ Cerro Catedral

Colonia

Río de la Plata

Montevideo

Punta del Este

OCÉANO ATLÁNTICO

Paraguay

La iguana verde se ve en México,
Centroamérica y una gran parte de
Sudamérica hasta Paraguay y Argentina.

Paraguay

Un jaguar, el felino
más grande de la
América del Sur

Uruguay

Una vista del puerto deportivo en el
balneario famoso de Punta del Este

Paraguay

Las cataratas del Iguazú en la frontera
entre Paraguay, Argentina y Brasil

SH61

GeoVista

Cuba 🏴

Músicos tocando en la Casa de las Tradiciones en Santiago de Cuba

República Dominicana 🏴

Una plaza en Puerto Plata, un balneario famoso

Cuba 🏴

El campanario de la Iglesia y Convento de San Francisco en Trinidad, Cuba

Puerto Rico 🏴

Unos alumnos en su uniforme escolar en Fajardo

Cuba 🏴

Una vista panorámica de La Habana, la capital de Cuba

(tl)Author's Image/PunchStock, (tr)M. Timothy O'Keefe/Alamy, (cl bl)Lissa Harrison, (cr)Hola Images/Getty Images

Go Online!

connectED.mcgraw-hill.com

Puerto Rico

La flor–leche de gallina–en el Bosque Nacional El Yunque

Puerto Rico

Muchas especialidades de la cocina puertorriqueña llevan jueyes (cangrejos de tierra).

Puerto Rico

El Yunque, una famosa selva tropical

República Dominicana

Bañadores en la Playa de Cabarete, una favorita entre los surfistas

GeoVista

New York 🇺🇸

Un señor boricua con su bicicleta y bandera puertorriqueña en el desfile que celebra el día puertorriqueño en la Ciudad de Nueva York

Michigan 🇺🇸

Mexicanoamericanos celebrando el Cinco de Mayo en Port Huron, Michigan

Texas 🇺🇸

El Paseo del Río en San Antonio →

Washington 🇺🇸

Noticieros latinos de televisión en Seattle

Florida 🇺🇸

Una vista del centro de San Agustín, la primera ciudad europea en EE.UU. fundada en 1565 por el español Pedro Menéndez de Avilés

RUSIA

Alaska CANADÁ

Mar de Bering

Golfo de Alaska

CANADÁ

Washington

Oregón Idaho

Montana

Dakota del Norte Minnesota

Wyoming

Nevada

Utah

California

Colorado

Arizona

Nuevo México

ESTADOS UNIDOS

Dakota del Sur

Nebraska

Kansas

Oklahoma

Texas

Wisconsin

Michigan

Iowa

Illinois Indiana

Misuri

Kentucky

Tennessee

Arkansas

Misisipí Alabama Georgia

Luisiana

New Hampshire

Vermont Maine

Nueva York

Ohio

Washington, D.C.

Virginia Occidental Virginia

Carolina del Norte

Carolina del Sur

Florida

Massachusetts
Rhode Island
Connecticut
Nueva Jersey
Delaware
Maryland

Pensilvania

OCÉANO PACÍFICO

Hawai

OCÉANO PACÍFICO

MÉXICO

Golfo de México

OCÉANO ATLÁNTICO

Arizona

Una quinceañera celebrando con su familia

Florida

El Festival de la Calle Ocho se celebra cada año en marzo en la Pequeña Habana en Miami.

LA LIBERTAD MARKET CARNICERIA
CAFETERIA 24

Florida

Un mercado en una calle de la Pequeña Habana en Miami

California

La Misión de San Antonio de Padua en Monterey

Go Online!
connectED.mcgraw-hill.com

Audio Video Práctica Repaso Diversiones eScape

ePals

Amigos, alumnos y parientes

Objetivos

In this chapter you will review:

- vocabulary associated with friends, family, and home
- the verb **ser**
- the use of nouns, articles, and adjectives
- the verb **tener**
- possessive adjectives

◀ Estos jóvenes están usando su móvil mientras toman un refresco en Asunción, Paraguay.

Vocabulario 🎧

Mariana es morena y bastante alta.
Ella es de Guanajuato.
Es alumna en el Colegio Rivera.

Manuel y Adela son alumnos en la misma escuela.
Son alumnos buenos. Son muy inteligentes.
Los dos son bastante cómicos.

Santiago tiene dieciséis años.
Su hermano menor tiene catorce.
Y su hermano mayor tiene dieciocho.
Ellos tienen una mascota—Chispa.

La familia Solís tiene una casa privada.
La casa tiene siete cuartos.

Práctica

HABLAR • ESCRIBIR

1 Parea y forma frases basado en la información en el vocabulario.

1. Santiago	**a.** amigos
2. Mariana	**b.** de Puerto Rico
3. Manuel y Adela	**c.** dos hermanos
4. Santiago	**d.** de nacionalidad mexicana

HABLAR

2 Contesta. Presta atención a la palabra interrogativa.

1. ¿De qué nacionalidad es Mariana Valdéz?
2. ¿De dónde es?
3. ¿Cómo es?
4. ¿Dónde es alumna?

LEER • ESCRIBIR

3 Corrige la información falsa.

1. Manuel y Adela son hermanos.
2. Son muy serios.
3. Son alumnos malos.
4. No son muy inteligentes.
5. Son alumnos en escuelas diferentes.

LEER • ESCRIBIR

4 Completa con una palabra apropiada.

1. Santiago Barros es de _____.
2. Tiene dos _____.
3. _____ hermano menor tiene catorce años.
4. Su hermano mayor tiene dieciocho _____.
5. Santiago y sus hermanos tienen una _____.
6. Su perro es _____.

5 Rompecabezas

Cambia una letra en cada palabra para formar una palabra nueva.

1. dos
2. hola
3. buen
4. tengo
5. baño

CULTURA

Estos señores mayores pasan un rato agradable sentados en el Parque de la Independencia en Quito, Ecuador. Tienen una conversación interesante.

Richard Brommer

PLANTA BAJA

PLANTA ALTA

HABLAR • ESCRIBIR

6 Describe la casa de los Solís.

7 **Comunicación**

With a classmate, look at these real estate ads. Describe your family and housing needs to your real estate agent (your partner). He or she will recommend a dwelling and will describe it to you. Take turns.

PROMOCIONES, FINANCIACION Y VENTAS, S.L.

MILENIUM

VALDELAGRANA
Piso 3 dormitorios, 2 baños, coc. amueb. 3 arm. empotr. parking privado.
Ref.- 7151

FUENTEBRAVÍA
Apartamento 1 dormitorio, 1 baño, coc. amueb. jardines, aparc. cerrado. A 100 metros de la playa.
Ref.- 7000

VALDELAGRANA
Unifamiliar 160 m2, 3 dormitorios, 2 baños, cocina amueb., aseo, buhardilla, trastero, piscina.
Ref.- 7083

FUENTEBRAVÍA
Unifamiliar 3 dormitorios, 1 baño, aseo, cocina amueblada, chimenea, cerca de la playa.
Ref.- 7009

C/ Almirante Cañas Trujillo, 17 B (Junto Avd. Libertad)
11500 El Puerto de Santa María

Conversación 🎧

¿De dónde son?

Julio	¡Hola!
Rosa	¡Hola! ¿Qué tal?
Julio	Bien, ¿y tú?
Rosa	Bien. Oye, eres un amigo de Teresa Irizarry, ¿no?
Julio	Sí, soy Julio Arenal.
Rosa	¿De dónde eres, Julio?
Julio	¿Yo? Soy de la Ciudad de México. Y tú eres de Puebla como Teresa, ¿no?
Rosa	Sí.
Julio	¿Cuántos años tienes, Rosa?
Rosa	Tengo dieciséis años.
Julio	¿Dieciséis? Tenemos la misma edad.

¿Comprendes?

A Contesta según la información en la conversación.

1. ¿Son mexicanos los dos muchachos?
2. ¿De dónde es Julio?
3. ¿Son amigos los dos muchachos?
4. ¿Quién es amigo de Teresa Irizarry?
5. ¿De dónde es Rosa?
6. ¿Cuántos años tiene ella?
7. Y, ¿cuántos años tiene Julio?
8. ¿Tienen ellos la misma edad?

B **Resumiendo** Cuenta toda la información sobre las tres personas en la conversación en tus propias palabras.

CULTURA

Rascacielos modernos en la Ciudad de México

Gramática

Presente del verbo ser

Review the forms of the irregular verb **ser.**

ser	
soy	somos
eres	*sois*
es	son

Práctica

HABLAR

❶ Personaliza. Da respuestas personales.

    1. ¿Quién eres?
    2. ¿De qué nacionalidad eres?
    3. ¿Dónde eres alumno(a)?
    4. ¿Cómo es tu escuela?

LEER • ESCRIBIR

❷ Completa con las formas apropiadas de **ser.**

    Yo __1__ un amigo de Andrés. Andrés __2__ muy simpático. Y él __3__ gracioso. Andrés y yo __4__ dominicanos. __5__ de la República Dominicana.

    La capital de la República Dominicana __6__ Santo Domingo. Nosotros __7__ alumnos en un colegio en Santo Domingo. Nosotros __8__ alumnos de inglés. La profesora de inglés __9__ la señorita White. Ella __10__ norteamericana. __11__ de Estados Unidos.

CULTURA

¿De qué nacionalidad son los jóvenes? Son dominicanos, ¿no?

❸ *Comunicación*

You are key pals with an exchange student from Peru (your partner). He or she wants to know about your school, your schedule, and your classes. Tell as much as you can about your school and then ask him or her about school life in Peru.

Larry Hamill

Sustantivos, artículos y adjetivos

Go Online!

connectED.mcgraw-hill.com

1. Spanish nouns are either masculine or feminine. Most nouns ending in **o** are masculine and most nouns ending in **a** are feminine. The definite articles **el** and **los** accompany masculine nouns; **la** and **las** accompany feminine nouns.

SINGULAR	PLURAL	SINGULAR	PLURAL
el alumno	**los alumnos**	**la amiga**	**las amigas**
el curso	**los cursos**	**la escuela**	**las escuelas**

2. An adjective must agree with the noun it describes or modifies. Adjectives that end in **o** have four forms.

el amigo sincero	**los amigos sinceros**
la amiga sincera	**las amigas sinceras**

3. Adjectives that end in **e** or a consonant have only two forms.

el curso interesante	**los cursos interesantes**
la clase interesante	**las clases interesantes**
el curso difícil	**los cursos difíciles**
la clase difícil	**las clases difíciles**

Práctica

Julia es una alumna seria, muy estudiosa.

HABLAR • ESCRIBIR

4 Describe a Julia. •

HABLAR • ESCRIBIR

5 Describe al grupo de amigos. •

HABLAR • ESCRIBIR

6 Describe tu clase favorita.

7 **Comunicación**

Work in groups of three or four. In each group, rate your courses as **fácil, difícil, regular, aburrido, fantástico.** Tally the results and report the information to the class.

CULTURA

Los amigos están en el patio de su escuela en Santo Domingo.

El verbo tener

1. Review the forms of the irregular verb **tener.**

tener	
tengo	tenemos
tienes	*tenéis*
tiene	tienen

2. You use **tener** to express age.

¿Cuántos años tienes?

3. Note that the expression **tener que** followed by an infinitive means *to have to.*

Tenemos que estudiar y aprender mucho.

Práctica

Una familia española en una placita en Palma de Mallorca, España

HABLAR

8 Personaliza. Da respuestas personales sobre tu familia.

1. ¿Tienes una familia grande o pequeña?
2. ¿Cuántos hermanos tienes?
3. ¿Cuántos años tienen ellos?
4. ¿Y cuántos años tienes tú?
5. ¿Tienen ustedes un perro o un gato?
6. ¿Tiene tu padre o tu madre un carro?
7. En la escuela, ¿tienes que estudiar mucho?
8. ¿Y tienen que trabajar mucho tus padres?

LEER • ESCRIBIR

9 Completa con las formas apropiadas de **tener.**

La familia Bravo __1__ un piso o apartamento en Madrid. Su piso __2__ seis cuartos. Está en Salamanca, una zona muy bonita de la ciudad. Muchas calles en la zona Salamanca __3__ los nombres de artistas famosos—la calle Goya, la calle Velázquez.

Hay cuatro personas en la familia Bravo. Teresa __4__ diecisiete años y su hermano __5__ quince años. Ellos __6__ un gato adorable.

EXPANSIÓN

Ahora, sin mirar el párrafo, cuenta toda la información sobre la familia Bravo en tus propias palabras. Si no recuerdas algo, un(a) compañero(a) te puede ayudar.

Andrew Payti

Adjetivos posesivos

Go Online!

connectED.mcgraw-hill.com

1. Review the forms of the possessive adjectives **mi, tu,** and **su.** These adjectives have only two forms.

> **¿Dan una fiesta tu hermana y tus primos?**
> **Sí, mi hermana y mis primos dan una fiesta.**
> **Todos sus amigos van a recibir una invitación a su fiesta.**

2. The possessive adjective **nuestro** has four forms.

> **Nuestro primo, nuestra tía, nuestras sobrinas**
> **y nuestros abuelos viven todos en Madrid.**

Práctica

HABLAR

10 Personaliza. Da respuestas personales sobre tu familia y casa.

1. ¿Dónde está tu casa o departamento?
2. ¿Cuántas personas hay en tu familia?
3. ¿Cuántos cuartos tiene tu casa o departamento?
4. ¿De dónde son tus abuelos?
5. ¿Tienes muchos primos?
6. ¿Quiénes son los padres de tus primos?

LEER • ESCRIBIR

11 Completa con el adjetivo posesivo apropiado.

—La casa de mi familia está en la calle Independencia. ___1___ casa tiene siete cuartos. Detrás de ___2___ casa hay un jardín.

—José, ¿tienen ___3___ padres un carro?

—Sí, y ___4___ carro es bastante nuevo. ___5___ carro está en el garaje. Y nosotros tenemos un perro. ___6___ perro no está en el garaje. Está en el jardín.

Comunicación

12 You are spending the summer with a family in Venezuela. Tell your Venezuelan "brother" or "sister" (your partner) all you can about your family. Answer any questions he or she may have. Then reverse roles.

13 Work with a classmate. Be good interviewers. Make up questions with the following question words.

> **¿Qué?**   **¿Quién?**   **¿Quiénes?**   **¿Dónde?**
> **¿De dónde?**   **¿Cómo?**   **¿Cuánto(s)?**

CULTURA 🇻🇪

Un parque en el centro de San Juan, Venezuela

Kelli Drummer-Avendaño

Go Online!
connectED.mcgraw-hill.com

Audio

Video

Práctica

Repaso

Diversiones

eScape

ePals

En casa y en la escuela

Objetivos

In this chapter you will review:

- vocabulary associated with home and school activities
- the present tense of regular verbs
- the present tense of **ir, dar, estar**
- contractions

◀ Unas casas bonitas en Mallorca, España—una de las islas Baleares en el mar Mediterráneo

Vocabulario 🎧

Los alumnos están en la escuela.
Ellos prestan atención al profesor.
El profesor habla.
Ramón tiene una pregunta y
    levanta la mano.

Después de las clases los alumnos van a casa.
Toman el bus escolar.

La familia de Andrés Salinas vive
    en Nicaragua.
Su familia está en la sala.
La señora Salinas lee un libro.
Su esposo (marido) ve la tele.
Andrés escucha música en su MP3.

La hermana de Andrés está en su cuarto
    (de dormir).
Ella recibe un correo electrónico. Ella
    usa su computadora.
Lee su e-mail.

Práctica

ESCUCHAR

1 Escucha las frases. Usa una tabla como la de abajo para indicar si la acción tiene lugar en casa o en la escuela.

casa	escuela

HABLAR • ESCRIBIR

2 Contesta.

1. ¿Cómo llegan los alumnos a la escuela? ¿Toman el bus, van en carro o van a pie?
2. ¿Con quién hablan los alumnos cuando entran en la sala de clase?
3. ¿Prestan ellos atención cuando el/la profesor(a) habla?
4. ¿Qué levanta un(a) alumno(a) cuando tiene una pregunta?
5. Los alumnos que estudian mucho, ¿sacan notas buenas o malas?
6. En la escuela, ¿quién da los exámenes y quiénes toman los exámenes?

LEER • ESCRIBIR

3 Parea para formar expresiones.

1. leer
2. escribir
3. vivir
4. aprender
5. vender
6. comer
7. ser
8. subir
9. beber

a. mucho en la escuela
b. al quinto piso
c. una novela
d. un alumno bueno y serio
e. la orden
f. una limonada
g. en una casa particular
h. CDs en una tienda
i. carne, ensalada y papas

CULTURA

Los jóvenes comen y conversan en la cafetería de su escuela en Barranquilla, Colombia. Una de las muchachas chequea mensajes en su móvil.

HABLAR • ESCRIBIR

4 **Juego** Divide the class into two teams. Your teacher will ask each team to give a word that pertains to a category: **cosas que comemos, bebemos, leemos o escribimos.** Your teacher will keep asking for words until one team is unable to think of a word that pertains to the given category.

Kelli Drummer-Avendaño

Conversación 🎧

Otro año en la escuela

Paco	Claudia, ¿cómo estás?
Claudia	Muy bien, Paco. ¿Y tú?
Paco	Bien. ¿Qué tal la escuela este año?
Claudia	Muy bien. Pero un poco difícil. Tengo seis cursos.
Paco	¡Seis cursos! Estudias mucho, ¿no?
Claudia	Sí, bastante. Y, a propósito, Paco, ¿dónde están tus primos Enrique y Sara? ¿Dónde viven ahora?
Paco	Pues, viven en la misma casa. ¿Por qué?
Claudia	Pues, no los veo casi nunca.

¿Comprendes?

Contesta según la información en la conversación.

1. ¿Quiénes hablan?
2. ¿Cómo está Paco?
3. ¿Y Claudia?
4. ¿Cuántos cursos toma Claudia?
5. ¿Tiene que estudiar mucho?
6. ¿Quiénes son los primos de Paco?
7. ¿Ve Claudia mucho a sus primos?
8. ¿Viven ellos en la misma casa que antes o no?

Gramática

Presente de los verbos regulares

1. Review the present tense forms of regular **-ar, -er,** and **-ir** verbs.

infinitive	mirar	comer	vivir
stem	mir-	com-	viv-
yo	miro	como	vivo
tú	miras	comes	vives
Ud., él, ella	mira	come	vive
nosotros(as)	miramos	comemos	vivimos
vosotros(as)	*miráis*	*coméis*	*vivís*
Uds., ellos, ellas	miran	comen	viven

2. Note that the **-er** and **-ir** verbs have the same endings except **nosotros(as)** and *vosotros(as).*

comemos   **vivimos**
coméis   *vivís*

3. Remember, to make a sentence negative, you put **no** before the verb.

> **No habla francés.**
> **No vivimos en Francia.**

4. Remember to use **tú** when talking to a friend, family member, or person your own age. Use **usted** when speaking to an adult, a person you do not know well, or someone to whom you wish to show respect. You use **ustedes** when talking to two or more people.

> **¿Tú estudias español, Roberto?**
> **¿Y usted, señora? ¿Usted también estudia español?**
> **Ustedes viven aquí, ¿no?**

CULTURA

Un puesto de comida en una calle de Oaxaca, México. ¿Qué forma usa la mamá con su hijito? ¿Tú o usted?

Andrew Payti

Práctica

HABLAR • ESCRIBIR

1 Personaliza. Da respuestas personales.

1. ¿En qué escuela estudias?

2. ¿Cómo llegas a la escuela por la mañana?

3. ¿Cuántos cursos tomas?

4. ¿En qué llevas los materiales escolares?

5. ¿Estudian mucho los alumnos de tu escuela?

6. ¿Sacan ustedes notas buenas?

7. ¿Toman ustedes muchos exámenes?

8. ¿Escuchan ustedes cuando el/la profesor(a) habla?

EXPANSIÓN

Ahora, sin mirar las preguntas, cuenta toda la información en tus propias palabras. Si no recuerdas algo, un(a) compañero(a) te puede ayudar.

LEER • ESCRIBIR

2 Completa con la forma apropiada del verbo.

1. Durante la fiesta todos nosotros _____. (bailar)

2. Felipe _____ el piano. (tocar)

3. Mientras él _____ el piano, Paz y Jaime _____. (tocar, cantar)

4. ¿_____ ustedes refrescos durante la fiesta? (preparar)

5. ¿_____ ustedes fotos durante la fiesta? (tomar)

6. Sí, y todos nosotros _____ las fotografías. (mirar)

HABLAR • ESCRIBIR

3 Personaliza. Da respuestas personales.

1. ¿Qué comes cuando tienes hambre?

2. ¿Qué bebes cuando tienes sed?

3. ¿Qué aprenden tú y tus amigos en la escuela?

4. ¿Qué leen ustedes en la clase de inglés?

5. ¿Qué escriben ustedes?

6. ¿Comprenden los alumnos cuando el/la profesor(a) de español habla?

7. ¿Reciben ustedes notas buenas en todos sus cursos?

CULTURA

Un cartel anunciando cursos de verano en un instituto de idiomas en Ceuta, una ciudad española en el norte de África

Andrew Payti

LEER • ESCRIBIR

4 Completa sobre una visita a un café.

En el café los clientes __1__ (ver) al mesero. Ellos __2__ (hablar) con el mesero. Los clientes __3__ (leer) el menú y __4__ (decidir) lo que van a tomar. Los meseros __5__ (tomar) la orden y __6__ (escribir) la orden en un cuaderno pequeño. Los meseros no __7__ (leer) el menú. Y los clientes no __8__ (escribir) la orden.

CULTURA 🏳️

Los clientes toman un refresco en un café al aire libre en Valencia, España.

5 *Comunicación*

Tell all the things you do in a typical school day. Present your information to the class. Do you or your classmates do anything different?

CULTURA 🏳️

El exterior del Colegio Francisco Febres Cordero La Salle en Quito, la capital de Ecuador

Andrew Payti

Los verbos ir, dar, estar

1. Note that the verbs **ir, dar,** and **estar** are the same as regular **-ar** verbs in all forms except **yo.**

	ir	dar	estar
yo	voy	doy	estoy
tú	vas	das	estás
Ud., él, ella	va	da	está
nosotros(as)	vamos	damos	estamos
vosotros(as)	*vais*	*dais*	*estáis*
Uds., ellos, ellas	van	dan	están

2. The preposition **a** often follows the verb **ir.** Remember that **a** contracts with **el** to form one word—**al.**

Voy al café. No voy a la tienda.

3. Remember, you can use **ir a** + infinitive to express a future idea.

Voy a tomar el bus.

Práctica

HABLAR

6 Personaliza. Da respuestas personales.

1. ¿Vas a la escuela?
2. ¿A qué hora vas a la escuela?
3. ¿Con quién vas a la escuela?
4. ¿Están ustedes en la escuela ahora?
5. ¿Cómo van ustedes a la escuela?
6. ¿Da el/la profesor(a) muchos exámenes?
7. ¿Dan los alumnos exámenes también?

CULTURA

Unos jóvenes atraviesan la plaza en San Pablo, Ecuador.

Andrew Payti

LEER • ESCRIBIR

7 Completa.

Yo __1__ (ir) a la tienda de ropa. Emilio __2__ (ir) también. Él y yo __3__ (estar) en la tienda. Yo __4__ (comprar) una camiseta y él __5__ (comprar) un blue jean. Nosotros no __6__ (necesitar) mucha ropa porque __7__ (llevar) uniforme a la escuela.

Laura y Tomás __8__ (llevar) uniforme a la escuela también. Ellos __9__ (ir) a una escuela en las afueras de Lima, en Miraflores.

Comunicación

8 Tell some things you're not going to do now because you have to do something else.

9 Work in groups of three or four. You're all friends from Mexico. After school you go to a café where you talk about lots of things—school, teachers, friends, home, family, etc. One of you will be the server. You have to interrupt the conversation once in a while to take the orders and serve. Take turns.

CULTURA

Los jóvenes están delante de un café Internet en Tepoztlán, México.

Andrew Payti

Go Online!

Audio

Video

Práctica

Repaso

Diversiones

eScape

Personalidad y salud

Objetivos

In this chapter you will review:

- vocabulary related to personality, health, and general well-being
- uses of **ser** and **estar**
- indirect object pronouns

◄ Estos jóvenes están jugando un juego de tira con una cuerda en Santa Marta, Colombia.

Vocabulario 🎧

Alberto no está bien.
Está enfermo.
Tiene fiebre y tiene
que guardar cama.

contento, alegre

triste, deprimida

El médico está en su
consulta (consultorio).
Examina al paciente
(enfermo).

lleno de energía

cansado

El médico le da
una receta.

Arturo está de mal humor. Algo le molesta (enoja).
Felipe está de buen humor.

(t)MOODBOARD/age fotostock, (tr b)David H. Brennan, (c)Heath Korvola/Getty Images, (cr)BananaStock/PunchStock

Práctica

ESCUCHAR

1 Escucha. Escoge la frase correcta. Usa una tabla como la de abajo para indicar tus respuestas.

a	b

HABLAR • ESCRIBIR

2 Contesta sobre una consulta médica.

1. César está enfermo. Tiene la temperatura alta. ¿Qué tiene?
2. ¿Adónde tiene que ir?
3. ¿Le da un examen físico el médico?
4. ¿Abre la boca César?
5. ¿Le examina la garganta el médico?
6. ¿Está roja la garganta?
7. ¿Tiene César dolor de garganta?
8. ¿Le duele mucho?

EXPANSIÓN

Ahora, sin mirar las preguntas, cuenta toda la información en tus propias palabras. Si no recuerdas algo, un(a) compañero(a) te puede ayudar.

LEER

3 Parea.

1. Es bien educado.
2. Es muy terco.
3. Tiene una sonrisa en la cara.
4. Tiene dolor de cabeza.
5. Él es perezoso.

a. Nunca trabaja.
b. Nunca presta atención.
c. Tiene buena conducta.
d. Está contento.
e. Le duele mucho.

HABLAR • ESCRIBIR

4 ¿Cuáles son todas las partes del cuerpo que puedes identificar en español? Usa la foto como guía.

5 **Comunicación**

Work with a classmate and discuss some traits or characteristics you look for in a good friend.

Conversación 🎧

¿Qué le pasa a Ana?

Enrique ¿Qué te pasa, Ana? Tienes la cara triste. ¿Estás enferma?

Ana Sí, me parece que sí. Tengo dolor de garganta y estoy muy cansada.

Enrique Pues, ¿por qué no vas a ver al médico?

Ana No, no tengo que ir al médico. Voy a tomar una siesta.

Enrique Eres muy terca, Ana. Debes ir al médico.

¿Comprendes?

A Contesta según la información en la conversación.

1. ¿Qué le pregunta Enrique a Ana?
2. ¿Cómo tiene la cara?
3. ¿Qué le duele a Ana?
4. ¿Está llena de energía?
5. ¿Debe ir a ver al médico?
6. ¿Va a ir?
7. ¿Qué va a tomar?
8. Según Enrique, ¿cómo es Ana?

B **Resumiendo** Resume toda la información en la conversación en tus propias palabras.

Gramática

Ser y estar

1. The verbs **ser** and **estar** both mean *to be.* **Ser** is used to tell where someone or something is from. It is also used to describe an inherent trait or characteristic.

> **Roberto es de Miami.**
> **Él es inteligente y guapo.**

2. **Estar** is used to tell where someone or something is located. It is also used to describe a temporary state or condition.

> **Roberto es de Miami pero ahora está en Madrid.**
> **Madrid está en España.**
> **Roberto está muy contento en Madrid.**

CULTURA

La Plaza Mayor en el centro del barrio viejo en Madrid.
La estatua de bronce que está en la plaza es de Felipe III.

Daniel Salsgiver

Repaso C

Práctica

HABLAR

1 Personaliza. Da respuestas personales.

1. ¿Estás en la escuela ahora?
2. ¿Dónde está la escuela?
3. ¿En qué clase estás?
4. ¿Está tu profesor(a) en clase también?
5. ¿Cómo es él o ella?
6. Y, ¿cómo es la clase de español?
7. ¿De dónde es el/la profesor(a)?
8. Y tú, ¿de dónde eres?
9. ¿Cómo estás hoy?

LEER • ESCRIBIR

2 Completa con **ser** o **estar**.

Ángel ___1___ de Caracas. Él ___2___ muy simpático. ___3___ gracioso también. Ahora Ángel ___4___ en Nueva York. ___5___ estudiante en la universidad allí. Ángel ___6___ muy contento en Nueva York.

Nueva York ___7___ en el nordeste de Estados Unidos. La Ciudad de Nueva York ___8___ muy grande y ___9___ muy interesante. A Ángel le gusta mucho Nueva York.

HABLAR • ESCRIBIR

3 Forma frases completas con **es** o **está**.

1. contento
2. de buen humor
3. serio
4. inteligente
5. lleno de energía
6. cansado
7. enfermo
8. estudioso
9. ambicioso
10. enojado

4 **Comunicación**

Tell some things about yourself. Where are you from? What kind of personality do you have? Are you a good student?

CULTURA

Una vista de los rascacielos y montañas en Caracas, la capital de Venezuela

El muchacho está contento y tiene una sonrisa agradable. Y es guapo, ¿no?

(t)Neil Beer/Getty Images. (b)moodboard/age fotostock

R26

REPASO C

Pronombres de complemento indirecto

Go Online!

connectED.mcgraw-hill.com

1. An indirect object is the indirect receiver of the action of a verb.

   El médico me da la receta.
   Yo le doy la receta al farmacéutico.

2. Review the indirect object pronouns.

me	nos
te	*os*
le	les

3. Since **le** and **les** can refer to different people they are often clarified with a prepositional phrase.

Le hablo {
  a él.
  a ella.
  a usted.
}

Les hablo {
  a ellos.
  a ellas.
  a ustedes.
}

Práctica

La muchacha les lee algo a los otros miembros de su clase de español. El profesor y los otros alumnos le prestan atención.

HABLAR

5 Personaliza. Da respuestas personales.
   1. ¿Te habla en español el/la profesor(a) de español?
   2. ¿Les da (a ustedes) muchos exámenes el/la profesor(a)?
   3. ¿Te envían correos electrónicos tus amigos?
   4. Cuando hablas, ¿te prestan atención tus amigos?

LEER • ESCRIBIR

6 Completa.
   1. _____ hablo casi todos los días a mis abuelos.
   2. _____ explico la lección a él.
   3. Guillermo _____ da un regalo a sus abuelos.
   4. La empleada _____ habla a sus clientes.
   5. Al pobre José _____ duele mucho la garganta.

7 *Comunicación*

Work with a classmate and describe people who have the following personality traits. Be creative!

Está lleno(a) de energía.	**Es dinámico(a) y ambicioso(a).**
Tiene mucha paciencia.	**Es bien educado(a).**
Es bastante perezoso(a).	**Siempre les enoja a sus amigos.**

Go Online!

connectED.mcgraw-hill.com

Audio

Video

Práctica

Repaso

Diversiones

eScape

ePals

Los deportes

Objetivos

In this chapter you will review:

- vocabulary related to sports
- the present tense of stem-changing verbs
- the verbs **aburrir, interesar, gustar**

◀ Estos jóvenes están jugando béisbol en un parque de La Habana, la capital de Cuba.

Vocabulario 🎧

Los dos equipos quieren ganar.
Pero no pueden.
Un equipo pierde.

Los dos equipos juegan (al) fútbol.
Empieza el segundo tiempo.
Los jugadores vuelven al campo de fútbol.

Es un partido de béisbol.
El jugador batea la pelota.
Luego corre de una base a otra.

(tl tr)Federico Gil, (b)PhotoLink/Getty Images

Práctica

ESCUCHAR • HABLAR

1 Contesta según se indica.

1. ¿Cuántos tiempos hay en un juego de fútbol? (dos)
2. ¿Cuántos jugadores hay en un equipo de fútbol? (once)
3. ¿Dónde juegan fútbol? (en el campo de fútbol)
4. ¿Quién guarda la portería? (el portero)
5. ¿Qué bloquea? (el balón)
6. ¿Quieren perder los dos equipos? (no, ganar)

LEER

2 **Cada uno en su sitio** Determina el deporte que cada frase describe.

1. El jugador lanza el balón con el pie.
2. Hay cinco jugadores en el equipo.
3. La pelota pasa por encima de la red.
4. El jugador corre de una base a otra.
5. Es un deporte de invierno.
6. El portero para o bloquea el balón.
7. El jugador tira el balón y encesta.
8. La jugadora usa una raqueta.

EL FÚTBOL	EL BÁSQUETBOL	EL BÉISBOL	EL TENIS	EL PATINAJE SOBRE EL HIELO

HABLAR

3 Personaliza. Da respuestas personales.

1. ¿Cuáles son los deportes que a ti te gustan?
2. ¿Cuáles son los comestibles que te gustan?
3. ¿Cuáles son los cursos que te interesan?
4. ¿Cuáles son algunas cosas que no te gustan, que te aburren?

4 **Juego** Work with a classmate. Give him or her some information about a sport. He or she has to guess what sport you're talking about. Take turns.

Conversación

Un partido importante

Tadeo   Isabel y Marta, ¿quieren ir al Café Selma?

Isabel   Gracias, Tadeo, pero no podemos. Queremos ver el partido.

Tadeo   ¿De qué partido hablas?

Isabel   El Real juega contra el Valencia.

Tadeo   ¿Cuál es tu equipo favorito? ¿Cuál te gusta más?

Isabel   Mi equipo favorito es el Real porque soy madrileña.

¿Comprendes?

Contesta según la información en la conversación.

1. ¿Adónde va Tadeo?
2. ¿Quieren ir con él Isabel y Marta?
3. ¿Por qué no pueden ir?
4. ¿Qué equipos juegan?
5. ¿Cuál es el equipo favorito de Isabel?

David H. Brennan

Gramática

Verbos de cambio radical

Go Online!

connectED.mcgraw-hill.com

1. Review the following forms of the stem-changing verbs. Remember that the **e** changes to **ie** in all forms except **nosotros(as)** and *vosotros(as).*

	empezar	perder
yo	empiezo	pierdo
tú	empiezas	pierdes
Ud., él, ella	empieza	pierde
nosotros(as)	empezamos	perdemos
vosotros(as)	*empezáis*	*perdéis*
Uds., ellos, ellas	empiezan	pierden

2. The following verbs change the **o** to **ue** in all forms except **nosotros(as)** and *vosotros(as).*

	volver	poder
yo	vuelvo	puedo
tú	vuelves	puedes
Ud., él, ella	vuelve	puede
nosotros(as)	volvemos	podemos
vosotros(as)	*volvéis*	*podéis*
Uds., ellos, ellas	vuelven	pueden

3. The verb **jugar** also has a stem change.

jugar			
yo	juego	nosotros(as)	jugamos
tú	juegas	*vosotros(as)*	*jugáis*
Ud., él, ella	juega	Uds., ellos, ellas	juegan

> ### Nota
>
> - Other verbs with the **e → ie** stem change like **empezar** and **perder** are: **sentarse, comenzar, pensar.**
> - Other **o → ue** verbs like **volver** and **poder** are: **acostarse, recordar, encontrar.**
> - **Sentir** is conjugated like **preferir.**

CULTURA

Los jóvenes juegan fútbol en una playa de Gijón, Asturias, en el norte de España.

Andrew Payti

Práctica

HABLAR • ESCRIBIR

1 Contesta.

1. ¿Quieres ir a la fiesta?
2. ¿Quieren ustedes bailar durante la fiesta?
3. ¿A qué hora empieza la fiesta?
4. ¿Puedes llegar a tiempo?
5. ¿Pueden ustedes tomar el bus a la fiesta?
6. ¿A qué hora vuelven ustedes a casa?

LEER • ESCRIBIR

2 Completa con la forma apropiada del verbo.

El juego de béisbol __1__ (empezar) a las tres y media.
Habla Teresa:

—Hoy yo __2__ (querer) ser la pícher.

La verdad es que Teresa __3__ (ser) una pícher muy
buena. Ella __4__ (jugar) muy bien. Nosotros __5__ (tener) un
equipo bueno. Todos nosotros __6__ (jugar) bien. Nuestro
equipo no __7__ (perder) mucho.

HABLAR

3 ¡Te toca a ti!

1. **Puedo...** Tell all that you can do.
2. **Quiero...** Tell all that you want to do.
3. **Quiero pero no puedo...** Tell all that you want to do
   but for some reason you cannot do.
4. **No quiero porque prefiero...** Tell something you don't
   want to do because you prefer to do something else.

4 ### Comunicación

Work with a classmate. Tell him or her what sport
you don't want to play because you don't like it. Tell
him or her what you prefer to play. Then ask your
classmate questions to find out what sports he or
she likes.

Una beisbolista que quiere ganar

Verbos como **aburrir, interesar** y **gustar**

1. The verbs **aburrir** and **interesar** function the same in Spanish and English.

¿Te aburre el arte?	*Does art bore you?*
¿Te aburren los deportes?	*Do sports bore you?*
No, los deportes me interesan.	*No, sports interest me.*

2. The verb **gustar** functions the same as **aburrir** and **interesar**. **Gustar** conveys the meaning *to like,* but it actually means *to be pleasing to.*

—**¿Te gusta el béisbol?**   —**¿Te gustan los deportes?**
—**Sí, me gusta mucho.**   —**Sí, me gustan.**

¿Te gustan
los camarones?

ESCUCHAR • HABLAR

5 Sigue el modelo.

 MODELO   **¿A mí? ¿Los tomates? →**
          —Me gustan mucho los tomates.
          Y, ¿a ti te gustan también?

1. ¿A mí? ¿El pescado?
2. ¿A mí? ¿Los vegetales?
3. ¿A mí? ¿La carne?
4. ¿A mí? ¿El jamón?
5. ¿A mí? ¿Los mariscos?

¿Te gustan
los mejillones?

HABLAR • ESCRIBIR

6 Personaliza. Da respuestas personales.

1. ¿Te interesan o te aburren las matemáticas? ¿Te gustan o no?
2. ¿Te interesa o te aburre la historia? ¿Te gusta o no?
3. ¿Te interesan o te aburren las ciencias? ¿Te gustan o no?
4. ¿Te interesa o te aburre la literatura? ¿Te gusta o no?
5. ¿Te interesa o te aburre la geografía? ¿Te gusta o no?

7 **Comunicación**

Work with a classmate. Tell him or her about your favorite team. Tell all about the sport and tell why you really like this team in particular. Then ask your classmate about his or her favorite team. Do you by chance have the same favorite team?

CULTURA

Los jóvenes celebran la victoria de su equipo. Marchan por una calle de Madrid.

(t)Getty Images/Jonelle Weaver, (c)Spike Mafford/Getty Images, (b)Corbis/age fotostock

Audio Video Práctica Repaso Diversiones eScape

ePals

De compras

Objetivos

In this chapter you will review:

- vocabulary related to shopping for food and clothing
- the verbs **saber** and **conocer**
- comparatives and superlatives

◀ Una vista del Mercado Central de Valencia, España. En el mercado hay puestos donde se vende todo tipo de comestibles—legumbres, frutas, carnes, pescado, mariscos. ¡Y todo está muy fresco!

Vocabulario 🎧

Una tienda de ropa

una blusa

una chaqueta

una camisa de manga larga

una falda

un pantalón largo

un par de zapatos

40

el número

Para conversar

¿Qué te parece?
¿Me queda bien?

No. Te queda grande.
¿No sabes tu talla?

No.

Un mercado

las zanahorias

el maíz

los guisantes

las judías verdes

las papas (patatas)

los plátanos

los tomates

las manzanas

las naranjas

Hay muchos puestos en el mercado.
La señora conoce a la vendedora.
En el mercado venden frutas y legumbres.
Las frutas y legumbres son más baratas en
   el mercado que en el supermercado.
Cuestan menos.

Práctica

HABLAR

1 Personaliza. Da respuestas personales.

1. ¿Qué llevas a la escuela?
2. ¿Prefieres una camisa o una blusa de mangas largas o de mangas cortas?
3. ¿Llevas un pantalón corto en verano o en invierno?
4. Cuando compras ropa, ¿cuáles son tus colores favoritos?
5. Si necesitas una camiseta, ¿qué talla usas?
6. Si necesitas zapatos, ¿qué número calzas?
7. ¿Te sale todo más barato o más caro cuando una tienda tiene una liquidación?

CULTURA

El escaparate de una tienda de ropa en Valencia, España

HABLAR • ESCRIBIR

2 Completa una tabla como la de abajo. ¡A ver cuántas palabras recuerdas o sabes!

ropa	colores	frutas	vegetales

Andrew Payti

LEER

3 Escoge la palabra apropiada.

1. En un mercado indígena hay muchos (puestos, carritos).
2. Los clientes conocen a los vendedores en el (supermercado, mercado).
3. En el supermercado los clientes llenan (un bote, un carrito) con todas sus compras.
4. —¿Quieres algo más?
   —No, (algo, nada) más, gracias.
5. Las sandalias y cerámicas son ejemplos de (utensilios domésticos, artesanía).

HABLAR • ESCRIBIR

4 Parea los antónimos.

1. blanco	**a.** barato
2. largo	**b.** aburrir
3. interesar	**c.** corto
4. algo	**d.** comprar
5. clientes	**e.** negro
6. caro	**f.** invierno
7. verano	**g.** nada
8. vender	**h.** empleados

LEER • ESCRIBIR

5 Completa con la palabra apropiada.

1. _____ de atún
2. _____ de agua mineral
3. _____ de zanahorias congeladas
4. _____ de mayonesa

6 *Comunicación*

 Work with a classmate. Discuss whether or not you like to go shopping for clothes. Also discuss the type of clothing you like and dislike. What's your favorite outfit? Do you know what size you wear?

¡Mira lo que acabo de comprar!

Elena acaba de comprar una camiseta. ¿Qué piensas?
¿A Antonio le gusta la camiseta?

Glowimages/age fotostock

Conversación 🎧

En una tienda de ropa

¿Comprendes?

A Contesta según la información en la conversación.

1. ¿Dónde está Jorge?
2. ¿Con quién va de compras?
3. ¿Qué quiere comprar Jorge?
4. ¿Necesita una talla más grande o más pequeña?
5. ¿Qué color prefiere Mariluz?
6. ¿Tienen una chaqueta en la talla que necesita Jorge?
7. ¿Cuánto cuesta?

B **Llegando a conclusiones** ¿Qué piensas? ¿Compra Jorge la chaqueta o no? ¿Por qué?

Gramática

Saber y conocer

1. The verbs **saber** and **conocer** both mean *to know*. Like many Spanish verbs, they have an irregular **yo** form in the present tense. All other forms are regular.

saber			
yo	sé	nosotros(as)	sabemos
tú	sabes	*vosotros(as)*	*sabéis*
Ud., él, ella	sabe	Uds., ellos, ellas	saben

conocer			
yo	conozco	nosotros(as)	conocemos
tú	conoces	*vosotros(as)*	*conocéis*
Ud., él, ella	conoce	Uds., ellos, ellas	conocen

2. The verb **saber** means *to know a fact* or *to have information about something*. It also means *to know how to do something.*

> **Yo sé donde está el mercado.**
> **No sabemos a qué hora sale el vuelo.**
> **Ellos saben regatear.**

3. The verb **conocer** means *to know* in the sense of *to be acquainted with*. It is used to talk about people and complex or abstract concepts rather than simple facts.

> **Yo conozco a Luis.**
> **Ella conoce a su hermano.**
> **Los alumnos conocen bien la literatura mexicana.**

Andrew Payti

CULTURA •
Estos jóvenes saben disfrutar de sus momentos libres jugando un juego espontáneo de fútbol en una playa de Puerto Madryn, Argentina.

Práctica

HABLAR • ESCRIBIR

1 Personaliza. Da respuestas personales.

1. ¿Sabes el número que calzas?
2. ¿Sabes la talla que usas cuando compras ropa?
3. ¿Sabes el número del celular de tu mejor amigo(a)?
4. ¿Sabes su dirección de correo electrónico también?
5. ¿Conoces a la familia de tu mejor amigo(a)?
6. ¿Conoces la cultura hispana?

HABLAR

2 Trabajen en grupos de tres. Indiquen todo lo que saben hacer.

HABLAR • ESCRIBIR

3 Completa cada frase con **saber** o **conocer.**

1. Yo _____ la palabra.
2. Nosotros _____ a María.
3. Carlos _____ esquiar.
4. Ellos _____ la lección.
5. Yo _____ leer.
6. ¿_____ tú a Enrique?
7. Ella _____ el arte de México.
8. Nosotros _____ que París es la capital de Francia.

ESCRIBIR

4 Escribe frases originales.

1. yo / saber…
2. y ellos / saber…
3. tú / conocer…
4. y nosotros / conocer…

5 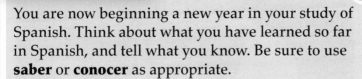 *Comunicación*

You are now beginning a new year in your study of Spanish. Think about what you have learned so far in Spanish, and tell what you know. Be sure to use **saber** or **conocer** as appropriate.

CULTURA

Los clientes saben que todo lo que se vende en esta tienda del Mercado Central en Valencia está fresco. Ellos conocen a la empleada.

Andrew Payti

Comparativo y superlativo

1. To form the comparative in Spanish you put **más** or **menos** before the adjective or adverb and **que** after it.

> **Ella es más (menos) ambiciosa que su hermana.**
> **Ella es más (menos) ambiciosa que yo y la verdad es que ella sabe más (menos) que nadie.**

Note that after **que** you use subject pronouns (**yo, tú,** etc.) or **nadie.**

2. You form the superlative by using the appropriate definite article plus **más** or **menos** and the adjective or adverb. The preposition **de** follows the superlative.

> **Es el joven más (menos) inteligente del grupo.**
> **Es el más (menos) inteligente del grupo.**

3. Study the following irregular comparative and superlative forms.

COMPARATIVE		SUPERLATIVE	
bueno	**mejor**	**el/la mejor**	**los/las mejores**
malo	**peor**	**el/la peor**	**los/las peores**
bien	**mejor**		
mal	**peor**		

> **Esta chaqueta te queda mejor que las otras.**
> **Elena es la mejor alumna de la clase.**

4. The adjectives **mayor** and **menor** most often refer to age.

> **Yo soy menor que mi hermana.**
> **Yo soy el/la menor de la familia.**
> **Mi abuelo es el mayor.**

Comparaciones

El inglés

To form the comparative in English, you add -er to short adjectives or adverbs. You put *more* before longer adjectives or adverbs.

> *He is smarter than the others.*
> *She is more intelligent than the others.*

To form the superlative in English, you add -est to short adjectives or adverbs and you put *most* before longer ones.

> *This is the largest size.*
> *This is the most popular color.*

Según Teresa, el libro que ella tiene es más interesante que los libros que tiene Paco.

Práctica

HABLAR • ESCRIBIR

6 Compara.

1. tu clase de español y tu clase de inglés
2. el equipo de fútbol y el equipo de béisbol
3. tu mejor amigo(a) y tu hermano(a)
4. tu escuela secundaria y tu escuela primaria

HABLAR • ESCRIBIR

7 Forma frases según el modelo.

MODELO **inteligente**
José / Carlos / Diego →
José es inteligente. Carlos es más inteligente
que José y Diego es el más inteligente de
los tres.

1. graciosa
Julia / Eva / Carla
2. simpático
Enrique / Tadeo / Alfonso
3. interesante
el curso de biología / el curso de historia / el curso
de español

HABLAR • ESCRIBIR

8 Personaliza. Da respuestas personales.

1. ¿Quiénes en tu familia son mayores que tú?
2. Y, ¿quiénes son menores?
3. ¿Quién es el/la menor de tu familia?
¿Quién es el/la mayor?
4. ¿En qué curso sacas la mejor nota?
5. ¿En qué curso sacas la peor nota?

HABLAR

9 **Juego** Work in groups of four. Create a
sentence that compares two people or things.
Have your classmates guess who or what you
are comparing. Take turns.

CULTURA
Unas muchachas en un bote de remos en el
lago de Nicaragua—el lago de agua dulce
(freshwater) más grande de Nicaragua

Andrew Payti

De vacaciones

Objetivos

In this chapter you will review:

- vocabulary related to summer resorts and activities

- vocabulary related to winter resorts and activities

- the preterite of regular verbs

- the preterite of **ir** and **ser**

- direct and indirect object pronouns

◀ Mucha gente está disfrutando de un día soleado en la playa de Gijón en Asturias. Aquí el agua del mar Cantábrico está un poco fría.

Vocabulario 🎧

Raúl pasó el verano en la playa.
Nadó en el mar.

Tomó el sol.
Volvió a casa muy bronceado.

Susana pasó una semana en una estación
  de esquí.
Tomó el telesilla para subir la montaña.
Subió en el telesilla.

Ella bajó la pista para expertos.
No bajó la pista para principiantes.

Práctica

HABLAR • ESCRIBIR

1 Contesta sobre un día en la playa.

1. ¿Fue Francisco a la playa?
2. ¿Nadó en el mar?
3. ¿Esquió en el agua?
4. ¿Tomó el sol?
5. ¿Volvió a casa muy bronceado?

EXPANSIÓN

Ahora, sin mirar las preguntas, cuenta toda la información en tus propias palabras. Si no recuerdas algo, un(a) compañero(a) te puede ayudar.

CULTURA

Esquiadores en Portillo, Chile

HABLAR • ESCRIBIR

2 Contesta sobre una estación de esquí.

1. ¿Fueron a una estación de esquí los amigos?
2. ¿Salieron ellos muy temprano por la mañana?
3. ¿Pasaron el día entero en las pistas?
4. ¿Subieron la montaña en el telesilla?
5. ¿Bajaron la pista para expertos o para principiantes?
6. ¿Volvieron a casa el mismo día?

EXPANSIÓN

Ahora, sin mirar las preguntas, cuenta toda la información en tus propias palabras. Si no recuerdas algo, un(a) compañero(a) te puede ayudar.

3 *Comunicación*

Work with a classmate. Look at these photos. Tell where you prefer to go and why. Take turns.

Conversación

¿Adónde fueron los amigos?

Nando   ¿Adónde fuiste ayer, Teresa?
Teresa   Fui a casa de Sofi.
Nando   ¿Y… ?
Teresa   Jugamos tenis.
Nando   ¿Tiene Sofi una cancha de tenis?
Teresa   No. Hay canchas en un parque cerca de su casa.
            Pero Sofi tiene una piscina.
Nando   ¿Sí? ¿Nadaron ustedes?
Teresa   Sí, nadamos después de jugar tenis.

¿Comprendes?

Usa una tabla como la de abajo para indicar si la información
es correcta o no.

	correcta	incorrecta
1. Nando fue con Teresa a casa de Sofi.		
2. La casa de Sofi tiene una cancha de tenis.		
3. Teresa y Sofi jugaron tenis.		
4. Jugaron en una cancha en un parque.		
5. Nadaron también.		
6. Nadaron en una piscina en el parque.		

Gramática

El pretérito

1. Review the forms of the preterite of regular verbs.

	nadar	comer	subir
yo	nadé	comí	subí
tú	nadaste	comiste	subiste
Ud., él, ella	nadó	comió	subió
nosotros(as)	nadamos	comimos	subimos
vosotros(as)	*nadasteis*	*comisteis*	*subisteis*
Uds., ellos, ellas	nadaron	comieron	subieron

Note that **-er** and **-ir** verbs have the same endings in the preterite.

2. The forms of the verbs **ir** and **ser** are the same in the preterite. The meaning is made clear by the context of the sentence.

ir, ser		
yo fui	nosotros(as)	fuimos
tú fuiste	*vosotros(as)*	*fuisteis*
Ud., él, ella fue	Uds., ellos, ellas	fueron

3. The preterite is used to express an event or action that began and ended at a definite time in the past.

> **Ellos pasaron el verano pasado en México.**
> **Fueron a Acapulco.**

4. Note the forms of the verbs **ver** and **dar.**

VER	vi	viste	vio	vimos	*visteis*	vieron
DAR	di	diste	dio	dimos	*disteis*	dieron

InfoGap For more practice with the preterite, do Activity R in the Student Resource section at the end of this book.

CULTURA

Ellos pasaron el verano pasado en México y fueron a la Ciudad de México.

Andrew Payti

Práctica

1 Personaliza. Da respuestas personales.

1. ¿Fuiste a la escuela ayer?
2. ¿A qué hora llegaste a la escuela?
3. ¿Hablaste con el/la profesor(a) de español?
4. ¿Tomaste un examen?
5. ¿En qué curso tomaste el examen?
6. ¿Saliste bien en el examen?
7. ¿Comiste en la cafetería de la escuela?
8. ¿A qué hora volviste a casa?

2 Contesta.

1. ¿Fuiste al cine ayer?
   ¿Viste una película?
   ¿Tomaste un refresco en el cine?
2. ¿Salieron ustedes anoche?
   ¿Fueron a una fiesta?
   ¿Bailaron y cantaron durante la fiesta?
3. ¿Esquió Sandra?
   ¿Subió la montaña en el telesilla?
   ¿Bajó la pista para expertos?
4. ¿Pasaron los amigos el fin de semana en la playa?
   ¿Te escribieron una tarjeta postal?
   ¿Nadaron y esquiaron en el agua?

Comunicación

3 Tell what you and your friends did last Friday night.

4 Tell what you did last night.

5 Tell what you or you and your family or friends did during your last vacation.

CULTURA

Una escuela de esquí y snowboard en la estación de esquí en Cerro Catedral en Bariloche, Argentina

Andrew Payti

Los pronombres de complemento

1. The object pronouns **me, te,** and **nos** can be either direct or indirect objects. Note that the object pronoun precedes the conjugated verb.

DIRECT
Él me miró.
¿Te invitó Carlos?
Ella nos vio.

INDIRECT
Él me habló por teléfono.
¿Te dio una invitación?
Mónica nos envió algo.

2. Lo, los, la, and **las** function as direct objects only. They can replace either persons or things.

Pablo compró el boleto.   **Pablo lo compró.**

Pablo compró los boletos.   **Pablo los compró.**

Teresa compró la raqueta.   **Teresa la compró.**

Teresa compró las raquetas.   **Teresa las compró.**

Yo vi a los muchachos.   **Yo los vi.**

3. Le and **les** function as indirect objects only.

Yo le escribí un correo electrónico (a él, a ella, a usted).
Yo les escribí (a ellos, a ellas, a ustedes).

Práctica

HABLAR

6 Contesta.

1. ¿Fuiste al médico?
2. ¿Te habló el médico?
3. ¿Te examinó?
4. ¿Te dio una diagnosis?
5. ¿Te recetó medicina?

ESCUCHAR • HABLAR

7 Sigue el modelo.

MODELO   **la toalla** →
               Aquí la tienes.

1. el anorak
2. la crema bronceadora
3. el traje de baño
4. los anteojos de sol
5. los boletos para el telesilla
6. las raquetas

LEER • ESCRIBIR

8 Completa con **le, lo** o **la.**

Pepe está en el consultorio del médico. Pepe __1__ explica al médico que __2__ duele el estómago. El médico __3__ examina. __4__ da una receta. En la farmacia el farmacéutico __5__ lee y __6__ da los medicamentos a Pepe.

CULTURA
Una farmacia en Baños, Ecuador

Go Online!

connectED.mcgraw-hill.com

Audio

Video

Práctica

Repaso

Diversiones

eScape

ePals

Aquí y Allí

Vamos a comparar Los medios de transporte más importantes varían de una región del mundo a otra. En España, por ejemplo, el servicio de trenes es excelente. No lo es en Latinoamérica donde mucha gente toma un autobús para ir de un lugar a otro. Pero vas a aprender por qué el avión es el medio de transporte más importante. Donde tú vives, ¿qué medios de transporte público hay? ¿Tienen muchos usuarios?

Objetivos

You will:

- talk about packing for a trip and getting to the airport
- tell what you do at the airport
- talk about being on an airplane
- discuss air travel in South America

You will use:

- verbs that have **g** in the **yo** form of the present tense
- the present progressive tense

◀ El avión está despegando de la pista del aeropuerto de La Romana en la República Dominicana.

¡PARE!
BARRERA AUTOMATIC
CARROS DE GOLF SOLAM
DESDE ESTE PUNTO

En avión

Look at these photographs to acquaint yourself with the theme of this chapter. Air travel is the most important means of transportation in the world today. As you learn to use your Spanish in an airport and on an airplane, you will also learn why air travel is so extremely important in Latin America.

Estados Unidos 🇺🇸

Aquí vemos una pantalla de salidas. ¿Para qué ciudades latinoamericanas hay vuelos?

Perú 🇬🇹

¡Qué bienvenida más simpática reciben los pasajeros que llegan al aeropuerto de Arequipa en el sur de Perú!

España 🔺

Pasajeros en el nuevo aeropuerto de Barajas en Madrid

Guatemala 🇬🇹

El mostrador de una línea aérea centroamericana en el aeropuerto de la Ciudad de Guatemala. Es de noche y hay muy poca gente.

Perú 🇵🇪

El avión está en el aeropuerto de Arequipa en el sur de Perú. En el fondo vemos los Andes.

Argentina 🇦🇷

Es una experiencia aterrizar o despegar en el aeropuerto de Ushuaia debido a la proximidad del mar, las montañas y los vientos fuertes que a veces son casi violentos.

Perú 🇵🇪

De esta parte del aeropuerto Jorge Chávez de Lima salen y llegan los vuelos que sirven a las otras ciudades y pueblos de Perú.
En la mayoría de los países se llaman «vuelos nacionales», pero a veces se oye «vuelos internos» o «vuelos domésticos». En Argentina son «vuelos de cabotaje».

Antes de salir para el aeropuerto 🎧

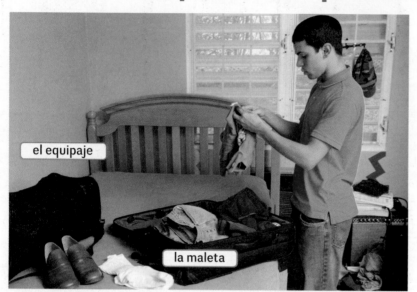

el equipaje

la maleta

Juan va a hacer un viaje.
Antes hace la maleta.
¿Qué pone en la maleta?

Pone la ropa que necesita
para el viaje.

¿Te acuerdas?

You will want to be able to discuss packing a suitcase. To review summer and winter clothing, see Repaso E.

Al aeropuerto

el baúl, la maletera

el taxi

Juan sale para el aeropuerto en taxi.
Trae su equipaje.

Pone su equipaje en la maletera del taxi.
El taxista lo ayuda con su equipaje.

David H. Brennan

En el aeropuerto

Nueva Generación de asientos de clase ejecutiva en el 767

AA

el boleto (billete) electrónico

el agente

el mostrador

Su tarjeta de embarque sale de un distribuidor automático.

la tarjeta de embarque

AEROMEXICO
aeromexico.com

el nombre del pasajero

NOMBRE/NAME
PAYTI/ANDREWMR
ORIGEN/ORIGIN
MEXICO CITY
DESTINO/DESTINATION
OAXACA

el número del vuelo

VUELO/FLIGHT CLASE FECHA/DATE
AM 2046 L 04JUN07
SALA/GATE HORA/TIME ASIENTO/SEA
-7A 1140
NON-SMOKING 5C
CONTROL 28
FTKT 704

la hora de salida

el número del asiento

Juan está en el mostrador de la línea aérea.
Está haciendo un viaje internacional en avión.
Tiene que facturar su equipaje.
Pero no tiene que facturar su equipaje de mano.

ESCUCHAR

1 Escucha las frases. Parea cada frase con el dibujo que describe.

a.   b.   c.

d.   e.   f.

CULTURA 🇲🇽

La señora está en el mostrador de la línea aérea. Va a volar a México.

HABLAR • ESCRIBIR

2 Contesta sobre un viaje que Teresa va a hacer a México.

1. ¿Hace Teresa un viaje a México?
2. Antes de hacer su viaje, ¿qué pone en la maleta?
3. ¿Para dónde sale Teresa para empezar su viaje?
4. ¿Cómo va al aeropuerto?
5. ¿Quién la ayuda con su equipaje?
6. ¿Dónde lo pone?

EXPANSIÓN

Ahora, sin mirar las preguntas, relata toda la información en tus propias palabras. Si no recuerdas algo, un(a) compañero(a) te puede ayudar.

LEER • ESCRIBIR

3 Elisa está en el aeropuerto. Va a las Galápagos. Completa con una palabra apropiada.

1. En el aeropuerto Elisa tiene que _____ su equipaje.
2. Va al mostrador de la _____.
3. Elisa tiene un _____ electrónico.
4. El agente le da su _____ para poder abordar el avión.

CULTURA

Una vista de las islas Galápagos, Ecuador

LEER • ESCRIBIR

4 Completa. Escoge del **banco de palabras.**

pone	sale	trae	hace

1. Eduardo _____ un viaje a España.
2. Él _____ su ropa en la maleta.
3. Eduardo no _____ mucho equipaje.
4. _____ solamente una maleta y una mochila.
5. _____ el equipaje en la maletera del taxi.
6. _____ para el aeropuerto.
7. Su vuelo para España _____ a las ocho y media de la tarde.

InfoGap For more practice using your new vocabulary, do Activity 1 in the Student Resource section at the end of the book.

HABLAR • ESCRIBIR

5 Prepara una pregunta sobre cada frase en la Actividad 4. Usa las siguientes palabras.

¿quién? ¿cuándo?
¿adónde? ¿qué? ¿dónde?

LEER • ESCRIBIR

6 Completa la tarjeta de embarque.

7 **Rompecabezas**

Unscramble the letters to reveal words related to airplane travel.

1. a l t a m e
2. n o t i s e a
3. j a q u e p i e
4. r a d o r o m t s
5. s o a r j e p a

En el control de seguridad 🎧

hacer cola

el pasaporte

Los pasajeros están pasando por el control de seguridad.
Su equipaje de mano tiene que pasar por el control de seguridad.
Hay que mostrar una forma de identidad con una fotografía.

En la puerta de salida

¡Así se dice!

- **Hay que** is a useful expression that means **Es necesario.**
- **A veces** and **de vez en cuando** are expressions to tell what you do every so often.

La pasajera está en la puerta de salida.
Está esperando la salida de su vuelo.
El avión está saliendo a tiempo. No sale tarde.
No hay un retraso (una demora).
Ella va a embarcar (abordar) dentro de poco.

David H. Brennan

A bordo del avión

el compartimiento superior

el servicio

la ventanilla

el asistente de vuelo

el pasillo

abrochados

el cinturón de seguridad

el asiento

la señal de no fumar

la máscara de oxígeno

Los pasajeros tienen que poner su equipaje de mano en el compartimiento superior o debajo del asiento.

Durante el despegue y el aterrizaje, los pasajeros tienen que tener sus cinturones abrochados.

el despegue

El avión está despegando.
Está despegando con destino a Madrid.
El avión acaba de despegar de la pista.

el aterrizaje

El avión está aterrizando.
Es un vuelo (procedente) de Lima.

(t)David H. Brennan, (bl br)Andrew Payti

ESCUCHAR • HABLAR • ESCRIBIR

1 Personaliza. Da respuestas personales.

1. ¿Tomas un vuelo de vez en cuando?
2. ¿Te gusta volar?
3. ¿Quieres tomar un vuelo un día?
4. ¿Quieres hacer un viaje nacional o internacional?
5. ¿Adónde quieres ir?
6. ¿Hay un aeropuerto cerca de tu casa? ¿Cuál?
7. ¿Es un aeropuerto nacional o internacional?
8. Si tienes que tomar un vuelo, ¿prefieres un asiento en el pasillo o en la ventanilla?

LEER

2 Escoge la palabra apropiada.

1. Los pasajeros hacen cola en (el asiento, la puerta) de salida.
2. Están (esperando, haciendo) la salida del vuelo.
3. El avión sale con un retraso de cinco minutos. Sale (tarde, a tiempo).
4. Los pasajeros toman su (pasillo, asiento) en el avión.
5. El avión despega de la (cola, pista).
6. Un vuelo (procedente de, con destino a) Panamá llega ahora.

LEER

3 Verifica. ¿Sí o no?

1. Los pasajeros tienen que pasar por el control de seguridad a bordo del avión.
2. Los pasajeros esperan la salida de su vuelo en la puerta de salida.
3. Los pasajeros embarcan después del aterrizaje.
4. Los pasajeros desembarcan después del aterrizaje.
5. Los pasajeros pueden poner su equipaje en el pasillo.
6. Los pasajeros tienen que tener sus cinturones de seguridad abrochados durante el despegue y el aterrizaje.
7. Un vuelo que sale tarde sale a tiempo.
8. En una cola o fila hay mucha gente.

CULTURA

Una señora aborda una avioneta en el aeropuerto de San José, Costa Rica.

Richard Brommer

4 ▸ **Comunicación**

Habla con un(a) compañero(a). Discutan todo lo que necesitan si hacen un viaje internacional.

LEER • ESCRIBIR

5 Pon las actividades en orden.

Llega al aeropuerto.

Toma su asiento.

Pone su ropa en la maleta.

Factura su equipaje y toma su tarjeta de embarque.

Sale de casa para ir al aeropuerto.

Espera el avión en la puerta de salida.

Pone su equipaje en la maletera del taxi.

Pasa por el control de seguridad.

Embarca en el avión.

El avión despega.

6 ▸ **Comunicación**

You are flying to Mexico to visit your key pal. You have never flown before. Once on the plane, you have some questions for the flight attendant (your partner) about the flight and where to put your things. Take turns.

7 ◗ **¡Manos a la obra!** Make up a name for a Spanish airline. Create a fun and colorful travel poster advertising the airline and where it flies. See how many new words you can include.

Andrew Payti

Presente de hacer, poner, traer, salir

1. The verbs **hacer** *(to do, to make)*, **poner** *(to put, to place)*, **traer** *(to bring)*, and **salir** *(to leave)* have an irregular **yo** form. The **yo** form has a **g**. All the other forms are regular.

	hacer	poner	traer	salir
yo	hago	pongo	traigo	salgo
tú	haces	pones	traes	sales
Ud., él, ella	hace	pone	trae	sale
nosotros(as)	hacemos	ponemos	traemos	salimos
vosotros(as)	hacéis	ponéis	traéis	salís
Uds., ellos, ellas	hacen	ponen	traen	salen

2. Remember that the verb **tener** has a **g** in the **yo** form. The verb **venir** *(to come)* follows the same pattern. Note the **g** and the stem change.

venir			
yo	vengo	nosotros(as)	venimos
tú	vienes	vosotros(as)	venís
Ud., él, ella	viene	Uds., ellos, ellas	vienen

CULTURA

Las señoritas tienen equipaje porque van a hacer un viaje de Puerto Rico a Nueva York. Salen pronto pero antes toman un refresco en un café en San Juan.

Rebecca Smith

Práctica

Go Online!

connectED.mcgraw-hill.com

HABLAR • ESCRIBIR

1 Imagina que vas a hacer un viaje a Ecuador. Contesta las preguntas.

1. ¿Haces un viaje?
2. ¿Haces un viaje a Ecuador?
3. ¿Haces el viaje con un grupo de tu escuela?
4. ¿Sales para el aeropuerto con tus padres?
5. ¿Traes mucho equipaje?
6. ¿Traes tu cámara digital?
7. ¿Pones tu boleto y tu pasaporte en tu mochila?

EXPANSIÓN

Ahora, sin mirar las preguntas, relata toda la información en tus propias palabras. Si no recuerdas algo, un(a) compañero(a) te puede ayudar.

CULTURA

La Plaza de Armas en el casco antiguo de Quito, Ecuador

HABLAR • ESCRIBIR

2 Personaliza. Da respuestas personales.

Cuando haces un viaje a la playa donde hace calor, ¿qué pones en la maleta? Y cuando haces un viaje a una estación de esquí, ¿qué pones en la maleta?

ESCUCHAR • HABLAR • ESCRIBIR

3 Sigue el modelo. Presta atención a las terminaciones **-emos, -imos.**

MODELO **Ellos hacen un viaje. →**
Sí, ellos hacen un viaje y nosotros también hacemos un viaje.

1. Ellos hacen un viaje a España.
2. Ellos salen para el aeropuerto.
3. Ellos traen mucho equipaje.
4. Ellos salen en el mismo vuelo.
5. Ellos vienen al aeropuerto en autobús.

Richard Brommer

LEER • ESCRIBIR

4 Completa con la forma correcta del presente del verbo. Ahora tienes que usar todas las formas.

Yo __1__ (hacer) un viaje a Palma. Palma __2__ (estar) en la isla de Mallorca en el Mediterráneo. __3__ (Estar) al este de España no muy lejos de Barcelona. Mi amiga Luisa __4__ (hacer) el viaje también. Nosotros __5__ (hacer) el viaje en avión hasta Barcelona y luego __6__ (ir) en barco, un ferry, desde Barcelona a Palma. Claro que podemos __7__ (hacer) el viaje en avión pero preferimos tomar el barco.

—¡Ay, Luisa! Pero tú __8__ (traer) mucho equipaje.

—No, yo no __9__ (traer) mucho. __10__ (Tener) solo dos maletas. Tú exageras. Tú también __11__ (venir) con mucho equipaje.

—¡Oye! ¿A qué hora __12__ (salir) nuestro vuelo para Barcelona?

—No __13__ (salir) hasta las seis y media. Nosotros __14__ (tener) mucho tiempo.

—¡Vamos ya! ¡Con permiso, señora!

5 *Comunicación*

Tell a friend all the things you do the day of a flight from packing your suitcase to boarding the plane. Your friend will then ask you questions.

HABLAR

6 **Juego** Play this **Diez preguntas** game with a partner. Think of something related to airline travel for your partner to guess. If your partner guesses in ten questions or less, he or she wins. Take turns.

CULTURA
Una playa en Palma de Mallorca. Mallorca es una de las islas Baleares en el mar Mediterráneo.

El presente progresivo

1. You use the present progressive tense in Spanish to express an action in progress, an action that is currently taking place.

2. To form the present progressive you use the verb **estar** and the present participle. Study the forms of the present participle.

INFINITIVE	hablar	comer	vivir	hacer	salir
STEM	habl-	com-	viv-	hac-	sal-
PARTICIPLE	hablando	comiendo	viviendo	haciendo	saliendo

The verbs **leer, traer, oír,** and **caer** have a **y.**

leyendo   trayendo   oyendo   cayendo

3. Study the following examples of the present progressive.

José está haciendo un viaje a México.
Ahora está esperando la salida de su vuelo.
José está mirando su tarjeta de embarque.

CULTURA

Una pantalla de llegadas y salidas en el aeropuerto de la Ciudad de Guatemala. Hace buen tiempo hoy y la mayoría de los vuelos salen a tiempo. ¡Qué suerte para todos!

Práctica

ESCUCHAR • HABLAR

7 Con un(a) compañero(a), practica la conversación en voz alta. Presta atención a todos los verbos en el tiempo progresivo.

Sandra, ¡qué sorpresa! ¿Qué estás haciendo aquí en el aeropuerto?

Estoy esperando a mi padre. Está volviendo de Puerto Rico. ¿Y tú, Julia? ¿Qué estás haciendo aquí?

Pues, estoy viajando a Costa Rica.

¡A Costa Rica! ¡Qué suerte tienes!

Sí, toda mi familia está haciendo el viaje para visitar a nuestros abuelos.

Ah, tus abuelos son de Costa Rica.

No, no. Son de aquí pero ahora están viviendo en Costa Rica. Les gusta mucho.

HABLAR • ESCRIBIR

8 Contesta según la conversación.

1. ¿Por qué está en el aeropuerto Sandra?
2. ¿De dónde está volviendo el padre de Sandra?
3. Y, ¿para dónde está saliendo Julia?
4. ¿Quién está viajando con ella?
5. ¿A quiénes van a visitar?
6. ¿Qué están haciendo sus abuelos en Costa Rica?

EXPANSIÓN

Ahora, sin mirar las preguntas, relata toda la información en tus propias palabras. Si no recuerdas algo, un(a) compañero(a) te puede ayudar.

David H. Brennan

ESCUCHAR • HABLAR • ESCRIBIR

 Contesta según se indica.

1. ¿Adónde están llegando los pasajeros? (al aeropuerto)
2. ¿Cómo están llegando? (en taxi)
3. ¿Adónde están viajando? (a Argentina en la América del Sur)
4. ¿Cómo están haciendo el viaje? (en avión)
5. ¿Dónde están facturando el equipaje? (en el mostrador de la línea aérea)
6. ¿Qué está mirando el agente? (los boletos y los pasaportes)
7. ¿De qué puerta están saliendo los pasajeros para Buenos Aires? (número siete)
8. ¿Qué están abordando? (el avión)

 ## *Comunicación*

Use the conversation between Julia and Sandra as a guide to role-play a conversation between two friends who run into each other at an airport. Be sure to use gestures and other nonverbal communication in your conversation.

CULTURA

La Casa Rosada en Buenos Aires. Es aquí donde tiene el presidente argentino sus oficinas.

Richard Brommer

SINGLE PICTURE FRAME
See the Foldables section of the Student Handbook at the beginning of this book for help with making this foldable. Work in groups. Each member of the group will make a foldable with a drawing (or magazine picture) related to airplane travel. Create a story about each picture by passing the picture around, with each person adding a sentence in the present progressive. An alternative would be to do this same activity as a writing activity.

HABLAR • ESCRIBIR

11 Forma frases según el modelo. Escoge palabras del **banco de palabras**.

MODELO   viajar →
   Sí, estoy viajando.
   No, no estoy viajando.

hablar español	usar mi móvil	hacer una tarea
leer una novela	estudiar	jugar fútbol
aprender mucho	salir ahora	comer

HABLAR

12 **Juego** Form small groups. Take turns pantomiming activities that might take place at an airport or on an airplane. The others will guess what you're doing, using the present progressive.

HABLAR • ESCRIBIR

13 Describe lo que ves en los dibujos. Usa el presente progresivo.

PRONUNCIACIÓN

La consonante r

When a word begins with **r** (initial position), the **r** is trilled in Spanish. Within a word, this trilled **r** sound is spelled **rr.** The Spanish trilled **r** sound does not exist in English. Repeat the following.

ra	re	ri	ro	ru
rápido	receta	Ricardo	Roberto	Rubén
raqueta	red	aterriza	rojo	rubio
párrafo	corre	río	perro	

The sound for a single **r** within a word (medial position) does not exist in English either. It is trilled less than the initial **r** or **rr.** Repeat the following.

ra	re	ri	ro	ru
verano	arena	boletería	número	Perú
maletera	quiere	consultorio	pasajero	Aruba
para		periódico	cinturón	

Pronounce the following sentences carefully. Then write them to prepare for a dictation.

El perro de Rubén corre en la arena.

El avión para Puerto Rico aterriza con un retraso de una hora.

El pasajero corre rápido por el aeropuerto.

Ricardo pone su raqueta en la maletera del carro.

Refrán

Can you guess what the following proverb means?

Mal hace quien nada hace.

Andrew Payti

CULTURA

El avión está aterrizando en el aeropuerto de Buenos Aires, Argentina.

¡Bravo!

You have now learned all the new vocabulary and grammar in this chapter. Continue to use and practice all that you know while learning more cultural information. **¡Vamos!**

En el aeropuerto 🎧 ↺

Susana	¡Oye, Pedro! Está saliendo nuestro vuelo.
Pedro	Sí, ¡vamos ya! Tenemos que pasar por el control de seguridad y siempre hay una cola larga.
Susana	¿Tienes nuestras tarjetas de embarque?
Pedro	Sí, sí. Las tengo. ¿Necesitas ayuda con tu equipaje de mano?
Susana	No, no traigo mucho. Lo puedo llevar. ¿De qué puerta salimos?
Pedro	De la puerta 11. ¿A qué hora empieza el embarque?
Susana	Ahora mismo. ¡Vamos!

¿Comprendes?

A Contesta según la información en la conversación.
1. ¿Dónde están Pedro y Susana?
2. ¿Qué están anunciando?
3. ¿Ya pasaron por el control de seguridad Pedro y Susana?
4. ¿Qué hay siempre en el control de seguridad?
5. ¿Quién tiene las tarjetas de embarque?
6. ¿De qué puerta de salida salen?
7. ¿Está empezando el embarque?

B Resumiendo Relata toda la información en la conversación en tus propias palabras.

C Prediciendo ¿Piensas que Susana y Pedro van a perder su vuelo? ¿Por qué contestas que sí o que no?

CULTURA

Una vista panorámica de San Juan de Puerto Rico desde el Viejo San Juan hasta el Condado

Lectura

READING STRATEGY

Antes de leer

Scan the reading to find the most important idea in each section. Look for topic sentences.

✔ **READING CHECK**

¿Cuál es un medio de transporte muy importante en Sudamérica?

✔ **READING CHECK**

¿Dónde es muy densa la vegetación? ¿En las montañas o en las selvas?

Durante la lectura

Note each topic sentence. Think about the one idea that all the sentences and sections are about.

Después de leer

What was the main idea of the reading and of each section? What do you think was the author's purpose here?

IDENTIFYING THE MAIN IDEA It is important to identify the main idea of a reading. Topic sentences—usually the first sentence in a paragraph—help you determine the main idea of a reading.

El avión en la América del Sur

El continente sudamericano es vasto. Las distancias entre ciudades son largas. Por eso el avión es un medio de transporte importante. A veces es imposible viajar por tierra[1] de un lugar a otro. ¿Por qué?

Montañas Una gran parte del oeste del continente es montañosa. Los altos picos nevados de los Andes parecen tocar el cielo[2]. Unas ciudades como Bogotá, Quito y La Paz están en los Andes. Y claro que hay también pequeños pueblos aislados en las montañas.

Selvas Al este de los Andes en Colombia, Ecuador, Perú, Bolivia y Brasil hay grandes selvas tropicales del río Amazonas. En las selvas la vegetación es muy densa y una gran parte de la cuenca[3] amazónica es inhóspita e impenetrable.

Desiertos La región a lo largo de la costa desde Perú hasta el centro de Chile es desierto. El Atacama en Chile es el desierto más árido (seco) del mundo—una región de arena y rocas (piedras).

Día y noche los aviones sobrevuelan los picos, selvas y desiertos para enlazar[4] las ciudades y pueblos de Sudamérica.

[1]por tierra *by land*
[2]cielo *sky*
[3]cuenca *basin*
[4]enlazar *connect*

CULTURA
Un pueblo aislado en los Andes de Venezuela

Kelli Drummer-Avendaño

¿Comprendes?

A Recordando hechos Contesta.

1. ¿Qué montañas corren del norte al sur a lo largo del océano Pacífico en la América del Sur?
2. ¿Qué hay al este de los Andes?
3. ¿Qué región de Sudamérica es desierto?

B Describiendo Describe.

1. los picos andinos
2. las selvas tropicales
3. el desierto

C Analizando Contesta.

1. ¿Por qué es el avión un medio de transporte muy importante?
2. En muchas regiones de Sudamérica, ¿por qué es difícil viajar por tierra?

D Categorizando Completa la tabla de abajo. Luego, relata la información en la tabla en tus propias palabras.

	a lo largo de la costa peruana y chilena	al este de las montañas	en las montañas
desiertos			
picos cubiertos de nieve			
selvas tropicales			
la cuenca amazónica			
vegetación densa			
tierra árida			
Bogotá, Quito, La Paz			

Lectura
UN POCO MÁS

Antes de leer

Vas a leer sobre un misterio famoso que hay en Perú. ¿Te gustan los misterios? ¿Hay algún misterio donde vives?

✔ **READING CHECK**

¿Qué son las líneas de Nazca?

Un viaje interesante 🎧 ↺

Un vuelo interesante Si quieres hacer un viaje interesante en avión tienes que sobrevolar las líneas de Nazca. ¿Qué son las líneas de Nazca? Pues, en el desierto árido del sur de Perú hay una serie de dibujos o figuras misteriosas. Hay figuras geométricas—rectángulos, triángulos y líneas paralelas. Hay también representaciones perfectas de varios animales. A pesar de[1] muchas investigaciones el origen de las líneas o figuras que tienen más de 1.500 años queda[2] un misterio.

Y son tan grandes que la única manera de ver las figuras es tomar un vuelo. Las avionetas salen de Lima o del aeropuerto de la pequeña ciudad de Ica, muy cerca de las figuras.

[1]A pesar de *In spite of*   [2]queda *remains*

CULTURA
Las líneas de Nazca

Glow Images

¿Comprendes?

Escoge o completa.

1. Las líneas de Nazca están _____ .
   a. en el pico de una montaña
   b. en una selva
   c. en un desierto

2. ¿Qué son las líneas?
   a. animales
   b. figuras misteriosas
   c. solamente figuras geométricas

3. El origen de las líneas de Nazca es _____ .

4. ¿Por qué es necesario ver las líneas desde un avión?
   a. porque hay avionetas que salen de Ica y Lima
   b. porque están en un desierto
   c. porque son tan inmensas

5. Un avión pequeño es _____ .

CULTURA

Las líneas de Nazca. Además de las líneas de Nazca, los arqueólogos descubrieron otras figuras delineadas en el costado rocoso no muy lejos de Nazca. Se cree que son aún más antiguas que las líneas de Nazca.

CULTURA

Una avioneta que sobrevuela las líneas de Nazca

(t)Glow Images, (b)Andrew Payti

Prepárate para el examen

↺ To review, see **Vocabulario 1** and **Vocabulario 2**.

Vocabulario

1 **Completa.**

1–2. El agente trabaja en el _____ de la línea aérea en el _____.

3. La tarjeta de embarque indica el número del _____ y el número del asiento del pasajero.

4. Antes de ir a la puerta de salida, los pasajeros tienen que pasar por el _____ donde inspeccionan su equipaje de mano.

5. El avión no sale a tiempo. Sale _____.

6. Los pasajeros tienen que _____ una forma de identidad.

7. A bordo del avión, hay que poner el equipaje en el _____.

8. Estamos esperando nuestro vuelo en la _____.

9. Antes de facturar mi equipaje, tomo mi tarjeta de embarque del _____.

10. Estás a bordo del avión. ¿Sabes el número de tu _____?

2 **Identifica.**

11.

12.

13.

14.

15.

③ Contesta.

16. ¿Haces un viaje?

17. ¿Vienes en junio para mi cumpleaños?

18. ¿Qué pones en tu maleta o mochila?

19. ¿A qué hora sales?

20. ¿Traes mucho equipaje?

↻ To review, see **Presente de hacer, poner, traer, salir.**

④ Completa con el presente.

21. Ellos _____ mañana. (venir)

22. Nosotros _____ mucho trabajo. (hacer)

23. José _____ su mochila debajo del asiento. (poner)

24. Yo lo _____. (oír)

25. ¿Tú _____ tu equipaje de mano? (traer)

26. Señor, ¿usted _____ esta mañana o esta tarde? (salir)

27. Nosotros _____ al aeropuerto con nuestros padres. (venir)

↻ To review, see **El presente progresivo.**

⑤ Escribe en el presente progresivo.

28. El avión despega.

29. Nosotros hacemos cola.

30. Ellos salen a tiempo.

31. Los pasajeros esperan en la puerta de salida.

32. Yo leo mi libro favorito.

33. Juan y Marisol, ¡ustedes nadan en el mar!

34. Tú vives cerca de mi casa ahora.

35. ¿Qué oyen tus primos?

⑥ Escoge.

36. El continente sudamericano es _____.

    a. pequeño   **b.** alto   **c.** inmenso

37. Hay selvas tropicales en _____.

    a. las montañas   **b.** el desierto   **c.** la cuenca amazónica

38. El Amazonas es _____.

    a. un pico andino   **b.** un río   **c.** un desierto

⑦ Contesta.

39. ¿Por qué es difícil viajar por tierra en muchas partes de la América del Sur?

40. ¿Cuáles son unas características geográficas de la América del Sur?

CULTURA 🇵🇪

Un barquito como este es un medio de transporte importante de la selva tropical en Latinoamérica. El barquito que vemos aquí está en el Amazonas cerca de Iquitos en Perú. Las aguas del Amazonas bajan y suben según la marea.

↻ To review this cultural information, see the **Lectura cultural.**

Prepárate para el examen

❶ Preparar para un viaje

Tell about packing for a trip

You're getting ready to leave on a trip. Tell what you're going to pack. Will you use a suitcase, carry-on, or backpack? Does the weather where you're going influence what you are going to pack?

❷ En el mostrador de la línea aérea

Converse with a ticket agent

You are at the ticket counter at the airport. You are talking with the ticket agent (your partner). You want to find out details about the flight and check your luggage. The ticket agent asks for confirmation of your e-ticket and passport and answers any questions you have.

❸ Un billete para Madrid

Buy an airplane ticket

Work with a classmate. You want to fly with your family from somewhere in the United States to Madrid and you will be returning from Barcelona. Call the airline to get a reservation. Your classmate will be the reservation agent. Before you call, think about all the information you will need to provide or get from the airline agent: your name, date of departure, departure time, arrival time in Madrid, flight number, and price.

❹ ¿Quién está haciendo qué?

Tell what people are doing in your classroom

Who's doing what? Look around you and tell what everyone is doing.

CULTURA 🇵🇷

La profesora está enseñando y los alumnos están prestando atención en una clase de matemáticas en San Juan, Puerto Rico.

❺ El continente sudamericano

Tell about travel in South America

Your aunt and uncle are thinking about traveling around South America. You have already been there. Make suggestions about where they should go, how they should get there, and what they should do and see. Tell them why it can be difficult to travel from one place to another by land. They will ask you questions for clarification.

David H. Brennan

Tarea

Write a letter to a service organization interested in international relations. Your goal is to win an all-expense-paid trip to spend two weeks living with a Spanish-speaking family in a country of your choice.

Writing Strategy

Answering an essay question Many types of applications contain or expect you to answer questions concerning your qualifications or reasons for applying. This requires you to write an essay that convinces that you are the right person.

❶ Prewrite

- Think of your overall goal—to convince all concerned why you are the right person to be sent to a foreign country.

- Look at the list of some types of questions you may have to answer. **¿Qué quieres visitar? ¿Por qué quieres ir allí? ¿Qué esperas hacer, ver o aprender allí? ¿Cómo quieres viajar? ¿Qué tipo de persona eres? ¿Qué estás haciendo ahora?**

- Think of other information the organization may want to know about you. Add those questions to the list.

❷ Write

You really want to go on this trip, so be sure to plan your essay carefully.

- Write an introduction that tells the organization a little about you and makes them want to find out more about you.

- Start a new paragraph for the answer to each question.

- When you finish writing, check your work. Check spelling, grammar, and verb endings. Make sure your sentences are complete and understandable.

- Read over your work again to make sure all errors are corrected and to make sure that you have effectively communicated your message to the organization.

Evaluate

Don't forget that your teacher will evaluate you on your organization, use of vocabulary and grammar, and on how clear, complete, and convincing your essay is.

Repaso del Capítulo 1

Gramática

Presente de hacer, poner, traer, salir

The verbs **hacer, poner, traer, salir,** and **oír** have a **g** in the **yo** form. All other forms are regular. Review the following forms.

| yo | **hago** | **pongo** | **traigo** | **salgo** | **oigo** |

Venir has a **g** in the **yo** form as well as a stem change just like the verb **tener,** which you have already learned.

venir	
vengo	**venimos**
vienes	*venís*
viene	**vienen**

Comparaciones

How is the present progressive expressed in English?

El presente progresivo

The present progressive expresses an action that is taking place at the moment. It is formed with the verb **estar** and the present participle. Review the following forms.

estoy				
estás				
está	**viajando**	**comiendo**	**saliendo**	**leyendo**
estamos				
estáis				
están				

La señorita está escuchando música en su MP3 mientras regresa a casa después de un viaje.

John Flournoy/McGraw-Hill Education

Juego There are a number of cognates in this list. See how many you and a partner can find. Who can find the most? Compare your list with those of your classmates.

Go Online!

connectED.mcgraw-hill.com

Vocabulario

Leaving for a trip

el equipaje de mano	el/la taxista	hacer
la maleta	la maletera, el baúl	un viaje
el taxi	poner	la maleta

Describing airport activities

el aeropuerto	la tarjeta de embarque	la puerta de salida
el avión	el pasaporte	facturar el equipaje
el/la agente	el nombre	pasar por el control de
el mostrador	el/la pasajero(a)	seguridad
la línea aérea	el número del vuelo	hacer cola
el boleto, el billete	la hora de salida	mostrar
(electrónico)	la hora de embarque	esperar
el distribuidor	el número del asiento	embarcar, abordar
automático	la forma de identidad	

Describing a flight

el/la asistente(a)	el cinturón de	despegar
de vuelo	seguridad	aterrizar
el asiento	la señal de no fumar	internacional
el pasillo	el servicio	a bordo
la ventanilla	un retraso, una	tarde
el compartimiento	demora	a tiempo
superior	el despegue	con destino a
la máscara de	el aterrizaje	procedente de
oxígeno	la pista	

Other useful words and expressions

hay que	dentro de poco	¡Con permiso!
a veces	debajo de	abrochado(a)
de vez en cuando		

Repaso cumulativo

Repasa lo que ya has aprendido

These activities will help you review and remember what you have learned so far in Spanish.

1 Escucha las expresiones. Indica en una tabla como la de abajo si tienes que usar el verbo saber o conocer.

saber	conocer

2 Completa con verbos apropiados.

Álvaro Irizarry __1__ un muchacho alto y guapo. Él __2__ de San Juan, la capital de Puerto Rico. Puerto Rico __3__ una isla tropical en el mar Caribe. En la isla siempre __4__ calor y el tiempo __5__ muy bueno con mucho sol. A Álvaro y a sus amigos les __6__ mucho ir a la playa donde __7__ una tarde agradable. Si __8__ hambre, __9__ a uno de los carritos que __10__ en la playa donde __11__ una empanada deliciosa.

CULTURA

Una playa en la isla de Vieques en Puerto Rico

3 Repasa tu vocabulario. Prepara una lista de todos los artículos de ropa que ya aprendiste en español.

4 Contesta.

1. Va a hacer calor. ¿Qué vas a llevar?
2. Va a hacer frío. ¿Qué vas a llevar?
3. ¿Qué te gusta comer cuando tienes hambre?
4. ¿Qué te gusta beber cuando tienes sed?

5 Escribe las frases y cambia las palabras indicadas por pronombres.

1. Juan vio *a Ana* después de las clases.
2. Él dio *los boletos* a Ana porque es su amiga buena.
3. Habló también *a Mateo y Gabriela*.
4. Ellos compraron un refresco *para Juan*.

Rebecca Smith

6 **Identifica el deporte.**

1. El portero quiere bloquear el balón.

2. Es posible bajar una pista fácil para principiantes o una pista difícil para expertos.

3. Los jugadores corren de una base a otra.

4. El balón tiene que pasar por encima de la red.

5. Juegan con una pelota y una raqueta y la pelota tiene que pasar por encima de la red.

7 **Rompecabezas**

El intruso Choose the word in each group that does not belong and tell why it is **el intruso.**

1. banda   avión   carro   autobús

2. siempre   a veces   nunca   nadie

3. mar   pelota   ola   piscina

4. cama   silla   falda   mesa

5. leer   patinar   escribir   estudiar

8 **Contesta.**

1. Ellos están jugando voleibol. ¿Tiene que pasar el balón por encima de la red o por debajo de la red?

2. Mi padre está trabajando en nuestro jardín. ¿Él está cerca de nuestra casa o lejos de nuestra casa?

3. La agente trabaja en el mostrador de la línea aérea en el aeropuerto. ¿Está delante del mostrador o detrás del mostrador?

4. La pasajera está facturando su equipaje en el aeropuerto. ¿Está delante del mostrador o detrás del mostrador?

5. A bordo del avión, ¿es necesario poner el equipaje de mano debajo del asiento o sobre el asiento?

CULTURA

Los pasajeros están embarcando un vuelo en el aeropuerto de Bilbao en el País Vasco en el norte de España.

¡Una rutina diferente!

Vamos a comparar ¿Qué haces cada día desde el momento en que te levantas hasta que te acuestas? Muchas cosas de la rutina diaria pueden ser aburridas, ¿no? Vas a ver si los jóvenes en España y Latinoamérica tienen la misma rutina. Pero vas a observar también que hay maneras de cambiar la rutina—sobre todo si decides viajar con un grupo de jóvenes por un país hispano.

Objetivos

You will:

- identify more parts of the body
- talk about your daily routine
- talk about backpacking and camping

You will use:

- reflexive verbs
- commands with **favor de**

◀ Estos mochileros lo están pasando bien dando una caminata en Costa Rica. Pasan unos días sin tener que seguir su rutina ordinaria.

¡Una rutina diferente!

Look at these photographs to acquaint yourself with the theme of this chapter. What activities are part of your daily routine? What activities do you enjoy doing occasionally? What do you think **una rutina diferente** refers to? In this chapter you will learn to talk about daily activities, but you will also see that many fun opportunities in Spain and Latin America await anyone with a spirit of adventure.

México 🇲🇽

La muchacha mexicana se cepilla. Tiene el pelo largo, ¿no?

Perú 🇵🇪

El cartel que vemos aquí se encuentra delante de un albergue juvenil en Barranco, un barrio de Lima, Perú.

México 🇲🇽

Mochileros en Oaxaca, México

España 🇪🇸

Aquí tenemos una vista de los Picos de Europa en Asturias en el norte de España. Es una región muy bonita y mucha gente da paseos o caminatas por la región.

OBELISCO CAMPING

- MOCHILAS
- BOLSAS de DORMIR
- CARPAS
- ART. P/ESCALADA
- ACCESORIOS

Argentina

Una mochila puede llevar muchas cosas—aun un saco de dormir o, como indica el cartel en una tienda de camping en Buenos Aires, una bolsa de dormir.

Chile

La muchacha tiene su saco de dormir y su carpa en un camping en una reserva natural en Chile.

Chile

El camping es bastante popular en muchas partes de Latinoamérica. Aquí vemos un campamento con muchas carpas o tiendas de campaña y caravanas en una playa de Arica, Chile.

El cuerpo humano 🎧

la cabeza

la espalda

el codo

el brazo derecho

el dedo

la pierna

la rodilla

el pie

la mano izquierda

Para mantenerse en forma, Cristina se estira.

La rutina diaria

despertarse

tomar una ducha

lavarse la cara

lavarse el pelo

cepillarse (lavarse) los dientes

peinarse

el espejo

mirarse

sentarse

Stockbyte/PictureQuest/Jupiter Images

¡Hola!
Me llamo Roberto.
¿Y tú? ¿Cómo te llamas?

El muchacho se llama Roberto.

Ana se levanta temprano.
No se queda en la cama.
Se levanta enseguida. Ella es madrugadora.
Le gusta levantarse temprano.

Roberto se acuesta tarde.
Se acuesta a las once y media de la noche.
Él se duerme enseguida.
Él duerme ocho horas.

Elena tiene frío.
Se pone un suéter.

Elena tiene calor.
Se quita el suéter.

McGraw-Hill Education

ESCUCHAR

1 Escucha las frases. Parea cada frase con el dibujo que describe.

a.

b.

c.

d.

e.

f.

HABLAR • ESCRIBIR

2 Contesta.

1. Cuando Marisol se despierta, ¿se levanta enseguida?
2. Cuando Carlos se despierta, ¿se queda en la cama?
3. Cuando Vicente se peina, ¿se mira en el espejo?
4. Cuando Juanita se lava el pelo, ¿usa agua caliente?
5. Cuando Tomás toma el desayuno, ¿se sienta a la mesa?
6. Cuando Julia se acuesta, ¿se duerme enseguida?
7. ¿Cuándo se levanta un madrugador? ¿Temprano por la mañana o tarde?
8. Cuando Ricardo se levanta, ¿se estira?

3 Rompecabezas

Cambia una letra en cada palabra para formar una palabra nueva.

1. como
2. dolor
3. cada
4. coche

5. tocar
6. peso
7. gano
8. hola

Go Online!

connectED.mcgraw-hill.com

4 Parea para hacer una frase larga.

1. Él se pone un suéter
2. Ella se lava las manos
3. Ella se cepilla los dientes
4. Él se mira en el espejo
5. Ella se quita el suéter

a. porque va a comer.
b. porque se peina.
c. porque tiene calor.
d. porque acaba de comer.
e. porque tiene frío.

InfoGap For more practice using your new vocabulary, do Activity 2 in the Student Resource section at the end of this book.

HABLAR • ESCRIBIR

5 **Juego** ¡Corrige todas las frases absurdas!

1. **Cada pierna tiene una mano y la mano tiene un dedo.**
2. **El codo está en la pierna y la rodilla está en el brazo.**
3. **La cara está en la espalda.**
4. Los dientes están en el pelo.
5. **La boca y los ojos están en la rodilla.**

6 **Comunicación**

Pick someone in your family and describe his or her weekday routine to the class.

LEER

7 **Juego** Race with a partner to see who can be the first to put José's activities in the correct order.

José se levanta.

José se duerme enseguida.

José se lava la cara y los dientes en el cuarto de baño.

José va al comedor y toma el desayuno.

José se despierta.

José se acuesta.

José se quita la ropa.

La muchacha se mira en el espejo para ver si el pantalón le queda bien.

El camping 🎧

una carpa, una tienda de campaña

un saco (una bolsa) de dormir

Los amigos van de camping.
Lo están pasando bien. Se divierten mucho.
Los jóvenes arman (montan) una carpa.

Para conversar

Alex, favor de venir acá. Favor de ayudarme con la carpa.

¡Ya voy!

En otras **partes**

- In addition to **una barra** you will also hear **una pastilla.** You will also hear **pasta dentífrica** as well as **crema dental.**
- Una **tienda de campaña** is more common in Spain, **una carpa** in Latin America.

¿Qué llevan en su mochila?

una barra de jabón

un peine

un cepillo

un rollo de papel higiénico

el champú

un tubo de crema dental

un cepillo de dientes

(t)Anne Ackerman/Getty Images, (b)McGraw-Hill Education

Los mochileros dan una caminata.
Dan una caminata por un parque nacional.

Andrea se acuesta en la carpa.
Duerme en un saco de dormir.

¡Así se dice!

Note that when someone calls and you want to respond *I'm coming* you say: **¡Ya voy!**

ESCUCHAR

1 Escucha las frases. Indica en una tabla como la de abajo si cada frase es correcta o no.

sí	no

HABLAR • ESCRIBIR

2 Contesta sobre un grupo de amigos que van de camping.

1. ¿Van de camping los amigos?
2. ¿Se divierten en el camping?
3. ¿Qué montan (arman)?
4. ¿En qué duermen?
5. ¿Dónde ponen sus sacos de dormir?
6. ¿Quiere José ayuda para montar la carpa?
7. ¿A ti te gusta el camping?

EXPANSIÓN

Sin mirar las preguntas, da toda la información que recuerdas en tus propias palabras. Si no recuerdas algo, un(a) compañero(a) te puede ayudar.

LEER • HABLAR • ESCRIBIR

3 Completa con una palabra apropiada.

1. María va a cepillarse los dientes. Necesita _____ y _____.
2. Tomás va a tomar una ducha. Necesita _____.
3. Carlos quiere peinarse. Necesita _____.
4. Julia quiere lavarse el pelo. Necesita _____.
5. Claudia va a cepillarse el pelo. Necesita _____.

LEER

4 Parea las palabras que significan lo mismo.

1. la carpa
2. armar
3. los que llevan una mochila
4. lo pasa bien
5. el paseo largo

a. los mochileros
b. se divierte
c. la tienda de campaña
d. montar
e. la caminata

Index Stock Imagery, Inc.

Comunicación

5 Vas a ir de camping este fin de semana con unos(as) amigos(as). Investiga unos campings que quieres visitar. Luego les debes escribir un e-mail a tus amigos(as) con una descripción de tu lugar preferido y una lista completa de todas las cosas necesarias para tu aventura.

6 Estás en una farmacia. Quieres comprar los siguientes objetos. Conversa con el/la empleado(a).

ESCRIBIR

7 **Rompecabezas**

Join two puzzle pieces to form a word. When you have finished, you should have nine words. Do not use any piece more than once.

jo — nata — ce — pa — espe — ro — cami — pú — pillo — ja — cham — recho — car — tes — dien — dilla — bón — de

CULTURA

El mochilero está esperando un autobús en una parada de buses en Valencia, España.

(t)Ken Cavanagh/McGraw-Hill Education, (tcl)Getty Images, (tcr)Rebecca Smith, (tr b)Andrew Payti

Verbos reflexivos

1. Read the following sentences as you look at the illustrations.

Federico lava el carro.
Federico lo lava.

Federico se lava.

Julia cepilla al perro.
Julia lo cepilla.

Julia se cepilla.

Pedro mira a su amigo.
Pedro lo mira.

Pedro se mira en el espejo.

In the sentences to the left, one person performs the action and another person or thing receives the action. In the sentences to the right, the same person performs and receives the action of the verb. For this reason the pronoun **se** must be used. **Se** is called a reflexive pronoun because it refers back to the subject—**Federico, Julia, Pedro.**

2. Study the forms of a reflexive verb. Pay particular attention to the pronoun that goes with each form of the verb. It is called a "reflexive pronoun."

lavarse			
yo	me lavo	nosotros(as)	nos lavamos
tú	te lavas	vosotros(as)	os laváis
Ud., él, ella	se lava	Uds., ellos, ellas	se lavan

levantarse			
yo	me levanto	nosotros(as)	nos levantamos
tú	te levantas	vosotros(as)	os levantáis
Ud., él, ella	se levanta	Uds., ellos, ellas	se levantan

3. In the negative form, **no** is placed before the reflexive pronoun.

> **¿No te lavas las manos?**
> **La familia Martínez no se levanta tarde.**

4. In Spanish, when you refer to parts of the body and articles of clothing in a reflexive sentence, you often use the definite article, not the possessive adjective.

> **Me lavo la cara.**
> **Ella se cepilla los dientes.**
> **Él se pone el suéter.**

5. Note that the reflexive pronoun is added to the infinitive.

> **El niño quiere acostarse.**
> **Voy a lavarme las manos.**
> **¿Quieres quitarte la chaqueta?**

CULTURA

Aquí vemos la entrada al parque de atracciones La Feria en el Bosque de Chapultepec en la Ciudad de México. La gente va a divertirse mucho.

Andrew Payti

Práctica

ESCUCHAR • HABLAR • ESCRIBIR

1 Contesta.

1. ¿Se levanta tarde o temprano Gregorio?
2. ¿Se lava por la mañana o por la noche?
3. ¿Se lava los dientes antes o después del desayuno?
4. ¿Se pone un suéter cuando hace frío?
5. ¿Se quita el suéter cuando tiene calor?

HABLAR • LEER

2 Completa las conversaciones con un pronombre.

1. ¿A qué hora _____ levantas?
   Soy madrugador(a). _____ levanto temprano,
   a las seis y media.
2. ¿_____ cepillas los dientes con frecuencia?
   Sí, _____ cepillo los dientes unas cuatro veces al día.
3. ¿_____ peinas con frecuencia?
   No, no _____ peino con frecuencia.
4. ¿A qué hora _____ despertaste esta mañana?
   _____ desperté a las siete.
5. Y, ¿a qué hora _____ acostaste anoche?
   Anoche _____ acosté a las diez y media.

HABLAR

3 Trabaja con un(a) compañero(a). Preparen una conversación según el modelo.

MODELO

—¿Te cepillas?
—Sí, me cepillo.

1.

2.

3.

4.

Conexiones

La salud

Aquí tienes unas sugerencias importantes para mantenerte en buena salud. Debes

- dormir entre siete y ocho horas cada noche
- tomar un buen desayuno
- lavarte las manos antes de comer
- cepillarte los dientes después de comer

Con un(a) compañero(a), habla de lo que puedes hacer para incorporar estas sugerencias en tu rutina diaria.

4 Personaliza. Da respuestas personales.

1. ¿Cómo te llamas?
2. Y tu(s) hermano(s), ¿cómo se llama(n)?
3. ¿Cómo se llama tu profesor(a) de español?

CULTURA

Es una clase de español en Santa Fe, Nuevo México. La profesora se llama señora Brown. Parece que los alumnos se divierten mucho en clase, ¿no?

LEER • ESCRIBIR

5 Completa con un pronombre reflexivo y la forma correcta del verbo.

Hola. Yo __1__ llam_2_ Jorge y mi amigo __3__ llam_4_ Felipe. Felipe y yo no __5__ levant_6_ a la misma hora porque él es madrugador y yo no. Él __7__ levant_8_ temprano y yo __9__ levant_10_ tarde. Y tú, ¿__11__ levant_12_ tarde como yo o __13__ levant_14_ temprano como Felipe?

LEER • ESCRIBIR

6 Completa con un pronombre.

1. Quiero levantar__ temprano.
2. Niño, tienes que peinar__.
3. Vamos a lavar__ las manos.
4. ¿No quieres poner__ un suéter? Está haciendo frío.
5. Tienen que cepillar__ los dientes después de cada comida.

HABLAR

7 **Juego** Think of an object from this chapter. Your partner will ask **sí/no** questions which you will answer in complete sentences. If your partner guesses it in five questions or less, he or she wins. If you stump your partner, you win. Then reverse roles.

BananaStock/PictureQuest/Jupiter Images

Verbos reflexivos de cambio radical

1. The reflexive verbs **acostarse (o → ue), dormirse (o → ue), sentarse (e → ie), despertarse (e → ie),** and **divertirse (e → ie)** are stem-changing verbs.

acostarse			
yo	me acuesto	nosotros(as)	nos acostamos
tú	te acuestas	*vosotros(as)*	*os acostáis*
Ud., él, ella	se acuesta	Uds., ellos, ellas	se acuestan

divertirse			
yo	me divierto	nosotros(as)	nos divertimos
tú	te diviertes	*vosotros(as)*	*os divertís*
Ud., él, ella	se divierte	Uds., ellos, ellas	se divierten

2. Many verbs in Spanish can be used with a reflexive pronoun. Often the reflexive pronoun gives a different meaning to the verb. Study the following examples.

Ana pone su blusa en su mochila.	*Ana puts her blouse in her backpack.*
Ana se pone la blusa.	*Ana puts on her blouse.*
Ana duerme ocho horas.	*Ana sleeps eight hours.*
Ana se duerme enseguida.	*Ana falls asleep immediately.*
Ana llama a Carlos.	*Ana calls Carlos.*
Ella se llama Ana.	*She calls herself Ana. (Her name is Ana.)*
Ana divierte a sus amigos.	*Ana amuses her friends.*
Ana se divierte.	*Ana amuses herself. (Ana has a good time.)*

La joven ciclista se divierte en el Parque de la Ciudadela en Barcelona.

Jessica Vilalta

Práctica

ESCUCHAR • HABLAR • ESCRIBIR

8 Personaliza. Da respuestas personales.

1. ¿Duermes en una cama o en un saco de dormir?
2. Cuando te acuestas, ¿te duermes enseguida?
3. Por la mañana, ¿te quedas en la cama cuando te despiertas?
4. A veces, ¿despiertas a tus hermanos?
5. ¿Ellos se enfadan cuando los despiertas?
6. ¿Te sientas a la mesa para tomar el desayuno?
7. ¿Te diviertes en la escuela?
8. ¿Diviertes a tus amigos?

LEER • ESCRIBIR

9 Completa sobre un día que María pasa en la playa.

1. María _____ su traje de baño en su mochila. Cuando llega a la playa ella _____ el traje de baño.
2. En la playa María ve a un amigo. Su amigo _____ Luis. Ella _____ a su amigo.
3. María y sus amigos lo pasan muy bien en la playa. Ellos _____ mucho y como María es muy cómica ella también _____ mucho a sus amigos.
4. Después de pasar el día en la playa, María está muy cansada. Cuando ella se acuesta, _____ enseguida y _____ más de ocho horas.

LEER • ESCRIBIR

10 Completa.

Cuando yo __1__ (acostarse), yo __2__ (dormirse) enseguida. Cada noche yo __3__ (dormir) ocho horas. Yo __4__ (acostarse) a las once y __5__ (levantarse) a las siete de la mañana. Cuando yo __6__ (despertarse), __7__ (levantarse) enseguida. Pero cuando mi hermana __8__ (despertarse), ella no __9__ (levantarse) enseguida. Y mi hermano, cuando él __10__ (acostarse), no __11__ (dormirse) enseguida. Él pasa horas escuchando música en la cama. Así él __12__ (dormir) solamente unas seis horas.

CULTURA

La playa de Nerja en el sur de España

11 **Comunicación**

Work with a partner and discuss your typical daily routines. Then create a schedule of your activities for the coming week that includes at least three workouts. Share your results with your classmates.

Andrew Payti

¡UNA RUTINA DIFERENTE!

Mandatos con favor de

1. The expression **favor de** followed by the infinitive is a very useful way to give a command to tell someone what to do. It is very polite and you can use **favor de** with a friend, an adult, or any group of people.

> **Favor de venir aquí (acá).**
> **Favor de no hablar.**
> **Favor de volver pronto.**

Favor de lavarse las manos

2. Whenever a pronoun is used with the infinitive, the pronoun is attached to it.

> **Favor de ayudarme.**
> **Favor de traerme el menú.**
> **Favor de darme el libro.**
> **Favor de levantarte.** *(to a friend)*
> **Favor de levantarse.** *(to an adult or group of friends)*

Práctica

MINIATURE MATCHBOOK
See the Foldables section of the Student Handbook at the beginning of this book for help with making this foldable. With a partner discuss your daily routines using reflexive verbs. On the front of each matchbook draw something you do every day. On the inside your partner will write a sentence about the picture using the appropriate reflexive verb.

LEER • HABLAR

12 Escoge.

> un amigo   un adulto o un grupo de personas

1. Favor de sentarte.
2. Favor de sentarse aquí.
3. Favor de quitarte las botas.
4. Favor de ponerte los zapatos.
5. Favor de quedarse aquí.
6. Favor de lavarte.
7. Favor de levantarse.

EXPANSIÓN

Ahora, usando la expresión «favor de», puedes decirle a un(a) compañero(a) de clase lo que él o ella debe hacer. Tu compañero(a) tiene que seguir tus mandatos. Luego, cambien de rol.

13 **Comunicación**

You and a friend are planning to do something, for example, take a trip. You need to get ready. Make a diagram similar to the one below and tell your partner what to do to help. Take turns.

buscar algo   llamar un taxi
comprar los boletos   hacer la maleta
hacer un viaje

Kerri Galloway

PRONUNCIACIÓN

La h, la y y la ll

H in Spanish is silent. It is never pronounced. Repeat the following.

hijo	**helado**	**higiénico**	**hola**
hace	**hermano**	**huevos**	**hispano**

Y in Spanish can be either a vowel or a consonant. As a vowel, it is pronounced exactly the same as the vowel **i.** Repeat the following.

el hijo y el hermano
el hotel y el hospital

Y is a consonant when it begins a word or a syllable. As a consonant, **y** is pronounced similarly to the *y* in the English word *yo-yo.* This sound has several variations throughout the Spanish-speaking world. Repeat the following.

ya	**desayuno**	**ayuda**	**playa**
yo	**oye**	**leyó**	

Ll is pronounced as a single consonant in Spanish. In many areas of the Spanish-speaking world, it is pronounced the same as the **y.** It too has several variations. Repeat the following.

llama	**botella**	**taquilla**	**toalla**	**lleva**
llega	**pastilla**	**llueve**	**rollo**	**cepillo**

Dictado

Pronounce the following sentences carefully. Then write them to prepare for a dictation.

> **La hermana habla hoy con su hermano en el hotel.**
> **Está lloviendo cuando ella llega a la calle Hidalgo.**
> **El hombre lleva una botella de agua a la playa bella.**
> **Él no lo oyó; lo leyó.**

Refrán

Can you guess what the following proverb means?

Quien mucho duerme, poco aprende.

¡Bravo!

You have now learned all the vocabulary and grammar in this chapter. Continue to use and practice all that you know while learning more cultural information. ¡Vamos!

De camping 🎧 ↺

Rafael	A ti te gusta mucho el camping, ¿no?
Pablo	A mí, sí.
Rafael	La verdad es que no me interesa mucho. ¿Dónde duermes? ¿Te acuestas al aire libre?
Pablo	No. Siempre voy con uno o dos amigos y montamos una carpa. Y dormimos en un saco de dormir.
Rafael	¿Qué hacen para comer?
Pablo	Muy fácil. Preparamos hamburguesas y salchichas en una barbacoa.
Rafael	Hay muchos insectos, ¿no?
Pablo	Pues, hay. Pero, ¡qué va! No nos molestan.
Rafael	¿Cómo pasan el día entero? ¿No se aburren?
Pablo	Al contrario, damos caminatas y nadamos en el lago. Nos acostamos temprano porque nos levantamos temprano también.
Rafael	Me parece que tienen que levantarse cuando se levanta el sol.
Pablo	Sí, pero no me molesta porque soy madrugador. Pero hay una cosa que no me gusta.
Rafael	¿Verdad? ¿Qué?
Pablo	Lavarme en agua fría.

Fuse

¿Comprendes?

A Completa según la información en la conversación.

1. A _____ le gusta el camping.
2. A _____ no le interesa mucho.
3. Cuando Pablo y su(s) amigo(s) van de camping, montan _____.
4. Duermen en _____.
5. Comen _____.
6. Las preparan en _____.
7. _____ no les molestan.
8. Durante el día _____.
9. Se acuestan temprano porque _____.
10. A Pablo no le gusta _____.

B **Resumiendo** Relata la información en la conversación en tus propias palabras.

C **Comparando** Compara y contrasta los gustos de Rafael y Pablo.

D **Dando opiniones** ¿Estás de acuerdo con las opiniones de Rafael o de Pablo sobre el camping? Explica.

CULTURA

Saltos del Petrohué cerca del lago Llanquihue en Chile

Andrew Payti

¡UNA RUTINA DIFERENTE!

Lectura

Antes de leer

Have you ever done any backpacking? When and where? If not, do you think you would like to? Think about it. Would you rather go camping or stay in a youth hostel? Explain why.

✓ READING CHECK

¿Llevan maletas los jóvenes?

Durante la lectura

How would you like to travel and make new friends from around the world? Would it be fun?

✓ READING CHECK

¿Por qué van a albergues juveniles?

✓ READING CHECK

¿Cuáles son algunas inconveniencias?

Después de leer

After reading, are your opinions the same about backpacking around the globe?

USING PRIOR KNOWLEDGE Prior knowledge is what you already know. Using what you have read, seen, or experienced will help you understand what you read.

Los mochileros

Si decides hacer un viaje por España o Latinoamérica con un grupo de amigos, vas a encontrar a muchos jóvenes de muchas nacionalidades haciendo turismo también. Todos tienen el deseo de ver y conocer el mundo. Pero como no tienen mucho dinero, tienen que viajar de una manera económica. ¿Tú no tienes mucho dinero tampoco? Pues, no hay problema. Como los otros aventureros, puedes poner todo lo que necesitas en una mochila grande y salir a ver el mundo.

Vamos a hablar con un mochilero típico. Se llama Antonio. Es de Texas.

—Me encanta viajar y ver el mundo y lo hago sin mucho dinero. Como en restaurantes económicos y a veces mis compañeros y yo vamos a un mercado donde compramos comida para un picnic. Por lo general pasamos la noche en un albergue juvenil. Son muy económicos pero sus facilidades son limitadas. No tienes baño privado. Te levantas por la mañana y a veces tienes que lavarte en agua fría porque no hay agua caliente. Pero a mí no me importan estas pequeñas inconveniencias. Lo importante es poder hacer nuevos amigos de todas partes del mundo y llegar a apreciar sus costumbres y manera de vivir. ¿Qué te parece? ¿Por qué no nos encontramos un día en México o Chile?

—¡Hola! Me llamo Antonio y soy de Texas. Me encanta viajar con mi mochila y ver el mundo. Soy un verdadero trotamundos.

¿Comprendes?

A **Recordando hechos** Contesta.
1. ¿De dónde vienen los mochileros que viajan por España o Latinoamérica?
2. ¿Cuál es una cosa que tienen en común?
3. ¿Dónde comen los mochileros?
4. ¿Dónde se quedan los mochileros?

B **Describiendo** Describe.
1. un albergue juvenil
2. a un mochilero
3. a Antonio

C **Analizando** Contesta.
¿Cuáles son las ventajas, o conveniencias, y desventajas, o inconveniencias, de quedarse en un albergue juvenil?

D **Explicando** Antonio piensa que los jóvenes se divierten mucho y al mismo tiempo aprenden a apreciar a gente de muchas culturas. Explica el significado de su opinión.

CULTURA
Un hostal o albergue en Punta Arenas en la Patagonia chilena

Andrew Payti

Lectura
UN POCO MÁS

Antes de leer

*¿Fuiste de camping una vez?
Si contestas que sí, ¿te gustó
o no? Piensa en tu experiencia. Si
contestas que no, que nunca fuiste
de camping, ¿qué crees? ¿Te
interesa el camping o no?
A ver si tienes la misma opinión
después de leer esta lectura.*

El camping

Hoy en día muchos turistas, sobre todo los mochileros jóvenes, llevan equipo para hacer camping. En Latinoamérica hay campings en los parques nacionales y reservas naturales. Pasar unas noches en un camping puede ser una experiencia agradable. Tienes la oportunidad de conocer a otros turistas y también a familias locales porque a muchas familias les gusta hacer camping. Es una manera económica de viajar.

Los campers se levantan temprano—cuando se levanta el sol. Pasan el día dando caminatas por unas regiones de una belleza natural increíble.

CULTURA
Carpas en una playa de Arica, Chile

De noche regresan al camping. Se sientan alrededor de una fogata[1] y preparan comida en la fogata o en una barbacoa. Después de un día de mucha actividad física y una buena comida todos están cansados y van a su carpa. Cada uno desenrolla su saco de dormir y enseguida se duerme. Y, ¿mañana? Otro día de experiencias nuevas.

Con solamente mochila, carpa y saco de dormir es posible disfrutar de[2] unas vacaciones estupendas rodeado de un paisaje espectacular.

[1]fogata   *bonfire*   [2]disfrutar de   *to enjoy*

Andrew Payti

¿Comprendes?

Escoge.

1. ¿Quiénes hacen camping?
   a. solo los mochileros
   b. solo los turistas de otros países
   c. los mochileros y otros turistas
   d. nadie

2. Los campings en Latinoamérica se
   encuentran en _____.
   a. las ciudades
   b. los alrededores de una ciudad
   c. zonas rurales
   d. caminatas

3. ¿Cuándo se levantan los campers?
   a. temprano por la mañana
   b. cuando regresan al camping
   c. cuando toman el sol
   d. de noche

4. Las montañas y los lagos ofrecen _____.
   a. una experiencia cultural
   b. un paisaje espectacular
   c. un viaje económico
   d. una comida estupenda

CULTURA

Los jóvenes dan una caminata por los Andes no muy lejos de Mérida, Venezuela.

Kelli Drummer-Avendaño

Prepárate para el examen

↻ To review, see **Vocabulario 1**.

↻ To review, see **Vocabulario 1** and **Vocabulario 2**.

↻ To review, see **Verbos reflexivos** and **Verbos reflexivos de cambio radical**.

Vocabulario

1 **Escoge la palabra apropiada.**

    1. Hay cinco (dedos, pies) en cada mano.

    2. Escribo con la (mano, pierna) izquierda.

    3. Ana estira (las piernas, los codos) antes de correr.

    4. Cuando tengo dolor de (dientes, cabeza) no puedo leer bien.

2 **Completa.**

    5. Los amigos van de camping. Arman una _____.

    6. Es mi amiga. ¿Quieres saber su nombre? Ella _____ _____ Susana.

    7–8. El joven _____ _____ a las diez y media de la noche. Pero no _____ _____ enseguida porque pasa una hora leyendo en la cama.

    9. Necesito _____. Voy a lavarme el pelo.

    10. No puedo hacerlo. ¿Me puedes _____?

    11. Los mochileros dan una _____ por el parque nacional.

Gramática

3 **Contesta.**

    12. ¿Cómo te llamas?

    13. ¿A qué hora te levantas?

    14. ¿A qué hora te acuestas?

4 **Completa.**

    15. Yo _____ a la mesa. (sentarse)

    16. ¿Tú _____ a qué hora? (acostarse)

    17. Ellos _____ Raúl y Magdalena. (llamarse)

    18. Nosotros _____ enseguida. (dormirse)

    19. Yo _____ las manos. (lavarse)

    20. Ustedes _____ en la sala. (sentarse)

    21. Ellos _____ mucho. (divertirse)

    22. Ella _____ temprano cada día. (despertarse)

5 Forma frases.

23. tú / sentarse / para comer

24. usted / acostarse / a las diez de la noche

25. mis primos / llamarse / Carlos y Felipe

26. yo / cepillarse / los dientes

27. nosotros / divertirse / durante una fiesta

28. ustedes / ponerse / los guantes

6 Completa con un pronombre si es necesario.

29. Ella _____ mira en el espejo cuando se peina.

30. Ella _____ mira a la profesora.

31. Yo _____ lavo a mi perro.

32. Yo _____ lavo antes de ir a la escuela.

7 Escribe un mandato con **favor de.** Sigue el modelo.

MODELO **No como.** →
Favor de comer.

To review, see **Mandatos con favor de.**

33. No salgo.

34. No leo las notas.

35. No escribo la tarea.

36. No paso la sal.

Cultura

8 Contesta.

37. ¿Cómo viajan muchos jóvenes en España y Latinoamérica?

38. ¿Dónde pasan la noche?

39. ¿Cómo son los albergues?

40. ¿Por qué a los jóvenes les gustan los albergues juveniles?

To review this cultural information, see the **Lectura cultural.**

CULTURA

Caballito de Totora es un hostal en Huanchaco, Perú. Es un balneario en el océano Pacífico. Un «caballito de totora» es un tipo de embarcación que usan los pescadores.

Andrew Payti

Prepárate para el examen

① Mi familia

Talk about family routines

Work with a classmate. Discuss your family routines. What things do you and your family typically do and at what times? Do your families have similar routines or are they quite different?

② No es siempre igual.

Compare your weekday and weekend routines

Most people like a change of pace on the weekend. Compare the things you do or do not do during the week with the things you do or do not do during the weekend.

CULTURA

Están tomando una siesta en hamacas en un camping en las afueras de Santa Marta, Colombia.

③ Una excursión de camping

Talk about a camping trip

Work with a classmate. A friend's family invited you both to join them on a camping trip. Discuss the things you will need to take. Also discuss some of the things you'll probably do during the camping trip.

④ Un día ideal

Talk about your ideal day

Interview a classmate to find out about his or her ideal day. Take turns. See who can come up with the most original ideas. Share the information with the class.

⑤ Favor de...

Ask someone to do something

Work with a classmate and tell each other to do things. Act out what you're told to do.

Kelli Drummer-Avendaño

Go Online! ➕

connectED.mcgraw-hill.com

Tarea

For the next week keep **un diario** (*diary*) in Spanish. Write down everything you do in the course of each day.

Writing Strategy

Writing in a journal There are many types of personal writing. One example of personal writing is keeping a journal. One type of journal writing involves writing about what you do each day, along with your thoughts and impressions about these events or activities. It's similar to "thinking out loud."

❶ Prewrite

- Find a notebook or journal in which you will feel comfortable writing.
- Decide what time of day you will write in your journal, preferably before you go to bed.
- Remember that journal writing is informal, but in this case you still want to use correct vocabulary, grammar, and sentence structure. Use as many reflexive verbs as you can. Don't try to write anything you haven't learned yet.

❷ Write

Keeping a diary should be an enjoyable, thoughtful experience.

- Write the date at the top of the page. Write down your activities, thoughts, and feelings for each day. Remember that your teacher will be reading it!
- To help refresh your memory, ask yourself questions such as the following: What did I do when I woke up? Did I go to school? What did I do at school? What did I do after school? Did I eat dinner with my family? What homework did I do? Did I wash my hair? Many activities will be different for the weekend days.
- Read over your diary. Check for correct vocabulary, verb forms, and grammar.

- **Expansion:** If you would like to expand this **Tarea** in order to track your progress, make a list of the goals that you would like to set for yourself with regard to this activity. Continue to write in your journal for as long as you would like or until you achieve the goals you want to achieve. Take note of the improvement you made in your writings. The improvements could include better use of descriptive words, increased use of newly learned vocabulary, or any other aspect of writing that you wish to improve. At the end of your journal writing, review your diary and make a note of the areas in which you have improved most and check that against your list of goals you set for yourself.

Evaluate

Don't forget that your teacher will evaluate you on your sequencing of events and activities, use of vocabulary, correctness of grammar and sentence structure, and the completeness of your message.

Gramática

Verbos reflexivos

Review the forms of the reflexive verbs. These verbs have an extra pronoun that refers back to the subject because the subject is both the performer (doer) and receiver of the action of the verb.

lavarse			
yo	me lavo	nosotros(as)	nos lavamos
tú	te lavas	vosotros(as)	os laváis
Ud., él, ella	se lava	Uds., ellos, ellas	se lavan

Verbos reflexivos de cambio radical

Some reflexive verbs have a stem change in the present. Review the following verbs.

acostarse			
yo	me acuesto	nosotros(as)	nos acostamos
tú	te acuestas	vosotros(as)	os acostáis
Ud., él, ella	se acuesta	Uds., ellos, ellas	se acuestan

divertirse			
yo	me divierto	nosotros(as)	nos divertimos
tú	te diviertes	vosotros(as)	os divertís
Ud., él, ella	se divierte	Uds., ellos, ellas	se divierten

Mandatos con favor de

You can use the expression **favor de** followed by the infinitive to tell someone what to do. Review the following.

Favor de empezar ahora.

Favor de no poner la ropa aquí.

Remember that when a pronoun is used with the infinitive, the pronoun is attached to it.

Favor de ayudarme.

CULTURA

Los jóvenes se divierten observando y escuchando la Catarata La Paz en Costa Rica. En el parque hay una serie de senderos y miradores de donde los turistas pueden apreciar el paisaje extraordinario.

Richard Brommer

Juego There are a number of cognates in this list. See how many you and a partner can find. Who can find the most? Compare your list with those of your classmates.

Vocabulario

Stating daily activities

la rutina diaria	lavarse	dormirse
despertarse	cepillarse	ponerse (la ropa)
estirarse	peinarse	quitarse (la ropa)
levantarse	mirarse	llamarse
quedarse	sentarse	
tomar una ducha	acostarse	

Identifying articles for grooming and hygiene

el espejo	el peine	la barra de jabón
el champú	el cepillo de dientes	el rollo de papel
el cepillo	el tubo de crema dental	higiénico

Identifying more parts of the body

el cuerpo humano	el brazo	la pierna
la cabeza	el codo	el pie
los dientes	el dedo	
la espalda	la rodilla	

Describing camping

el parque	el saco (la bolsa)	montar, armar
el camping	de dormir	dar una caminata
la carpa, la tienda	el/la mochilero(a)	divertirse,
de campaña	ir de camping	pasarlo bien

Other useful words and expressions

derecho(a)	el suéter	acá
izquierdo(a)	tener frío (calor)	¡Ya voy!
el/la madrugador(a)	Favor de (+ *infinitive*)	

Repaso cumulativo

Repasa lo que ya has aprendido

These activities will help you review and remember what you have learned so far in Spanish.

1 Escucha las frases. Indica si la frase ocurre en el presente o en el pasado.

en el presente	en el pasado

2 Cambia al presente progresivo.

1. Él compra un juego de computadora.
2. Ellos hacen un álbum de fotografías electrónicas.
3. Compro un regalo para mi papá.
4. ¿Qué lees?
5. No comprendemos nada.
6. Ellos viven en Caracas.
7. ¡Vamos! Sale nuestro vuelo.
8. Hacen cola.

3 Completa con una palabra apropiada.

1. Tengo que _____ una composición para mi clase de inglés.
2. Mañana voy a _____ a la playa donde voy a _____ en el mar.
3. No tengo hambre porque acabo de _____.
4. Mis amigos acaban de _____ de Colombia donde pasaron sus vacaciones.
5. Yo voy a _____ a la tienda porque tengo que _____ un regalo para el cumpleaños de Teresa.

4 Forma frases en el presente.

1. nosotros / poder
2. nosotros / jugar
3. yo / querer
4. ella / pensar que sí
5. ellos / preferir
6. nosotros / querer
7. nosotros / volver
8. ustedes / volver
9. tú / tener que

Una playa en la costa del Caribe en Colombia

Kelli Drummer-Avendaño

⑤ Completa con ser o estar.

1. Quiero acostarme. _____ cansado(a).

2. José tiene que prepararse para un examen. _____ un poco nervioso.

3. Teresa no se siente bien. _____ enferma.

4. La muchacha se baña. El jabón que usa _____ muy bueno.

5. Los alumnos se duermen porque el profesor _____ muy aburrido y ellos _____ aburridos.

⑥ Escribe el contrario.

1. El niño tiene algo en la boca.

2. Ellos siempre se acuestan muy temprano.

3. Yo siempre me duermo enseguida.

4. Alguien va a pie y alguien va en bicicleta.

5. Tenemos algo en la mochila.

⑦ Mira los dibujos. Describe todo lo que ves.

¡UNA RUTINA DIFERENTE!

En tren

Go Online!

Audio Video Práctica Repaso Diversiones eScape

ePals

Aquí y Allí

Vamos a comparar Donde tú vives, ¿hay mucho servicio ferroviario—servicio de trenes? ¿Hay solo trenes locales o hay también trenes de larga distancia? En algunas partes de Estados Unidos, el tren es un medio de transporte importante. En otras no hay servicio ferroviario. Existe la misma situación en el mundo hispano. Vamos a ver donde es importante.

Objetivos

You will:

- use vocabulary related to train travel
- discuss interesting train trips in Peru and Mexico

You will use:

- the preterite of irregular verbs
- the verb **decir**
- prepositional pronouns

◄ El tren azul en los Andes peruanos es un tren de lujo que corre desde Machu Picchu a Cuzco, al lago Titicaca, Puno y otros sitios. Durante estos viajes hay vistas magníficas de los Andes.

En tren

El tema de este capítulo es el viajar en tren. En unas regiones el tren es un medio de transporte muy importante y en otras no es importante. Sin embargo como vas a ver en este capítulo hay unas excursiones espectaculares que puedes hacer en tren en varias partes del mundo hispanohablante.

Chile 🇨🇱

La antigua estación de ferrocarril Arica–La Paz en el norte de Chile es un monumento histórico. Hoy en día la estación sirve de museo ferroviario.

Panamá

Estas jóvenes trabajan en el coche cafetería del tren que enlaza la Ciudad de Panamá con Colón. Los pasajeros que tuvieron la experiencia inolvidable de observar la vegetación tropical a lo largo del canal de Panamá desde las ventanillas del tren hacen cola para bajar(se) en Colón.

Cuba 🇨🇺

Qué contraste entre esta locomotora antigua de un tren de turismo en la provincia de Camagüey en Cuba y otros trenes modernos como el AVE.

Nicaragua

Una vieja locomotora en un museo ferroviario en Granada, Nicaragua

OJO · PARE · CRUCE · TREN

Chile

La antigua estación de trenes en Poconchile, Chile, cerca de Arica

México

Un trencito en el Bosque de Chapultepec en la Ciudad de México

España

Hay muchos jóvenes que viajan por España y aprovechan el excelente servicio de trenes para ir de una ciudad a otra.

España

Si no quieres hacer cola delante de la ventanilla para sacar tu billete (comprar tu boleto), lo puedes sacar de un distribuidor automático como este en la estación de Atocha en Madrid.

Billetes
Venta Automática

(br)Digital Vision/Getty Images, (others)Andrew Payti

En la estación de ferrocarril (tren) 🎧

el hall

la sala de espera

el horario

Los pasajeros esperan su tren en la sala de espera.
El horario indica las llegadas y salidas de los trenes.

el distribuidor automático

Puedes insertar tu tarjeta de crédito
o dinero, seleccionar tu destino y
tarifa y el billete te sale
automáticamente.

el billete (boleto)

la tarifa

el billete sencillo

el billete de ida y vuelta,
el boleto de ida y regreso

Para conversar

Un billete para
Madrid, por favor.

¿En primera clase
o en segunda?

En segunda, por favor,
de ida y vuelta.

el quiosco

los libros de bolsillo

las revistas

los periódicos

el vagón, el coche

el andén

la vía

Los amigos hicieron un viaje en tren.
Tomaron el tren.
No quisieron tomar el autobús.
Los amigos estuvieron en el andén.
Esperaron el tren en el andén.

La señora hizo un viaje en tren.
No pudo poner su equipaje en el tren.
Un joven la ayudó.

ESCUCHAR

1 Escucha las frases. Parea cada frase con la foto que describe.

a.

b.

HABLAR • ESCRIBIR

2 Contesta.

1. La señora no sabe a qué hora sale su tren. ¿Qué consulta?
2. La señora quiere sacar un billete para el tren. ¿Adónde va?
3. La señora piensa volver. ¿Qué tipo de billete (boleto) necesita?
4. Los trenes tienen dos clases. ¿En qué clase es más alta la tarifa? ¿En primera o en segunda?
5. La señora no quiere hacer cola delante de la ventanilla. ¿Dónde puede sacar su billete?
6. ¿Dónde esperan los pasajeros el tren?
7. En el hall de la estación de tren hay un quiosco. ¿Qué venden en el quiosco?

ESCRIBIR

3 Da una palabra relacionada.

la ventana   esperar   salir

ir   llegar   volver

(tl)David H. Brennan, (tr)Steve Mason/Getty Images, (b)Andrew Payti

HABLAR • ESCRIBIR

4 Contesta según la información en el billete.

1. ¿De qué estación en Madrid sale el tren?
2. ¿Cuál es el destino del tren?
3. ¿A qué hora sale?
4. ¿A qué hora llega?
5. ¿Es un billete sencillo o de ida y vuelta?

ESCUCHAR • HABLAR • ESCRIBIR

5 Contesta según se indica.

1. ¿Quiso José hacer el viaje en bus? (no)
2. ¿Cómo hizo el viaje? (en tren)
3. ¿Pudo llevar su equipaje? (no)
4. ¿Quién lo ayudó? (su amigo)
5. ¿Dónde esperó el tren? (en el andén)
6. ¿Estuvo mucho tiempo en el andén? (no)

EXPANSIÓN

Ahora, sin mirar las preguntas, cuenta la información en tus propias palabras. Si no recuerdas algo, un(a) compañero(a) te puede ayudar.

LEER • ESCRIBIR

6 **Juego** **Cada uno en su sitio** Pon cada palabra en el lugar apropiado.

el vagón   el horario   la vía
la sala de espera   el distribuidor automático
el tren   el quiosco   la ventanilla

EN EL HALL	EN EL ANDÉN
_____	_____
_____	_____
_____	_____

CULTURA

Una vista parcial de la estación de ferrocarril de Atocha en Madrid

Comunicación

7 Trabaja con un(a) compañero(a) de clase. Tu compañero(a) va a ser el/la agente en la ventanilla. Preparen una conversación para comprar un billete.

8 Tienes un(a) amigo(a) que está en la estación de Atocha en Madrid. Explícale lo que tiene que hacer para sacar su billete de un distribuidor automático.

¡Así se dice!

If while speaking you realize that you have made a grammatical error, just stop and say, **Perdón, digo...**, and restate correctly what you meant to say.

Andrew Payti

En el tren 🎧

subir al tren

bajar(se) del tren

el asiento, la plaza
libre
el revisor
ocupado
el pasillo

El revisor revisó los billetes.
El tren no está completo. Hay asientos libres.

el coche comedor, el coche cafetería, la bufetería

En otras partes

In Spain **el revisor** is a *train conductor.* The term is used in Latin America as well, but you will also hear **el cobrador,** particularly on buses or trains where one actually pays the fare on board. **El asiento** is used throughout Latin America, and **la plaza** is used in Spain.

Horarios

	LLAN
Clase de tren	961
Número de tren	**(1)(N)**
Observaciones	
Días de circulación	LMXJ
MADRID Puerta de Atocha	07:0
CIUDAD REAL	-
PUERTOLLANO	-
CÓRDOBA	08:4
SEVILLA Santa Justa	09:2
Restauración	

El tren salió a tiempo.
No salió tarde.
No salió con retraso (con una demora).

el cañón

una senda

el caballo

el risco

Estos jóvenes estuvieron en México.
Cuando (se) bajaron del tren, alquilaron (rentaron) unos caballos.
Anduvieron a caballo por los riscos del cañón.

Los pasajeros van a bajar(se) en la próxima
parada (estación).

Para conversar

¿Este tren va a Barcelona?

No, señor. Tiene que transbordar (cambiar de tren).

Ay, ¿sí? ¿Dónde?

Puede bajar(se) en la próxima parada (estación).

Tienen que transbordar (cambiar de tren).

(t)Glowimages/Getty Images, (c b)David H. Brennan

EN TREN

1 Escucha. Escoge la frase correcta. Usa una tabla como la de abajo para indicar tus respuestas.

a	b

2 Contesta.

1. Cuando el tren sale a tiempo, ¿hay una demora o no?
2. ¿Pasa el revisor por los pasillos del tren?
3. ¿Revisa los boletos de los pasajeros?
4. Cuando el tren está completo, ¿hay asientos libres?
5. Si los pasajeros tienen hambre, ¿pueden ir a la bufetería?

3 Identifica. Luego usa cada palabra en una frase original.

Conexiones

Las matemáticas

Si tienes que leer un anuncio de un evento o el horario en un país hispano, vas a ver que dan la hora usando las veinticuatro horas. La una es la una de la mañana y las doce es el mediodía. Las trece es una hora después del mediodía—es la una de la tarde. Las veinticuatro horas es la medianoche.

HORARIO DE TRENES

JULIO, JULIOL JULY, JULI	AGOSTO, AGOST AUGUST, AUGUST	SEPTIEMBRE, SETEMBRE SEPTEMBER, SEPTEMBER

SÓLLER - PALMA	PALMA - SÓLLER
8 00	8 00
9 15	10 40 TREN TURÍSTICO
11 50	13 00
14 10	15 15
19 00	20 05
19 35	

1.

2.

3.

4.

Go Online!

connectED.mcgraw-hill.com

LEER

4 Parea las palabras que tienen el mismo significado.

1. una plaza
2. desocupado
3. el coche cafetería
4. rentar
5. con retraso
6. transbordar

a. la bufetería
b. con una demora
c. cambiar de tren
d. un asiento
e. libre
f. alquilar

HABLAR • ESCRIBIR

5 Contesta las preguntas sobre unos amigos que hicieron un viaje interesante por un cañón famoso.

1. ¿Tomaron los amigos el tren?
2. ¿Pagaron una tarifa estudiantil?
3. Cuando (se) bajaron del tren, ¿dieron una caminata?
4. ¿Rentaron caballos?
5. ¿Por dónde anduvieron?
6. ¿Adónde hicieron una excursión?
7. ¿Fueron solos o tuvieron que ir acompañados de un guía?
8. ¿Vieron todo el cañón?

CULTURA
Los jóvenes van a cabalgar.

ESCRIBIR

6

Rompecabezas

Forma palabras con las siguientes letras. Luego descubre el mensaje secreto.

1. rfíbuteea

◯ ◯ ◯ ____ ◯ ____ ____ ____
1 2 3   4

2. ilasplo

◯ ◯ ____ ◯ ____
5 6   7

3. rrsantdabor

◯ ____ ____ ◯ ____ ____ ◯ ____ ____ ◯
8   9   10   11

4. serrivo

____ ____ ◯ ◯ ____ ____ ____
      12 13

El mensaje secreto

____ ____ ____ ____ ____ ____ ____ ____ ____ ,
2   9   1   13 7   7   4   8   4

____ ____ ____ ____ ____ ____ ____ ____ .
5   10 11   3   6   12 10 11

InfoGap For more practice using your new vocabulary words, do Activity 3 in the Student Resource section at the end of this book.

ImageSource/age fotostock

Pretérito de los verbos irregulares

1. The verbs **hacer, querer,** and **venir** are irregular in the preterite. Note that they all have an **i** in the stem. Note too that the endings for **yo** and **usted (él, ella)** are different from the endings of regular verbs.

	hacer	querer	venir
yo	hice	quise	vine
tú	hiciste	quisiste	viniste
Ud., él, ella	hizo	quiso	vino
nosotros(as)	hicimos	quisimos	vinimos
vosotros(as)	*hicisteis*	*quisisteis*	*vinisteis*
Uds., ellos, ellas	hicieron	quisieron	vinieron

2. The verbs **poder, poner,** and **saber** all have a **u** in the stem.

	poder	poner	saber
yo	pude	puse	supe
tú	pudiste	pusiste	supiste
Ud., él, ella	pudo	puso	supo
nosotros(as)	pudimos	pusimos	supimos
vosotros(as)	*pudisteis*	*pusisteis*	*supisteis*
Uds., ellos, ellas	pudieron	pusieron	supieron

3. The verbs **estar, andar,** and **tener** all have a **uv** in the stem.

	estar	andar	tener
yo	estuve	anduve	tuve
tú	estuviste	anduviste	tuviste
Ud., él, ella	estuvo	anduvo	tuvo
nosotros(as)	estuvimos	anduvimos	tuvimos
vosotros(as)	*estuvisteis*	*anduvisteis*	*tuvisteis*
Uds., ellos, ellas	estuvieron	anduvieron	tuvieron

CULTURA

Los peatones anduvieron por la Plaza de la Independencia en Montevideo, Uruguay.

Andrew Payti

4. Many of these verbs are not used frequently in the preterite. When they are, they take on a special meaning. Observe the following.

Quise ayudar.	*I tried to help.*
No quiso ir en carro.	*He refused to go by car.*
Yo lo supe ayer.	*I found out yesterday.*
No pude terminar.	*(I tried but) I couldn't finish.*
Pude terminar.	*(After much effort) I managed to finish.*

Práctica

HABLAR • ESCRIBIR

1 Imagina que estuviste en una estación de tren. Contesta.

1. ¿Cómo viniste a la estación de tren?
2. ¿Hiciste el viaje en tren?
3. ¿Lo hiciste en tren porque no quisiste ir en carro?
4. ¿Pudiste poner todo tu equipaje en el tren?
5. ¿Tuviste que buscar un asiento libre?
6. ¿Anduviste de un vagón a otro para buscar un asiento?

EXPANSIÓN

Ahora, sin mirar las preguntas, cuenta la información en tus propias palabras. Si no recuerdas algo, un(a) compañero(a) te puede ayudar.

LEER • ESCRIBIR

2 Completa las conversaciones en el pretérito.

1. —Ellos no _____ (querer) hacer el viaje.
   —¿No lo _____ (querer) hacer?
   —No, de ninguna manera.
   —Pues, ¿qué pasó entonces? ¿Lo _____ (hacer) o no lo _____ (hacer)?
   —No lo _____ (hacer).

2. —¿Por qué no _____ (venir) ustedes esta mañana?
   —Nosotros no _____ (venir) porque no _____ (hacer) reservación.
   —¿Ustedes no _____ (tener) reservación?

3. —Carlos no _____ (querer) hacer la cama.
   —Entonces, ¿quién la _____ (hacer)?
   —Pues, la _____ (hacer) yo.
   —¡Qué absurdo! ¿Tú la _____ (hacer) porque él no la _____ (querer) hacer?

CATEGORY BOOK See the Foldables section of the Student Handbook at the beginning of this book for help with making this foldable. Make a *category book* foldable with ten tabs. On the top tab, write the infinitive of a verb that is irregular in the preterite. On the following tabs, write the subject pronouns: **yo, tú, Ud., él, ella, nosotros(as), Uds., ellos, ellas.** Exchange foldables with your partner. Open each tab and write the correct form of the verb.

LEER • ESCRIBIR

3 Completa con el pretérito del verbo indicado.

El otro día yo __1__ (estar) en un mercado en Perú. Rafael __2__ (estar) allí también. Nosotros __3__ (andar) por el mercado pero no __4__ (poder) comprar nada. No es que no __5__ (querer) comprar nada, es que no __6__ (poder) porque __7__ (ir) al mercado sin dinero.

CULTURA
Un mercado indígena en un pueblo andino de Perú

ESCUCHAR • HABLAR • ESCRIBIR

4 Sigue el modelo.

MODELO **No puedo ahora. →**
No puedo ahora y no pude ayer tampoco.

1. No pueden ahora.
2. No tenemos que hacerlo ahora.
3. No lo haces ahora.
4. Ellos no están ahora.
5. Él no viene ahora.

CULTURA
Carlos es un joven peruano. Como los jóvenes en todas partes, Carlos no pudo salir anoche porque tuvo que estudiar.

5 *Comunicación*

Habla con un(a) compañero(a) de clase. Dile lo que no pudiste o no quisiste hacer porque tuviste que hacer otra cosa. Dile lo que hiciste. Luego tu compañero(a) va a decir lo que no pudo o no quiso hacer porque tuvo que hacer otra cosa.

(t)Richard Brommer, (b)©Photodisc/PunchStock

El verbo **decir**

The verb **decir** (*to say*) is irregular in the present and preterite tenses. Study the following forms.

PRESENTE			
yo	digo	nosotros(as)	decimos
tú	dices	*vosotros(as)*	*decís*
Ud., él, ella	dice	Uds., ellos, ellas	dicen

PRETÉRITO			
yo	dije	nosotros(as)	dijimos
tú	dijiste	*vosotros(as)*	*dijisteis*
Ud., él, ella	dijo	Uds., ellos, ellas	dijeron

Práctica

HABLAR

6 Personaliza. Da respuestas personales.

1. ¿Qué dices? ¿Quieres dar una caminata? Digo que…
2. ¿Qué dices? ¿Quieres subir hasta las ruinas?
3. ¿Qué dices? ¿Quieres hacer una excursión al cañón?
4. ¿Qué dices? ¿Quieres alquilar un caballo?

LEER • ESCRIBIR

7 Completa con el presente de **decir.**

—Yo __1__ que quiero ir en tren pero Elena me __2__ que prefiere tomar el avión. Ella y Tomás también __3__ que no hay mucha diferencia entre la tarifa del avión y la tarifa del tren. ¿Qué __4__ tú?

—Yo __5__ que es mejor ir en tren.

—Bueno. Tú y yo __6__ la misma cosa. Estamos de acuerdo.

LEER • ESCRIBIR

8 Completa con el presente y el pretérito de **decir.**

1. Yo lo _____ pero ellos no lo _____.
2. Ellos lo _____ pero nosotros no lo _____.
3. Él lo _____ pero ustedes no lo _____.
4. Nosotros lo _____ pero ustedes no lo _____.
5. Tú lo _____ pero yo no lo _____.

Nota

- Note the use of **que** after the verb **decir.**

  Yo digo que sí y ellos dicen que no.

- Note that the verb **traer** follows the same pattern as the verb **decir** in the preterite: **traje.**

LEER • ESCRIBIR

9 Completa con el pretérito de **decir.**

1. Tomás me _____ que le gusta mucho la ciudad de Montevideo.
2. Yo le _____ que a mí me gusta también.
3. Nosotros _____ que nos gusta porque es una ciudad bonita.
4. ¿No me _____ (tú) que está cerca del mar?
5. Sí, y (yo) te _____ que en la ciudad misma hay playas.

CULTURA

Montevideo, la capital de Uruguay, es una ciudad cosmopolita. Dentro de la ciudad, hay muchos barrios residenciales.

HABLAR • ESCRIBIR

10 ¿Quién dijo que sí? Contesta usando cada sujeto.

yo
mi amigo
¿Quién dijo que sí?
tú
usted

nosotros
Pilar y yo
¿Quiénes dijeron que sí?
Miguel y Andrés
ustedes

Andrew Payti

Pronombres después de una preposición

Go Online!

connectED.mcgraw-hill.com

1. You already know all the pronouns you use after a preposition. Remember they are the same as the subject pronouns except for **mí** and **ti. Mí** takes an accent mark to differentiate it from the possessive adjective **mi—mi casa.**

Para $\left\{ \begin{array}{l} \text{mí} \\ \text{ti} \\ \text{usted} \\ \text{él} \\ \text{ella} \\ \text{nosotros(as)} \\ \text{ustedes} \\ \text{ellos} \\ \text{ellas} \end{array} \right\}$ está bien, ¿no?

2. Note what happens to **mí** and **ti** when used with **con.**

—¿Vienes **conmigo**?
—Sí, voy **contigo**.

—¿Quién hizo el viaje **contigo**?
—Carolina lo hizo **conmigo**.

Práctica

HABLAR • ESCRIBIR

11 Contesta.

1. ¿De quién es el boleto? ¿Es de él o de ella?
2. ¿Para quién es la cámara digital? ¿Es para ti?
3. ¿Qué piensas de mí? Puedes ser honesto(a).
4. ¿Quiere Julia hacer una caminata con ustedes?
5. ¿Quieres ir conmigo?
6. ¿Quiénes van a hacer el viaje contigo?
7. ¿A ti te gusta más leer libros de bolsillo o artículos en una revista?

ESCRIBIR

12 Escribe en el singular.

1. No es para *ellos*.
2. Ellos quieren ir con *nosotros*.
3. Es de *ustedes*, ¿no?
4. Estamos pensando en *ellas*.
5. ¿Por qué no lo están discutiendo con *nosotros*?

Refrán

Can you guess what the following proverb means?

Querer y poder,
hermanos
vienen a ser.

¡Bravo!

You have now learned all the new vocabulary and grammar in this chapter. Continue to use and practice all that you know while learning more cultural information. **¡Vamos!**

EN LA VENTANILLA

UN BILLETE PARA CÓRDOBA, POR FAVOR.

¿SENCILLO O DE IDA Y VUELTA?

DE IDA Y VUELTA, POR FAVOR.

¿PARA CUÁNDO, SEÑORITA?

PARA HOY.

¿EN QUÉ CLASE? ¿PRIMERA O SEGUNDA?

EN SEGUNDA, POR FAVOR. ¿HAY UNA TARIFA REDUCIDA PARA ESTUDIANTES?

SÍ. ¿TIENE USTED SU TARJETA DE IDENTIDAD ESTUDIANTIL?

SÍ, AQUÍ LA TIENE USTED.

CON EL DESCUENTO SON VEINTISIETE EUROS.

¿A QUÉ HORA SALE EL PRÓXIMO TREN?

SALE A LAS VEINTE DIEZ DEL ANDÉN OCHO.

GRACIAS.

¿Comprendes?

Go Online!

connectED.mcgraw-hill.com

A Completa según la información en la conversación. Indica tus respuestas en una tabla como la de abajo.

el billete				
tipo	clase	destino	tipo de tarifa	precio (tarifa)

B Completa según la información en la conversación. Indica tus respuestas en una tabla como la de abajo.

el viaje		
medio de transporte	hora de salida	andén

¿Lo sabes?

Muchos alumnos toman el tren. Hay tarifas escolares (estudiantiles) reducidas.

C Corrige toda la información falsa.
1. La pasajera compra un billete para Sevilla.
2. Quiere un billete sencillo.
3. Necesita el billete para mañana.
4. Quiere viajar en primera.
5. La pasajera es profesora.
6. El tren sale a las seis y diez de la tarde.

D **Resumiendo** Cuenta todo lo que pasa en la conversación en tus propias palabras.

CULTURA

Córdoba, a orillas del río Guadalquivir, es una ciudad de mucho interés histórico. Aquí vemos el puente romano y la famosa Mezquita.

Lectura
CULTURAL

ESTRATEGIA DE LECTURA

▶ Antes de leer

Mira y estudia todos los elementos visuales que acompañan la lectura.

✔ READING CHECK

¿Dónde es más importante el servicio de trenes?

✔ READING CHECK

¿Quién descubrió Machu Picchu?

▶ Durante la lectura

Al leer cierto párrafo, estudia el elemento visual específico que clarifica la información en el párrafo.

USANDO ELEMENTOS VISUALES Antes de empezar a leer una lectura es importante mirar todos los elementos visuales que la acompañan—fotografías, ilustraciones, tablas, etc. Estos elementos visuales te dan una idea del contenido de la lectura y te facilitan la comprensión.

Viajes ferroviarios fabulosos

El servicio de trenes El tren es un medio de transporte importante y cómodo en España. Hay trenes que sirven casi todas las ciudades y pueblos del país con salidas frecuentes y muy pocas demoras.

En Latinoamérica el bus y el avión son los medios de transporte más importantes. En muchas regiones el servicio ferroviario no existe. No obstante[1] hay unos recorridos o viajes en tren que son fantásticos. Uno es el viaje de Cuzco a Machu Picchu en los Andes de Perú.

De Cuzco a Machu Picchu Cuzco es una ciudad andina famosa por sus magníficos edificios coloniales. Al borde de un cañón en una región remota no muy lejos de Cuzco está Machu Picchu—una ciudad construida por los incas. Un hecho[2] histórico increíble es que los españoles no descubrieron la ciudad durante su conquista de Perú. Fue el senador estadounidense Hiram Bingham quien la descubrió en 1911.

[1]No obstante   *Nevertheless*   [2]hecho   *fact*

CULTURA

Plaza de Armas, Cuzco, Perú

Richard Brommer

¿Quiénes toman el tren de Cuzco a Machu Picchu? La mayoría son turistas, entre ellos muchos mochileros jóvenes, que quieren tener la experiencia de visitar las famosas ruinas incaicas. El tren sale de Cuzco y para llegar a Machu Picchu tiene que bajar unos 1.200 metros. Corre al borde mismo de[3] muchos riscos escarpados[4]. Los pasajeros observan que, al bajar, el clima y la vegetación cambian mucho. A pesar de[5] su altura, Machu Picchu se encuentra en la región amazónica. Es una región semitropical de densa vegetación. En Machu Picchu es necesario llevar ropa ligera[6] y un impermeable[7] es imprescindible (obligatorio).

La Barranca del Cobre Otra excursión espectacular es la de la línea de ferrocarril Pacífico-Chihuahua por la Sierra Madre de México. El tren hace parada en Divisadero. De allí los pasajeros pueden contemplar la vista de la Barranca del Cobre, un cañón más profundo que el Gran Cañón de Colorado. Si algún día haces el viaje, debes bajar(te) del tren en Divisadero y pasar unos días dando caminatas por esta región espectacular. Si eres más aventurero(a), puedes rentar un caballo y con un guía hacer excursiones por los riscos del cañón.

[3]al borde mismo de   *right on the edge of*
[4]escarpados   *steep*
[5]A pesar de   *In spite of*
[6]ligera   *light*
[7]impermeable   *raincoat*

CULTURA
Ruinas en Machu Picchu

READING CHECK
¿Dónde hace más frío? ¿En Cuzco o en Machu Picchu?

CULTURA
La Barranca del Cobre en el estado de Chihuahua, México

READING CHECK
¿De dónde pueden ver la Barranca del Cobre los pasajeros del tren?

Lectura
CULTURAL

☑ **READING CHECK**

¿Cómo es la vida de los tarahumaras?

Después de leer

Explica como los elementos visuales te ayudaron a comprender la lectura.

En la región del cañón viven los tarahumaras. Una vez los tarahumaras ocuparon todo el estado de Chihuahua pero muchos de ellos murieron[8] por el duro trabajo forzado que tuvieron que hacer en las minas y más tarde en la construcción del ferrocarril. Para sobrevivir se fueron a vivir en los lugares más recónditos (aislados) de la barranca. Hoy son seminómadas y algunos viven en cuevas. En verano vagan (andan) por las mesetas de la Sierra Madre y en invierno bajan al fondo del cañón.

[8]murieron   *died*

CULTURA 🇲🇽
Una vista de la Barranca del Cobre en Divisadero, México

Steven dosRemedios/Getty Images

¿Comprendes?

A **Confirmando información** Indica si la información es correcta o no.

	correcta	incorrecta
1. El tren es un medio de transporte importante en España.		
2. El tren es un medio de transporte importante en todas partes de Latinoamérica.		
3. Hay ruinas de una ciudad azteca en Cuzco.		
4. Cuzco es una ciudad colonial en los Andes peruanos.		
5. Machu Picchu se encuentra al borde de un cañón.		
6. Machu Picchu está a una altura más baja que Cuzco.		
7. Por su altura Machu Picchu está en una zona muy fría.		
8. Nunca llueve en Machu Picchu.		

B **Describiendo** En tus propias palabras describe el viaje en tren de Cuzco a Machu Picchu.

C **Infiriendo** La lectura no indica de una manera directa que llueve mucho en Machu Picchu. Pero, ¿qué información en la lectura indica que llueve bastante en Machu Picchu?

D **Recordando hechos** Contesta.
  1. ¿Cuál es una excursión espectacular en México?
  2. ¿Qué es posible ver desde Divisadero?
  3. ¿Qué es la Barranca del Cobre?
  4. Hay dos maneras de visitar la Barranca del Cobre. ¿Cuáles son?

E **Describiendo** Contesta.
  1. ¿Cuáles son unas características de los tarahumaras?
  2. ¿Cómo fue su vida en el pasado y cómo es su vida actual?

CULTURA
Un edificio incaico en Machu Picchu

Richard Brommer

Lectura
UN POCO MÁS

Antes de leer

Utiliza lo que se llama «lo ya aprendido». Piensa en lo que ya aprendiste en el curso de español sobre las regiones tropicales de las Américas. Trata de imaginar el paisaje que ve un(a) pasajero(a) en un viaje a lo largo de un canal en una zona tropical.

CULTURA

Vista desde la estación de ferrocarril en Colón, Panamá

CULTURA

Ferrocarril del canal de Panamá en la estación de Colón

De Panamá a Colón en tren

Colón es la segunda ciudad más grande de Panamá. La primera es la capital, la Ciudad de Panamá. Colón está en el Atlántico y Panamá está en el Pacífico.

Si uno quiere ir de la Ciudad de Panamá a Colón, puede tomar el tren. El boleto o el pasaje es bastante barato y el viaje es interesante. El tren corre a lo largo del famoso canal de Panamá y durante el viaje los pasajeros pueden observar los muchos barcos que usan el canal para hacer la travesía desde el Atlántico hasta el Pacífico o viceversa. Es una zona tropical de vegetación densa y paisaje espectacular.

El tren pasa también por la pequeña isla de Barro Colorado. El Instituto Smithsonian mantiene la isla donde hacen investigaciones importantes sobre enfermedades tropicales.

Es muy fácil hacer el viaje de ida y regreso el mismo día porque dura (toma) solamente una hora y media.

¿Comprendes?

Escoge.

1. ¿Cómo sabemos que Colón no es la ciudad más grande de Panamá?
   a. No es la capital.
   b. Está en el Atlántico.
   c. La lectura indica que es la segunda ciudad del país.
   d. Hay solo dos ciudades grandes en Panamá.

2. ¿Cómo puede uno ir de Colón a Panamá?
   a. por el canal
   b. en tren
   c. por la isla de Barro Colorado
   d. observando los barcos

3. ¿Por qué es importante el canal de Panamá?
   a. Los barcos pueden hacer la travesía entre el Atlántico y el Pacífico en muy poco tiempo.
   b. Está en una zona tropical con una vegetación densa.
   c. En una de sus islas hay un instituto que hace investigaciones médicas importantes.
   d. Empalma o enlaza la Ciudad de Panamá con Colón.

4. ¿Cuál es la frase que expresa la misma idea que la siguiente?

   Los pasajeros pueden observar los muchos barcos que usan el canal.

   a. Los pasajeros pueden estudiar los muchos barcos que usan el canal.
   b. Los pasajeros pueden servir los muchos barcos que usan el canal.
   c. Los pasajeros pueden ver los muchos barcos que usan el canal.
   d. Los pasajeros pueden describir los muchos barcos que usan el canal.

5. ¿Cuál es un buen título para esta lectura?
   a. La Ciudad de Panamá
   b. El canal de Panamá
   c. Una región tropical
   d. Un viaje interesante en tren

Cultura

Investiga como la construcción del canal de Panamá afectó el comercio internacional.

CULTURA
Vista de unas esclusas del canal de Panamá

Andrew Payti

Prepárate para el examen

Un tren en el desierto de Atacama cerca de Arica, Chile

↻ To review, see **Vocabulario 1** and **Vocabulario 2.**

Vocabulario

1 **¿Sí o no?**

1. El revisor trabaja en la ventanilla en la estación de ferrocarril.

2. Un boleto sencillo es para un(a) pasajero(a) que no piensa volver al mismo lugar (sitio).

3. Si no sabes la hora de salida de tu tren tienes que consultar el quiosco.

4. Cuando quieres comer en el tren, vas al coche comedor.

5. Venden los boletos en el andén.

6. Un tren que sale tarde tiene una demora.

2 **Da otra palabra o expresión.**

7. cambiar de tren

8. con retraso

9. de ida y vuelta

10. la bufetería

3 **Completa con palabras apropiadas.**

11–12. Si quieres leer algo puedes comprar _____ y _____ en el quiosco.

13. El tren está completo. No hay _____ libres.

Gramática

↻ To review, see **Pretérito de los verbos irregulares.**

4 **Completa con el pretérito.**

14. Yo _____ que salir. (tener)

15. Nosotros no _____ esperar más. (poder)

16–17. Él _____ ir pero no _____. (querer, poder)

18. ¿Cuánto tiempo _____ ustedes allí? (estar)

19. Ellos _____ juntos, ¿no? (venir)

20. ¿Por qué no _____ tú la revista en la mochila? (poner)

21–22. Él no _____ porque no _____ vernos. (estar, querer)

Andrew Payti

Go Online!

connectED.mcgraw-hill.com

5 Escribe las frases en el pretérito.

23. Hacemos una excursión interesante.

24. Tengo que hacer las maletas.

25. Ustedes ven todo, ¿no?

26. ¿Por qué no quieres ir?

↻ To review, see **Pretérito de los verbos irregulares.**

6 Completa con la letra que falta.

27–28. Él lo hi_o pero yo no lo hi_e.

7 Completa con decir.

29–30. Yo lo _____ ahora y lo _____ ayer también.

31–32. Ellos lo _____ ahora y lo _____ ayer también.

33–34. Nosotros lo _____ ahora y lo _____ ayer también.

↻ To review, see **El verbo decir.**

Cultura

8 Contesta.

35. ¿Dónde es el tren un medio de transporte importante?

36. ¿Qué hay en Machu Picchu?

37. ¿Cómo van muchos turistas de Cuzco a Machu Picchu?

38. ¿Qué es la Barranca del Cobre?

39. ¿Dónde está?

40. ¿Quiénes son los tarahumaras?

↻ To review this cultural information, see the **Lectura cultural.**

CULTURA
Aguas Calientes, la última parada entre Cuzco y Machu Picchu

Richard Brommer

Prepárate para el examen

① Un viaje en avión o en tren

Compare train and plane travel

Trabaja con un(a) compañero(a) de clase. Van a comparar un viaje en tren con un viaje en avión. Cada uno(a) va a dar su preferencia.

② En la boletería

Talk about buying a train ticket

Prepara una conversación en la boletería de una estación de ferrocarril para comprar el tipo de boleto que necesitas.

③ Un lugar que conozco

Talk about a trip you took

Escoge un lugar que visitaste con unos amigos o parientes. Describe el lugar.

CULTURA

De compras en un mercado al aire libre en San Telmo en Buenos Aires, Argentina

④ El viaje más interesante

Discuss train trips in Spanish-speaking countries

De los viajes en tren en las lecturas de este capítulo, ¿cuál te interesa más? ¿Por qué? Habla con un(a) compañero(a) para determinar si ustedes tienen la misma opinión.

Andrew Payti

Go Online! ➕

connectED.mcgraw-hill.com

Tarea

You are going to write about a fabulous trip you took to a place that you love. The place can be real or imaginary. Be sure to write in such a way that your readers will also want to make that same trip.

Writing Strategy

Describing When writing a descriptive essay, use words that enable your reader to visualize the scene you are describing. Choose details and organize them in a way that creates an impression. Use vivid adjectives to make your writing more alive. Think of some adjectives you know in Spanish that you consider "vivid."

CULTURA 🔊

Estos dos mochileros en Oaxaca están viajando por México.

❶ Prewrite

Use a diagram like the one below to help you organize your writing.

❷ Write

- Read the sentences you wrote in the graphic organizer. Decide the best order for your composition. Each topic could be one paragraph. Give order to the sentences that develop each topic.

- In your description, try to make your readers understand what it is about the place that makes you think it is so great.

- **Expansion:** If you are a person who loves to travel and would like to expand this **Tarea** in order to track your progress, make a list of the goals that you would like to set for yourself with regard to this activity. You will learn about many other interesting places you might like to visit as you continue with your study of Spanish. Review this activity and what you wrote and determine how you could improve your writing. Continue to write about other places you might like to visit as you gain more knowledge of Spanish. Take note of the improvement you make in your writings. The improvements could include better use of descriptive words, the use of more newly learned vocabulary, or any other aspect of writing that you wish to improve. When you are ready, review and make a note of the areas in which you have improved most, then check that against the list of goals you set for yourself.

Evaluate

Don't forget that your teacher will evaluate you on organization, use of vocabulary, correctness of grammar, and completeness of information.

EN TREN

noventa y siete **97**

Andrew Payti

Repaso del Capítulo 3

Gramática

Pretérito de los verbos irregulares

Note the irregular preterite stems of the following verbs.

hacer → hic-   poder → pud-   estar → estuv-

querer → quis-   poner → pus-   andar → anduv-

venir → vin-   saber → sup-   tener → tuv-

venir	poner	tener
vine	puse	tuve
viniste	pusiste	tuviste
vino	puso	tuvo
vinimos	pusimos	tuvimos
vinisteis	*pusisteis*	*tuvisteis*
vinieron	pusieron	tuvieron

Remember the spelling of **hacer.**

hice, hizo

El verbo decir

Decir is irregular in the present and in the preterite.

presente		pretérito	
digo	decimos	dije	dijimos
dices	*decís*	dijiste	*dijisteis*
dice	dicen	dijo	dijeron

Traer is conjugated the same as **decir** in the preterite.

Pronombres después de una preposición

Except for **mí** and **ti,** prepositional pronouns are the same as subject pronouns.

mí, ti, usted, él, ella, nosotros(as), ustedes, ellos, ellas

With **con, mí** and **ti** become **conmigo** and **contigo.**

CULTURA

La pantalla de salidas en la estación de ferrocarril de Atocha en Madrid

Daniel Salsgiver

Juego There are a number of cognates in this list. See how many you and a partner can find. Who can find the most? Compare your list with those of your classmates.

Go Online!

connectED.mcgraw-hill.com

Vocabulario

Getting around a train station

la estación de
  ferrocarril (tren)
el hall
la sala de espera
el horario
la llegada
la salida
la ventanilla,
  la boletería

el billete, el boleto
  sencillo
  de ida y vuelta
  de ida y regreso
en primera
  (segunda) clase
la tarifa
  escolar
  (estudiantil)
  reducida

la tarjeta de crédito
el distribuidor
  automático
el tren
el vagón, el coche
el andén
la vía
el destino
subir al tren
bajar(se) del tren

At a kiosk

el quiosco
el periódico

la revista
el libro de bolsillo

On board the train

el pasillo
el asiento, la plaza
el revisor
el coche comedor,
  el coche cafetería,
  la bufetería

la parada
libre
ocupado(a)
completo(a)
próximo(a)
revisar los billetes

transbordar
  (cambiar de tren)

Describing an excursion

el cañón
el risco

una senda
el caballo

andar a caballo
alquilar, rentar

Other useful words and expressions

a tiempo
tarde

insertar
seleccionar

LA PRACTICE Refer to the Language Arts Practice section and use your Spanish to practice Language Arts skills.

Literary Reader

You may wish to read the adaptation of the Spanish classic *El Quijote*, found in the Literary Reader at the end of this book.

Repaso cumulativo

Repasa lo que ya has aprendido

These activities will help you review and remember what you have learned so far in Spanish.

1 Escucha las palabras. Haz un diagrama como el de abajo. Indica si cada palabra se relaciona con un viaje en tren o en avión o los dos.

el tren — los dos — el avión

CULTURA

Hay muchos trenes que salen de la estación General Belgrano para los suburbios de Buenos Aires.

2 Completa en el presente con la forma yo.

1. _____ un viaje en tren. (hacer)
2. _____ a las ocho. (salir)
3. _____ mucho equipaje. (tener)
4. _____ tres maletas. (traer)
5. _____ mucha ropa en mis maletas. (poner)
6. _____ en tren. (venir)
7. _____ que _____ el viaje en tren. (decir, hacer)
8. _____ que me voy a divertir. (saber)
9. _____ a viajar por Argentina. (ir)
10. _____ Argentina. (conocer)

3 Cambia las frases en la Actividad 2 a María.

4 Parea los contrarios.

1. el despegue	a. largo
2. la llegada	b. subir
3. bajar	c. temprano
4. sentarse	d. el aterrizaje
5. volver, regresar	e. vender
6. corto	f. la salida
7. comprar	g. salir
8. tarde	h. levantarse

Andrew Payti

100 *cien*

CAPÍTULO 3

⑤ Escoge la palabra apropiada del banco de palabras para contestar cada pregunta.

el mostrador de la línea aérea	el cinturón de seguridad
la tarjeta de embarque	el control de seguridad
el boleto electrónico	en el pasillo
la puerta de salida	en la pista

1. ¿Dónde se presenta Felipe para facturar su equipaje en el aeropuerto?
2. ¿De dónde sale el vuelo?
3. ¿Por dónde tienen que pasar los pasajeros antes de ir a la puerta de salida?
4. ¿Qué necesitan los pasajeros para poder abordar el avión?
5. ¿Qué tienen que abrochar los pasajeros a bordo del avión?
6. El asiento de José no está en la ventanilla. ¿Dónde está?

⑥ ¿Qué pone José en su maleta?

⑦ Personaliza. Da respuestas personales.

1. Cuando estás de vacaciones, ¿a qué hora te despiertas?
2. ¿Te levantas enseguida?
3. Si vas de camping, ¿duermes en una carpa?
4. ¿Te duermes enseguida si tienes que dormir en un saco de dormir?
5. ¿A qué hora te acuestas?
6. ¿Te diviertes cuando estás de vacaciones?

En el restaurante

Vamos a comparar ¿Come tu familia a veces en un restaurante? ¿Qué tipo de restaurantes hay donde tú vives? ¿Hay restaurantes elegantes y restaurantes económicos? ¿Hay restaurantes étnicos o no? Vamos a ver los muchos tipos de restaurantes que hay en España y Latinoamérica y lo que uno debe esperar cuando come en un restaurante en un país hispano.

Objetivos

You will:

- order and pay for a meal at a restaurant
- identify more foods
- identify eating utensils and dishes
- discuss restaurants in Spain and Latin America

You will use:

- stem-changing verbs in the present and preterite
- adjectives of nationality
- the passive voice with **se**

◀ El restaurante Casa Duque en Segovia, España

En el restaurante

Mira las fotografías para familiarizarte con el tema del capítulo—experiencias en restaurantes en varias partes del mundo hispano. Consulta los menús y observa unos platos deliciosos regionales para decidir los que te apetecen. Y, ¡buen provecho!

México

¿Te apetece comer algo? ¿Qué quieres pedir de esta lista delante de una cafetería en Guadalajara, México?

¡RICAS!
TORTAS AHOGADAS $17.⁰⁰
LONCHES
JAMON.....$17.⁰⁰
PANELA.....$17.⁰⁰
CARNITAS...$20.⁰⁰
TOSTADAS
CUERITOS...$11.⁰⁰
JAMON.....$13.⁰⁰
PANELA.....$13.⁰⁰
CARNITAS...$16.⁰⁰
TACOS
Vapor 5 x $11.⁰⁰
Dorados 5 x $10.⁰⁰

Ecuador

Es la terraza de un restaurante en Baños, Ecuador. A mucha gente le gusta comer al aire libre.

España

La paella es una especialidad de Valencia. Es un plato rico y como vemos aquí lleva arroz amarillo con un surtido de mariscos. Es el azafrán, un condimento caro, que le da el color amarillo al arroz.

Guatemala

El mesero sirve la comida en un restaurante elegante en la Ciudad de Guatemala.

```
Unid. Descripción
recio        Total          P

1 BOC  TORTILLA 100G    3,35    3,35
1 AGUA 0.5 L (PC)       1,35    1,35

TOTAL Euro              4,70
  ENTREGADO                   20,00
  CAMBIO                      15,30


        I.V.A Incluido
  GRACIAS POR SU VISITA
```

(tr)Kerri Galloway, (cl cr)Andrew Payti, (bl)Lori Ernfridsson, (br)McGraw-Hill Education

Perú

Entrada a un restaurante en Lima que tiene unas especialidades interesantes. ¿Qué te apetece?

ESPECIALIDAD
TAPAS VARIADAS
RABO DE TORO
PERDIZ
COCHINILLO
PATA DE CORDERO

RESTAURANTE
Hnos.
MACIAS
HOSTAL
Bodega
La Verdad

HORCHATERIA DE SANTA CATALINA
Casa con dos siglos de tradición

España

El restaurante Horchatería de Santa Catalina en Valencia, España. Este restaurante tiene un menú variado, pero una horchata es una bebida popular en España. Es una bebida hecha a base de almendras machadas con agua y azúcar. Se toma muy fría.

Mesa en la que fue servida S.A.R. la Infanta D.ª Isabel en sus respectivas visitas a esta casa

España

¿Quién fue servida en este restaurante?

Costa Rica

El casado es una comida típica de los ticos, o costarricenses. Lleva arroz, frijoles, una rodaja de plátano frito y pollo acompañado de una ensalada. El casado puede llevar también yuca y patacones con un filete de carne de res o pescado.

Chile

Los meseros tienen unos momentos libres para tomar un poco de aire fresco delante de su restaurante en Vicuña, Chile. Vicuña es el pueblo natal de la famosa autora chilena Gabriela Mistral.

HALLEY
Cabrito asado
Porotos Granad
Humitas
Pastel de Choclo
Escabecha

En el restaurante 🎧

Carlos y Alicia están en el restaurante.
Alicia pide el menú.

En otras partes

- **El mesero** is used throughout Latin America. **El camarero** is used in Spain.
- **El cerdo** is the general word for *pork* and **chuletas de cerdo** means *pork chops.* Roast suckling pig is a very popular dish— **el cochinillo asado** in Spain, **el lechón asado** in most of Latin America but particularly in the Caribbean. The word **chancho** is also used in several Latin American countries.
- **El biftec** as well as **el bistec** is used. Both are correct.

Carlos pidió un biftec.
El mesero lo sirvió.

Alicia pide la cuenta.
Carlos deja una propina.

David H. Brennan

Más comestibles
La carne

Los mariscos

la carne de res

el cordero

la chuleta de cerdo

la langosta

los mejillones

las almejas

el aceite

la sal

el vinagre

la pimienta

poner la mesa

levantar (quitar) la mesa

¡Así se dice!

When you are really starving you can say **Me muero de hambre,** which literally means *I'm dying of hunger.*

el platillo

la taza

la servilleta

la cucharita

la cuchara

el tenedor

el plato

el cuchillo

el mantel

(tl tr c b)David H. Brennan, (tc)Kelli Drummer-Avendaño

1 Escucha. Indica en una tabla como la de abajo si ves en la foto la información que oyes.

sí	no

2 **Juego** **Cada uno en su sitio** Determina a qué categoría pertenece cada palabra.

el jamón   la pimienta   el aceite   el cordero
los mejillones   la sal   los camarones
el biftec   el pollo   la langosta

CARNE	MARISCOS	CONDIMENTOS
_____	_____	_____
_____	_____	_____
_____	_____	_____
_____	_____	_____

3 Contesta sobre un restaurante.

1. ¿Quién sirve la comida en un restaurante?
2. ¿Qué pide el cliente para seleccionar o escoger lo que quiere comer?
3. Después de la comida, ¿qué pide para pagar?
4. ¿Deja una propina a veces?
5. ¿Para quién es la propina?

EXPANSIÓN

Ahora, sin mirar las preguntas, cuenta la información en tus propias palabras. Si no recuerdas algo, un(a) compañero(a) te puede ayudar.

4 **¡Te toca a ti!** Vas a poner la mesa. ¿Qué pones en la mesa?

CULTURA

El mesero sirve los refrescos que pidieron las jóvenes en un restaurante al aire libre en Manta, Ecuador.

Andrew Payti

LEER • HABLAR

5 Rompecabezas

¡Adivina! ¿Qué es?

1. Se usa para cubrir la mesa.
2. Se usa para tomar agua o leche.
3. Se usa para beber café o té.
4. Se usa para comer sopa.
5. Se usa para cortar la carne.

HABLAR • ESCRIBIR

6 Personaliza. Da respuestas personales.

1. ¿Te gusta comer en un restaurante?
2. ¿Te gusta más la carne o el pescado?
3. ¿Te gustan las legumbres?
4. Para tu ensalada, ¿te gusta una salsa de aceite y vinagre?
5. ¿Te gusta la carne bien hecha, a término medio o casi cruda?
6. En tu casa, ¿quién pone la mesa?
7. ¿Quién lava los platos?
8. Y, ¿quién levanta o quita la mesa?

CULTURA
Un restaurante con una terraza al aire libre en Guadalajara, México

Conexiones

El lenguaje

Ya sabes que en el mundo hispano hay diferencias regionales en cuanto al uso de ciertas palabras. Los nombres de los comestibles tienden a variar de una región a otra. Aquí tenemos unos ejemplos.

• Las judías verdes tienen muchos nombres. Se llaman también «habichuelas tiernas», «chauchas», «vainitas», «ejotes» y «porotos».

• En casi todas partes el maíz es «el maíz» pero en México también se dice «el elote» y en Chile y otros países latinos se dice «el choclo». Un plato chileno delicioso es «el pastel de choclo».

Presente de los verbos de cambio radical e → i

PAPER FILE FOLDER See the Foldables section of the Student Handbook at the beginning of this book for help with making this foldable. Use this foldable to help you review the different tenses of the verbs that you have learned. Make a *paper file folder* for a verb. On separate pieces of paper, write the conjugations of the verb. Continue to file new conjugations in your *paper file folder.*

1. The verbs **pedir, servir, repetir, freír** *(to fry),* **seguir** *(to follow),* and **vestirse** *(to get dressed)* are stem-changing verbs. The **e** of the infinitive stem changes to **i** in all forms of the present tense except **nosotros(as)** and *vosotros(as).* Study the following forms.

pedir			
yo	pido	nosotros(as)	pedimos
tú	pides	vosotros(as)	pedís
Ud., él, ella	pide	Uds., ellos, ellas	piden

servir			
yo	sirvo	nosotros(as)	servimos
tú	sirves	vosotros(as)	servís
Ud., él, ella	sirve	Uds., ellos, ellas	sirven

2. Note the spelling of **seguir.**

sigo, sigues, sigue, seguimos, *seguís,* **siguen**

3. Note that the present participle of these verbs also has **i.**

No estoy pidiendo nada.
El mesero nos está sirviendo.

Práctica

HABLAR • ESCRIBIR

1. Personaliza. Da respuestas personales.

    1. ¿Qué pides cuando vas a un restaurante?
    2. Si te gusta un plato, ¿lo repites?
    3. ¿Sigues una dieta o un régimen?
    4. ¿Te vistes antes de salir para la escuela?
    5. ¿Sigues un horario fijo en la escuela o varía de un día a otro tu horario?

CULTURA

Un restaurante callejero en Valencia, España

Andrew Payti

ESCUCHAR • HABLAR

2 Conversa según el modelo.

MODELO —**A Juan le gusta la carne de res. ¿Qué pide él?**
—**Él pide carne de res.**

1. A Marta le gustan las legumbres. ¿Qué pide ella?
2. A Andrés le gusta el biftec. ¿Qué pide él?
3. A mis amigos les gustan los mariscos. ¿Qué piden ellos?
4. A mis padres les gusta mucho el postre. ¿Qué piden ellos?
5. Nos gusta la ensalada. ¿Qué pedimos?
6. Nos gustan las tortillas. ¿Qué pedimos?

ESCRIBIR

3 Completa la tabla.

yo	nosotros	usted	tú	ellos
		pide		
sirvo				
	seguimos			
				se visten
			repites	

HABLAR • ESCRIBIR

4 Personaliza. Da respuestas personales.

1. Cuando vas a un restaurante, ¿qué pides?
2. ¿Pides papas? Si no pides papas, ¿pides arroz?
3. ¿Qué más pides con la carne y las papas o el arroz?
4. ¿Quién te sirve en el restaurante?
5. Si te sirve bien, ¿qué le dejas?

LEER • ESCRIBIR

5 Escribe en el plural.

1. Siempre pido postre.
2. No repito nada.
3. Él se viste bien.
4. Sigo un plan definido.
5. ¿Qué repites?
6. Ella fríe las papas.

6 **Comunicación**

Trabaja con un(a) compañero(a). Preparen una conversación entre un(a) cliente(a) y un(a) camarero(a). El/La cliente(a) va a leer el menú para decidir lo que quiere comer. El/La camarero(a) contesta las preguntas que el/la cliente(a) tiene sobre los platos y luego escribe la orden. Presenten la conversación a la clase.

POTROS RESTAURANTE-BAR 24-HORAS

Menú

Lunes
- Sopa de Pastas
- Pollo al Horno ó Carne ASADA
- Arroz Blanco
- Frijoles
- Patacones ó Yuca
- Ensalada de Lechuga, Zanahoria, Tomate
- Jugos

Martes
Sopa de Guineo
Chuleta Ahumada ó Corvina
Apanada
Arroz Blanco
Ensalada de Lechuga
Torrejas de Trigo ó Patacones
Jugos

3.00

Miércoles
- Sopa de Cebada
- Pechuga Apanada o Lomo de Cerdo Jamonado
- Arroz c/guandú
- Lentejas
- Papa hervida picada en trocitos
- Plátano Asado
- Jugos

Jueves
Sopa de Mondongo
Arroz Blanco
Muchacho Relleno,
Carne en su Salsa
Yuca Frita o Tajadas
Ensalada Roja
Jugos

Viernes
Bandeja PAISA y Sancocho Colombiano
Jugos

4.00

Sábado
Arroz con Pollo (tajada, ensalada de aguacate)
Frijolada, Pollo frito,
arroz blanco y ensalada de aguacate, Jugos

3.00

Pretérito de los verbos de cambio radical e → i, o → u

1. The verbs **pedir, repetir, freír, servir, seguir,** and **vestirse** have a stem change in the preterite. The **e** of the infinitive stem changes to **i** in the **él** and **ellos** forms.

repetir			
yo	repetí	nosotros(as)	repetimos
tú	repetiste	vosotros(as)	repetisteis
Ud., él, ella	repitió	Uds., ellos, ellas	repitieron

vestirse			
yo	me vestí	nosotros(as)	nos vestimos
tú	te vestiste	vosotros(as)	os vestisteis
Ud., él, ella	se vistió	Uds., ellos, ellas	se vistieron

2. The verbs **preferir, divertirse,** and **dormir** also have a stem change in the preterite. The **e** in **preferir** and **divertirse** changes to **i** and the **o** in **dormir** changes to **u** in the **él** and **ellos** forms. The verb **morir** (*to die*) follows the same pattern as **dormir—murió, murieron.**

preferir			
yo	preferí	nosotros(as)	preferimos
tú	preferiste	vosotros(as)	preferisteis
Ud., él, ella	prefirió	Uds., ellos, ellas	prefirieron

dormir			
yo	dormí	nosotros(as)	dormimos
tú	dormiste	vosotros(as)	dormisteis
Ud., él, ella	durmió	Uds., ellos, ellas	durmieron

CULTURA

Los amigos pasaron un rato en un café en Cádiz, España. Alguien pidió un refresco y el mesero lo está sirviendo ahora.

Andrew Payti

Práctica

HABLAR • ESCRIBIR

7 Contesta según se indica.

1. ¿Te vestiste elegantemente para ir al restaurante? (no)
2. ¿Qué pediste en el restaurante? (una ensalada)
3. ¿Cómo la pediste? (sin aceite y vinagre)
4. ¿Cuántas veces le repetiste «sin aceite y vinagre»? (dos veces)
5. Y, ¿cómo sirvió el mesero la ensalada? (con aceite y vinagre)
6. ¿Qué hiciste? (pedí otra ensalada)
7. ¿Qué pidió tu amigo? (puré de papas)
8. ¿Y qué pasó? (ellos frieron las papas)
9. ¿Qué sirvió el mesero? (papas fritas)
10. ¿Le dieron ustedes una propina al mesero? (no)

EXPANSIÓN

Ahora, sin mirar las preguntas, cuenta la información en tus propias palabras. Si no recuerdas algo, un(a) compañero(a) te puede ayudar.

Después contesta la pregunta, ¿Por qué no le dieron una propina al mesero?

LEER • ESCRIBIR

8 Completa con el pretérito.

Anoche mi amigo Ángel y yo ___1___ (ir) a un restaurante. Ángel ___2___ (pedir) pescado—más específicamente ___3___ (pedir) corvina, un pescado delicioso del Pacífico. Ángel lo ___4___ (pedir) frito y el cocinero lo ___5___ (freír) muy bien. El mesero ___6___ (servir) la corvina en una salsa de mantequilla y limón.

Yo no ___7___ (pedir) pescado. Yo ___8___ (pedir) mariscos—un plato delicioso de mejillones, almejas y camarones. El mesero ___9___ (servir) el plato muy caliente. Luego nosotros ___10___ (pedir) un postre rico, delicioso. Nosotros ___11___ (divertirse) mucho.

Cuando yo volví a casa ___12___ (dormirse) enseguida. No sé si Ángel ___13___ (dormirse) enseguida o no.

CULTURA

Un restaurante popular en una esquina de San Telmo, un barrio interesante de Buenos Aires, la capital de Argentina

Andrew Payti

InfoGap For more practice with stem-changing verbs, do Activity 4 in the Student Resource section at the end of this book.

⑨ ¡Te toca a ti! Completa la palabra.

1. rep_tió
2. s_rvieron
3. se v_stieron
4. p_dió
5. se div_rtió
6. d_rmieron
7. m_rió
8. pref_rió
9. fr_eron
10. p_dieron

Adjetivos de nacionalidad

1. Adjectives of nationality that end in **o** or **e** follow the same pattern as any other adjective. Those that end in **o** have four forms and those that end in **e** have two forms.

un restaurante cubano	**una comida cubana**
unos restaurantes cubanos	**unas comidas cubanas**

un plato nicaragüense	**una comida nicaragüense**
unos platos nicaragüenses	**unas comidas nicaragüenses**

2. Adjectives of nationality that end in a consonant have four forms rather than two.

un restaurante español	**una comida española**
unos restaurantes españoles	**unas comidas españolas**

3. Adjectives of nationality that end in **s** or **n** have a written accent in the masculine singular. The accent is dropped in all other forms.

francés	**francesa**	**catalán**	**catalana**
franceses	**francesas**	**catalanes**	**catalanas**

Some other common adjectives of nationality that end in a consonant are: **inglés, portugués, irlandés, japonés, alemán.**

4. Note that with an article the adjective becomes a noun.

Los portugueses son de Portugal y los brasileños son de Brasil.

CULTURA 🇫🇷

Una joven francesa delante de un monumento francés—la famosa Torre Eiffel

CULTURA 🇲🇽

Un plato mexicano

Práctica

10 Contesta según el modelo.

MODELO —¿**Son de España las muchachas?**
—**Sí, son españolas.**

1. ¿Son de España los muchachos?
2. ¿Es de Colombia el café?
3. ¿Son de Nicaragua las profesoras?
4. ¿Son de Inglaterra los libros?
5. ¿Es de Francia tu amigo?

LEER • ESCRIBIR

11 Completa según se indica.

1. En el restaurante sirven comida _____. (mexicano)
2. La cocina _____ no es como la cocina _____.
   (catalán, francés)
3. Las rosas _____ son las más bonitas. (ecuatoriano)
4. Los pasajeros _____ comprenden el español. (portugués)
5. Los _____ hablan inglés. (irlandés)
6. Hay muchos restaurantes _____ y _____ en
   Latinoamérica. En Perú los restaurantes _____ se llaman
   «chifas». (japonés, chino, chino)

CULTURA
Estos jóvenes venezolanos están comiendo comida japonesa
auténtica en un restaurante japonés en Caracas, Venezuela.

Kelli Drummer-Avendaño

La voz pasiva con se

1. When you talk about something being done without saying who does it, you use the passive voice in English.

Fish is sold at the fish market.

2. In Spanish, the pronoun **se** is used to express this idea.

Se vende pescado en la pescadería.
Se venden papas en la verdulería.

3. You will often see the **se** construction used to express ideas such as:

They speak Spanish here.
Spanish is spoken here.
One speaks Spanish here. ⎫ **Aquí se habla español.**
People speak Spanish here.

¡Así se dice!

A very useful expression is
¿Cómo se dice en español?

DENTISTAS Y MEDICOS
SE ACEPTAN ASEGURANZAS
MD. MARCO A. TAMAYO MENDEZ
DR. MARCO ANTONIO TAMAYO
DR. JUAN CARLOS GONZALEZ LOCAL 11-B

Práctica

ESCUCHAR • HABLAR • ESCRIBIR

12 Contesta. Presta atención a la forma de **vender.**

1. ¿Se vende pan en la panadería?
2. ¿Se venden suéteres en la tienda de ropa?
3. ¿Se vende carne en la carnicería?
4. ¿Se venden guisantes en la verdulería?
5. ¿Se vende fruta en la frutería?
6. ¿Se venden productos congelados en el supermercado?
7. ¿Se vende pescado en la pescadería?
8. ¿Se venden camisas en la tienda de ropa?

CULTURA

Se venden frutas en este puesto en Tepoztlán, México.

Andrew Payti

HABLAR • ESCRIBIR

13 ¿Qué se habla y dónde? Sigue el modelo.

MODELO

—¿Qué lengua se habla en España?
—Se habla español en España.

1.

2.

3.

4.

5.

6.

HABLAR • ESCRIBIR

14 Contesta.

1. ¿Se deja una propina (en un restaurante) cuando el servicio está incluido?
2. ¿Se sirve mucha carne en un restaurante argentino?
3. ¿Se usa mucho aceite en España?
4. ¿Se pone el cuchillo a la derecha o a la izquierda del plato?
5. ¿Se pone la taza en un platillo?
6. ¿Se comen muchos mariscos en los restaurantes cerca de la costa?
7. Los tostones son populares en el Caribe. ¿Se sirven tostones con muchas comidas cubanas?
8. ¿Se dice «menú» de la misma manera en inglés y español?

Refrán

Can you guess what the following proverb means?

Con mal vinagre y peor aceite, buen gazpacho no se puede hacer.

¡Bravo!

You have now learned all the new vocabulary and grammar in this chapter. Continue to use and practice all that you know while learning more cultural information. **¡Vamos!**

Jennifer Thermes/Getty Images

Una comida muy buena 🎧 ↻

Adela	Anoche fuimos a un restaurante argentino.
Felipe	Sí, ¿qué pediste?
Adela	Yo pedí un biftec o como dicen en Argentina «bife de lomo».
Felipe	¿Qué tal te gustó?
Adela	Mucho. Lo pedí casi crudo porque yo sé que en Argentina se sirve el bife bien hecho.
Felipe	¿Qué te sirvieron con el bife?
Adela	Papas fritas. Y pedí una ensalada aparte.
Felipe	Se dice que en Argentina se sirven porciones grandes.
Adela	Sí, es verdad. Y después de comer tanto todos pedimos flan.
Felipe	¿Flan? Es un postre español, ¿no?
Adela	Sí, lo es pero es popular en Latinoamérica también.
Felipe	Pues me parece que te divertiste.
Adela	Mucho. Y cuando volví a casa, me dormí enseguida—como se dice «con la panza llena».

¿Comprendes?

A Contesta según la información en la conversación.

1. ¿Qué pidió Adela en el restaurante argentino?
2. ¿Le gustó?
3. ¿Cómo pidió el bife?
4. ¿Cómo lo sirven en Argentina?
5. ¿Qué más comió Adela?
6. ¿Cómo son las porciones que se sirven en Argentina?
7. ¿Qué pidió Adela de postre?
8. ¿Qué hizo Adela cuando volvió a casa?

B **Resumiendo** Cuenta la información en la conversación en tus propias palabras.

C **Identificando** Indica todo lo que Adela comió en el restaurante argentino.

D **Llegando a conclusiones** Según la información en la conversación, ¿cuáles son unas características típicas de una comida en Argentina?

CULTURA

El mesero sirve a sus clientes en la terraza de un café en la Recoleta, Buenos Aires, Argentina.

Andrew Payti

Lectura
CULTURAL

ESTRATEGIA DE LECTURA

COMPARANDO Cuando lees algo es importante hacer comparaciones. Cuando comparas algo identificas lo que es diferente y lo que es lo mismo o semejante. Hacer comparaciones mentales te ayuda a recordar la información que estás leyendo.

Antes de leer

Piensa en una visita a un restaurante. ¿Qué comes? ¿Quién te sirve? ¿Dejas una propina?

Restaurantes de España y Latinoamérica 🎧 ↻

Algún día vas a tener la oportunidad de visitar un país hispano. Y como tienes que comer unas tres veces al día, debes saber algo sobre los restaurantes.

✓ READING CHECK

¿Dónde se puede comer económicamente?

¿Comer dónde? En todas las grandes ciudades hay restaurantes elegantes y económicos. Si quieres solamente una merienda puedes ir a un café. Si quieres una comida es mejor ir a un restaurante o una cafetería. Pero una cafetería no es de autoservicio[1]. Es un restaurante generalmente modesto donde se sirve comida en una barra[2] igual que en una mesa. Comer en la barra cuesta menos que en una de las mesas.

[1]autoservicio   *self-service*
[2]barra   *counter*

Durante la lectura

Prepara una lista mental de las cosas que son las mismas en un restaurante aquí en Estados Unidos y las cosas que son diferentes.

CULTURA 🇪🇸

Mucha gente pasa un domingo por la tarde en un restaurante como este en Cádiz, España.

Andrew Payti

¿Servir cómo? Por lo general una comida, sobre todo una comida española, consiste en varios platos—primer plato, plato principal y postre. En muchas partes el plato principal se llama «el plato fuerte». En España no se sirve una mezcla[3] de cosas en el mismo plato como aquí en Estados Unidos. Si pides judías verdes o alcachofas salteadas[4], el camarero te va a servir estas legumbres como un primer plato o entrada. Pero como sabemos, siempre hay excepciones. En unos restaurantes modestos o cafeterías se sirve lo que se llama «un plato combinado» que lleva, por ejemplo, carne, papas y una legumbre en el mismo plato.

En Latinoamérica las costumbres varían de país en país. En Puerto Rico y otras islas del Caribe, por ejemplo, la carne o el pescado viene acompañado de arroz blanco o amarillo con frijoles (habichuelas) y tostones o maduros[5]. En México muchos platos llevan arroz y frijoles refritos.

[3]mezcla   *mixture*
[4]alcachofas salteadas   *sautéed artichokes*
[5]maduros   *fried sweet bananas*

✔ **READING CHECK**

¿Cuál es una característica de una comida española?

✔ **READING CHECK**

¿Qué acompaña una comida en los países del Caribe?

CULTURA

Unos mariscos de un restaurante en Barcelona y una comida de pescado en un restaurante en Maracay, Venezuela.

(tl)Andrew Payti, (tr)Daniel Salsgiver, (b)McGraw-Hill Education

✔ **READING CHECK**

¿Qué es la sobremesa?

Después de leer

*Decide si hay más semejanzas
(cosas similares) o diferencias al
comer en un restaurante aquí
en Estados Unidos y en un
restaurante en un país hispano.*

¿Tomar el postre? A muchos les gusta terminar una comida
con un postre. Una vez la palabra «sobremesa» era sinónimo
de «postre», pero hoy en día no se usa así. Pero el fenómeno
de sobremesa continúa. En España y muchos países de
Latinoamérica la comida puede durar unas horas. Después
del postre empieza la sobremesa. Los comensales[6] se quedan
y la conversación comenzada durante la comida sigue. ¿Por
cuánto tiempo? Pues, no se sabe cuánto tiempo durará la
sobremesa.

Muchos turistas le preguntan al mesero si el servicio está
incluido. La respuesta es casi siempre «sí» y no es necesario
dejar una propina.

¿Se puede? ¡Un punto muy importante! Si no comes toda la
comida, por lo general no pides llevar las sobras[7] a casa. Hasta
recientemente la etiqueta no lo permitía, pero es algo que está
cambiando. Pero la costumbre de llevar las sobras a casa para
el «perrito» no es tan común como aquí, en Estados Unidos.

¡Otro punto importante! Después de comer bien en un
restaurante, a mucha gente le gusta ir a otro local para tomar
su cafecito, un local que se especializa en el café.

¡Buen apetito!

CULTURA

Los cafés al aire libre son muy populares en
la Recoleta, un barrio bonito de Buenos Aires.

Andrew Payti

¿Comprendes?

A Confirmando información Indica si la información es correcta o no.

	correcta	incorrecta
1. En las ciudades españolas y latinoamericanas hay solo restaurantes elegantes.		
2. Una cafetería es siempre de autoservicio.		
3. En una cafetería cuesta más comer en una mesa que en la barra.		
4. En España siempre ponen muchas cosas diferentes en el mismo plato.		
5. En España una comida típica comprende (consiste en) varios platos.		

B Describiendo Describe.

    1. lo que acompaña una típica comida puertorriqueña
    2. lo que acompaña una típica comida mexicana
    3. lo que es la sobremesa

C Explicando Explica.

    1. la diferencia entre un café, un restaurante y una cafetería
    2. como se sirve la comida en España
    3. lo que es un plato combinado

D Comparando Compara tu experiencia en restaurantes estadounidenses con lo que aprendiste de los restaurantes en los países hispanos.

E Identificando ¿Cuál es la idea principal de esta lectura? Da unos detalles que apoyan (*support*) esta idea.

F Analizando ¿Qué piensas? ¿Por qué quiere compartir el autor esta información con sus lectores? ¿Cuál es su propósito?

CULTURA

¿Quieres pedir algo del menú de este restaurante en Guatemala?

Richard Brommer

Lectura
UN POCO MÁS

Antes de leer
Piensa en unas experiencias personales en un restaurante. ¿Cómo es el servicio? ¿Son corteses los meseros? Una vez, ¿te dio un servicio malo un mesero? Si contestas que sí, recuerda lo que pasó. Si contestas que no, piensa en algunas cosas que pueden pasar.

CULTURA
Es la terraza de un restaurante popular en Miraflores en Lima, Perú.

Sé lo que pedí

Anoche Julio y un grupo de sus amigos fueron a cenar en un restaurante. Se divirtieron porque les gusta estar en su grupo pero la verdad es que no comieron bien. Fue un desastre. Nada anduvo bien. Todo salió mal.

Por ejemplo, Julio pidió un bistec a término medio. Y lo repitió dos veces al mesero: «a término medio». Pidió también papas fritas y una ensalada de lechuga y tomates. Y, ¿qué le sirvió el mesero? Es verdad que le sirvió un bistec, pero no a término medio. Le sirvió el bistec casi crudo y a Julio no le gusta la carne muy roja. ¿Le sirvió las papas fritas? No. Le puso un plato de arroz y le dio una ensalada pero sin tomates. ¿Qué piensas? ¿Dejó Julio una buena propina para el mesero? Tú puedes decidir. Pero, te digo una cosa. Cuando salió del restaurante Julio dijo: «¡Increíble! Yo le pedí una cosa y él me sirvió otra. No sé si él me comprendió o no».

¿Tuviste alguna mala experiencia en un restaurante como la de Julio y sus amigos? ¿Te enfadaste? ¿Le dijiste algo al mesero?

Andrew Payti

¿Comprendes?

Escoge o completa.

1. ¿Se divirtieron Julio y sus amigos?
   a. Sí, porque fueron a cenar en un restaurante.
   b. Sí, porque el mesero les dio un servicio bueno.
   c. Sí, porque les gusta pasar tiempo juntos.
   d. Sí, porque fue un desastre.

2. ¿Quién o qué causó el problema?
   a. el mesero
   b. Julio
   c. los amigos de Julio
   d. la propina

3. Los comestibles mencionados en la lectura son _____.

4. ¿Qué no comprendió Julio?
   a. por qué no le dio una buena propina al mesero
   b. por qué él pidió una cosa y el mesero le sirvió otra
   c. por qué el mesero no lo comprendió
   d. por qué decidieron ir al restaurante

5. ¿Cuál es un buen título para la lectura?
   a. Mis amigos
   b. Nos gusta pasar tiempo juntos.
   c. Una comida
   d. Una comida desastrosa

CULTURA

Este restaurante en Antigua, Guatemala tiene el nombre de una famosa artista mexicana. ¿Quién es?

Lori Ernfridsson

Prepárate para el examen

↻ To review, see **Vocabulario**.

1 Identifica.

2 Completa con una palabra apropiada.

6. Se puede preparar una salsa para una ensalada con _____ y vinagre.

7. El cordero no es un pescado. Es _____.

8. Se sirve el café en _____.

9–10. Los clientes en un restaurante piden _____ antes de comer y piden _____ después de comer.

11. La langosta es _____. No es una carne.

3 ¿Sí o no?

12. Patricia pide el menú porque sabe lo que quiere comer.

13. Si el servicio no está incluido el cliente deja una propina para el mesero.

14. El cerdo es un pescado.

15. El flan es un postre.

16. Tomás necesita un tenedor para tomar la sopa.

17. Levantamos la mesa antes de comer.

18. Antonio pide el bistec casi crudo porque no le gusta la carne muy roja.

Gramática

4 Completa con el presente.

19. El mesero les _____ a los clientes en el restaurante. (servir)

20. Yo siempre _____ la misma cosa, un bistec. (pedir)

21. Ellas _____ elegantemente para ir al restaurante. (vestirse)

22. Nosotros no lo _____. (repetir)

23. El cocinero _____ las papas. (freír)

24. El postre _____ el plato principal. (seguir)

↺ To review, see **Presente de los verbos de cambio radical e → i.**

5 Completa con el pretérito.

25. Ellos se divirtieron. Y yo _____ también.

26. Yo dormí bien. Y él _____ bien también.

27. Tú lo repetiste. Y nosotros lo _____ también.

28. Ellos lo prefirieron. Y su amigo lo _____ también.

29. Nos vestimos. Y ellos _____ también.

30. Abuela les sirvió la comida. Y tú les _____ la comida también.

↺ To review, see **Pretérito de los verbos de cambio radical e → i, o → u.**

6 Completa.

31. En los restaurantes _____ se sirve comida _____. (japonés)

32. La blusa _____ es preciosa. (guatemalteco)

33. Unos _____ hablan inglés y francés. (canadiense)

↺ To review, see **Adjetivos de nacionalidad.**

7 Completa.

34. _____ sirv_ el postre después del plato principal.

35. _____ com_ muchos mariscos en Chile y en España.

36. _____ habl_ mucho español en Estados Unidos.

↺ To review, see **La voz pasiva con se.**

Cultura

8 Escoge la información correcta.

37. Se sirven porciones (grandes, pequeñas) de comida en Argentina.

38. En España (ponen, no ponen) muchas cosas en el mismo plato.

39. En España y (Latinoamérica, Estados Unidos) la gente no lleva las sobras a casa.

40. Los tostones o maduros, arroz y frijoles negros acompañan muchas comidas (mexicanas, caribeñas).

↺ To review this cultural information, see the **Lectura cultural.**

Prepárate para el examen

De estas tapas españolas, ¿cuáles te apetecen?

1 **¡Al restaurante!**

Order a meal and chat with friends at a restaurant

Imagínate que tu clase de español está en un restaurante donde se sirve comida española y latinoamericana. Todos los meseros hablan español. Pide lo que quieres en español. Con unos compañeros de clase prepara una conversación que tiene lugar en el restaurante. Luego presenta la conversación a la clase.

2 **Una comida típica**

Talk about foods

Ya sabes mucho sobre las comidas latinas. Habla de un plato o de una comida que te gusta o que quieres probar o comer por primera vez.

3 **Preferencias**

Discuss where you prefer to eat

Con un(a) compañero(a) indica si prefieres comer en casa o en un restaurante. ¿Por qué? A ver si tu compañero(a) tiene la misma opinión.

4 **En casa**

Talk about a meal at home

Describe una comida en casa y todo lo que tienes que hacer cuando comes en casa. Mira el diagrama abajo para ayudarte.

5 **Semejanzas y diferencias**

Compare restaurants where you live with restaurants in Spanish-speaking countries

Compara y contrasta algunas cosas interesantes sobre restaurantes aquí en Estados Unidos y en los países hispanos.

Go Online!
connectED.mcgraw-hill.com

Tarea

You are going to write a letter of complaint to a restaurant you went to where you had a very bad experience. Write a letter to the management. Include the following details.

¿Cuándo fuiste?
¿Con quiénes?
¿Qué pidieron ustedes?
¿Qué tal la comida?
¿Cómo fue el servicio?

Writing Strategy

Writing a letter of complaint When you write a letter of complaint your goal is to get a problem corrected. You might be angry when you write the letter; however, to be effective, you must control your emotions and use a businesslike tone. Clearly state the problems you had and suggest what the restaurant should do in order to solve each problem. In addition, it is important that the letter be addressed to the person who has the most authority.

CULTURA
Un restaurante pintoresco en Colonia, Uruguay

❶ Prewrite

Use a flow chart like the one below to help you organize the sequence of events in your letter.

¿Cuándo fuiste? → ¿Qué pidieron ustedes?

¿Qué tal la comida? → ¿Qué tal el servicio?

❷ Write

- An appropriate opening to a business letter in Spanish is **Estimado(a) señor(a).**
- Use the information organized in your prewriting charts to compose your letter.
- An appropriate closing to a business letter is **Atentamente.**

Evaluate

Don't forget that your teacher will evaluate you on the businesslike presentation of your letter, your ability to present solutions to the problems you raise, use of vocabulary, and correctness of grammar.

Gramática

Presente de los verbos de cambio radical e → i

The verbs **pedir, servir, repetir, freír, seguir,** and **vestirse** have a stem change in the present tense. Review the following forms.

pedir			
yo	pido	nosotros(as)	pedimos
tú	pides	*vosotros(as)*	*pedís*
Ud., él, ella	pide	Uds., ellos, ellas	piden

Pretérito de los verbos de cambio radical e → i, o → u

The verbs **pedir, servir, repetir, seguir, freír, vestirse, preferir, divertirse,** and **dormir** have a stem change in the preterite. Review the following forms.

pedir	preferir	dormir
pedí	preferí	dormí
pediste	preferiste	dormiste
pidió	prefirió	durmió
pedimos	preferimos	dormimos
pedisteis	*preferisteis*	*dormisteis*
pidieron	prefirieron	durmieron

Adjetivos de nacionalidad

Unlike other adjectives, adjectives of nationality that end in a consonant have four forms.

un libro español   **una canción española**
unos libros españoles   **unas canciones españolas**

La voz pasiva con se

The passive voice can be expressed in Spanish with the pronoun **se.**

Se habla español en Chile.
Se venden calcetines en la tienda de ropa.

¿En qué piso se vende?

Andrew Payti

Juego
There are a number of cognates in this list. See how many you and a partner can find. Who can find the most? Compare your list with those of your classmates.

Go Online!

connectED.mcgraw-hill.com

Vocabulario

Getting along at a restaurant

el restaurante	el/la mesero(a),	el menú	la propina
la mesa	el/la camarero(a)	la cuenta	

Identifying a place setting

la taza	el tenedor	la cuchara
el platillo	el cuchillo	el mantel
el plato	la cucharita	la servilleta

Identifying more foods

los comestibles	los mariscos	el aceite
la carne	los mejillones	el vinagre
la carne de res,	las almejas	casi crudo
el biftec, el bistec	la langosta	a término medio
la chuleta de cerdo	la sal	bien hecho
el cordero	la pimienta	

Describing some restaurant activities

poner la mesa	pedir	repetir
levantar (quitar)	servir	freír
la mesa	dejar una propina	

Other useful words and expressions

seguir	divertirse	Me muero de hambre.
vestirse	morir	

Repaso cumulativo

Repasa lo que ya has aprendido

These activities will help you review and remember what you have learned so far in Spanish.

1 Escucha las frases. Indica en una tabla como la de abajo si la persona viaja en tren o en avión.

tren	avión

2 Parea los contrarios.

1. grande
2. después
3. alto
4. aburrido
5. gordo
6. siempre
7. debajo de
8. triste
9. cerca
10. detrás
11. fácil
12. corto

a. lejos
b. interesante
c. contento
d. nunca
e. pequeño
f. antes
g. difícil
h. encima de
i. largo
j. flaco
k. bajo
l. delante

3 Personaliza. Da respuestas personales.

1. ¿Qué comes cuando tienes hambre?
2. ¿Qué bebes cuando tienes sed?
3. ¿Qué haces cuando estás cansado(a) o tienes sueño?
4. ¿Qué te pones cuando tienes frío?
5. ¿Qué ropa llevas cuando tienes calor?

CULTURA

Una panadería en el patio de comedores en una estación de ferrocarril en Buenos Aires

Andrew Payti

4 Escribe una lista de todos los comestibles (alimentos) que puedes decir en español.

legumbres	frutas	carne	pescado y mariscos	postres

5 Cambia al pretérito.

1. Ellos viven en San Francisco.

2. Su hermano asiste a la escuela secundaria en San Francisco.

3. Yo aprendo mucho en la escuela.

4. Nosotros comemos en la cafetería de la escuela.

5. ¿Comprendes lo que lees?

6 Sigue el modelo.

MODELO   yo / matemáticas →

Yo estudié matemáticas y aprendí mucho.

1. tú / biología

2. nosotros / historia

3. Carmen / geografía

4. ellos / álgebra

5. yo / español

6. ustedes / geometría

7 Escribe en la forma negativa.

1. Alguien llama a la puerta.

2. Él siempre hace algo.

3. Ella siempre tiene hambre.

4. Quiero comer algo.

5. Siempre quiere decir algo a alguien.

CULTURA 🇪🇸
Tapas en un café en Barcelona

Daniel Salsgiver

terry harris just greece photolibrary/Alamy

Go Online!
connectED.mcgraw-hill.com

Audio
Video
Práctica
Repaso
Diversiones
eScape

ePals

Vamos a comparar El mundo hispano es famoso por sus ferias y fiestas. Hay ferias para celebrar muchas ocasiones. Algunas duran solamente un día y otras una semana entera. ¿Hay ferias y fiestas donde tú vives? ¿Qué celebran o conmemoran? ¿Tienes una fiesta favorita? ¿Cuál es?

Objetivos

You will:

- talk about several Hispanic holidays
- compare holidays that you celebrate with those in some Spanish-speaking countries

You will use:

- regular and irregular forms of the imperfect tense

◀ Las jóvenes están tomando parte en las celebraciones para Carnaval en Puerto Plata en la República Dominicana.

¿Qué se celebra?

Mira las fotos para familiarizarte con el tema de este capítulo, un tema alegre: fiestas, festivales y celebraciones. El mundo hispano es famoso por sus fiestas. A mucha gente le gusta participar en las festividades en la plaza de su ciudad o pueblo o en su propio barrio.

México 🇲🇽

Aquí vemos a una joven oaxaqueña vestida con un traje tradicional durante la Guelaguetza, una fiesta popular que se celebra cada julio en Oaxaca.

Chile 🇨🇱

Un grupo de jóvenes chilenos vestidos con trajes regionales haciendo un baile tradicional en Poconchile en el norte de Chile

Ecuador

Aquí vemos a unos niños con disfraces en Cotacachi durante unas festividades para celebrar la Navidad.

Venezuela

Máscaras tradicionales para el festival Los Diablos Danzantes del Yare en el pueblo de San Francisco de Yare en Venezuela

Perú

Un desfile durante una
fiesta en Cuzco, Perú

España

Celebración del Baztandarren
Biltzarra, una fiesta tradicional
del valle de Baztán en Navarra

México

Calaveras de
azúcar para
la celebración
del Día de los
Muertos

Cuba

El señor va a andar sobre
zancos (stilts) durante una
fiesta en La Habana, Cuba.

España

Unas señoras vestidas con trajes
tradicionales cantando y tocando panderetas
durante una fiesta en el pueblo de Torrelavega
en Cantabria, España

(tl cl)Dave Moyer, (tr b)©Melba Photo Agency/PunchStock. (cr)Siede Preis/Getty Images

Una feria

una fiesta patronal

la santa patrona

una procesión

Había una procesión.
Todo el mundo desfilaba (caminaba) por
   las calles.
Llevaban una estatua del santo patrón
   (de la santa patrona).

el camposanto, el cementerio

un mausoleo

una ofrenda

Los difuntos (muertos) están enterrados en el camposanto.
Los parientes ponen coronas de flores en las tumbas.
En el cementerio hay también mausoleos familiares.

(t)Author's Image/PunchStock, (b)HECTOR GUERRERO/AFP/Getty Images

El Día de los Muertos

una máscara

un disfraz

Go Online!

connectED.mcgraw-hill.com

¡Ojo!

Note the spelling.
**un disfraz →
dos disfraces**

Para celebrar el Día de los Muertos, algunos
llevaban disfraz.
Llevaban también una máscara.
La máscara cubría la cara.

una calavera, un cráneo

un esqueleto

un hueso

Confeccionaba (elaboraba) bizcochos.
Los bizcochos tenían la forma
de las personas muertas.
Los bizcochos son dulces.

(t)©Erica Simone Leeds, (bl)Kelli Drummer-Avendaño, (br)Creatas/age fotostock

ESCUCHAR

1 Escucha las frases. Parea cada frase con la foto que describe.

a.   b.

HABLAR • ESCRIBIR

2 Personaliza. Da respuestas personales.

1. ¿Tiene un santo patrón el pueblo o la ciudad donde ustedes viven?
2. ¿Visitas a veces la tumba de un pariente difunto en el cementerio?
3. ¿Es una costumbre o tradición poner una corona de flores en la tumba?
4. ¿Hay una fiesta cuando se llevan disfraces? ¿Cuál es?
5. A veces, ¿tenemos figuras de cráneos o esqueletos? ¿Cuándo?
6. ¿Tenemos bizcochos o dulces en forma de cráneos o esqueletos?

LEER

3 Completa con una palabra del **banco de palabras.**

elaboraba	llevaba	caminaba	tenía	había

1. _____ una procesión en la calle.
2. Mucha gente _____ un disfraz.
3. Todo el mundo _____ detrás del santo patrón.
4. Abuelita _____ bizcochos.
5. Un bizcocho _____ la forma de una calavera.

CULTURA

Bizcochos en forma de calaveras

McGraw-Hill Education

LEER • ESCRIBIR

4 Expresa de otra manera.

1. Lleva *un disfraz.*
2. Todo el mundo *marchaba* hacia el cementerio.
3. Todo el mundo marchaba hacia *el cementerio.*
4. Todo el mundo *andaba* hacia atrás.
5. La señora *hacía* bizcochos.
6. *Los muertos* están enterrados en el cementerio.
7. Hacía bizcochos en forma de *una calavera.*

ESCRIBIR

5 Completa con la letra que falta.

1. una pro_e_ión
2. un disfra_
3. dos disfra_es
4. un bi_cocho
5. un _ueso

6 **Comunicación**

Habla con un(a) compañero(a) de clase. Describan todo lo que ustedes hacen o no hacen para celebrar *Halloween.* ¿Es una fiesta que les gusta o no?

7 Rompecabezas

Escoge la palabra en cada grupo que no pertenece.

1. el hueso   el esqueleto   el dulce   el cráneo

2. el camposanto   el muerto   el santo patrón   la tumba

3. la ofrenda   la corona de flores   el bizcocho   el mausoleo

4. la procesión   enterrar   desfilar   caminar por la calle

La Navidad, Las Navidades

el árbol de Navidad

la chimenea

un aguinaldo

La Nochebuena es el 24 de diciembre.
Los niños decoraban el árbol de Navidad.
Había aguinaldos debajo del árbol.

los Reyes Magos

el camello

la paja

Los niños sabían que iban a venir
los Reyes Magos.

¡Feliz Hanuka!

la vela

la menora

La familia siempre celebraba la fiesta de
las luces, Hanuka.
La familia encendía una vela de la menora.
Hanuka es una fiesta hebrea (judía).

los fuegos artificiales

La fiesta celebraba la llegada del
Año Nuevo.
Durante la fiesta había fuegos artificiales.
Los fuegos artificiales iluminaban el cielo.

un desfile

Todos bailaban mientras tocaba la banda.
Todo el mundo estaba contento.
Lo pasaban bien. Se divertían.

La piñata

La piñata es una vasija de cartón o barro. Se llena de dulces y durante muchas fiestas familiares los niños, con los ojos vendados *(blindfolded)*, tratan de romper la piñata con un palo o bastón. Si tienen éxito, la piñata se rompe y todos los niños corren a recoger *(gather)* los dulces.

ESCUCHAR

1 Escucha. Escoge la frase correcta. Usa una tabla como la de abajo para indicar tus respuestas.

a	b

HABLAR • ESCRIBIR

2 Contesta.

1. ¿Tienen muchas familias cristianas un árbol de Navidad?
2. ¿Decoran el árbol?
3. ¿Quién les trae aguinaldos a los niños?
4. ¿Dónde los pone?
5. ¿Celebran Hanuka las familias judías?
6. ¿Qué hay en la menora?

CULTURA

Estos niños están caminando por los jardines de un parque durante una fiesta en Cotacachi, Ecuador.

LEER • ESCRIBIR

3 Rompecabezas

¡Adivina! ¿Qué es?

1. un animal del desierto
2. lo que comen ciertos animales
3. un regalo de Navidad
4. lo que hay en una menora
5. lo que hacía la gente mientras tocaba la banda

ESCUCHAR • HABLAR • ESCRIBIR

4 Contesta según se indica.

1. ¿Cuántos Reyes Magos hay? (tres)
2. ¿Cuántas velas hay en una menora? (nueve)
3. ¿Cuándo hay fuegos artificiales? (de noche después del desfile)
4. ¿Cuándo toca la banda municipal? (durante el desfile)
5. ¿Qué decoran los niños? (el árbol de Navidad)
6. ¿Qué reciben los niños para la Navidad? (aguinaldos)

InfoGap For more practice using your new vocabulary, do Activity 5 in the Student Resource section at the end of this book.

5 **Comunicación**

Con un grupo de amigos, describe una fiesta típica que se celebra el 4 de julio en Estados Unidos.

¡Así se dice!

If while speaking you realize that you have made a grammatical error or know that you haven't been clear in your explanation, just stop and say, **o sea...,** and continue from where you left off.

HABLAR • ESCRIBIR

6 Corrige la información falsa.

1. La Navidad es en junio.
2. Un aguinaldo es un regalo que se recibe para el Año Nuevo.
3. Hay cuatro Reyes Magos.
4. Hanuka se llama también la fiesta de los fuegos.

Cultura

El weekend o el fin de semana libre es una costumbre anglosajona. En el mundo hispano mucha gente tiene que trabajar los sábados. No tienen todo el fin de semana libre. Pero tienen muchos días festivos durante el año. Cada país tiene sus propias fiestas o ferias. Y si la fiesta es el martes, el lunes debe ser un día festivo también, ¿no? Incluir un día adicional para tener más días festivos se llama «un puente».

Alan Crosthwaite/Alamy

¿QUÉ SE CELEBRA?

¡Ojo!

There are no verbs with a stem change in the imperfect.

PRESENTE		IMPERFECTO
juego	→	jugaba
empiezo	→	empezaba

Imperfecto de los verbos en -ar

1. In Spanish there are two simple past tenses—the preterite and the imperfect. You have already learned the preterite. You use the preterite to state an action that began and ended at a definite time in the past.

2. You will now learn the imperfect. The imperfect is used to describe a habitual or repeated past action. The exact time the action began and/or ended is not important.

3. Observe the imperfect forms of regular **-ar** verbs.

infinitive	hablar	mirar
stem	habl-	mir-
yo	hablaba	miraba
tú	hablabas	mirabas
Ud., él, ella	hablaba	miraba
nosotros(as)	hablábamos	mirábamos
vosotros(as)	*hablabais*	*mirabais*
Uds., ellos, ellas	hablaban	miraban

4. Some common time expressions used with the imperfect are:

siempre	con frecuencia
a veces	a menudo
de vez en cuando	todos los días (años)

Ellos siempre desfilaban detrás de la banda.
A veces bailaban al son de la banda.
De vez en cuando llevaban disfraces.
Lo pasaban bien.

Práctica

HABLAR • ESCRIBIR

1 Contesta.

1. En la Nochebuena, ¿se acostaban bastante temprano los niños?
2. ¿Qué esperaban ellos? ¿Esperaban la llegada de Santa Claus?
3. ¿Escuchaban cuando hablaban sus padres?
4. ¿Quiénes decoraban el árbol? ¿Los niños o sus padres?
5. Y en los países hispanos, ¿a quiénes esperaban los niños?

CULTURA

Esta muchacha guatemalteca regresaba a casa cada día después de sus clases. Siempre llevaba sus materiales escolares en su mochila.

HABLAR • ESCRIBIR

2 Personaliza. Da respuestas personales.

1. Cuando estabas en la escuela primaria, ¿cómo llegabas a la escuela? ¿Llegabas a pie o tomabas el bus escolar?
2. ¿Estaba tu casa lejos o cerca de tu escuela?
3. ¿Con quiénes jugabas?
4. ¿Qué jugaban ustedes?
5. ¿Tomabas el almuerzo con tus amigos en la cafetería de la escuela?

HABLAR • ESCRIBIR

3 Da la frase con el nuevo sujeto.

Ellas jugaban fútbol.

1. él
2. nosotros
3. yo
4. ustedes
5. tú
6. Javier

LEER • ESCRIBIR

4 Completa con el imperfecto sobre unos veranos en la playa.

Cada año cuando __1__ (llegar) el verano, yo __2__ (estar) contento(a). Mi familia siempre __3__ (pasar) el mes de julio en la playa. Por la mañana mi hermano y yo __4__ (levantarse) y __5__ (tomar) el desayuno. Pero después de tomar el desayuno, no __6__ (caminar) a la escuela. Nosotros __7__ (pasar) el día en la playa.

Yo siempre __8__ (nadar) en el mar. Me __9__ (gustar) las olas altas. De vez en cuando mi hermano __10__ (alquilar) un barquito y nosotros __11__ (esquiar) en el agua.

Cada tarde a eso de las tres __12__ (llegar) algunos amigos y (nosotros) __13__ (formar) un equipo de voleibol. Si digo la verdad (nosotros) __14__ (jugar) muy bien.

El mismo equipo no __15__ (ganar) siempre pero lo importante es que (nosotros) lo __16__ (pasar) bien.

—Y tú, ¿__17__ (pasar) los veranos en la playa o __18__ (quedarse) en casa?

CULTURA 🇺🇸

La muchacha norteamericana jugaba «soccer» con el equipo de su escuela. Su equipo ganaba casi siempre.

5 **Comunicación**

Trabajen en grupos de cuatro o cinco. Un miembro del grupo es el/la entrevistador(a) que va a preguntar a los otros dónde pasaban los veranos. Presenten las respuestas a la clase.

Eyewire/Getty Images

¡Ojo!

There are no verbs with a stem change in the imperfect.

PRESENTE		IMPERFECTO
quiero	→	quería
vuelvo	→	volvía

Imperfecto de los verbos en -er, -ir

1. Regular **-er** and **-ir** verbs have the same endings in the imperfect tense.

infinitive	leer	escribir
stem	le-	escrib-
yo	leía	escribía
tú	leías	escribías
Ud., él, ella	leía	escribía
nosotros(as)	leíamos	escribíamos
vosotros(as)	*leíais*	*escribíais*
Uds., ellos, ellas	leían	escribían

2. The imperfect of **hay** is **había.** Note that either a singular or plural noun follows **había.**

> **Había un concierto durante la fiesta.**
> **Había fuegos artificiales durante la fiesta.**

Práctica

HABLAR • ESCRIBIR

6 Personaliza. Da respuestas personales.

1. ¿Vivías en la misma casa cuando tenías doce años?
2. ¿A qué escuela asistías?
3. ¿Recibías buenas o malas notas?
4. ¿Tenías muchos amigos donde vivías?
5. ¿Leías muchos libros de bolsillo?
6. ¿Aprendías mucho?
7. ¿Sabías usar la computadora?
8. ¿Escribías muchos correos electrónicos?
9. ¿Recibías muchos también?

EXPANSIÓN

Ahora, sin mirar las preguntas, relata en tus propias palabras lo que dijo tu compañero(a). Si no recuerdas algo o si no comprendiste algo que te dijo, tu compañero(a) te puede ayudar.

CULTURA

Un grupo de jóvenes haciendo un baile folklórico en el desierto de Atacama en el norte de Chile

Andrew Payti

LEER • ESCRIBIR

7 Completa con el imperfecto.

Yo recuerdo que durante la fiesta __1__ (haber) fuegos artificiales que __2__ (iluminar) el cielo. Todo el mundo __3__ (divertirse). Todos nosotros __4__ (beber) y __5__ (comer). __6__ (Haber) muchos puestos de comida donde se __7__ (vender) perros calientes, hamburguesas, pizza y papas fritas.

__8__ (Haber) un desfile. Durante el desfile algunos __9__ (ponerse) máscaras. Yo no __10__ (poder) reconocer a varios amigos porque __11__ (llevar) disfraces.

Nosotros __12__ (tener) mucha suerte. Durante la fiesta __13__ (hacer) buen tiempo y no __14__ (llover).

Yo tengo muy buenos recuerdos (memorias) de esta fiesta.

CULTURA

Grupos de músicos se reúnen los sábados y domingos para dar conciertos en las calles de San Telmo en Buenos Aires, Argentina.

FOLDABLES
Study Organizer

MINIBOOK
See the Foldables section of the Student Handbook at the beginning of this book for help with making this foldable. Use this foldable to illustrate and tell about things you did frequently. On each page, draw a picture of an activity you enjoyed. Below each picture, write a few sentences in Spanish describing what was happening. Remember to use the imperfect tense and to stick to the words that you already know in Spanish.

HABLAR • ESCRIBIR

8 Forma frases en el imperfecto con los siguientes verbos.

comer	beber	aprender	conocer	saber	volver
vivir	subir	recibir	salir	escribir	tener

9 ***Comunicación***

Dile a un(a) compañero(a) las cosas que hacías a menudo cuando eras alumno(a) en la escuela primaria. Tu compañero(a) va a hacerte preguntas para saber más.

Andrew Payti

Imperfecto de los verbos irregulares

The verbs **ser, ir,** and **ver** are the only verbs that are irregular in the imperfect tense.

	ser	ir	ver
yo	era	iba	veía
tú	eras	ibas	veías
Ud., él, ella	era	iba	veía
nosotros(as)	éramos	íbamos	veíamos
vosotros(as)	*erais*	*ibais*	*veíais*
Uds., ellos, ellas	eran	iban	veían

CULTURA

Los niños se divertían en el patio de su escuela primaria en Antigua, Guatemala.

Práctica

HABLAR • ESCRIBIR

10 Personaliza. Da respuestas personales.

1. Cuando eras alumno(a) en la escuela primaria, ¿eras amigo(a) de tus vecinos?
2. A veces, ¿ibas al parque con tus amigos?
3. ¿Adónde iban ustedes los sábados?
4. ¿Quién era tu maestro(a) en el tercer grado?
5. ¿Cómo ibas a la escuela?
6. Cuando volvías a casa, ¿veías la televisión?

ESCUCHAR • LEER • ESCRIBIR

11 Cambia al imperfecto.

1. Ellos son de la República Dominicana.
2. Veo a mis parientes con frecuencia.
3. Vamos muy a menudo a la República Dominicana.
4. La casa de mis parientes es bonita.
5. Cuando estás allí, ¿vas a la playa?
6. ¿Quién va a la playa contigo?
7. ¿Ven ustedes a otros amigos en la playa?

CULTURA

Los niños de la primaria hacían una excursión escolar al Parque Güell en Barcelona, España. Sus maestros los acompañaban.

(t)Lori Ernfridsson, (b)Courtney Brown

Usos del imperfecto

Go Online!

connectED.mcgraw-hill.com

In addition to expressing repeated, habitual actions or events in the past, the imperfect is used to describe persons, places, objects, events, weather, dates, and time in the past.

APPEARANCE	**Eloísa era alta y bonita.**
AGE	**Tenía trece años.**
PHYSICAL CONDITION	**Siempre estaba llena de energía.**
EMOTIONAL STATE	**Y estaba muy contenta.**
ATTITUDES AND DESIRES	**Le gustaban las fiestas.**
LOCATION	**Estaba en una fiesta en casa de Lucio.**
DATE	**Era el ocho de octubre.**
TIME	**Eran las diez de la noche.**
WEATHER	**Hacía bastante frío.**

Práctica

ESCUCHAR • HABLAR • ESCRIBIR

12 Contesta según se indica.

1. ¿Quién era alto? (don Quijote)
2. ¿Quién era bajo? (Sancho Panza)
3. ¿Quién tenía un asno? (Sancho Panza)
4. ¿Quién tenía un caballo? (don Quijote)
5. ¿Quién era idealista? (don Quijote)
6. ¿Quién era realista? (Sancho Panza)
7. ¿Quién quería viajar? (don Quijote)
8. ¿Quién quería volver a casa? (Sancho Panza)
9. ¿Quién quería conquistar los males del mundo? (don Quijote)
10. ¿Quién estaba loco? (don Quijote)

HABLAR • ESCRIBIR

13 Personaliza. Da respuestas personales.

1. ¿Quién era tu mejor amigo(a) en la escuela elemental?
2. ¿Cómo era?
3. ¿Cuántos años tenían ustedes cuando eran amigos?
4. ¿Qué tipo de personalidad tenía él o ella?
5. ¿Son ustedes amigos ahora?

14 **Comunicación**

Describe el tiempo que hacía ayer.

Refrán

Can you guess what the following proverb means?

Con sus libros, los muertos abren los ojos a los vivos.

¡Bravo!

You have now learned all the new vocabulary and grammar in this chapter. Continue to use and practice all that you know while learning more cultural information. **¡Vamos!**

El Día de San Juan 🎧 ↺

Patricia	José, eres de Puerto Rico, ¿no?
José	Sí, ¿por qué?
Patricia	Pues, ¿me puedes decir lo que es una fiesta patronal?
José	¡Cómo no! Es una fiesta en honor del santo patrón de un lugar. El santo patrón de Puerto Rico, por ejemplo, es San Juan Bautista.
Patricia	¿Hay una fiesta en su honor?
José	Sí, el 24 de junio. Durante toda una semana hay fiestas.
Patricia	¿Qué hacen para celebrar la fiesta?
José	Pues, hay una tradición interesante. El Día de San Juan todos vamos a la playa y a la medianoche entramos en el mar.
Patricia	¿Siempre nadan el Día de San Juan?
José	No dije que nadamos. Dije que entramos en el mar. ¿Sabes cómo? Caminamos hacia atrás hasta llegar al mar.
Patricia	Y, ¿por qué andan hacia atrás?
José	Entrar en el mar así nos trae buena suerte durante el año.

Carlos Fernandez/Moment Open/Getty Images

¿Comprendes?

A Completa según la información en la conversación.

    1. José es de _____.

    2. Una fiesta patronal rinde honor a _____.

    3. El santo patrón de Puerto Rico es _____.

    4. Su fiesta patronal es _____.

    5. Todo el mundo va _____.

    6. _____ para entrar en el mar.

    7. Si entran en el mar así, van a tener _____.

B **Resumiendo** Cuenta la información en la conversación en tus propias palabras.

CULTURA

Maite preparaba a su amigo del continente para las celebraciones del Día de San Juan. Le enseñaba como andar hacia atrás.

C **Analizando** Los sanjuaneros tienen una costumbre interesante. ¿Qué hacen? ¿Por qué lo hacen?

David H. Brennan

Lectura

ESTRATEGIA DE LECTURA

Antes de leer

Visualiza unas fiestas o ferias que tienen lugar donde tú vives—la Navidad, el Año Nuevo, el Cuatro de Julio, etc.

✔ READING CHECK

¿Por qué celebraba la familia de Carmencita el Día de los Muertos?

Durante la lectura

Pinta un cuadro mental de lo que está haciendo la gente—lo que todos están llevando, lo que preparan, adónde van.

VISUALIZANDO Es importante visualizar lo que estás leyendo. Al leer, pinta un cuadro mental de la información. Este cuadro mental te permite apreciar más la información y recordar mejor lo que estás leyendo.

Unas fiestas hispanas

El Día de los Muertos Carmencita Dávila es alumna en nuestra clase de español. Cuando ella era niña, vivía en México y asistía a la primaria en Guadalajara. Ella nos quiere hablar de los recuerdos que tiene de una fiesta mexicana que le gustaba mucho.

—Cuando yo era niña en México me encantaban todas las festividades que tenían lugar[1] para celebrar el Día de los Muertos, el primero y el dos de noviembre. Celebrábamos para rendirles honor a todos nuestros parientes difuntos.

Mi mamá y abuelita siempre tenían que hacer muchos preparativos. Confeccionaban calaveras, un tipo de dulce en forma de cara de muerto. Elaboraban también el delicioso pan de muerto, un pan dulce en forma de huesos. Unos días antes de la fiesta íbamos al cementerio o camposanto donde limpiábamos[2] y decorábamos con coronas de flores las tumbas de nuestros parientes difuntos. Durante las fiestas las tumbas servían de altar.

[1]tenían lugar *took place*   [2]limpiábamos *we cleaned*

Mamá y abuelita preparaban también lo que eran las comidas favoritas de los difuntos. El primero de noviembre la familia entera se reunía e íbamos juntos al cementerio. Colocábamos las calaveras, las coronas de flores, unas velas y la comida en las tumbas como una ofrenda. Algunos parientes llevaban calacas de madera[3], o sea, figuras en forma de esqueletos. En el cementerio teníamos un gran picnic. Comíamos con los difuntos.

✓ READING CHECK

¿Qué hacían en el cementerio?

CULTURA

Una ofrenda con calacas y calaveras para el Día de los Muertos

Roberto Jones levanta la mano y le hace una pregunta a Carmencita.

—Carmencita, me parece que la fiesta que nos describes es una ocasión mórbida, bastante triste.

Contesta Carmencita: —No, Roberto. La verdad es que es una ocasión festiva. Tiene sus orígenes entre los indígenas en la época precolombina. Los indígenas no consideran la muerte el final de la vida[4] sino la continuación de la vida. Creen también que las almas[5] de los muertos vuelven cada año para visitar a sus parientes vivos. Luego, ¿por qué no reunirnos con ellos para tener una fiesta?

✓ READING CHECK

¿Por qué no es una fiesta triste?

[3]de madera *wooden*
[4]vida *life*

[5]almas *souls*

D. Normark/PhotoLink/Getty Images

Lectura

CULTURAL

☑ **READING CHECK**

¿Cómo reciben los niños sus aguinaldos en los países hispanos?

CULTURA

Los Reyes Magos en el escaparate de una tienda por departamentos durante la temporada navideña en Madrid, España

☑ **READING CHECK**

¿Qué reciben los niños durante Hanuka? ¿Cuántas veces?

Después de leer

De las tres fiestas, ¿cuáles podías visualizar mejor? ¿Por qué?

La Navidad Y ahora la señora Salas, nuestra profesora de español, nos describe otra fiesta—una fiesta celebrada en todos los países hispanos.

Dice la señora Salas: —La mayoría de los niños en los países hispanos no reciben sus regalos de Navidad, sus aguinaldos, el 25 de diciembre. Los reciben el 6 de enero, el Día de los Reyes. La fiesta conmemora la llegada de los tres Reyes Magos al establo en Belén.

Los niños hispanos escriben sus cartas a los Reyes, no a Santa Claus, porque saben que son los Reyes quienes les traen los aguinaldos. Así, en sus cartas ponen una lista de los regalos que quieren recibir. La noche del 5 de enero, antes de acostarse, los niños dejan sus zapatos a la puerta de la casa, delante de la chimenea o debajo de su cama. Llenan sus zapatos de heno, paja o hierba porque saben que los animales de los Reyes van a querer comer. Y saben que los Reyes van a dejar los regalos que quieren en sus zapatos. Pero saben algo más. Si no se comportan bien durante el año los Reyes van a llenar sus zapatos de carbón[6].

Hanuka Isaac del Olmo tiene familia que vive en Panamá.

Dice la señora Salas: —Isaac, ¿sabes cómo celebra tu familia Hanuka en Panamá?

—Sí. Ellos celebran Hanuka de la misma manera que nosotros aquí en Estados Unidos. Es una fiesta alegre que empieza el 25 del mes hebreo de *Kislev* y dura ocho días. La primera noche un miembro de la familia enciende dos velas en la menora. Cada noche después se enciende una vela más. Cada noche los niños reciben regalos y bombones[7]. Y a todos les gusta comer *latkes*, panqueques de papas.

[6]carbón *coal*   [7]bombones *candies*

Esta familia judía abría sus regalos durante el festival de Hanuka.

(t)Andrew Paytt, (b)Corbis/Alamy

¿Comprendes?

A Recordando hechos Contesta.

1. ¿Dónde vivía Carmencita Dávila cuando era niña?
2. ¿Qué día de fiesta le encantaba?
3. ¿Quiénes hacían muchos preparativos?
4. ¿Adónde iban todos durante la fiesta?

B Describiendo Describe.

1. una calavera
2. una calaca

C Categorizando Completa la tabla.

lo que hacía la familia de Carmencita en casa	lo que hacía la familia de Carmencita en el cementerio

D Analizando Contesta.

¿Por qué no se considera el Día de los Muertos una ocasión mórbida?

E Recordando hechos Contesta.

1. ¿Cuándo reciben la mayoría de los niños hispanos sus aguinaldos?
2. ¿Qué se conmemora el Día de los Reyes?
3. ¿De quiénes reciben sus aguinaldos los niños hispanos?
4. ¿Qué ponen en sus zapatos?
5. ¿Dónde dejan sus zapatos la noche del 5 de enero?
6. ¿Qué les dan los Reyes a los niños que no se comportan bien durante el año?

F Buscando información Completa.

1. Hanuka es _____.
2. Hanuka dura _____.
3. _____ enciende una vela en la menora.
4. Cada una de las ocho noches de Hanuka los niños reciben _____.
5. Los *latkes* son _____.

Lectura
UN POCO MÁS

Antes de leer

Piensa en unas cosas que haces el 31 de diciembre para celebrar la llegada del Año Nuevo. En la Ciudad de Nueva York, por ejemplo, miles y miles de personas van a Times Square para ver caer un gran balón a la medianoche. Al leer esta lectura, compara las actividades en Madrid con las de Nueva York. Compáralas también con tus actividades tradicionales.

¡Así se dice!

If you want to wish someone Happy New Year, you say **¡Próspero Año Nuevo!**

La Nochevieja en España

En España el día final del año es «la Nochevieja» y en los otros países hispanos es «la víspera del Año Nuevo». Fernando Orjales nació en Madrid, la capital de España, y ahora está viviendo con su familia en Nueva York. Es la noche del 31 de diciembre y Fernando va con su familia a *Times Square* para celebrar la llegada del Año Nuevo. Mientras está en *Times Square*, Fernando piensa en lo que él hacía para celebrar la Nochevieja cuando estaba en Madrid.

Dice: —Recuerdo que nosotros, como casi todos los madrileños, íbamos a la Puerta del Sol, una gran plaza en el centro mismo de la ciudad. Nos reuníamos frente a una campana[1]. Recuerdo que casi siempre hacía frío y soplaba[2] un viento bastante fuerte de la Sierra de Guadarrama. Todo el mundo estaba bien abrigado[3] para protegerse del frío.

Pero a pesar del[4] frío todos tenían la mirada fija en la campana. Y en la mano cada uno tenía su racimo de doce uvas. Estábamos listos para recibir el Año Nuevo. Esperábamos las doce campanadas que anunciaban la llegada del Año Nuevo.

Fernando dice que recuerda bien que él comía una uva con cada una de las campanadas. Y por cada uva pedía un deseo. Por eso se llaman «las doce uvas de la felicidad».

[1]campana   *bell tower*
[2]soplaba   *blew*
[3]abrigado   *wrapped up*
[4]a pesar del   *in spite of the*

CULTURA 🇪🇸

¿Quién va a comer las doce uvas de la felicidad para celebrar el Año Nuevo, una costumbre española?

Burazin/Photographer's Choice RF/Getty Images

¿Comprendes?

Escoge.

1. ¿De dónde es Fernando?
   a. de Nueva York
   b. de Madrid
   c. de la Nochevieja

2. ¿Adónde va Fernando ahora para celebrar la llegada del Año Nuevo?
   a. a *Times Square*
   b. a la Puerta del Sol
   c. a la Sierra de Guadarrama

3. ¿Qué hay en la Puerta del Sol?
   a. el sol
   b. un parque
   c. una campana

4. ¿Por qué estaban todos bien abrigados?
   a. Siempre llevaban un abrigo nuevo.
   b. Hacía mucho frío.
   c. Estaban en la Sierra de Guadarrama.

5. ¿Cómo comía Fernando las uvas?
   a. todo un racimo
   b. doce a la vez
   c. una a una

6. ¿Cuándo las comía?
   a. al llegar a la Puerta del Sol
   b. al oír cada campanada
   c. al anunciar la llegada del Año Nuevo

CULTURA

Una vista de la Puerta del Sol donde se celebra la llegada del Año Nuevo en Madrid. Es de este campanario que las campanas dan las doce.

Prepárate para el examen

↺ To review, see **Vocabulario 1** and **Vocabulario 2**.

Vocabulario

1 Identifica.

1.

2.

3.

4.

5.

2 Da otra palabra.

6. el muerto

7. un tipo de desfile

8. confeccionar

9. el cementerio

10. un disfraz

11. un regalo de Navidad

12. pasarlo bien

3 Completa.

13. Todo el mundo _____ hacia el cementerio.

14. Abuelita _____ bizcochos.

15. La familia pone _____ de flores en la tumba.

16. La noche de la fiesta había _____ que iluminaban el cielo.

17. _____ es la fiesta de las luces.

Gramática

4 **Completa con el imperfecto.**

18. La banda _____. (tocar)

19. Todos nosotros _____. (bailar)

20. _____ muy buen tiempo. (hacer)

21. Ellos _____. (celebrar)

22. Y tú, ¿qué _____? (hacer)

23–24. Yo _____ y _____. (comer, beber)

25. ¿Qué hora _____? (ser)

26–27. Yo _____ quedarme pero ellos _____ salir. (querer, preferir)

28. La gente _____. (divertirse)

5 **Escribe en el imperfecto.**

29. Yo sé hacerlo.

30. Ellos pueden ir.

31. Es alumno en la primaria.

32. ¿Qué va a decir?

33. Tienes quince años.

34. Antonia ve el desfile.

↺ To review, see **Imperfecto de los verbos en -ar, Imperfecto de los verbos en -er, -ir, Imperfecto de los verbos irregulares**, and **Usos del imperfecto.**

↺ To review this cultural information, see the **Lectura cultural.**

Cultura

6 **Contesta.**

35. Cuando Carmencita vivía en México, ¿qué ponían los miembros de la familia en las tumbas de sus parientes difuntos?

36. El Día de los Muertos no es una ocasión triste ni mórbida. ¿Por qué?

37. ¿Cuándo reciben la mayoría de los niños hispanos sus regalos de Navidad?

38. ¿Quiénes traen los regalos a los niños y dónde los dejan?

39. ¿Por qué ponen los niños paja en los zapatos?

40. ¿Durante qué fiesta se comen *latkes*?

CULTURA

La tumba de Eva Perón y su familia en el cementerio de la Recoleta, Buenos Aires, Argentina

Richard Brommer

Prepárate para el examen

1 Una fiesta latina

Describe a Hispanic holiday

Escoge una de las siguientes fiestas. Describe la fiesta a un(a) amigo(a).

el Día de los Muertos	**el Día de los Reyes**
el Día de San Juan	**la Nochevieja**

2 Mi fiesta favorita

Talk about your favorite holiday

De todas las fiestas en la lectura, ¿cuál es tu predilecta (favorita)? Explica por qué.

3 Comparaciones

Compare holidays in the United States with Hispanic holidays

Compara el Día de los Muertos con *Halloween*. También compara el día de Navidad con el Día de los Reyes.

4 Recuerdos

Talk about your childhood

Relata unos recuerdos placenteros (agradables) que tienes de los años de tu niñez. Empieza con «Cuando yo era niño(a)... ».

CULTURA

Estas niñas de Cotacachi, Ecuador, llevan trajes para celebrar las Navidades.

Andrew Payti

Tarea

Write a journal entry in which you reminisce about a holiday you enjoyed as a youngster. Describe the general characteristics of that holiday, such as when you would celebrate it, how it was celebrated, what would often happen, who would always be there, and why you always enjoyed it.

Writing Strategy

Reminiscing One technique frequently used in journal writing is reminiscing. When you reminisce, you use your memory to recall how things were in the past. The primary source of information will be the thoughts and images that your mind produces of "the way things were back then." Use what you have learned about the imperfect and the vocabulary from this chapter to make your journal entry as descriptive and lively as possible.

❶ Prewrite

Make a list of the thoughts and images that come to mind when you reminisce about your favorite holiday. Think about when it would take place, who would be there, what the scene would be like, what would often happen, why it was always fun, how you felt, etc.

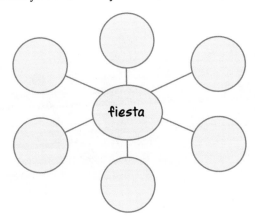

❷ Write

- Be sure to stick to vocabulary that you already know.
- Remember to incorporate time expressions often used to indicate habitual or repeated actions in the past, such as **siempre, cada, a menudo, con mucha frecuencia, a veces,** etc.
- Use descriptive adjectives and include as many details as possible to make the memory of your favorite holiday come alive.

It is important to keep in mind that you are not writing about specific events that took place one time during your favorite holiday. Your goal is to capture the overall essence of this habitual or repeated event from your childhood as you remember it.

Evaluate

Don't forget that your teacher will evaluate you on use of vocabulary, correctness of grammar, and the vivid description of details.

©Lars A. Niki

Repaso del Capítulo 5

Gramática

Imperfecto de los verbos regulares

The imperfect is used to describe a habitual or repeated action in the past. Some words commonly used with the imperfect are **siempre, con frecuencia, a menudo,** and **todos los días.** Review the imperfect forms of regular verbs.

bailar	beber	vivir
bailaba	bebía	vivía
bailabas	bebías	vivías
bailaba	bebía	vivía
bailábamos	bebíamos	vivíamos
bailabais	*bebíais*	*vivíais*
bailaban	bebían	vivían

Imperfecto de los verbos irregulares

Ser, ir, and **ver** are irregular in the imperfect. Review the following forms.

ser	ir	ver
era	iba	veía
eras	ibas	veías
era	iba	veía
éramos	íbamos	veíamos
erais	*ibais*	*veíais*
eran	iban	veían

Usos del imperfecto

The imperfect is used to express a continuous action in the past and to describe persons, places, objects, events, weather, and time in the past.

> **Ellos siempre hacían mucho.**
> **Dolores estaba muy contenta.**
> **Llovía mucho en la primavera.**
> **Era el seis de enero y nevaba.**

CULTURA

Un baile folklórico chileno

Andrew Payti

Vocabulario

Talking about a patron saint's day

una feria	la santa patrona	patronal
una fiesta	una procesión,	desfilar
el santo patrón	un desfile	caminar

Talking about the Day of the Dead

los muertos,	una ofrenda	un esqueleto
los difuntos	una corona de	un hueso
el camposanto,	flores	un disfraz
el cementerio	una calavera,	una máscara
el mausoleo	un cráneo	enterrado(a)
la tumba		

Talking about Christmas and Three Kings Day

la Navidad, las	un aguinaldo	la paja
Navidades	los Reyes Magos	el árbol de Navidad
la Nochebuena	el camello	decorar
la chimenea		

Talking about Hanukkah

Hanuka	la menora	hebreo(a)
¡Feliz Hanuka!	la vela	encender
la fiesta de las luces	judío(a)	

Talking about Independence Day

un desfile	los fuegos artificiales	bailar
una banda municipal	el cielo	iluminar

Other useful words and expressions

el bizcocho	celebrar	elaborar
todo el mundo	confeccionar	mientras
dulce		

These activities will help you review and remember what you have learned so far in Spanish.

1 Escucha las frases. Indica en una tabla como la de abajo si la frase describe una acción en el presente o el pasado.

presente	pasado

2 Personaliza. Da respuestas personales.

1. ¿A qué escuela fuiste el año pasado?
2. ¿Cuántos cursos tomaste?
3. ¿En qué curso recibiste la nota más alta?
4. ¿Qué curso te gustó más?
5. El año pasado, ¿trabajaste después de las clases?
6. Y este año, ¿a qué escuela vas?
7. ¿Cuántos cursos tienes?
8. ¿En qué curso recibes la nota más alta?
9. ¿Qué curso te gusta más?
10. ¿Trabajas después de las clases?

CULTURA

El corredor de un colegio en Rawson en la Patagonia argentina

Andrew Payti

Vamos a comparar ¿Puedes imaginar el mundo sin computadoras? ¿Usas tu computadora con frecuencia? ¿Para qué la usas? ¿Qué piensas? ¿Tienen computadora los jóvenes de España y Latinoamérica? Vamos a ver la influencia de la tecnología en su vida diaria.

Objetivos

You will:

- talk about computers, the Internet, and e-mail
- talk about a digital camera and an MP3 player
- make and receive phone calls
- discuss technology in Hispanic countries

You will use:

- the preterite and imperfect tenses

◀ La gente está usando sus aparatos electrónicos para sacar fotos de unas obras arquitectónicas de Antoni Gaudí en el Parque Güell en Barcelona, España. Aquí vemos una serie de viaductos que construyó Gaudí para poder andar por el parque.

Tecnomundo

Mira estas fotos para familiarizarte con el tema de este capítulo—la tecnología hoy en día. No hay duda de que los avances tecnológicos en el campo de la informática cambian rápidamente y siguen influyendo la vida de muchos en todos los rincones del mundo.

Venezuela

Las dos jóvenes están caminando en San Juan, Venezuela. A una le gusta la conversación en su móvil.

TARJETA CHIP, TU OTRO MÓVIL

Siempre es bueno tener un teléfono a mano

Telefónica

www.telefonica.es/telecomunicacionespublicas

España

El teléfono público sigue siendo un medio de comunicación corriente en muchas partes del mundo hispano. Aquí vemos unos teléfonos públicos en Arrecife, Lanzarote, en las islas Canarias.

CENTRO DE LLAMADA

Agente Autorizado

Costa Rica 20 ¢
Colombia 15 ¢
República Dominicana 25 ¢
USA 20 ¢
Resto del mundo 25 ¢
Nicaragua 30 ¢
Ecuador 23 ¢

INTERNET 1.500k
ABIERTO

Estados Unidos

Esta joven de ascendencia mexicana se divertía escuchando música en su MP3 después de las clases.

Panamá

De este centro de llamadas en Panamá se puede hacer llamadas telefónicas a muchas partes del mundo. ¿Qué tal te parecen las tarifas? ¿Son altas o no?

Argentina

Una muchacha argentina usa su computadora portátil en un parque de Buenos Aires.

Nicaragua

Esta tienda en León, Nicaragua, ofrece muchos servicios.

LLAMADAS
NACIONALES E INTERNACIONALES

IMPRESIONES A COLOR
BLANCO Y NEGRO

QUEMADO EN DVD-R Y CD-ROM

LEVANTADO DE TEXTO

VENTA DE DISKS - CD

ENVIO Y RECIBO DE FAX

SALA DE VIDEO JUEGOS PLAYSTATION 2

México

Aquí vemos una cartelera en la Plaza de la tecnología en el centro histórico de la Ciudad de México. En esta zona hay muchos comercios dedicados a la compra y venta de dispositivos tecnológicos.

Nicaragua

Los jóvenes están jugando juegos de video en este salón de videos en León, Nicaragua.

La computadora, El ordenador 🎧

la página de inicio (inicial, frontal)

la pantalla de escritorio

la alfombrilla

el ratón

el teclado

el botón regresar (retroceder)

Atrás

Cristina navegaba la red (el Internet).
Quería regresar a un sitio Web anterior.
Hizo clic en el botón regresar.

Cristina estaba sentada delante de su computadora.
Prendió la computadora.
Quería entrar en línea.
Por eso, hizo clic con el ratón.
Cuando terminó, apagó la computadora.

En otras partes

La computadora is used in all of Latin America. **El ordenador** is used in Spain.

la carpeta

oprimir, pulsar

José no quería guardar cierto archivo.
Ya no lo necesitó y lo borró.
Oprimió (Pulsó) el botón borrador.

David H. Brennan

el correo electrónico, el e-mail

el icono

la barra de herramientas

la bandeja de entrada

la dirección de correo electrónico (e-mail)

la bandeja de enviados

el documento adjunto

el/la destinatario(a)

la libreta de direcciones

Hoy Paco recibió muchos correos electrónicos.
Los leyó todos pero no contestó todos.
Había tres que no le interesaron y los borró.
Enviaba un correo cuando sonó su móvil (celular).

¿Lo sabes?

Así se lee o se da una dirección de e-mail en español.
josésalas@terra.es
José Salas arroba terra punto España
Observa que además de *com, net, org,* etc., se usa el país.

la impresora

El padre de José Luis recibió un boleto aéreo electrónico por correo electrónico.
Quería una copia dura de su boleto y lo imprimió.
La sacó de la impresora.

(t)McGraw-Hill Education, (c b)David H. Brennan

HABLAR • ESCRIBIR

1 Identifica las partes de la computadora.

LEER

2 Verifica. ¿Sí o no?

	sí	no
1. Cada sitio Web tiene su página inicial.		
2. Si quieres volver a un sitio, haz clic en el botón retroceder.		
3. Dentro de (En) un archivo hay varias carpetas.		
4. Si quieres guardar un documento lo tienes que borrar.		
5. Cada correo electrónico tiene un documento adjunto.		
6. Para hacer una copia dura de un documento necesitas una impresora.		
7. Si quieres leer de nuevo (una vez más) un correo electrónico que enviaste ayer tienes que abrir tu bandeja de entrada.		

HABLAR • ESCRIBIR

3 Personaliza. Da respuestas personales.
1. ¿Tienes una computadora portátil?
2. ¿Eres muy aficionado(a) a la computadora?
3. ¿Usas la computadora para hacer tus tareas escolares? ¿Cómo?
4. ¿Para qué navegas el Internet (la red)?
5. ¿Recibes y envías muchos correos electrónicos?
6. ¿Cuál es tu dirección de e-mail?
7. ¿Recibes muchos correos electrónicos que borras enseguida?
8. ¿Cuándo tienes que consultar tu libreta de direcciones?
9. ¿Apagas la computadora cuando no la usas?

EXPANSIÓN

Ahora, sin mirar las preguntas, cuenta la información en tus propias palabras. Si no recuerdas algo, un(a) compañero(a) te puede ayudar.

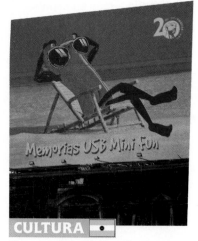

CULTURA

Una cartelera divertida en Buenos Aires

Andrew Payti

connectED.mcgraw-hill.com

LEER

④ **¡Te toca a ti!** Parea cada verbo con una palabra o expresión apropiada.

1. sonar   **a.** en línea
2. imprimir   **b.** el correo electrónico
3. enviar   **c.** el botón
4. borrar   **d.** una copia
5. entrar   **e.** el archivo
6. oprimir   **f.** el móvil

HABLAR • ESCRIBIR

⑤ Usa cada expresión de la Actividad 4 en una frase original.

LEER • ESCRIBIR

⑥ Completa con una palabra apropiada.

1. César quería abrir su bandeja de entrada e hizo clic con el _____.
2. Había muchos _____ nuevos en su bandeja de entrada. Los recibió hoy.
3. Él los leyó. Había tres que no le interesaron y los _____.
4. Recibió uno de un buen amigo. Él lo contestó enseguida y guardó la respuesta en su _____.
5. César _____ la computadora cuando empezó a trabajar y la _____ cuando terminó.

LEER • ESCRIBIR

⑦ Expresa de otra manera.

1. Ella siempre está sentada delante de su *ordenador*.
2. El sitio tiene una página *de inicio* interesante.
3. Ella navegaba *el Internet*.
4. Tienes que *pulsar* el botón borrador.
5. ¿Cuál es tu dirección de *e-mail*?

Comunicación

⑧ Trabaja con un(a) compañero(a) de clase. Usando el vocabulario y expresiones que ya conocen, discutan lo que hacen con su computadora. ¿Quién la usa más?

⑨ Usa el Internet para buscar eventos y actividades culturales de la región donde vives. Luego, busca eventos y actividades de una ciudad hispanohablante. Comparte lo que descubriste con tus compañeros(as) de clase. ¿Quién descubrió el evento cultural más interesante? ¿Dónde y cuándo tiene lugar?

Fotos y música 🎧

una cámara digital

A Cristina le encanta la fotografía.
Siempre descarga (baja) las fotos que
toma con su cámara digital o su móvil
a su computadora.

A Anita le encanta la música.
Siempre baja sus canciones favoritas
a su MP3.

Llamadas telefónicas

¡Ah!
Es mi amigo Paco.

el timbre (sonoro)

un móvil,
un (teléfono) celular

Sonó el móvil de Patricia.
Sabía quien la llamaba por el timbre.
Es el timbre que asignó a su mejor amigo.

Para conversar

¡Hola! Pepe, ¿eres
tú? No te oigo bien.
Se está cortando. ¿Me
escuchas?

¡Hola!

Ah, se nos cortó la
línea. Una llamada
perdida (caída).

David H. Brennan

la tarjeta telefónica

Bs. 4.000

¡Aló...
teléfonos públicos
DIGITEL TIM

la guía telefónica

el número de teléfono

el teléfono público

la clave de área

Juan y Teresa estaban en España.
Usaron un teléfono público para
    llamar a casa.
Para llamar a Estados Unidos,
    tenían que marcar el
    prefijo del país.

Descolgó (el
auricular).

Introdujo su tarjeta
en la ranura.

Esperó el tono.

Marcó el número
que deseaba.

Como contestar el teléfono

¡Hola!

Sí, está. ¿De
parte de quién,
por favor?

Un momento,
por favor.

¿Está Teresa,
por favor?

De Rafael. Rafael
Lugones.

¡Hola!

Lo siento,
pero no está.

Cómo no,
Señor.

¿Está Teresa,
por favor?

¿Le puedo dejar
un mensaje?

ENVELOPE FOLD

See the Foldables section of the Student Handbook at the beginning of this book for help with making this foldable. Use this study organizer with a partner to help you practice your new words. Draw a picture of a word on the top of each flap. Then pass the foldable to your partner who will write the word that corresponds with each picture on the reverse side of each flap. Take turns.

ESCUCHAR

1 Escucha y decide. Escucha cada frase y decide si la información es correcta o no. Usa una tabla como la de abajo para indicar tus respuestas.

correcta	incorrecta

HABLAR

2 Personaliza. Da respuestas personales.

1. ¿Tienes una cámara digital?
2. A veces, ¿bajas (descargas) las fotos que tomas en tu computadora?
3. ¿Qué bajas más en tu computadora? ¿Fotografías o canciones?
4. ¿Te gusta jugar videojuegos? ¿Cuál es tu favorito?
5. ¿Tienes un móvil?
6. ¿Cuál es el número de tu móvil?
7. ¿Tiene tu móvil un solo timbre o varios timbres?
8. ¿Tienes a veces llamadas perdidas cuando usas tu móvil?
9. ¿Hay muchos teléfonos públicos donde vives?
10. ¿Tiene tu familia un teléfono en casa? ¿Cuál es el número de su teléfono?

LEER • ESCRIBIR

3 Parea los sinónimos.

1. un celular
2. un ordenador
3. le gusta mucho
4. bajar
5. el código de área
6. una llamada perdida
7. ¡Bueno! (al contestar el teléfono)

a. descargar
b. una llamada caída
c. un móvil
d. le encanta
e. ¡Dígame!
f. la clave de área
g. una computadora

LEER • HABLAR

4 Contesta.

¿Para qué producto es el anuncio? ¿Qué significa **prepago**?

HABLAR • ESCRIBIR

5 Estás hablando por teléfono. ¿Qué vas a decir?

1. Quieres saber si alguien está.
2. Quieres saber quién está llamando.
3. Quieres saber si la persona con quien hablas (tu interlocutor) te puede oír.
4. Quieres decirle que la conexión es mala.
5. Quieres decirle a la persona con quien hablas que alguien no está.
6. Quieres dejarle un mensaje a una persona que no está.
7. Quieres decirle a otra persona que tuviste una llamada perdida.

LEER • ESCRIBIR

6 Completa.

Para hacer una llamada de un teléfono público en España o Latinoamérica debes comprar una __1__. Primero tienes que __2__ el auricular y luego __3__ la tarjeta en la ranura. Es necesario esperar __4__ antes de __5__ el número que deseas. Si haces una llamada de larga distancia tienes que marcar primero __6__ y si haces una llamada internacional tienes que marcar __7__ también. Si no sabes un número de teléfono lo puedes buscar en __8__.

7 ### Comunicación

Trabaja con un(a) compañero(a) de clase. Uno(a) de ustedes hace una llamada telefónica y el/la otro(a) contesta. Conversen. Recuerda, si cometes un error gramatical, puedes decir, **«Perdón, digo... »** para clarificar.

CULTURA

Mamá está haciendo una llamada telefónica en Miraflores, Perú. ¿Está introduciendo el niño una tarjeta en la ranura o está jugando?

InfoGap For more practice using your new vocabulary, do Activity 6 in the Student Resource section at the end of this book.

Una joven hablaba en su móvil mientras la otra leía un mensaje de texto.

Verbos como **querer, creer** en el pasado

Since most mental processes involve duration or continuance, verbs that deal with mental activities or conditions are most often expressed in the imperfect tense in the past. The most common of these verbs are:

creer	**pensar**
desear	**preferir**
querer	**poder**
tener ganas de (*to feel like*)	**saber**
sentir	**gustar**

Él sabía lo que preferíamos.
Yo tenía ganas de salir.

Práctica

CULTURA

Esta señorita guatemalteca siempre tenía ganas de ser artista y ahora tiene su propio taller en Antigua, Guatemala.

HABLAR • ESCRIBIR

1 Personaliza. Da respuestas personales.

1. ¿Te gustaba jugar videojuegos cuando eras joven?
2. ¿Sabías usar la computadora cuando eras muy joven?
3. ¿Siempre querías salir o preferías quedarte en casa?
4. ¿Siempre sabías lo que preferías hacer?
5. ¿Creías que siempre tenías razón o no?

LEER • ESCRIBIR

2 Completa en el pasado con el imperfecto del verbo indicado.

1. Yo _____ que sí pero no sé por qué, pero ellos _____ que no. (creer, creer)
2. Yo _____ que a ellos les _____ mucho hablar en su móvil. (saber, gustar)
3. Ella _____ lo mismo. (pensar)
4. Nosotros _____ ganas de hacer el viaje. (tener)
5. Nosotros _____ que ellos _____ salir. (saber, preferir)

3

Comunicación

Cuenta algunas cosas que tú siempre querías hacer pero que tu hermano(a) o mejor amigo(a) casi nunca quería hacer. Casi siempre prefería hacer otra cosa. ¿Qué prefería hacer él o ella?

Lori Ernfridsson

El pretérito y el imperfecto

1. The choice of whether to use the preterite or imperfect depends upon whether the speaker is describing an action completed in the past or a continuous, recurring action in the past.

2. You use the preterite to express actions or events that began and ended at a specific time in the past.

> Anoche **volví** a casa y **envié** unos correos electrónicos.
> Luego **pasé** un rato navegando la red.
> Y a eso de las nueve **fui** a ver la tele.

3. You use the imperfect to talk about a continuous, habitual, or repeated action in the past. The moment when the action began or ended is unimportant.

> Cada noche **volvía** a casa y **enviaba** unos correos electrónicos.
> Luego **pasaba** un rato navegando la red.
> Y después **iba** a la sala donde **veía** la tele.

4. Compare the following sentences.

REPEATED, HABITUAL ACTION
Él hablaba con sus abuelos cada semana.
Ella siempre navegaba la red.
Yo siempre me acostaba tarde.

COMPLETED ACTION
Él habló con sus abuelos la semana pasada.
Ella navegó la red anoche.
Pero anoche **me acosté** temprano.

Práctica

ESCUCHAR

4 Escucha. Usa una tabla como la de abajo para indicar si es una acción repetida o terminada.

repetida	terminada

CULTURA
El señor hablaba en su móvil mientras caminaba hacia la playa en Cádiz, España.

ESCUCHAR • HABLAR

5 Contesta. Presta atención a la expresión de tiempo.

1. ¿Jugaron los niños un videojuego anoche?
   ¿Cuándo jugaron un videojuego?
   ¿Jugaban los niños videojuegos todos los días?
   ¿Cuándo jugaban videojuegos?

2. ¿Compraste algo en línea ayer? ¿Qué compraste?
   ¿Cuándo lo/la compraste?
   ¿Siempre hacías compras en línea?
   ¿Cuándo hacías compras en línea?

3. ¿Fue José a España el año pasado?
   ¿Cuándo fue a España?
   ¿Iba José a España cada año?
   ¿Cuándo iba a España?

LEER • ESCRIBIR

6 Cambia **todos los sábados** a **el sábado pasado** y haz los cambios necesarios.

Todos los sábados Juan Antonio se levantaba muy temprano. Bajaba a la cocina y él mismo preparaba el desayuno. Después de comer, subía a su cuarto y prendía su computadora. Cuando se conectaba a Internet mandaba un correo electrónico a un buen amigo en España. En pocos segundos se comunicaba con su amigo. Los dos escribían de muchas cosas durante horas.

HABLAR • ESCRIBIR

7 Contesta.

1. Por lo general, ¿guardabas la mayoría de los correos electrónicos que recibías o los borrabas?
2. ¿Guardaste el correo que recibiste anoche o lo borraste?
3. ¿Abría Teresa su bandeja de entrada con frecuencia?
4. ¿La abrió ayer o no?
5. ¿Enviabas mensajes de texto a tus amigos muy a menudo?
6. ¿A quién le enviaste un mensaje de texto ayer?
7. ¿Usabas el Internet muy a menudo?
8. ¿Usaste el Internet anoche?

CULTURA

Muchos españoles recuerdan que visitaban molinos de viento cuando eran jóvenes. Les interesaban los molinos porque pensaban en la aventura de don Quijote con los molinos de viento.

Andrew Payti

HABLAR • ESCRIBIR

8 Mira la fotografía y contesta las preguntas.

CULTURA

¿Qué piensas? ¿Eran fanfarrones los que tomaban parte en este encierro durante las fiestas en San Sebastián de los Reyes, España?

1. ¿Había muchos espectadores que asistían al encierro?
2. ¿Corrían los toros en una plaza o en una calle?
3. ¿Corrían detrás de los toros o delante de los toros los corredores?
4. Mira bien la foto. ¿Tocó uno de los corredores a un toro?
5. ¿Obedecieron todos los corredores?
6. ¿Eran jóvenes los corredores?
7. ¿Qué opinas? ¿Eran bravos también? ¿Tenían miedo algunos?
8. ¿Querían impresionar a sus amigos?

EXPANSIÓN

Se dice que las personas como estas son fanfarrones. ¿Qué significa «fanfarrón»?

HABLAR • ESCRIBIR

9 Personaliza. Da respuestas personales.

¿Conocías a un niño fanfarrón cuando eras más joven? ¿Qué hacía? ¿Veías lo que hacía? ¿Qué hacías tú mientras él cometía sus tonterías? Una vez, ¿hizo algo que le causó un problema? ¿Qué hizo y qué pasó? Y, ¿qué hiciste (tú)?

Cultura

El encierro
El encierro se celebra durante muchas fiestas en España. Generalmente los toros corren en un área cerrada pero a veces corren en la calle misma. Durante un encierro no les hacen daño a los toros. Según las reglas aun no deben tocarlos.

10 **Comunicación**

Di algunas cosas que hacías con frecuencia cuando eras niño(a) y que hiciste ayer también.

Daniel Salsgiver

Dos acciones pasadas en la misma frase

1. Often a sentence may have two or more verbs in the past. The verbs may be in the same tense or in different tenses. In the sentence below, both verbs are in the preterite. Both describe simple actions that began and ended at a specific time in the past.

> **Laura llegó ayer y Pepe la vio.**

2. In the sentence below, the two verbs are in the imperfect because they both describe habitual or continuous actions. The moment when the actions began or ended is unimportant.

> **Durante el invierno, Adela iba a las montañas a esquiar, pero yo trabajaba.**

3. In the sentence below, the verb **estudiaba** is in the imperfect; it describes the background—what was going on. The verb in the preterite, **entró,** expresses the action or event that interrupted the ongoing action.

> **Yo estudiaba cuando Julia entró.**

El joven estudiaba mientras su hermana hablaba por teléfono.

Práctica

HABLAR • ESCRIBIR

11 Contesta.

1. ¿Enviaba José un correo electrónico cuando sonó su móvil? ¿Contestó el móvil?
2. Mientras ellos hablaban, ¿se estaba cortando la línea?
3. Mientras ellos hablaban, ¿se les cortó la línea?
4. ¿Estaba Teresa en casa cuando Rafael la llamó?
5. ¿Navegaba Anita el Internet cuando su hermanito apagó la computadora?
6. ¿Se puso furiosa Anita cuando él la apagó?

LEER • ESCRIBIR

12 Completa con la forma apropiada del pretérito o imperfecto.

1. Él _____ cuando yo le _____. (enfadarse, hablar)
2. Yo _____ su e-mail cuando él me _____ en mi móvil. (leer, llamar)
3. La conexión no _____ muy buena. Se _____ cortando y finalmente se nos _____ la línea. (ser, estar, cortar)
4. Mi hermanita no _____ que yo _____ la red y cuando (yo) _____ de mi cuarto ella _____ la computadora. (saber, usar, salir, apagar)

HABLAR • ESCRIBIR

13 Di lo que hacías cuando algo te interrumpió. Forma frases según el modelo.

MODELO leer →
Yo leía cuando sonó el teléfono.

leer	correr	ver	jugar	beber	hablar	sonar
llamar	bailar	comer	subir	servir	llover	pagar

Comunicación

14 Trabaja con un(a) compañero(a) de clase. Dile lo que hacía cada miembro de tu familia anoche mientras tú hacías otra cosa. Di también lo que tú hacías. Luego comparen sus actividades.

15 Habla con un(a) compañero(a) de clase. Dile algo que hacías ayer. Tu compañero(a) te va a decir algo que ocurrió e interrumpió lo que hacías. Luego en una sola frase, describe lo que hacías y lo que pasó (ocurrió).

Refrán

Can you guess what the following proverb means?

No me importa nada. No están maduras.

Así dijo la zorra a las uvas: que no estaban maduras.

¡Bravo!

You have now learned all the new vocabulary and grammar in this chapter. Continue to use and practice all that you know while learning more cultural information. **¡Vamos!**

Se cortó la línea.

David H. Brennan

¿Comprendes?

A Contesta según la información en la conversación.

1. ¿Cómo sabe Andrés que es Alejandra quien lo llama cuando suena su móvil?
2. ¿Qué pasó anoche?
3. ¿Por qué no contestó ella?
4. ¿Sabemos si Andrés dejó un mensaje?
5. ¿Qué problema están teniendo?
6. ¿Cómo terminó la llamada?

B **Analizando** ¿Por qué es conveniente dar un timbre diferente a cada uno de tus amigos o miembros de la familia que te llaman con frecuencia?

C **Personalizando** ¿Tienes a veces unos problemas con tu móvil como los que tenían (experimentaban) Andrés y Alejandra en la conversación? Describe los problemas. Luego habla con tus compañeros para ver si ellos tienen las mismas dificultades.

100% REVERSIBLE

FANTÁSTICO DESDE CUALQUIER ÁNGULO

Francisco Monroy

Lectura

ESTRATEGIA DE LECTURA

Antes de leer

Piensa en todo lo que tú haces con tu computadora y otros aparatos electrónicos.

Durante la lectura

Compara las actividades de los jóvenes hispanos en la lectura con tus propias actividades.

☑ **READING CHECK**

¿Qué información buscaba Manuel?

☑ **READING CHECK**

¿Cuál es un pasatiempo favorito de Julia?

☑ **READING CHECK**

¿Por qué es interesante la información que envió el hermano de Raúl?

Después de leer

¿Con qué actividades te identificas más? ¿Usan estos jóvenes sus computadoras y otros aparatos de la misma manera que tú?

PERSONALIZANDO Una buena estrategia de lectura es personalizar la información que estás leyendo. Determina cuáles son las cosas que tú también haces o las cosas que no haces. Cuando personalizas, puedes identificarte más con la información.

En un mundo tecnológico 🎧 ↺

Vamos a hablar con unos amigos hispanohablantes.

—¡Hola! Me llamo Manuel Ramos. Tengo dieciséis años y vivo en la Ciudad de México. Anoche navegaba el Internet para buscar información sobre Simón Bolívar para mi clase de historia. Yo no sabía que Bolívar era de una familia acomodada, una familia que tenía mucho dinero, y que desde su niñez le interesaban mucho las condiciones en que vivían los pobres. Creo que esta información es correcta pero antes de incluirla en mi composición tengo que verificar su confiabilidad[1]. Todos sabemos que hay sitios que no son confiables.

—¡Hola! Me llamo Julia González y soy de Ponce, Puerto Rico. A mí me encanta la música. Anoche bajé (descargué) unas ocho canciones más en mi computadora y en mi MP3. Me encanta escuchar mis canciones favoritas en cualquier[2] momento del día. ¡Una cosa importante! Siempre verifico si es legal bajar las canciones.

— ¡Hola! Soy Raúl Torres. Soy de Málaga, España. Anoche recibí una noticia interesante. Mi hermano mayor está estudiando en la Universidad de Salamanca. Me envió un correo electrónico y me dijo que algunos de sus profesores ponen sus conferencias en el Internet. Si un(a) estudiante no puede asistir a clase puede escuchar la conferencia en su MP3. ¿Qué piensas de tal idea? Vale, ¿no?

---

[1]confiabilidad   *reliability*   [2]cualquier   *any*

¿Comprendes?

A Hojeando Hojea la lectura para determinar quién hace las siguientes actividades.

	Manuel Ramos	Julia González	Raúl Torres
1. descarga su música favorita			
2. navega el Internet buscando datos para una tarea escolar			
3. lee un correo electrónico que acaba de recibir			

B Buscando información Da la información para cada persona—Manuel, Julia, Raúl—usando frases completas.
   1. de donde es
   2. lo que tiene
   3. detalles sobre sus actividades

C Recordando hechos Contesta.
   1. ¿Qué aprendió Manuel Ramos mientras navegaba el Internet?
   2. ¿Qué tiene que verificar Manuel? ¿Por qué?
   3. Y Julia, ¿qué tiene ella que verificar?
   4. ¿Qué noticia interesante recibió Raúl Torres de su hermano?

D Identificando ¿Cuál es la idea principal de esta lectura? Identifica unos detalles que apoyan (support) esta idea.

E Pronosticando Contesta.
   1. ¿Cuáles son unos avances tecnológicos no mencionados en esta lectura?
   2. ¿Cuáles son otros avances que piensas que van a ocurrir en el futuro?

Lectura
UN POCO MÁS

Antes de leer

Piensa en como la tecnología moderna te afecta casi a diario (todos los días). ¿Cuáles son unos aparatos que usas tanto que los consideras indispensables? ¿Cómo te ayudan estos aparatos? En tu opinión, ¿cómo era la vida de tus abuelos sin la tecnología que tienes a tu disposición?

La tecnología de hoy y ayer

Tomás Navarro vive en Martínez, un suburbio de Buenos Aires, la capital de Argentina. Nos va a hablar de su nuevo juguete[1] que le gusta mucho.

—Ayer me compré un móvil. Es increíble la cantidad de opciones que tiene. Claro que puedo hacer y recibir llamadas y para saber quién me está llamando puedo personalizar los timbres asignando canciones u otros sonidos a mis amigos y familiares. Además mi móvil me permite enviar mensajes de texto, acceder mi correo electrónico y bajar música y videojuegos. Tiene otra opción que se llama fotomensajería. Puedo tomar fotografías digitales con mi móvil y enviarlas instantáneamente a mis amigos. Y puedo grabar y enviar un videomensaje con sonido. Las opciones no tienen límite.

Tú tienes un móvil, ¿no? ¿Te ofrece otras opciones que no me ofrece el mío? ¿Cuáles?

Sí, la tecnología está cambiando el mundo de una manera rápida y radical. Si no lo crees, debes hablar con tus abuelos. Cuando ellos eran niños, ¿tenían computadora y móvil? De ninguna manera. Si querían escuchar música ponían la radio o ponían un disco[2] en un tocadiscos. Cuando querían comunicarse con alguien escribían una carta o usaban el teléfono. Hoy día, en Estados Unidos, España y Latinoamérica la gente se comunica por medio de la comunicación electrónica. Pero en España y Latinoamérica, además de los móviles, sigue siendo popular y conveniente el teléfono público. Para usarlo compras una tarjeta telefónica que contiene una cantidad de unidades. La tarjeta que se introduce en la ranura del teléfono te permite hacer llamadas locales, interurbanas, de larga distancia y hasta[3] internacionales. Mientras hablas, se deduce automáticamente el número apropiado de unidades. ¡Otro ejemplo de la tecnología!

[1]juguete *toy*
[2]disco *record*
[3]hasta *even*

CAPÍTULO 6

¿Comprendes?

A Escoge.

1. ¿Qué compró Tomás?
   a. un juguete
   b. un móvil
   c. una cámara

2. Tomás asigna timbres personales para _____.
   a. poder hacer y recibir llamadas
   b. poder oír sus canciones favoritas
   c. poder identificar quien lo está llamando

3. ¿Qué no puede hacer Tomás con su móvil?
   a. escuchar la radio
   b. tomar fotos
   c. enviar mensajes de texto

4. ¿Cómo se comunicaban nuestros abuelos cuando eran jóvenes?
   a. Usaban la radio.
   b. Usaban su tocadiscos.
   c. Usaban el teléfono.

5. ¿Qué contiene una tarjeta telefónica?
   a. números de teléfono
   b. unidades que te permiten hacer una llamada de un teléfono público
   c. un teléfono público

6. Una llamada interurbana es una llamada _____.
   a. local, dentro de la misma ciudad
   b. de una ciudad a otra en la misma región
   c. de larga distancia

B Prepara una presentación visual que compare y contraste la manera en que Tomás emplea la tecnología con tu uso de la tecnología.

CULTURA

Es un teléfono público en una calle de Buenos Aires, la capital de Argentina. ¿Qué se puede usar para hacer una llamada de este teléfono?

Andrew Payti

Prepárate para el examen

↺ To review, see **Vocabulario 1.**

↺ To review, see **Vocabulario 1** and **Vocabulario 2.**

A esta pareja les gusta usar su móvil pero no tenían móvil cuando eran jóvenes.

Vocabulario

1 Identifica.

2 Completa.

6. La muchacha quiere entrar en línea y _____ con su ratón.

7–8. Si estás navegando y quieres regresar a un sitio anterior tienes que _____ en el _____ regresar.

9. Una _____ contiene varios archivos.

10. Si quieres saber si tienes correos electrónicos tienes que abrir tu _____.

11. No quiero guardar el correo. Lo voy a _____.

12. Si necesitas una copia dura de un correo o de una página del Internet, tienes que tener _____.

13. Puedes tener diferentes _____ en tu móvil para identificar quienes te llaman.

3 Parea.

14. un móvil	**a.** bajar
15. la computadora	**b.** punto
16. descargar	**c.** guardar
17. llamada perdida	**d.** un celular
18. @	**e.** pulsar
19. regresar	**f.** llamada caída
20. oprimir	**g.** el ordenador
	h. arroba
	i. retroceder

Gramática

4 **Escribe en el pasado.**

21. Quiero comprarme un nuevo móvil.

22. A mis abuelos les gusta usar un teléfono fijo.

23. Él está contento cuando recibe la buena noticia.

5 **Completa con el imperfecto o el pretérito.**

24–25. Él _____ muy a menudo y _____ ayer también.
(ir, ir)

26–27. Ellos me _____ correos casi todos los días pero ayer yo no _____ ninguno. (enviar, recibir)

28–29. Cuando yo _____ niño(a) mis abuelos siempre me _____ en español. (ser, hablar)

6 **Completa con el imperfecto o el pretérito.**

30–31. Teresa _____ en el supermercado cuando _____ su móvil. (estar, sonar)

32–33. Yo _____ en mi móvil cuando el empleado me _____ una pregunta. (hablar, hacer)

34–35. Él _____ canciones en su MP3 mientras yo _____ fotografías en el mío. (bajar, bajar)

36–37. Mientras ellos _____ nosotros _____. (divertirse, trabajar)

Cultura

7 **Corrige las frases falsas.**

38. En algunas universidades si un(a) estudiante no puede ir a clase, puede mirar las conferencias de sus profesores en la televisión.

39. Siempre sabemos que la información que leemos en el Internet es correcta.

40. Se pueden bajar canciones sin permiso.

To review, see **Verbos como querer, creer en el pasado.**

To review, see **El pretérito y el imperfecto.**

To review, see **Dos acciones pasadas en la misma frase.**

To review this cultural information, see the **Lectura cultural.**

Kerri Galloway

TECNOMUNDO

Prepárate para el examen

① La tecnología

Talk about your opinion of technology

¿A ti te gusta la tecnología? Explica por qué dices que sí o que no. Si conoces a alguien que habla español, puedes preguntarle su opinión. ¿Tiene la misma opinión que tú?

② Mi móvil

Discuss your new cell phone

Imagínate que acabas de comprar un nuevo móvil con todas las opciones más avanzadas. Dile a un(a) compañero(a) todo lo que puedes hacer con tu móvil. Luego discutan las opciones que les gustan más o que consideran las más interesantes.

③ El uso de los celulares

Debate the use of cell phones

Trabajen en grupos y debatan sus ideas sobre el uso de los celulares. ¿Deben permitir el uso de celulares en la escuela, a bordo de un avión, mientras uno maneja (conduce) un carro, en el teatro o cine, etc.? Defiendan sus opiniones.

④ Cuando mis abuelos eran jóvenes

Tell about what your grandparents had and didn't have

Habla con tus abuelos. Ellos te van a decir las muchas cosas que tú tienes que ellos no tenían cuando eran niños. Te van a decir lo que tenían. Comparte los resultados de tus conversaciones con unos(as) compañeros(as) de clase y decidan si sus abuelos dicen más o menos la misma cosa.

CULTURA 🇪🇸

Estas dos señoras mayores están disfrutando del tiempo con una conversación importante en una calle de Gijón en Asturias.

⑤ Interrupciones

Talk about one activity interrupting another in the past

Trabaja con un(a) compañero(a) de clase. Ayer ustedes hacían muchas cosas. Pero siempre había interrupciones. Hablen de todo lo que hacían y todo lo que interrumpió lo que hacían.

Andrew Payti

Tarea

You have just received an e-mail message from a Spanish-speaking friend who hasn't heard from you in awhile and wants to know what's up. Write a reply informing him or her of how you are doing and what you did today. Use this opportunity to impress your friend with some of the grammar and vocabulary that you have learned recently, and don't forget to follow the rules of *netiquette.*

Writing Strategy

Netiquette E-mail is a quick and fun way to communicate with friends all over the world. Still, it is important to ensure that your message is not carelessly written. Tone of voice can easily be misunderstood, especially when sarcasm is used, and misspelled words or incorrect grammar can lead to confusion. To avoid hurt feelings and misunderstandings, it is important to adhere to net etiquette, or *netiquette,* and to always check your message for errors before sending it.

❶ Prewrite

Although e-mail between friends is an informal means of expression, your message should still follow a logical structure so that it is both easy to understand and fun to read. As you think about what you want your message to contain, categorize the information in terms of whether it belongs in the introduction, in the body or main part of the text, or in the conclusion.

❷ Write

Be sure to adhere to the following rules of *netiquette.*

- Be certain that you have typed the correct e-mail address. Sending a personal message to the wrong person can be embarrassing!
- Make sure that your subject line reflects the content of your e-mail.
- Use the correct spelling of words and proper grammar.
- Be cautious when using sarcasm as it can easily be misunderstood.
- Use capital letters appropriately. Words with all capital letters are read as SHOUTING and can be interpreted as rude.
- Remember that good manners are just as important in cyberspace as they are in real life.
- Always re-read your message carefully before sending it.

Evaluate

Don't forget that your teacher will evaluate you on correct use of vocabulary, proper spelling and grammar, logical structure, and good *netiquette.*

Repaso del Capítulo 6

Gramática

Verbos como querer, creer en el pasado

Verbs that express mental processes or conditions in the past are usually expressed in the imperfect tense.

> **Tenía ganas de ver a mis amigos.**
> **Mi abuela sabía lo que preferíamos comer.**

El pretérito y el imperfecto

The choice of whether to use the preterite or imperfect depends upon whether the action began and ended at a specific time in the past or if it was a continuous, habitual, or repeated action in the past. Compare the following sentences.

PRETERITE	IMPERFECT
Ella habló con su madre anoche.	**Ella hablaba con su madre cada día.**
El sábado fuiste al cine.	**Siempre ibas al cine.**
Comieron en el restaurante una vez.	**Comían en el restaurante a menudo.**

Dos acciones pasadas en la misma frase

A sentence may have two or more verbs in the past. In the sentence below, both verbs are in the preterite because they both tell of events that began and ended at a specific point in the past.

> **Pablo escribió el e-mail y lo envió.**

In the following sentence, both verbs are in the imperfect because they describe continuous actions in the past.

> **En el verano Tito siempre iba a la playa y yo me quedaba en casa.**

Some sentences contain both the preterite and the imperfect. In this case, the preterite expresses an action that interrupted an ongoing action in the past.

> **Mamá y papá hablaban cuando sonó el teléfono.**

CULTURA

Los jóvenes venezolanos se divertían mientras una amiga les leía un textomensaje que alguien le envió en su móvil. ¿Qué crees? ¿Es gracioso o serio el mensaje que recibió?

Kelli Drummer-Avendaño

CAPÍTULO 6

Vocabulario

Describing a computer

la computadora, el ordenador	el ratón	un sitio Web	el botón borrador
la pantalla de escritorio	el teclado	la página de inicio, (inicial, frontal)	el archivo
la alfombrilla	el icono	el botón regresar (retroceder)	la carpeta
	la barra de herramientas		la impresora
			una copia dura

Discussing e-mail

el correo electrónico, el e-mail	la dirección de correo electrónico (de e-mail)	punto	la bandeja de enviados
el/la destinatario(a)	arroba	la libreta de direcciones	el documento adjunto
		la bandeja de entrada	

Describing computer activities

prender	hacer clic	borrar	bajar, descargar
apagar	oprimir, pulsar	navegar la red (el Internet)	imprimir
entrar en línea	guardar		

Discussing cell phones and other technology

el móvil, el celular	una llamada perdida (caída)	la cámara digital	sonar
el timbre (sonoro)		el MP3	asignar

Making a phone call

el teléfono público	llamar	introducir la tarjeta telefónica	marcar el número
la ranura	descolgar (el auricular)	esperar el tono	¿Está...?
un mensaje			¿De parte de quién?

Discussing telephone numbers

la guía telefónica	el número de teléfono	el prefijo del país	la clave de área

Other useful words and expressions

Se está cortando.	Se nos cortó la línea.	cierto(a)
¿Me escuchas?	anterior	encantar

LA PRACTICE Refer to the Language Arts Practice section for activities that will strengthen your Language Arts skills as you continue to use your Spanish.

Literary Reader

You may wish to read the excerpts from the famous poem *Versos sencillos,* found in the Literary Reader at the end of this book.

Repaso cumulativo

Repasa lo que ya has aprendido

These activities will help you review and remember what you have learned so far in Spanish.

1 Escucha las frases. Parea cada frase con el dibujo que describe.

 a.

 b.

2 Completa con el imperfecto.

1. _____ una fiesta. (haber)
2. Todo el mundo _____ durante la fiesta. (bailar)
3. Una banda _____. (tocar)
4. Nosotros _____. (divertirse)
5. Yo no _____ ir a casa. (querer)
6. Me _____ los fuegos artificiales. (gustar)
7. Mucha gente _____ mientras _____ los fuegos artificiales. (comer, mirar)

3 Completa con cada verbo que falta.

1. Él lo hizo y tú lo _____ pero ellos no lo _____.
2. Ellos vinieron y nosotros _____ pero tú no _____.
3. Yo estuve y él _____ pero tú no _____.
4. Tú lo supiste y yo lo _____ pero los otros no lo _____.

4 Sigue el modelo.

MODELO   **Lo pido. →**
             Lo pedí.

1. Juan lo pide.
2. Tú lo sirves.
3. Nosotros lo repetimos.
4. Ella lo prefiere así.
5. El cocinero fríe las papas.
6. Usted lo sigue.

⑤ Identifica. Usa un diagrama como el de abajo para escribir palabras relacionadas con una estación de tren.

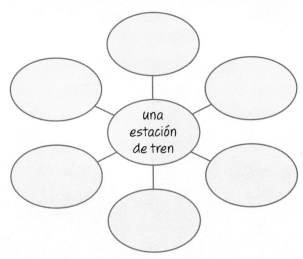

una estación de tren

⑥ Escribe una frase original con cada una de las palabras de la Actividad 5.

⑦ Escribe una pregunta.

1. *Juan* fue al restaurante.
2. Juan fue *al restaurante.*
3. El mesero trabajaba *en el restaurante.*
4. Juan pidió *un menú.*
5. El mesero era *de México.*
6. El mesero era *muy simpático.*
7. *Todos* comieron muy bien.
8. Todos comieron *mucho.*
9. Juan volvió a casa *en bus.*
10. Juan volvió *tarde.*

⑧ Rompecabezas

Cambia una letra en cada palabra para formar una nueva palabra.

1. base
2. peso
3. jamón
4. piso
5. llenar
6. fue
7. hay
8. cada

En el hotel

Go Online!
connectED.mcgraw-hill.com

Audio

Video

Práctica

Repaso

Diversiones

eScape

ePals

Aquí y Allí

Vamos a comparar ¿Has pasado una noche en un hotel aquí en Estados Unidos? ¿Cuándo? Y, ¿cómo era el hotel? ¿Hay muchas categorías de hoteles en Estados Unidos? En este capítulo vas a aprender algo sobre los muchos tipos de hoteles que hay en los países hispanos. Algunos son muy interesantes.

Objetivos

You will:

- check into a hotel or hostel
- ask for things you may need while at a hotel or hostel
- discuss hotel stays in Latin America and Spain

You will use:

- the present perfect tense
- double object pronouns

◀ Aquí ves la piscina o la alberca del Hotel Atitlán en el lago Atitlán en Guatemala. Desde la terraza de la alberca hay vistas estupendas del lago y de los volcanes Tolimán, San Pedro y Atitlán.

Introducción al tema

En el hotel

¿Te has alojado una vez en un hotel? ¿Por cuántas noches? Mira estas fotos para familiarizarte con el tema de este capítulo—una estadía en un hotel en un país hispano. Como vas a observar hay muchos tipos de hoteles—de los más económicos a los más elegantes.

Perú

El hostal La Rivera en el balneario de Huanchaco en el norte de Perú

España

Una antigua llave que se usaba mucho antes de las llaves magnéticas. En unos hoteles pequeños siguen usando llaves como esta y los clientes siempre tienen que dejarlas en la recepción.

Venezuela

El hotel Los Frailes en las montañas de Mérida en Venezuela. ¿Qué tal te parece pasar una hora andando a caballo?

Ecuador

La recepción y el hall en un hotel en Manta, Ecuador

Favor de Arreglar la Habitación

Please Make Up room
Prière De Faire La Chambre

Hoteles Calinda
Hotels, Suites, Resorts
Mexico

Puerto Rico

Es un hotel bonito en la isla de Vieques.

España

Es el patio de un hotel en la Costa de la Luz en la provincia de Huelva. La provincia está en Andalucía en el suroeste de España.

Nicaragua

El hall de entrada de un hotel bonito en Granada

México

Un hotel elegante en Tepoztlán adonde va mucha gente de la Ciudad de México a pasar el fin de semana

Una estadía en un hotel 🎧

la recepcionista

la recepción

la llave (magnética)

el cliente, el huésped

un hotel

un albergue juvenil, un hostal

José está en la recepción.
Él ha hecho una reservación en línea.
Ha reservado un cuarto sencillo, no doble.
El huésped va a hospedarse en el hotel.

Un desayuno continental

la mermelada

el pan dulce

la mantequilla

el panecillo

el café

el ascensor

1 2 3

el mozo

El mozo ha subido el equipaje en el ascensor.

Un desayuno americano

el pan tostado

el tocino, el bacón, el lacón

el jugo de naranja

huevos revueltos

El cuarto, La habitación

la percha, el colgador

la almohada

la sábana

el armario

la manta, la frazada

la cama

La camarera ha limpiado el cuarto.
Ha hecho la cama.

El cuarto de baño

la ducha

una toalla limpia

el jabón

la bañera

el lavabo

el inodoro, el váter

una toalla sucia

Para conversar

Necesitamos toallas limpias. ¿Nos las ha cambiado la camarera?

No, no nos las ha cambiado.

El huésped va a salir.
Ha abandonado el cuarto.

En otras partes

In addition to **la camarera**, you will also hear **la mucama**, especially in Mexico.

el aire acondicionado

David H. Brennan

1 Escucha las frases. Parea cada frase con la foto que describe.

a.

b.

c.

Nota

Hoy en día muchos hoteles tienen un gimnasio y una sauna para sus clientes. A mucha gente le gusta ir al gimnasio por la mañana antes de ir a su trabajo o por la tarde después de volver de su trabajo. Todos quieren mantenerse en forma.

HABLAR • ESCRIBIR

2 Contesta sobre la llegada a un hotel.

1. ¿Ha reservado el señor un cuarto?
2. ¿Adónde va el cliente cuando llega al hotel?
3. ¿Quién lo saluda en la recepción?
4. ¿Quién lo va a ayudar con sus maletas?
5. ¿Qué le da el recepcionista para abrir la puerta de su cuarto?

EXPANSIÓN

Ahora, sin mirar las preguntas, cuenta la información en tus propias palabras. Si no recuerdas algo, un(a) compañero(a) te puede ayudar.

(tl b)Andrew Payti, (tr)Joshua Ets-Hokin/Getty Images

LEER

③ Escoge la palabra apropiada.

1. (Una manta, Una almohada) cubre la cama.
2. Hay (perchas, sábanas) en el armario.
3. (El mozo, La camarera) ha hecho la cama.
4. Me gusta dormir con dos (camas, almohadas).
5. Es necesario cambiar las toallas (limpias, sucias).
6. El desayuno (continental, americano) incluye huevos.
7. La huéspeda ha (abandonado, reservado) el cuarto porque va a salir.
8. Necesito (jabón, champú) para lavarme la cara.

CULTURA

Es una habitación en un hotel en Madrid, España. Identifica todo lo que ves en la habitación.

ESCRIBIR

④ **Rompecabezas**

Usa las letras en la tabla para formar palabras de este capítulo. Puedes usar unas letras más de una vez. Luego, escribe frases originales con tus palabras.

a	r	e
p	i	s
t	d	v
l	n	c
o	b	m

HABLAR • ESCRIBIR

⑤ Describe.

1. el cuarto de un hotel
2. un desayuno continental
3. un desayuno americano
4. las actividades en la recepción de un hotel

Carreras

Si conoces el español y lo sabes hablar por lo menos un poquito, hay muchas oportunidades para trabajar en la industria hotelera. Además de los muchos hispanohablantes que viven aquí, hay miles de turistas de España y Latinoamérica que visitan Estados Unidos cada año. Si es posible, visita un hotel en tu ciudad y observa a los clientes y habla con los empleados. ¿Hablan español?

El presente perfecto

1. The present perfect tense is called a compound tense because it consists of two parts—the present tense of the verb **haber** and the past participle.

2. The past participle is formed by adding **-ado** to the stem of **-ar** verbs and **-ido** to the stem of **-er** and **-ir** verbs.

   llegar → llegado   comer → comido   subir → subido
   cambiar → cambiado tener → tenido   vivir → vivido

3. Study the forms of regular present perfect verbs.

	llegar	comer	salir
yo	he llegado	he comido	he salido
tú	has llegado	has comido	has salido
Ud., él, ella	ha llegado	ha comido	ha salido
nosotros(as)	hemos llegado	hemos comido	hemos salido
vosotros(as)	habéis llegado	habéis comido	habéis salido
Uds., ellos, ellas	han llegado	han comido	han salido

4. The present perfect tense is used when speaking of a past event without reference to any particular time. It brings the action right up to the present. Some time expressions frequently used with the present perfect are:

ya	already, yet
todavía no	not yet
hasta ahora	until now, so far
jamás	ever, never
nunca	never

   —En tu vida, ¿has viajado a México?
   —No. No he ido nunca a México.
   —Yo sí. Hasta ahora he estado tres veces.

5. The verb **haber** and the past participle are never separated.

   Ella ha llegado pero sus amigos no han llegado.
   Y ella no les ha hablado.

CULTURA

Es una calle peatonal en Guadalajara, México. ¿Jamás has viajado a México?

Práctica

ESCUCHAR • HABLAR • ESCRIBIR

1 Contesta sobre la visita de Sofía a un hotel.

1. ¿Ha llegado Sofía al hotel?
2. ¿Ha ido a la recepción?
3. ¿Ha hablado con la recepcionista?
4. ¿Le ha dado su llave la recepcionista?
5. ¿Ha subido a su cuarto?
6. ¿Ha subido la escalera o ha tomado el ascensor?
7. ¿La ha ayudado el mozo?

EXPANSIÓN

Ahora, sin mirar las preguntas, cuenta la información en tus propias palabras. Si no recuerdas algo, un(a) compañero(a) te puede ayudar.

HABLAR

2 Personaliza. Da respuestas personales.

1. ¿Has viajado por Ecuador?
2. ¿Te has hospedado en un albergue juvenil?
3. ¿Jamás has comido tacos o enchiladas?
4. ¿Has asistido a un concierto de rock?
5. Tú y tus amigos, ¿han ido a un museo?
6. ¿Han viajado ustedes en avión?

LEER • ESCRIBIR

3 Completa con el presente perfecto.

Los huéspedes ___1___ (llegar) al hotel y ___2___ (presentarse) en la recepción. El recepcionista les ___3___ (dar) su llave pero (ellos) no ___4___ (subir) a su cuarto todavía. ¿Tú ___5___ (ir) a un hotel recientemente?

CULTURA

Si quieres estar cerca del mercado en Otavalo, Ecuador, puedes hospedarte en este hostal.

4 *Comunicación*

Tus tíos y primos están visitando tu ciudad. Están hospedándose en un hotel. Llama al hotel por teléfono y habla con el/la recepcionista (tu compañero[a]). Quieres saber si ya han llegado tus parientes y si ya han subido a su cuarto. Después cambien de rol.

InfoGap For more practice using the present perfect, do Activity 7 in the Student Resource section at the end of this book.

Richard Brommer

Conexiones

El inglés

There are very few verbs that have an irregular past participle in Spanish. Such is not the case in English. There are many verbs with irregular past participles and many people learning English, as well as native speakers, have trouble with them. Can you give the past participle of the following verbs? *be, begin, bite, break, bring, buy, catch, come, eat, fall, find, fly, go, hear, hide, leave, make, meet, ride, run, see, sing, sit, speak, stand, swim, throw, write*

Participios irregulares

The following verbs have irregular past participles.

decir → dicho	volver → vuelto
hacer → hecho	devolver → devuelto
ver → visto	morir → muerto
escribir → escrito	abrir → abierto
poner → puesto	cubrir → cubierto (*covered*)
romper → roto (*broken*)	freír → frito

Práctica

HABLAR

5 Conversa según el modelo.

MODELO —¿Van a verlo?

—Pero, ya lo hemos visto.

1. ¿Van a abrirlo?
2. ¿Van a ponerlo?
3. ¿Van a devolverlo?
4. ¿Van a escribirlo?
5. ¿Van a decirlo?
6. ¿Van a cubrirlo?

HABLAR

6 Contesta según el modelo.

MODELO ¿Hacer tal cosa? →

¿Hacer tal cosa? ¡Vaya, hombre! ¿Yo?
En mi vida he hecho tal cosa.

1. ¿Ver tal cosa?
2. ¿Decir tal cosa?
3. ¿Leer tal cosa?
4. ¿Escribir tal cosa?

HABLAR • ESCRIBIR

7 Contesta según se indica.

1. ¿Ustedes se han ayudado? (sí)
2. ¿Quién ha hecho la cama? (yo)
3. ¿Quién ha frito los huevos? (Elena y Tomás)
4. ¿Quién ha abierto la lata? (yo)
5. ¿Quién ha puesto la mesa? (yo)
6. ¿Quién no ha hecho nada? (tú)

CULTURA 🎥

¿Quién ha puesto esta mesa en un restauránte en Guatemala?

8 **Comunicación**

Hay muchas cosas que queremos hacer algún día que hasta ahora no hemos hecho. Con un(a) compañero(a) de clase, hablen de las cosas que quieren hacer pero que todavía no han hecho. Cuando posible, expliquen por qué no las han hecho o no las han podido hacer.

Lori Ernfridsson

Dos complementos me lo, te lo, nos lo

1. Many sentences have both a direct and an indirect object pronoun. In Spanish the indirect object pronoun always precedes the direct object pronoun. Both pronouns precede the conjugated form of the verb.

2. Study the following sentences.

Ella **nos** sirvió **el helado**.	Ella **nos lo** sirvió.
El mozo **me** dio **la llave**.	El mozo **me la** dio.
Él **me** vendió **los libros**.	Él **me los** vendió.
Papá **te** hizo **las reservaciones**.	Papá **te las** hizo.

FOLDABLES
Study Organizer

LARGE SENTENCE STRIPS
See the Foldables section of the Student Handbook at the beginning of this book for help with making this foldable. Use this study organizer to help you practice object pronouns. Write a sentence with a direct and indirect object on the front of each flap. Then pass the foldable to your partner who will open each flap and rewrite the sentences using pronouns. When you're finished, switch roles.

Práctica

HABLAR

9 Conversa según el modelo.

MODELO los videos →
—¿Quién te dio los videos?
—Mi tío Julio me los dio.

1. la raqueta
2. los esquís
3. las botas
4. el boleto
5. las gafas para el sol
6. la computadora

HABLAR • ESCRIBIR

10 Contesta con **la camarera** o **el mozo** y los pronombres apropiados.

1. ¿Quién te ha traído las perchas?
2. ¿Quién te ha cambiado las toallas?
3. ¿Quién te ha limpiado el baño?
4. ¿Quién te ha subido el equipaje?
5. ¿Quién te ha abierto la puerta?
6. ¿Quién te ha servido el desayuno?

CULTURA

Es un cuarto con dos camas en un hotel bonito en Cotacachi, Ecuador. La camarera ha limpiado el cuarto y ha puesto las batas en la cama para los huéspedes.

Andrew Payti

Refrán

Can you guess what the following proverb means?

Sobre gustos no hay nada escrito.

HABLAR

11 Conversa según el modelo.

MODELO cámara nueva →
—¿Quieres ver mi cámara nueva?
—¿Quién te la compró?
—Me la compró mi tía Adela.

1. zapatos nuevos   3. mochila nueva
2. casco nuevo   4. botas nuevas

ESCUCHAR • HABLAR • ESCRIBIR

12 Contesta con **nuestra profesora** y los pronombres apropiados.

MODELO —¿Quién les dio (a ustedes) el examen?
—Nuestra profesora nos lo dio.

1. ¿Quién les explicó (a ustedes) la regla?
2. ¿Quién les enseñó la gramática?
3. ¿Quién les explicó las diferencias?
4. ¿Quién les presentó el vocabulario?
5. ¿Quién les leyó los poemas?

13 ### Comunicación

Habla con un(a) compañero(a) de clase. Tu compañero(a) está llevando unas cosas que te gustan y quieres saber quién se las dio. Sigue el modelo.

MODELO — _____, me gusta mucho tu camisa. ¿Quién te la dio?
— _____ me la dio. **or** No me la dio nadie. Me la compré.

CULTURA

El Hospedaje Sunset en Huanchaco, Perú. Este hospedaje tiene tarifas económicas.

Dos complementos con se

Go Online!

connectED.mcgraw-hill.com

1. The indirect object pronouns **le** and **les** change to **se** when used with **lo, la, los,** or **las.** Note that the indirect object **se** always precedes the direct object.

El mozo **les** subió **el equipaje.**   El mozo **se lo** subió.

El recepcionista **le** dio **las llaves** a José.   El recepcionista **se las** dio.

2. Because the pronoun **se** can refer to many different people, it is often clarified with a prepositional phrase.

Yo se lo di $\begin{cases} \text{a él.} \\ \text{a ella.} \\ \text{a usted.} \end{cases}$ Yo se lo di $\begin{cases} \text{a ellos.} \\ \text{a ellas.} \\ \text{a ustedes.} \end{cases}$

Práctica

ESCUCHAR • HABLAR

14 Conversa según el modelo.

MODELO —¿Quién le compró el regalito?
—Su abuela se lo compró.

1. ¿Quién le compró la bicicleta?
2. ¿Quién le compró las entradas?
3. ¿Quién le compró la tabla hawaiana?
4. ¿Quién le compró los esquís acuáticos?
5. ¿Quién le compró el balón?

LEER • ESCRIBIR

15 Contesta con los pronombres apropiados.

1. ¿Les abrió la puerta a los huéspedes el mozo?
2. ¿Les subió las maletas el mozo?
3. ¿Le dio la llave a la cliente el recepcionista?
4. ¿Le dieron su nombre al recepcionista los huéspedes?
5. ¿Les ha cambiado las toallas sucias la camarera?

16 *Comunicación*

Alguien que conoces acaba de recibir algo nuevo. Decide lo que es. Con un(a) compañero(a) de clase, prepara una conversación como la siguiente.

MODELO —¿Viste el carro nuevo de Isabel?
—Sí, lo vi. ¿Quién se lo dio?
—No sé si alguien se lo dio o si se lo compró.

CULTURA
Parece que a la niña le gusta mucho el dulce. ¿Quién se lo compró?

¡Bravo!

You have now learned all the new vocabulary and grammar in this chapter. Continue to use and practice all that you know while learning more cultural information. **¡Vamos!**

Andrew Payti

¿Comprendes?

A Contesta según la información en la conversación.

1. ¿Con quién están hablando las muchachas? ¿Dónde?
2. ¿Han hecho una reservación las dos muchachas?
3. ¿Hay una habitación disponible?
4. ¿Cuál es la tarifa?
5. ¿Cuánto tiempo piensan estar en el hotel las muchachas?
6. ¿Por qué están cansadas?
7. ¿Han abandonado la habitación los otros clientes?
8. ¿Qué está incluido en la tarifa?

B Resumiendo Cuenta la información en la conversación en tus propias palabras.

C Llegando a conclusiones ¿Qué piensas? ¿Van a tomar un desayuno continental o un desayuno americano las muchachas? ¿Por qué has llegado a esta conclusión?

D Investigando En línea o en el periódico busca el tipo de cambio del dólar al euro. Luego, calcula el precio de la habitación en dólares.

Comparaciones

Los hoteles
En España y Latinoamérica todavía hay hoteles económicos que no tienen baño privado pero menos que en el pasado. Hasta recientemente había muchos que no lo tenían y un cuarto con baño privado costaba mucho. Cuando vas a un hotel, ¿prefieres un baño privado?

CULTURA
La entrada a un hotel en Gijón, Asturias

Andrew Payti

Lectura

Antes de leer

Imagina que tienes unos amigos que están disfrutando de un viaje en un país hispano pero no tienen mucho dinero. ¿Cuáles son unas cosas que pueden hacer para economizar?

Durante la lectura

Identifícate con lo que tus amigos están haciendo. ¿Encuentras unas cosas bastante graciosas? ¿Cuáles?

✓ **READING CHECK**

¿Por qué se hospedan los viajeros en un albergue juvenil?

CULTURA

Un hostal en la estación de esquí Los Penitentes en Argentina, no muy lejos de Mendoza

✓ **READING CHECK**

¿Cómo han botado la casa por la ventana los amigos? Y, ¿por qué?

LEYENDO ALGO PERSONAL Un e-mail de un(a) amigo(a) es un ejemplo de lectura personal. En este tipo de textos, la persona que escribe comparte sucesos, proyectos y experiencias de su vida. Al leer estos textos, usa las mismas estrategias que con otros y simplemente disfruta de lo que tu amigo(a) te está contando.

Un hostal y un parador

De: Verónica Valverde
A: maripaz.contador@estrella.com
Asunto: Viaje a Latinoamérica

Queridos amigos:

Ya hemos viajado bastante y no pueden imaginar todo lo que hemos visto y hecho. ¡El Perú! ¡Una maravilla! Y aquí estamos en Bariloche, después de un vuelo de cinco horas de Lima a Buenos Aires y dos más a Bariloche. Son largos, ¿no? Como siempre, hemos decidido hospedarnos en un albergue juvenil porque cuestan mucho menos que un hotel. La mayoría de los albergues son bastante cómodos pero en algunos hasta ocho personas duermen en un solo cuarto. A veces no hay agua caliente pero nos hemos acostumbrado a tomar una ducha con agua fría. Todos han estado limpios y baratos. Además hemos conocido a estudiantes de todas partes del mundo.

Besitos,
Verónica

De: Agustín Echevarría
A: maripaz.contador@estrella.com
Asunto: Viaje por España

Queridos amigos:

Saludos de Galicia en el norte de España. Ya hemos visitado a lo menos diez ciudades españolas y después de muchas noches en albergues juveniles hemos decidido botar la casa por la ventana. Estamos pasando una noche en el parador de los Reyes Católicos en Santiago de Compostela. En España, los paradores son del gobierno. Casi todos son antiguos castillos o monasterios. Son elegantes y NO baratos. Somos los únicos clientes del hotel con mochilas. Pero, ¡qué va!

Hemos elegido a Phil rey del castillo. Como él es rey, él va a pagar la cuenta. ¡Ja, ja! Dice Phil que si él es el rey es también el dueño del castillo y no tiene que pagar nada. Ustedes conocen a Phil, ¿no?

Agustín

Andrew Payti

¿Comprendes?

A **Buscando información** Da la siguiente información.

Verónica y sus amigos	
por donde viajan	
donde están ahora	
donde se hospedan	
por qué les gustan los albergues	
como son los albergues	

Agustín, Phil y sus amigos	
por donde viajan	
donde están ahora	
donde se hospedan en este momento	
cuantas noches van a estar	
como son los paradores	

B **Explicando** Explica lo que es un parador nacional en España.

C **Comparando** Compara un albergue juvenil con un parador nacional.

D **Resumiendo** En tus propias palabras, cuenta el episodio entre Phil y sus compañeros de viaje en el parador de los Reyes Católicos.

E **Llegando a conclusiones** Basado en el episodio entre Phil y sus compañeros, ¿qué concluyes sobre la personalidad de Phil? ¿Qué tipo de persona es?

CULTURA

El exterior de un parador en Cáceres, España. Los paradores son del gobierno español y muchos de ellos son joyas arquitectónicas como conventos, monasterios y palacios.

Andrew Payti

Lectura
UN POCO MÁS

Antes de leer

¿Te interesa hacer un viaje si tienes que caminar muchos kilómetros cada día por una semana entera o más? ¿Por qué contestas que sí o que no? Luego decide si el viaje en la lectura es para ti o no.

El Camino de Santiago

Durante la Edad Media[1] había unas peregrinaciones[2] importantes. Una era la peregrinación a Santiago de Compostela.

Santiago de Compostela está en Galicia, una región en el noroeste de España que se parece mucho a Irlanda. Llueve mucho en Galicia y todo es muy verde. Además hay mucha influencia de los celtas, como en Irlanda. Muchos gallegos son rubios o pelirrojos y tienen ojos azules o verdes.

Los peregrinos de la Edad Media iban a Santiago porque creían que allá estaba enterrado el apóstol Santiago. El Camino empezaba en Francia. Cruzaba los Pirineos y todo el norte de España, una región de altos picos montañosos. Los peregrinos viajaban a pie de un pueblo a otro. Cada día cubrían un trecho[3] fijo. Al final de cada trecho había un hostal donde los peregrinos podían comer y pasar la noche. Aun[4] en el siglo XI había industria hotelera.

Una vez más el Camino de Santiago es muy popular. A muchos turistas les gusta seguir el mismo camino que los peregrinos de la Edad Media. Muchos de ellos son mochileros jóvenes. Unos siguen andando a pie pero hay también quienes van en bicicleta o aun en carro.

[1]Edad Media *Middle Ages*
[2]peregrinaciones *pilgrimages*
[3]trecho *stretch*
[4]Aun *Even*

CULTURA

Una escena idílica en Navarra, España. Navarra es la puerta del Camino de Santiago en la Península ibérica.

©Melba Photo Agency/PunchStock

¿Comprendes?

Escoge.

1. ¿Qué es una peregrinación?
   a. un viaje al extranjero
   b. un viaje por motivo religioso
   c. un viaje por las montañas

2. ¿Por qué son rubios y pelirrojos muchos gallegos?
   a. Son de ascendencia celta.
   b. Son irlandeses.
   c. Tienen ojos azules.

3. ¿Por qué hacían los peregrinos el viaje?
   a. Querían ver la catedral de Santiago de Compostela.
   b. Querían ver la tumba del apóstol Santiago.
   c. Querían cruzar el norte de España.

4. ¿Qué hay hoy en día?
   a. un interés nuevo en el Camino de Santiago
   b. un nuevo Camino de Santiago
   c. hostales del siglo XI

5. ¿Cuál es una diferencia entre la peregrinación durante la Edad Media y hoy?
   a. Hoy no hay hostales.
   b. Hoy todos los peregrinos no van a pie.
   c. La ruta ha cambiado.

CULTURA

Una vista de Burgos, España

Sami Sarkis/Getty Images

Prepárate para el examen

↻ To review, see **Vocabulario.**

1 Identifica siete cosas que están en una habitación y en un cuarto de baño de un hotel.

2 Completa.

8. Cecilia y Gloria han llegado al hotel. Han reservado un cuarto doble con _____.

9. Necesito _____ para abrir la puerta.

10. _____ te puede ayudar con tu equipaje en un hotel.

11. La camarera tiene que cambiar las toallas porque están _____.

12. Los clientes del hotel tienen que _____ su cuarto al mediodía.

13. Es más caro pasar una noche en un hotel que en un _____.

14. Para subir al piso doce de un hotel, los clientes usan _____.

3 Describe.

15–16. un desayuno continental

17–18. un desayuno americano

Gramática

To review, see **El presente perfecto**.

4 Completa con el presente perfecto.

19. Ellos _____ al hotel. (llegar)

20. ¿Todavía no _____ (tú) el desayuno? (tomar)

21. ¿_____ ustedes en el hotel? (comer)

22. No, (nosotros) no _____ todavía. (salir)

23. Yo _____ en tres estados. (vivir)

24. Mónica ya _____ con este libro. (terminar)

To review, see **Participios irregulares**.

5 Sigue el modelo.

MODELO   ¿Hacerlo? →
          Ya lo he hecho.

25. ¿Decirlo?

26. ¿Verlo?

27. ¿Escribirlo?

28. ¿Abrirlo?

29. ¿Devolverlo?

6 Contesta con pronombres.

30. ¿Te ha devuelto el dinero Tomás?

31. ¿Te ha dado las llaves la recepcionista?

32. ¿Le has enviado el correo electrónico a Tomás?

33. ¿Les has escrito la carta a tus padres?

34. ¿Les has dicho la información a tus tíos?

To review, see **Dos complementos me lo, te lo, nos lo**, and **Dos complementos con se**.

7 Completa con pronombres.

35. El profesor les explicó la gramática a los alumnos.
    El profesor _____ explicó _____.

36. Yo le di los boletos a Teresa. Yo _____ di _____.

37. ¿Te ha cambiado las toallas la camarera? Sí, _____ ha cambiado.

38. ¿Les ha abierto la puerta el mozo a ustedes? Sí, el mozo _____ ha abierto.

Cultura

To review this cultural information, see the **Lectura cultural**.

8 Contesta.

39. ¿Por qué a muchos viajeros jóvenes les gustan los albergues juveniles?

40. ¿Qué es un parador nacional en España?

Prepárate para el examen

1 Una extravagancia

Discuss a time when you splurged on something

En tu vida, ¿has botado la casa por la ventana? ¿Qué has hecho?

2 Experiencias interesantes

Talk about interesting experiences you have had

Habla con un(a) compañero(a). Dile a tu compañero(a) las cosas que tú has hecho en la vida que consideras interesantes. Tu compañero(a) te va a decir lo que ha hecho él/ella. Van a llegar a una conclusión. ¿Quién ha tenido las experiencias más interesantes?

3 Todavía no lo he hecho.

Talk about things you have not done yet

Habla con un(a) compañero(a). Los dos van a hablar de algunas cosas que todavía no han hecho pero que quieren hacer un día.

4 Una estadía personal

Describe a stay at a hotel

¿Te has hospedado o pasado unas vacaciones en un hotel? ¿En qué hotel? Describe tu experiencia. Si nunca has estado en un hotel, da una descripción ficticia.

5 Una habitación, por favor.

Make a hotel reservation

Tú has llegado a Burgos, España. Necesitas una habitación en un hotel. Llama a un hotel y habla con el/la recepcionista (tu compañero[a]). Quieres saber si tienen una habitación disponible, la tarifa, lo que está incluido en la tarifa, etc.

6 Las preferencias de un(a) viajero(a) joven

Compare and contrast travel preferences

Por lo general un viaje fabuloso para una persona joven no es un viaje fabuloso para una persona mayor y viceversa. Describe lo que para ti es un viaje ideal. ¿Cuáles son las necesidades que tú consideras importantes y las que no son importantes? ¿Qué buscas en un hotel? ¿Qué piensas? ¿Tienen tus abuelos las mismas opiniones que tú? ¿Tienen ellos los mismos deseos o las mismas necesidades que tú?

Tarea

You and your classmates are on an educational tour of a Spanish-speaking country and your teacher has given everyone the assignment of keeping a travel journal in Spanish. Write about everything you have done since you arrived there. You will need to use the library and/or the Internet to find out more about the country you have chosen to visit.

Writing Strategy

Transition Words To make your writing flow more smoothly, it is a good idea to use a variety of transition words, because they help connect different ideas. Some useful transition words in Spanish are listed below:

antes (de)	luego
después (de)	por último
primero	también
segundo	sobre todo
tercero	por eso

As you research, answer the questions with information you want to include in your travel narrative. You should consult multiple sources to ensure that your information is accurate.

❷ Write

- Use the present perfect tense and vocabulary from the textbook to describe what you and your classmates have done on the trip.
- Use your outline as a guide to help keep your information organized.
- Incorporate transition words so that your writing flows smoothly.

❶ Prewrite

Create a rough outline using the following questions.

¿Adónde han ido?

¿Qué han visto?

¿Qué han hecho?

el viaje

¿Qué han comido?

¿Qué han aprendido?

Evaluate

Your teacher will evaluate you on correct use of vocabulary and grammar, organization, accuracy and completeness of information, and effective use of transition words.

Repaso del Capítulo 7

Gramática

El presente perfecto

The present perfect tense is used to speak about a past event without reference to any particular time. It is formed with the present tense of the verb **haber** and a past participle. The past participle of an **-ar** verb is formed by adding **-ado** to the stem, and the past participle of an **-er** or **-ir** verb is formed by adding **-ido** to the stem. Review the following forms.

hablar	beber	asistir
he hablado	he bebido	he asistido
has hablado	has bebido	has asistido
ha hablado	ha bebido	ha asistido
hemos hablado	hemos bebido	hemos asistido
habéis hablado	*habéis bebido*	*habéis asistido*
han hablado	han bebido	han asistido

Participios irregulares

Review the verbs that have irregular past participles.

decir → dicho	poner → puesto
hacer → hecho	volver → vuelto
romper → roto	devolver → devuelto
escribir → escrito	morir → muerto
freír → frito	abrir → abierto
ver → visto	cubrir → cubierto

CULTURA

Los huéspedes han pasado unos días agradables en la piscina de este hotel en Manta, Ecuador.

Dos complementos en la misma frase

When a sentence has two object pronouns, the indirect object always precedes the direct object. The indirect object pronouns **le, les** change to **se** when used with **lo, la, los,** or **las.**

Teodoro me vendió el carro.	**Teodoro me lo vendió.**
Tu padre te dio los regalos.	**Tu padre te los dio.**
El cliente le devolvió las llaves a la recepcionista.	**El cliente se las devolvió.**

Andrew Payti

Juego There are a number of cognates in this list. See how many you and a partner can find. Who can find the most? Compare your list with those of your classmates.

Go Online!

connectED.mcgraw-hill.com

Vocabulario

Making a hotel reservation

una reservación	un cuarto sencillo	reservar
un cuarto, una habitación	un cuarto doble	

Arriving at/leaving a hotel

el hotel	el/la recepcionista	el mozo
el albergue juvenil, el hostal	el/la cliente(a), el/la huésped(a)	el ascensor
la recepción	la llave (magnética)	hospedarse
		abandonar el cuarto

Having breakfast in a hotel

el desayuno continental	la mantequilla	el pan tostado
el panecillo	el café	el tocino, el bacón, el lacón
el pan dulce	el desayuno americano	
la mermelada	los huevos revueltos	el jugo de naranja

Talking about a hotel room

la cama	la almohada	la percha, el colgador
la sábana	el armario	el aire acondicionado
la manta, la frazada		

Talking about a bathroom

el cuarto de baño	el inodoro, el váter	una toalla
la bañera	el lavabo	sucio(a)
la ducha	el jabón	limpio(a)

Talking about cleaning a hotel room

la camarera	hacer la cama	cambiar
limpiar		

David H. Brennan

Repaso cumulativo

Repasa lo que ya has aprendido

These activities will help you review and remember what you have learned so far in Spanish.

1 Escucha las frases. Indica si la frase describe el dibujo o no.

2 Imagina que vas de camping por una noche. ¿Qué vas a poner en tu mochila?

3 Completa con el pronombre reflexivo.

1. Cuando voy de camping, _____ acuesto en una carpa.
2. Marcos _____ duerme enseguida en su saco de dormir.
3. Nosotros _____ lavamos con agua fría.
4. Ellos _____ divierten mucho cuando van de camping.
5. ¿Por qué no _____ peinas? Tienes el pelo desarreglado.

4 Completa con el pronombre apropiado.

1. Él tiene que levantar_____.
2. Voy a cepillar_____ los dientes.
3. Y yo voy a vestir_____.
4. ¿A qué hora tenemos que reunir_____?
5. Ellos quieren acostar_____ temprano porque tienen que levantar_____ mañana a las cinco y media.
6. ¿Quieres sentar_____ aquí?

Unos *campers* con sus caravanas y carpas en una playa cerca de Arica, Chile

5 **Escoge.**

1. _____ llave que tengo no es para mi puerta.

   a. Esta   **b.** Esa   **c.** Aquella

2. _____ muchacho que ves allá es el primo de Esteban.

   a. Este   **b.** Ese   **c.** Aquel

3. Carlos, _____ novela que estás leyendo, ¿te gusta?

   a. esta   **b.** esa   **c.** aquella

6 **Cambia al plural.**

1. ¿De quién es *este libro de bolsillo*?

2. ¿Quiénes han dejado *aquella mochila* allí?

3. Me gusta mucho *ese juego* que tiene José.

4. ¿Es caro *aquel carro*?

7 **¿Sí o no?**

1. Hay muchas tiendas en un centro comercial.

2. Los precios son más bajos cuando hay un saldo.

3. Si una camisa no te queda bien necesitas otra talla.

4. Venden objetos de artesanía en una tienda de ropa.

5. Mucha gente regatea en una tienda elegante.

6. En un mercado municipal hay muchos puestos diferentes.

CULTURA

Una tienda en un mercado callejero en Catarina, Nicaragua

8 **Tienes que comprar mucho. Decide en qué tienda vas a comprar las siguientes cosas. Puedes comprar algunas cosas en más de una tienda.**

lo que necesitas	la tienda de ropa	la frutería	la verdulería	el supermercado	el mercado indígena
1. el papel higiénico					
2. la artesanía					
3. el maíz					
4. un vestido					
5. un paquete de judías verdes congeladas					
6. un racimo de uvas					

Andrew Payti

Ciudad y campo

Andrew Payti

Go Online!
connectED.mcgraw-hill.com

Audio

Video

Práctica

Repaso

Diversiones

eScape

Vamos a comparar La vida en el campo es muy diferente que la vida en una ciudad. Los problemas que existen en el campo y en la ciudad son diferentes también. Piensa en las zonas urbanas y rurales donde tú vives. Vas a observar si en Latinoamérica hay muchas diferencias entre la vida en una ciudad y la vida en el campo. Y aprenderás también si hay diferencias entre Latinoamérica y Estados Unidos.

Objetivos

You will:

- describe life in the city
- describe life in the country
- discuss the differences between the city and the country in Latin America

You will use:

- the future tense
- object pronouns with infinitives and gerunds

◄ Un gaucho joven con su caballo trabajando en la estancia Ombú en las pampas argentinas

Ciudad y campo

Mira estas fotos para familiarizarte con el tema de este capítulo—ciudad y campo. Vas a observar que hay unas diferencias interesantes entre la vida urbana y la vida rural en las muchas regiones del mundo hispanohablante.

Perú 🏴

El Jirón de la Unión en el centro de Lima es una calle peatonal comercial.

España 🏴

Se cultivan deliciosas naranjas en los naranjos de los naranjales de Andalucía. A los españoles les gusta beber «zumo de naranja» y a los latinoamericanos les gusta tomar un «jugo de naranja» o, en Puerto Rico, «jugo de china».

Venezuela 🏴

Santo Domingo es un pueblo idílico en los Andes venezolanos. Las casas se parecen a los chalets en los Alpes suizos.

Ecuador 🏴

Unos niños andan con su rebaño de ovejas. Están al lado de una carretera en un pueblo en las afueras de Riobamba, Ecuador.

Argentina 🇦🇷

La famosa Avenida 9 de Julio en Buenos Aires tiene fama de ser la avenida más ancha del mundo.

España 🇪🇸

Un mimo vestido de oro entretiene a los peatones en una calle de Madrid en espera de recibir una propina por su talento.

Argentina 🇦🇷

El gaucho conduce (lleva) al caballo por las riendas. En muchas estancias los visitantes tienen la oportunidad y el placer de andar (montar) a caballo.

México 🇲🇽

La Ciudad de México tiene cada día más y más rascacielos modernos de un estilo arquitectónico reconocido y apreciado en el mundo entero.

Costa Rica 🇨🇷

Los bueyes están tirando una carreta llena de café. Están tirándola por un pueblo de Costa Rica. El pueblo de Sarchí cerca de Alajuela tiene fama por la fábrica de estas carretas de diferentes colores y diseños.

En el centro de la ciudad

un rascacielos

una oficina

la plaza

una avenida ancha, un paseo

el casco (el barrio) antiguo

la esquina

una calle angosta (estrecha)

Para conversar

¿Vas al centro mañana? Es viernes y habrá mucho tráfico. Si tomas el carro, no podrás aparcar en la calle. Tendrás que buscar un parking.

un parking, un parqueo

En otras partes

- In Spain you will hear both **estacionar** and **aparcar.** These terms are also used in Latin America as well as **parquear.** A parking spot or lot can be **el parking, el parqueo, el aparcamiento,** or **el estacionamiento.**

- There are many words used for **autobús.** It is not necessary for you to learn them all. In general **el autobús** is used in Spain, **el camión** in Mexico, and **la guagua** in the Caribbean and in the Canary Islands. You will also frequently hear **el bus.**

un semáforo

los peatones

la acera

una calle

el cruce

(tr)Courtney Brown, (others)Andrew Payti

Medios de transporte urbanos

la estación de metro

la boca del metro

la escalera mecánica

el autobús, el camión, la guagua

Los pasajeros esperan el autobús en la parada de autobús.

El señor no subirá la escalera. Tomará la escalera mecánica.

el mimo

El parque de atracciones

la montaña rusa

el zoológico

la noria

El sábado los jóvenes irán al parque de atracciones.

el tiovivo

PARQUE ZOOLÓGICO

(tc)image 100/PunchStock, (br)Kelli Drummer-Avendaño, (others)Andrew Payti

ESCUCHAR

1 Escucha cada frase y decide si la información es correcta o no. Usa una tabla como la de abajo para indicar tus respuestas.

correcta	incorrecta

Conexiones

La ecología

El término «ecología» significa el equilibrio entre los seres humanos y la naturaleza. Hoy en día hay grandes problemas ecológicos en todas partes del mundo. Muchos consideran la contaminación del aire el número uno. En las zonas urbanas el aire que se respira está contaminado principalmente por las emisiones de gases que escapan de los automóviles, los camiones y las chimeneas de las fábricas.

HABLAR

2 Contesta sobre unos jóvenes en un parque en Latinoamérica.

1. ¿Está en la ciudad el parque?
2. ¿Irán los jóvenes al parque el sábado?
3. ¿Caminarán por las sendas del parque?
4. ¿Irán al parque de atracciones?
5. ¿Subirán a la montaña rusa?
6. ¿Visitarán el zoológico?
7. ¿Verán los animales?
8. ¿Les darán de comer a los animales?

CULTURA

Las jóvenes están mirando a sus perros en un parque de Buenos Aires, Argentina.

Andrew Payti

LEER • ESCRIBIR

3 Expresa de otra manera.

1. una avenida ancha
2. el casco antiguo
3. parquear
4. un parking
5. el autobús
6. una calle estrecha

LEER • ESCRIBIR

4 Completa con una palabra del **banco de palabras.**

la esquina	mimos	peatones	el parque de
un rascacielos	estrechas	la escalera	atracciones
el zoológico	la parada	la boca	

1. Hay un semáforo en _____ de la calle para controlar la circulación del tráfico.
2. Una calle peatonal es solo para _____.
3. La entrada al metro en la calle se llama _____.
4. Él bajó _____ para ir a la estación de metro.
5. Un edificio muy alto de muchos pisos es _____.
6. Hay calles _____ en el casco antiguo de la ciudad.
7. Mucha gente está esperando el bus en _____.
8. Muchas veces los _____ tienen la cara pintada.
9. Hay una montaña rusa y una noria en _____.
10. Hay elefantes, tigres, leones y cocodrilos en _____.

CULTURA

Un edificio interesante con una torre alta en la Plaza de la Independencia en el centro de Montevideo, la capital de Uruguay

ESCRIBIR

5 **Rompecabezas**

Join two puzzle pieces to form a word. When you have finished you should have six words. Do not use any piece more than once.

ción   rada   es   bús

quina   esta   rasca   pa

auto   pea   cielos   tones

6 **Comunicación**

Describe la ciudad en que vives. Si no vives en una ciudad describe una que está cerca de donde tú vives.

En el campo

una finca, una granja, una chacra

una casa de campo

el campesino, el peón

la cosecha

el trigo

Los peones cultivan (labran, trabajan) la tierra.
Están cultivando trigo.
Siembran el trigo en la primavera.
¿Cuándo será la cosecha?
Cosecharán el trigo en el otoño.

la huerta

la vaca

la hierba

la gallina

el cordero

el cerdo

En una huerta cultivan legumbres o frutas.

(l to r: t to b)Andrew Payti, FRILET Patrick/age fotostock, Andrew Payti, ©Goodshoot/PunchStock, G.K. & Vikki Hart/Getty Images, ©Brand X Pictures/PunchStock, McGraw-Hill Education

un granero

un establo

el heno

un corral

Los caballos están en el corral.
Las muchachas montarán (andarán) a caballo.
Les gusta mucho la equitación.

En otras **partes**

- The words **finca** and **granja** both mean *farm* and are used in Spain and many areas of Latin America. **Chacra** is used only in certain areas of Latin America. In many areas of Latin America, **la hacienda** is *a ranch*. In Spain it is **una finca**. **El rancho** is used in Mexico. In Chile, Argentina, and Uruguay **una estancia** is *a cattle ranch*.

- Another word for **cosechar** (**la cosecha**) is **recolectar** (**la recolección**).

el ganado

El ganado pace en el campo.

la hacienda, el rancho, la estancia

El verano que viene Enrique y su hermana
  visitarán a sus primos en el campo.
Pasarán un mes con ellos.

FOLDABLES
Study Organizer

FORWARD-BACKWARD

BOOK See the Foldables section of the Student Handbook at the beginning of this book for help with making this foldable. On the front cover, write **la ciudad.** Open your book. On the right-hand page list words that you have learned that pertain to the city. On the next right-hand page, draw a picture illustrating the words on your list. Close your book and flip it over. On the back cover, write **el campo** and do the same.

ESCUCHAR

1 Escucha cada frase y decide si la información es correcta o no. Usa una tabla como la de abajo para indicar tus respuestas.

correcta	incorrecta

LEER

2 Parea los sinónimos.

1. cultivar la tierra
2. persona del campo
3. practicar la equitación
4. una finca grande
5. recoger o recolectar el trigo
6. el rancho

  a. cosechar
  b. una estancia
  c. trabajar, labrar la tierra
  d. la hacienda
  e. montar a caballo
  f. un(a) campesino(a)

HABLAR • ESCRIBIR

3 Contesta.

1. ¿Dónde trabajan los campesinos?
2. ¿Qué hay en una finca?
3. ¿Qué hay en una huerta?
4. ¿Cuáles son algunos animales que producen carne?
5. Ella es aficionada a la equitación. ¿Qué hace ella?

LEER • ESCRIBIR

4 Completa con una palabra apropiada.

1. La _____ es verde y el trigo es amarillo.
2. El ganado _____ en el campo.
3. Las _____ ponen huevos.
4. Las _____ dan leche.
5. Cuando los caballos no están en el establo, están en _____.
6. Guardan el trigo y el heno en _____.
7. Los _____ trabajan la tierra.
8. Una _____ produce vegetales y frutas.

CULTURA

Estos caballos están comiendo heno en una granja cerca de Córdoba, España.

Emily Lowry

ESCRIBIR

5 Usa diagramas como los de abajo para categorizar las palabras que ya sabes en español.

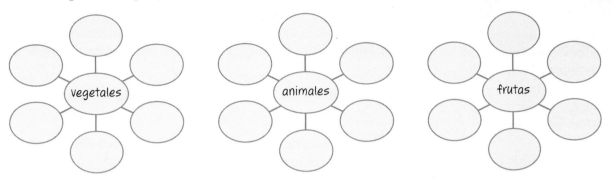

vegetales

animales

frutas

HABLAR • ESCRIBIR

6 Utiliza cada palabra en una frase original.

la finca   una estancia   el ganado

una casa de campo   la huerta

cosechar   el corral

7 ## Comunicación

Con unos compañeros de clase, preparen una encuesta (*survey*) para determinar si la mayoría de los alumnos en su clase aprecian más o conocen mejor la vida urbana o la vida rural. Basado en los resultados de su encuesta, analicen y expliquen el porqué.

LEER

8 Rompecabezas

Choose the word in each group that does not belong. Then switch the wrong words to make each group correct.

1. la vaca   la gallina   la hacienda

2. el trigo   una granja   el heno

3. el rancho   el cordero   la estancia

4. una finca   una chacra   sembrar

5. la hierba   cosechar   labrar

InfoGap For more practice using your new vocabulary, do Activity 8 in the Student Resource section at the end of this book.

Futuro de los verbos regulares

El inglés

English, the same as Spanish, very often uses the present tense or the expression *to be going to* to express the future.

They leave tomorrow.

They're (They are) leaving tomorrow.

They are going to leave tomorrow.

They'll (They will) leave tomorrow.

1. The future tense is used to tell what will take place in the future. The endings for the future tense come from the verb **haber.**

he	has	ha	hemos	habéis	han

2. You add these endings to the entire infinitive to form the future tense of regular verbs.

infinitive	estudiar	leer	escribir
stem	estudiar-	leer-	escribir-
yo	estudiaré	leeré	escribiré
tú	estudiarás	leerás	escribirás
Ud., él, ella	estudiará	leerá	escribirá
nosotros(as)	estudiaremos	leeremos	escribiremos
vosotros(as)	*estudiaréis*	*leeréis*	*escribiréis*
Uds., ellos, ellas	estudiarán	leerán	escribirán

Algún día él irá a la América del Sur.
Visitará Perú y otros países.
Yo estaré en Bogotá en el mes de julio.

3. The future tense is not used a great deal in Spanish. It is more common to use **ir a** + *the infinitive* or the present tense.

Voy a salir mañana.   **Salgo mañana.**
Ellos van a volver en   **Ellos vuelven en**
    dos meses.   **dos meses.**

4. The future tense can be used to express what is called the future of probability.

¿Cuántos años tendrá él?   *How old can he be?*
    No sé.   *I don't know.*
¿Qué hora será?   *What time can it be?*
Serán las once.   *It must be about*
                                        eleven o'clock.

CULTURA

Los peatones cruzan la calle en Buenos Aires, Argentina. ¿Adónde irán?

Andrew Payti

Práctica

HABLAR

1 Contesta sobre un viaje futuro de Mónica.

1. ¿Irá Mónica a Quito el año que viene?
2. ¿Pasará unos días en Quito?
3. ¿Visitará el casco antiguo?
4. ¿Irá al Museo de Arte Moderno?
5. ¿Caminará por el parque el Ejido?
6. ¿Verá una exposición de arte en el parque?
7. ¿Comerá ceviche?
8. ¿Asistirá a un concierto?

ESCUCHAR • HABLAR • ESCRIBIR

2 Sigue el modelo.

MODELO **Tomaré el carro. →**
Voy a tomar el carro.

1. Aparcaré el carro en un parking.
2. Tomaremos el metro para llegar al centro.
3. ¿Visitarán ustedes el barrio viejo?
4. ¿Andarás por las calles estrechas del barrio viejo?
5. ¿Tú irás al parque de atracciones?
6. Pasaré unas horas en el zoológico.

CULTURA

¿Caminarás un día por una de estas pintorescas calles en el barrio de Panecillo en Quito, Ecuador?

ESCUCHAR • HABLAR • ESCRIBIR

3 Sigue el modelo.

MODELO **Voy a ir al campo. →**
Iré al campo.

1. Van a cultivar trigo.
2. Vamos a comer vegetales de la huerta.
3. ¿Vas a montar a caballo?
4. ¿Quién va a limpiar el establo?
5. Voy a visitar una estancia.

LEER • ESCRIBIR

4 Completa con el futuro.

1. Ellos _____ dentro de poco. (volver)
2. Yo los _____. (ver)
3. Nosotros _____ de muchas cosas. (hablar)
4. ¿Tú los _____ a tu casa? (invitar)
5. Sí, (yo) _____ una comida y (nosotros) _____ juntos. (preparar, comer)
6. El postre _____ el plato principal. (seguir)

Richard Brommer

Futuro de los verbos irregulares

1. Study the following forms of verbs that have an irregular stem in the future tense. Note that the endings for all irregular verbs are the same as those for the regular verbs.

infinitive	tener	salir	venir
stem	tendr–	saldr–	vendr–
yo	tendré	saldré	vendré
tú	tendrás	saldrás	vendrás
Ud., él, ella	tendrá	saldrá	vendrá
nosotros(as)	tendremos	saldremos	vendremos
vosotros(as)	tendréis	saldréis	vendréis
Uds., ellos, ellas	tendrán	saldrán	vendrán

2. Other verbs that follow the same pattern are **poner, saber,** and **poder.**

poner → pondré   saber → sabré   poder → podré

3. The verbs **decir, hacer,** and **querer** also have an irregular future stem.

infinitive	decir	hacer	querer
stem	dir–	har–	querr–
yo	diré	haré	querré
tú	dirás	harás	querrás
Ud., él, ella	dirá	hará	querrá
nosotros(as)	diremos	haremos	querremos
vosotros(as)	diréis	haréis	querréis
Uds., ellos, ellas	dirán	harán	querrán

4. Note that the future of **hay (haber)** is **habrá.**

¿Cuántos habrá?
Habrá más de uno.
Habrá por lo menos cuatro.

¿Harás un viaje a Ecuador algún día para conocer mejor el país?

Richard Brommer

Práctica

HABLAR

5 Personaliza. Da respuestas personales.

1. Algún día, ¿tendrás la oportunidad de viajar a Latinoamérica?
2. ¿Podrás visitar varias ciudades?
3. ¿Harás el viaje en avión?
4. ¿Podrás tomar fotos digitales?
5. ¿Las podrás descargar a tu computadora?
6. ¿Las imprimirás y las pondrás en un álbum?

ESCUCHAR • HABLAR

6 Conversa según el modelo.

MODELO —**Beatriz no vino hoy.**
—**No, pero vendrá mañana.**

1. Ella no salió de casa a tiempo.
2. Él no me lo dijo.
3. No lo hice.
4. No tuvimos tiempo.
5. Antonio no sabía hacerlo.
6. Ellos no podían decirlo.

CULTURA
Un paseo en el casco histórico de la Ciudad de Panamá

LEER • ESCRIBIR

7 Completa sobre Ricardo en Panamá.

El invierno que viene Ricardo Rojas ___1___ (tener) dos semanas de vacaciones. Él y su familia ___2___ (hacer) un viaje a Panamá. Allí ellos ___3___ (poder) pasar unos días con sus parientes. El padre de Ricardo ___4___ (llamar) a Panamá y les ___5___ (decir) a sus parientes la hora de su llegada. Todos los parientes de Ricardo ___6___ (querer) ir al aeropuerto a recibirlos. Ricardo y sus padres ___7___ (salir) en el vuelo de las once. El vuelo ___8___ (hacer) escala en Miami antes de llegar a Panamá.

8 *Comunicación*

Tu familia va a hacer un viaje a un país latinoamericano. Trabajando en pequeños grupos, (o sea, con los miembros de tu «familia») hagan investigaciones para escribir un plan detallado para su viaje. Incluyan detalles esenciales sobre las necesidades y deseos específicos de los varios miembros de su grupo. Luego compartan su plan e itinerario con otros grupos.

Andrew Payti

Los pronombres con el infinitivo y el gerundio

1. You have already learned that the pronoun is attached to the infinitive in the expression **favor de** and with the reflexive verbs.

Favor de darme el menú.	**¿Quieres levantarte?**
Favor de pasarle el pan.	**¿Puedo sentarme aquí?**
Favor de decírmelo.	**Vamos a divertirnos.**

2. When the object pronouns are used with the infinitive and a helping verb, the object pronouns can either be placed before the helping verb or attached to the infinitive.

Voy a tomar el metro.	**Quiero mostrar la finca a mi primo.**
Lo voy a tomar.	**Se la quiero mostrar a él.**
Voy a tomarlo.	**Quiero mostrársela a él.**

3. When the object pronouns are used with the present participle, they may also precede the helping verb or they may be attached to the present participle.

Está visitando el parque de atracciones.
Lo está visitando.
Está visitándolo.

4. To maintain the same stress, a participle carries a written accent with either one or two attached pronouns. The infinitive carries a written accent only when two pronouns are attached to it.

PARTICIPLE	INFINITIVE
Está sirviéndolo.	**Quiero darle el plano.**
Está sirviéndomelo.	**Quiero dárselo.**

Práctica

ESCUCHAR • HABLAR • ESCRIBIR

9 Sigue el modelo.

MODELO la fecha →
No la puedo recordar.
No puedo recordarla.

1. el día
2. la hora
3. el número de teléfono
4. las direcciones
5. los nombres

En todas partes, como en esta calle de Buenos Aires, a los niños les fascinan los títeres. Parece que este niño está preguntándose si puede o debe tocarlos o no.

Andrew Payti

10 Contesta con pronombres.

1. ¿Acabas de comprar el periódico?
2. ¿Acabas de leer el periódico?
3. ¿Acabas de dar el periódico a Pedro?
4. ¿Acabas de hacer tus planes finales?
5. ¿Acabas de comunicarlos a tus padres?

11 Sigue el modelo.

MODELO   **Los campesinos están labrando la tierra.** →
Los campesinos están labrándola.
Los campesinos la están labrando.

1. Están cultivando el trigo.
2. Están cosechando las legumbres.
3. Están limpiando el corral.
4. Los corderos están comiendo la hierba.
5. Los caballos están comiendo el heno.

12 Escribe las frases con pronombres.

1. En la clase de español los alumnos están aprendiendo *la gramática.*
2. Ahora algunos están escuchando *los CDs.*
3. Todos están prestando atención *a la profesora.*
4. Carlos está revisando *su composición.*
5. León está enviando *el correo electrónico a un amigo.*
6. El profesor está devolviendo *los exámenes a los alumnos.*

13 Contesta con **sí** usando pronombres.

1. ¿Quiere ver la película Marisol?
2. ¿Va a ver la película?
3. ¿Está comprando las entradas ahora?
4. ¿Está comprando las entradas en la taquilla del cine?
5. ¿Quiere Marisol ver la película desde la primera fila o está demasiado cerca de la pantalla?
6. Desde la primera fila, ¿puede ver bien la película?

Refrán

Can you guess what the following proverb means?

Alegría ten, y vivirás bien.

¡Bravo!

You have now learned all the new vocabulary and grammar in this chapter. Continue to use and practice all that you know while learning more cultural information. **¡Vamos!**

Un verano en el campo

Clara ¿Vas a pasar el verano en la casa de campo de tus primos?

Julio Sí, estaré dos meses en su estancia.

Clara ¡Dos meses en el campo! ¿Qué harás? ¿No te aburrirás?

Julio ¡Aburrirme! ¿Estás loca? Hay un montón de cosas que hacer. Montamos a caballo, limpiamos los establos, recogemos verduras y frutas frescas, damos caminatas, nadamos en un lago o río…

Clara Eso no es para mí. Me quedaré en la ciudad.

Julio Sí, con el calor, el tráfico, el ruido de las sirenas, la contaminación…

Clara Eso no me molesta nada. Iré a un concierto, visitaré un museo y a veces iré a la piscina en el parque municipal. Habrá mucho que hacer.

Julio Pues, cada uno a su gusto.

Larry Hamill

¿Comprendes?

A Contesta según la información en la conversación.

    1. ¿Quién va a pasar el verano en el campo?

    2. ¿A quiénes visitará?

    3. ¿Qué tienen sus primos en el campo?

    4. ¿Por qué a Julio no le gusta la ciudad en el verano?

    5. ¿Se aburrirá Clara en el campo?

B Completa la tabla según la conversación.

actividades en el campo	actividades en la ciudad

C **Explicando** Contesta.

    1. ¿Cuál es la diferencia de opinión entre Clara y Julio?

    2. ¿Qué significa «Cada uno a su gusto»?

CULTURA

Los alumnos están esperando un bus en una parada
en una esquina de Quito, Ecuador. ¿Qué piensas?
¿Tomarán el bus que está pasando ahora?

Andrew Payti

Go Online!

connectED.mcgraw-hill.com

Lectura
CULTURAL

ESTRATEGIA DE LECTURA

> **Antes de leer**
> *Reflexiona sobre lo que ya sabes de la vida urbana y rural según tus experiencias personales.*

CULTURA

Plaza de Armas, Quito

☑ READING CHECK

¿Cuáles son características del casco viejo y del barrio moderno?

REPASANDO Al leer una selección que tiene muchos detalles, es importante volver a leer unos trozos (la misma parte) para ayudarte a recordar los detalles.

La ciudad y el campo 🎧 ↺

La ciudad Si vas algún día a una ciudad latinoamericana, observarás que en el centro mismo de casi todas hay un casco antiguo. En el centro del casco antiguo se encuentra una gran plaza que muchas veces se llama «la Plaza de Armas». En la plaza verás la catedral y algunos edificios gubernamentales que datan de la época colonial. De la plaza salen callecitas pintorescas.

Cada ciudad tiene también barrios modernos con grandes rascacielos que tienen oficinas y condominios donde vive la gente de las clases media y alta. En los barrios modernos hay avenidas anchas y paseos bonitos. Hay también calles peatonales donde no se permite entrar el tráfico vehicular.

CULTURA

Hay muchos peatones en la Plaza de Armas en Lima. Les gusta andar por la plaza sobre todo cuando hace buen tiempo.

Andrew Payti

Cada ciudad tiene uno o más parques donde los habitantes disfrutan del aire libre y espacio abierto. Los fines de semana dan un paseo por el parque y se divierten mirando a los mimos. En muchos parques hay un parque de atracciones y a veces un zoológico.

Las afueras Desafortunadamente en las afueras de casi todas las ciudades verás los barrios bajos. Sus nombres varían de país en país—ranchos, villas miseria, pueblos jóvenes, etc. No importa el nombre. En todos viven los pobres en chozas o casuchas[1] sin luz (electricidad), gas ni agua corriente[2]. Para saber una de las razones por las que tanta gente vive en tales condiciones iremos al campo.

[1]chozas, casuchas   *shacks*   [2]agua corriente   *running water*

Durante la lectura

Al leer, toma notas o apuntes sobre los detalles que consideras importantes y que crees que debes recordar.

✔ **READING CHECK**

¿Qué hay en las afueras de las ciudades?

CULTURA

Mucha gente va al Bosque de Chapultepec los domingos. Es un parque muy grande en la Ciudad de México.

Andrew Payti

Lectura
CULTURAL

CULTURA

El cultivo de flores, como estas orquídeas, es una industria importante en Ecuador.

✓ **READING CHECK**

¿Siguen existiendo problemas económicos en las zonas rurales?

Después de leer

Los detalles pueden ser interesantes o aburridos. De los detalles en esta lectura, ¿cuáles consideras interesantes? ¿Cuáles te interesan menos?

El campo La vida de muchos campesinos es difícil. Los problemas rurales tienen una larga historia. Desde la época de los españoles había grandes extensiones de tierras llamadas latifundios. Sus dueños o propietarios eran grandes terratenientes[3] ricos y más tarde grandes compañías de Estados Unidos y Europa. Debido a reformas agrarias estos latifundios han sido divididos en parcelas pequeñas y distribuidas entre los campesinos pobres que antes las tenían que trabajar para los terratenientes. Pero los campesinos no tienen suficiente dinero para comprar lo que necesitan para labrar la tierra de una manera productiva. Así toman la decisión de salir para la ciudad en busca de una vida mejor y añaden al problema de la sobrepoblación[4] que ya existe en las ciudades latinoamericanas.

Sí, hay problemas pero hay que señalar[5] que al viajar por Latinoamérica verás paisajes de una belleza increíble—montañas, volcanes, jardines, estancias o ranchos—todo.

[3]terratenientes *landowners*
[4]sobrepoblación *overpopulation*
[5]señalar *point out*

CULTURA

Una campesina cuidando de sus ovejas en el campo en Sabandía, Perú

(t)Richard Brommer, (b)Andrew Payti

¿Comprendes?

A **Confirmando información** Corrige la información falsa.

1. Muy pocas ciudades latinoamericanas tienen un casco antiguo.
2. La gran plaza que se encuentra en el centro de muchas ciudades latinoamericanas se llama la Catedral.
3. Casi todos los edificios en el casco viejo datan de la época de las civilizaciones indígenas o precolombinas.
4. Los barrios bajos donde viven los pobres se encuentran en el centro de las ciudades.

B **Describiendo y analizando** Describe un parque de una ciudad latinoamericana y explica por qué los parques son importantes y populares.

CULTURA
Es la entrada a un rancho en Cozumel, México.

C **Recordando hechos** Contesta.

1. ¿Cómo es la vida de muchos campesinos?
2. ¿Qué es un latifundio?
3. ¿Quiénes eran sus dueños o propietarios?
4. ¿Cuál es el resultado de muchas reformas agrarias?
5. ¿Por qué no pueden labrar bien la tierra?
6. ¿Adónde van?
7. ¿Cuál es un problema que ya existe en muchas ciudades latinoamericanas?

D **Describiendo y categorizando** Completa las tablas.

la ciudad en Latinoamérica		
el barrio antiguo	el barrio moderno	problemas en las afueras

el campo en Latinoamérica		
distribución de la tierra en el pasado	distribución de la tierra actualmente	problemas en las zonas rurales

E **Explicando** Completa.

Visitar el campo en Latinoamérica puede ser una experiencia fabulosa porque…

M. Timothy O'Keefe/Alamy

Lectura
UN POCO MÁS

Antes de leer

Durante toda la historia de Estados Unidos ha habido ciudades con grandes poblaciones de gente de otros países. ¿Conoces tal ciudad?

Una ciudad interesante

La ciudad de Miami en la Florida empezó a desarrollarse[1] en 1895 cuando Henry Flagler tomó la decisión de extender el ferrocarril hacia el sur. Hoy la aglomeración de Miami tiene casi dos millones quinientos mil habitantes y está aumentando cada día. Es uno de los grandes focos latinos de Estados Unidos. Empezó una gran migración de cubanos a fines de los años cincuenta cuando Fidel Castro derrocó[2] la dictadura de Fulgencio Batista. Hoy en día sigue llegando y estableciéndose en Miami gente de casi todas partes de Centroamérica, Sudamérica y del Caribe.

Una zona típicamente cubana de Miami se llama «la Pequeña Habana». Aquí se oye más español que inglés. El corazón[3] de la Pequeña Habana es la calle Ocho. Aquí hay muchos cafés, restaurantes y tiendas cubanas tradicionales. Si quieres comprarte una guayabera no hay problema. Hay una cantidad de tiendas de ropa. Si tienes sed, puedes sentarte en un café para tomar un guarapo, un café con leche o un típico cafecito cubano—un expreso muy fuerte con mucho azúcar. A los cubanos les gusta su cafecito muy dulce.

En una calle llamada *Cuban Memorial Boulevard,* hay una serie de monumentos dedicados a patriotas cubanos que lucharon[4] por la libertad de su país. Hay también un mapa de relieve de Cuba. Es imposible pasar un día en Miami sin observar la influencia y las contribuciones de los cubanos y otros hispanos o latinos a la vitalidad y personalidad de esta gran ciudad cosmopolita.

[1]desarrollarse *develop*
[2]derrocó *brought down*
[3]corazón *heart*
[4]lucharon *fought*

CULTURA

El parque de Máximo Gómez se conoce como el Parque Dominó porque a muchos cubanos de mayor edad les gusta reunirse allí para jugar dominó.

Dennis MacDonald/Alamy

¿Comprendes?

A Escoge o completa.

1. ¿Cuál es el mejor título para esta lectura?
   a. El establecimiento de Miami
   b. Un parque interesante
   c. La Pequeña Habana
   d. Miami, ayer y hoy

2. ¿Qué tuvo mucha importancia en el desarrollo de Miami?
   a. el Parque Dominó
   b. el ferrocarril
   c. la calle Ocho
   d. Cuba

3. ¿Por qué es Miami uno de los grandes focos hispanos o latinos de Estados Unidos?
   a. Hay muchos inmigrantes de Cuba y de todo Latinoamérica.
   b. Castro derrocó la dictadura de Fulgencio Batista.
   c. Está en el mar Caribe.
   d. Ya había muchos hispanos en Miami cuando llegó Henry Flagler.

4. ¿Cuál es una característica de la Pequeña Habana?
   a. Está en el corazón de la ciudad.
   b. Es la única zona donde hay restaurantes y cafés.
   c. Allí se oye más español que inglés.
   d. Nadie habla inglés.

5. Sabemos que podemos comprar una guayabera porque la lectura dice _____.

6. ¿Cuál de los siguientes es una bebida?
   a. un dominó
   b. un guarapo
   c. el azúcar
   d. una guayabera

B Analiza.

¿Por qué quiere compartir el autor esta información con sus lectores? En tu opinión, ¿cuál es su propósito?

CULTURA 🇺🇸
Una vista bonita de la ciudad de Miami

Andrew Payti

Prepárate para el examen

↻ To review, see **Vocabulario 1.**

To review, see **Vocabulario 1** and **Vocabulario 2.**

To review, see **Vocabulario 2.**

Vocabulario

1 **Completa con una palabra apropiada.**

    1. Puedes aparcar en la calle o en un _____.

    2. Los peatones deben cruzar la calle en _____.

    3. Hay _____ para bajar a la estación de metro.

    4. Un _____ es un edificio alto que tiene muchos pisos.

    5–6. _____ y _____ son dos atracciones en el parque de atracciones.

    7. Hay animales exóticos en el _____.

CULTURA

Llamas en una hacienda cerca de Puerto Montt, Chile

2 **Corrige.**

    8. El semáforo está en la boca del metro.

    9. Un paseo es una calle angosta.

    10. Tienes que aparcar el carro en la parada de autobús.

    11. El ganado cosecha en el campo.

    12. Los caballos están en el granero.

    13. Los campesinos cultivan trigo en la huerta.

3 **Identifica.**

    14. contrario de «sembrar»

    15. los que cultivan o trabajan la tierra

    16–17. dos cosas que comen unos animales

Andrew Payti

Gramática

4 Escribe en el futuro.

18. Visitamos Lima.

19. Él va a la Plaza de Armas.

20. Ellos comen en el Café Haití.

21. ¿Tú nos reservas un cuarto en el hotel?

22. No vivo en Lima.

23. Ellos no rentan un departamento.

To review, see **Futuro de los verbos regulares.**

5 Completa con el futuro.

24. Yo _____ mañana. (salir)

25. Ellos _____ todo en orden. (poner)

26. ¿Tú me _____ ayudar? (poder)

27. Él me lo _____. (decir)

28. Nosotros _____ el viaje juntos. (hacer)

29. Yo _____ que recordar los billetes. (tener)

To review, see **Futuro de los verbos irregulares.**

6 Escribe con pronombres.

30. Acabo de comprar el plano de la ciudad.

31. ¡Bueno! Ahora puedes consultar el plano.

32. Estoy mirando el plano ahora.

33. Voy a darte las direcciones.

34. Estoy escribiendo las direcciones.

35. Tenemos que llamar a nuestros amigos.

36. Quiero darles la hora de nuestra llegada.

To review, see **Los pronombres con el infinitivo y el gerundio.**

Cultura

7 Describe.

37. el casco antiguo de una ciudad latinoamericana

38. un parque típico en una ciudad latinoamericana

39. un barrio bajo

40. el problema agrario en el campo

To review this cultural information, see the **Lectura cultural.**

CULTURA
Una calle típica del Casco Viejo en la Ciudad de Panamá

Andrew Payti

Prepárate para el examen

El bus local de León a Managua, Nicaragua

1 La ciudad

Describe a city that you know
Describe una ciudad que has visitado y que te gusta. Explica por qué volverás a esta ciudad.

2 Una ciudad hispana

Describe a Latin American city
Describe una típica ciudad latinoamericana. Luego mira las fotos que salen en el libro o en el Internet y escoge la ciudad que a ti te gusta más. Explica por qué te gusta.

3 Transporte público

Talk about modes of transportation
Describe los medios de transporte que existen en muchas ciudades.

4 El campo

Describe what you like about the country
Describe algunos aspectos del campo que a ti te gustan.

5 ¿El campo o la ciudad?

Compare and contrast the city and the country
Trabajen en grupos. Van a preparar una encuesta (survey) contestando las siguientes preguntas:
    ¿Prefieres vivir en la ciudad o en el campo? ¿Por qué?
    ¿Cuáles son las ventajas y desventajas de cada lugar?
Después de terminar las entrevistas para la encuesta, presentarán los resultados a la clase.

6 En el futuro

Talk about what you will do in the future
Habla de todo lo que harás en el futuro. Luego habla con un(a) compañero(a) y comparen sus deseos o planes.

La campesina está cosechando heno a mano en la isla Taquile en el lago Titicaca en Perú.

Tarea

Think about all you have learned so far about the countryside and the city in parts of Latin America. Using vocabulary and information contained in the textbook, write a short essay comparing and contrasting life in the countryside with life in the city. Conclude your essay with a paragraph in which you predict what the city and the countryside will be like in fifty years. In what ways do you think they will change and why?

Writing Strategy

Comparing and contrasting When you write an essay that compares and contrasts, you write about similarities and differences between two things. To start organizing the main ideas of your essay, ask yourself a few questions. How does life in the countryside differ from life in the city? What similarities are there? What aspects of city and country life do I want to focus on and do I have enough information to compare and contrast them?

❶ Prewrite

Create a Venn diagram like the one below to help you illustrate the similarities and differences between the city and the countryside. List the similarities in the area where the two circles intersect. List the differences in the main body of each circle.

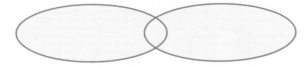

Try to maintain a balance of the details that you would like to include in your essay. In other words, for each detail that you provide for life in the city, you should also provide a detail about the countryside.

❷ Write

- Be sure to include a topic sentence that presents the purpose of your essay to the reader.
- Use the information from your Venn diagram to present the similarities and differences in an organized way.
- Use the future tense in your concluding paragraph to predict what you think the city and the countryside will be like in fifty years.

Evaluate

Your teacher will evaluate you on correct use of vocabulary and grammar, organization, completeness of information, and presence of comparable and contrastable details.

Andrew Payti

Futuro de los verbos regulares

Review the forms of regular **-ar, -er,** and **-ir** verbs in the future tense.

bailar	comer	vivir
bailaré	comeré	viviré
bailarás	comerás	vivirás
bailará	comerá	vivirá
bailaremos	comeremos	viviremos
bailaréis	*comeréis*	*viviréis*
bailarán	comerán	vivirán

Futuro de los verbos irregulares

The following verbs have irregular stems in the future.

tener → tendr-	poner → pondr-	decir → dir-
salir → saldr-	saber → sabr-	hacer → har-
venir → vendr-	poder → podr-	querer → querr-

Los pronombres con el infinitivo y el gerundio

Note that object pronouns can be added to an infinitive or present participle, or they can precede the helping verb.

Voy a comer la manzana.
Voy a comerla.
La voy a comer.

Estoy preparando la comida.
Estoy preparándola.
La estoy preparando.

Los jóvenes están comprando entradas. Están comprándolas en las taquillas a la entrada del parque de atracciones en el Bosque de Chapultepec en la Ciudad de México.

Andrew Payti

Go Online!

connectED.mcgraw-hill.com

Vocabulario

Talking about the city

la ciudad	la avenida,	el/la peatón(ona)	el parking, el parqueo
el centro	el paseo	el cruce	ancho(a)
el casco (el barrio)	la calle	el rascacielos	angosto(a), estrecho(a)
antiguo	el semáforo	la oficina	urbano(a)
la plaza	la esquina	el tráfico	aparcar, estacionar
		la acera	

Talking about public transportation

el medio de transporte	la boca del metro	el autobús, el camión, la
la estación de metro	la escalera	guagua
	la escalera mecánica	la parada de autobús

Talking about an amusement park and a zoo

el parque de	el tiovivo	la montaña rusa	el zoológico
atracciones	la noria	el mimo	

Talking about the country

el campo	el/la campesino(a), el	el granero	la hacienda, el rancho,
la finca, la granja, la	peón	el heno	la estancia
chacra	el establo	la hierba	montar (andar)
la casa de campo	el corral	la equitación	a caballo

Talking about farming

la tierra	la huerta	cosechar	cultivar, labrar
el trigo	la cosecha	sembrar	

Talking about some farm animals

el cerdo	la gallina	el ganado	pacer
el cordero	la vaca		

Repaso cumulativo

These activities will help you review and remember what you have learned so far in Spanish.

1 Escucha las frases. Indica en una tabla como la de abajo si la acción ocurrió en el pasado o si va a ocurrir en el futuro.

pasado	futuro

2 Parea los antónimos.

1. derecho	**a.** delante
2. sencillo	**b.** viejo
3. guardar	**c.** izquierdo
4. detrás	**d.** encima, sobre
5. bajar	**e.** de ida y vuelta
6. ancho	**f.** estrecho
7. largo	**g.** borrar
8. joven	**h.** subir
9. debajo	**i.** corto

3 Completa con el imperfecto o el pretérito.

1. Yo _____ ayer pero él _____ todos los días. (ir, ir)
2. Él lo _____ ayer pero nosotros lo _____ todos los días. (ver, ver)
3. Tú le _____ ayer pero yo le _____ todos los días. (hablar, hablar)
4. Ellas lo _____ con frecuencia y tú lo _____ solamente una vez. (hacer, hacer)
5. Yo _____ el verano pasado en el campo y él _____ todos los veranos allí. (pasar, pasar)
6. Mi abuelita _____ todo lo que _____ cada día. (comprar, necesitar)
7. Yo _____ hablar con José y lo _____ ayer pero él no _____. (querer, llamar, contestar)
8. ¿_____ tú hacer lo que _____ el profesor? (poder, querer)

Richard Brommer

4 **Cambia al pasado.**

1. Hace buen tiempo.

2. Hay sol.

3. La niña es adorable.

4. Tiene solo quince meses.

5. Está muy contenta.

6. Tiene una sonrisa grande.

7. Su papá la adora.

8. Él sabe que yo los conozco.

5 **Usa cada palabra en una frase original.**

1. el cine

2. el museo

3. un concierto

6 **Describe el dibujo.**

Go Online!
connectED.mcgraw-hill.com

Audio Video Práctica Repaso Diversiones eScape

ePals

Vamos a comparar Piensa en la importancia del carro como medio de transporte donde tú vives. ¿Qué problemas crean los carros? Ahora vas a aprender algo sobre el tráfico vehicular en Latinoamérica. Leerás también sobre una carretera famosa de Latinoamérica—la carretera más larga del mundo.

Objetivos

You will:

- talk about cars and driving
- give directions
- discuss the Pan American Highway

You will use:

- **tú** affirmative commands
- the conditional

◀ Intersección donde convergen la Castellana, el Paseo de Recoletos, la calle de Alcalá y la Gran Vía en el centro de Madrid en la famosa Plaza de Cibeles

¿Vas en carro?

Mira las fotos para familiarizarte con el tema del capítulo—el carro y la carretera. Como observarás hay mucho tráfico vehicular en todas partes del mundo hispanohablante. Hay autopistas modernas y pintorescos caminos rurales.

España 🏳

Un camino rural en la Mancha

Venezuela 🏳

Hay mucho tráfico en Caracas, ¿no? Los embotellamientos como este que ves aquí son frecuentes.

PUERTO RICO
DYA 525
Isla Del Encanto

VENEZUELA
LAS·668·

Argentina 🏳

Estos dos turistas jóvenes (se) bajan de un taxi en Buenos Aires.

España

Muchos peatones están cruzando
la calle en el Passeig de Gràcia en
Barcelona. En esta avenida bonita
se pueden ver muchos ejemplos de la
arquitectura modernista de Barcelona.

España

Esta gasolinera en
Estepona ofrece un
servicio excelente a los
dueños de mascotas—un
lugar donde pueden lavar
a su perro mientras llenan
de gasolina el tanque de
su coche.

Ecuador

Si uno no tiene carro y no quiere
tomar el bus, puede tomar un taxi.

En la carretera 🎧

En otras partes

- **La autopista, la autovía, la garita**, and **la cabina** are widely used.
- **El peaje** is the most common word for *toll* but you will also hear **la cuota**.
- The word for *lane*, **el carril**, has many variations.
- Another word for **derecho** is **recto**.

el rótulo

la garita (la cabina) de peaje

la autopista, la autovía

una línea continua

k m
68

el carril

la velocidad máxima

el arcén, el acotamiento

En la carretera nacional hay solo un carril en cada sentido.

Está prohibido pasar (adelantar, rebasar) otro carro cuando hay una línea continua.

Hay que quedarse en su carril.

Para conversar

PEAJE

Carolina, paga el peaje. Después de pagar el peaje, sal de la autopista en la próxima salida.

Para conversar

Yo tomaría la autopista porque llegaríamos en menos tiempo.

Yo la tomaría también, pero José no. Él no pagaría el peaje. Es muy tacaño.

En la ciudad

una calle de sentido único

la luz roja

Al llegar a una bocacalle (donde se cruzan dos calles) debes reducir la velocidad. Debes ir más despacio.

Para conversar

¡Mira! Hay una luz roja. Párate.

el parabrisas

el parquímetro

una moneda

—Mete una moneda en el parquímetro. Te saldrá un tiquete. Pon el tiquete en el parabrisas. ¡Ten cuidado! Si no metes el tiquete, te clavarán (darán) una multa.

Pidiendo direcciones

el plano de la ciudad

derecho

una cuadra, una manzana

Para llegar al Hotel Condes de Barcelona:
Da la vuelta.
Sigue derecho dos cuadras.
En el segundo cruce (la segunda bocacalle), dobla a la izquierda.
A cien metros, verás el Hotel Condes de Barcelona.

Conexiones

La ecología

La contaminación del aire es un problema serio en casi todas las áreas urbanas del mundo. España y Latinoamérica no son ninguna excepción. El aire de muchas de sus ciudades está contaminado. Los gases que salen de los tubos de escape de los automóviles, camiones y buses son una causa principal de la contaminación. ¿Está contaminado el aire donde tú vives? Si contestas que sí, ¿cuál es la causa de la contaminación?

ESCUCHAR

1 Escucha cada frase y decide si la información es correcta o no. Usa una tabla como la de abajo para indicar tus respuestas.

correcta	incorrecta

HABLAR • ESCRIBIR

2 Contesta.

1. ¿Tiene varios carriles en cada sentido una autopista?
2. Por lo general, ¿hay que pagar un peaje para tomar la autopista?
3. ¿Dónde se paga el peaje?
4. Si hay una línea continua en el medio de una carretera de solo dos carriles, ¿es posible adelantar un carro que anda despacio?
5. En las autopistas, ¿hay rótulos que indican la velocidad máxima?

LEER • ESCRIBIR

3 Completa con las palabras apropiadas.

1. Hay _____ en muchas esquinas de una ciudad.
2. Donde se cruzan dos calles es _____.
3. Para aparcar el carro, debes tomar el tiquete que sale del _____ y ponerlo en el _____ del carro.
4. Si excedes la velocidad máxima o si no pagas para aparcar el carro, el policía te dará _____.
5. No puedes entrar porque es una calle de _____ único.
6. Si buscas una calle en la ciudad debes consultar _____.
7. José no tomaría la autopista porque tendría que pagar _____.
8. No lo (la) pagaría porque es muy _____. No le gusta gastar dinero.

CULTURA

Aquí ves un rótulo en una esquina de Quito, Ecuador. ¿Cómo se dice «sentido único» en Ecuador?

Andrew Payti

4 Parea las expresiones que tienen el mismo significado.

1. ir en el sentido contrario
2. ni a la izquierda ni a la derecha
3. una cuadra
4. un cruce
5. el arcén
6. adelantar
7. el sentido

a. derecho
b. rebasar
c. una manzana
d. la dirección
e. dar la vuelta
f. el acotamiento
g. una bocacalle

5 Escribe de otra manera.

1. Tienes que pagar *el peaje* en *la cabina*.
2. El rótulo indica que estamos llegando a la entrada de *la autovía*.
3. *El arcén* está a cada lado de la carretera.
4. No se puede *rebasar* cuando hay una línea continua entre los carriles.
5. Debes reducir la velocidad al llegar a *un cruce*.
6. Debes *reducir la velocidad*.
7. Tienes que seguir *unas* cinco *manzanas* más.
8. Te *darán* una multa.

6 *Comunicación*

Conversa con un(a) compañero(a) sobre las reglas de la calle—lo que uno puede y no puede hacer. Luego imaginen que están en la carretera. Inventen unos escenarios en que tú y tu compañero(a) discuten lo que pasa y lo que ven—rótulos, señales, etc. Usen voz animada y gestos al describir las situaciones. Presenten los escenarios a la clase.

El coche, El carro

el permiso de conducir, la licencia, el carnet

el conductor

la maletera, el baúl

las direccionales, las intermitentes

la guantera

la puerta

el capó

los frenos

el volante

las luces

un descapotable, un convertible

un coche deportivo

un sedán a cuatro puertas

un SUV

un camión

Para conversar

¡Cuánto me gustaría tener un coche deportivo! Me compraría uno pero no puedo.

¿Por qué no?

Porque no tengo bastante dinero.

(tl)David H. Brennan, (others)McGraw-Hill Education

En la estación de servicio (la gasolinera)

El tanque está casi vacío.
La señorita llena el tanque.

¡Ay! Tengo un pinchazo. Tengo que cambiar la llanta. Tengo una rueda de repuesto y un(a) gato(a) en la maletera.

la llanta, la goma, el neumático

el/la gato(a)

una rueda (llanta) de repuesto (recambio)

(tl)Image Source/age fotostock, (tr b)David H. Brennan

HABLAR • ESCRIBIR

1 Identifica.

LEER

2 Indica si la información es correcta o no.

	correcta	incorrecta
1. Para conducir (manejar) un carro es necesario tener un permiso de conducir.		
2. Un descapotable es más bien un coche deportivo.		
3. Antes de doblar el conductor debe poner las direccionales.		
4. Por si acaso tienes un pinchazo, siempre debes tener una gata y una rueda de repuesto en la guantera.		
5. Para parar el carro tienes que poner los frenos.		
6. El motor del carro está en la maletera.		
7. Tienes que llenar el tanque de gasolina cuando está lleno.		

Conexiones

Las finanzas

Muchas veces cuando uno quiere comprar un carro no tiene suficiente dinero para pagar el precio total. Así tiene que pedir un préstamo. Pero hay que tener cuidado porque la tasa de interés de un préstamo a corto plazo (por poco tiempo) es más alta que la tasa de interés de un préstamo a largo plazo. Un(a) consumidor(a) inteligente siempre tiene que verificar la tasa de interés que tiene que pagar.

Calculadora de Pagos Mensuales

Ingresa el precio del vehículo que estás considerando y otras variables para calcular una estimación del pago mensual. Este cálculo refleja montos en dólares aproximados al valor entero más cercano. Esta estimación de pagos mensuales no incluye licencia, documentación, cobros por emisiones u otros posibles pagos extra.

Precio	25000
Pago adelantado	5000
Tasa de interés	6.0 %

Calcular

HABLAR • ESCRIBIR

3 Personaliza. Da respuestas personales.

1. ¿Tienes un carro?
2. ¿Tienes tu permiso de conducir?
3. En tu estado, ¿a qué edad puedes conseguir (tener) un permiso de conducir?
4. En tu estado, ¿son de autoservicio las gasolineras?

David H. Brennan

4 *Conexiones*

El lenguaje Como el mundo hispano es tan grande, hay muchas maneras de decir la misma cosa. Puedes familiarizarte con los siguientes términos relacionados con un carro o una carretera pero no tienes que aprenderlos todos. En esta lista debes saber por lo menos la primera palabra.

- el carril, la pista, la vía, la banda, el canal
- el arcén, el acotamiento, la banquina, la berma, el hombrillo
- adelantar, pasar, rebasar
- el tráfico, el tránsito
- estacionar, aparcar, parquear
- el permiso de conducir, la licencia, el carnet
- la llanta, el neumático, la goma, el caucho
- el pinchazo, la llanta desinflada, la llanta pinchada
- de repuesto, de recambio, de refacción
- la gasolina, la nafta, la benzina

Si hay unos alumnos latinos en tu clase, pregúntales cuáles son las palabras que ellos usan. Pregúntales también si usan otra palabra para expresar la misma idea.

LEER

5 Parea para crear una historia.

1. A Alejandra le gustaría tener
2. Lo compraría pero
3. No puede porque
4. Para comprarlo
5. Para ganar bastante dinero

a. necesitaría mucho dinero.
b. no tiene bastante dinero.
c. un carro nuevo.
d. tendría que trabajar mucho.
e. no puede.

EXPANSIÓN

Ahora, sin mirar las frases, cuenta la historia en tus propias palabras. Si no recuerdas algo, tu compañero(a) te puede ayudar.

HABLAR

6 **Juego** Trabaja con un(a) compañero(a). Piensa en una palabra relacionada con los carros. Tu compañero(a) te va a hacer unas preguntas para adivinar la palabra en que estás pensando. Después, cambien de rol. ¡A ver quién hace menos preguntas antes de adivinar la palabra!

CULTURA

Entrada a un servicio para autos en la Ciudad de México

Andrew Payti

Imperativo familiar—formas regulares

1. Just as in English, you use the imperative in Spanish to give a command. You use the **tú** command when speaking to a friend, a family member, someone you know well, or a child. The regular **tú** form of the command is the same as the **usted** form of the present tense of the verb.

PRESENT (UD.)	IMPERATIVE (TÚ)
Usted habla.	**¡Habla!**
Usted conduce.	**¡Conduce!**
Usted escribe.	**¡Escribe!**
Usted comienza.	**¡Comienza!**
Usted vuelve.	**¡Vuelve!**
Usted sigue.	**¡Sigue!**

2. The object pronouns are added to this command form and the verb takes a written accent.

> **Quédate en el carril izquierdo.**
> **El plano, por favor. Dámelo.**

Nuestra responsabilidad es conservar y proteger el Bosque.

- Evita encender fogatas, hornillas, explosivos o cohetes.
- Está prohibido introducir armas.
- Se prohíbe consumir bebidas alcohólicas.
- No alimentes a los animales del Bosque.
- Deposita la basura en su lugar.
- Respeta las señales.
- Evita traer mascotas.

Práctica

ESCUCHAR • HABLAR

1 Conversa según el modelo.

MODELO —¿Debo hablar?
—Sí, Pepe. ¡Habla!

1. ¿Debo parar?
2. ¿Debo doblar?
3. ¿Debo dar la vuelta?
4. ¿Debo doblar a la derecha?
5. ¿Debo leer el rótulo?
6. ¿Debo seguir derecho?
7. ¿Debo volver?
8. ¿Debo pedir direcciones?

¿Qué es el programa Hoy No Circula?

Si visitas la Ciudad de México o el Área Metropolitana, tienes que cumplir con el Programa Hoy No Circula, el cual prohíbe la circulación de vehículos algunos días de la semana. Opera de lunes a viernes de las 05:00 a las 22:00 horas, de acuerdo con el último número de placa de tu vehículo. Revisa qué día no circula tu auto:

Lunes 5 y 6
Martes 7 y 8
Miércoles 3 y 4
Jueves 1 y 2
Viernes 9 y 0, así como permisos y placas personalizadas que no cuenten con números.

AZ 0004

Muévete en bici, patineta o caminando

Domingo 13 de mayo
7 Am a 2 Pm

Disfruta el Paseo de la Reforma desde la Puerta de los leones de Chapultepec hasta el Zócalo

Llega en bici o llévala en metro o metrobús

Ciudad México

Andrew Payti

LEER • ESCRIBIR

2 Completa con el imperativo familiar del verbo indicado.

1. Oye, Magda, _____ a la derecha. (doblar)
2. _____ derecho. (seguir)
3. _____ derecho hasta el tercer cruce. (seguir)
4. _____ a la izquierda. (mirar)
5. A mano izquierda, verás la tienda. _____. (entrar)
6. _____ el ascensor. (tomar)
7. _____ al sexto piso. (subir)
8. _____ allí. (esperar)

HABLAR

3 Mira las ilustraciones. Usa el imperativo para decirle a tu compañero(a) lo que debe hacer.

1. 2. 3. 4.

HABLAR

4 **Juego** Escoge a un(a) compañero(a) para jugar «Simón dice».

ESCUCHAR • HABLAR • ESCRIBIR

5 Sigue el modelo.

MODELO la mantequilla →
Pásame la mantequilla, por favor.

1. el pan
2. el vaso
3. la taza
4. la botella
5. los panecillos

ESCUCHAR • HABLAR • ESCRIBIR

6 Sigue el modelo.

MODELO la toalla →
Ramón, dámela, por favor.

1. la cámara
2. el jabón
3. el peine
4. los boletos
5. las entradas

VOCABULARY BOOK See the Foldables section of the Student Handbook at the beginning of this book for help with making this foldable. Use this study organizer to practice your informal commands. On the front of each flap, write the infinitive form of a verb. Then open each flap and write the informal (**tú**) command of the verb. For extra practice, exchange *vocabulary book* foldables with a partner.

InfoGap For more practice with affirmative commands, do Activity 9 in the Student Resource section at the end of this book.

Imperativo familiar—formas irregulares

The following verbs are irregular in the **tú** form of the command.

INFINITIVE	IMPERATIVE (**TÚ**)
decir	**di**
ir	**ve**
ser	**sé**
salir	**sal**
hacer	**haz**
tener	**ten**
venir	**ven**
poner	**pon**

Práctica

ESCUCHAR • HABLAR • ESCRIBIR

7 Contesta con **sí** y el imperativo.

1. ¿Debo venir mañana?
2. ¿Debo salir temprano?
3. ¿Debo hacer el viaje en carro?
4. ¿Debo poner aire en las llantas?
5. ¿Debo decir «adiós» a mi hermano?
6. ¿Debo ir por la carretera vieja?
7. ¿Debo tener cuidado?

ESCUCHAR • HABLAR

8 Tu compañero(a) no sabe lo que debe hacer. Conversa según el modelo.

MODELO ir →
—**No sé si debo ir.**
—**Sí, ve.**

1. hacer el viaje
2. salir de la ciudad
3. manejar
4. ir por la autopista
5. pedir un día libre
6. volver tarde

CULTURA

El monumento a la Independencia en el famoso Paseo de la Reforma en la Ciudad de México

Andrew Payti

Comunicación

9 Escríbele las direcciones a un(a) amigo(a) diciéndole como llegar a tu casa del aeropuerto. Tu amigo(a) leerá las direcciones y preparará un mapa para verificar que las comprendió.

10 Habla con un(a) compañero(a) de clase. Dale direcciones para ir de la escuela a tu casa. Luego tu compañero(a) te dirá como ir a su casa. Deben hacerse preguntas si no comprenden algo.

El condicional

1. As with the future, the infinitive serves as the stem for the conditional of regular verbs. The endings added to the infinitive to form the conditional are the same endings you use for the imperfect of **-er** and **-ir** verbs.

	llegar	ver	ir
yo	**llegaría**	**vería**	**iría**
tú	**llegarías**	**verías**	**irías**
Ud., él, ella	**llegaría**	**vería**	**iría**
nosotros(as)	**llegaríamos**	**veríamos**	**iríamos**
vosotros(as)	*llegaríais*	*veríais*	*iríais*
Uds., ellos, ellas	**llegarían**	**verían**	**irían**

CULTURA

¿Te gustaría nadar en esta alberca en Tepoztlán, México?

2. Verbs that have an irregular stem in the future have the same irregular stem in the conditional.

INFINITIVE	FUTURE STEM	CONDITIONAL
tener	**tendr–**	**tendría**
poner	**pondr–**	**pondría**
salir	**saldr–**	**saldría**
venir	**vendr–**	**vendría**
poder	**podr–**	**podría**
saber	**sabr–**	**sabría**
hacer	**har–**	**haría**
decir	**dir–**	**diría**
querer	**querr–**	**querría**

3. You use the conditional in Spanish the same as you do in English. The conditional expresses what would take place under certain conditions.

> **Ellos podrían llegar en menos tiempo, pero no quieren tomar la autopista.**
> **Él adelantaría el otro carro, pero no quiere exceder el límite de velocidad.**
> **No excederíamos el límite porque no queremos tener una multa.**

4. You can also use the conditional to soften requests.

> **¿Me pasaría usted la sal, por favor?**
> **¿Me dirías cómo llegar a la Plaza de Armas?**

Práctica

CULTURA

Una joven está conduciendo su moto en una calle de Madrid. Esta joven es muy sabia porque está llevando casco. No es el caso entre muchos motociclistas en España y Latinoamérica.

ESCUCHAR

11 Escucha. Indica el tiempo del verbo.

futuro	condicional

HABLAR • ESCRIBIR

12 Personaliza. Da respuestas personales.

1. ¿Te gustaría ser millonario(a) o no?
2. ¿Vivirías en el campo o en la ciudad?
3. ¿Tendrías una casa de verano?
4. ¿Viajarías mucho?
5. ¿Adónde irías?
6. ¿Con quién harías tus viajes?

Andrew Payti

LEER • ESCRIBIR

13 Completa con el condicional.

1. Yo sé que él no lo hará, pero yo lo _____.
2. Yo sé que a ellos les gustará la idea, pero a mí no me _____ nada.
3. Yo sé que ellos no lo dirán, pero tú se lo _____ a todos.
4. Yo sé que ella irá, pero ustedes no _____.
5. Yo sé que tú contestarás, pero ella no _____.
6. Nosotros sabemos que él comerá el pescado pero nosotros no lo _____.

ESCUCHAR • HABLAR

14 Conversa según el modelo.

MODELO —¿Se quedará tu hermano?
—Dijo que se quedaría.

1. ¿Estará tu hermano?
2. ¿Hará el viaje?
3. ¿Vendrá mañana?
4. ¿Saldrá con Elena?
5. ¿Tendrá mucho tiempo?

ESCUCHAR • HABLAR • ESCRIBIR

15 Sigue el modelo para ser más cortés.

MODELO Pásame la sal, por favor. →
¿Me pasarías la sal, por favor?

1. Pásame el pan, por favor.
2. Ayúdame, por favor.
3. Llámame mañana, por favor.
4. Repítelo, por favor.

16 **Comunicación**

¿Hay muchas cosas que te gustaría hacer pero que no puedes porque tienes otras obligaciones? Ten una conversación con un(a) compañero(a). Discutan todo lo que les gustaría hacer pero que no pueden. Expliquen por qué no pueden.

Refrán

Can you guess what the following proverb means?

Si ves las estrellas brillar, sal, marinero, a la mar.

¡Bravo!

You have now learned all the new vocabulary and grammar in this chapter. Continue to use and practice all that you know while learning more cultural information. **¡Vamos!**

¿Comprendes?

A Contesta según la información en la conversación.

1. ¿Por qué no puede Gregorio aparcar el carro donde lo quiere aparcar?
2. ¿Qué hay en la esquina donde tiene que doblar a la derecha?
3. ¿Hasta dónde debe seguir derecho?
4. ¿Qué hay en la plaza?
5. ¿Qué indica su entrada?

B Busca todas las direcciones que Carmen le da a Gregorio para llegar a la plaza.

C Resumiendo Cuenta la información en la conversación en tus propias palabras.

TARIFA
0.05 €hora o fracción
10.20 €24 horas
PERDIDA DE TIQUE
10.20 €
Exceptuando a 24 horas

HORARIO
DE LUNES A SÁBADO
DOMINGOS Y FESTIVOS
DE 7 a las HORAS

CAJA ↘

CAJA DEL PARKING

LABORABLES DE 9 A 20 H.
SÁBADOS DE 9 A 14 H.

ZONA DE ESTACIONAMIENTO
LIMITADO Y CONTROLADO
TARJETA DE CONTROL OBLIGATORIO

CULTURA

Es la caja de un parking en Tenerife en las islas Canarias de España.

Lectura

Antes de leer

Piensa en las carreteras donde vives. ¿Son anchas con muchos carriles en cada sentido o son más bien caminos estrechos con solo un carril en cada sentido?

✓ **READING CHECK**

¿Entre qué países se extiende la carretera Panamericana?

✓ **READING CHECK**

¿Por qué es muy importante la carretera Panamericana?

Durante la lectura

Escribe a lo menos dos frases sobre cada párrafo. Al terminar cada párrafo lee todos tus apuntes.

RESUMIENDO Hacer un resumen de lo que estás leyendo te permite recordar información. Tomar notas o apuntes también te puede ayudar a preparar para una prueba o un examen.

La Panamericana

¿Te gustaría rentar un carro y explorar a lo menos una o más regiones de Latinoamérica? Sería una experiencia que no olvidarías nunca. Pues, ¡al volante! ¡Empieza tu aventura! Tendrías que tomar, sin duda, una parte de la carretera Panamericana—pero solo una parte pequeña porque la Panamericana es la carretera más larga del mundo—cubre 47.516 kilómetros.

La Panamericana es una red o sistema de carreteras y caminos que se extiende desde la frontera de Estados Unidos y México hasta la ciudad de Puerto Montt en la Patagonia chilena. En unos lugares la carretera enlaza también la costa occidental con la costa oriental de la América del Sur. La carretera es una ruta importante para el transporte de todo tipo de mercancías y productos agrícolas. Muchos camiones están tan cargados que parecen[1] que se van a volcar[2]. Cuando llegan a una pendiente[3] su peso[4] no les permite agarrar velocidad[5] y los sigue una larga cola (fila) de vehículos que querrían adelantarlos.

[1]parecen   *they seem*
[2]volcar   *flip over*
[3]pendiente   *incline*
[4]peso   *weight*
[5]agarrar velocidad   *to pick up speed*

CULTURA

Una garita de peaje en la carretera Panamericana en Perú

Unas partes de la Panamericana son modernas con dos o más carriles en cada sentido. La mayor parte de la carretera está pavimentada—a veces en buenas condiciones y otras veces no. Por eso tendrías que manejar con mucho cuidado sobre todo de noche. En las áreas remotas no hay luces pero hay baches[6] que frecuentemente no puedes ver. De repente puede terminar el pavimento y la carretera se convierte en un camino de rocas, piedras[7] y lodo[8].

[6]baches   *ruts, potholes*   [8]lodo   *mud*
[7]piedras   *stones*

✓ READING CHECK

¿Cómo cambia la carretera de una región a otra?

CULTURA

Este rótulo en el centro de Cotacachi indica como ir a Quito vía la Panamericana.

CULTURA

Un tramo de la carretera Panamericana al llegar a Buenos Aires, Argentina

Andrew Payti

¿VAS EN CARRO?

✔ READING CHECK

¿Qué pone el conductor en la carretera cuando hay una avería?

¡Ten cuidado! Hay otro peligro[9] posible. Una gran parte de la carretera no tiene acotamiento. Cuando un carro, camión o bus tiene una avería[10], el conductor coloca unas ramas de árboles o plantas unos metros detrás del vehículo. Estas ramas les avisan a los otros conductores que hay cerca un vehículo averiado que está bloqueando el camino. Y después de cambiar una llanta o reparar el vehículo, ¿qué hace el conductor? Pues, sale y deja en su lugar las ramas. Y de noche es difícil verlas.

Como te he dicho, en muchas áreas la Panamericana es una carretera moderna y conveniente. Pero en unas zonas remotas, tomar la Panamericana es una aventura.

[9]peligro   *danger*
[10]avería   *breakdown*

Después de leer

Lee todos tus apuntes. Añade algunos detalles o descripciones que quieres recordar. Puedes consultar tus apuntes antes de tomar un examen.

CULTURA 🇵🇪

Es un rótulo en el sur de Perú. Hay que ir derecho (recto) si quieres ir a Pisco. Pero si quieres seguir la Panamericana tienes que doblar a la derecha en el siguiente cruce.

Andrew Payti

¿Comprendes?

A Recordando hechos Contesta.

1. ¿Cuál es la carretera más larga del mundo?
2. ¿Qué es la Panamericana?
3. ¿Dónde empieza (nace) y dónde termina (muere) la Panamericana?
4. ¿Cómo es la carretera en algunas partes?
5. ¿Cómo es en otras partes?

B Confirmando información Verifica. ¿Sí o no?

1. Toda la carretera Panamericana es una carretera moderna con muchos carriles en cada sentido.
2. De noche la carretera está bien iluminada.
3. Una gran parte de la Panamericana no tiene acotamiento.
4. No se puede usar la Panamericana en ninguna parte para viajar de la costa occidental a la costa oriental de la América del Sur.
5. La Panamericana es una ruta usada exclusivamente por razones turísticas.

C Describiendo Describe.

1. unas características de la Panamericana
2. los posibles peligros en la Panamericana

D Analizando Contesta.

¿Por qué es muy importante la carretera Panamericana?

E Describiendo y categorizando Completa la tabla.

la Panamericana		
por donde pasa	**su condición**	**unos peligros**

Antes de leer

Piensa en el tráfico donde tú vives. ¿Hay mucho o no? ¿Es un problema o no? ¿Tiene la mayoría de las familias carros que usan casi siempre o hay un buen sistema de transporte público?

CULTURA

Hay mucho tráfico en las calles en el centro de Caracas, Venezuela.

Tráfico y más tráfico

Hay muchos que dicen que hay más tráfico en Caracas, Buenos Aires o México que en Chicago, Jacksonville o Dallas, y puede ser verdad. En estas ciudades el tráfico es denso y hay muchos embotellamientos o tapones[1]. Se observará también que muchos carros son bastante viejos. Son viejos pero en su mayoría están en buenas condiciones. En Latinoamérica los carros suelen ser muy caros. Los gobiernos les imponen impuestos[2] altos a los automóviles. Un carro de ocasión, es decir un carro usado, que ya tiene más de diez años puede costar unos quince mil dólares o más. ¿Cuánto cuesta un carro nuevo? Depende, pero puede costar casi el doble de lo que cuesta en Estados Unidos. Por eso, los dueños de los carros los cuidan bien y los reparan frecuentemente para mantenerlos en excelentes condiciones.

No hay duda de que los vehículos viejos contaminan el aire. Por eso, la contaminación del aire es un problema serio en muchas ciudades latinoamericanas. Tan grave es el problema que en algunas ciudades el gobierno no permite circular todos los vehículos todos los días. Algunos pueden circular los días pares[3] y otros los días impares[4].

Como los carros cuestan tanto, los autobuses son el medio de transporte más popular en los países latinoamericanos. Viajar en bus, sea en bus municipal o en el de una compañía privada, resulta muy barato. Y es interesante notar que la palabra «autobús» no es universal en el mundo hispanohablante. Otros términos son el autocar, el bus, el camión, la guagua, el ómnibus, la camioneta, el micro y el colectivo.

[1]tapones *traffic jams*
[2]impuestos *taxes*
[3]pares *even*
[4]impares *odd*

CULTURA

El bus es un medio de transporte importante en Latinoamérica. El bus que vemos aquí está en la Ciudad de Panamá.

(l)Kelli Drummer-Avendaño, (r)Andrew Payti

¿Comprendes?

Escoge o completa.

1. ¿Por qué hay muchos carros viejos en Latinoamérica?
   a. Nadie tiene el dinero para comprarse un carro nuevo.
   b. Los carros son muy caros.
   c. La gente prefiere carros de ocasión.
   d. A mucha gente le gusta repararlos.

2. ¿Por qué cuestan tanto dinero los carros en Latinoamérica?
   a. Los gobiernos les imponen impuestos altos.
   b. La mayoría de la gente es muy rica.
   c. Pueden costar hasta el doble de lo que cuestan en Estados Unidos.
   d. Los dueños los cuidan bien.

3. Los carros viejos causan mucha _____.

4. ¿Qué hacen algunos gobiernos para tratar de eliminar la contaminación del aire?
   a. Imponen impuestos altos cada vez que el dueño usa su vehículo.
   b. No permiten circular todos los vehículos todos los días.
   c. Imponen impuestos altos para los carros viejos.
   d. No permiten circular los carros en malas condiciones.

5. En inglés se dice *bottleneck* al hablar de un problema de mucho tráfico. Hay dos palabras en español que también tienen que ver con una botella y que expresan la misma idea. Estas dos palabras son _____.

CULTURA

Muchos carros y taxis pasan delante del monumento a la Revolución en la Ciudad de México.

Andrew Payti

Prepárate para el examen

↻ To review, see **Vocabulario 1.**

Vocabulario

1 **Completa.**

1–2. En una autopista hay varios _____ en cada _____.

3. El _____ indica donde está la salida.

4. Quiero _____ el carro delante de mí porque va muy despacio.

5. En muchas autopistas hay que pagar _____.

6. Hay _____ en el cruce que indica que tienes que pararte.

7. El museo está a tres _____ de aquí.

8. Para llegar al hotel tienes que _____ a la derecha en el segundo cruce.

2 **Identifica.**

9. donde se ponen las maletas en el carro

10. lo que se usa en el carro de noche

11. lo que se usa para indicar a otros conductores que vas a doblar

12. un vehículo que transporta muchas cosas

13. adonde vas cuando necesitas llenar el tanque de gasolina

14. lo que se usa para levantar el carro cuando hay un pinchazo

15. cada carro tiene cuatro y uno de recambio

16. lo que necesitas para conducir un carro; tiene una foto del/de la conductor(a)

↻ To review, see **Vocabulario 2.**

Gramática

3 **Completa con el imperativo familiar.**

17. José, _____ la vuelta. (dar)

18. _____ dos cuadras. (seguir)

19. Luego _____ a la izquierda. (doblar)

20. Si te pierdes, _____ el plano de la ciudad. (consultar)

21. _____ una moneda en el parquímetro. (introducir)

22. _____ si necesitas gasolina. (verificar)

23. _____ antes de las seis de la tarde. (volver)

24. _____ con el agente de policía. (hablar)

↻ To review, see **Imperativo familiar—formas regulares.**

4 Completa con el imperativo familiar.

25. _____ cuidado. (tener)

26. _____ las direccionales para indicar que vas a doblar. (poner)

27. _____ de la autopista en la próxima salida. (salir)

28. _____ el viaje en carro. (hacer)

29. _____ la verdad. (decir)

↻ To review, see **Imperativo familiar—formas irregulares.**

5 Completa con el condicional.

30. Yo tomaré la autovía, pero Lupe no la _____ porque no quiere pagar el peaje.

31. Estaremos muy cansados, pero Nando y Eduardo no _____ cansados porque siempre se acuestan temprano.

32. Aunque no debes exceder la velocidad máxima, yo sé que ella la _____.

33. Mis padres no asistirán al concierto, pero yo sí _____.

34. Luis no lo hará, pero tú lo _____.

35. El niño le tendrá miedo al perro, pero nosotros no _____ miedo.

36. Yo iré pero sé que tú no _____.

↻ To review, see **El condicional.**

Cultura

6 Contesta.

37. ¿Qué es la Panamericana?

38. ¿Cómo es la Panamericana en algunas áreas remotas?

39–40. ¿Por qué tienes que tener cuidado cuando conduces en la carretera Panamericana? Puedes dar más de una respuesta.

↻ To review this cultural information, see the **Lectura cultural.**

CULTURA

Un tramo de la carretera Panamericana en un área muy árida en el sur de Perú cerca de Ica. ¿Cuántos carriles tiene la carretera aquí en cada sentido o dirección?

Andrew Payti

Prepárate para el examen

Un tapón en una calle del centro de la Ciudad de Panamá

1 Leyendo el mapa

Create and describe a travel route through Spain

Con un(a) compañero(a), mira un mapa de España. Han alquilado un coche y quieren ir de Madrid a otra ciudad que ustedes dos han escogido. Discutan como van a ir y las carreteras que van a tomar. ¡A ver si pueden adivinar cuánto tiempo tardará (*will take*) el viaje!

2 Las carreteras de tu estado

Describe highways in your state

Describe las carreteras de tu estado. ¿Cómo son? ¿Adónde van? ¿Hay mucho tráfico?

3 ¿Qué piensas de la Panamericana?

Explain your opinion

Algún día, ¿quieres tener la experiencia de tomar la Panamericana? Explica por qué dices que sí o que no.

4 Uno de tus padres te habla.

Tell what needs to be done

Imagínate que eres tu madre o padre. Imita como habla él o ella. Dile a un(a) compañero(a) las tareas que te da con frecuencia. Usa el imperativo familiar.

5 ¿Yo? ¿Millonario(a)?

Talk about what you would do with a million dollars

Tú y un(a) compañero(a) acaban de recibir un millón de dólares. Cada uno de ustedes hará una lista de todo lo que haría con tal cantidad de dinero. Comparen sus listas y decidan quién haría las cosas más interesantes.

6 Una encuesta

Prepare a survey and present the results

Trabaja con un(a) compañero(a). Van a hacer una encuesta. Esta es la situación. Hay un billete de cien dólares en la calle. Cada uno(a) de ustedes preguntará a cinco compañeros lo que harían al encontrar los cien dólares. Luego organicen las respuestas para informar a la clase sobre los resultados.

Tarea

A Spanish-speaking friend who is always getting lost calls to tell you he or she is coming to visit but doesn't remember how to get to your house. Write a dialogue of a phone conversation between you and your friend in which you are trying to give directions but he or she keeps getting mixed up.

Writing Strategy

Dialogue Composing a dialogue between two or more people is a good way to practice the way language is naturally spoken. Although a conversation between friends involves informal speech, when writing dialogue, it is important to use correct spelling and punctuation, appropriate vocabulary, and proper grammar. This is especially true in the context of giving directions, because you don't want misunderstandings or confusion to cause your friend to get lost!

❶ Prewrite

Give your Spanish-speaking friend an identity and decide where he or she will be coming from. Then use the vocabulary from this chapter to make a list of the information you will need to know in order to give accurate directions. Break the information down in steps.

❷ Write

- Be sure to review the information in Chapter 6 on how to make and receive phone calls.
- Use the affirmative **tú** commands when giving directions.
- Make sure your phone conversation flows smoothly and sounds natural.
- Remember that your friend keeps getting mixed up. Be creative!

Evaluate

Your teacher will evaluate you on correct spelling and punctuation, proper vocabulary and grammar, organization, and completeness of information.

Gramática

Imperativo familiar—formas regulares

You use the **tú** command when speaking to a friend, family member, a child, or someone you know well. The **tú** form of the command is the same as the **usted** form of the present tense.

PRESENT (UD.)	IMPERATIVE (TÚ)
Usted habla.	**¡Habla!**
Usted come.	**¡Come!**
Usted sigue.	**¡Sigue!**

Object pronouns are added to the imperative.

Dame la mano.   **Devuélvemelo.**

Imperativo familiar—formas irregulares

Review the following irregular forms of the **tú** command.

decir → di	**venir → ven**	**salir → sal**
ir → ve	**tener → ten**	**hacer → haz**
ser → sé	**poner → pon**	

El condicional

To form the conditional of regular verbs, you add the endings of the imperfect tense of **-er** and **-ir** verbs to the infinitive.

pagar	comer	seguir
pagaría	comería	seguiría
pagarías	comerías	seguirías
pagaría	comería	seguiría
pagaríamos	comeríamos	seguiríamos
pagaríais	*comeríais*	*seguiríais*
pagarían	comerían	seguirían

Verbs that have an irregular stem in the future tense have the same irregular stem in the conditional. Review the following forms.

tener → tendría	**poner → pondría**	**hacer → haría**
salir → saldría	**venir → vendría**	**decir → diría**
poder → podría	**saber → sabría**	**querer → querría**

The conditional is used the same in Spanish as in English.

Juego There are a number of cognates in this list. See how many you and a partner can find. Who can find the most? Compare your list with those of your classmates.

Go Online!

connectED.mcgraw-hill.com

Vocabulario

Talking about driving on the highway

la carretera	el sentido	la salida	el arcén, el acotamiento
la autopista, la autovía	el peaje	el rótulo	una línea continua
el carril	la garita (la cabina) de peaje	la velocidad máxima	conducir

Giving directions

el plano de la ciudad	quedarse en el carril	adelantar, rebasar, pasar	estar prohibido
dar la vuelta	doblar	parar(se)	
seguir derecho			

Talking about the city

la cuadra, la manzana	el parquímetro	una calle de sentido único	reducir la velocidad
el cruce, la bocacalle	una moneda	despacio	cruzar
la luz roja	el tiquete	clavar	
	una multa		

Talking about cars

el coche, el carro	el SUV	la estación de servicio, la gasolinera	llenar
el descapotable, el convertible	el camión	el/la gato(a)	cambiar la llanta
el coche deportivo	el/la conductor(a)	el tanque	vacío(a)
el sedán a cuatro puertas	el permiso de conducir, la licencia, el carnet	un pinchazo	

Identifying parts of a car

el capó	las luces	la guantera	la llanta (la rueda) de repuesto (de recambio)
la puerta	los frenos	el volante	
la maletera, el baúl	las direccionales, las intermitentes	la llanta, la goma, el neumático	
el parabrisas			

Other useful words and expressions

tacaño(a)	tener cuidado

LA PRACTICE Refer to the Language Arts Practice section for activities that will strengthen your Language Arts skills as you continue to use your Spanish.

 Literary Reader
You may wish to read the adapted version of *Marianela*, found in the Literary Reader at the end of this book.

Repaso cumulativo

Repasa lo que ya has aprendido

These activities will help you review and remember what you have learned so far in Spanish.

1 Escucha las frases. Indica si la frase describe el dibujo o no.

2 Personaliza. Da respuestas personales.

1. ¿Cuántos años tienes?
2. ¿Haces mucho trabajo cada día?
3. ¿Te pones un suéter cuando hace frío?
4. ¿A qué hora sales de casa por la mañana?
5. ¿Conoces a muchos compañeros de clase?
6. ¿Conduces un carro?

3 Da la forma de yo en el presente.

1. hacer	**6.** decir
2. poner	**7.** venir
3. traer	**8.** conocer
4. salir	**9.** conducir
5. tener	**10.** oír

4 Categoriza las siguientes palabras.

	legumbres	frutas	carnes	productos lácteos	pescado o mariscos
1. el jamón					
2. el queso					
3. la lechuga					
4. el helado					
5. la naranja					
6. el pollo					
7. los camarones					
8. las judías verdes					
9. la piña					
10. las almejas					

5 **Personaliza. Da respuestas personales.**

1. ¿A qué escuela ibas cuando tenías siete años?
2. ¿Quiénes eran algunos de tus maestros en la escuela primaria?
3. ¿Te gustaba ir a un parque de atracciones cuando eras niño(a)?
4. ¿Había un parque de atracciones cerca de donde vivías?
5. ¿Qué atracciones te gustaban más?
6. ¿Ibas de vez en cuando a un zoológico?
7. ¿Qué animales veías?
8. ¿Podías darles de comer a los animales o estaba prohibido?

CULTURA

Mucha gente está haciendo cola para comprar tickets para subirse a la montaña rusa en el Parque de Chapultepec en la Ciudad de México.

6 **Completa con el adjetivo posesivo.**

1. La hermana de mi padre es _____ tía y _____ hermano es _____ tío.
2. Los hijos de mis tíos son _____ primos y _____ hijos son los sobrinos de mis padres.
3. Mi hermano y yo queremos mucho a los abuelos. Los adoramos. _____ abuelos son los padres de _____ padres.
4. Dime algo de _____ familia. ¿Tienes hermanos? ¿Cuántos años tienen _____ hermanos?

Andrew Payti

Cocina hispana

Go Online!

connectED.mcgraw-hill.com

Audio

Video

Práctica

Repaso

Diversiones

eScape

ePals

Vamos a comparar Ya has aprendido que las sobras son la comida que queda después de comer. Has aprendido también que las sobras de una comida en un restaurante de Latinoamérica o España no se llevan a casa «para el perrito». Ahora vamos a ver si las familias hispanas elaboran unos platos sirviéndose de las sobras en vez de botarlas. Y en tu casa, ¿usan las sobras para preparar algunos platos?

Objetivos

You will:

- talk about foods and food preparation
- talk about a Hispanic recipe

You will use:

- the subjunctive
- formal commands
- negative informal commands

◀ Esta señora está preparando una salsa de mole en Puebla, México. El mole es una exquisita salsa confeccionada con varios chiles, especias y condimentos. Se sirve típicamente sobre pollo o cerdo.

Cocina hispana

Mira estas fotos para familiarizarte con el tema de este capítulo—la cocina hispana. Al mirar las fotos, ¿qué piensas? Hay una gran variedad de platos. ¿Hay algunos que quieres probar?

Cuba

Un vendedor o cocinero callejero está haciendo churros en La Habana Vieja. A muchos españoles y a mucha gente de varias partes de Latinoamérica les encanta comer churros frescos para el desayuno. Los adultos los comen con café y los niños con chocolate.

Costa Rica

Un cuenco de chiles—un tipo de pimiento o ají. Se usan los chiles para añadir un sabor picante a muchas comidas.

México

Un plato de chiles rellenos acompañado de arroz y aguacate en un restaurante en Tepoztlán

Guatemala

El señor está asando carne en Tikal, Guatemala. ¿Quieres que él te prepare la carne bien hecha o a término medio?

LA PAELLA

INGREDIENTES

3 tomates
2 cebollas grandes
2 pimientos (uno verde y uno rojo)
4 dientes de ajo
1/2 kilo de camarones

4 calamares
12 almejas
12 mejillones
langosta (opcional)
1 pollo en partes
3 chorizos

1 paquete de guisantes congelados
1 bote de pimientos morrones
1 1/2 tazas de arroz
3 tazas de consomé de pollo
4 pizcas de azafrán
1/4 taza de aceite de oliva

PREPARACIÓN

1. Pique los tomates, los pimientos, las cebollas y el ajo.
2. Lave las almejas y los mejillones en agua fría.
3. Limpie y pele los camarones.
4. Limpie y corte en rebanadas los calamares.
5. Corte en rebanadas los chorizos.
6. Fría o ase el pollo aparte.

España

Una paella valenciana con camarones y mejillones. La paella es un plato popular en España y también en muchas partes de Latinoamérica. Hay muchas recetas diferentes para preparar una paella deliciosa.

España

El cocinero está asando cochinillos y corderos en un horno viejo de un restaurante muy antiguo y famoso de Madrid.

Perú

Aquí vemos dos teteras sobre un tipo de estufa u horno de barro colocado sobre una superficie de piedras en el pueblo de Uros en una de las islas flotantes cerca de Puno, Perú.

Latinoamérica y España

El cochinillo asado en España o el lechón asado en muchas partes de Latinoamérica es un plato muy apreciado. Se sirve durante una gran variedad de fiestas—fiestas populares y fiestas elegantes—para celebrar eventos familiares.

(t)Daniel Salsgiver, (c)Glow Images, (cr b)Andrew Payti

La cocina

el congelador

el horno de microondas

la estufa, la cocina

el refrigerador, la nevera

el horno

el lavaplatos

freír las papas

el/la sartén

asar la carne

la parrilla

hervir el agua

la tapa

la olla, la cacerola

la cazuela

revolver la salsa

En otras partes

- **El aguacate** is **la palta** in Chile, Bolivia, Peru, Argentina, and Uruguay.
- There are many terms that mean *slice*. Some general guidelines are:
  rebanada (de pan, pastel)
  tajada (de carne)
  lonja, loncha (de jamón)
  rodaja (de limón, pepino)
  raja (de melón)
- **Pedazos** and **trozos** (**trocitos**) refer to pieces.

Para conversar

¿Quiere usted que yo ase el pollo o que lo fría?

Fríalo, por favor. Me gusta el pollo frito.

el ajo

las zanahorias

los pimientos

el pepino

el aguacate

la cebolla

SOPA DE POLLO
una receta

INGREDIENTES
1 taza de cebolla picada
1 taza de apio
1 taza de zanahorias
  cortadas en rebanadas
3 dientes de ajo machacados

½ cucharadita de
  pimienta negra
10 tazas de caldo de pollo
1½ tazas de pollo cortado
  en cubitos (¾ de una libra)

RECETA
Poner la cebolla, el apio, las zanahorias, el ajo y el caldo de pollo en un horno holandés. Poner a hervir; remover una o dos veces. Bajar el fuego y dejarlo cocer a fuego lento sin tapar por 15 minutos. Añadir el pollo; dejar cocer a fuego lento de 5 a 10 minutos.

cortar en pedacitos

cortar en rebanadas

picar

pelar

Pique usted el ajo.

Pele usted las zanahorias.

la chuleta de cerdo

el muslo de pollo

la pechuga de pollo

las alitas

el escalope de ternera

Cuando el cocinero cocina algo tiene que añadir condimentos.
Los condimentos le dan sabor a la comida.

Para conversar

¿Quiere usted que yo ponga la cacerola al fuego?

Sí, póngala, por favor. Pero, cocínela (cuézala) a fuego lento. No quiero que se queme.

COCINA HISPANA

Conexiones

Las matemáticas

Si lees una receta en español tienes que comprender los pesos métricos. La onza y la libra no existen en el sistema métrico que es un sistema decimal. Las medidas para el peso se basan en el kilogramo o kilo. Hay mil gramos en un kilo.

El kilo es igual a 2,2 libras. Una libra inglesa o estadounidense es un poco menos de medio kilo.

ESCUCHAR

1 Escucha cada frase y decide si la información es correcta o no. Usa una tabla como la de abajo para indicar tus respuestas.

correcta	incorrecta

LEER

2 Escoge.

1. Antes de hervirlas, debes (freír, pelar) las zanahorias.
2. Puedes freír las pechugas de pollo en (una cacerola, una sartén).
3. Tienes que (revolver, asar) la salsa.
4. Favor de poner los vasos sucios en (la nevera, el lavaplatos).
5. Si lo quieres cocinar rápido lo debes poner en (el horno, el horno de microondas).
6. ¿Quiere usted que yo ponga la olla (al agua, al fuego)?
7. ¿Quiere usted que yo pele (las zanahorias, los pimientos)?
8. Voy a cortar el pan en (rebanadas, pedacitos).

ESCRIBIR

3 ¡Manos a la obra! Good nutrition is an important part of staying healthy. Working in groups, make a food pyramid. You can either create it digitally or by using a piece of poster board and markers. Label the pyramid with each of the food groups: grains, vegetables, fruits, oils, milk, and meat/beans. Within each food group, label the foods that you know. Then present your pyramid to the class and suggest a healthy meal based on the foods you listed in each group.

Kerri Galloway

HABLAR • ESCRIBIR

4 Personaliza. Da respuestas personales.

1. Cuando comes pollo, ¿prefieres el muslo o la pechuga?
2. ¿Te gusta más una chuleta de cerdo o un escalope de ternera?
3. ¿Prefieres el pescado asado o frito?
4. ¿Prefieres tus legumbres muy cocidas o casi crudas?
5. ¿Te gusta la carne con una salsa o sin salsa?
6. ¿Te gusta la comida salada o no? ¿Añades mucha sal?

LEER

5 Usa una tabla como la de abajo para indicar si se pueden poner los siguientes ingredientes en una ensalada.

sí	no

1. la lechuga
2. el ajo
3. la carne cruda
4. el aguacate

5. las zanahorias
6. el aceite
7. el café
8. una cebolla

CULTURA

El señor está asando carne en un puesto de comida en una calle de la Ciudad de Panamá.

HABLAR • ESCRIBIR

6 Describe.

1. tu comida favorita
2. las legumbres que te gustan
3. los ingredientes de una buena ensalada
4. algunos alimentos que pones en el refrigerador
5. unas cosas que se preparan a la parrilla
6. una cocina moderna

▲ Unos platos populares ▼

7 *Comunicación*

 Trabajen en grupos de cuatro y discutan sus platos o comidas favoritas. ¿Tienen ustedes los mismos gustos o no?

(t)Andrew Payti, (c)John A. Rizzo/Getty Images, (b)©Ingram Publishing/Alamy

El subjuntivo

1. All verbs you have learned so far are in the indicative mood. The indicative mood is used to express actions that actually do, did, or will take place. The indicative is used to express real events.

> **Juan es un alumno bueno.**
> **Estudia mucho.**
> **Recibe buenas notas.**

All the preceding information is factual.

> *Juan is a good student, he studies a lot, and he gets good grades.*

2. You are now going to learn the subjunctive mood. The subjunctive is used to express something that is not necessarily factual or real. It expresses things that might happen. Compare the following.

> **Juan estudia mucho y recibe buenas notas.**
> **Los padres de Juan quieren que él estudie mucho y que reciba buenas notas.**

The first sentence tells you that Juan studies a lot and gets good grades. The information is factual, and for this reason you use the indicative. The second sentence states that Juan's parents want him to study a lot and get good grades, but that doesn't mean that Juan will actually do it even though his parents want him to. The second sentence tells what may happen. It does not present facts, and for this reason you must use the subjunctive in the clause that depends upon **quieren.** Such a clause is called a dependent clause.

3. To form the present tense of the subjunctive of regular verbs, you drop the **o** ending of the **yo** form of the present indicative. This is also true for verbs that have an irregular form in the present tense of the indicative. Add **e** endings to all **-ar** verbs and **a** endings to all **-er** and **-ir** verbs.

La profesora ayuda a una alumna porque quiere que salga bien en su examen y que tenga éxito.

¿Te acuerdas?

Remember that you just reviewed the present tense in the previous chapter.

INFINITIVE	PRESENT (YO)	STEM	PRESENT SUBJUNCTIVE (YO)
mirar	**miro**	**mir–**	**mire**
comer	**como**	**com–**	**coma**
vivir	**vivo**	**viv–**	**viva**
salir	**salgo**	**salg–**	**salga**
hacer	**hago**	**hag–**	**haga**
decir	**digo**	**dig–**	**diga**
conducir	**conduzco**	**conduzc–**	**conduzca**

4. Study the forms for the present tense of the subjunctive.

	mirar	comer	vivir	salir
yo	mire	coma	viva	salga
tú	mires	comas	vivas	salgas
Ud., él, ella	mire	coma	viva	salga
nosotros(as)	miremos	comamos	vivamos	salgamos
vosotros(as)	*miréis*	*comáis*	*viváis*	*salgáis*
Uds., ellos, ellas	miren	coman	vivan	salgan

5. The following are the only verbs that do not follow the regular pattern for the formation of the present subjunctive.

	dar	estar	ir	saber	ser
yo	dé	esté	vaya	sepa	sea
tú	des	estés	vayas	sepas	seas
Ud., él, ella	dé	esté	vaya	sepa	sea
nosotros(as)	demos	estemos	vayamos	sepamos	seamos
vosotros(as)	*deis*	*estéis*	*vayáis*	*sepáis*	*seáis*
Uds., ellos, ellas	den	estén	vayan	sepan	sean

Práctica

ESCUCHAR • HABLAR • ESCRIBIR

1 Sigue el modelo.

MODELO estudiar mucho →
Los padres de Mateo quieren que
él estudie mucho.

1. trabajar
2. leer mucho
3. comer bien
4. aprender mucho
5. asistir a la universidad
6. recibir buenas notas
7. hacer el trabajo
8. poner todo en orden
9. salir bien en todo
10. ir a clase
11. estar aquí
12. ser bueno

CULTURA

Los señores están preparando una paella grande en Tenerife, España. Quieren que salga deliciosa y que a todos les guste.

Andrew Payti

Esta muchacha está preparando tortillas en Chichicastenango, Guatemala. La tortilla sirve de base de muchas comidas en México y Centroamérica.

LEER • ESCRIBIR

2 Forma una frase completa usando el subjuntivo.

Yo quiero que Luis…

1. preparar la comida
2. cortar las cebollas
3. asar la carne
4. leer la receta
5. pelar los tomates
6. picar el ajo
7. poner la mesa
8. hacer una ensalada

HABLAR • ESCRIBIR

3 Completa la frase con tus propias ideas usando los siguientes nombres y pronombres.

Yo quiero que…

1. tú
2. Justina y Roberto
3. todos ustedes
4. ella
5. todos nosotros
6. mi profesor

LEER • ESCRIBIR

4 Completa con la forma apropiada del verbo.

1. Yo quiero que tú le _____ y ellos quieren que nosotros le _____. (hablar)
2. Yo quiero que él _____ el postre y él quiere que yo lo _____. (comer)
3. Ellos quieren que yo _____ el paquete y yo quiero que ellos lo _____. (abrir)
4. Tú quieres que yo lo _____ y yo quiero que tú lo _____. (hacer)
5. Ellos quieren que nosotros _____ la mesa y nosotros queremos que ellos la _____. (poner)
6. Él quiere que yo lo _____ pero no quiere que tú lo _____. (saber)
7. Ellos quieren que tú _____ pero no quieren que yo _____. (ir)
8. Yo quiero que ustedes se lo _____ y ellos quieren que nosotros se lo _____. (dar)

InfoGap For more practice with the subjunctive, do Activity 10 in the Student Resource section at the end of this book.

5 *Comunicación*

Trabajen en grupos y discutan todo lo que tu profesor(a) de español quiere que ustedes hagan.

Lori Ernfridsson

El imperativo formal

CULTURA
En un parque en San Pablo, Ecuador

1. The formal commands **(usted, ustedes),** both affirmative and negative, use the subjunctive form of the verb.

(no) prepare usted	**(no) preparen ustedes**
(no) lea usted	**(no) lean ustedes**
(no) sirva usted	**(no) sirvan ustedes**
(no) haga usted	**(no) hagan ustedes**
(no) salga usted	**(no) salgan ustedes**
(no) conduzca usted	**(no) conduzcan ustedes**
(no) vaya usted	**(no) vayan ustedes**
(no) sea usted	**(no) sean ustedes**

2. You have already learned that object pronouns can be attached to an infinitive or gerund or come before the helping verb. In the case of commands, the object pronouns must be added to the affirmative command, as you already know from the **tú** commands. They must come before the negative command.

AFFIRMATIVE
Háblele.
Démelo.
Levántense.

NEGATIVE
No le hable usted.
No me lo dé usted.
No se levanten ustedes.

Práctica

ESCUCHAR • HABLAR • ESCRIBIR

6 Contesta según el modelo.

MODELO —¿**Preparo la comida?**
—**Sí, prepare usted la comida.**

1. ¿Preparo el postre?
2. ¿Aso la carne?
3. ¿Pelo los tomates?
4. ¿Pico el ajo?
5. ¿Frío el pollo?
6. ¿Pongo la mesa?
7. ¿Hago la ensalada?
8. ¿Pongo la cacerola al fuego?

PROJECT BOARD WITH TABS
See the Foldables section of the Student Handbook at the beginning of the book for help with making this foldable. Think of the food words you know in Spanish and use them to create a recipe of your own. Draw a small picture of each ingredient on the front of each tab in the order you will use it. Next, lift each tab and write instructions about how to prepare your recipe using formal commands.

(t)Andrew Payti, (b)Kelli Drummer-Avendaño

Esta señora cocina en una calle de Oaxaca, México. Como se ve, tiene un negocio próspero. Muchos clientes quieren saborear sus comidas.

ESCUCHAR • HABLAR • ESCRIBIR

7 Contesta según el modelo.

MODELO —¿Preparamos la comida?
—No, no preparen ustedes la comida. Yo la voy a preparar.

1. ¿Preparamos el postre?
2. ¿Lavamos la lechuga?
3. ¿Pelamos las papas?
4. ¿Cortamos el pepino?
5. ¿Hacemos la ensalada?
6. ¿Ponemos la mesa?

ESCUCHAR • HABLAR • ESCRIBIR

8 Contesta según el modelo.

MODELO —¿Quiere usted que yo ase la chuleta?
—No, no la ase usted. Fríala.

1. ¿Quiere usted que yo ase el pollo?
2. ¿Quiere usted que yo ase las papas?
3. ¿Quiere usted que yo ase las chuletas de cordero?
4. ¿Quiere usted que yo ase los pimientos?
5. ¿Quiere usted que yo ase el pescado?
6. ¿Quiere usted que yo ase los camarones?

ESCUCHAR • HABLAR • ESCRIBIR

9 Sigue el modelo.

MODELO Páseme la sal, por favor. →
Pásemela, por favor.

1. Páseme la pimienta, por favor.
2. Páseme el pan, por favor.
3. Páseme la ensalada, por favor.
4. Páseme los platos, por favor.
5. Páseme el tenedor, por favor.
6. Páseme las zanahorias, por favor.

¿Te acuerdas?

Remember other polite ways you learned to express a command.

Favor de pasarme la sal.

¿Me pasaría usted la sal, por favor?

LEER • ESCRIBIR

10 Completa la tabla.

sí	no
Démelo.	
	No me lo diga usted.
Cocínelo a fuego lento.	
	No la revuelva usted.
Léamela.	

Andrew Payti

El imperativo familiar— formas negativas

Go Online!

connectED.mcgraw-hill.com

1. The negative **tú** or informal command uses the **tú** form of the verb in the subjunctive.

No hables más.	**No salgas.**
No comas más.	**No vayas.**
No sirvas más.	**No conduzcas.**

2. As with the formal commands, object pronouns are added to the affirmative command and come before the negative command.

Háblame.	**No me hables.**
Dímelo.	**No me lo digas.**

Práctica

ESCUCHAR • HABLAR • ESCRIBIR

11 Contesta según el modelo.

MODELO —¿Miro ahora o no?

—**No, no mires ahora.**

1. ¿Hablo ahora o no?
2. ¿Como ahora o no?
3. ¿Subo ahora o no?
4. ¿Sirvo ahora o no?
5. ¿Salgo ahora o no?
6. ¿Voy ahora o no?

LEER • ESCRIBIR

12 Completa la tabla.

sí	no
Ponlo allí.	
Dámelo.	
Dímelo.	
	No me hables.
	No lo hagas.
Llámala.	

13 **Comunicación**

Acabas de recibir un gatito para tu cumpleaños. Como todos los gatitos, es muy curioso. Dale un nombre al gatito y dile que no haga cosas peligrosas y destructivas.

¿Te acuerdas?

You have already learned the familiar **tú** command in the affirmative.

Refrán

Can you guess what the following proverb means?

Espinacas, cómelas a sacas.

¡Bravo!

You have now learned all the new vocabulary and grammar in this chapter. Continue to use and practice all that you know while learning more cultural information. **¡Vamos!**

¿Yo? ¿En la cocina? 🎧 ↻

David H. Brennan

¿Comprendes?

A Contesta según la información en la conversación.

1. ¿A quién le gusta cocinar?
2. ¿Quién es un desastre en la cocina?
3. Algún día, ¿qué quiere ser Jorge?
4. ¿Cuál es el plato que más le gusta preparar?
5. ¿De qué región de España es la paella una especialidad?
6. ¿A Alicia le va a gustar una paella?
7. ¿Son caros los mariscos?

B Identifica a quien describe.

	Jorge	Alicia
1. Le gusta cocinar y sabe cocinar.		
2. No sabe si le gustan los mariscos.		
3. Es un desastre en la cocina.		
4. Come mariscos.		

C **Analizando** Contesta.

1. ¿De qué país es Jorge? ¿Cómo lo sabes?
2. ¿Es Alicia de España?

D **Personalizando** ¿Qué piensas? ¿A ti te gustaría la paella o no? ¿Por qué?

CULTURA

En esta tienda en Valencia, España, se venden utensilios para elaborar una buena paella.

Andrew Payti

COCINA HISPANA

Lectura
CULTURAL

ESTRATEGIA DE LECTURA

Antes de leer

Dale una ojeada a la receta para familiarizarte con los ingredientes y la preparación.

Durante la lectura

Al leer asegúrate que comprendes el orden de cada procedimiento durante la elaboración del plato.

✔ **READING CHECK**

¿Por qué es amarillo el arroz?

CULTURA

Los ingredientes para hacer arroz con pollo

Después de leer

Trata de contar la receta de la manera más detallada posible a un(a) compañero(a) de clase.

LEYENDO INFORMACIÓN DETALLADA A veces cuando lees algo como una receta es necesario prestar atención a muchos detalles. Para hacerlo debes leer o consultar la selección más de una vez siempre concentrándote y prestando mucha atención.

Una receta hispana ↻

Otro plato delicioso y muy apreciado en España y otros países hispanohablantes es el arroz con pollo. Hay muchas variaciones en las recetas para elaborar un buen arroz con pollo pero aquí tiene usted una receta bastante sencilla. Decida si a usted le gustaría comer este plato delicioso.

Antes de leer la receta hay que saber algo más. En el arroz con pollo el arroz es amarillo como el arroz de la paella. El azafrán, de origen árabe, es la hierba que le da el color amarillo al arroz. Pero el azafrán es muy caro y como colorante se puede usar cúrcuma o cártamo que se venden en muchos supermercados.

Arroz con pollo

Ingredientes
- 3 tomates
- 2 cebollas grandes
- 2 pimientos (uno verde y uno rojo)
- 4 dientes[1] de ajo
- 1 pollo en partes
- 3 chorizos[2]
- 1 paquete de guisantes congelados
- 1 frasco de (pimientos) morrones (rojos)
- 1 ½ tazas de arroz
- 3 tazas de consomé de pollo
- unas pizcas[3] de azafrán o bujol
- ¼ (un cuarto de) taza de aceite de oliva
- una pizca de sal y pimienta

Preparación
1. Pique los tomates, pimientos, cebollas y ajo.
2. Corte en rodajas los chorizos.
3. Fría o ase el pollo aparte (se puede preparar el pollo en partes [muslos, media pechuga, piernas] o se puede cortarlo en pedazos deshuesados[4]).

Elaboración
Use una sartén o una olla grande.
1. Fría ligeramente[5] en el aceite los pimientos y las cebollas picadas.
2. Agregue (Añada) a la misma sartén el ajo y los tomates y fría ligeramente a fuego lento unos dos o tres minutos.
3. Agregue el arroz.
4. Revuelva el arroz con los tomates, cebollas, morrones y ajo.
5. Añada el pollo.
6. Agregue la consomé de pollo y llévelo a ebullición[6].
7. Agregue el azafrán o bujol.
8. Ponga sal y pimienta a su gusto.
9. Tape[7] la sartén o la olla y cocine a fuego lento encima de la estufa unos treinta minutos.
10. Al final agregue los guisantes y pimientos morrones.

[1]dientes *cloves*
[2]chorizos *Spanish sausage*
[3]pizcas *pinches*
[4]deshuesados *deboned*

[5]ligeramente *lightly*
[6]a ebullición *to a boil*
[7]Tape *Cover*

(l)Purestock/SuperStock, (r)©Iconotec/Alamy

¿Comprendes?

A **Buscando palabras específicas** ¿Cuál es la palabra? Completa según la receta.

1. una _____ para hacer (elaborar) arroz con pollo
2. un _____ de guisantes congelados
3. cuatro _____ de ajo
4. una _____ de sal
5. tres _____ de consomé de pollo

B **Recordando detalles importantes** Lee la receta una vez más. Luego, sin consultar la receta, escribe una lista de todos los ingredientes necesarios. Luego consulta la receta para verificar si has omitido algo.

C **Confirmando información** Verifica. ¿Sí o no?

	sí	no
1. Se puede cocinar el arroz con pollo encima de la estufa.		
2. El arroz con pollo lleva muchas papas.		
3. Hay muchos mariscos en un arroz con pollo.		
4. El arroz se pone amarillo.		
5. El chorizo es un tipo de salchicha española.		

Comparaciones

La historia y la geografía influyen la comida de una región. La geografía dicta los productos que pueden crecer en un lugar y la historia indica lo que a los antiguos habitantes les gustaba comer. Investiga estas influencias en varios países latinos y discute el impacto que tienen ahora en nuestra propia cultura.

A veces no podemos comer todo lo que está en nuestro plato. Lo que no comemos y dejamos en el plato son «las sobras». Piensa en alguna receta familiar que se prepara con sobras.

Una receta para «la ropa vieja» ↺

Aquí tienes otra receta para un plato que es popular en muchas partes de Latinoamérica—sobre todo en Cuba. Se llama «ropa vieja»—un nombre divertido, ¿no? Se llama «ropa vieja» porque se puede elaborar con muchas sobras. Este plato tan conocido se originó en las islas Canarias.

Ropa vieja

Ingredientes

½ kg de carne (de ternera, bife) picada
1 cebolla
1 pimiento verde y un pimiento rojo
3 dientes de ajo
1 cucharadita de orégano
una pizca de pimienta
½ taza de tomate cocido (o enlatado)
3 cucharadas de aceite de oliva
½ taza de caldo (consomé de pollo)

Preparación o cocción

Corte los pimientos, las cebollas y los ajos en trocitos. Fría los pimientos, las cebollas y los ajos en el aceite de oliva con una pizca de pimienta y el orégano. Añada la carne picada y revuelva todos los ingredientes (unos dos minutos). Añada el caldo y cueza (cocine) a fuego medio hasta que se evapore el caldo. Sirva con arroz blanco.

Emily Lowry

¿Comprendes?

Escoge o completa.

1. La ropa vieja viene de _____.
   a. Latinoamérica
   b. Cuba
   c. las islas Canarias

2. Se llama «ropa vieja» porque se puede elaborar (hacer) con _____.
   a. ropa
   b. comida que queda
   c. ingredientes divertidos

3. _____ es una cantidad muy pequeña.

4. Hay que _____ los pimientos verdes y rojos, la cebolla y los dientes de ajo en trocitos.
   a. cortar
   b. picar
   c. freír

5. Dos especias que lleva el plato son _____ y _____.

6. Cueza los ingredientes hasta que se evapore _____.
   a. el aceite
   b. el tomate
   c. el caldo

7. La ropa vieja se sirve acompañada de _____.
   a. caldo
   b. azafrán
   c. arroz blanco

8. Un amigo vegetariano comerá la ropa vieja si no pones _____.

COCINA HISPANA

trescientos quince **315**

Prepárate para el examen

↺ To review, see **Vocabulario.**

1 **Parea.**

1. hervir
2. freír
3. revolver
4. pelar
5. cortar en rebanadas
6. añadir

a. la salsa
b. el pan
c. las zanahorias
d. el agua
e. sal y pimienta
f. el pollo

2 **Identifica.**

7.

8.

9.

10.

11.

12.

Gramática

3 **Completa.**

13–14. Él quiere que yo _____ y yo quiero que él _____. (hablar)

15–16. Tú quieres que nosotros lo _____ y nosotros queremos que tú lo _____. (leer)

17–18. Yo quiero que tú lo _____ y tú quieres que yo lo _____. (escribir)

19–20. Tú quieres que yo lo _____ y él quiere que tú lo _____. (hacer)

21–22. Nosotros queremos que ellos _____ y ellos quieren que nosotros _____. (ir)

To review, see **El subjuntivo.**

4 **Completa con el imperativo formal.**

23. _____ usted la comida. (preparar)

24. _____ usted la receta. (leer)

25. _____ usted la lata. (abrir)

26. _____ usted ahora. (salir)

27. Y _____ usted mañana. (regresar)

28. No me lo _____ usted. (decir)

29. No _____ usted más. (añadir)

To review, see **El imperativo formal.**

5 **Escribe con el pronombre.**

30. Prepare usted *la ensalada*.

31. No prepare usted *el postre*.

32. Deme *las direcciones*.

6 **Escribe en la forma negativa.**

33. Luis, habla.

34. Jacinta, come más.

35. Carlos, levántate.

36. Teresa, ven.

To review, see **El imperativo familiar—formas negativas.**

Cultura

7 **Contesta.**

37–40. ¿Cuáles son algunos ingredientes que lleva el arroz con pollo?

To review this cultural information, see the **Lectura cultural.**

Prepárate para el examen

❶ Yo en la cocina

Talk about cooking

Habla con un(a) compañero(a) de clase. Dile si te gusta cocinar o no. Explícale por qué. Luego verifica si tu compañero(a) tiene las mismas opiniones que tú.

❷ Comidas étnicas

Discuss and describe a restaurant and the food it serves

¿Hay restaurantes étnicos, restaurantes que sirven comida de otras partes del mundo, en tu comunidad? Si hay, con un(a) compañero(a) preparen una lista de estos restaurantes y el tipo de comida que sirven. Luego describan un plato típico de uno de los restaurantes que les gusta.

❸ ¡Qué comida más deliciosa!

Describe a delicious meal

Estás viajando por México. Anoche fuiste a cenar en un restaurante y pediste algo que resultó delicioso, muy rico. Te gustó mucho. Llama a tus padres y descríbeles el restaurante y el plato que te gustó tanto. Si puedes, explícales como crees que el cocinero preparó el plato.

❹ Simón dice...

Give and receive commands

Trabajen en grupos de cinco. Van a jugar «Simón dice». Cada líder dará cinco órdenes a todos los miembros del grupo y luego escogerá a otro líder.

❺ Mis padres

Discuss what your parents want you to do

Tus padres quieren que hagas muchas cosas, ¿no? Dile a un(a) compañero(a) todo lo que quieren tus padres que hagas. Tu compañero(a) te dirá si sus padres quieren que él o ella haga las mismas cosas. Luego discutan como se sienten cuando sus padres quieren que ustedes hagan algo que no quieren hacer.

CULTURA

La gente está sentada en la terraza de un café en Puebla, México.

Tarea

Your teacher wants to know the recipe for the warm quesadillas and chilled fresh tomato salsa that you brought to the last Spanish Club meeting. Use the ingredients listed below or research other recipes for quesadillas and salsa to give your teacher instructions on how to make this delicious, easy-to-prepare Mexican snack.

Quesadillas	**Salsa de tomate**
unas tortillas de harina	tomates
queso triturado	pimientos verdes
(shredded cheese)	cebolla
aceite de oliva	chiles jalapeños
	ajo
	cilantro
	jugo de lima

Writing Strategy

Giving Instructions When giving instructions, it is important to present the details accurately, clearly, and in logical order. This is especially true when writing a recipe because directions that are incorrect, unclear, or out of order could cause the dish to taste bad or be ruined altogether.

❶ Prewrite

Make a list of the steps for completing the recipe and put them in chronological order. Also think about what utensils and/or appliances will be used, and remember that timing and presentation are very important. What should be prepared first? What should be prepared last? How will the dish be served?

❷ Write

• Use formal commands since this is a recipe for your teacher.

• Make sure all of the steps follow a logical order.

• Use transition words to help you present your information in an organized way.

• Remember to stick to vocabulary you already know and don't attempt to translate from English to Spanish.

Evaluate

Your teacher will evaluate you on accurate and logical presentation of details, correct use of vocabulary and grammar, and completeness of information.

Getty Images/Blend Images

Gramática

El subjuntivo

The subjunctive expresses that which is not necessarily factual or real. It expresses things that might happen.

El profesor quiere que los alumnos lean el libro.

Review the following forms of the present subjunctive.

hablar	beber	escribir	poner
hable	beba	escriba	ponga
hables	bebas	escribas	pongas
hable	beba	escriba	ponga
hablemos	bebamos	escribamos	pongamos
habléis	*bebáis*	*escribáis*	*pongáis*
hablen	beban	escriban	pongan

Review the following irregular verbs in the present subjunctive.

dar	estar	ir	saber	ser
dé	esté	vaya	sepa	sea
des	estés	vayas	sepas	seas
dé	esté	vaya	sepa	sea
demos	estemos	vayamos	sepamos	seamos
deis	*estéis*	*vayáis*	*sepáis*	*seáis*
den	estén	vayan	sepan	sean

El imperativo

The affirmative and negative formal commands and the negative familiar commands use the subjunctive form of the verb.

(no) mire usted	(no) miren ustedes	no mires
(no) coma usted	(no) coman ustedes	no comas
(no) asista usted	(no) asistan ustedes	no asistas
(no) salga usted	(no) salgan ustedes	no salgas
(no) vaya usted	(no) vayan ustedes	no vayas

Object pronouns are attached to affirmative commands but must come before negative commands. Review the following sentences.

Mírelo.	**No lo mire usted.**	**No lo mires.**
Démelas.	**No me las dé usted.**	**No me las des.**
Levántenlas.	**No las levanten ustedes.**	**No las levantes.**

¿Te acuerdas?

You learned the affirmative **tú** command in the previous chapter.

Juego There are a number of cognates in this list. See how many you and a partner can find. Who can find the most? Compare your list with those of your classmates.

Vocabulario

Talking about some kitchen appliances and utensils

la cocina	el horno	la olla, la cacerola
el refrigerador, la nevera	el horno de microondas	la tapa
el congelador	el lavaplatos	la cazuela
la estufa, la cocina	el/la sartén	la parrilla

Talking about food preparation

la receta	cortar	quemarse
el/la cocinero(a)	en pedacitos	hervir
el sabor	en rebanadas	freír
pelar	añadir	asar
picar	poner al fuego	revolver
	cocinar, cocer a fuego lento	

Identifying more foods

la chuleta de cerdo	la pechuga de pollo	el aguacate
el escalope de ternera	la cebolla	el ajo
el muslo de pollo	la zanahoria	el condimento
las alitas de pollo	el pepino	
	el pimiento	

Andrew Payti

COCINA HISPANA

Repaso cumulativo

These activities will help you review and remember what you have learned so far in Spanish.

1 Escucha las frases. Indica en una tabla como la de abajo si la información en cada frase es correcta o no.

sí	no

2 Identifica.

1. todas las legumbres que ya conoces en español
2. todas las carnes que ya conoces en español
3. todo lo que necesitas para poner la mesa
4. la diferencia entre un desayuno continental y un desayuno americano

3 Completa con el presente.

1. Yo _____ bife y Anita _____ pescado y nosotros dos _____ flan. (pedir)
2. Nosotros no nos _____. El mesero nos _____. (servir)
3. Yo _____ esto y él _____ el otro. Nosotros nunca _____ la misma cosa. (preferir)

4 Describe las siguientes fiestas.

1. el Día de los Muertos
2. el Día de los Reyes
3. el Cuatro de Julio en Estados Unidos

5 Completa con el imperativo.

1. José, _____ más. (comer)
2. Rosario, _____ el correo electrónico. (leer)
3. Manuel, _____ tu regalo. (abrir)
4. Adela, _____ acá. (venir)
5. Alberto, _____ pronto. (volver)
6. Federico, _____ la mesa. (poner)
7. Magda, _____ la verdad. (decir)
8. Gabriel, _____ la comida. (servir)

CULTURA 🇺🇸

Una barbacoa para celebrar el Cuatro de Julio en Estados Unidos

6 **Categoriza según el deporte.**

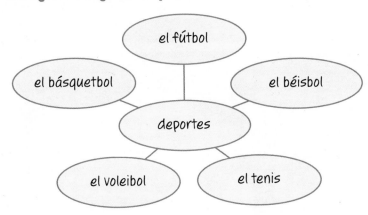

el fútbol

el básquetbol

el béisbol

deportes

el voleibol

el tenis

1. Un jugador lanza el balón y quiere que entre en la portería.
2. El portero no pudo bloquear el balón y el balón entró en la portería.
3. Un jugador corre de una base a otra.
4. Para marcar un tanto hay que meter el balón en el cesto.
5. El jugador corre y dribla con el balón.
6. La jugadora atrapa la pelota con el guante.
7. El balón o la pelota tiene que pasar por encima de la red.
8. Podemos jugar dobles o individuales.
9. Los jugadores juegan con un balón.
10. Los jugadores juegan con una pelota.

7 **Usa las siguientes palabras en frases originales.**

el campo   **la cancha**   **el balón**

la pelota   **el segundo tiempo**

el tanto   **devolver**   **marcar**

lanzar

8 **Prepara una lista de lo que tienes que comprar para preparar un plato favorito. Da las cantidades también.**

CULTURA

Un mercado en Tepoztlán, México

Andrew Payti

Go Online!

connectED.mcgraw-hill.com

Audio Video Práctica Repaso Diversiones eScape

ePals

Vamos a comparar Hoy en día todos quieren cuidarse y mantenerse en forma. No importa que sea aquí en Estados Unidos o en España o Latinoamérica—todos van a un parque o gimnasio para hacer ejercicio. Pero, a veces, ¿qué tenemos? ¡Un accidente pequeño!

Objetivos

You will:

- identify more parts of the body
- talk about exercise
- talk about having a minor accident and a trip to the emergency room
- discuss physical fitness

You will use:

- the subjunctive with impersonal expressions
- **ojalá, quizás, tal vez**
- the subjunctive of stem-changing verbs
- the comparison of like things

◄ Todos sabemos que es necesario que nos mantengamos en forma. Estos jóvenes lo saben también y aquí los vemos haciendo jogging en Santa Cruz de Tenerife. El jogging es un ejercicio bueno.

¡Cuídate bien!

Mira estas fotos para familiarizarte con el tema de este capítulo—cuídate bien. ¿Qué haces para cuidarte? ¿Hay algunas actividades que ves aquí que tú también practicas o que te gustan? Y, ¿puedes simpatizar con la joven argentina que ha tenido un accidente?

España 🏴

Estos corredores están participando en un maratón en Santa Cruz de Tenerife. En un maratón hay participantes de todas las edades—los mayores y los menores.

Argentina 🏴

Mucha gente toma agua mineral porque la consideran buena para la salud.

Chile 🏴

El joven anda en bici por las montañas. Nota que él también lleva casco. La seguridad siempre es importante, ¿no?

Venezuela 🏴

Estos andinistas pasan un día agradable haciendo una caminata por las montañas en la región de Mérida, Venezuela.

España 🇪🇸

Este joven está divirtiéndose andando en monopatín en una calle cerca de las famosas Ramblas de Barcelona.

México

Un hospital privado en Oaxaca, México

Guatemala

Una ambulancia en Antigua, Guatemala

Argentina

Siempre es necesario tener cuidado cuando haces ejercicio para evitar tener un accidente como tuvo esta joven en Trelew, Argentina. Acaba de salir de un centro médico y tiene que andar con muletas. ¡Ojalá que se mejore pronto!

CORRÉ HASTA QUEDAR CON LA LENGÜETA AFUERA.

CORRÉ CON NOSOTROS EL 10K EL 11 DE NOVIEMBRE

Argentina

Aquí hay un anuncio en Buenos Aires. ¿Cuál es el significado del juego de palabras? Para ayudarte en la solución te damos una pista: la lengua está en la boca y la lengüeta está en el zapato.

327

Más partes del cuerpo 🎧

la frente
el cuello
el pecho
el hombro
la muñeca
el dedo del pie
el tobillo

Los amigos están practicando yoga.
Hacen ejercicios de respiración.
Hacen movimientos lentos.
Liberan su espíritu de tensiones.

En el gimnasio

estirar los brazos
hacer planchas
levantar pesas

La muchacha está haciendo ejercicio.
El señor anda en bicicleta.
El muchacho levanta pesas.
Es necesario que él tenga cuidado.
Es importante que todos hagamos ejercicio.

(tl b)David H. Brennan, (tr)GoGo Images/age fotostock

el casco

las rodilleras

el monopatín

un buzo

descansar

hacer jogging

Las jóvenes están patinando en línea.
Es importante que lleven casco y rodilleras.

Los corredores participan en un maratón.

Están corriendo una carrera de relevos.
Cada corredora corre una vuelta.

Es una carrera a campo traviesa.
Una carrera a campo traviesa es de larga distancia.

(tl)Doug Menuez/Getty Images, (tc)Pixtal/age fotostock, (tr)David H. Brennan, (c)Andrew Payti

ESCUCHAR

1 Escucha las frases. Parea cada frase con la foto que describe.

a.   b.   c.

HABLAR

2 Personaliza. Da respuestas personales.

1. ¿Haces mucho ejercicio?
2. ¿Haces ejercicios aeróbicos o abdominales?
3. ¿Estiras los brazos y las piernas?
4. ¿Levantas pesas?
5. ¿Andas en bicicleta?
6. ¿Haces jogging?
7. ¿Participas en carreras?
8. ¿Corres vueltas?
9. ¿Practicas yoga?
10. ¿Has participado en un maratón?

LEER • ESCRIBIR

3 Completa con una palabra apropiada.

1. Uno se pone _____ cuando va al gimnasio o cuando hace jogging.
2. Es importante ponerse _____ para proteger el cráneo al andar en bicicleta.
3. Es importante llevar _____ al patinar en línea.
4. ¿Cuántas _____ puedes correr sin descansar?
5. El yoga ayuda a liberar el espíritu de _____.
6. Muchas ciudades y organizaciones tienen _____ que son carreras de muy larga distancia.
7. Dos tipos de carreras son _____ y _____.

LEER • ESCRIBIR

4 Pon las siguientes partes del cuerpo en orden desde la parte más alta del cuerpo hasta la más baja.

el pecho   la mano   el dedo del pie

la frente   el hombro

el tobillo   el cuello   la rodilla

HABLAR

5 Dramatiza. Trabajen en grupos. Escojan a un líder. El líder va a dramatizar un ejercicio o un deporte. Los otros miembros del grupo adivinarán la actividad. Cambien de líder.

HABLAR • ESCRIBIR

6 Usa las siguientes expresiones en frases originales.

hacer ejercicio	patinar en línea	hacer jogging
practicar yoga	correr vueltas	hacer planchas

CULTURA

Equipo para hacer ejercicio en un gimnasio en un hotel en Montelimar, Nicaragua

ESCRIBIR

7 Completa con lo que falta.

1. el cue_o
2. las rodi_eras
3. el tobi_o
4. el _imnasio
5. los _óvenes
6. un bu_o
7. el bra_o

8 *Comunicación*

Trabajen en grupos y discutan las actividades que practican en su clase de educación física. Indiquen las actividades que les gustan y que no les gustan. Expliquen por qué.

Andrew Payti

Unos accidentes

una herida

Pilar se cortó el dedo.
Tiene una herida.
Pero no es seria. No se ha hecho mucho daño.

José corría y se torció el tobillo.
El tobillo está hinchado.
Le duele mucho.

El joven se cayó.
¿Se rompió (Se quebró) la pierna?

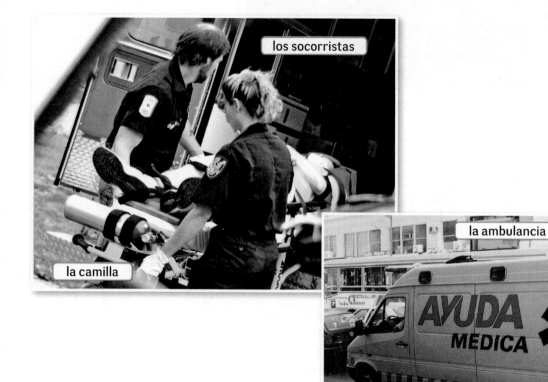

los socorristas

la camilla

la ambulancia

AYUDA MEDICA

(t)David H. Brennan, (c)VStock/Alamy, (b)Andrew Payti

En la sala de emergencia

una radiografía

una silla de ruedas

Le toman (hacen) una radiografía.

Nota

In addition to **hacerse daño**, you will hear **lastimarse**. Another term for **radiografía** is **rayos equis**.

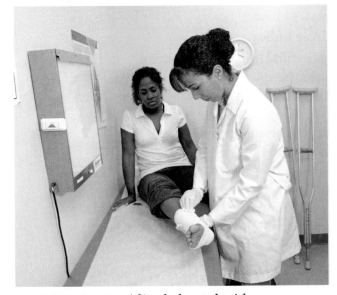

La cirujana ortopédica le ha reducido (acomodado) el hueso.
Le ha puesto la pierna en un yeso.
Paula tendrá que andar con muletas.

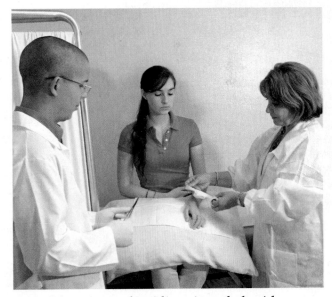

Es necesario que el médico cierre la herida.
El médico pone unos puntos (unas suturas).
La enfermera le va a poner una venda.

(inset)Ingram Publishing, (others)David H. Brennan

¡CUÍDATE BIEN!

ESCUCHAR

1 Escucha cada frase y decide si la información es correcta o no. Usa una tabla como la de abajo para indicar tus respuestas.

correcta	incorrecta

HABLAR • ESCRIBIR

2 Contesta sobre un accidente que tuvo Mariana.

1. Mariana ha tenido un accidente. ¿Se cayó ella?
2. ¿Se torció el tobillo?
3. ¿Le duele mucho el tobillo?
4. ¿Está hinchado el tobillo?
5. ¿Le duele mucho cuando anda a pie?
6. ¿Tendrá que andar con muletas?
7. ¿Se ha hecho mucho daño o no?

EXPANSIÓN

Ahora, sin mirar las preguntas, cuenta la información en tus propias palabras. Si no recuerdas algo, un(a) compañero(a) te puede ayudar.

ESCUCHAR • HABLAR • ESCRIBIR

3 Contesta según se indica.

1. ¿Qué tuvo Tomás? (un accidente serio)
2. ¿Qué le pasó? (se quebró la pierna)
3. ¿Qué le causó la pierna quebrada? (mucho dolor)
4. ¿Adónde fue? (a la sala de emergencia)
5. ¿Cómo fue? (en ambulancia)
6. ¿Quiénes lo ayudaron? (los socorristas)
7. ¿En qué lo pusieron? (una camilla)
8. ¿Qué le tomaron en el hospital? (radiografías)
9. ¿A qué médico llamaron? (al cirujano ortopédico)
10. Al salir del hospital, ¿qué necesitará Tomás? (una silla de ruedas)

EXPANSIÓN

Ahora, sin mirar las preguntas, cuenta la información en tus propias palabras. Si no recuerdas algo, un(a) compañero(a) te puede ayudar.

CULTURA

Un hospital grande y moderno en Barcelona, España

Andrew Payti

4 Trabajen en grupos. Describan unas actividades que tienen lugar en esta sala de emergencia.

ESCRIBIR

5 Completa con lo que falta.

1. una _erida
2. un tobi_o _inchado
3. el _ospital
4. la cami_a y la si_a de ruedas
5. se ca_ó
6. el _eso
7. el _ueso
8. una _enda

ESCRIBIR

6 Rompecabezas

Pon las palabras en orden para formar frases. Luego, pon las frases en orden para crear una historia.

1. dijo no que le la necesitaba enfermera suturas
2. corrió la de cerca bicicleta perro muy un
3. calle la andaba por en Catalina bicicleta
4. de sala fue la a emergencia
5. rodilla enfermera venda la le en la puso una
6. ella perro a le cayó el se sorprendió y Catalina
7. rodilla cayó cortó se se la cuando

InfoGap For more practice with your new vocabulary, do Activity 11 in the Student Resource section at the end of this book.

El subjuntivo con expresiones impersonales

The subjunctive is used after each of the following impersonal expressions because it is not known if the information in the clause that follows will actually take place. It may or may not.

es importante	**es fácil**
es necesario	**es difícil**
es imposible	**es bueno**
es posible	**es probable**
es mejor	**es improbable**

Es probable que él esté bien.
Pero es necesario que vea al médico.
Es importante que sepa lo que tiene.

Práctica

ESCUCHAR • HABLAR • ESCRIBIR

1 Sigue el modelo.

MODELO **Tú haces ejercicio. →**
Es necesario que tú hagas ejercicio.

1. Hablas con el entrenador.
2. Vas al gimnasio.
3. Haces jogging.
4. Corres por lo menos cinco vueltas.
5. Participas en el maratón.

HABLAR • ESCRIBIR

2 Prepara una lista de cosas que es probable que tú hagas con frecuencia porque es fácil hacerlas. Prepara otra lista que indica lo que es difícil que tú hagas. Luego compara tus listas con las listas que ha preparado un(a) compañero(a).

LEER • ESCRIBIR

3 Sigue el modelo.

MODELO **es necesario / saber la receta →**
Es necesario que el cocinero sepa la receta.

1. es importante / lavar las ollas
2. es fácil / pelar las papas
3. es probable / freír el pescado
4. es mejor / asar el cordero
5. es posible / servir la comida

CULTURA

Papi corre en un maratón con sus dos niños en Tenerife en las islas Canarias. Es posible que ganen, ¿no?

CULTURA

¿Es posible que el cocinero esté aprendiendo a cocinar algo en esta escuela culinaria en España?

(t)Andrew Payti, (b)Javier Larrea/age fotostock

HABLAR

4 Contesta.

1. ¿Es importante que los jóvenes de Estados Unidos estudien una lengua?
2. ¿Es necesario que ellos sepan hablar otra lengua?
3. ¿Es bueno que ellos hablen otra lengua?
4. ¿Es necesario que ellos conozcan otra cultura?
5. ¿Es posible que algún día ellos tengan la oportunidad de visitar otros países?
6. ¿Es probable que ellos vayan a otros países?

EXPANSIÓN

Ahora, sin mirar las preguntas, cuenta la información en tus propias palabras. Si no recuerdas algo, un(a) compañero(a) te puede ayudar.

LEER • ESCRIBIR

5 Completa.

Abuelito está un poco nervioso. Es posible que sus nietos __1__ (llegar) mañana por la mañana. Es importante que Abuelito __2__ (saber) cuándo van a llegar. Pero es difícil que Abuelita le __3__ (decir) la hora precisa de la llegada de los nietos. Es posible que mañana __4__ (hacer) mal tiempo. Como los nietos vienen en carro será necesario que __5__ (conducir) despacio y con mucho cuidado si hay nieve. Es mejor que ellos __6__ (llegar) un poco tarde. Abuelito no quiere que ellos __7__ (tener) un accidente. Es mejor que __8__ (llegar) tarde pero sanos y salvos.

6 *Comunicación*

Trabaja con un(a) compañero(a) de clase. Dile cosas que haces. Tu compañero(a) te dará su opinión sobre las cosas que haces usando las siguientes expresiones: **es importante, es bueno, es necesario, es mejor.**

FOLDABLES Study Organizer

TAB BOOK See the Foldables section of the Student Handbook at the beginning of this book for help with making this foldable. Use this study organizer to help you practice the subjunctive. On the top of each tab, write an expression that requires the subjunctive, for example, **Es imposible que...** Then open each tab and write a sentence using that expression with the subjunctive.

¡Ojalá! ¡Quizás! ¡Tal vez!

The expression **¡Ojalá!** or **¡Ojalá que!** comes from Arabic and it means *Would that* . . . Since the information that follows **ojalá** may or may not happen, it is followed by the subjunctive. The expressions **¡Quizás!** and **¡Tal vez!** mean *perhaps* or *maybe* and can also be followed by the subjunctive.

> **¡Ojalá que vengan!**
> **¡Quizás lleguen mañana!**
> **¡Tal vez estén aquí!**

Práctica

ESCUCHAR • HABLAR

7 Contesta con **quizás** según el modelo.

MODELO   **¿Carla lo va a saber?** →
            ¡Quizás lo sepa!

1. ¿Carla va a estar aquí?
2. ¿Va a ir al parque?
3. ¿Va a participar en la carrera?
4. ¿Va a salir primero?
5. ¿Va a romper un récord?
6. ¿Va a ganar un trofeo?

LEER • ESCRIBIR

8 Sigue el modelo.

MODELO   **tener cuidado** →
            ¡Ojalá que tengan cuidado!

1. prestar atención
2. no tomar una decisión ridícula
3. ponerse el casco
4. llevar rodilleras
5. no tener ningún accidente
6. no ir al hospital

9   **Comunicación**

Trabaja con un(a) compañero(a). Los dos van a hablar de eventos que quieren que ocurran durante su vida. Introduzcan sus ideas con **¡ojalá!**

CULTURA

¡Quizás te guste comer una golosina! ¿Qué color o sabor prefieres?

Andrew Payti

El subjuntivo de los verbos de cambio radical

Go Online!

connectED.mcgraw-hill.com

1. Verbs that have a stem change in the present indicative also have a stem change in the present subjunctive.

E → IE			
cerrar			
yo	**cierre**	**nosotros(as)**	**cerremos**
tú	**cierres**	*vosotros(as)*	*cerréis*
Ud., él, ella	**cierre**	**Uds., ellos, ellas**	**cierren**

O → UE			
encontrar			
yo	**encuentre**	**nosotros(as)**	**encontremos**
tú	**encuentres**	*vosotros(as)*	*encontréis*
Ud., él, ella	**encuentre**	**Uds., ellos, ellas**	**encuentren**

2. The verbs **preferir (e → ie)**, **dormir (o → ue)**, and **pedir (e → i)** have a stem change in every person of the present subjunctive.

	E → IE, I	O → UE, U	E → I
	preferir	**dormir**	**pedir**
yo	**prefiera**	**duerma**	**pida**
tú	**prefieras**	**duermas**	**pidas**
Ud., él, ella	**prefiera**	**duerma**	**pida**
nosotros(as)	**prefiramos**	**durmamos**	**pidamos**
vosotros(as)	*prefiráis*	*durmáis*	*pidáis*
Uds., ellos, ellas	**prefieran**	**duerman**	**pidan**

Nota

- Other verbs with the **e → ie** stem change like **cerrar** are: **perder, sentarse, comenzar, empezar, pensar.**
- Other **o → ue** verbs like **encontrar** are: **acostarse, recordar, poder, volver.**
- **Sentir** is conjugated like **preferir.**
- Other verbs with the **e → i** stem change like **pedir** are: **repetir, freír, seguir, servir.**

HABLAR • ESCRIBIR

10 Contesta.

1. ¿Dónde quieres que yo me siente?
2. ¿Es importante que yo no pierda el juego?
3. ¿Quieres que yo vuelva temprano?
4. ¿Es posible que yo duerma aquí?
5. ¿Es necesario que yo se lo repita?

Según los jóvenes, es importante que todos sigamos una dieta sana.

Olive/age fotostock

Práctica

LEER • ESCRIBIR

11 Sigue el modelo.

 MODELO **Quiere que tú lo cierres. →**
Quiere que nosotros lo cerremos.

1. Quiere que te sientes aquí.
2. Quiere que tú pierdas.
3. Quiere que tú lo encuentres.
4. Quiere que tú vuelvas pronto.
5. Quiere que duermas aquí.
6. Quiere que lo pidas.
7. Quiere que lo sigas.
8. Quiere que tú no lo repitas.

HABLAR • LEER • ESCRIBIR

12 Cambia el segundo verbo al verbo indicado.

1. Yo quiero que ellos lo cierren. (empezar, perder, encontrar, recordar, devolver, preferir, pedir, repetir)
2. Es posible que yo lo encuentre. (cerrar, perder, recordar, devolver, servir, pedir, repetir)
3. Es necesario que nosotros volvamos. (comenzar, sentarnos, recordar, dormir, seguir)

Comparación de igualdad

1. In Spanish you use **tanto... como** to compare quantities. Because **tanto** is an adjective, it has to agree with the noun it modifies.

   Elena tiene tanta energía como yo.
   Pero ella no tiene tantos accidentes como yo.

2. In Spanish you use **tan... como** to compare qualities with either an adjective or adverb.

   Él está tan enfermo como su amiga.
   Él se va a curar tan rápido como ella.

3. The subject pronoun always follows the comparison of equality.

   Él es tan bueno como tú.
   Y tiene tanto dinero como yo.

Conexiones

El inglés

To compare equal quantities in English you use:
   as much money as I
   as many problems as I
To compare equal qualities you use:
   as smart as she
   as tall as he

Práctica

HABLAR

13 Personaliza. Da respuestas personales.

1. ¿Eres tan inteligente como tus amigos?
2. ¿Eres tan cómico(a) como tus amigos?
3. ¿Eres tan ambicioso(a) como tus amigos?
4. ¿Eres tan aficionado(a) a los deportes como tus amigos?
5. ¿Tienes tanta paciencia como tus amigos?
6. ¿Tienes tanto éxito como tus amigos?
7. ¿Tienes tanto trabajo como tus amigos?
8. ¿Tienes tantas ambiciones como tus amigos?

LEER • ESCRIBIR

14 Completa con **tan...** o **tanto... como**.

1. Ella corre en _____ carreras _____ yo.
2. Y ella va _____ rápido _____ yo.
3. Él puede levantar _____ pesas _____ yo.
4. Pero él no es _____ fuerte _____ yo.
5. Yo no hago _____ ejercicio _____ tú.
6. Yo no soy _____ aficionado(a) a los ejercicios físicos _____ tú.

CULTURA

Un grupo de gente mayor (de la tercera edad) está jugando voleibol en un gimnasio en Oaxaca, México.

Refrán

Can you guess what the following proverb means?

La mejor almohada es la conciencia sana.

15

Comunicación

Trabaja con un(a) compañero(a). Piensen en algunas personas que ustedes conocen que, en su opinión, tienen mucho en común o que tienen las mismas características físicas. Comparen a estas personas.

¡Bravo!

You have now learned all the new vocabulary and grammar in this chapter. Continue to use and practice all that you know while learning more cultural information. **¡Vamos!**

Andrew Payti

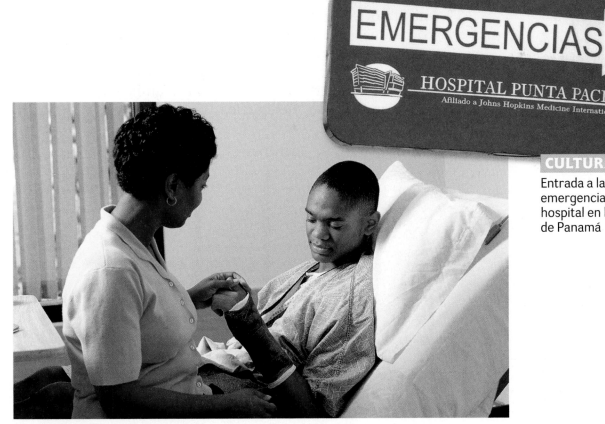
¿Comprendes?

A Contesta según la información en la conversación.

1. ¿Qué hacía Enrique cuando se cayó?
2. ¿Qué le duele?
3. ¿Cómo está el tobillo?
4. ¿Qué crees? ¿Quiere Enrique que Catalina lo lleve a la sala de emergencia? ¿Le gusta la idea?
5. Según Catalina, ¿por qué debe ir Enrique a la sala de emergencia?
6. ¿Es posible que no tenga el tobillo quebrado?

B Resumiendo Cuenta todo lo que pasó en la conversación en tus propias palabras.

C Prediciendo Predice lo que va a pasar a Enrique y Catalina en la sala de emergencia. Prepara una conversación que tiene lugar en el hospital. Debes incluir a otros en la conversación como el médico o el enfermero. ¡Usa tanta imaginación posible!

EMERGENCIAS →

HOSPITAL PUNTA PACIFICA
Afiliado a Johns Hopkins Medicine International

CULTURA
Entrada a la sala de emergencias en un hospital en la Ciudad de Panamá

Es necesario que él se cuide bien.
Es posible que le duela mucho el brazo, ¿no?

(l)Photodisc Collection/Getty Images. (r)Andrew Payti

Lectura

ESTRATEGIA DE LECTURA

▶ Antes de leer

Dale una ojeada a la lectura y busca palabras que consideres desconocidas. No habrá muchas.

☑ READING CHECK

¿Qué hacen todos en el gimnasio?

▶ Durante la lectura

Busca clarificaciones—si hay una palabra que no sabes, tal vez haya un sinónimo en la frase.

☑ READING CHECK

¿Cuál es la ventaja de los parques?

ADIVINANDO Hay dos estrategias que te pueden ayudar a comprender lo que lees en español: reconocer o adivinar el significado de palabras aparentadas con una palabra inglesa y adivinar el significado de una palabra desconocida por medio del contexto en que se usa. Las otras palabras en la frase te pueden ayudar a determinar el significado de la palabra desconocida.

Vida activa y buena salud 🎧 ↺

Hoy en día el interés que tenemos en nuestra salud y forma física es fenomenal. Y este interés existe en España y Latinoamérica igual que en Estados Unidos.

Como es importante que uno haga ejercicio por lo menos tres veces a la semana, hay una gran proliferación de gimnasios. Estos gimnasios tienen muchos socios[1]. En el gimnasio hacen ejercicios aeróbicos y abdominales. Estiran los brazos y las piernas. Hacen planchas. Algunos levantan pesas. ¡Todo para mantenerse en forma!

Además de los gimnasios los parques son inmensamente populares, y para ir a un parque no hay que ser socio o miembro. Un parque es un buen lugar para hacer jogging o correr unas vueltas. A muchos les gusta dar un paseo por el parque en bicicleta. Andar en bicicleta es una forma excelente de ejercicio. Otros se sientan en un lugar aislado del parque donde disfrutan del silencio y de la tranquilidad. Se relajan practicando yoga y meditando.

[1]socios *members*

CULTURA ⬧

El ciclista está haciendo ejercicio en un parque en Viña del Mar, Chile.

Andrew Payti

Muchas ciudades tienen un maratón a lo menos una vez al año. Muchos maratones tienen un propósito benévolo[2] y atraen a muchos participantes. Además atraen a muchos espectadores que animan a los corredores que tienen que correr largas distancias.

Entre los jóvenes el patinaje en línea y el monopatín son muy apreciados. Tienen muchos aficionados. Pero, una advertencia[3]: al practicar estas formas de patinaje hay que tener mucho cuidado porque puedes lastimarte fácilmente. Siempre tienes que llevar casco y rodilleras. Nadie quiere que te hagas daño y que te encuentres en una sala de emergencia.

[2]propósito benévolo *charitable purpose*   [3]advertencia *warning*

 READING CHECK

¿Quiénes animan a los corredores en el maratón?

 READING CHECK

¿Qué hay que tener al practicar el patinaje o el monopatín? ¿Por qué?

Después de leer

Prepara una lista de palabras emparentadas que encontraste en la lectura.

¿Comprendes?

A   Categorizando Completa la tabla según la información en la lectura.

actividades en un gimnasio	actividades en el parque	actividades durante un maratón	actividades populares entre los jóvenes

B   Personalizando   Contesta.
¿En qué actividades de la Actividad A participas? Explica por qué te gustan.

C   Analizando   Contesta.
¿Por qué son populares los gimnasios y los parques?

CULTURA
Los jóvenes están patinando en línea en el Parque Tres de Febrero en Buenos Aires, Argentina.

Andrew Payti

Lectura
UN POCO MÁS

▶ **Antes de leer**

*Piensa en unas organizaciones
benévolas o caritativas donde
vives. ¿Qué tipo de trabajo hacen?
¿Has oído de* Médicos Sin
Fronteras, *una famosa
organización internacional?*

Médicos Sin Fronteras

Hay gente que se cuida bien y también hay gente que cuida de otros como los *Médicos Sin Fronteras.* La organización *Médicos Sin Fronteras* tuvo su origen en Francia en 1971. Un grupo de médicos y periodistas franceses fueron a África con la Cruz Roja donde vieron morir a millones de biafranos[1] por la guerra[2] y de hambre. Su situación era tan desesperada que a su regreso a Francia este grupo de médicos creó una organización pequeña, *Médecins Sans Frontières.* Hoy es una organización internacional independiente con más de dos mil quinientos voluntarios en más de setenta países, incluyendo unos en Latinoamérica. La organización tiene proyectos en zonas de guerra, campos de refugiados y en regiones devastadas por desastres naturales o epidemias como el sida[3].

Entre los voluntarios hay médicos, cirujanos, enfermeros y técnicos. Hay también personas que se responsabilizan por los materiales que necesitan y la administración de los proyectos. Todos reciben muy poco dinero por el trabajo maravilloso que hacen.

En 1999 *Médicos Sin Fronteras* ganó el prestigioso Premio Nobel de la Paz.

[1]biafranos   *people from Biafra*   [3]sida   *AIDS*
[2]guerra   *war*

▶ **Después de leer**

Investiga la organización Médicos
Sin Fronteras. *Escoge uno de los
países hispanohablantes donde hace
la organización proyectos de ayuda
médico-humanitaria. Prepara un
informe sobre el trabajo que hacen
los voluntarios de* Médicos Sin
Fronteras *en aquel país.*

Doctors Without Borders/Médecins Sans Frontières (MSF)

¿Comprendes?

A Escoge.

1. Los *Médicos Sin Fronteras* _____.
   a. se cuidan bien
   b. cuidan de otros
   c. no tienen país
   d. son todos franceses

2. La organización *Médicos Sin Fronteras* tuvo su origen en _____.
   a. Francia
   b. Biafra, África
   c. la Cruz Roja
   d. una situación desesperada

3. ¿Quiénes establecieron la organización?
   a. miembros de la Cruz Roja
   b. un grupo internacional independiente
   c. un grupo de médicos y periodistas franceses
   d. un grupo de voluntarios

4. Los biafranos morían _____.
   a. de un desastre natural
   b. de una epidemia
   c. de malnutrición y guerra
   d. a causa del calor

5. Por lo general, ¿quiénes toman refugio en los campos de refugiados?
   a. las víctimas de guerra
   b. los voluntarios
   c. los enfermos
   d. los soldados

6. Los voluntarios que trabajan con la organización _____.
   a. son todos personal médico
   b. tienen un salario
   c. reciben muy poco dinero
   d. viven de proyectos

B Identifica.
¿Cuál es la idea principal de esta lectura? Da unos detalles que apoyan (*support*) esta idea.

C Analiza.
¿Qué piensas? ¿Por qué quiere compartir el autor esta información con sus lectores? ¿Cuál es su propósito?

EL TRATAMIENTO MÉDICO NO DEBERÍA SER UN LUJO

8.000 personas mueren cada día por no tener acceso a tratamientos que existen. Son enfermos de malaria, tuberculosis, sida pediátrico, Chagas, kala azar y enfermedad del sueño.

www.hazquellegue.org

CULTURA

Aquí tienes un cartel de los *Médicos Sin Fronteras* en Valencia, España. ¿Cuál es el mensaje en el cartel?

Andrew Payti

Prepárate para el examen

↺ To review, see **Vocabulario 1.**

↺ To review, see **Vocabulario 2.**

Vocabulario

1 **Identifica.**

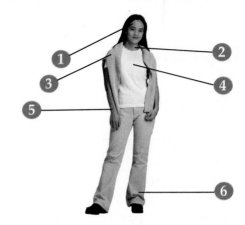

2 **Corrige.**

7. Es importante que uno lleve casco y rodilleras si levanta pesas.

8. A mucha gente le gusta andar en monopatín en el hospital.

9. Un maratón es una carrera de corta distancia.

10. Antes de correr, los corredores estiran los dedos y los pies.

11. Cuando practicas yoga, haces muchas planchas.

3 **Identifica.**

12.

13.

14.

15.

4 **Completa.**

16. El niño se _____ el tobillo y lo tiene muy hinchado.

17. Se _____ la pierna y el cirujano ortopédico la tiene que poner en un yeso.

18. Los socorristas pusieron a la víctima en una camilla y la llevaron al hospital en _____.

19. José necesita ayuda para andar. Anda con _____.

Gramática

5 Completa.

20. Es importante que nosotros _____ ejercicio. (hacer)

21. Es necesario que ellos nos _____. (acompañar)

22. Es posible que ella _____. (estar)

23. Es probable que yo _____. (ir)

24. Es imposible que tú lo _____. (saber)

To review, see **El subjuntivo con expresiones impersonales.**

6 Completa formando una frase.

25. Es necesario que…

26. Es posible que…

27. Es difícil que…

7 Completa.

28. ¡Ojalá _____ su equipo! (ganar)

29. ¡Quizás _____ ellos! (venir)

30. ¡Tal vez _____ (ellos) en el gimnasio! (estar)

31. ¡Ojalá _____ (tú) los resultados mañana! (tener)

To review, see **¡Ojalá! ¡Quizás! ¡Tal vez!**

8 Completa las frases con **nosotros.**

32. Ellos quieren que tú se lo pidas a Javier.

Ellos quieren que nosotros…

33. Ella quiere que yo me siente aquí.

Ella quiere que nosotros…

To review, see **El subjuntivo de los verbos de cambio radical.**

9 Completa con **tan… como** o **tanto… como.**

34. A veces los hospitales en las zonas rurales no son _____ buenos _____ los de las grandes ciudades.

35. Esta clínica es _____ moderna _____ la otra.

36. Ella tiene _____ paciencia _____ yo.

37. Yo hago _____ ejercicio _____ tú.

To review, see **Comparación de igualdad.**

Cultura

10 Contesta.

38. ¿Por qué hay gimnasios que tienen muchos socios?

39. ¿Cuáles son algunas actividades atléticas que practica la gente en un parque?

40. ¿Qué propósito tienen muchos maratones?

To review this cultural information, see the **Lectura cultural.**

Prepárate para el examen

1 **Actividades atléticas**

Discuss which sports you play
Trabajen en grupos de tres o cuatro. Discutan todas las actividades atléticas en que participan ustedes. Determinen si tienen los mismos intereses o no.

EL DEPORTE LE PIDE MINERALES A TU CUERPO.

Villavicencio. Tu vida necesita minerales.

2 **Peligros**

Talk about avoiding danger
Las actividades atléticas pueden ser buenas para la salud pero cuando practicas ciertas actividades hay que tener cuidado de no lastimarte. ¿Cuáles son algunas cosas que debes hacer para evitar (no tener) accidentes?

3 **Un accidente**

Describe an accident you had when you were young
Explica si tú eres propenso(a) a accidentes o si lo eras de niño(a). ¿Has tenido unos accidentes? Descríbelos. Si nunca has tenido un accidente explica como es posible que tengas tanta suerte.

4 **Importante y necesario**

Talk about what is important for you to do and what is necessary for you to do
Completa una tabla como la de abajo y presenta la información a tu clase.

Es importante que yo	Y es necesario que yo
porque	

5 **En la sala de emergencia**

Helping someone out after an accident
Estás en la sala de espera de la sala de emergencia en un hospital. Entran los padres con su hijo que ha tenido un accidente y se ha hecho daño. Los padres están nerviosos y solo hablan español. Ayúdalos.

Andrew Payti

Tarea

You have learned about many sports in Spanish. You have also learned about the parts of the body and physical fitness. Now you are going to write a research paper that discusses the physical benefits of some sports. Use the library and the Internet to find out more about how your body stays fit by doing each sport. Be sure to cite your sources.

Writing Strategy

Researching As you prepare to write your research paper, you will be consulting many sources for information. It is important that your sources be reliable, especially when they are found on the Internet. It is advisable to consult more than one source for any fact you present. If your two sources disagree, consult a third.

CULTURA

El andinista venezolano tiene todo el equipo necesario para escalar montañas.

❶ Prewrite

• Before you begin your research, create a rough outline of your paper. This will help you identify the topics you need to research.

Título
A. El fútbol
1. ¿Cómo se mantiene uno en forma jugando fútbol?
a.
b.
2. ¿Cuáles son algunas desventajas o peligros del fútbol?
a.
b.
B. El jogging
1. ¿Cómo se mantiene uno en forma haciendo jogging?

• As you research, fill the holes in your outline. Make an effort to consult written as well as video resources to practice both your reading and listening skills.

❷ Write

• Use your outline as a guide while you write. It will ensure your information is organized and that nothing is omitted.

• It is very important to cite the sources you used to obtain information. This will add validity to your paper and it will also ensure that you do not plagiarize.

Evaluate

Your teacher will evaluate you on organization of information, correctness of grammar, and proper citation.

Kelli Drummer-Avendaño

Repaso del Capítulo 11

Gramática

El subjuntivo con expresiones impersonales

The subjunctive is used after many impersonal expressions when it is not known if the information that follows will or will not take place.

> **Es importante que tengas cuidado cuando levantas pesas.**
> **Es necesario que la niña lleve casco cuando anda en bicicleta.**
> **Es probable que ellos lleguen a tiempo.**

¡Ojalá! ¡Quizás! ¡Tal vez!

The expressions **¡Ojalá!**, **¡Quizás!**, and **¡Tal vez!** are also followed by the subjunctive. Review the following sentences.

> **¡Ojalá no te hagas daño!**
> **Quizás vengan mañana.**

El subjuntivo de los verbos de cambio radical

Verbs that have a stem change in the present indicative also have a stem change in the present subjunctive.

cerrar		encontrar	
cierre	cerremos	encuentre	encontremos
cierres	*cerréis*	encuentres	*encontréis*
cierre	cierren	encuentre	encuentren

Preferir and **sentir (e → ie, i)**, **dormir (o → ue, u)**, and **pedir, repetir, freír, seguir,** and **servir (e → i, i)** have a stem change in every person of the subjunctive. Review the following forms.

preferir		dormir		pedir	
prefiera	prefiramos	duerma	durmamos	pida	pidamos
prefieras	*prefiráis*	duermas	*durmáis*	pidas	*pidáis*
prefiera	prefieran	duerma	duerman	pida	pidan

Comparación de igualdad

You use **tanto... como** to compare like quantities and **tan... como** to compare like qualities.

> **Yo tengo tanta paciencia como mi padre.**
> **Anita hace tanto ejercicio como yo.**

> **La señora Mayo es tan simpática como la señora Hernández.**
> **Manolo corre tan rápido como tú.**

CULTURA

Los jóvenes están haciendo jogging en Barcelona, España.

Rafael Campillo/age fotostock

Juego There are a number of cognates in this list. See how many you and a partner can find. Who can find the most? Compare your list with those of your classmates.

Go Online!

connectED.mcgraw-hill.com

Vocabulario

Identifying more parts of the body

la frente
el cuello
el hombro

el pecho
la muñeca

el tobillo
el dedo del pie

Talking about physical fitness

el gimnasio
el buzo
el casco
las rodilleras
los ejercicios
las planchas
las pesas
el movimiento

la respiración
el monopatín
el jogging
el/la corredor(a)
una carrera
  de relevos
  a campo traviesa
  de larga distancia

una vuelta
un maratón
estirarse
patinar
  en línea
practicar yoga
descansar
liberar

Talking about an accident

una herida
hinchado(a)
cortarse

torcerse
caerse
romperse, quebrarse

doler
hacerse daño

Talking about medical emergencies and a hospital

la ambulancia
el/la socorrista

la camilla
la sala de emergencia

la silla de ruedas
andar con muletas

Talking about medical care

el/la cirujano(a)
  ortopédico(a)
el/la enfermero(a)

una radiografía
un yeso
un hueso

los puntos, las suturas
una venda
reducir, acomodar

Other useful words and expressions

el espíritu

la tensión

lento(a)

Repaso cumulativo

Repasa lo que ya has aprendido

These activities will help you review and remember what you have learned so far in Spanish.

1 Escucha las frases. Indica en una tabla como la de abajo a quien habla el joven en cada frase.

a un(a) amigo(a)	a su profesor(a)	a sus padres

2 Sigue el modelo.

MODELO　—Son mis zapatos nuevos.
　　　　　—¿Quién te los compró?

1. Es mi cámara nueva.
2. Es mi casco nuevo.
3. Son mis gafas nuevas.
4. Son mis esquís nuevos.
5. Son mis botas nuevas.

3 Completa con los pronombres.

1. Yo le di los CDs a Anita.
   Yo _____ di a ella.
2. Carlos le devolvió el dinero a Juan.
   Carlos _____ devolvió a él.
3. Sara le dio las direcciones a usted.
   Sara _____ dio.
4. Yo le leí la receta a Susana.
   Yo _____ leí a ella.
5. Yo no le preparé la comida.
   Yo no _____ preparé.

4 **Completa cada serie de frases con el presente, el pretérito y el imperfecto.**

hablar

1. **a.** Yo _____ con Juan todos los días.

   b. Yo _____ con Juan ayer.

   c. Yo _____ mucho con Juan cuando éramos niños.

vender

2. **a.** Mi padre _____ carros.

   b. Ayer él _____ dos.

   c. Pero cuando yo era niño él no _____ carros.

escribir

3. **a.** Ahora nosotros le _____ un correo electrónico todos los días.

   b. Nosotros le _____ un correo electrónico el otro día.

   c. Nosotros le _____ correos electrónicos casi a diario cuando estaba en España.

hacer

4. **a.** No lo _____ yo.

   b. No lo _____ yo ayer.

   c. Yo no lo _____ nunca.

poner

5. **a.** ¿Por qué no _____ (tú) las maletas en la maletera?

   b. ¿Por qué no _____ (tú) las maletas en la maletera cuando fuiste al aeropuerto?

   c. Cada vez que hacías un viaje _____ las maletas en la maletera.

decir

6. **a.** Yo siempre _____ la verdad.

   b. Yo no te _____ una mentira. Fue la verdad.

   c. Yo nunca _____ mentiras—siempre la verdad.

poder

7. **a.** Ellos _____ hacerlo ahora.

   b. Ellos intentaron pero no _____ hacerlo.

   c. Ellos _____ hacerlo cuando eran más jóvenes.

CULTURA

Cada día los señores pasaban mucho tiempo en la terraza de este café en San Juan. Les gustaba leer el periódico y hablar.

Literary Reader

Contenido

Literatura 1
El Quijote 358
Miguel de Cervantes Saavedra

Literatura 2
Versos sencillos 364
José Martí

Literatura 3
Marianela 368
Benito Pérez Galdós

The literary selections in the pages that follow will introduce you to Hispanic literature while helping you to develop reading skills and a better understanding of Hispanic culture. These selections have been carefully adapted to match your developing language skills. As you draw on your knowledge of Spanish grammar and vocabulary and apply the reading strategies you have learned, you will discover that you are able to comprehend and enjoy the selections. **¡A leer!**

Una vista exterior de
El Escorial con sus jardines.
El Escorial es un monasterio
y palacio construido en el
siglo XVI cerca de Madrid.

El Quijote

de Miguel de Cervantes Saavedra

flaco

la lanza

el caballo

gordo

Vocabulario

Estudia las siguientes palabras y sus definiciones.

el mal lo contrario de «bien»; una desgracia, un daño

una tontería una cosa absurda

la guerra una larga serie de batallas

espantable horrible

sabio(a) muy inteligente

desviar disuadir, apartar o alejar a alguien de su camino

hacerle caso a alguien prestarle atención

a toda prisa rápido

Práctica

A Contesta.

1. ¿Tiene escudero don Quijote? ¿Quién es su escudero?
2. ¿Monta don Quijote a caballo o en un asno?
3. ¿Existen males en el mundo o es todo bueno?
4. ¿Hay una guerra en este momento?
5. ¿Son espantables las guerras?

B Expresa de otra manera.

1. Él siempre está haciendo *cosas ridículas*.
2. No hay duda. Es un señor *muy inteligente*.
3. Ellos tenían miedo y salieron *rápido*.
4. Él nunca quiere *prestarle atención* a nadie.
5. Cuando quiere hacer algo es difícil *disuadirlo*.

C Da la palabra cuya definición sigue.

1. a toda velocidad
2. de mucha inteligencia
3. una estupidez
4. espantoso, asqueroso
5. vicio, imperfección

INTRODUCCIÓN

La obra más famosa de todas las letras hispanas es la novela *El ingenioso hidalgo don Quijote de la Mancha* de Miguel de Cervantes Saavedra.

Los dos personajes principales de la novela son don Quijote y Sancho Panza. Don Quijote, un hombre alto y delgado, es un caballero andante. Es un idealista que quiere conquistar todos los males del mundo. Su escudero, Sancho Panza, es un hombre bajo y gordo. Él es un realista puro. Siempre trata de° desviar a don Quijote de sus ilusiones y aventuras.

trata de *he tries*

El Quijote
⌘ 1 ⌘

Un día, don Quijote salió de su pueblo en la región de la Mancha. Un idealista sin par°, don Quijote salió en busca de aventuras para conquistar los males del mundo. Es el trabajo de un verdadero caballero andante. Pero después de unos pocos días, don Quijote volvió a casa porque hizo su primera expedición sin escudero. No hay caballero andante sin escudero—sobre todo un caballero andante de la categoría de don Quijote.

Cuando volvió a su pueblo, empezó a buscar un escudero. Por fin encontró a un vecino, Sancho Panza, un hombre bajo y gordo. Salió por segunda vez, esta vez acompañado de su escudero. Don Quijote montó a su caballo, Rocinante, y Sancho lo siguió montado en su asno.

sin par *without equal*

Conexiones

La literatura
Busca en el Internet algo sobre las obras de Miguel de Cervantes Saavedra. Examina su impacto en la literatura española.

CULTURA
El ingenioso hidalgo don Quijote de la Mancha, el famoso caballero andante

Andrew Payti

Literatura 1

Vuestra Merced *Your Highness*
loco *crazy*
dejamos *we put an end to*

consejos *advice*

así como *as soon as*

parecen *appear to be*

～ 2 ～

Los dos hicieron muchas expediciones por la región de la Mancha. El idealista don Quijote hizo muchas cosas que no quiso hacer el realista Sancho Panza. Más de una vez Sancho le dijo: —Pero, don Quijote, noble caballero y fiel compañero, Vuestra Merced° está loco°. ¿Por qué no dejamos° estas tonterías? ¿Por qué no volvemos a casa? Yo quiero comer. Y quiero dormir en mi cama.

Don Quijote no hizo mucho caso a los consejos° de Sancho. Uno de los episodios más famosos de nuestro estimado caballero es el episodio de los molinos de viento.

～ 3 ～

Del buen suceso que el valeroso don Quijote tuvo en la espantable y jamás imaginada aventura de los molinos de viento.

En esto descubrieron treinta o cuarenta molinos de viento que hay en aquel campo; y así como° don Quijote los vio, dijo a su escudero: —¡Sancho! ¡Mira! ¿Tú ves lo que veo yo?

—No, Vuestra Merced. No veo nada.

—Amigo Sancho, ¿no ves allí unos treinta o más gigantes que vienen hacia nosotros a hacer batalla?

—¿Qué gigantes?

—Aquellos que allí ves, de los brazos largos.

—Don Quijote. No son gigantes. Son simples molinos de viento. Y lo que en ellos parecen° brazos son aspas.

—Bien parece, Sancho, que tú no sabes nada de aventuras. Ellos son gigantes. Y si tienes miedo...

—¡Don Quijote! ¿Adónde va Vuestra Merced?

CULTURA
Los molinos de viento tienen aspas.

©PhotoLink/Photodisc/Getty Images

⌐∾ 4 ∾⌐

¿Adónde fue don Quijote? Él fue a hacer batalla con los terribles gigantes. Gigantes como estos no deben ni pueden existir en el mundo. En nombre de Dulcinea, la dama de sus pensamientos°, don Quijote los atacó. Puso su lanza en el aspa de uno de los molinos. En el mismo instante vino un viento fuerte. El viento movió las aspas. El viento las revolvió con tanta furia que hizo pedazos° de la lanza de don Quijote y levantó a don Quijote en el aire.

A toda prisa el pobre Sancho fue a socorrer° a su caballero andante. Lo encontró en el suelo muy mal herido°.

—Don Quijote, le dije a Vuestra Merced que no vio gigantes. Vio simples molinos de viento. No puedo comprender por qué los atacó.

—Sancho, tú no sabes lo que dices. Son cosas de guerra que tú no comprendes. Tú sabes que tengo un enemigo. Mi enemigo es el horrible pero sabio monstruo Frestón. Te dije las cosas malas que él hace. Y ahora convirtió a los gigantes en molinos de viento.

—Yo no sé lo que hizo vuestro enemigo, Frestón. Pero yo sé lo que le hizo el molino de viento.

Sancho levantó a don Quijote del suelo. Don Quijote subió de nuevo sobre Rocinante. Habló más de la pasada aventura pero Sancho no le hizo caso. Siguieron el camino hacia Puerto Lápice en busca de otras aventuras jamás imaginadas.

dama de sus pensamientos *lady of his dreams*

pedazos *pieces*

socorrer *help*
herido *injured*

CULTURA 🇪🇸
El letrero de la Calle de Cervantes en el barrio de Lavapiés en Madrid. La calle lleva el nombre del autor porque Cervantes pasó una parte de su vida viviendo en esta calle.

EL QUIJOTE

¿Comprendes?

∼ 1 ∼

A **Recordando hechos** Escoge.

1. Don Quijote es _____.
   a. un realista
   b. un idealista
   c. un escudero
2. Don Quijote salió de su pueblo _____.
   a. en busca de la Mancha
   b. en busca de un escudero
   c. en busca de aventuras
3. Don Quijote volvió a casa para _____.
   a. comenzar su primera expedición
   b. buscar un escudero
   c. ver a Dulcinea
4. Sancho Panza es _____.
   a. un caballero andante también
   b. un idealista sin par
   c. un vecino de don Quijote
5. Sancho Panza tiene _____.
   a. un asno
   b. un caballo
   c. una lanza

CON ESTO, POCO A
POCO, LLEGVE AL PVERTO,
A QVIEN LOS DE
CARTAGO DIERON NOMBRE.

CERRADO A TODOS
VIENTOS Y ENCVBIERTO,
A CVYO CLARO Y
SINGVLAR RENOMBRE

SE POSTRAN CVANTOS
PVERTOS EL MAR BAÑA,
DESCVBRE EL SOL Y HA
NAVEGADO EL HOMBRE.

M. DE CERVANTES.

CULTURA

Un azulejo con unos versos de Cervantes en la pared de un edificio en Cartagena, España

∼ 2 ∼

B **Confirmando información** Usa una tabla como la de abajo para indicar si la información es correcta o no.

	correcta	incorrecta
1. Don Quijote y Sancho Panza hicieron solo dos expediciones.		
2. Sancho le dice a don Quijote que está loco.		
3. Don Quijote siempre quiere volver a casa.		
4. Un episodio famoso del *Quijote* es el episodio de los molinos de viento.		

Andrew Payti

~⌁ **3** ⌁~

C **Buscando información** Busca la información en la lectura para completar cada frase.

1. Hay unos _____ molinos de viento en el campo.
2. Don Quijote le dice a Sancho que ve unos _____.
3. Estos vienen hacia don Quijote y Sancho para _____.
4. Don Quijote dice que tienen _____.
5. Pero Sancho no ve _____, solamente _____.

~⌁ **4** ⌁~

D **Recordando hechos** Contesta.

1. ¿Contra quiénes fue don Quijote a hacer batalla?
2. ¿En dónde puso su lanza?
3. ¿Qué hizo mover el aspa?
4. ¿Se revolvió rápidamente el aspa?
5. ¿Adónde levantó a don Quijote?
6. ¿Dónde encontró Sancho a don Quijote?
7. ¿Quién convirtió a los gigantes en molinos de viento?
8. Cuando Sancho levantó a don Quijote del suelo, ¿volvieron a casa?
9. Después de este episodio, ¿admite don Quijote que los gigantes son molinos de viento?

E **Causa y efecto** When an event or action causes other things to happen it is called a *cause-and-effect relationship*. In English, explain the cause and effect of Don Quijote's actions.

F **Comparando y contrastando** When you describe how two or more things are similar, you are *comparing* them. When you describe how they are different, you are *contrasting* them. Compare and contrast Sancho Panza's reasoning with that of Don Quijote.

CULTURA

Una librería en León, Nicaragua, que lleva el nombre de don Quijote

Andrew Payti

Versos sencillos

de José Martí

Vocabulario

Estudia las siguientes palabras y sus definiciones.

el monte   elevación natural de terreno, montaña

las joyas   adornos de oro, plata, diamantes, esmeraldas, etc.

el joyero   el que vende joyas

el corazón   órgano vital muscular que impulsa la sangre

arrancar   sacar o quitar con violencia

Práctica

Completa con la palabra apropiada.

1. Me causó tanto dolor y tristeza que me _____ el corazón.
2. El _____ y los pulmones son órganos vitales.
3. Un anillo de oro con diamantes es una _____.
4. El _____ vende anillos, brazaletes (pulseras) y pendientes (aretes) en su joyería.
5. No hay muchos _____ en un estado como Kansas o Nebraska.

INTRODUCCIÓN

José Martí (1853–1895) nació en Cuba de padres españoles. Dedicó su vida a la causa de la independencia de su país. Fue deportado dos veces a España por sus actividades políticas. Martí vivió también en México, Guatemala, Honduras y Venezuela. Dice que en cada país se encontró en casa—lo que le hizo proclamar «De América soy hijo». Pasó catorce años en Estados Unidos donde organizó un grupo revolucionario. Martí murió en el campo de batalla en Cuba en 1895. Murió sin realizar su sueño de ver a su Cuba libre e independiente.

Además de ser político y revolucionario, la gran pasión de Martí durante toda su vida era la poesía. Escribió sus famosos *Versos sencillos* durante su estadía en Nueva York.

Las palmas crecen en regiones tropicales.

Versos sencillos

I

Yo soy un hombre sincero

de donde crece la palma;

y antes de morirme, quiero

echar mis versos del alma°.

alma *soul*

Conexiones

La literatura
Investiga las obras de José Martí. Determina si la época en que escribió influyó sus obras.

5   Yo vengo de todas partes

y hacia todas partes voy:

arte soy entre las artes;

en los montes, monte soy.

. . .

Si dicen que del joyero

10 tome la joya mejor,

tomo a un amigo sincero

y pongo a un lado el amor°.

amor *love*

La rosa es una flor
bonita.

XXXIX

Cultivo una rosa blanca

en julio como en enero,

para el amigo sincero

que me da su mano franca.

5   Y para el cruel que me arranca

del corazón con que vivo

cardo° ni ortiga° cultivo

cultivo la rosa blanca.

cardo *thistle*
ortiga *nettle*

Andrew Payti

¿Comprendes?

A Interpretando ¿Cómo lo dice José Martí?

1. Soy de un país tropical.
2. Quiero ser poeta.
3. Me siento o me encuentro en casa en muchos lugares diferentes.
4. Quiero ver el mundo.
5. Puedo adaptarme a muchas situaciones.

B Buscando hechos Contesta.

1. ¿Cuál es la mejor joya para Martí?
2. ¿Cuál prefiere? ¿A un amigo sincero o el amor?
3. ¿Qué cultiva para un amigo?
4. ¿Cómo trata a una persona que no lo trata bien?

C Personalizando En estos versos aprendemos mucho sobre la personalidad y las aspiraciones del poeta José Martí. Compara tres ideas y opiniones tuyas con las de José Martí.

CULTURA

El Morro, La Habana, Cuba

VERSOS SENCILLOS

Marianela

de Benito Pérez Galdós

CULTURA
El pueblo de Erronkari en las montañas de Navarra

Vocabulario

Estudia las siguientes palabras y sus definiciones.

una colina   elevación de terreno menor que un monte o una montaña

un buen mozo   un joven guapo

la estrella   lo que brilla en el cielo de noche

una tontería   una cosa absurda

bello(a)   bonito, hermoso

desconocido(a)   no conocido

feliz   contento, alegre

acercarse a   ir cerca de algo

despedirse de   salir y decirles «adiós» a todos

huir   escapar

ladrar   lo que hace el perro

ponerse a   empezar

a lo lejos   en la distancia

a menudo   con frecuencia

a solas   solo, sin nadie, no acompañado

lentamente   despacio, no rápido

Práctica

A Contesta.

1. ¿Es el hermano de Teresa un buen mozo?
2. ¿Comete una persona inteligente y sabia muchas tonterías?
3. ¿Te sientes feliz cuando te ocurre algo agradable?
4. ¿Tienes miedo cuando te acerca una persona desconocida?
5. ¿Brillan las estrellas en el cielo de día o de noche?
6. ¿Te despides de tus amigos cuando tienes que salir?
7. ¿Ladra el perro si quiere atención?

B Expresa de otra manera.

1. Ella es una persona *alegre*.
2. Ellos lo hacen *con frecuencia*.
3. Yo sé que van a *escapar*.
4. ¡Qué *cosa más ridícula!*
5. Vi las colinas *en la distancia*.
6. Andaba *despacio*.
7. Él lo hizo *solo*.
8. Tiene paisajes *hermosos*.

C Da el contrario.

1. feo
2. triste
3. famoso
4. rápido
5. de cerca
6. alejarse de

CULTURA 🏛
Las Palmas de Gran Canaria, ciudad natal de Benito Pérez Galdós

INTRODUCCIÓN

Benito Pérez Galdós es uno de los mejores novelistas de España. Nació en Las Palmas de Gran Canaria en 1843 pero pasó casi toda su vida en Madrid donde murió en 1920. Un escritor fecundo, Galdós escribió setenta y siete novelas y veintidós obras teatrales. Dijo Galdós en un discurso «la novela es la imagen de la vida y su arte consiste en reproducir sus caracteres humanos; pasiones, debilidades, grandezas y bajezas».

Una de sus novelas más populares es *Marianela*. En esta novela Galdós trata el problema social de la miseria y del trabajo en las minas del norte de España. De todas sus novelas *Marianela* es la más sentimental como observarás al conocer a los dos protagonistas—Pablo Penáguilas y Marianela.

Benito Perez Galdos

Conexiones

La literatura
Se dice que la influencia de las novelas de Galdós es universal. Haz unas investigaciones para aprender algo de esta idea.

nacimiento *birth*

Marianela

∽ 1 ∾

Un día se acercó cierto Teodoro Golfín al pueblo de Socartes. En el camino él se perdió. Andaban por la región un joven, Pablo Penáguilas, y su perro Choto. Pablo era un muchacho guapo. Tenía unos veinte años. Pablo y Choto oyeron al señor y lo ayudaron a encontrar su camino. Como el pueblo de Socartes está situado en la región de las minas es fácil desorientarse. Para llegar a Socartes hay que bajar y subir muchas colinas y pasar por una cueva misteriosa.

Cuando Pablo y el señor Golfín salieron de la cueva oscura el señor observó algo en el muchacho que le hizo preguntar a Pablo:

—Chico, ¿eres ciego?

—Sí, señor. No tengo vista. No puedo ver. Soy ciego desde mi nacimiento° —contestó Pablo.

—¡Qué pena!—pensó el señor Golfín—un buen mozo como este y no tiene el don de ver.

Los dos seguían el camino de Socartes cuando a lo lejos oyeron una voz muy bella. Era la voz de Marianela. Pablo le explicó al señor Golfín que Marianela era una muchacha muy buena que siempre lo acompañaba por las minas.

Cuando el señor Golfín vio a Marianela observó enseguida que la pobre muchacha era muy fea. Era muy pequeña de estatura. Sus ojos negros le daban una expresión de mujer pero tenía el cuerpo de una niña. Marianela tenía dieciséis años pero parecía° menor.

El señor Golfín le habló a Pablo. Le dijo que era el hermano de Carlos Golfín, el ingeniero de las minas.

—Ah, don Carlos es muy amigo de mi padre y sé que le espera a usted desde ayer—dijo Pablo.

Por fin el joven tuvo que despedirse del grupo para volver a casa. Sabía que su padre le esperaba. El señor Golfín, guiado por Marianela, continuó su viaje hacia la casa de su hermano. Mientras caminaban hacia la casa, Marianela le hablaba al señor Golfín de su vida.

—Soy una muchacha pobre. No tengo ni padre ni madre. Soy huérfana. Mi padre fue el primero que encendía y limpiaba faroles en este pueblo. Cada día él me ponía en un cesto y yo lo acompañaba en su trabajo. Un día tenía que subir a un farol que había en un puente. Puso el cesto sobre el antepecho del puente. Yo me salí fuera° y me caí° al río. Me caí sobre unas piedras. Antes del accidente yo era bonita pero ahora soy fea. Poco después del accidente mi padre se puso enfermo y fue al hospital donde se murió. Mi madre fue a trabajar en las minas y un día ella se cayó en una cueva y no ha vuelto a salir. Y ahora yo vivo con los Centeno. Ellos tienen una casa aquí en las minas.

Después de caminar un rato más, los dos llegaron a la casa del hermano de Teodoro Golfín.

Marianela le dice «adiós» al señor Golfín y vuelve a la casa de los Centeno. Antes de salir el señor le da una moneda.

parecía *she seemed*

Un farol

me salí fuera *fell out*
me caí *I fell*

Un cesto

Un puente en el pueblo de Aribe en la provincia de Navarra

MARIANELA

∽ **2** ∽

Cuando salió el señor Golfín, Marianela, que se llama también la Nela, fue a la casa de los Centeno.

La casa de los Centeno es bastante humilde. Viven en la casa el señor Centeno, la señora Centeno, sus cuatro hijos y la pobre Marianela. La señora Centeno es una persona cruel. Le encanta contar su dinero pero no se lo da a nadie. Trata a la Nela peor que a un animal. La hace dormir en una cesta en un rincón° de la cocina. A pesar de° toda la miseria en que vive la Nela, ella es muy generosa. En cuanto° vuelve a casa, ella le da la moneda del señor Golfín a Celipín.

Celipín es el hijo menor de los Centeno. Él no quiere seguir viviendo como está viviendo ahora. Quiere salir de Socartes para ir a estudiar en Madrid para hacer algo de su vida. Quiere ser un hombre importante. Marianela le dice que siempre tiene que ser bueno para con sus padres y que les debe escribir a menudo.

Al día siguiente, igual que todos los días, Marianela sale de casa y va a buscar a su amigo Pablo Penáguilas. Como el joven no tiene vista hay muchas cosas que le son desconocidas. La pobre Marianela no tiene educación alguna pero siempre quiere explicarle a Pablo como son las cosas del mundo. Mientras andan a diario por los campos discuten muchas tonterías. La Nela le dice que las estrellas en el cielo son las sonrisas de los muertos que están en el cielo.

Durante sus muchas conversaciones Pablo promete a Marianela que un día va a casarse con° ella. Una muchacha tan buena como ella tiene que ser bonita. Cada vez que Pablo le dice a Marianela que es bonita, ella se mira en el agua de un arroyo° y una vez más ve que es fea.

rincón *corner*
A pesar de *In spite of*
En cuanto *As soon as*

casarse con *marry*

arroyo *brook*

CULTURA
Casas con balcones típicos en Gijón, Asturias

Andrew Payti

Teodoro Golfín es médico y después de observar mucho a Pablo, toma la decisión de operarle de los ojos. No sabe si la operación tendrá éxito o no pero quiere intentar darle vista al hijo del mejor amigo de su hermano. Pablo le dice a Marianela que después de la operación él se casará con ella.

Todos se preparan para la operación. Llega a Socartes Florentina, la prima de Pablo. Florentina es una muchacha muy bonita y es además una persona buena y generosa. Cuando ve por primera vez a Marianela, se pone triste. No puede comprender como algunas personas como ella y su familia tienen mucho y otras no tienen nada. La pobre Marianela no tiene zapatos. Florentina le dice a Marianela que le comprará un vestido y un par de zapatos. Promete que cuidará° de Marianela para siempre. La Nela cree que Florentina es una santa. Una persona tan buena tiene que ser santa.

cuidará *she will take care*

~ 3 ~

Ha llegado el día de la operación. Todo el mundo está muy ansioso por saber los resultados. ¿Pablo tendrá vista o no? ¡Es la cuestión! Pasan unos días y el médico decide que ha llegado la hora de quitarle° las vendas a Pablo. ¿Puede ver o no? Sí, puede ver. Todos se alegran° con una sola excepción. La única persona que no es feliz es la Nela. Está contenta porque sabe que Pablo tiene vista pero está triste porque sabe que Pablo querrá casarse con Florentina y no con ella.

quitarle *to take off*
se alegran *rejoices*

La pobre Marianela no sabe qué hacer. No quiere estar con nadie. Quiere estar a solas con sus pensamientos°. Decide vagar por los campos.

pensamientos *thoughts*

A lo lejos, Marianela oye un ruido°. ¿Quién puede ser? Es Florentina.

ruido *noise*

Habla Florentina:

—Pero, Nela, ¿dónde has estado? ¿No sabes que Pablo tiene vista? La operación ha sido un éxito.

—Sí, lo sé —contesta la Nela.

—Pablo te quiere ver. Siempre pregunta dónde está la Nela. Tú sabes que él te quiere mucho.

La pobre Nela se cayó al suelo.

—Florentina, usted ha sido muy buena conmigo. La quiero mucho y no quiero ser ingrata. Y adoro a Pablo. Pero no puedo, no puedo.

—¿No puedes qué? —preguntó Florentina. De repente° la Nela se levantó y empezó a correr.

De repente *Suddenly*

Gritó: —No, no puedo, Florentina. Perdóneme, pero no puedo hablar más con usted. ¡Adiós! ¡Adiós!

Con estas palabras la Nela desapareció entre los árboles. Tomó la decisión de huir. No quiso pasar más tiempo en Socartes.

Durante la noche la Nela oyó otro ruido. Oyó a Celipín, el hijo de los Centeno.

—¿Adónde vas, Celipín?—preguntó Marianela.

—Nela, por fin voy a Madrid. Pero me tienes que hacer una promesa. No vas a decir nada a mis padres.

—De acuerdo, Celipín. No les voy a decir nada. Pero les escribirás, ¿no? Tienes que ser bueno para con tus padres.

—Sí, les escribiré. Te lo prometo. Pero, Nela, ¿por qué no vienes conmigo a Madrid? No tienes que quedarte aquí en Socartes. Podemos salir juntos.

—¡Buena idea! Te acompaño—contestó la Nela.

Luego se puso a° pensar. La Nela pensó en su madre enterrada en una cueva de Socartes. Por fin le dijo a Celipín:

—Celipín. Lo siento pero no puedo ir contigo. No puedo salir de Socartes. Tengo mis razones. Tú tienes que ir solo. Y, ¡escribe mucho! Adiós, Celipín y ¡buena suerte!

—No me olvidaré° de mis padres ni de ti que me has ayudado tanto… Adiós, Nelilla. Siento pasos°… Me voy—dijo Celipín.

se puso a *she began*

No me olvidaré *I will not forget*
Siento pasos *I hear steps*

CULTURA
Picos de Europa, Asturias

Andrew Payti

Entrada a una mina

✦ 4 ✦

Celipín desapareció entre las sombras° de la noche. Los pasos que había sentido eran de Choto, el perro de Pablo. Al ver a Marianela, Choto saltó alrededor de ella acariciándola con sus patas°. Luego empezó a correr hacia la casa de los Penáguilas.

A la misma hora que Choto llegaba a la casa, Teodoro Golfín salía de la casa. Cuando el perro lo vio dio unas cuarenta vueltas en torno de él y no dejó de ladrar. El señor Golfín sabía que el perro trataba de decirle algo. Choto empezó a correr y el doctor Golfín decidió seguirlo. Lo siguió y el perro lo llevó hasta donde estaba la Nela delante de la cueva donde está enterrada su madre.

El doctor gritó:

—Nela, ¿qué haces allí? Te quiero hablar.

—No puedo—contestó la Nela.

—Sí—insistió el doctor.

Marianela subió de la cueva. Le dijo al doctor que quería estar con su madre. No quería ver a Pablo porque él creía que era bonita y ella sabía que no lo era.

Por fin el doctor levantó a la Nela, la puso en sus hombros y la llevó a la casa de Pablo.—¡Ay! Marianela, ¡qué enferma estás!— pensó el médico.

Cuando llegaron a la casa, el doctor puso a la Nela en el sofá. Todos cuidaron de ella—Florentina, el padre de Pablo, el doctor Golfín.

sombras *shadows*

acariciándola con sus patas
caressing her with its paws

Al día siguiente Pablo salió de su cuarto para hablar con Florentina. Consideró a Florentina la muchacha más bonita del mundo. Cuando vio a Florentina le dijo:

—Florentina, no te vi esta mañana. ¿Por qué no viniste a hablar conmigo?

Pablo vio solo a Florentina—a nadie más. Luego miró hacia el sofá y vio la cara de una pobre muchacha fea con los ojos cerrados y la boca abierta.

—¡Ah!—dijo Pablo. Florentina ha encontrado a una pobre fea y la quiere ayudar. ¡Qué buena es Florentina!

Pablo se acercó al sofá. Extendió una mano hasta tocar aquella cabeza en la cual veía una expresión de dolor y tristeza. Entonces la Nela movió los ojos y los fijó en Pablo. Sacó de entre las mantas una mano flaca y tomó la mano de Pablo. Al sentir° su contacto Pablo se estremeció° de pies a cabeza y gritó.

Con voz temblorosa°, Marianela le dijo:

—Sí, señorito mío, yo soy la Nela.

Lentamente ella llevó a sus secos labios la mano de Pablo y le dio un beso°… después un segundo beso… y al darle el tercero, sus labios se quedaron inertes.

El primero que dijo algo fue Pablo.

—Eres tú… , eres tú.

Pablo la llamó repetidas veces.

—No responde—dijo con terror.

Pablo se inclinó sobre ella y acercando sus labios al oído de Marianela, gritó:

—Nela, Nela, amiga querida°, que tanto me has ayudado y ahora estás muerta. Adiós, Nelilla. Adiós.

Al sentir *Upon feeling*

se estremeció *shook*

temblorosa *trembling*

beso *kiss*

querida *dear, beloved*

CULTURA 🏚

Fíjate en el montañoso terreno de Extremadura, al sur de Asturias. Aun en las regiones del centro y del sur de España hay montañas. España es el segundo país más montañoso de Europa después de Suiza.

Andrew Payti

¿Comprendes?

∽ 1 ∽

A Identificando Identifica quien es.

	Pablo Penáguilas	Teodoro Golfín	don Carlos	los Centeno	Marianela
1. un señor que se perdió un día en el camino de Socartes					
2. un muchacho ciego que vive en Socartes y que ayudó al señor que se perdió					
3. una muchacha fea que siempre ayuda al joven ciego y que guió al señor que se perdió					
4. el ingeniero de las minas a quien iba a visitar el señor que se perdió					
5. la familia con quien vive la muchacha					

B Describiendo Escoge las frases que describen a Marianela.

1. Es una muchacha muy buena.
2. Es ciega.
3. Su madre y su padre trabajan en las minas de Socartes.
4. Es muy fea.
5. Tiene ojos azules.
6. Es muy alta.
7. Tiene una estatura baja.
8. Ayuda mucho al muchacho ciego.
9. Sufrió un accidente horrible cuando era niña.

C Describiendo Describe a los siguientes personajes.

1. Pablo Penáguilas
2. Marianela
3. Teodoro Golfín

D Analizando Contesta.

1. El camino de Socartes es un camino difícil y es fácil perderse en el camino. ¿Por qué?
2. ¿Qué indica que el señor Golfín es un hombre generoso?
3. ¿Por qué quiere compartir el autor esta historia con sus lectores? En tu opinión, ¿cuál es su propósito?

E **Aumentando tu vocabulario** Parea.

1. se perdió	**a.** se encuentra
2. andaba	**b.** guapo
3. está situado	**c.** sin padres
4. oscura	**d.** bonito
5. ser ciego	**e.** se desorientó
6. buen mozo	**f.** caminaba, iba
7. bello	**g.** sin luz
8. huérfano	**h.** poco tiempo
9. un rato	**i.** no tener vista

F **Identificando** Usa una tabla como la de abajo para indicar quien es.

1. un señor que es médico y que le puede operar a Pablo de los ojos

2. un joven de unos veinte años que es guapo

3. el hijo menor de la familia Centeno que no quiere seguir viviendo como está viviendo ahora

4. una muchacha generosa que no tiene nada pero que siempre quiere ayudar a los otros

5. una muchacha bonita y generosa que viene a Socartes antes de la operación de Pablo

6. una señora cruel que nunca le da nada a nadie

Marianela	Pablo Penáguilas	Celipín	Teodoro Golfín	la Sra. Centeno	Florentina	don Carlos

~ 2 ~

G Recordando hechos Contesta.

1. ¿Con quién vive Marianela?
2. ¿Cómo la trata la señora?
3. ¿En qué cuarto de la casa duerme Marianela?
4. ¿En qué duerme ella?
5. ¿A quién le da Marianela la moneda del señor Golfín?
6. ¿Quién es Celipín?
7. ¿Por qué quiere él ir a Madrid?
8. ¿Qué le dice siempre Marianela?

H Analizando Contesta.

1. El autor dice que Marianela le dice muchas tonterías a Pablo. ¿Por qué son tonterías la información que Marianela le da?
2. Pablo siempre le dice a Marianela que va a casarse con ella. ¿Por qué quiere Pablo casarse con ella?
3. Marianela dice que Florentina es una santa. ¿Por qué?

I Describiendo Describe.

Describe a Florentina. En tu descripción indica por qué se le considera una persona generosa y compasiva.

CULTURA

Paisaje cerca de Santillana del Mar en el norte de España

MARIANELA

trescientos setenta y nueve **379**

∽ **3** ∽

J Analizando Contesta.

1. Unos días después de la operación, el médico le quita las vendas a Pablo y todos se alegran. ¿Por qué?
2. La única persona que no es feliz es la Nela. ¿Por qué?
3. Florentina le dice a Marianela que Pablo la quiere ver. ¿Por qué quiere verla?
4. La pobre Marianela no puede hablar más con Florentina. ¿Por qué?
5. Cuando Celipín invita a Marianela a acompañarlo a Madrid, Marianela cree que es una buena idea. Luego dice que no, que ella no puede ir con él. ¿Por qué?
6. Marianela le dice a Florentina que no quiere ser ingrata. ¿Por qué le dice tal cosa a Florentina?

K Confirmando información Usa una tabla como la de abajo para indicar si la información es correcta o no.

	correcta	incorrecta
1. Marianela no quiere ir a la casa de Pablo porque sabe que todos son muy felices.		
2. Marianela está triste porque Pablo puede ver.		
3. Marianela quiere estar sola con sus pensamientos porque está muy triste.		
4. Está muy triste porque sabe que Pablo va a casarse con Florentina.		

L Creando un diálogo El diálogo, una conversación entre dos personas, es un elemento importante en muchas novelas. Prepara una conversación que tiene lugar entre Celipín y Marianela cuando él se despide de ella.

M Llegando a conclusiones ¿Qué opinión tienes? ¿Se casará Pablo con Florentina o no? Explica.

⟿ 4 ⟿

N Recordando hechos Contesta.

1. ¿De quién eran los pasos que oyó Celipín?
2. ¿Hacia dónde corrió el perro?
3. ¿Qué hizo el perro cuando llegó a la casa de Pablo?
4. ¿Quién siguió al perro?
5. ¿Adónde lo llevó el perro?
6. ¿Quería Marianela hablar con el doctor?
7. ¿Qué hizo el doctor?
8. ¿Adónde la llevó?
9. ¿Dónde la puso?
10. Al día siguiente, ¿quién salió de su cuarto?
11. ¿Con quién habló?

O Confirmando información Usa una tabla como la de abajo para indicar si la información es correcta o no.

	correcta	incorrecta
1. Cuando Pablo mira hacia el sofá, sabe que la muchacha en el sofá es Marianela. La reconoce enseguida.		
2. Pablo cree que la muchacha en el sofá es otra pobre a quien ayudaba Florentina.		
3. Pablo reconoció a Marianela cuando le tocó la cabeza y vio la expresión en su cara.		
4. Pablo no reconoció a Marianela hasta que ella le tomó la mano.		

P Interpretando Explica el significado de la siguiente frase.

«Al sentir su contacto Pablo se estremeció de pies a cabeza y gritó».

Q Interpretando y analizando En la novela *Marianela*, el doctor Teodoro Golfín representa la ciencia. Él da nueva vida a Pablo al darle vista. Pero, ¿qué le pasa a Marianela? Lee el siguiente párrafo. ¿Qué opinión tienes? ¿Han triunfado la ciencia y el progreso? Defiende tu opinión.

Después de la muerte de Marianela el doctor Teodoro Golfín dice:

—La realidad ha sido para él nueva vida; para ella ha sido dolor y asfixia, la humillación, la tristeza, el dolor… ¡la muerte!

En realidad, ¿qué nos está diciendo el doctor? ¿Es posible que sea también la opinión del autor Galdós?

Vista de la Catedral de Nuestra Señora de Guadalupe desde un balcón en Puerto Vallarta, México

Contents

Language Arts Practice 1
El arte 384

Language Arts Practice 2
La ecología. 388

Language Arts Practice 3
César Chávez 390

The pages that follow contain both informational and authentic selections designed to help you develop your Language Arts skills while using your Spanish. As you draw on your knowledge of Spanish grammar and vocabulary and apply the reading and writing strategies you have learned, you will discover that you can indeed improve your Language Arts skills through your study of Spanish.

El arte

Para apreciar una visita al museo o solo para apreciar una obra de arte es necesario tener a lo menos un conocimiento elemental del arte: la pintura, la escultura y el dibujo.

La pintura

Antes de empezar a pintar, el pintor o artista tiene que tener su lienzo[1] preparado. Tiene que tensarlo y colocarlo[2] en el caballete[3]. El pintor escoge su medio. Los tres medios que más emplean los pintores son la acuarela, el óleo y el acrílico. La espátula se usa para mezclar[4] los colores y a veces para aplicarlos. Por lo general el artista aplica los colores con un pincel[5], sobre todo cuando pinta con acuarelas.

Elementos de composición

Al mirar una pintura hay que fijarse en[6] la composición. Hay algunos elementos de composición muy importantes. La perspectiva es la representación de los objetos en tres dimensiones—alto, ancho, profundo—sobre una superficie plana. El pintor tiene que tomar en cuenta su alejamiento—su posición en el espacio con respecto a la del observador.

[1]lienzo *canvas*
[2]colocarlo *place it*
[3]caballete *easel*
[4]mezclar *mix*
[5]pincel *brush*
[6]fijarse en *pay attention to*

Pablo Picasso pintando en su taller

Un sello que conmemora la batalla en el pequeño pueblo de Guernica

El tema o motivo de una obra de arte es el principal elemento de interés para el observador. Es la materia que pinta el artista. El estilo es el modo o la expresión del artista. El estilo puede clasificarse en términos básicos en figurativo y abstracto. A las obras de arte que enfatizan la importancia de los elementos y principios de diseños a favor de asunto o de la materia se les llama obras de arte abstracto. Una obra figurativa presenta una rendición más literal, o sea, más realista de la materia.

La escultura

El escultor crea objetos o formas bellas en tres dimensiones o en relieve. Puede servirse de varios materiales como barro, yeso, madera, piedra o bronce. Unas esculturas, las de piedra o madera, por ejemplo, pueden ser talladas[7] con cincel[8]. Otras, de materiales blandos como el yeso, barro o bronce fundido pueden ser modeladas sobre un esqueleto o armadura. La cocción[9] y la fundición[10] en un horno son dos procesos que prolongan la duración de (hacen más duraderas) las esculturas.

El relieve

Un relieve es cualquier cosa que resalta sobre una superficie plana. Una escultura de relieve es una escultura hecha sobre una superficie de modo que las figuras están talladas solamente en parte. Bajorrelieve significa que la figura tallada es menos de la mitad del bulto[11] natural de la figura. Y altorrelieve significa que es más de la mitad del bulto de la figura. Se ven muchas esculturas de relieve en las catedrales, iglesias y otros edificios monumentales.

[7]talladas *carved*
[8]cincel *chisel*
[9]cocción *cooking*
[10]fundición *melting*
[11]bulto *shape*

Andrew Payti

Esta estatua del oso y del madroño es una escultura de bronce ubicada en la Puerta del Sol en Madrid.

Actividades

A En forma gráfica indica lo que tiene que hacer el pintor cuando decide pintar algo.

B Si tú tienes interés en el arte, sobre todo la pintura, explica a unos amigos tu medio favorito. Diles por qué.

C Estás hablando con un amigo que no sabe nada del arte. Explícale la diferencia entre el medio y la composición. Explícale también la diferencia entre el medio y el tema o motivo.

D Explica la diferencia entre una obra figurativa y una obra abstracta.

E Determina las ideas centrales sobre la información presentada en el texto. Da un resumen de las ideas más importantes y explica como se desarrollan en el texto.

F Describe en la manera más precisa posible lo que es una escultura.

G Prepara un cartel en el cual divides y presentas el vocabulario específico que se necesita al hablar de la pintura y de la escultura.

H Alguien dice que un relieve es una escultura. Habla con la persona y de una manera cortés y en un tono objetivo explícale que lo que está diciendo no es completamente correcto. Ayúdale a ampliar lo que ha dicho para dar una definición o descripción más precisa de un relieve.

I Trabajando en grupos divídanse una vez más en dos grupos—los que prefieren el arte abstracto y los que prefieren el arte figurativo. Abran la sesión con una definición de cada uno. Presenten sus opiniones sobre sus predilecciones y expliquen por qué ustedes tienen tales opiniones. Si alguien quiere una clarificación de la aserción de otro(a), puede pedirle más información. Todos deben señalar lo que consideran exageraciones o conclusiones erróneas de los otros. Al final, trabajen juntos para presentar una conclusión a las perspectivas e ideas del grupo.

Las Bellas Artes

UN PROYECTO

Busca y estudia varios cuadros de artistas españoles o latinoamericanos y decide cuales son obras que te interesan, que te pican el interés o que encuentras bonitas.

   Escribe un reportaje sobre el cuadro que selecciones. Luego da tus ideas personales sobre los aspectos de la obra que te pican el interés. Da también una descripción de lo que encuentras bonito en la obra y por qué te gusta tanto. Luego, presenta tu proyecto a la clase.

Aquí tienes una lista de algunos artistas famosos.

España	Latinoamérica
Murillo	Botero
Goya	Kahlo
El Greco	Rivera
Velázquez	Orozco
Dalí	

San Ildefonso de El Greco

Marquesa de Pontejos
de Francisco de Goya.

La ecología

El medio ambiente

El problema de la contaminación del medio ambiente[1] ha dado lugar al movimiento ecologista. El término «ecología», el equilibrio entre los seres vivientes y la naturaleza, ha llegado a ser[2] sinónimo de supervivencia[3] para muchos seres humanos.

La contaminación del aire

La contaminación de todos tipos es la plaga de nuestros tiempos. Buques[4] petroleros derraman[5] quién sabe cuántos litros de petróleo cada año en nuestros mares y océanos. El aire que respiramos está contaminado, mayormente por las emisiones de gases de los tubos de escape de los automóviles y camiones y de las fábricas[6] que queman[7] sustancias químicas. Es la responsabilidad de todos evitar que se expulsen al aire sustancias tóxicas.

La contaminación del agua

Los ríos son las venas de una gran parte de la humanidad y desgraciadamente muchos de ellos están tan contaminados que son portadores de enfermedades. En las zonas industriales, sobre todo en el este de Europa y China, la situación es catastrófica. Los desechos[8] industriales que las fábricas echan en las aguas cercanas son casi imposibles de eliminar. A estos se añaden los desechos que están enterrados[9] y que son transportados por las corrientes de agua subterráneas o los que simplemente vuelven a la superficie para contaminar la tierra. Siempre volvemos al mismo problema, el de los desechos y la manera de deshacernos de ellos. Hoy en día hay grandes campañas de reciclaje. El reciclaje consiste en recoger los desechos de papel, vidrio y hierro para transformarlos y poder utilizarlos de nuevo.

Como dijo el astronauta estadounidense John E. Blaha: «El planeta Tierra es un lugar absolutamente bello. Uno se da cuenta cuando lo ve desde aquí arriba. Ciertamente necesitamos cuidarlo».

[1]medio ambiente *environment*
[2]ha llegado a ser *has become*
[3]supervivencia *survival*
[4]Buques *ships*
[5]derraman *spill*

[6]fábricas *factories*
[7]queman *burn*
[8]desechos *waste*
[9]enterrados *buried*

Actividades

A Explica de una manera concisa lo que es el medio ambiente.

B Trabajen en grupos y respondan a diversas perspectivas de lo que sus colegas consideran los problemas más serios en cuanto a la destrucción del medio ambiente. Al terminar su discusión preparen un resumen de los puntos en que hay acuerdo y desacuerdo y preséntenlo a la clase.

C Hoy en día hay artículos casi a diario en los periódicos sobre el medio ambiente. Léelos y después de leer a lo menos tres prepara un reportaje sobre lo que el gobierno está considerando asuntos serios. ¿Hay mucho acuerdo o desacuerdo entre los varios grupos políticos? ¿Cuáles son los asuntos que tú personalmente consideras importantes? ¿Por qué los consideras tan importantes? Y, ¿cuáles para ti no tienen tanta importancia?

D Haz un reportaje en el cual comparas la contaminación del aire y la contaminación del agua. En tu opinión, ¿cuál es el problema más serio? Busca datos y evidencia para apoyar tus opiniones.

E Usando los recursos sobre el medio ambiente que tienes a tu disponibilidad, escribe una carta a un miembro gubernamental estatal diciéndole lo que tú propones como acciones que él debe realizar para mejorar el medio ambiente en tu estado. Escribe tu carta en un estilo formal y un tono objetivo. Cuando necesario da información para apoyar tus ideas y conclusiones.

F Trabajando en grupos preparen y presenten un debate sobre los problemas ambientales que existen en la región donde ustedes viven. Después de identificar los problemas discutan lo que ustedes creen que el gobierno está haciendo o no para enfrentar los problemas. Al terminar el debate, lleguen a una conclusión. Incluyan material que apoye su conclusión y que explique de una manera clara el significado y las posibles consecuencias del tema.

POR SIGLOS, EL HOMBRE DE ESTAS TIERRAS CONVIVIÓ CON LA NATURALEZA. RESTABLECER ESA ARMONÍA ES UNA TAREA QUE NOS CORRESPONDE A TODOS

G Describe la importancia del mensaje en esta cartelera. Explica lo que tú haces personalmente para tratar de conformarte con el aviso. ¿Qué hacen otros que rehúsan seguir el aviso?

César Chávez

César Chávez nació en 1927 en Yuma, Arizona, en una familia de campesinos. César recibió el nombre de su querido abuelo. Al perder su tierra la familia Chávez se trasladó a California donde el joven César recogía algodón, vegetales y uvas cuando podía encontrar trabajo. Dice Chávez que recuerda haber asistido a sesenta y cinco escuelas elementales en un solo año escolar—a veces por solamente un día.

Durante la Segunda Guerra mundial Chávez sirvió en la Marina. Al salir de la Marina se estableció de nuevo en California con su esposa, Helen Fabela. Cuando tenía solo veinticinco años César empezó a organizarse para ayudar a «su gente» a mejorar las lamentables condiciones laborales que habían aceptado durante generaciones. A principios de los años 60 Chávez fundó el primer sindicato para obreros[1] migratorios. Este sindicato se fusionó más tarde con otro para formar la primera gran organización de campesinos. César incitó a los campesinos mexicanoamericanos a inscribirse para votar e inauguró una huelga[2] contra las grandes empresas vinícolas[3]. La huelga atrajo mucha atención nacional y ayudó a informar a la nación de las grandes injusticias que enfrentaban los campesinos mexicanoamericanos.

Les informó también de las pésimas condiciones en que vivían durante décadas. En su lucha[4] llamada «La Causa», Chávez se aprovechó de algunas tácticas del movimiento de derechos civiles tales como marchas y protestas o manifestaciones pacíficas incluyendo un ayuno[5] de veinticinco días. Pero los cultivadores de uva no sucumbieron. Por fin el modesto pero carismático y determinado Chávez les rogó[6] a todos los americanos boicotear las empresas cultivadoras de uvas en California. Más de diecisiete millones de habitantes oyeron su petición y apoyaron a La Causa rehusando comprar uvas de California. El boicoteo duró cinco años. Las empresas perdieron millones de dólares y por fin el 30 de julio de 1970 los cultivadores de uvas de California accedieron[7] a firmar un contrato que por primera vez otorgó[8] algunos derechos a los recogedores[9] de uvas y les concedió un pequeño aumento de sueldo[10]. Fue el primero de muchos boicoteos exitosos organizados por Chávez para ayudar a mejorar la vida de todos los obreros agrícolas.

Chávez fue un hombre sencillo de una espiritualidad profunda. Era vegetariano. Sus símbolos fueron la virgen de Guadalupe, la santa patrona de México, y un águila azteca negra en un paisaje norteamericano. Su causa enfrentó muchas

CULTURA 🇺🇸

César Chávez hablando con unos obreros en California

Uvas

dificultades y obstáculos pero Chávez no dejó la lucha. Él será para siempre no solo el líder de los campesinos mexicanoamericanos sino de todos los campesinos. Chávez murió tranquilamente en su sueño a los sesenta y seis años en Yuma, no muy lejos de la casita de adobe donde había nacido. Había en su cara una sonrisa y en la mano un libro de artesanía del sudoeste. La muerte de Chávez suscitó elogios[11] de líderes nacionales e internacionales. Robert F. Kennedy describió a este humilde campesino mexicanoamericano con su ideal de justicia e igualdad para todos como *one of the heroic figures of our time.*

¡Qué descanse en paz y que sigamos realizando su sueño!

[1]obreros *workers*
[2]huelga *strike*
[3]empresas vinícolas *wine producers*
[4]lucha *fight*
[5]ayuno *fast*
[6]rogó *begged*

[7]accedieron *agreed*
[8]otorgó *gave*
[9]recogedores *pickers*
[10]sueldo *pay*
[11]elogios *tributes, praises*

Actividades

A Cita razones por las cuales César Chávez se considera, como lo dijo Roberto Kennedy, una figura histórica de nuestra época. Después de citar las razones, provee evidencia para sostener las razones.

B Da algunos datos personales sobre la vida de Chávez y describe el tipo de persona que era.

C Según todos los recursos que tienes a tu disponibilidad, defiende o refuta la siguiente declaración «Las grandes empresas estaban muy contentas con el trabajo que hacía César Chávez y sus seguidores». Explica el porqué.

D Hoy en día siguen problemas de inmigración y derechos de los trabajadores. Trabajen en grupos de tres o cuatro y comparen todo lo que saben de estos problemas y den sus opiniones sobre unas soluciones para resolverlos.

CULTURA
Plaza de César Chávez en San José, California

¿Quién sabe?

de José Santos Chocano

INTRODUCCIÓN

En muchas partes del mundo ha habido y todavía hay problemas de que sufren los labradores, sobre todo los labradores agrícolas. Muchos de ellos trabajan muchas horas al día y en la mayoría de los casos no son dueños de la tierra que labran. Aquí tenemos un poema de José Santos Chocano (1875–1934), el famoso poeta peruano, en el cual le habla al indígena peruano.

¿Quién sabe?

—Indio que labras[1] con fatiga
tierras que de otros dueños son:
¿Ignoras tú que deben tuyas
ser, por tu sangre y tu sudor[2]?
5   ¿Ignoras tú que audaz codicia[3],
siglos atrás te las quitó?
¿Ignoras tú que eres el Amo[4]?
—¡Quién sabe, señor!

—Indio de frente taciturna
10   y de pupilas sin fulgor[5]
¿Qué pensamiento es el que escondes
en tu enigmática expresión?
¿Qué es lo que buscas en tu vida?
¿Qué es lo que imploras a tu Dios?
15   ¿Qué es lo que sueña tu silencio?
—¡Quién sabe, señor!

[1]labras   *work*   [4]Amo   *owner*
[2]sudor   *sweat*   [5]sin fulgor   *without sparkle*
[3]audaz codicia   *bold greed*

Actividades

A Escribe un resumen sobre lo que aprendiste del indígena a quien habla José Santos Chocano. Indica las transiciones que hace el autor en su obra.

B Hablando en grupos discutan por qué usa el autor tantas preguntas en su poema. ¿Tendrá un sentido o mensaje especial? ¿Cuál será? ¿Cuál será la razón?

C Llega a una conclusión sobre el poema explicando la respuesta repetida del indígena: «¡Quién sabe, señor!»

CULTURA En muchos casos los agricultores se sirven de métodos antiguos para cultivar la tierra como vemos en este campo en Puno, Perú.

Student Resources

Daniel Salsgiver

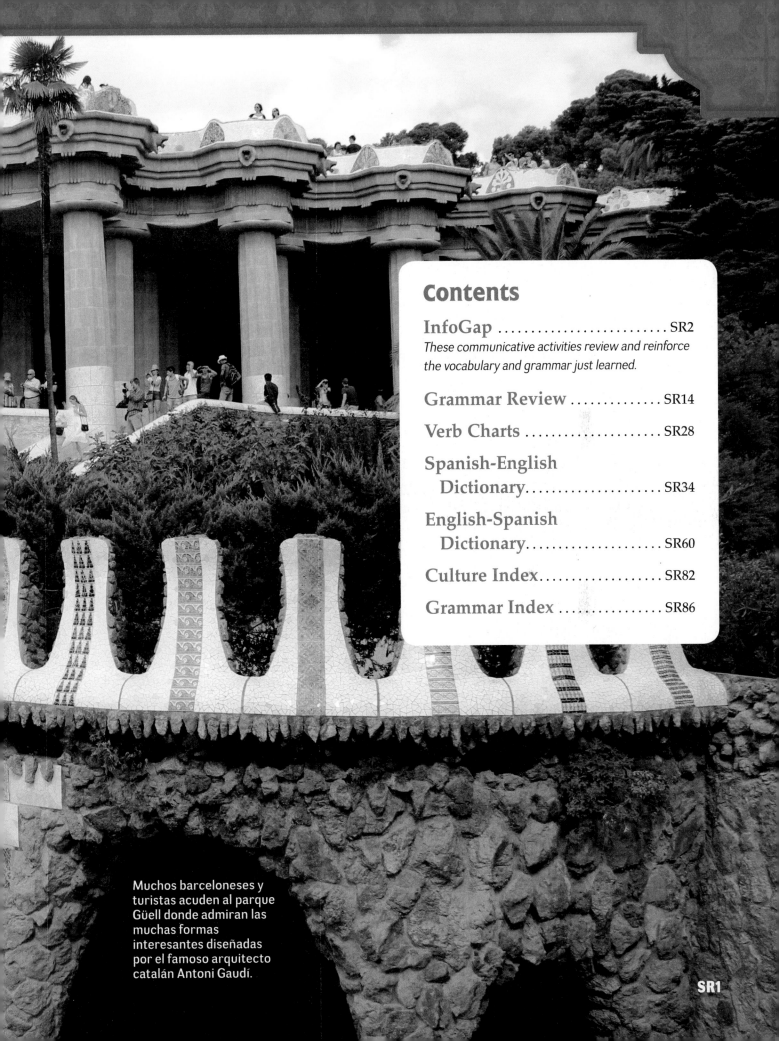

Contents

InfoGap SR2
*These communicative activities review and reinforce
the vocabulary and grammar just learned.*

Grammar Review SR14

Verb Charts SR28

**Spanish-English
  Dictionary** SR34

**English-Spanish
  Dictionary** SR60

Culture Index SR82

Grammar Index SR86

Muchos barceloneses y
turistas acuden al parque
Güell donde admiran las
muchas formas
interesantes diseñadas
por el famoso arquitecto
catalán Antoni Gaudí.

InfoGap

Alumno A Ask your partner the following questions. Correct answers are in parentheses.

1. ¿Dónde nadaste? (*Nadé en el mar.*)
2. ¿Adónde fueron ustedes? (*Fuimos al mercado.*)
3. ¿Qué viste? (*Vi una película.*)
4. ¿Qué comieron ustedes? (*Comimos una tortilla a la española.*)
5. ¿Dónde viviste? (*Viví en El Salvador.*)

Alumno A Use the clues below to answer your partner's questions.

1. el telesilla
2. una camisa roja
3. una exposición de arte colombiano
4. yo
5. no

Alumno B Use the clues below to answer your partner's questions.

1. el mar

2. al mercado

3. una película

4. una tortilla a la española

5. El Salvador

Alumno B Ask your partner the following questions. Correct answers are in parentheses.

1. ¿Cómo subieron la montaña ustedes? (*Subimos la montaña en el telesilla.*)

2. ¿Qué le compraste a Sofi? (*Le compré una camisa roja.*)

3. ¿Qué vieron ustedes? (*Vimos una exposición de arte colombiano.*)

4. ¿Quién fue el/la ganador(a)? (*Yo fui el/la ganador[a].*)

5. ¿Tomaron mucho sol ustedes? (*No, no tomamos mucho sol.*)

Alumno A Ask your partner the following questions. Correct answers are in parentheses.

Alumno A Answer your partner's questions based on the pictures below.

1. ¿Es una tarjeta de embarque o un carnet de identidad?
   (Es una tarjeta de embarque.)

2. ¿Qué hace Gil?
   (Gil factura su equipaje.)

3. ¿Quién espera a los pasajeros?
   (El taxista espera a los pasajeros.)

4. ¿Dónde están la madre y su hija? *(La madre y su hija están en el aeropuerto.)*

Alumno B Answer your partner's questions based on the pictures below.

1.
3.
2.
4.

Alumno B Ask your partner the following questions. Correct answers are in parentheses.

1. ¿Dónde pone el padre el equipaje? *(El padre pone el equipaje en la maletera [el baúl].)*

2. ¿Dónde están las pasajeras? *(Las pasajeras están en el mostrador de la línea aérea.)*

3. ¿El avión acaba de despegar o de aterrizar? *(El avión acaba de aterrizar.)*

4. ¿Cuál es el número del asiento del pasajero? *(El número del asiento del pasajero es 1C.)*

InfoGap

InfoGap

Activity 2

Alumno A Ask your partner the following questions. Correct answers are in parentheses.

Alumno A Answer your partner's questions based on the photos below.

Mateo

Elisa

Federico

la muchacha

1. ¿Qué hace Catalina? *(Catalina se cepilla los dientes.)* or *(Catalina se lava los dientes.)*

2. ¿Se acuesta Mateo o se estira? *(Mateo se acuesta.)*

3. ¿Qué hace Celia? *(Celia se pone un suéter.)*

4. ¿Se sienta la joven a la mesa o se cepilla el pelo? *(La joven se sienta a la mesa.)*

Alumno B Answer your partner's questions based on the photos below.

la joven

Celia

Mateo

Catalina

Alumno B Ask your partner the following questions. Correct answers are in parentheses.

1. ¿Qué hace Elisa? *(Elisa se despierta.)* or *(Elisa se estira.)* or *(Elisa se levanta.)*

2. ¿Qué hace Mateo? *(Mateo se lava la cara.)*

3. ¿Qué hace la muchacha? *(La muchacha se peina.)* or *(La muchacha se mira en el espejo.)*

4. ¿Se mira en el espejo Federico o se lava el pelo? *(Federico se lava el pelo.)*

InfoGap

Alumno A Ask your partner the following questions. Correct answers are in parentheses.

1. ¿Dónde compra el señor su billete? (*el señor compra su billete en la ventanilla [la boletería].*)

2. ¿Dónde comen Marcos y Mariana? (*Marcos y Mariana comen en el coche comedor [el coche cafetería].*)

3. ¿Dónde están los pasajeros? (*Los pasajeros están en el vagón [el coche].*) or (*Los pasajeros están en el tren.*)

4. ¿Qué lee el muchacho? (*El muchacho lee una revista.*) or (*El muchacho lee un periódico.*)

Alumno A Answer your partner's questions based on the pictures below.

4.

2-3.

1.

Alumno B Answer your partner's questions based on the pictures below.

1.

3-4.

2.

Alumno B Ask your partner the following questions. Correct answers are in parentheses.

1. ¿Dónde compras tu billete? (*Compro mi billete en el distribuidor automático.*)

2. ¿A quién le da su billete la muchacha? (*La muchacha le da su billete al revisor.*)

3. ¿Está el revisor en la plaza o en el pasillo? (*El revisor está en el pasillo.*)

4. ¿Van a bajar del tren los pasajeros o van a subir al tren? (*Los pasajeros van a subir al tren.*)

InfoGap

Activity 4

Alumno A Ask your partner the following questions. Correct answers are in parentheses.

1. ¿Qué piden ustedes? (*Nosotros pedimos los mariscos.*)

2. ¿Quién repitió la orden? (*El mesero repitió la orden.*)

3. ¿Cuántas horas durmieron los muchachos? (*Los muchachos durmieron cinco horas.*)

4. ¿Qué prefieres tomar? (*Prefiero tomar jugo.*)

5. ¿Cuántas veces repetí yo «el postre»? (*Tú repetiste «el postre» tres veces.*)

Alumno A Use the clues below to answer your partner's questions.

1. José Luis

2. los tostones

3. el arroz con frijoles

4. sí

5. el cocinero

Alumno B Use the clues below to answer your partner's questions.

1. los mariscos

2. el mesero

3. cinco horas

4. jugo

5. tres veces

Alumno B Ask your partner the following questions. Correct answers are in parentheses.

1. ¿Quién se viste? (*José Luis se viste.*)

2. ¿Qué prefirieron comer tus amigos? (*Mis amigos prefirieron comer los tostones.*)

3. ¿Qué pediste tú? (*Pedí el arroz con frijoles.*)

4. ¿Se divierten ustedes? (*Sí, nosotros nos divertimos.*)

5. ¿Quién frió las papas? (*El cocinero frió las papas.*)

InfoGap

Alumno A Answer your partner's questions based on the pictures below.

Alumno A Ask your partner the following questions. Correct answers are in parentheses.

1. ¿Qué celebraba la familia?
   (La familia celebraba Hanuka [la fiesta de las luces].)

2. ¿Qué había en el puesto? (Había esqueletos en el puesto.)

3. ¿Qué hay en los zapatos?
   (Hay paja en los zapatos.)

4. ¿Qué llevaba la muchacha?
   (La muchacha llevaba una máscara.)

Alumno B Answer your partner's questions based on the pictures below.

Alumno B Ask your partner the following questions. Correct answers are in parentheses.

1. ¿Qué hay en la sala?
   (Hay un árbol de Navidad en la sala.)
   or (Hay muchos aguinaldos en la sala.)

2. ¿Qué enciende el joven?
   (El joven enciende una vela de la menora.)

3. ¿Quiénes son ellos? (Ellos son los Reyes Magos.)

4. ¿Es un desfile o una tumba?
   (Es un desfile.)

InfoGap

Activity 6

Alumno A Ask your partner the following questions. Correct answers are in parentheses.

1. ¿La muchacha navega el Internet o asigna timbres a sus amigos? *(La muchacha navega el Internet.)*

2. ¿Qué compraste ayer? *(Compré un móvil [un (teléfono) celular].)*

3. ¿Cuál es el prefijo del país? *(El prefijo del país es 34.)*

4. ¿Cuál es la clave de área? *(La clave de área es 952.)*

Alumno A Answer your partner's questions based on the pictures below.

4.

2–3.

1.

Alumno B Answer your partner's questions based on the pictures below.

1.

3–4.

(+34) 952-001-0001

2.

Alumno B Ask your partner the following questions. Correct answers are in parentheses.

1. ¿Qué hace el muchaco? *(El muchacho baja fotos de su cámara digital.)*

2. ¿Qué usa el muchacho? *(El muchacho usa el teléfono público.)*

3. ¿Usa una tarjeta telefónica o unas monedas para hacer la llamada? *(Usa una tarjeta telefónica.)*

4. ¿Qué va a comprar Felipe para su computadora? *(Felipe va a comprar una impresora para su computadora.)*

Alumno A Ask your partner the following questions. Correct answers are in parentheses.

1. ¿Adónde no has ido todavía?
(Todavía no he ido al museo.)

2. ¿Quién ya ha llegado? (El mozo ya ha llegado.)

3. ¿Quién te ha ayudado?
(Mi padre me ha ayudado.)

4. ¿Qué ha comido Sara? (Sara ha comido el desayuno continental.)

5. ¿Qué han bebido ustedes?
(Hemos bebido un café.)

Alumno A Use the clues below to answer your partner's questions.

1. el huésped

2. Colombia

3. Francisco

4. en el restaurante nuevo

5. Fernando

Alumno B Use the clues below to answer your partner's questions.

1. al museo

2. el mozo

3. mi padre

4. el desayuno continental

5. un café

Alumno B Ask your partner the following questions. Correct answers are in parentheses.

1. ¿Quién ha abandonado el cuarto? (El huésped ha abandonado el cuarto.)

2. ¿Adónde ya han viajado ustedes? (Ya hemos viajado a Colombia.)

3. ¿Con quién has hablado? (He hablado con Francisco.)

4. ¿Dónde hemos comido ya? (Ya hemos comido en el restaurante nuevo.)

5. ¿Quién te ha dado un regalo? (Fernando me ha dado un regalo.)

InfoGap

InfoGap

Alumno A Ask your partner the following questions. Correct answers are in parentheses.

1. ¿Dónde entran los jóvenes?
   (Los jóvenes entran en la boca del metro.)

2. ¿Qué cosecha el campesino?
   (El campesino cosecha el trigo.)

3. ¿Es un cordero o es un cerdo?
   (Es un cerdo.)

4. ¿Dónde está la gente?
   (La gente está en la parada de autobús.)

Alumno A Answer your partner's questions based on the pictures below.

1.

2.

3.

4.

Alumno B Answer your partner's questions based on the pictures below.

1.

2.

3.

4.

Alumno B Ask your partner the following questions. Correct answers are in parentheses.

1. ¿Es una vaca o es una gallina?
   (Es una vaca.)

2. ¿Dónde están los caballos?
   (Los caballos están en el establo.)

3. ¿Adónde van los jóvenes este fin de semana? *(Los jóvenes van al parque de atracciones este fin de semana.)*

4. ¿Dónde vive la familia, en la ciudad o en el campo?
   (La familia vive en el campo.)

Alumno A Ask your partner the following questions. Correct answers are in parentheses.

1. ¿Debo tomar el ascensor o las escaleras? *(Toma el ascensor.)*

2. ¿Quieres el vaso? *(Sí, pásame el vaso, por favor.)* or *(Sí, pásamelo, por favor.)*

3. ¿Quieres saber el secreto? *(Sí, dime el secreto.)* or *(Sí, dímelo.)*

4. ¿Qué hago con los libros? *(Pon los libros en la mesa.)* or *(Ponlos en la mesa.)*

5. ¿Adónde debo ir el viernes? *(Ve a la fiesta.)*

Alumno A Answer your partner's questions with an affirmative command based on the cues and the verbs given below.

1. llevar / a la playa

2. venir / aquí

3. sí / pasarme

4. estudiar / todos los días

5. salir / conmigo

Alumno B Answer your partner's questions with an affirmative command based on the cues and the verbs given below.

1. tomar / el ascensor

2. sí / pasarme

3. sí / decirme

4. poner / en la mesa

5. ir / a la fiesta

Alumno B Ask your partner the following questions. Correct answers are in parentheses.

1. ¿Qué hago con la cámara digital? *(Lleva la cámara digital a la playa.)* or *(Llévala a la playa.)*

2. ¿Adónde debo ir? *(Ven aquí.)*

3. ¿Quieres el pan? *(Sí, pásame el pan, por favor.)* or *(Sí, pásamelo, por favor.)*

4. ¿Qué debo hacer para sacar notas buenas? *(Estudia todos los días.)*

5. ¿Con quién debo salir? *(Sal conmigo.)*

InfoGap

Activity 10

Alumno A Ask your partner the following questions. Correct answers are in parentheses.

1. ¿Qué quiere Marisa que su primo haga? *(Marisa quiere que su primo se acueste.)*

2. ¿Qué quieren sus amigos que Marta haga? *(Sus amigos quieren que Marta salga este fin de semana.)*

3. ¿Qué quieres que hagamos esta noche? *(Quiero que miremos la tele esta noche.)*

4. ¿Qué quiere la madre de Diego que él haga? *(La madre de Diego quiere que él limpie la casa.)*

Alumno A Answer your partner's questions based on the clues below.

1. jugar tenis

2. preparar la comida

3. conducir con cuidado

4. decir la verdad

Alumno B Answer your partner's questions based on the clues below.

1. acostarse

2. salir este fin de semana

3. mirar la tele

4. limpiar la casa

Alumno B Ask your partner the following questions. Correct answers are in parentheses.

1. ¿Qué quieren los padres que sus hijos hagan? *(Los padres quieren que sus hijos jueguen tenis.)*

2. ¿Qué quieres que yo haga? *(Quiero que tú prepares la comida.)*

3. ¿Qué quiere Olivia que su hermana haga? *(Olivia quiere que su hermana conduzca con cuidado.)*

4. ¿Qué quiere el profesor que sus alumnos hagan? *(El profesor quiere que sus alumnos digan la verdad.)*

Alumno A Ask your partner the following questions. Correct answers are in parentheses.

1. ¿Qué se ha cortado la joven?
   (La joven se ha cortado la frente.)

2. ¿Ella está en la ambulancia?
   (No, ella no está en la ambulancia.)

3. ¿El médico le pone unas suturas?
   (Sí, el médico le pone unas suturas [unos puntos].)

4. ¿Qué le va a poner la enfermera?
   (La enfermera le va a poner una venda.)

Alumno A Answer your partner's questions based on the photo below.

Alumno B Answer your partner's questions based on the photos below.

Alumno B Ask your partner the following questions. Correct answers are in parentheses.

1. ¿Qué se rompió el joven?
   (El joven se rompió el tobillo.) or
   (El joven se rompío el pie.)

2. ¿Habla el joven con los socorristas?
   (No, el joven no habla con los socorristas.)

3. ¿Con quién habla el joven?
   (El joven habla con la médica.)

4. ¿Está en una silla de ruedas?
   (Sí, está en una silla de ruedas.)

Grammar Review

Nouns and articles

Nouns and definite articles

A noun is the name of a person, place, or thing. Unlike English, all nouns in Spanish have a gender—either masculine or feminine. Almost all nouns that end in **-o** are masculine and almost all nouns that end in **-a** are feminine. Note that the definite article **el** is used with masculine nouns. The definite article **la** is used with feminine nouns.

MASCULINE	FEMININE
el muchacho	**la muchacha**
el libro	**la escuela**
el curso	**la sala**

Nouns that end in **-e** can be either masculine or feminine. It is necessary for you to learn the gender.

MASCULINE	FEMININE
el padre	**la madre**
el restaurante	**la carne**
el nombre	**la leche**
el norte	**la gente**
el billete	**la nube**

Many nouns that end in **-e** and refer to a person can be either masculine or feminine.

el paciente	**la paciente**

It is also necessary to learn the gender of nouns that end in a consonant.

el comedor	**la flor**
el animal	**la capital**
el jamón	**la mujer**

Note, however, that nouns that end in **-ción, -dad, -tad** are always feminine.

la habitación	**la universidad**	**la dificultad**

Irregular nouns

There are not many irregular nouns in Spanish. The ones you have learned so far are:

la mano   **el problema**   **la foto** (from **la fotografía**)

Plural of nouns

To form the plural of nouns you add **-s** to nouns that end in a vowel. You add **-es** to nouns that end in a consonant. Note, too, that the definite articles **el** and **la** become **los** and **las** in the plural.

MASCULINE PLURAL	FEMININE PLURAL
los libros	**las novelas**
los cuartos	**las casas**
los coches	**las carnes**
los comedores	**las flores**

Nouns that end in **-z** change the **-z** to **-c** and add **-es.**

el lápiz   **los lápices**

Nouns that end in **-ción** drop the accent in the plural.

la estación   **las estaciones**
la conversación   **las conversaciones**

Indefinite articles

The indefinite articles are *a, an,* and *some* in English. They are **un, una, unos, unas** in Spanish. Note that the indefinite article, like the definite article, must agree with the noun it modifies in both gender (masculine or feminine) and number (singular or plural).

SINGULAR		PLURAL	
un alumno	**una alumna**	**unos alumnos**	**unas alumnas**
un café	**una clase**	**unos cafés**	**unas clases**
un árbol	**una flor**	**unos árboles**	**unas flores**

Contractions

The prepositions **a** *(to, at)* and **de** *(of, from)* contract (combine) with the definite article **el** to form one word, **al** or **del.** There is no contraction with **la, los,** or **las.**

> **Voy al mercado; no vuelvo del mercado.**
> **Es el dinero del empleado, no del cliente.**

A personal

Remember that whenever a person is the direct object of the verb, it must be preceded by **a.** This **a personal** also contracts with **el.**

> **Conozco a Juan.**
> **Pero no conozco al hermano de Juan.**

Nouns and adjectives

Agreement of nouns and adjectives

An adjective is a word that describes a noun. An adjective must agree in gender (masculine or feminine) and number (singular or plural) with the noun it describes or modifies.

Adjectives that end in **-o** have four forms, the same as nouns that end in **-o.**

	SINGULAR	PLURAL
MASCULINE	**el muchacho simpático**	**los muchachos simpáticos**
FEMININE	**la muchacha simpática**	**las muchachas simpáticas**

Adjectives that end in **-e** have only two forms—singular and plural.

	SINGULAR	PLURAL
MASCULINE	**un alumno inteligente**	**los alumnos inteligentes**
FEMININE	**una alumna inteligente**	**las alumnas inteligentes**

Adjectives that end in a consonant have only two forms—singular and plural. Note that the plural ends in **-es.**

	SINGULAR	PLURAL
MASCULINE	**un curso fácil**	**dos cursos fáciles**
FEMININE	**una tarea fácil**	**dos tareas fáciles**

Adjectives of nationality

Adjectives of nationality that end in a consonant have four forms. Observe the following.

> **un joven francés**   **unos jóvenes franceses**
> **una joven francesa**   **unas jóvenes francesas**

Note that adjectives of nationality that end in **-s, -n (francés, inglés, japonés, tailandés, alemán, catalán)** drop the written accent in all forms except the masculine singular.

Possessive adjectives

A possessive adjective tells who owns or possesses something—*my* book and *your* pencil. Like other adjectives in Spanish, possessive adjectives agree with the noun they modify. Note that only **nuestro** and *vuestro* have four forms.

MASCULINE SINGULAR	FEMININE SINGULAR	MASCULINE PLURAL	FEMININE PLURAL
mi tío	**mi tía**	**mis tíos**	**mis tías**
tu tío	**tu tía**	**tus tíos**	**tus tías**
su tío	**su tía**	**sus tíos**	**sus tías**
nuestro tío	**nuestra tía**	**nuestros tíos**	**nuestras tías**
vuestro tío	*vuestra tía*	*vuestros tíos*	*vuestras tías*

Since **su** can refer to many different people, it is often accompanied by a phrase that gives clarification.

su familia

la familia de Juan	**la familia de él**
la familia de María	**la familia de ella**
la familia de Juan y María	**la familia de ellos**

la familia de usted

la familia de ustedes

Demonstrative adjectives

Until recently the demonstrative pronoun (*this one, that one, these, those*) had to carry a written accent to differentiate it from a demonstrative adjective. That is no longer the case and the pronouns are the same as the adjectives.

In Spanish there are three demonstrative adjectives (pronouns): **este** (*this*), **ese** (*that*), and **aquel** (*that, farther away*). Each of the demonstratives has four forms and must agree in gender and number with the nouns they modify or replace.

MASCULINE SINGULAR	FEMININE SINGULAR	MASCULINE PLURAL	FEMININE PLURAL
este libro	**esta chaqueta**	**estos libros**	**estas chaquetas**
ese libro	**esa chaqueta**	**esos libros**	**esas chaquetas**
aquel libro	**aquella chaqueta**	**aquellos libros**	**aquellas chaquetas**

Comparative and superlative

Regular forms

You use the comparative *(more, -er)* and the superlative *(most, -est)* to compare people or things.

To form the comparative in Spanish you use **más** (or **menos**) before the adjective. The comparative is followed by **que: más… que.**

> **Él es más (menos) inteligente que los otros.**
> **Ella es más ambiciosa que los otros.**

To form the superlative you use the definite article with **más.** Note that **de** follows the superlative: **el/la más… de.**

> **Él es el más ambicioso de todos.**
> **Ella es la alumna más inteligente de todos.**

Irregular forms

The adjectives **bueno** and **malo** and the adverbs **bien** and **mal** have irregular comparative and superlative forms.

	COMPARATIVE	SUPERLATIVE
bueno	mejor	el/la mejor
malo	peor	el/la peor
bien	mejor	el/la mejor
mal	peor	el/la peor

> **Él es mejor jugador que su hermano.**
> **Pero su hermana Teresa es la mejor jugadora de los tres.**
> **La verdad es que ella juega mejor que nadie.**
> **Ella juega mejor que yo.**

Note that the comparative is followed by the subject pronoun or a negative word.

> **más alto que yo (tú, él, nosotros)**
> **más alto que nadie**

(El) mayor and **(el) menor** are also comparative and superlative forms. They most often refer to age and sometimes size.

> **Mi hermano menor tiene trece años.**
> **Y mi hermana mayor tiene diecisiete.**
> **La Ciudad de México tiene el mayor número de habitantes.**

Comparison of equality

To compare things that have equal qualities *as . . . as* you use **tan... como** in Spanish. Note that **tan** can precede an adjective or an adverb.

> **Ella es tan inteligente como sus hermanos.**
> **Sus hermanos son tan inteligentes como ella.**
> **Ella habla tan rápido como los otros.**

To compare equal quantities *as much . . . as, as many . . . as* you use **tanto... como.** Since **tanto** is an adjective it must agree with the noun it modifies.

> **Él tiene tanta paciencia como su hermana.**
> **Susana no tiene tantos primos como yo.**

Note that the subject pronouns follow **como.**

Pronouns

A pronoun is a word that replaces a noun. Review the forms of the pronouns that you have learned so far.

SUBJECT PRONOUNS	DIRECT OBJECT PRONOUNS	INDIRECT OBJECT PRONOUNS	REFLEXIVE PRONOUNS	PREPOSITIONAL PRONOUNS
yo	me	me	me	mí
tú	te	te	te	ti
Ud., él, ella	lo, la	le	se	Ud., él, ella
nosotros(as)	nos	nos	nos	nosotros(as)
vosotros(as)	os	os	os	vosotros(as)
Uds., ellos, ellas	los, las	les	se	Uds., ellos, ellas

Remember that an object pronoun comes right before the conjugated form of the verb.

> **Ella me ve.**   **Ella nos habla.**   **Ella lo ha escrito.**

The direct object pronoun is the direct receiver of the action of the verb. The indirect object is the indirect receiver of the action of the verb.

The direct object pronouns **lo, la, los, las** can refer to a person or a thing.

> **Ellos tiraron la pelota.**   **Ellos la tiraron.**
> **Ellos vieron a sus amigos.**   **Ellos los vieron.**

The indirect object pronouns **le, les** refer to people only. They are often accompanied by a phrase for clarification.

> **Ella le habló**
> > a él.
> > a ella.
> > a usted.
>
> **Yo les hablé**
> > a ellos.
> > a ellas.
> > a ustedes.

Note that the prepositional pronouns **mí** and **ti** form one word with **con.**

> **Yo voy contigo y tú vas conmigo.**

Double object pronouns

When there are two object pronouns in the same sentence, the indirect object pronoun always precedes the direct object pronoun.

Él me lo dijo.
Nuestros padres nos los dan.
¿Quién te lo dio?

The indirect object pronouns **le** and **les** change to **se** when used with a direct object pronoun **(lo, la, los, las).**

El profesor se lo explica muy bien.
¿Quién se las compró?

Se is often accompanied by a prepositional phrase to clarify its meaning.

Yo se lo di
{
a usted.
a él.
a ella.
a ustedes.
a ellos.
a ellas.

Position of object pronouns

The object pronouns always precede the conjugated form of the verb.

José me vio.
El profesor se lo explicó a ustedes.
Ellos no lo han hecho.

With the progressive tenses or the infinitive the pronouns can either come before the helping verb or can be added to the present participle or the infinitive.

Ellos nos están ayudando.   **Ella te lo va a explicar.**
Ellos están ayudándonos.   **Ella va a explicártelo.**

Ella se la está vendiendo a ellos.   **Ellos nos quieren ayudar.**
Ella está vendiéndosela a ellos.   **Ellos quieren ayudarnos.**

Note that in order to maintain the same stress you add a written accent mark to the present participle with either one or two pronouns. You add an accent to the infinitive with two pronouns only.

The object pronouns are added to an affirmative command. They precede the negative command.

AFFIRMATIVE	NEGATIVE
Háblame.	**No me hables.**
Dáselo.	**No se lo des.**
Invítelos usted.	**No los invite.**
Díganmelo.	**No me lo digan.**

Note that in order to maintain the same stress, you add a written accent to the command with a pronoun.

Negative expressions

To make a sentence negative, you merely put **no** before the verb or before the object pronoun that precedes the verb.

El gato no está en el jardín.
No lo veo.

Review the following affirmative and negative expressions.

AFFIRMATIVE	NEGATIVE
algo	**nada**
alguien	**nadie**
siempre	**nunca**

Nadie está aquí.

Note that in Spanish, unlike in English, more than one negative word can be used in the same sentence.

No ves a nadie.
Ellos nunca hablan a nadie de nada.

The negative of **también** is **tampoco**.

A Juan le gusta. A mí también.
A Juan no le gusta. Ni a mí tampoco.

Grammar Review

Verbs such as interesar, aburrir, gustar

Note the construction with verbs such as **interesar** and **aburrir.**

La historia me interesa.
Me interesa la historia.

History interests me.

Los deportes no les aburren.
No les aburren los deportes.

Sports don't bore them.

Gustar functions the same as **interesar** and **aburrir.** It conveys the meaning *to like,* but it literally means *to please.*

Me
Te
Le
Nos
Les
gusta el helado.

Me
Te
Le
Nos
Les
gustan los vegetales.

Expressions with the infinitive

The infinitive is the form of the verb that ends in **-ar, -er,** or **-ir.** The infinitive often follows another verb.

Ellos quieren salir.
Yo debo estudiar más.
Me gusta leer.

Three very common expressions that are followed by the infinitive are **tener que** *(to have to),* **ir a** *(to be going to),* and **acabar de** *(to have just).*

Tengo que trabajar y estudiar más.
Y voy a trabajar y estudiar más.
Acabo de recibir una nota mala.

You can use the expression **favor de** followed by an infinitive to ask someone in a polite way to do something.

Favor de escribir tu nombre.
Favor de ayudarme.

Note that the object pronoun is added to the end of the infinitive.

Ser and estar

Spanish has two verbs that mean *to be*. They are **ser** and **estar** and each one has distinct uses.

Ser

You use **ser** to express a characteristic, where someone or something is from, or what something is made of.

> **Él es guapo. Es inteligente también.**
> **Ellos son de Nuevo México.**
> **Su casa es de adobe.**

Estar

You use **estar** to express a condition or location.

> **Él está muy cansado y está triste también.**
> **Madrid está en España.**
> **Sus amigos están en Madrid.**

Saber and conocer

Both **saber** and **conocer** mean *to know.*

Saber means to know a fact or to have information about something. With an infinitive it expresses *to know how to do something.*

> **Yo sé su número de teléfono.**
> **Sabemos que ella va a viajar.**
> **Todos saben usar el Internet.**

Conocer means *to know* in the sense of *to be familiar with.* It is used with people or complex, abstract concepts.

> **Yo conozco a su amigo Tadeo.**
> **Ellos conocen bien la historia de España.**

Reflexive verbs

When the subject is both the doer and receiver of the action of the verb, you have to use a reflexive pronoun with the verb. Study the following examples of the reflexive construction.

REFLEXIVE	NONREFLEXIVE
Ella se levanta.	**Ella levanta al niño.**
Él se divierte.	**Él divierte a sus amigos.**
Me cepillo.	**Cepillo a mi perro.**

When the reflexive is followed by an article of clothing or a part of the body, you use a definite article in Spanish. (In English the possessive adjective is used.)

> **Me lavo la cara y las manos.**
> **Ella tiene frío y se pone el suéter.**

Verbs

See the charts on pages SR28–SR33 for the verb forms you have learned.

Verb tense usage

Present

You use the present tense to state what is taking place now or what always takes place.

Hablamos español.
Juegan fútbol en el otoño.
Siempre hacen la misma cosa.

You can also use the present tense to express a future action.

Salen mañana.
Vamos a México en julio.

Preterite

You use the preterite to express an action that began and ended at a specific time in the past.

Ellos salieron la semana pasada.
Nosotros llegamos ayer.
Los árabes invadieron España en 711.

Imperfect

You use the imperfect to describe a continuous, habitual action in the past. The time at which the action began or ended is not important.

Ellos siempre hacían la misma cosa.
Yo los veía de vez en cuando.
Ellos iban a España con frecuencia porque tenían una casa allí.

You use the imperfect to describe things in the past.

Él era joven.
Tenía solo dos años.
Hacía buen tiempo.
Su hermana era muy simpática.

You use the imperfect to reminisce about past events.

Cuando yo era niño vivíamos en Puerto Rico y siempre celebrábamos el Día de los Reyes. Yo recuerdo bien que recibíamos nuestros regalos el seis de enero.

You use the imperfect with verbs to express mental activities or emotions in the past.

Él lo creía.
Querían hacerlo.
Estaban contentos.

Future

The true future *will* is used less frequently in Spanish than in English.

Le hablaré a él mañana.
Volverán la semana que viene.

The present tense and the **ir a** + *infinitive* construction are often used to convey the future.

Le hablo a él mañana.   **Le voy a hablar mañana.**
Vuelven la semana que viene.   **Van a volver la semana que viene.**

Conditional

You use the conditional in Spanish the same as in English. It tells what would or could happen.

¿Iría él?   **Sí, él iría.**
¿Lo sabrían ellos?   **Sí, ellos lo sabrían.**
¿Estarías contento?   **Sí, yo estaría contento.**

Present perfect

The present perfect is used to describe an action without reference to a specific past time. It is accompanied by time expressions such as **ya, todavía no, jamás, nunca.**

> **Nunca hemos hecho tal cosa.**
> **En mi vida he tenido un accidente.**
> **Todavía no han llegado.**

Progressive tense

The progressive tense is formed by using the verb **estar** (or **ir, seguir**) and the present participle. You use the progressive to indicate that the action is actually taking place.

> **Estamos pasando tiempo en la playa.**
> **Estoy mirando a los niños.**
> **Están nadando en el mar.**

Subjunctive

You use the subjunctive in a dependent clause. As the word *subjunctive* implies, it is used to express a subjective action that is not necessarily a fact. It may or may not take place. So far you have learned the following uses of the subjunctive.

You use the subjunctive in a clause introduced by **querer.**

> **Quiero que ellos salgan ahora.**
> **Ellos quieren que estudiemos y que tengamos éxito.**

You use the subjunctive following many impersonal expressions.

> **Es importante que lleguemos a tiempo.**
> **Es necesario que ellos lo sepan.**
> **Es mejor que tú lo hagas.**

The subjunctive follows the expressions **ojalá, quizás,** and **tal vez.**

> **¡Ojalá vengan a la fiesta!**
> **¡Quizá(s) vayan!**
> **¡Tal vez lo sepan!**

Passive voice with se

The pronoun **se** is used to express something being done without saying by whom.

Se habla español en México.	*Spanish is spoken in Mexico.*
	One speaks Spanish in Mexico.
	They speak Spanish in Mexico.

> **¿A qué hora se abre el restaurante?**
> **Se sirven comidas mexicanas y peruanas.**

Imperative (commands)

You use the subjunctive form of the verb for all formal **(usted, ustedes)** commands and the negative familiar **(tú)** command.

Hable Ud.	**No hable Ud.**	**Hablen Uds.**	**No hablen Uds.**	**No hables.**
Coma Ud.	**No coma Ud.**	**Coman Uds.**	**No coman Uds.**	**No comas.**

You use the **usted** form of the present indicative for the familiar **(tú)** command.

Habla.
Come.

Note that you add the object pronouns to affirmative commands. The pronouns come before the negative command.

AFFIRMATIVE	NEGATIVE
Prepárelo.	**No lo prepare.**
Escríbanlo Uds.	**No lo escriban Uds.**
Háblame.	**No me hables.**

There are no irregular formal commands. You will find any irregular familiar **(tú)** commands in the following verb charts.

Verb Charts

	Regular verbs		
INFINITIVO	hablar *to speak*	comer *to eat*	vivir *to live*
PARTICIPIO PRESENTE	hablando	comiendo	viviendo
PARTICIPIO PASADO	hablado	comido	vivido
PRESENTE	hablo hablas habla hablamos *habláis* hablan	como comes come comemos *coméis* comen	vivo vives vive vivimos *vivís* viven
PRETÉRITO	hablé hablaste habló hablamos *hablasteis* hablaron	comí comiste comió comimos *comisteis* comieron	viví viviste vivió vivimos *vivisteis* vivieron
IMPERFECTO	hablaba hablabas hablaba hablábamos *hablabais* hablaban	comía comías comía comíamos *comíais* comían	vivía vivías vivía vivíamos *vivíais* vivían
FUTURO	hablaré hablarás hablará hablaremos *hablaréis* hablarán	comeré comerás comerá comeremos *comeréis* comerán	viviré vivirás vivirá viviremos *viviréis* vivirán
CONDICIONAL	hablaría hablarías hablaría hablaríamos *hablaríais* hablarían	comería comerías comería comeríamos *comeríais* comerían	viviría vivirías viviría viviríamos *viviríais* vivirían
PRESENTE PERFECTO	he hablado has hablado ha hablado hemos hablado *habéis hablado* han hablado	he comido has comido ha comido hemos comido *habéis comido* han comido	he vivido has vivido ha vivido hemos vivido *habéis vivido* han vivido

Regular verbs (continued)

SUBJUNTIVO: PRESENTE	hable	coma	viva
	hables	comas	vivas
	hable	coma	viva
	hablemos	comamos	vivamos
	habléis	*comáis*	*viváis*
	hablen	coman	vivan

Stem-changing verbs (-ar and -er verbs)

INFINITIVO	empezar (e→ie) *to begin*	perder (e→ie) *to lose*	recordar (o→ue) *to remember*	volver (o→ue) *to return*
PRESENTE	empiezo	pierdo	recuerdo	vuelvo
	empiezas	pierdes	recuerdas	vuelves
	empieza	pierde	recuerda	vuelve
	empezamos	perdemos	recordamos	volvemos
	empezáis	*perdéis*	*recordáis*	*volvéis*
	empiezan	pierden	recuerdan	vuelven
SUBJUNTIVO: PRESENTE	empiece	pierda	recuerde	vuelva
	empieces	pierdas	recuerdes	vuelvas
	empiece	pierda	recuerde	vuelva
	empecemos	perdamos	recordemos	volvamos
	empecéis	*perdáis*	*recordéis*	*volváis*
	empiecen	pierdan	recuerden	vuelvan

e→ie

Other verbs conjugated like **empezar** and **perder** are: **cerrar, comenzar, despertar, pensar, defender, entender, querer.**

o→ue

Other verbs conjugated like **recordar** and **volver** are: **acordar, almorzar, contar, costar, probar, acostar(se), jugar (u→ue), devolver, mover, poder.**

Stem-changing verbs (-ir verbs)

INFINITIVO	preferir (e→ie, i) *to prefer*	dormir (o→ue, u) *to sleep*	pedir (e→i, i) *to ask for*
PARTICIPIO PRESENTE	prefiriendo	durmiendo	pidiendo
PRESENTE	prefiero	duermo	pido
	prefieres	duermes	pides
	prefiere	duerme	pide
	preferimos	dormimos	pedimos
	preferís	*dormís*	*pedís*
	prefieren	duermen	piden

Verb Charts

Stem-changing verbs (-ir verbs) *(continued)*

PRETÉRITO	preferí preferiste prefirió preferimos *preferisteis* prefirieron	dormí dormiste durmió dormimos *dormisteis* durmieron	pedí pediste pidió pedimos *pedisteis* pidieron
SUBJUNTIVO: PRESENTE	prefiera prefieras prefiera prefiramos *prefiráis* prefieran	duerma duermas duerma durmamos *durmáis* duerman	pida pidas pida pidamos *pidáis* pidan

e→ie, i
Other verbs conjugated like **preferir** are: **sentir, sugerir.**

o→ue
Another verb conjugated like **dormir** is **morir.**

e→i, i
Other verbs conjugated like **pedir** are: **repetir, servir, seguir, vestirse.**

Irregular verbs

PARTICIPIO PASADO	**abrir** *to open* **abierto**					
PRETÉRITO	**andar** *to walk* anduve	anduviste	anduvo	anduvimos	*anduvisteis*	anduvieron
PRESENTE	**conocer** *to know, to be familiar with* conozco	conoces	conoce	conocemos	*conocéis*	conocen
PARTICIPIO PASADO	**cubrir** *to cover* cubierto					
PRESENTE	**dar** *to give* doy	das	da	damos	*dais*	dan
PRETÉRITO	di	diste	dio	dimos	*disteis*	dieron
SUBJUNTIVO	dé	des	dé	demos	*deis*	den

Irregular verbs *(continued)*

decir *to say*						
PARTICIPIO PRESENTE	diciendo					
PARTICIPIO PASADO	dicho					
PRESENTE	digo	dices	dice	decimos	*decís*	dicen
PRETÉRITO	dije	dijiste	dijo	dijimos	*dijisteis*	dijeron
FUTURO	diré	dirás	dirá	diremos	*diréis*	dirán
CONDICIONAL	diría	dirías	diría	diríamos	*diríais*	dirían
IMPERATIVO FAMILIAR	di					

devolver *to return (bring back)*	
PARTICIPIO PASADO	devuelto

escribir *to write*	
PARTICIPIO PASADO	escrito

estar *to be*						
PRESENTE	estoy	estás	está	estamos	*estáis*	están
PRETÉRITO	estuve	estuviste	estuvo	estuvimos	*estuvisteis*	estuvieron
SUBJUNTIVO	esté	estés	esté	estemos	*estéis*	estén

freír *to fry*	
PARTICIPIO PASADO	frito

haber *to have (in compound tenses)*						
PRESENTE	he	has	ha	hemos	*habéis*	han

hacer *to do, to make*						
PARTICIPIO PASADO	hecho					
PRESENTE	hago	haces	hace	hacemos	*hacéis*	hacen
PRETÉRITO	hice	hiciste	hizo	hicimos	*hicisteis*	hicieron
FUTURO	haré	harás	hará	haremos	*haréis*	harán
CONDICIONAL	haría	harías	haría	haríamos	*haríais*	harían
IMPERATIVO FAMILIAR	haz					

ir *to go*						
PARTICIPIO PRESENTE	yendo					
PRESENTE	voy	vas	va	vamos	*vais*	van
PRETÉRITO	fui	fuiste	fue	fuimos	*fuisteis*	fueron
IMPERFECTO	iba	ibas	iba	íbamos	*ibais*	iban
SUBJUNTIVO	vaya	vayas	vaya	vayamos	*vayáis*	vayan
IMPERATIVO FAMILIAR	ve					

morir *to die*	
PARTICIPIO PASADO	muerto

Verb Charts

Irregular verbs (continued)

oír *to hear*						
PRESENTE	oigo	oyes	oye	oímos	*oís*	oyen
poder *to be able to*						
PARTICIPIO PRESENTE	pudiendo					
PRETÉRITO	pude	pudiste	pudo	pudimos	*pudisteis*	pudieron
FUTURO	podré	podrás	podrá	podremos	*podréis*	podrán
CONDICIONAL	podría	podrías	podría	podríamos	*podríais*	podrían
poner *to put*						
PARTICIPIO PASADO	puesto					
PRESENTE	pongo	pones	pone	ponemos	*ponéis*	ponen
PRETÉRITO	puse	pusiste	puso	pusimos	*pusisteis*	pusieron
FUTURO	pondré	pondrás	pondrá	pondremos	*pondréis*	pondrán
CONDICIONAL	pondría	pondrías	pondría	pondríamos	*pondríais*	pondrían
IMPERATIVO FAMILIAR	pon					
querer *to want*						
PRETÉRITO	quise	quisiste	quiso	quisimos	*quisisteis*	quisieron
FUTURO	querré	querrás	querrá	querremos	*querréis*	querrán
CONDICIONAL	querría	querrías	querría	querríamos	*querríais*	querrían
romper *to break*						
PARTICIPIO PASADO	roto					
saber *to know (how)*						
PRESENTE	sé	sabes	sabe	sabemos	*sabéis*	saben
PRETÉRITO	supe	supiste	supo	supimos	*supisteis*	supieron
FUTURO	sabré	sabrás	sabrá	sabremos	*sabréis*	sabrán
CONDICIONAL	sabría	sabrías	sabría	sabríamos	*sabríais*	sabrían
SUBJUNTIVO	sepa	sepas	sepa	sepamos	*sepáis*	sepan
salir *to leave, to go out*						
PRESENTE	salgo	sales	sale	salimos	*salís*	salen
FUTURO	saldré	saldrás	saldrá	saldremos	*saldréis*	saldrán
CONDICIONAL	saldría	saldrías	saldría	saldríamos	*saldríais*	saldrían
IMPERATIVO FAMILIAR	sal					
ser *to be*						
PRESENTE	soy	eres	es	somos	*sois*	son
PRETÉRITO	fui	fuiste	fue	fuimos	*fuisteis*	fueron
IMPERFECTO	era	eras	era	éramos	*erais*	eran
SUBJUNTIVO	sea	seas	sea	seamos	*seáis*	sean
IMPERATIVO FAMILIAR	sé					

Verb Charts

Irregular verbs (continued)

tener *to have*

PRESENTE	tengo	tienes	tiene	tenemos	*tenéis*	tienen
PRETÉRITO	tuve	tuviste	tuvo	tuvimos	*tuvisteis*	tuvieron
FUTURO	tendré	tendrás	tendrá	tendremos	*tendréis*	tendrán
CONDICIONAL	tendría	tendrías	tendría	tendríamos	*tendríais*	tendrían
IMPERATIVO FAMILIAR	ten					

traer *to bring*

PRESENTE	traigo	traes	trae	traemos	*traéis*	traen
PRETÉRITO	traje	trajiste	trajo	trajimos	*trajisteis*	trajeron

venir *to come*

PARTICIPIO PRESENTE	viniendo					
PRETÉRITO	vine	viniste	vino	vinimos	*vinisteis*	vinieron
FUTURO	vendré	vendrás	vendrá	vendremos	*vendréis*	vendrán
CONDICIONAL	vendría	vendrías	vendría	vendríamos	*vendríais*	vendrían
IMPERATIVO FAMILIAR	ven					

ver *to see*

PARTICIPIO PASADO	visto					
PRESENTE	veo	ves	ve	vemos	*veis*	ven
PRETÉRITO	vi	viste	vio	vimos	*visteis*	vieron
IMPERFECTO	veía	veías	veía	veíamos	*veíais*	veían

volver *to return*

PARTICIPIO PASADO	vuelto

Verb Charts

Spanish-English Dictionary

The Spanish-English Dictionary contains all productive and receptive vocabulary from Levels 1 and 2. The numbers following each productive entry indicate the chapter and vocabulary section in which the word is introduced. For example, 3.2 in dark print means that the word was first taught in **Capítulo 3, Vocabulario 2.** *A light print number means that the word was introduced in ¡Así se dice! Level 1. LP refers to the* Lecciones preliminares *in Level 1. If there is no number following an entry, this means that the word or expression is there for receptive purposes only.*

a at; to
> **a eso de las tres (cuatro, diez, etc.)** at around three (four, ten, etc.) o'clock
> **a fines de** at the end of
> **a la una (a las dos, a las tres…)** at one o'clock (two o'clock, three o'clock), LP
> **a lo lejos** in the distance
> **a lo menos** at least
> **a menudo** often
> **a pesar de** in spite of
> **a pie** on foot, 3.2
> **¡A propósito!** By the way!, 8.2
> **¿a qué hora?** at what time?, LP
> **a solas** alone
> **a tiempo** on time, 10.2; **1.2**
> **a veces** at times, sometimes, 6.1; **1.2**
> **a ver** let's see

a bordo aboard, on board, 10.2; **1.2**

abajo down; below
> **de abajo** below
> **(ir) para abajo** (to go) down

abandonar el cuarto to check out *(hotel)*, **7**

el **abono** fertilizer

abordar to board, 10.2; **1.2**

abreviado(a) abbreviated, shortened

abrigado(a) wrapped up

el **abrigo** coat

abril April, LP

abrir to open, 4.2

abrochado(a) fastened, 10.2; **1.2**

la **abuela** grandmother, 2.1

el **abuelo** grandfather, 2.1

los **abuelos** grandparents, 2.1

abundoso(a) abundant

aburrido(a) boring, 1.2

aburrir to bore, 5.2

acá here, 11.2; **2.2**

acabar de to have just (done something), 4.2

la **academia** school

acaso: por si acaso just in case

acceder to access

el **accidente** accident, **11.2**

el **aceite** oil, **4**

la **aceituna** olive, 4.2

el **acento** accent

la **acera** sidewalk, **8.1**

acercarse to approach

acomodado(a) wealthy, well-off

acomodar to set *(bone)*, **11.2**

acordarse (ue) to remember
> **¿Te acuerdas?** Do you remember?

acostarse (ue) to go to bed, 11.1; **2.1**

acostumbrarse to get used to

el **acotamiento** shoulder *(road)*, **9.1**

la **actividad** activity

actual present-day, current

actuar to act, to take action

acudir to go to

acuerdo: estar de acuerdo con to agree with

adelantar(se) to pass *(car)*, **9.1**

adelante ahead
> **ir hacia adelante** to move forward, ahead

además furthermore, what's more; besides

además de in addition to, besides

¡Adiós! Good-bye!, LP

adivinar to guess

adjunto: el documento

adjunto attached file, **6.1**

admitir to admit

¿adónde? (to) where?, 3.2

la **advertencia** warning

advertir (ie, i) to warn

aérea: la línea aérea airline, 10.1; **1.1**

aeróbico(a) aerobic

el **aeropuerto** airport, 10.1; **1.1**

aficionado(a): ser aficionado(a) a to like, to be a fan of

el/la **aficionado(a)** fan, 5.1

afine: la palabra afine cognate

las **afueras** suburbs, 2.2; outskirts

agarrar velocidad to pick up speed

el/la **agente** agent, 10.1; **1.1**

la **aglomeración** big city

agosto August, LP

agradable pleasant, friendly, agreeable

agrario(a) agrarian

agresivo(a) aggressive

agrícola agricultural

el **agua** *(f.)* water, 4.1
> **el agua mineral (con gas)** (sparkling) mineral water, 4.2
> **el agua corriente** running water

el **aguacate** avocado, **10**

el **aguinaldo** Christmas gift, **5.2**

ahora now

el **aire** air
> **al aire libre** open-air, outdoor

el **aire acondicionado** air conditioning, **7**

aislado(a) isolated

el **ají** chili pepper

el **ajo** garlic, **10**

al to the, on the, in the
> **al aire libre** open-air, outdoor

al borde mismo de right on the edge of

al contrario on the contrary

al lado de beside, next to, 2.2

la alberca swimming pool, 7.1

el albergue juvenil youth hostel, 7

la albóndiga meatball, 4.2

el álbum album

la alcachofa artichoke

las alcachofas salteadas sautéed artichokes

alcanzar to reach

la alcoba bedroom

la aldea small village

alegrarse to rejoice

alegre happy, 6.1

la alegría happiness, joy

alemán(ana) German

los alemanes Germans

la alfombrilla mouse pad, 6.1

el álgebra algebra

algo something, 4.1; anything, 9.2

¿Algo más? Anything else?, 9.2

alguien someone, somebody, 8.2

algunos(as) some

el alimento food

las alitas wings, 10

allá over there, 9.1

allí there

el alma (f.) soul

las almejas clams, 4

la almohada pillow, 7

el almuerzo lunch, 4.1

tomar el almuerzo to have lunch, 4.1

¡Aló! Hello! (on the phone)

alpino: el esquí alpino downhill skiing, 7.2

alquilar to rent, 7.1; 3.2

alrededor de around, 2.2

los alrededores outskirts, surroundings

altivo(a) arrogant

alto(a) tall, 1.1; high, 3.1; upper

la clase alta upper class

la nota alta high grade, 3.1

la altura altitude

el/la alumno(a) student, 1.2

amarillo(a) yellow, 5.1

la ambición ambition

ambicioso(a) hard-working, 1.2

el ambiente atmosphere, environment

la ambulancia ambulance, 11.2

la América del Sur South America

americano(a) American

el/la amigo(a) friend, 1.1

el amor love

amurallado(a) walled

anaranjado(a) orange (color), 5.1

ancho(a) wide, broad, 8.1

andar to go, to walk; to ride, 3.2

andar a caballo to ride a horse, 3.2

andar en bicicleta to ride a bike, 11.1

el andén (railway) platform, 3.1

andino(a) Andean, of the Andes

angosto(a) narrow, 8.1

la angustia distress, anguish

animado(a) lively

el animal animal

animar to cheer (somebody, something) on

anoche last night, 7.1

anónimo(a) anonymous

el anorak anorak, ski jacket, 7.2

los anteojos de sol sunglasses, 7.1

el antepecho parapet

anterior previous, 6.1

antes de before, 10.1; 1.1

los antibióticos antibiotics

antiguo(a) ancient, old, 8.1; former

el casco (barrio) antiguo the old city, 8.1

antipático(a) unpleasant, not nice 1.1

los antojitos snacks, nibbles, 4.2

anunciar to announce

el anuncio announcement

añadir to add, 10

el año year, LP

el Año Nuevo New Year

el año pasado last year, 7.1

¿Cuántos años tiene? How old is he (she)?, 2.1

cumplir... años to be (turn) ... years old

apagar to turn off, 6.1

el aparato device

aparcar to park, 8.1

aparentado(a) related

la apariencia appearance, looks

¿Qué apariencia tiene? What does he (she) look like?

el apartamento apartment, 2.2

la casa de apartamentos apartment house

el apartamiento apartment, 2.2

aparte apart, on the side

apetecer to feel like, to crave

apetito: ¡Buen apetito! Bon appétit! Enjoy your meal!

aplaudir to applaud, to clap, 5.1

el aplauso applause, 5.1

recibir aplausos to be applauded, 5.1

apreciado(a) appreciated, liked

aprender to learn, 4.2

apropiado(a) appropriate

aproximadamente approximately

aquel(la) that, 9.1

aquí here, 9.1

Aquí lo (las, etc.) tienes. Here it (they) is (are).

el/la árabe Arab

aragonés(esa) from Aragon (Spain)

el árbol tree, 2.2

el árbol de Navidad Christmas tree, 5.2

el arcén shoulder (road), 9.1

el archivo file, 6.1

la arena sand, 7.1

argentino(a) Argentine

árido(a) dry, arid

la aritmética arithmetic

armar to put up (tent), 11.2; 2.2

el armario closet, 7

la arqueología archaeology

el arroyo brook

la arroba the @ sign, 6.1

el arroz rice, 4.1

el arte art, 1.2

arterial: la tensión arterial blood pressure, 6.2

la artesanía crafts, 9.2

el/la artista artist

asar to grill, to roast, 10

la ascendencia heritage, background

el ascensor elevator, 7

asegurarse to make sure

así thus, so, in this way

el asiento seat, 10.1; 1.1

el número del asiento seat number, 10.1; 1.1

asignar to assign, 6.2

la asistencia médica medical care

el/la asistente de vuelo flight attendant, 10.2; 1.2

Spanish-English Dictionary

asistir a to attend, 8.1
el asno donkey
el aspa (f.) sail (windmill)
astuto(a) astute, smart
atacar to attack
la atención attention
¡Atención! Careful!
prestar atención to pay attention, 3.1
el aterrizaje landing, 10.2; **1.2**
aterrizar to land, 10.2; **1.2**
el/la atleta athlete
las atracciones rides (amusement park), **8.1**
el parque de atracciones amusement park, **8.1**
atraer to attract
atrapar to catch, 5.2
atrás: hacia atrás backwards
el atún tuna, 9.2
aumentar to grow, to increase, to enlarge
aun even
aún still
aunque although, even though
el auricular (phone) receiver, **6.2**
ausente absent
auténtico(a) authentic, real
el autobús bus, 8.1; **8.1**
perder el autobús to miss the bus, 8.1
automático(a) automatic, 10.2; **1.2**
el distribuidor automático boarding pass kiosk, 10.2; **1.2**; automatic dispenser, **3.1**
la autopista highway, **9.1**
el/la autor(a) author
el autoservicio self-service (restaurant, gas station)
la autovía highway, **9.1**
avanzado(a) difficult, 7.2; advanced
la avenida avenue, **8.1**
la aventura adventure
la avería breakdown
averiado(a) broken down
el avión airplane, 10.1; **1.1**
la avioneta small airplane
ayer yesterday, 7.1
ayer por la tarde yesterday afternoon, 7.1
la ayuda help, assistance
ayudar to help, 10.1; **1.1**

el azafrán saffron
el azúcar sugar
azul blue, 2.1
el azulejo glazed tile, floor tile

B
---

el bache pothole
el bacón bacon, 4.1; **7**
el/la bailador(a) dancer
bailar to dance, **5.2**
bajar to go down, 7.2; to download, **6.2**
bajar(se) to get off (train), **3.2**
la bajeza baseness
bajo(a) short, 1.1; low, 3.1; poor, lower-class
la nota baja low grade, 3.1
el balcón balcony
el balneario seaside resort, beach resort, 7.1
el balón ball, 5.1
el baloncesto basketball, 5.2
la banda band, 8.1; **5.2**; lane (highway)
la banda municipal municipal band, **5.2**
la bandeja de entradas inbox (e-mail), **6.1**
la bandeja de enviados sent mailbox (e-mail), **6.1**
la bandera flag
el bañador swimsuit, 7.1
bañarse to take a bath, to bathe oneself
la bañera bathtub, **7**
el baño bath; bathroom
el cuarto de baño bathroom, 2.2; **7**
barato(a) inexpensive, cheap, 9.1
Todo te sale más barato. It's all a lot cheaper., 9.1
la barbacoa barbecue
barbaridad: ¡Qué barbaridad! That's awful!
¡Bárbaro! Great!, Awesome!, 5.2
el barco boat
el barquito small boat, 7.1
la barra bar (soap), 11.2; **2.2**; counter, bar (restaurant)
la barra de jabón bar of soap, 11.2; **2.2**
la barra de herramientas toolbar, **6.1**

el barrio neighborhood, area, quarter, district, **8.1**
la base base, 5.2
el básquetbol basketball, 5.2
la cancha de básquetbol basketball court, 5.2
bastante rather, quite, 1.2; enough
el bastón ski pole, 7.2
la batalla battle
el bate bat, 5.2
el/la bateador(a) batter, 5.2
batear to hit, to bat, 5.2
batear un jonrón to hit a home run, 5.2
el batido shake, smoothie, 4.2
el baúl trunk (car), 10.1; **1.1**
beber to drink, 4.1
la bebida beverage, drink, 4.1
el béisbol baseball, 5.2
el/la beisbolista baseball player, 5.2
el campo de béisbol baseball field, 5.2
el/la jugador(a) de béisbol baseball player, 5.2
la belleza beauty
bello(a) beautiful
la benzina gas(oline)
el beso kiss
los biafranos people from Biafra
la biblioteca library
la bicicleta bicycle, 2.2
andar en bicicleta to ride a bike, **11.1**
bien well, fine, LP
bien educado(a) polite, well-mannered, 6.1
bien hecho(a) well-done (meat), 4
estar bien to be (feel) well, fine, 6.2
Muy bien. Very well., LP
la bienvenida: dar la bienvenida to greet, to welcome
bienvenido(a) welcome
el bife beef
el biftec steak, 4
el billete ticket, 10.1; **1.1**
el billete electrónico e-ticket, 10.1; **1.1**
el billete de ida y vuelta round-trip ticket, 3.1
el billete sencillo one-way ticket, 3.1
la biología biology
el/la biólogo(a) biologist

el **bizcocho** cake, **5.1**
blanco(a) white, 5.1
blando(a) soft
bloquear to block, 5.1
el **blue jean** jeans, 9.1
la **blusa** blouse, 3.1
la **boca** mouth, 6.2
la **boca del metro** subway entrance, **8.1**
la **bocacalle** intersection, **9.1**
el **bocadillo** sandwich, 4.1
los **bocaditos** snacks
la **boda** wedding
la **bodega** grocery store
la **boletería** ticket window, 7.2; **3.1**
el **boleto** ticket, 7.2; **3.1**
   el boleto de ida y regreso round-trip ticket, **3.1**
   el boleto electrónico e-ticket, 10.1; **1.1**
   el boleto sencillo one-way ticket, **3.1**
el **bolígrafo** pen, 3.1
el **bolívar** bolivar (*currency of Venezuela*)
la **bolsa de dormir** sleeping bag, 11.2; **2.2**
bolsillo: el libro de bolsillo paperback, **3.1**
la **bombilla** (*drinking*) container
los **bombones** candy
bonito(a) pretty, 1.1
el **borde** side (*of a street, sidewalk*)
   al borde mismo de right on the edge of
borrador: el botón borrador delete key, **6.1**
borrar to delete, **6.1**
el **bosque** woods
la **bota** boot, 7.2
botar to throw out
   botar la casa por la ventana to splurge
el **bote** can, 9.2
la **botella** bottle, 9.2
el **botón** button, key (*computer*), **6.1**
   el botón borrador delete key, **6.1**
   el botón regresar (retroceder) back button, **6.1**
Brasil Brazil
brasileño(a) Brazilian
bravo(a) rough, stormy
el **brazo** arm, 11.1; **2.1**
brillar to shine
bronce: de bronce bronze (*adj.*), 8.2

bronceador(a): la loción bronceadora suntan lotion, 7.1
bucear to go snorkeling, 7.1; to scuba dive
el **buceo** snorkeling, 7.1; scuba diving
buen good, LP
   estar de buen humor to be in a good mood, 6.1
   Hace buen tiempo. The weather is nice., LP
   tener un buen sentido de humor to have a good sense of humor, 6.1
bueno(a) good, 1.1; Hello! (*on the phone*)
   Buenas noches. Good evening., LP
   Buenas tardes. Good afternoon., LP
   Buenos días. Good morning., Hello., LP
   sacar notas buenas to get good grades, 3.1
la **bufetería** dining car, **3.2**
el **burrito** burrito
el **bus** bus
   el bus escolar school bus, 3.2
   perder el autobús to miss the bus, 8.1
   tomar el autobús to take the bus
busca: en busca de seeking, in search of
buscar to look for, to seek, 3.2
el **buzo** sweat suit, warm-ups, **11.1**

C

el **caballero** gentleman
   el caballero andante knight errant
el **caballo** horse, 3.2
   andar a caballo to ride a horse, 3.2
   montar a caballo to go horseback riding, 8.2
la **cabeza** head, 6.2; **2.1**
   tener dolor de cabeza to have a headache, 6.2
la **cabina de mando** cockpit (*airplane*)
la **cabina de peaje** tollbooth, **9.1**
el **cacahuate** peanut, 8.1
el **cacahuete** peanut
la **cacerola** saucepan, **10**
el **cacique** leader, chief
cada each, every, 2.2

caer to fall
caerse to fall, **11.2**
el **café** café, 3.1; coffee, 4.1; **7**
la **cafetería** cafeteria, 4.1
   el coche cafetería dining car, **3.2**
la **caída** drop
   la llamada caída dropped call (*cell phone*), **6.2**
la **caja** cash register, 3.2
la **calavera** skull, **5.1**; sweet cake made for the Day of the Dead
los **calcetines** socks, 5.1
la **calculadora** calculator, 3.1
el **caldo** broth
caliente hot, 4.1
   el chocolate caliente hot chocolate, 4.1
la **calle** street, 8.1
   la calle de sentido único one-way street, **9.1**
calmo(a) calm, 6.1
el **calor** heat
   Hace calor. It's hot., LP
   tener calor to be hot, 11.1; **2.1**
calzar to wear, to take (*shoe size*), 9.1
   ¿Qué número calzas? What size shoe do you wear (take)?, 9.1
la **cama** bed, 2.2; **7**
   guardar cama to stay in bed (*illness*), 6.2
   hacer la cama to make the bed, **7**
   quedarse en la cama to stay in bed, 11.1; **2.1**
la **cámara digital** digital camera, 7.1; **6.2**
el/la **camarero(a)** server, waiter (waitress), **4**; (*hotel*) housekeeper, **7**
los **camarones** shrimp, 4.2
cambiar to change, 3.2
el **camello** camel, 5.2
la **camilla** stretcher, **11.2**
caminar to walk, 5.1
la **caminata: dar una caminata** to take a hike, 11.2; **2.2**
el **camino** road
   tomar el camino to set out for
el **camión** bus (*Mexico*), 8.1; truck, 9.2
la **camisa** shirt, 3.1
   la camisa de manga corta (larga) short- (long-) sleeved shirt, 9.1

Spanish-English Dictionary

la **camiseta** T-shirt, 5.1
la **campana** bell tower
la **campanada** peal of the bell
el/la **campeón(ona)** champion
el/la **campesino(a)** farmer, peasant, **8.2**
el **camping** camping, 11.2; **2.2**; campsite
   ir de camping to go camping, 11.2; **2.2**
el **campo** field, 5.1; **8.2**; country, countryside, **8.2**
   el campo de béisbol baseball field, 5.2
   el campo de fútbol soccer field, 5.1
   la carrera a campo traviesa cross-country race, **11.1**
   la casa de campo country house, **8.2**
el **camposanto** cemetery, **5.1**
  canadiense Canadian
el **canal** lane *(highway)*
la **canasta** basket, 5.2
la **cancha** court, 5.2
   la cancha de básquetbol (tenis) basketball (tennis) court, 5.2
   la cancha de voleibol volleyball court, 7.1
la **candela** candle
el **cangrejo de río** crayfish
el **cañón** canyon, **3.2**
  cansado(a) tired, 6.1
el/la **cantante** singer, 8.1
  cantar to sing, 8.1
la **cantidad** quantity, amount, number of
la **cantina** cafeteria
la **capital** capital
el **capítulo** chapter
el **capó** hood *(car)*, **9.2**
la **cara** face, 6.1
la **característica** feature, trait
el **carbón** coal
el **cardo** thistle
  cargado(a) thrown (over one's shoulders); loaded
el **Caribe** Caribbean
   el mar Caribe Caribbean Sea
  cariñoso(a) adorable, affectionate, 2.1
  caritativo(a) charitable
la **carne** meat, 4.1; **4**
la **carne de res** beef, **4**
el **carnet** driver's license, **9.2**

el **carnet de identidad** ID card, 10.2; **1.2**
la **carnicería** butcher shop
  caro(a) expensive, 9.1
la **carpa** tent, 11.2; **2.2**
   armar (montar) una carpa to put up a tent, 11.2; **2.2**
la **carpeta** folder, 3.2; **6.1**
la **carrera** race, 11.1; career
   la carrera a campo traviesa cross-country race, **11.1**
   la carrera de larga distancia long-distance race, **11.1**
   la carrera de relevos relay race, **11.1**
la **carretera** highway, 9.1
el **carril** lane *(highway)*, 9.1
el **carrito** shopping cart, 9.2
el **carro** car, 2.2; **9.2**
   en carro by car
la **carta** letter
la **casa** house, 2.2
   la casa de apartamentos apartment building, 2.2
   la casa de campo country house, **8.2**
   en casa at home
   regresar a casa to go home, 3.2
  casarse to get married
el **casco** helmet, 7.2; **11.1**
el **casco antiguo** the old city, **8.1**
  casi almost, practically, 8.2; **4**
   casi crudo rare *(meat)*, **4**
el **caso** case
   hacer caso to pay attention
  castaño(a) brown, chestnut *(eyes, hair)*, 2.1
el **castillo** castle
la **casucha** shack
  catarro: tener catarro to have a cold, 6.2
el/la **cátcher** catcher, 5.2
la **catedral** cathedral
la **categoría** category
  catorce fourteen, LP
el **caucho** tire
  cautivar to captivate, to charm
la **cazuela** saucepan, pot, **10**
el **CD** CD
la **cebolla** onion, 9.2; **10**
  celebrar to celebrate, 5.2
el **celular** cell phone, 3.2; **6.1**
el **cementerio** cemetery, **5.1**

la **cena** dinner, 4.1
  cenar to have dinner, 4.1
el **cenote** natural water well
el **centro** downtown, **8.1**; center
el **centro comercial** shopping center, mall, 9.1
  cepillarse to brush, 11.1; **2.1**
   cepillarse los dientes to brush one's teeth, 11.1; **2.1**
el **cepillo** brush, 11.2; **2.2**
   el cepillo de dientes toothbrush, 11.2; **2.2**
las **cerámicas** ceramics, 9.2
  cerca (de) near, 3.2
el **cerdo** pig, **8.2**
   la chuleta de cerdo pork chop; **4**
el **cereal** cereal, 4.1
  cero zero, LP
  cerrar (ie) to close, 11.2; **2.2**
la **cesta** basket
el **cesto** basket, 5.2
la **chacra** farm, **8.2**
el **champú** shampoo, 11.2; **2.2**
  ¡Chao! Good-bye!, Bye!, LP
la **chaqueta** jacket, 9.1
   la chaqueta de esquí ski jacket, anorak, 7.2
las **chauchas** green beans
el **chico** boy
  chileno(a) Chilean
la **chimenea** fireplace, **5.2**
el **chipotle** smoked jalapeño pepper
el **chiringuito** refreshment stand
el **chisme** rumor, gossip
el **choclo** corn
el **chocolate** chocolate, 4.1
   el chocolate caliente hot chocolate, 4.1
el **chorizo** Spanish sausage
la **choza** shack
la **chuleta de cerdo** pork chop, **4**
el **churro** (type of) doughnut
  ciego(a) blind
el/la **ciego(a)** blind man (woman)
el **cielo** sky, **5.2**
  cien(to) one hundred, LP
la **ciencia** science, 1.2
  cierto(a) true, certain, **6.1**
  cinco five, LP
  cincuenta fifty, LP
el **cine** movie theater, movies, 8.2
   ir al cine to go to the movies, 8.2

el   **cinturón de seguridad** seat belt, 10.2; **1.2**

el/la   **cirujano(a) ortopédico(a)** orthopedic surgeon, **11.2**

la   **ciudad** city, 2.2; **8.1**

la   **civilización** civilization

  claro(a) clear

  claro que of course

la   **clase** class (*school*), 1.2; class (*ticket*), **3.1**

    en primera (segunda) clase first-class (second-class), **3.1**

    la sala de clase classroom, 3.1

  clavar una multa to give (someone) a ticket, **9.1**

la   **clave de área** area code, **6.2**

  clic: hacer clic to click (*computer*), **6.1**

el/la   **cliente(a)** customer, 4.2; **7**

el   **clima** climate

la   **clínica** clinic

la   **cocción** cooking

  cocer (ue) to cook, **10**

el   **coche** car, 9.2; train car, **3.1**

    el coche deportivo sports car, **9.2**

el   **coche comedor (cafetería)** dining car, **3.2**

el   **cochinillo asado** roast suckling pig

la   **cocina** kitchen, 2.2; **10**; stove, **10**; cooking, cuisine

  cocinar to cook, **10**

el/la   **cocinero(a)** cook, **10**

el   **cocodrilo** crocodile

el   **codo** elbow, 11.1; **2.1**

la   **cola** cola (soda) 4.1; line (*of people*), 10.2; **1.2**

    hacer cola to wait in line, 10.2; **1.2**

el   **colegio** secondary school, high school

el   **colgador** hanger, **7**

  colgar (ue) to hang up

la   **colina** hill

la   **colocación** placement

  colocar to place, to put

  colombiano(a) Colombian

  colonial colonial

el   **color** color, 5.1

    de color marrón brown, 5.1

    ¿De qué color es? What color is it?

el   **comando** command

  combinado: el plato combinado combination plate

el   **comedor** dining room, 2.2

  el coche comedor dining car, **3.2**

el/la   **comensal** diner

  comenzar (ie) to begin

  comer to eat, 4.1

    dar de comer a to feed

los   **comestibles** food, **4**

  cómico(a) funny, comical, 1.1

la   **comida** meal, 4.1; food

  como like, as; since

  ¿cómo? how?; what?, 1.1

    ¿Cómo es él? What's he like? What does he look like?, 1.1

    ¿Cómo está… ? How is…?

    ¡Cómo no! Sure! Of course!

  cómodo(a) comfortable

el/la   **compañero(a)** companion

  comparar to compare

el   **compartimiento superior** overhead bin, 10.2; **1.2**

  compartir to share

  completar to complete, to fill in

  completo(a) full, **3.2**

el   **comportamiento** behavior, conduct, 6.1

  comportarse to behave

la   **composición** composition

la   **compra** purchase, 9.2

el/la   **comprador(a)** shopper, customer

  comprar to buy, 3.2

  compras: ir de compras to shop, to go shopping, 9.1

  comprender to understand, 4.2; to include

la   **computadora** computer, 3.2; **6.1**

  comunicarse to communicate with each other

  con with

    con frecuencia often

    con retraso (una demora) late, delayed, 10.2; **1.2**

el   **concierto** concert, 8.1

el   **condimento** condiment, **10**

el   **condominio** condominium

  conducir to drive, **9.2**

la   **conducta** conduct, behavior, 6.1

    tener buena conducta to be well-behaved, 6.1

el/la   **conductor(a)** driver, **9.2**

  conectado(a) on-line, connected

  conectar to connect

la   **conexión** connection

  confeccionar to make, to prepare, **5.1**

la   **conferencia** lecture

  confiabilidad reliability

  confiable reliable, trustworthy

  conforme: estar conforme to agree, to be in agreement

  confortar to soothe

  congelado(a) frozen, 9.2

    los productos congelados frozen food, 9.2

el   **congelador** freezer, **10**

el   **conjunto** band, musical group, 8.1

  conocer to know, to be familiar with, 9.1; to meet

  conocido(a) known

el   **conquistador** conqueror

  conquistar to conquer

  consecuencia: por consecuencia as a result, consequently

el/la   **consejero(a)** counselor

el   **consejo** advice

  considerar to consider

  consiguiente: por consiguiente consequently

el   **consomé** bouillon, consommé

la   **consonante** consonant

  constar (de) to consist of, to be made up of

la   **consulta** doctor's office, 6.2

  consultar to consult

el   **consultorio** doctor's office, 6.2

el/la   **consumidor(a)** consumer

  contagioso(a) contagious

la   **contaminación del aire** air pollution

  contaminar to pollute

  contar (ue) to tell, to count

  contemporáneo(a) contemporary

el   **contenido** contents

  contento(a) happy, 6.1

  contestar to answer, 3.1

  continental: el desayuno continental Continental breakfast, **7**

el   **continente** continent

  continua: la línea continua solid line (*road*), **9.1**

  continuar to continue

  contra against

  contrario(a) opposite; opposing

    al contrario on the contrary

  contrastar to contrast

Spanish-English Dictionary

contribuir to contribute

el **control de seguridad** security (checkpoint), 10.2; **1.2**

pasar por el control de seguridad to go through security, 10.2; **1.2**

la **conversación** conversation

conversar to converse

el **convertible** convertible, **9.2**

convertir to convert, to transform

copa: la Copa Mundial World Cup

la **copia** copy, **6.1**

la copia dura hard copy, **6.1**

el **corazón** heart

la **corbata** tie, 9.1

el **cordero** lamb, **4**

la **corona** wreath, **5.1**

el **corral** corral, **8.2**

el/la **corredor(a)** runner

el **correo electrónico** e-mail, 3.2; **6.1**

correr to run, 5.2

cortar to cut off, **6.2**; to cut, to chop, **10**

cortar en pedacitos to cut in small pieces, to dice, **10**

cortar en rebanadas to slice, **10**

Estás cortando. You're breaking up. (telephone), **6.2**

Se nos cortó la línea. We've been cut off. (telephone), **6.2**

cortarse to cut oneself, **11.2**

la **cortesía** courtesy, LP

corto(a) short, 9.1

de manga corta short-sleeved, 9.1

el pantalón corto shorts, 5.1

la **corvina** corbina, drumfish

la **cosa** thing, 3.1

la **cosecha** harvest, **8.2**

cosechar to harvest, **8.2**

cosmopolito(a) cosmopolitan

la **costa** coast

costar (ue) to cost, 9.1

¿Cuánto cuesta? How much does it cost?, 3.2

costarricense Costa Rican

la **costumbre** custom

el **cráneo** skull, **5.1**

crear to create

crecer to grow

creer to believe, to think

Creo que sí (que no). I (don't) think so.

la **crema dental** toothpaste, 11.2; **2.2**

la **crema solar** suntan lotion, 7.1

el/la **criado(a)** housekeeper

cristiano(a) Christian

criticar to criticize

el **cruce** crosswalk, pedestrian crossing, **8.1**; intersection, **9.1**

crudo(a) raw, 8.1

casi crudo rare (meat), **4**

los vegetales crudos raw vegetables, crudités, 8.1

cruzar to cross; to intersect, **9.1**

el **cuaderno** notebook, 3.1

la **cuadra** (city) block, **9.1**

el **cuadro** painting, 8.2

¿cuál? which? what?, LP

¿Cuál es la fecha de hoy? What is today's date?, LP

¿cuáles? which ones? what?

cualquier(a) any

cualquier otro(a) any other

cuando when, 3.1

¿cuándo? when?, 3.2

cuanto: en cuanto as soon as

cuanto: en cuanto a in terms of, as far as . . . is concerned

¿cuánto? how much?

¿A cuánto está(n)... ? How much is (are) . . . ?, 9.2

¿Cuánto es? How much is it (does it cost)?, LP

¿cuántos(as)? how many?, 2.1

¿Cuántos años tiene? How old is he (she)?, 2.1

cuarenta forty, LP

el **cuarto** room, 2.2; **7**; quarter

el cuarto de baño bathroom, 2.2; **7**

el cuarto de dormir bedroom, 2.2

el cuarto sencillo (doble) single (double) room, **7**

y cuarto a quarter past (the hour), LP

cuatro four, LP

cuatrocientos(as) four hundred

el/la **cubano(a)** Cuban

el/la **cubanoamericano(a)** Cuban American

cubierto(a) covered; indoor

cubrir to cover

la **cuchara** tablespoon, **4**

la **cucharada** tablespoonful

la **cucharadita** teaspoonful

la **cucharita** teaspoon, **4**

el **cuchillo** knife, **4**

el **cuello** neck, **11.1**

la **cuenca** basin (river)

la **cuenta** check (restaurant), 4.2; **4**; account

darse cuenta to realize

por su cuenta on its own

tomar en cuenta to take into account

el **cuento** story

el **cuerdo** string

el **cuerpo** body, 11.1; **2.1**

la **cueva** cave

cuidado: con (mucho) cuidado (very) carefully

tener cuidado to be careful, **9.1**

cuidar to take care of, to care for

¡Cuídate! Take care of yourself!

la **culpa** blame, guilt

cultivar to work (land); to grow, **8.2**

la **cultura** culture

el **cumpleaños** birthday, 8.1

cumplir... años to be (turn) . . . years old

cumplir un sueño to fulfill a wish, to make a wish come true

la **cuota** toll

curarse to get better, to recover

el **curso** class, course, 1.2

cuyos(as) whose

D

daño: hacerse daño to harm oneself, to get hurt, **11.2**

dar to give, 3.1

dar de comer a to feed

dar la vuelta to turn around, **9.1**

dar un examen (una prueba) to give a test, 3.1

dar una caminata to take a hike, 11.2; **2.2**

dar una fiesta to throw a party, 8.1

darse cuenta to realize

datar to date *(time)*

los **datos** data, facts

de of, from, LP

¿**de dónde?** from where?, 1.1

De nada. You're welcome., LP

¿**De parte de quién, por favor?** Who's calling, please?, 6.2

¿**de qué nacionalidad?** what nationality?, 1.1

de vez en cuando from time to time, 10.2; **1.2**

No hay de qué. You're welcome., LP

debajo de below, underneath, 10.2; **1.2**

deber should, 4.2

debido a owing to

la **debilidad** weakness

decidir to decide

decir to say, to tell

la **decisión** decision

tomar una decisión to make a decision

decorar to decorate, 5.2

dedicado(a) devoted

el **dedo** finger, 11.1; **2.1**

el **dedo del pie** toe, **11.1**

deducirse to deduct

el **defecto** defect

defender (ie) to defend

definido(a) definite

dejar to leave (something), **4**; to let, to allow

dejar con to put an end to

dejar un mensaje to leave a message, **6.2**

dejar una propina to leave a tip, **4**

del of the, from the

delante de in front of, 2.2

delantero(a) front *(adj.)*, 8.1

delgado(a) thin

demás: lo(s) demás the rest

demasiado too *(adv.)*, too much

la **demora** delay, 10.2; **1.2**

con una demora late, 10.2; **1.2**

dental: el tubo de crema dental tube of toothpaste, 11.2; **2.2**

dentífrica: la pasta dentífrica toothpaste

dentro de within

dentro de poco soon, shortly thereafter, 10.2; **1.2**

el **departamento** apartment, 2.2

el **departamento de orientación** guidance office

el/la **dependiente(a)** salesperson, employee

el **deporte** sport, 5.1

el deporte de equipo team sport

el deporte individual individual sport

deportivo(a) *(related to)* sports

el coche deportivo sports car, 9.2

deprimido(a) sad, depressed, 6.1

derecho(a) right, 11.1; **2.1**

a la derecha on the right, 9.1

derecho straight (ahead), 9.1

derrocar to bring down

desafortunadamente unfortunately

desagradable unpleasant, not nice

desaparecer to disappear

desarrollarse to develop

el **desastre** disaster

desastroso(a) disastrous, catastrophic

el **desayuno** breakfast, 4.1; **7**

el desayuno americano American breakfast, **7**

el desayuno continental Continental breakfast, **7**

tomar el desayuno to have breakfast, 4.1

descansar to rest, **11.1**

el **descapotable** convertible, 9.2

descargar to download, 6.2

descolgar (el auricular) to unhook (the telephone receiver), 6.2

desconocido(a) unknown

desconsolado(a) very sad

describir to describe

la **descripción** description

el **descuento** discount

desde since; from

desear to want, to wish, 4.2

¿**Qué desean tomar?** What would you like *(to eat, drink)*?, 4.2

desembarcar to deplane, disembark, 10.2; **1.2**

desembocar to lead, to go (from one street into another), to come out onto

el **deseo** wish, desire

desesperado(a) desperate

desfilar to walk (in a parade or procession), 5.1

el **desfile** parade, 5.2

desgraciadamente unfortunately

deshuesado(a) deboned

el **desierto** desert

desinflada: la llanta desinflada flat tire, 9.2

despacio slow, slowly, 9.1

despedirse (i, i) to take leave

despegar to take off *(plane)*,10.2; **1.2**

el **despegue** takeoff, 10.2; **1.2**

despertarse (ie) to wake up, 11.1; **2.1**

después (de) after, 3.1; later

el/la **destinatario(a)** addressee, recipient, **6.1**

el **destino** destination, 3.1

destino: con destino a (going) to; for, 10.2; **1.2**

las **desventajas** disadvantages

el **detalle** detail

detrás de in back of, behind, 2.2

devolver (ue) to return *(something)*, 5.2

el **día** day

Buenos días. Good morning., LP

el Día de los Muertos Day of the Dead, 5.1

el Día de los Reyes Epiphany (January 6), 5.1

hoy en día nowadays

¿**Qué día es hoy?** What day is it today?, LP

el **diablo** devil

el **diagnóstico** diagnosis

el **diálogo** dialogue

diaria: la rutina diaria daily routine, 11.1; **2.1**

el **dibujo** drawing, illustration

diciembre December, LP

el **dictado** dictation

diecinueve nineteen, LP

dieciocho eighteen, LP

dieciséis sixteen, LP

diecisiete seventeen, LP

el **diente** clove (of garlic)

los **dientes** teeth, 11.1; **2.1**

cepillarse (lavarse) los dientes to brush one's teeth, 11.1; **2.1**

la **dieta** diet

Spanish-English Dictionary

diez ten, LP
   de diez en diez by tens
la **diferencia** difference
diferente different
difícil difficult, 1.2
la **dificultad** difficulty
   sin dificultad easily
difunto(a) dead, deceased, **5.1**
el/la **difunto(a)** deceased, dead person, **5.1**
   ¡Diga! Hello! *(on the phone)*
   ¡Dígame! Hello! *(on the phone)*
dinámico(a) dynamic, 6.1
el dinero money, 3.2
la **dirección** address, **6.1;** direction
   la dirección de correo electrónico (e-mail) e-mail address, **6.1**
las **direccionales** turn signals, 9.2
el **disco** record
el **disfraz** disguise, costume, **5.1**
disfrutar (de) to enjoy
disponible available
distancia: de larga distancia long-distance *(race)*, **11.1**
distinto(a) different
el **distribuidor automático** boarding pass kiosk, 10.1; **1.1;** ticket dispenser, **3.1**
el **distrito** district, area, section
divertido(a) fun, funny, amusing
divertir (ie, i) to amuse, 11.2; **2.2**
divertirse (ie, i) to have a good time, to have fun, 11.2; **2.2**
divino(a) divine, heavenly
doblar to turn, 9.1
doble: el cuarto doble double *(hotel room)*, 7
dobles doubles *(tennis)*, 5.2
doce twelve, LP
la **docena** dozen
el **documento adjunto** attached file, **6.1**
el **dólar** dollar
doler (ue) to ache, to hurt, 6.2; **11.2**
   Le (Me, etc.) duele mucho. It hurts him (me, etc.) a lot., **11.2**
   Me duele(n)... My . . . ache(s)., 6.2

el **dolor** pain, ache, 6.2
   tener dolor de cabeza to have a headache, 6.2
   tener dolor de estómago to have a stomachache, 6.2
   tener dolor de garganta to have a sore throat, 6.2
domesticado(a) domesticated
el **domingo** Sunday, LP
dominicano(a) Dominican
   la República Dominicana Dominican Republic
el **dominó** dominos
donde where
¿dónde? where?, 1.1
   ¿de dónde? from where?, 1.1
dormir (ue, u) to sleep
   la bolsa de dormir sleeping bag, 11.2; **2.2**
   el cuarto de dormir bedroom, 2.2
   el saco de dormir sleeping bag, 11.2; **2.2**
dormirse (ue, u) to fall asleep, 11.1; **2.1**
el **dormitorio** bedroom, 2.2
dos two
doscientos(as) two hundred
driblar to dribble, 5.2
la **ducha** shower, 11.1; **2.1**
   tomar una ducha to take a shower, 11.1; **2.1**
la **duda** doubt
el/la **dueño(a)** owner
dulce sweet, **5.1**
   el pan dulce pastry, 7
el **dulce** sweet
durante during, 3.2
durar to last
duro(a) hard, difficult, 1.2
   la copia dura hard copy, **6.1**
el **DVD** DVD, 3.2

la **ebullición** boiling
echar to throw, to expel
económico(a) inexpensive
ecuatoriano(a) Ecuadoran, 1.1
la **edad** age
   la Edad Media Middle Ages
el **edificio** building, 2.2

la **educación** education
   la educación física physical education, 1.2
educado(a) mannered
   estar bien (mal) educado(a) to be polite (rude), 6.1
egoísta selfish, egotistical
el **ejemplo** example
   por ejemplo for example
los **ejercicios** exercises, **11.1**
   ejercicios de respiración breathing exercises, **11.1**
   hacer ejercicios to exercise, **11.1**
los **ejotes** green beans
el **el** the *(m. sing.)*, 1.1
él he, 1.1
elaborar to make, to produce, **5.1**
electrónico(a) electronic, 10.1; **1.1**
   el boleto (billete) electrónico e-ticket, 10.1; **1.1**
   el correo electrónico e-mail, 3.2; **6.1**
el **elefante** elephant
elegante elegant, fancy
elegir (i, i) to elect
elemental elementary
ella she, 1.1
ellos(as) they, 1.2
el **elote** corn
el **e-mail** e-mail, **6.1**
embarcar to board, 10.2; **1.2**
el **embarque** boarding, 10.1; **1.1**
   la hora de embarque boarding time, 10.1; **1.1**
el **embotellamiento** traffic jam
emergencia: la sala de emergencia emergency room, **11.2**
emocionante moving; exciting
la **empanada** meat pie, 4.2
empezar (ie) to begin, 5.1
el/la **empleado(a)** salesperson, employee, 3.2
empujar to push
en in; on; at
   en casa at home
el/la **enamorado(a)** sweetheart
   enamorado(a) de in love with
encantar to love, to adore, 6.2
encender (ie) to light, 5.2

encerrar (ie) to enclose

encestar to make a basket (*basketball*), 5.2

la **enchilada** enchilada

encima: por encima de above, over, 5.2

encontrar (ue) to find, to encounter

encontrarse (ue) to be found; to meet

la **encuesta** survey

el/la **enemigo(a)** enemy

energético(a) energetic, 6.1

la **energía** energy, 6.1

enero January, LP

  el primero de enero January 1, LP

enfadado(a) angry, mad, 6.1

enfadar to make angry, 6.1

la **enfermedad** sickness, disease

el/la **enfermero(a)** nurse, 6.2; **11.2**

enfermo(a) ill, sick, 6.2

el/la **enfermo(a)** patient, sick person

enfrente de in front of

enlatado(a) canned

enlazar to connect

enojado(a) angry, mad, annoyed, 6.1

enojar to make angry, to annoy, 6.1

enorme enormous

la **ensalada** salad, 4.1

enseguida right away, 4.2

enseñar to teach, 3.1; to show

entender (ie) to understand, 8.2

entero(a) entire, whole

enterrado(a) buried, **5.1**

enterrar (ie) to bury

la **entrada** ticket, 8.1; entrée (*meal*); entrance

entradas: la bandeja de entradas e-mail inbox, **6.1**

entrar to enter, to go into, 5.1

  entrar en línea to go online, **6.1**

entre between, among

el/la **entrenador(a)** coach, manager

el/la **entrevistador(a)** interviewer

entusiasmado(a) enthusiastic

el **entusiasmo** enthusiasm, 6.1

enviados: la bandeja de enviados sent mailbox, **6.1**

enviar to send, 3.2

el **episodio** episode

la **época** times, period

el **equilibrio** balance

el **equipaje** luggage, baggage, 10.1; **1.1**

  el equipaje de mano hand luggage, carry-on bags, 10.2; **1.2**

el **equipo** team, 5.1; equipment

  el deporte de equipo team sport

la **equitación** horseback riding, **8.2**

escala: hacer escala to stop over, to make a stop

la **escalera** stairs, staircase, **8.1**

  la escalera mecánica escalator, **8.1**

el **escalope de ternera** veal cutlet, **10**

el **escaparate** store window, 9.1

la **escena** scene

escoger to choose

escolar (*related to*) school

  el bus escolar school bus, 3.2

  los materiales escolares school supplies, 3.1

  la tarifa escolar student fare

escribir to write, 4.2

escrito(a) written

el **escrito** document, paper

escritorio: la pantalla de escritorio (*computer*) screen, 6.1

escuchar to listen (to), 3.2

  ¿Me escuchas? Can you hear me? (*telephone*), **6.2**

el **escudero** squire

la **escuela** school, 1.2

  la escuela primaria elementary school

  la escuela secundaria secondary school, high school, 1.2

el/la **escultor(a)** sculptor

la **escultura** sculpture

ese(a) that, that one

eso: a eso de at about (*time*)

  por eso for this reason, that is why

esos(as) those

la **espalda** back, 11.1; **2.1**

espantable horrendous

España Spain

español(a) Spanish (*adj.*)

el/la **español(a)** Spaniard

el **español** Spanish (*language*), 1.2

la **especia** spice

la **especialidad** specialty

especialmente especially

específico(a) specific

espectacular spectacular

el **espectáculo** show, spectacle

el/la **espectador(a)** spectator

el **espejo** mirror, 11.1; **2.1**

espera: la sala de espera waiting room, **3.1**

esperar to wait (for), 10.2; **1.2**; to hope; to expect

el **espíritu** mind, spirit, **11.1**

la **esplendidez** splendor

espontáneo(a) spontaneous

la **esposa** wife, 2.1

el **esposo** husband, 2.1

el **esqueleto** skeleton, **5.1**

el **esquí** ski; skiing, 7.2

  el esquí acuático (naútico) waterskiing, 7.1

  el esquí alpino downhill skiing

  el esquí nórdico cross-country skiing

el/la **esquiador(a)** skier, 7.2

esquiar to ski, 7.2

  esquiar en el agua to water-ski, 7.1

la **esquina** corner, **8.1**

¿Está… , por favor? Is . . . there, please?, **6.2**

establecer(se) to establish; to settle

el **establecimiento** establishment, settling

el **establo** stable, **8.2**; manger

la **estación** season, LP; resort, 7.1; station, **3.1**

  la estación de esquí ski resort, 7.2

  la estación de ferrocarril (tren) railroad (train) station, **3.1**

  la estación de metro subway (metro) station, **8.1**

  la estación de servicio gas station, **9.2**

  ¿Qué estación es? What season is it?, LP

estacionar to park

la **estadía** stay

el **estadio** stadium

Estados Unidos United States

estadounidense from the United States

la **estancia** ranch, **8.2**

estar to be, 3.1

  ¿Está…? Is . . . there?, **6.2**

  estar bien to feel fine, 6.2

  estar cansado(a) to be tired, 6.1

  estar contento(a) (triste, nervioso[a], etc.) to be happy (sad, nervous, etc.), 6.1

Spanish-English Dictionary

estar de buen (mal) humor
to be in a good (bad)
mood, 6.1

estar enfermo(a) to be sick,
6.2

la **estatua** statue, 8.2

la **estatura** stature, height

este(a) this, this one, 9.1

el **este** east

estereofónico(a) stereo

el **estilo** style

estimado(a) esteemed

estirarse to stretch, 11.1; **2.1**

el **estómago** stomach, 6.2

el dolor de estómago
stomachache, 6.2

estos(as) these

la **estrategia** strategy

estrecho(a) narrow, **8.1**

la **estrella** star

estremecerse to shake

el **estrés** stress, 6.2

la **estructura** structure

el/la **estudiante** student

**estudiantil: la tarifa
estudiantil** student fare

estudiar to study, 3.1

el **estudio** study

los estudios sociales social
studies, 1.2

la **estufa** stove, **10**

estupendo(a) terrific,
stupendous

la **etnia** ethnicity, ethnic group

étnico(a) ethnic

el **euro** euro (currency of most of
the countries of the European
Union)

Europa Europe

el **evento** event

evitar to avoid

el **examen** test, exam, 3.1

el examen físico physical,
6.2

examinar to examine, 6.2

exceder to go over (speed limit)

excelente excellent

la **excepción** exception

la **excursión** excursion, outing

el/la **excursionista** hiker

existir exist

el **éxito** success, 6.1

tener éxito to succeed, to be
successful, 6.1

exótico(a) exotic

experimentar to try, to try out

el/la **experto(a)** expert

explicar to explain

el/la **explorador(a)** explorer

la **exposición de arte** art show,
exhibition, 8.2

la **expresión** expression

extenderse (ie) to extend

extranjero(a) foreign

al extranjero abroad

extraordinario(a)
extraordinary

la **fábrica** factory

fabuloso(a) fabulous

fácil easy, 1.2

la **factura** bill

facturar el equipaje to check
luggage, 10.1; **1.1**

la **falda** skirt, 3.1

falso(a) false

faltar to lack, not to have, 6.1

Le falta paciencia. He
(She) has no patience., 6.1

la **familia** family, 2.1

familiar (related to) family

los **familiares** family members

famoso(a) famous

la **fantasía** fantasy

fantástico(a) fantastic

el/la **farmacéutico(a)** druggist,
pharmacist

la **farmacia** pharmacy,
drugstore, 6.2

el **favor** favor

Favor de (+ infinitive).
Please (do something).,
11.2; **2.2**

por favor please, LP

favorito(a) favorite

febrero February, LP

la **fecha** date, LP

¿Cuál es la fecha de hoy?
What is today's date?, LP

fecundo(a) prolific

la **felicidad** happiness

feliz happy, **5.2**

¡Felices Pascuas! Happy
Easter!

¡Feliz Hanuka! Happy
Hanukkah!, **5.2**

¡Feliz Navidad! Merry
Christmas!, **5.2**

feo(a) unattractive, ugly, 1.1

la **feria** festival, fair, **5.1**

**ferrocarril: la estación de
ferrocarril** train station,
railroad station, **3.1**

festivo: el día festivo holiday

la **fiebre** fever, 6.2

tener fiebre to have a fever,
6.2

fiel loyal, faithful

la **fiesta** party, 8.1; holiday, **5.1**

dar una fiesta to throw a
party, 8.1

la fiesta de las luces
festival of lights
(Hanukkah), **5.2**

fijo(a) fixed, unchanging

la **fila** line (of people); row (of
seats)

estar en fila to wait in line

el **film** film, movie

el **filme** film, movie, 8.2

el **fin** end

el fin de semana weekend,
7.1

por fin finally

final: al final de at the end of

la **finca** farm, **8.2**

fines: a fines de at the end of

fingir to pretend

físico(a) physical

la apariencia física
physical appearance, looks

la educación física physical
education, 1.2

flaco(a) thin

el **flan** flan, custard, 4.1

la **flauta** flute

la **flecha** arrow

flexible open-minded,
flexible, 6.1

la **flor** flower, 2.2

el **foco** center, focal point

la **fogata** bonfire, campfire

fondo: al fondo to the bottom

los **fondos** funds, money

la **forma** form, piece, 10.2; **1.2;**
shape

la forma de identidad
piece of ID, 10.2; **1.2**

formar to form, to make up;
to put together

el **formulario** form

forzado(a) forced

la **foto(grafía)** photo, 7.1

la **fractura** fracture

el **francés** French, 1.2

el **franciscano** Franciscan

franco(a) frank, sincere,
candid

el **frasco** jar, 9.2

la **frase** sentence

la **frazada** blanket, **7**

frecuencia: con frecuencia often, frequently

freír (i, i) to fry, **4**

los **frenos** brakes, **9.2**

la **frente** forehead, **11.1**

frente a in front of

fresco(a) cool, LP

Hace fresco. It's cool (*weather*)., LP

los **frijoles** beans, 4.1

frío(a) cold, 4.2

Hace frío. It's cold (*weather*)., LP

tener frío to be cold, 11.1; **2.1**

el **frío** cold

frito(a) fried

las patatas (papas) fritas french fries, 4.1

frontal: la página frontal home page, **6.1**

la **frontera** border

la **fruta** fruit, 9.2

el puesto de frutas fruit stand, 9.2

la **frutería** fruit stand, 9.2

el **fuego** flame, heat, **10**

a fuego lento on low heat, **10**

los **fuegos artificiales** fireworks, **5.2**

la **fuente** fountain

fuera de outside

fuerte strong; substantial

las **fuerzas** (armed) forces

fumar: la señal de no fumar no-smoking sign, 10.2; **1.2**

el **fútbol** soccer, 5.1

el campo de fútbol soccer field, 5.1

el fútbol americano football

el/la **futbolista** soccer player

el **futuro** future

las **gafas para el sol** sunglasses, 7.1

el **galán** elegant man, heartthrob

gallardo(a) brave, dashing

las **galletas** crackers, 8.1

la **gallina** hen, **8.2**

la **gamba** shrimp, prawn

el **ganado** cattle, livestock, **8.2**

ganar to win, 5.1; to earn

ganas: tener ganas de to feel like

el **garaje** garage, 2.2

la **garganta** throat, 6.2

el dolor de garganta sore throat, 6.2

la **garita de peaje** tollbooth, **9.1**

el **gas: el agua mineral con gas** carbonated (sparkling) mineral water, 4.2

la **gaseosa** soda, carbonated drink, 4.2

la **gasolina** gas

la **gasolinera** gas station, **9.2**

gastar to spend; to waste

el/la **gato(a)** cat, 2.1; jack (*car*), **9.2**

el/la **gemelo(a)** twin, 2.1

general general

en general in general

por lo general usually, as a rule

generalmente usually, generally

generoso(a) generous

la **gente** people, 9.1

la **geografía** geography

la **geometría** geometry

el **gigante** giant

el **gimnasio** gym(nasium), **11.1**

la **gitanilla** little gypsy

el **gobierno** government

el **gol** goal, 5.1

meter un gol to score a goal, 5.1

golpear to hit (*ball*), 5.2

la **goma** tire, **9.2**

gordo(a) fat

el **gorro** ski hat, 7.2

gozar de to enjoy

grabar to record

Gracias. Thank you., LP

dar gracias a to thank

gracioso(a) funny, 1.1

la **gramática** grammar

gran, grande big, large, 1.2

la **grandeza** greatness, grandeur

el **granero** barn, 8.2

la **granja** farm, 8.2

gratis for free

gratuito(a) free

grave serious

gris gray, 5.1

gritar to yell, to shout

el **grupo** group, 8.1

la **guagua** bus (*Puerto Rico, Cuba*), 8.1

el **guante** glove, 5.2

la **guantera** glove compartment, **9.2**

guapo(a) attractive, good-looking, 1.1

guardar to guard, 5.1; to save, to keep, 6.1

guardar cama to stay in bed (*illness*), 6.2

la **guardería** shelter

guatemalteco(a) Guatemalan

la **guerra** war

el **guerrero** warrior

la **guía** guidebook

la guía telefónica phone book, **6.2**

guiar to guide

el **guisante** pea, 9.2

la **guitarra** guitar

gustar to like, to be pleasing to, 5.1

el **gusto** pleasure; like; taste

Mucho gusto. Nice (*It's a pleasure*) to meet you. 1.2

H

haber to have (*in compound tenses*)

las **habichuelas** beans

las habichuelas tiernas green beans, string beans

la **habitación** bedroom; hotel room, **7**

el/la **habitante** inhabitant

hablar to speak, to talk, 3.1

hablar en el móvil to talk on the cell phone

hablar por teléfono to talk on the phone

¿Hablas en serio? Are you serious?

hace: Hace... años ... years ago

Hace buen tiempo. The weather is nice., LP

Hace (mucho) calor. It's (very) hot (*weather*)., LP

Hace fresco. It's cool (*weather*)., LP

Hace frío. It's cold (*weather*)., LP

Hace mal tiempo. The weather is bad., LP

Hace sol. It's sunny., LP

Hace viento. It's windy., LP

hacer to do, to make, 10.2; **1.2**

hacer clic to click (*computer*), **6.1**

hacer cola to stand (wait) in line, 10.2; **1.2**

Spanish-English Dictionary

hacer ejercicios to exercise, **11.1**

hacer jogging to go jogging, **11.1**

hacer la cama to make the bed, **7**

hacer la maleta to pack, 10.1; **1.1**

hacer planchas to do push-ups, **11.1**

hacer un viaje to take a trip, 10.1; **1.1**

hacerse daño to hurt oneself, **11.2**

hacia toward

hacia atrás backwards

la **hacienda** ranch, **8.2**

el **hall** concourse (*train station*), **3.1**

el **hambre** (*f.*) hunger

   Me muero de hambre. I'm starving., **4**

   tener hambre to be hungry, **4.1**

la **hamburguesa** hamburger, **4.1**

el **Hanuka** Hanukkah, **5.2**

   ¡Feliz Hanuka! Happy Hanukkah!, **5.2**

la **harina** flour

hasta until; up to; as far as; even

   ¡Hasta luego! See you later!, **LP**

   ¡Hasta mañana! See you tomorrow!, **LP**

   ¡Hasta pronto! See you soon!, **LP**

hay there is, there are, **2.2**

   hay que it's necessary to (do something), one must, 10.2; **1.2**

   Hay sol. It's sunny., **LP**

   No hay de qué. You're welcome., **LP**

   ¿Qué hay? What's new (up)?

la **hazaña** achievement

hebreo(a) Jewish, Hebrew, **5.2**

el **hecho** fact

hecho(a): bien hecho(a) well-done (*meat*), **4**

el **helado** ice cream, **4.1**

el **heno** hay, **8.2**

la **herida** wound, injury, **11.2**

el/la **herido(a)** injured person

la **hermana** sister, **2.1**

la **hermanastra** stepsister, **2.1**

el **hermanastro** stepbrother, **2.1**

el **hermano** brother, **2.1**

hermoso(a) beautiful

el **héroe** hero

la **heroína** heroine

herramientas: la barra de herramientas toolbar, **6.1**

hervir (ie, i) to boil, **10**

el **hielo** ice, **7.2**

   el patinaje sobre el hielo ice-skating, **7.2**

la **hierba** grass, **8.2**

las **hierbas** herbs

el **hígado** liver

higiénico: el rollo de papel higiénico roll of toilet paper, 11.2; **2.2**

la **hija** daughter, **2.1**

el **hijo** son, child, **2.1**

   el hijo único only child, **2.1**

los **hijos** children, **2.1**

hinchado(a) swollen, **11.2**

hincharse to get swollen, to swell

hispano(a) Hispanic

hispanohablante Spanish-speaking

el/la **hispanohablante** Spanish speaker

la **historia** history, **1.2**

el/la **historiador(a)** historian

la **hoja de papel** sheet of paper, **3.1**

hojear to skim, to scan

¡Hola! Hello!, **LP**

el **hombre** man

el **hombro** shoulder, **11.1**

honesto(a) honest

la **hora** hour; time, 10.1; **1.1**

   ¿a qué hora? at what time?, **LP**

   la hora de embarque boarding time, 10.1; **1.1**

   la hora de salida departure time, 10.1; **1.1**

   ¿Qué hora es? What time is it?, **LP**

el **horario** (*train*) schedule, timetable, **3.1**

el **horno** oven, **10**

el **horno de microondas** microwave oven, **10**

hospedarse to stay (*in a hotel*), **7**

el **hospital** hospital

el **hostal** hostel, small (inexpensive) hotel, **7**

el **hotel** hotel, **7**

hoy today, **LP**

   ¿Cuál es la fecha de hoy? What's today's date?, **LP**

   hoy en día nowadays

   ¿Qué día es hoy? What day is it today?, **LP**

la **huerta** orchard, **8.2**

el **hueso** bone, **5.1**

el/la **huésped(a)** guest, **7**

el **huevo** egg, 4.1; **7**

   los huevos pasados por agua soft-boiled eggs

   los huevos revueltos scrambled eggs, **7**

huir to flee

humanitario(a) humanitarian

humano(a) human, 11.1; **2.1**

   el ser humano human being

humilde humble

el **humor** mood; humor

   estar de buen (mal) humor to be in a good (bad) mood, **6.1**

   tener un buen sentido de humor to have a good sense of humor, **6.1**

el **huso horario** time zone

el **icono** icon, **6.1**

ida y vuelta (regreso): un boleto (billete) de ida y vuelta (regreso) round-trip ticket, **3.1**

la **idea** idea

la **identidad** identification, 10.2; **1.2**

   el carnet de identidad ID card, 10.2; **1.2**

identificar to identify

la **iglesia** church

igual que as well as; like; just as

iluminar to light up, to illuminate, **5.2**

la **imagen** picture, image

impaciente impatient, **6.1**

impares odd (*numeric*)

impermeable raincoat

importa: No importa. It doesn't matter.

la **importancia** importance

importante important

la imposible impossible

la impresora printer, **6.1**

imprimir to print, **6.1**

el impuesto tax

incluir to include

¿**Está incluido el servicio?** Is the tip included?, 4.2

increíble incredible

indicar to indicate

indígena native, indigenous, 9.2

el/la indígena indigenous person

individual: el deporte individual individual sport

individuales singles (tennis), 5.2

industrializado(a) industrialized

la infinidad infinity

la influencia influence

la información information, 3.2

el inglés English, 1.2

el ingrediente ingredient

inhóspito(a) inhospitable, desolate

inicial: la página inicial home page, **6.1**

inicio: la página de inicio home page, **6.1**

inmenso(a) immense

el inodoro toilet, 7

insertar to insert, **3.1**

inteligente intelligent, 1.2

el interés interest

interesante interesting, 1.2

interesar to interest, 5.1

las intermitentes turn signals, **9.2**

el Internet Internet, 3.2; **6.1**

navegar el Internet to surf the Net, 3.2; **6.1**

interurbano(a) city-to-city

intervenir (ie) to intervene

la introducción introduction

introducir to insert, **6.2**

el invierno winter, LP

la invitación invitation

el/la invitado(a) guest

invitar to invite

ir to go, 3.2

ir a (+ infinitive) to be going to (do something), 4.2

ir a casa to go home, 3.2

ir a pie to go on foot, 3.2

ir al cine to go to the movies, 8.2

ir de camping to go camping, 11.2; **2.2**

ir de compras to go shopping, 9.1

la irlandés(esa) Irish

la isla island

el istmo isthmus

italiano(a) Italian

izquierdo(a) left, 11.1; **2.1**

a la izquierda to the left, **9.1**

el jabón soap, 11.2; **2.2**

la barra (pastilla) de jabón bar of soap, 11.2; **2.2**

jamás never

el jamón ham, 4.1

el sándwich de jamón y queso ham and cheese sandwich, 4.1

el jardín garden, 2.2

el/la jardinero(a) outfielder, 5.2

jogging: hacer jogging to go jogging, **11.1**

el jonrón home run

batear un jonrón to hit a home run

joven young

el/la joven young person, 1.1

la joya jewel, piece of jewelry

las judías verdes green beans, 9.2

judío(a) Jewish, **5.2**

el juego game, 5.1

el jueves Thursday, LP

el/la jugador(a) player, 5.1

jugar (ue) to play, 5.1

jugar (al) fútbol (béisbol, básquetbol) to play soccer (baseball, basketball), 5.1

el jugo juice, 4.1

el jugo de naranja orange juice, 4.1; **7**

el juguete toy

julio July, LP

junio June, LP

juntos(as) together

el kilo kilogram (2.2 lbs.), **9.2**

el kilómetro kilometer

la the (f. sing.), **1.1**; it, her (pron.)

el labio lip

el laboratorio laboratory

laborioso(a) hardworking

labrar to work (land), **8.2**

el lacón bacon, 7

lácteo(a): productos lácteos dairy products

el lado side

al lado de beside, next to, 2.2

ladrar to bark

el lago lake

la lámpara lamp, 2.2

la langosta lobster, **4**

la lanza lance

el/la lanzador(a) pitcher, 5.2

lanzar to kick, to throw, 5.1

el lapicero ballpoint pen

el lápiz pencil, 3.1

largo(a) long, 5.1

a lo largo de along

las the (f. pl.); them (pron.)

lastimarse to harm oneself, to get hurt

la lata can, 9.2

latino(a) Latino

Latinoamérica Latin America

el/la latinoamericano(a) Latin American

el lavabo washbasin, sink, **7**

el lavaplatos dishwasher, **10**

lavar to wash, 11.2; **2.2**

lavarse to wash oneself, 11.1; **2.1**

lavarse el pelo (la cara, las manos) to wash one's hair (face, hands), 11.1; **2.1**

lavarse los dientes to clean (brush) one's teeth, 11.1; **2.1**

le to him, to her; to you (formal) (pron.)

la lección lesson

la leche milk, 4.1

el café con leche coffee with milk, café au lait

el lechón asado roast suckling pig

la lechuga lettuce, 4.1

la lectura reading

leer to read, 4.2

la legumbre vegetable, 4.1

lejos (de) far (from), 3.2

a lo lejos in the distance

la lengua language

lentamente slowly

lento(a) slow, 11.1; low (heat), **10**

a fuego lento on low heat, **10**

el león lion

les to them; to you (formal) (pron.)

Spanish-English Dictionary

la letra letter *(of alphabet)*

las letras literature

levantar to raise, 3.1; to clear, 4; to lift, **11.1**

  levantar la mano to raise one's hand, 3.1

  levantar la mesa to clear the table, **4**

  levantar pesas to lift weights, **11.1**

levantarse to get up, 11.1; **2.1**

la leyenda legend

liberar to free, to rid, **11.1**

la libertad freedom

la libra pound *(weight)*

libre free, unoccupied, 4.2; **3.2**

  al aire libre outdoor, open-air

  el tiempo libre spare time, 8.1

la libreta de direcciones (e-mail) address book, **6.1**

el libro book, 3.1

  el libro de bolsillo paperback, **3.1**

la licencia driver's license, **9.2**

el líder leader

la liga league

  las Grandes Ligas Major Leagues

ligeramente lightly

ligero(a) light

el límite de velocidad speed limit

el limón lemon

la limonada lemonade

limpiar to clean, **7**

limpio(a) clean, **7**

lindo(a) beautiful

la línea *(telephone)* line, **6.2**; *(road)* line, **9.1**

  la línea continua solid line, **9.1**

  Se nos cortó la línea. We've been cut off. *(phone)*, **6.2**

línea: en línea online, **6.1**

  entrar en línea to go online, **6.1**

la línea aérea airline, 10.1; **1.1**

la liquidación sale, 9.1

listo(a) ready

la litera bunk

la literatura literature

la llama llama

la llamada *(telephone)* call, **6.2**

la llamada perdida (caída) dropped call *(cell phone)*, **6.2**

llamar to call, 11.2; **2.2**

llamarse to call oneself, to be called, named, 11.1; **2.1**

  Me llamo… My name is . . . , 11.1; **2.1**

la llanta tire, **9.2**

  la llanta de repuesto (recambio) spare tire, **9.2**

la llave key, **7**

  la llave magnética magnetic key, **7**

la llegada arrival, **3.1**

llegar to arrive, 4.1

llenar to fill, **9.2**

lleno(a) de full of, 6.1

llevar to carry; to wear, 3.1; to take; to bear; to have

llorar to cry

llover (ue) to rain

  Llueve. It's raining., LP

lluvioso(a) rainy

lo it, him, you *(formal) (pron.)*

lo que what

la loción bronceadora suntan lotion, sunblock, 7.1

loco(a) crazy

el lodo mud

lógico(a) logical

la loncha slice *(ham)*

la lonja slice *(ham)*

el loro parrot

los them *(m. pl.) (pron.)*

el lote lot

las luces lights, 5.2; headlights, **9.2**

  la fiesta de las luces festival of lights *(Hanukkah)*, **5.2**

luchar to fight

luego later, LP; then, 3.2

  ¡Hasta luego! See you later!, LP

el lugar place

  tener lugar to take place

lujoso(a) luxurious

el lunes Monday, LP

la luz light, **5.2**

  la luz roja red light, **9.1**

M

---

la madera wood

  de madera wooden

la madrastra stepmother, 2.1

la madre mother, 2.1

los madrileños citizens of Madrid

el/la madrugador(a) early riser, 11.1; **2.1**

los maduros fried sweet bananas

magnético(a) magnetic, **7**

magnífico(a) magnificent, splendid

Magos: los Reyes Magos the Three Wise Men, **5.2**

el maíz corn, 9.2

mal bad

  estar de mal humor to be in a bad mood, 6.1

  Hace mal tiempo. The weather is bad., LP

  mal educado(a) ill-mannered, rude, 6.1

el malecón boardwalk (seafront)

los males the evil (things), the ills

la maleta suitcase, 10.1; **1.1**

  hacer la maleta to pack, 10.1; **1.1**

la maletera trunk *(car)*, 10.1; **1.1**

malicioso(a) malicious

malo(a) bad, 1.2

  sacar notas malas to get bad grades, 3.1

mamá mom, mommy

mandar to send

el mandato command

mando: la cabina de mando cockpit

manejar to drive

la manera manner, way

  de ninguna manera in no way, by no means

  manga: de manga corta (larga) short- (long-) sleeved, 9.1

el maní peanut, 8.1

la mano hand, 3.1

  el equipaje de mano carry-on luggage, 10.2; **1.2**

  levantar la mano to raise one's hand, 3.1

manso(a) gentle

la manta blanket, **7**

el mantel tablecloth, **4**

mantener to maintain

  mantenerse en forma to stay in shape

la mantequilla butter, 4.1; **7**

la manzana apple, 9.2; (city) block, **9.1**

la **mañana** tomorrow, LP

   ¡Hasta mañana! See you tomorrow!, LP

la **mañana** morning

   de la mañana A.M.

   por la mañana in the morning

el **mapa** map

la **máquina** machine

la **maquinaria** machinery, equipment

el **mar** sea, ocean, 7.1

   el mar Caribe Caribbean Sea

el **maratón** marathon, **11.1**

  marcar to score, 5.1; to dial, **6.2**

   marcar el número to dial the number, **6.2**

   marcar un tanto to score a point, 5.1

la **marcha** march

   en marcha working

  marchar to march

el **marido** husband, 2.1

el **marinero** sailor

los **mariscos** shellfish, seafood, **4**

  marrón: de color marrón brown, 5.1

el **martes** Tuesday, LP

  marzo March, LP

  más more, 9.1

   ¡Qué... más... ! What a . . . !

la **máscara** mask, **5.1**

la **máscara de oxígeno** oxygen mask, 10.2; **1.2**

la **mascota** pet, 2.1

las **matemáticas** mathematics, math, 1.2

los **materiales escolares** school supplies, 3.1

el **mausoleo** mausoleum, **5.1**

  máximo(a) highest, top

   la velocidad máxima speed limit, top speed

  mayo May, LP

la **mayonesa** mayonnaise, 9.2

  mayor older

el/la **mayor** the oldest; the greatest

la **mayoría** majority

  mayoritario(a) (related to) majority

  me me (pron.)

  mediano(a) medium, medium-size

la **medianoche** midnight

el **medicamento** medicine, 6.2

la **medicina** medicine, 6.2

el/la **médico(a)** doctor, 6.2

la **medida** measurement

las **medidas** measures

  medio(a) half; middle

   a término medio medium (meat), **4**

   la clase media middle class

   y media half past (the hour), LP

el **medio** means; middle

   el medio de transporte means of transport, **8.1**

el **mediodía** noon

los **mejillones** mussels, **4**

  mejor better

el/la **mejor** the best

  menor younger; lesser

el/la **menor** the youngest; the least

la **menora** menorah, **5.2**

  menos less, 9.1

   a lo menos at least

   menos cuarto a quarter to (the hour)

el **mensaje** message, **6.2**

el **menú** menu, 4.2; **4**

  menudo: a menudo often

el **mercado** market, 9.2

la **mercancía** merchandise

la **merienda** snack, 4.2

la **mermelada** jam, marmalade, **7**

el **mes** month, LP

la **mesa** table, 2.2; **4**

   levantar la mesa to clear the table, **4**

   poner la mesa to set the table, **4**

   quitar la mesa to clear the table, **4**

el/la **mesero(a)** waiter (waitress), server, 4.2; **4**

la **meseta** meseta, plateau

la **mesita** table, 2.2; **4**

  meter to put, to place

   meter un gol to score a goal, 5.1

el **metro** subway, metro, **8.1**; meter

   la boca del metro subway station entrance, **8.1**

   la estación de metro subway station, **8.1**

el **metrópoli** metropolis, big city

  mexicano(a) Mexican, 1.2

la **mezcla** mixture

  mi(s) my

  mí me

el **miedo** fear

   tener miedo to be afraid, 7.2

el **miembro** member, 2.1

  mientras while, **5.2**

el **miércoles** Wednesday, LP

  mil (one) thousand

el **millón** million

el/la **millonario(a)** millionaire

  mimado(a) spoiled (person)

el **mimo** mime, **8.1**

la **mina** mine

el **minuto** minute

  ¡Mira! Look! 3.1

la **mirada** gaze, look

   tener la mirada fijada to keep one's eyes fixed on

  mirar to look at, 3.2

  mirarse to look at oneself, 11.1; **2.1**

la **miseria** poverty

  mismo(a) same, 1.2; own; very

  misterioso(a) mysterious

  mixto(a) co-ed

la **mochila** backpack, knapsack, 3.1

el/la **mochilero(a)** backpacker, hiker, 11.2; **2.2**

   viajar de mochilero to go backpacking, hiking

los **modales** manners, 6.1

   tener buenos (malos) modales to have good (bad) manners, to be well-behaved (rude), 6.1

  moderno(a) modern

  modesto(a) inexpensive

  molestar to bother, to annoy, 6.1

el **molino de viento** windmill

el **monasterio** monastery

la **moneda** coin, 9.1

el **mono** monkey

el **monopatín** skateboard, **11.1**

el **monstruo** monster

la **montaña** mountain, 7.2

la **montaña rusa** roller coaster, **8.1**

  montañoso(a) mountainous

  montar to put up (tent), 11.2; **2.2**; to ride, 8.2

   montar a caballo to go horseback riding, 8.2

el **montón** bunch, heap

el **monumento** monument

  mórbido(a) morbid

  morder (ue) to bite

  moreno(a) dark-haired, brunette, 1.1

  morir (ue, u) to die, **4**

el **morrón** sweet red pepper

el **mostrador** (ticket) counter, 10.1; **1.1**

  mostrar (ue) to show, 10.2; **1.2**

Spanish-English Dictionary

el **motivo** theme; reason, motive

el **móvil** cell phone, 3.2; **6.1**

el **movimiento** movement, **11.1**

el **mozo** bellhop, **7**

el **MP3** MP3 player, **6.2**

la **muchacha** girl, 1.1

el **muchacho** boy, 1.1

mucho a lot, many, much, 2.2; very, LP

  Hace mucho calor (frío). It's very hot (cold)., LP

  Mucho gusto. Nice to meet you.

los **muebles** furniture, 2.2

la **muerte** death

muerto(a) dead

el/la **muerto(a)** dead person, deceased, **5.1**

  el Día de los Muertos the Day of the Dead, **5.1**

la **mujer** wife, 2.1

la **mula** mule

las **muletas** crutches, **11.2**

  andar con muletas to walk on crutches, **11.2**

la **multa** fine, **9.1**

mundial: la Copa Mundial World Cup

el **mundo** world

  todo el mundo everyone

la **muñeca** wrist, **11.1**

el **mural** mural

el/la **muralista** muralist

el **muro** wall

el **museo** museum, 8.2

la **música** music, 1.2

el/la **músico(a)** musician, 8.1

el **muslo** thigh, **10**

muy very, LP

  muy bien very well, LP

nacer to be born

el **nacimiento** birth

nacional national

la **nacionalidad** nationality 1.1

  ¿de qué nacionalidad? what nationality?, 1.1

nada nothing, not anything, 8.2

  De nada. You're welcome., LP

  Nada más. Nothing else., 9.2

  Por nada. You're welcome., LP; for no reason

nadar to swim, 7.1

nadie nobody, not anybody, 8.2

la **nafta** gasoline

la **naranja** orange *(fruit)*, 4.1

natal pertaining to where someone was born

la **naturaleza** nature

navegar la red (el Internet) to surf the Web (the Internet), 3.2; **6.1**

la **Navidad** Christmas, **5.2**

  el árbol de Navidad Christmas tree, **5.2**

  ¡Feliz Navidad! Merry Christmas!

necesario: Es necesario. It's necessary., **11.2**

necesitar to need, 3.2

negativo(a) negative

negro(a) black, 2.1

nervioso(a) nervous, 6.1

el **neumático** tire, **9.2**

nevado(a) snowy, snow-covered

nevar (ie) to snow

  Nieva. It's snowing., LP

la **nevera** refrigerator, **10**

ni neither, nor

  Ni idea. No idea.

nicaragüense Nicaraguan

la **nieta** granddaughter, 2.1

el **nieto** grandson, 2.1

la **nieve** snow, 7.2

ninguno(a) none, not any

  de ninguna manera in no way, by no means

la **niñez** childhood

el/la **niño(a)** boy, girl, child, 6.2

el **nivel** level

no no

  No hay de qué. You're welcome., LP

  no obstante nevertheless

la **noche** night, evening

  Buenas noches. Good evening., LP

  esta noche tonight, 4.1

  por la noche in the evening

la **Nochebuena** Christmas Eve, **5.2**

la **Nochevieja** New Year's Eve

nombrar to name

el **nombre** name, 2.1; **10.1**

la **noria** Ferris wheel, **8.1**

normal normal, 6.2

el **norte** north

norteamericano(a) American, North American

nos us (*pron.*)

nosotros(as) we

la **nota** grade, mark, 3.1

  sacar notas buenas (malas) to get good (bad) grades, 3.1

la(s) **noticia(s)** news, piece of news

novecientos(as) nine hundred, 9.2

la **novela** novel

noventa ninety, LP

noviembre November, LP

la **nube** cloud, 7.1

nublado(a) cloudy, 7.1

nuestro(a) our

nueve nine, LP

nuevo(a) new, 1.1

  de nuevo again

el **número** shoe size, 9.1; number, 10.1; **1.1**

  el número del asiento seat number, 10.1; **1.1**

  el número de teléfono telephone number, **6.2**

  el número del vuelo flight number, 10.1; **1.1**

  ¿Qué número calzas? What size shoe do you wear (take)?, 9.1

nunca never, not ever, 8.2

o or

objetivo objective

obligatorio(a) required, obligatory

la **obra** work; work of art

observar to observe, to notice

el **obstáculo** obstacle

obstinado(a) obstinate, stubborn, 6.1

occidental western

el **océano** ocean

ochenta eighty, LP

ocho eight, LP

ochocientos(as) eight hundred, 9.2

octubre October, LP

ocupado(a) occupied, 4.2; **3.2**

el **oeste** west

la **oficina** office, **8.1**

ofrecer to offer

la **ofrenda** offering, **5.1**

el **oído** ear

oír to hear, 8.1

Ojalá que... Would that . . . , I hope . . . , **11.2**

ojeada: dar una ojeada to take a look at

¡Ojo! Watch out! Be careful!

el **ojo** eye, 2.1

tener mucho ojo to be very careful

tener ojos azules (castaños, verdes) to have blue (brown, green) eyes, 2.1

la **ola** wave, 7.1

oliva: el aceite de oliva olive oil

la **olla** pot, **10**

olvidar to forget

once eleven, LP

la **onza** ounce

la **opinión** opinion

la **oportunidad** opportunity

el/la **opresor(a)** oppressor

oprimir to press, to push (*button, key*), **6.1**

opuesto(a) opposite

la **oración** sentence

la **orden** order (*restaurant*), 4.2

el **orden** order

el **ordenador** computer, 3.2; **6.1**

la **orfebrería** craftsmanship in precious metals

organizar to organize, to set up

el **órgano** organ

oriental eastern

el **origen** origin, background

originarse to come from

las **orillas** banks, shores

a orillas de on the shores of

el **oro** gold

la **orquesta** orchestra, band

la **orquídea** orchid

ortopédico(a): el/la cirujano(a) ortopédico(a) orthopedic surgeon, **11.2**

oscuro(a) dark

el **otoño** autumn, fall, LP

otro(a) other, another

otros(as) others

el **oxígeno: la máscara de oxígeno** oxygen mask, 10.2; **1.2**

¡Oye! Listen!, 1.2

P

pacer to graze, **8.2**

la **paciencia** patience

paciente patient (*adj.*), 6.1

el/la **paciente** patient, 6.2

el **padrastro** stepfather, 2.1

el **padre** father, 2.1

los **padres** parents, 2.1

pagar to pay, 3.2

la **página** page

la **página de inicio (inicial, frontal)** home page, **6.1**

el **país** country

el **paisaje** landscape

la **paja** straw, **5.2**

el **pájaro** bird

la **palabra** word

la **palabra afine** cognate

el **palacio** palace

la **palma** palm tree

la **paloma** pigeon

la **palta** avocado

el **pan** bread

el **pan dulce** pastry, **7**

el **pan tostado** toast, 4.1; **7**

la **panadería** bakery

el **panecillo** roll, 4.1; **7**

el **panqueque** pancake

la **pantalla de escritorio** (computer) screen, monitor, **6.1**

el **pantalón** pants, 3.1

el **pantalón corto** shorts, 5.1

el **pantalón largo** long pants, 9.1

la **panza** belly

la **papa** potato, 4.1

las **papas fritas** french fries, 4.1

el **papel** paper, 3.1; role

la **hoja de papel** sheet of paper, 3.1

el **rollo de papel higiénico** roll of toilet paper, 11.2; **2.2**

el **paquete** package, 9.2

el **par** pair, 9.1

el **par de zapatos** pair of shoes, 9.1

para for; in order to

el **parabrisas** windshield, **9.1**

la **parada** stop, station, 3.2

la **parada de autobús** bus stop, 8.1

el **parador** inn

el **paraíso** paradise

parar(se) to stop, 9.1

parear to match

parecer to seem, to look like

a mi (tu, su) parecer in my (*your, his*) opinion

¿Qué te parece? What do you think?

pares even (*numeric*)

el/la **pariente** relative, 2.1

el **parking** parking lot, 8.1

el **parque** park, 11.2; **2.2**

el parque de atracciones amusement park, **8.1**

parquear to park

el **parqueo** parking lot, **8.1**

el **parquímetro** parking meter, **9.1**

el **párrafo** paragraph

la **parrilla** grill, **10**

la **parte** part; place

¿De parte de quién, por favor? Who's calling, please?, **6.2**

en muchas partes in many places

la mayor parte the greatest part, the most

participar to participate, to take part in

el **partido** game, 5.1

el **pasabordo** boarding pass

pasado(a) last, 7.1

el año pasado last year, 7.1

la semana pasada last week, 7.1

el/la **pasajero(a)** passenger, 10.1; **1.1**

el **pasaporte** passport, 10.2; **1.2**

pasar to pass, to go, 5.2; to spend (*time*), 7.1; to pass (*car*), **9.1**

pasarlo bien to have a good time, to have fun, 11.2; **2.2**

pasar por el control de seguridad to go through security, 10.2; **1.2**

¿Qué pasa? What's going on? What's happening?

¿Qué te pasa? What's the matter (with you)?

la **Pascua (Florida)** Easter

el **paseo** broad street, avenue, **8.1**

dar un paseo to take a walk

dar un paseo en bicicleta to take a (bike) ride

el **pasillo** aisle, 10.2; **1.2**

la **pasta dentífrica** toothpaste

el **pastel** cake

Spanish-English Dictionary

la **pastilla** bar *(soap)*

los **patacones** slices of fried plantain

la **patata** potato, 4.1

    las patatas fritas french fries, 4.1

el **patín** ice skate, 7.2

el/la **patinador(a)** ice-skater, 7.2

el **patinaje** skating, 7.2; **11.1**

    el patinaje en línea in-line skating, **11.1**

    el patinaje sobre hielo ice-skating, 7.2

    patinar to skate, to go skating, 7.2; **11.1**

    patinar en línea to go in-line skating, **11.1**

    patinar sobre el hielo to ice-skate, 7.2

el/la **patrón(ona)** patron, 5.1

    el/la santo(a) patrón(ona) patron saint, 5.1

    patronal pertaining to a patron saint, 5.1

    pausado(a) slow, deliberate

    pavimentado(a) paved

el **pavimento** pavement

el **peaje** toll, **9.1**

    la cabina (garita) de peaje tollbooth, **9.1**

el/la **peatón(ona)** pedestrian, **8.1**

    peatonal related to pedestrians, **8.1**

el **pecho** chest, **11.1**

la **pechuga (de pollo)** (chicken) breast, **10**

el **pedacito** little piece, **10**

el **pedazo** piece

    pedir (i, i) to ask for, to request, **4**

    peinarse to comb one's hair, **11.1**; **2.1**

el **peine** comb, 11.2; **2.2**

    pelar to peel, **10**

la **película** movie, film, 8.2

el **peligro** danger

    peligroso(a) dangerous

    pelirrojo(a) redheaded, 1.1

el **pelo** hair, 2.1

    tener el pelo rubio (castaño, negro) to have blond (brown, black) hair, 2.1

la **pelota** ball *(baseball, tennis)*, 5.2

    la pelota vasca jai alai

la **pena** pain, sorrow

    ¡Qué pena! What a shame!, 5.1

    pendiente steep

la **pendiente** incline

el **pensamiento** thought

    pensar (ie) to think, 5.1

    pensar en to think about

    ¿Qué piensas? What do you think?, 5.1

el **peón** peasant, farm laborer, **8.2**

    peor worse

el/la **peor** worst

el **pepino** cucumber, **10**

    pequeño(a) small, little, 1.2

la **percha** hanger, **7**

    perder (ie) to lose, 5.1; to miss, 8.1

    perdida: la llamada perdida dropped call *(cell phone)*, **6.2**

    perdón pardon me, excuse me

la **peregrinación** pilgrimage

    perezoso(a) lazy, 1.2

el **periódico** newspaper, **3.1**

    permiso: Con permiso. Excuse me., 10.1; **1.1**

el **permiso de conducir** driver's license, **9.2**

    permitir to permit

    pero but

el/la **perro(a)** dog, 2.1

la **persona** person

el **personaje** character *(in a novel, play)*

la **personalidad** personality, 6.1

    pertenecer to belong

    peruano(a) Peruvian

la **pesa** weight, **11.1**

    levantar pesas to lift weights, **11.1**

    pesar: a pesar de in spite of

la **pescadería** fish market

el **pescado** fish, 4.1

el **peso** peso *(monetary unit of several Latin American countries)*; weight

    picar to nibble on; to chop; to mince, **10**

    picaresco(a) picaresque

el/la **pícher** pitcher, 5.2

el **pico** mountain top, peak, 7.2

el **pie** foot, 5.1; **2.1**

    a pie on foot, 3.2

    de pie standing

la **piedra** stone

la **pierna** leg, 11.1; **2.1**

la **pieza** bedroom; piece

la **pila** swimming pool

el **pimentón** pepper *(vegetable)*

la **pimienta** pepper *(spice)*, **4**

el **pimiento** bell pepper, 9.2; **10**

el **pinchazo** flat tire, **9.2**

los **pinchitos** kebabs, 4.2

    pintado(a) painted

    pintar to paint

el/la **pintor(a)** painter, artist, 8.2

    pintoresco(a) picturesque

la **piña** pineapple, 9.2

la **piscina** swimming pool, 7.1

el **piso** floor, 2.2; apartment *(Spain)*

la **pista** ski slope, 7.2; runway, 10.2; **1.2**; lane *(highway)*

    la pista de patinaje ice-skating rink, 7.2

la **pizca** pinch

la **pizza** pizza, 4.1

    placentero(a) pleasant

la **plancha de vela** windsurfing; sailboard, 7.1

    practicar la plancha de vela to windsurf, to go windsurfing, 7.1

    planchas: hacer planchas to do push-ups, **11.1**

el **plano** map, **9.1**

la **planta** plant, 2.2

la **plata** silver

el **plátano** banana, 9.2

el **platillo** saucer, **4**

el **plato** dish *(food)*; plate, **4**; home plate, 5.2; course *(meal)*;

la **playa** beach, 7.1

la **plaza** square, plaza, **8.1**; seat *(train)*, **3.2**

la **pluma** (fountain) pen

la **población** population

    pobre poor

el/la **pobre** poor boy (girl)

    poco(a) a little; few, 2.2

    dentro de poco soon; shortly thereafter

    un poco más a little more

    poder (ue) to be able, 5.1

el **poema** poem

el/la **policía** police officer

el **pollo** chicken, 4.1; **10**

    poner to put, to place, to set, 10.2; **1.2**

poner al fuego to heat, **10**

poner la mesa to set the table, **4**

poner unos puntos (unas suturas) to give (someone) stitches, **11.2**

ponerse to put on *(clothes)*, 11.1; **2.1;** to become

popular popular

por for, by

  por ejemplo for example

  por encima de over, 5.2

  por eso that's why, for this reason

  por favor please, LP

  por fin finally

  por la mañana in the morning

  por la noche at night, in the evening

  por la tarde in the afternoon

  por lo general in general

  Por nada. You're welcome., LP; for no reason

  ¿por qué? why?, 3.2

los **porotos** green beans *(Chile)*

porque because, 3.2

el/la **porrista** cheerleader

portátil: la computadora portátil laptop computer

el/la **porteño(a)** person from Buenos Aires

la **portería** goal *(box)*, 5.1

el/la **portero(a)** goalie, 5.1

portugués(esa) Portuguese

poseer to possess

posible possible

positivo(a) positive

el **postre** dessert, 4.1

practicar to practice *(sport)*

  practicar la plancha de vela (la tabla hawaiana) to go windsurfing (surfing), 7.1

  practicar yoga to do yoga, **11.1**

el **precio** price, 9.1

precolombino(a) pre-Columbian

la **preferencia** preference

preferir (ie, i) to prefer

el **prefijo del país** country code, **6.2**

la **pregunta** question, 3.1

preguntar to ask (a question)

el **premio** prize, award

prender to turn on, **6.1**

preparar to prepare; to get ready

la **prepa(ratoria)** high school

presentar to introduce

el **préstamo** loan

  el préstamo a corto (largo) plazo short- (long-) term loan

prestar: prestar atención to pay attention, 3.1

el **pretendiente** suitor

primario(a): la escuela primaria elementary school

la **primavera** spring, LP

primero(a) first, LP

  el primero de enero (febrero, etc.) January (February, etc.) 1, LP

  en primera clase first-class, **3.2**

el/la **primo(a)** cousin, 2.1

la **princesa** princess

principal main

el/la **principiante** beginner, 7.2

prisa: de prisa fast, hurriedly

  a toda prisa with full speed

privado(a) private, 2.2

probable probable, likely

el **problema** problem

  No hay problema. No problem.

procedente de coming, arriving from, 10.2; **1.2**

el **procedimiento** step *(recipe)*

la **procesión** procession, parade, **5.1**

producir to produce

el **producto** product; food, 9.2

  los productos congelados frozen food, 9.2

la **profesión** profession, occupation

profesional professional

el/la **profesor(a)** teacher, 1.2

profundo(a) deep

prohibido(a) forbidden, **9.1**

prometer to promise

el **pronombre** pronoun

pronto: ¡Hasta pronto! See you soon!, LP

propenso(a) prone to

la **propina** tip *(restaurant)*, 4

propio(a) own, 5.1

propósito: ¡A propósito! By the way!, 8.2

el **propósito benévelo** charitable purpose

protectora: la loción protectora suntan lotion, sunblock, 7.1

próximo(a) next, **3.2**

la **prueba** test, exam, 3.1

el **pueblo** town

el **puente** bridge

la **puerta** gate *(airport)*, 10.2; **1.2;** door, 9.2

  la puerta delantera (trasera) front (back) door *(bus)*

  la puerta de salida gate *(airport)*, 10.2; **1.2**

el **puerto** port

puertorriqueño(a) Puerto Rican

pues well

el **puesto** market stall, 9.2

los **pulmones** lungs

pulsar to press *(button, key)*, **6.1**

la **pulsera** bracelet

pulso: tomar el pulso to take someone's pulse, 6.2

el **punto** point; dot *(Internet)*, **6.1;** stitch, **11.2**

  poner puntos (a alguien) to give (somebody) stitches, **11.2**

el **pupitre** desk, 3.1

que that; who

¿qué? what? how?, LP

  ¿a qué hora? at what time?, LP

  ¿de qué nacionalidad? what nationality?

  No hay de qué. You're welcome., LP

  ¿Qué desean tomar? What would you like (to eat)?, 4.2

  ¿Qué día es hoy? What day is it today?, LP

  ¿Qué hay? What's new (up)?

  ¿Qué hora es? What time is it?, LP

  ¡Qué… más… ! What a . . . !

  ¿Qué pasa? What's going on? What's happening?

  ¡Qué pena! What a shame!, 5.1

  ¿Qué tal? How are things? How are you?, LP

  ¿Qué tal le gustó? How did you like it? *(formal)*

  ¿Qué tiempo hace? What's the weather like?, LP

quebrarse to break, **11.2**

quedar (bien) to fit, to look good on, 9.1

Spanish-English Dictionary

Esta chaqueta no te queda bien. This jacket doesn't fit you., 9.1

quedar(se) to remain, to stay, 11.1; **2.1**

quemarse to burn, **10**

querer (ie) to want, to wish, 5.1; to love

querido(a) dear, beloved

el **queso** cheese, 4.1

    el sándwich de jamón y queso ham and cheese sandwich, 4.1

el **quetzal** quetzal (*currency of Guatemala*)

¿quién? who?, 1.1

    ¿De parte de quién, por favor? Who's calling, please?, **6.2**

¿quiénes? who? (*pl.*), 1.2

quince fifteen, LP

la **quinceañera** fifteen-year-old girl

quinientos(as) five hundred

el **quiosco** kiosk, newsstand, **3.1**

quitar la mesa to clear the table, 4

quitarse to take off (*clothes*), 11.1; **2.1**

quizá(s) maybe, perhaps, 7.2

R

el **racimo** bunch (*grapes*)

la **radiografía** X ray, **11.2**

    Le toman (hacen) una radiografía. They're taking an X ray of him (her)., **11.2**

la **raja** slice (*melon*)

la **rama** branch

el **rancho** ranch, **8.2**

la **ranura** slot, **6.2**

rápidamente quickly

rápido(a) fast

la **raqueta** (*tennis*) racket, 5.2

raro(a) rare

el **rascacielos** skyscraper, **8.1**

el **rato** time, while

el **ratón** mouse, **6.1**

la **raza** breed

la **razón** reason

    tener razón to be right

el/la **realista** realist

rebajar to lower (*prices*), 9.1

la **rebanada** slice (*bread*), **10**

    cortar en rebanadas to slice, **10**

rebasar to pass (*car*), **9.1**

la **recámara** bedroom, 2.2

recambio: la rueda (llanta) de recambio spare tire, **9.2**

la **recepción** front desk (*hotel*), 7

el/la **recepcionista** hotel clerk, 7

el/la **receptor(a)** catcher, 5.2

la **receta** prescription, 6.2; recipe, **10**

recetar to prescribe, 6.2

recibir to receive, 4.1; to catch

    recibir aplausos to be applauded, 5.1

reclamar to claim

recoger to collect, to gather

reconocer to recognize

recordar (ue) to remember

el **recorrido** trip, route

los **recuerdos** memories

recuperar to claim, to get back

la **red** the Web, 3.2; **6.1**; net, 5.2

    navegar la red to surf the Web, 3.2; **6.1**

    pasar por encima de la red to go over the net, 5.2

reducido(a) reduced

reducir to reduce; to set (*bone*), **11.2**

    reducir la velocidad to reduce speed, **9.1**

refacción: la rueda (llanta) de refacción spare tire

el **refresco** soft drink, 4.2

el **refrigerador** refrigerator, **10**

refrito(a) refried

el **refugio** refuge

el **regalo** gift, present, 8.1

regatear to bargain, 9.2

el **régimen** diet

la **región** region

la **regla** rule

regresar to go back, to return, 3.2

    el botón regresar back button, back key, **6.1**

    regresar a casa to go home, 3.2

regreso: el boleto de ida y regreso round-trip ticket, **3.1**

regular regular, average

la **reina** queen

reinar to rule, to reign

relacionado(a) related

relevos: la carrera de relevos relay race, **11.1**

religioso(a) religious

rendir (i, i) honor to honor

renombrado(a) famous

rentar to rent, 7.1; **3.2**

repartido(a) distributed, split up among

repasar to review

el **repaso** review

repente: de repente suddenly, all of a sudden

repetir (i, i) to repeat, to have seconds (*meal*), 4

la **república** republic

    la República Dominicana Dominican Republic

repuesto: la rueda (llanta) de repuesto spare tire, **9.2**

la **reserva** reservation

la **reservación** reservation, 7

reservar to reserve, 7

resfriado(a) stuffed up (*cold*), 6.2

respetado(a) respected

respetar to respect

la **respiración** breathing, **11.1**

respirar to breathe

responsable responsible

la **respuesta** answer

el **restaurante** restaurant, 4

resultar to turn out to be

el **retraso** delay, 10.2; **1.2**

    con retraso late, 10.2; **1.2**

el **retrato** portrait

retroceder: el botón retroceder back button, back key, **6.1**

la **reunión** meeting, get-together

reunirse to meet, to get together

revisar to check (*ticket*), **3.2**

el/la **revisor(a)** conductor, **3.2**

la **revista** magazine, **3.1**

revolver (ue) to stir, **10**

revueltos: los huevos revueltos scrambled eggs, 7

el **rey** king

    el Día de los Reyes Epiphany (January 6), **5.2**

    los Reyes Magos the Three Wise Men, **5.2**

rico(a) rich; delicious

    ¡Qué rico! How delicious!

el **rincón** corner

los **riñones** kidneys

el **río** river

el **risco** cliff, **3.2**

el **ritmo** rhythm

robar to steal

la **roca** rock, stone

la **rodaja** slice (lemon, cucumber)

rodeado(a) surrounded

la **rodilla** knee, 11.1; **2.1**

la **rodillera** kneepad, **11.1**

rojo(a) red, 5.1

la luz roja red light, **9.1**

el **rol** role

el **rollo de papel higiénico** roll of toilet paper, 11.2; **2.2**

el **rompecabezas** puzzle

romper(se) to break, **11.2**

Se rompió la pierna. He (She) broke his (her) leg., **11.2**

la **ropa** clothing, 9.1

la **rosa** rose

rosado(a) pink, 5.1

roto(a) broken

el **rótulo** sign, **9.1**

rubio(a) blonde, 1.1

la **rueda** tire, **9.2**

la rueda de repuesto (recambio) spare tire, **9.2**

la silla de ruedas wheelchair, **11.2**

el **ruido** noise

las **ruinas** ruins

la **ruta** route

la **rutina diaria** daily routine, 11.1; **2.1**

S

el **sábado** Saturday, LP

la **sábana** sheet, **7**

saber to know, 9.1

sabio(a) wise

el **sabor** flavor, **10**

sacar to get, 3.1; to take, 7.1

sacar fotos to take pictures, 7.1

sacar notas buenas (malas) to get good (bad) grades, 3.1

el **saco de dormir** sleeping bag, 11.2; **2.2**

el **sacrificio** sacrifice

la **sal** salt, **4**

la **sala** living room, 2.2

la sala de clase classroom, 3.1

la sala de emergencia emergency room, **11.2**

la **sala de espera** waiting room, **3.1**

salado(a) salty

el **saldo** sale, 9.1

la **salida** departure, 10.1; **1.1**; exit, **9.1**

la hora de salida time of departure, 10.1; **1.1**

la puerta de salida gate (airport), 10.2; **1.2**

salir to leave; to go out, 8.1; to turn out, to result

Todo te sale más barato. Everything costs a lot less.; It's all a lot less expensive., 9.1

la **salsa** sauce, gravy, **10**; dressing

saltar to jump (over)

salteado(a) sautéed

la **salud** health, 6.1

saludar to greet

el **saludo** greeting

salvar to save

la **sandalia** sandal, 9.2

el **sándwich** sandwich, 4.1

el sándwich de jamón y queso ham and cheese sandwich, 4.1

sano(a) healthy

el/la **santo(a)** saint

el/la santo(a) patrón(ona) patron saint, 5.1

el **sarape** blanket

el/la **sartén** skillet, frying pan, **10**

satisfacer to satisfy

el **sato** a type of dog from Puerto Rico

seco(a) dry

secundario(a): la escuela secundaria high school, 1.2

la **sed** thirst, 4.1

tener sed to be thirsty, 4.1

el **sedán** sedan, 9.2

seguir (i, i) to follow, **4**; to continue, 9.1

según according to

segundo(a) second

el segundo tiempo second half (soccer), 5.1

en segunda clase second-class (ticket), 3.1

seguramente surely, certainly

seguridad: el control de seguridad security (airport), 10.2; **1.2**

el cinturón de seguridad seat belt, 10.2; **1.2**

seguro(a) sure; safe

seguro que certainly

seis six, LP

seiscientos(as) six hundred

seleccionar to choose, **3.1**

la **selva** jungle, forest

el **semáforo** traffic light, 8.1

la **semana** week, LP

el fin de semana weekend, 7.1

la semana pasada last week, 7.1

sembrar (ie) to plant, to sow, **8.2**

el **seminómada** seminomad

sencillo one-way, 3.1; single (hotel room), **7**; simple

el billete (boleto) sencillo one-way ticket, 3.1

el cuarto sencillo single room, **7**

la **senda** path, **3.2**

sentado(a) seated

sentarse (ie) to sit down, 11.1; **2.1**

el **sentido** direction, **9.1**; sense, 6.1

la calle de sentido único one-way street, 9.1

sentir (ie, i) to be sorry; to feel

Lo siento mucho. I'm very sorry.

sentirse (ie, i) to feel

la **señal** sign, 10.2; **1.2**

la señal de no fumar no-smoking sign, 10.2; **1.2**

señalar to point out

el **señor** sir, Mr., gentleman, LP

la **señora** Ms., Mrs., madam, LP

los **señores** Mr. and Mrs.

la **señorita** Miss, Ms., LP

septiembre September, LP

ser to be

el **ser** being

los seres humanos human beings

los seres vivientes living beings

serio(a) serious, 1.1

¿Hablas en serio? Are you serious?

el **servicio** tip, 4.2; restroom, 10.2; **1.2**; service, 9.2

¿Está incluido el servicio? Is the tip included?, 4.2

la estación de servicio gas station, 9.2

la **servilleta** napkin, **4**

servir to serve, **4**

servir de to serve as

sesenta sixty, LP

Spanish-English Dictionary

setecientos(as) seven hundred

setenta seventy, LP

severo(a) harsh, strict

si if

sí yes, LP

siempre always, 8.2

siento: Lo siento mucho. I'm very sorry., 5.1

la **siesta** nap

siete seven, LP

el **siglo** century

significar to mean

siguiente following

la **silla** chair, 2.2

    la silla de ruedas wheelchair, **11.2**

similar similar

simpático(a) nice, 1.1

sin without

sincero(a) sincere

sino but rather

el **síntoma** symptom

el **sistema** system

el **sitio** space (parking)

el **sitio Web** Web site, **6.1**

el/la **snowboarder** snowboarder, 7.2

las **sobras** leftovers

sobre on, on top of; about

    sobre todo above all, especially

la **sobremesa** dessert; after-dinner conversation

la **sobrepoblación** overpopulation

sobrevivir to survive

sobrevolar (ue) to fly over

la **sobrina** niece, 2.1

el **sobrino** nephew, 2.1

social social

    los estudios sociales social studies, 1.2

la **sociedad** society

el/la **socio(a)** member

socorrer to help

el/la **socorrista** paramedic, **11.2**

el **sofá** sofa, 2.2

el **sol** sun

    Hace (Hay) sol. It's sunny., LP

    tomar el sol to sunbathe, 7.1

solamente only

solar: la crema solar suntan lotion, 7.1

solas: a solas alone

el **soldado** soldier

soler (ue) to be used to, to do something usually

solo(a) single; alone

solo only

el/la **soltero(a)** single, unmarried person

el **sombrero** hat

sonar (ue) to ring, **6.1**

el **sonido** sound

la **sonrisa** smile, 6.1

la **sopa** soup

soplar to blow (wind)

la **sorpresa** surprise, 4.1

su(s) his, her, their, your (formal)

subir to go up, 7.2; to get on (train, etc.), **3.1**

subterráneo(a) underground

los **suburbios** suburbs, 2.2

sucio(a) dirty, 7

Sudamérica South America

sudamericano(a) South American

el/la **suegro(a)** father- (mother-) in-law

el **suelo** ground, floor

el **sueño** dream

    tener sueño to be sleepy

la **suerte** luck

    ¡Buena suerte! Good luck!

    ¡Qué suerte tengo! How lucky I am!, 9.1

el **suéter** sweater, 11.1; **2.1**

sufrir to suffer

superior upper, top

    el compartimiento superior overhead bin (airplane), 10.2; **1.2**

el **supermercado** supermarket, 9.2

el **sur** south

    la América del Sur South America

el **surtido** assortment

sus his, her, their, your (formal)

el **susto** fear

la **sutura** stitch, **11.2**

suturar to give (someone) stitches

el **SUV** SUV, 9.2

T

---

la **tabla** chart, table

la **tabla hawaiana** surfboard, 7.1

    practicar la tabla hawaiana to surf, to go surfing, 7.1

tacaño(a) stingy, cheap, **9.1**

el **taco** taco

la **tajada** slice (ham, meat), 9.2

tal such

    ¿Qué tal? How are things? How are you?, LP

    ¿Qué tal tu clase de español? How's your Spanish class?

tal vez maybe, perhaps, 7.2

la **talla** size, 9.1

    ¿Qué talla usas? What size do you take?, 9.1

el **tamaño** size

también also, too, 1.2

el **tambor** drum

el **tamborín** small drum

tampoco either, neither

tan so

tan... como as . . . as

el **tanque** gas tank, **9.2**

el **tanto** score, point, 5.1

    marcar un tanto to score a point, 5.1

tanto(a) so much

    tanto(a)... como as much . . . as

    tantos(as)... como as many . . . as

la **tapa** lid, 10

tapar to cover (pot)

las **tapas** snacks, nibbles, 4.2

el **tapón** traffic jam

la **taquilla** box office, ticket window, 8.2

tarde late, 10.2; **1.2**

la **tarde** afternoon

    ayer por la tarde yesterday afternoon, 7.1

    Buenas tardes. Good afternoon., LP

la **tarea** homework; task

la **tarifa** fare, **3.1**; price

la **tarjeta** card; pass

    la tarjeta de abordar boarding pass

    la tarjeta de crédito credit card, 3.1

    la tarjeta de embarque boarding pass, 10.1; **1.1**

    la tarjeta telefónica telephone card, **6.2**

la **tarta** cake, 8.1

la **tasa de interés** interest rate

el **taxi** taxi, 10.1; **1.1**

el/la **taxista** taxi driver, 10.1; **1.1**

la **taza** cup, 4.1; **4**

te you *(fam. pron.)*

el **té** tea

el **teclado** keyboard, **6.1**

el/la **técnico(a)** technician

la **tecnología** technology

tejano(a) Texan

los **tejidos** fabrics, 9.2

la **tele** TV

telefónico(a) *(related to)* phone, **6.2**

   la guía telefónica phone book, **6.2**

   la tarjeta telefónica phone card, **6.2**

el **teléfono** telephone

   el número de teléfono phone number, **6.2**

   el teléfono celular cell phone, **6.1**

   el teléfono público pay phone, **6.2**

   hablar por teléfono to speak on the phone

la **telenovela** serial, soap opera

el **telesilla** chairlift, ski lift, 7.2

el **telesquí** ski lift, 7.2

la **televisión** television

el **tema** theme

tembloroso(a) trembling

la **temperatura** temperature, 7.2

temprano(a) early, 11.1; **1.2**

el **tenderete** market stall, 9.2

el **tenedor** fork, **4**

tener (ie) to have, 2.1

   tener... años to be ... years old, 2.1

   tener calor (frío) to be hot (cold), 11.1; **2.1**

   tener catarro to have a cold, 6.2

   tener cuidado to be careful, **9.1**

   tener dolor de... to have a(n) ... -ache, 6.2

   tener el pelo rubio (castaño, negro) to have blond (brown, black) hair, 2.1

   tener éxito to be successful, 6.1

   tener fiebre to have a fever, 6.2

   tener ganas de to feel like

   tener hambre to be hungry, 4.1

   tener lugar to take place

   tener miedo to be afraid, 7.2

   tener ojos azules (castaños, verdes) to have blue (brown, green) eyes, 2.1

   tener que to have to *(do something)*, 4.2

   tener sed to be thirsty, 4.1

el **tenis** tennis

   la cancha de tenis tennis court, 5.2

   jugar (al) tenis to play tennis, 5.2

los **tenis** sneakers, tennis shoes, 9.1

el/la **tenista** tennis player

la **tensión** tension, stress, **11.1**

   la tensión arterial blood pressure, 6.2

tercer(o)(a) third

terco(a) stubborn, 6.1

terminar to end, finish

término: a término medio medium *(meat)*, **4**

el **término** term

la **ternera** veal, 10

   el escalope de ternera veal cutlet, **10**

el/la **terrateniente** landowner

la **terraza** terrace, balcony

el **terremoto** earthquake

el **tesoro** treasure

ti you

la **tía** aunt, 2.1

el **ticket** ticket, 7.2

el **tiempo** weather, LP; half *(soccer)*, 5.1

   a tiempo on time, 10.2; **1.2**

   a tiempo completo (parcial) full- (part-) time

   el segundo tiempo second half *(soccer)*, 5.1

   Hace buen (mal) tiempo. The weather is nice (bad)., LP

   ¿Qué tiempo hace? What's the weather like?, LP

la **tienda** store, 3.2

   la tienda de ropa clothing store, 9.1

la **tienda de campaña** tent, 11.2; **2.2**

la **tierra** land, 8.2

el **tigre** tiger

los **timbales** small drums, kettledrums

el **timbre (sonoro)** ringtone, **6.2**

tímido(a) shy

el **tío** uncle, 2.1

los **tíos** aunt and uncle, 2.1

el **tiovivo** merry-go-round, **8.1**

típico(a) typical

el **tipo** type, 6.1

el **tiquete** ticket, **9.1**

tirar to throw, 5.2

el **título** title

la **toalla** towel, 7.1; **7**

el **tobillo** ankle, **11.1**

el **tocadiscos** record player

tocar to touch, 5.1; to play *(musical instrument)*, 8.1; **5.2**

   ¡Te toca a ti! It's your turn!

el **tocino** bacon, 4.1; **7**

todavía still; yet

todo(a) everything; all

   sobre todo above all, especially

   todo el mundo everyone, **5.2**

todos(as) everyone, 8.1; everything; all

   en todas partes everywhere

tomar to take, 3.1; to have *(meal)*, 4.1

   tomar el almuerzo (el desayuno) to have lunch (breakfast), 4.1

   tomar el bus to take the bus

   tomar el pulso to take someone's pulse, 6.2

   tomar el sol to sunbathe, 7.1

   tomar fotos to take pictures, 7.1

   tomar la tensión arterial to take someone's blood pressure, 6.2

   tomar un examen to take a test, 3.1

   tomar una ducha to take a shower, 11.1; **2.1**

   tomar una radiografía to take an X ray of someone, **11.2**

el **tomate** tomato, 4.1

la **tonelada** ton

el **tono** dial tone, **6.2**

las **tonterías** foolish things

tonto(a) foolish, crazy

torcerse (ue) to sprain, to twist, **11.2**

   Se torció el tobillo. He (She) sprained his (her) ankle., **11.2**

torcido(a) sprained, twisted

la **torta** cake, 4.1; sandwich

la **tortilla** tortilla

la **tos** cough, 6.2

   tener tos to have a cough, 6.2

toser to cough, 6.2

la **tostada** tostada

Spanish-English Dictionary

las **tostadas** toast, 4.1
tostado(a) toasted
   el pan tostado toast, 4.1; **7**
los **tostones** slices of fried
   plantain, 4.2
trabajar to work, 3.2; **8.2**
el **trabajo** work
tradicional traditional
traer to carry, to bring,
   to take, 10.1; **1.1**
el **tráfico** traffic, **8.1**
el **traje** suit
el **traje de baño** swimsuit, 7.1
tranquilo(a) calm, 6.1
transbordar to transfer
   (*trains*), **3.2**
el **tránsito** traffic
**transporte: los medios de
   transporte** means of
   transportation, **8.2**
trasero(a) back
el **tratamiento** treatment
tratar to treat
tratar de to try to
   (do something)
   tratar de desviar to try to
   dissuade
la **travesía** crossing
**traviesa: a campo
   traviesa** cross-country
   (*race*), **11.1**
el **trayecto** stretch (of road)
trece thirteen, LP
el **trecho** stretch (*distance*)
treinta thirty, LP
treinta y uno thirty-one, LP
el **tren** train, **3.1**
tres three, LP
trescientos(as) three hundred
el **trigo** wheat, **8.2**
triste sad, 6.1
el **trocito** little piece
la **trompeta** trumpet
las **tropas** troops
tropical tropical
el **trotamundos** globe-trotter
el **trozo** piece
el **T-shirt** T-shirt
tu(s) your (*fam.*)
tú you (*sing. fam.*)
el **tubo de crema dental** tube of
   toothpaste, 11.2; **2.2**
la **tumba** grave, tomb, **5.1**
el **turismo** tourism
el/la **turista** tourist

u or (*used instead of o before
   words beginning with o or ho*)
Ud., usted you (*sing.*) (*formal*)
Uds., ustedes you (*pl.*)
   (*formal*)
último(a) last; final
un(a) a, an, 1.1
la **una** one o'clock, LP
único(a) only, 2.1;
   one-way, **9.1**
   la calle de sentido único
      one-way street, **9.1**
   el/la hijo(a) único(a) only
      child, 2.1
la **unidad** unit
el **uniforme** uniform, 3.1
la **universidad** university
uno(a) one, LP
unos(as) some
urbano(a) urban, **8.1**
usar to use, 3.2; to wear (*size*),
   9.1
   ¿Qué talla usas? What size
      do you wear (take)?, 9.1
el **uso** use
el/la **usuario(a)** user
la **uva** grape, 9.2

la **vaca** cow, **8.2**
las **vacaciones** vacation, 7.1
   estar de vacaciones to be
      on vacation
vacante vacant
vacío(a) empty, **9.2**
vagar to wander, to roam
el **vagón** train car, **3.1**
la **vainilla** vanilla
las **vainitas** green beans
Vale. It's a good idea.
   No vale. It's not worth it.,
      7.1
valeroso(a) brave
el **valle** valley
¡Vamos! Let's go!
varios(as) several
el **varón** man, boy
vasco(a) Basque
   la pelota vasca jai-alai

el **vaso** glass, 4.1
el **váter** toilet, **7**
veces: a veces at times,
   sometimes, 6.1
el/la **vecino(a)** neighbor
el **vegetal** vegetable, 4.1
   los vegetales crudos raw
      vegetables, crudités, 8.1
vegetariano(a) vegetarian, 4.1
veinte twenty, LP
veinticinco twenty-five, LP
veinticuatro twenty-four, LP
veintidós twenty-two, LP
veintinueve twenty-nine, LP
veintiocho twenty-eight, LP
veintiséis twenty-six, LP
veintisiete twenty-seven, LP
veintitrés twenty-three, LP
veintiuno twenty-one, LP
la **vela** candle, 8.1; **5.2**
vela: la plancha de vela
   windsurfing; sailboard, 7.1
la **velocidad** speed, **9.1**
   la velocidad máxima speed
      limit, **9.1**
la **venda** bandage, **11.2**
el/la **vendedor(a)** merchant, 9.2
vender to sell, 6.2
venezolano(a) Venezuelan
venir (ie) to come
   **el verano (año, mes) que
      viene** next summer (year,
      month), **8.2**
la **venta** small hotel
las **ventajas** advantages
la **ventanilla** ticket window, 7.2,
   3.1; window (*plane*), 10.2; **1.2**
ver to see, 4.2
el **verano** summer, LP
el **verbo** verb
la **verdad** truth
   Es verdad. That's true
      (right)., 9.1
   ¿Verdad? Right?
verdadero(a) real, true
verde green, 2.1
   las judías verdes green
      beans, 9.2
la **verdulería** greengrocer
   (vegetable) store, 9.2
la **verdura** vegetable, 4.1
verificar to check
el **vestido** dress, 9.1
   el vestido de novia
      wedding dress

la **vestirse (i, i)** to get dressed, to dress, **4**

la **vez** time

    a veces at times, sometimes, 6.1; **1.2**

    cada vez each time, every time

    de vez en cuando from time to time, occasionally, 10.2; **1.2**

    en vez de instead of

    una vez más (once) again, one more time

la **vía** track, **3.1;** lane *(highway)*

viajar to travel

    viajar en avión (tren) to travel by plane (train)

el **viaje** trip, voyage 10.1; **1.1**

    hacer un viaje to take a trip, 10.1; **1.1**

la **víctima** victim

la **vida** life

el **video** video

viejo(a) old, 2.2

el **viento** wind, LP

    Hace viento. It's windy., LP

el **viernes** Friday, LP

el **vinagre** vinegar, **4**

el **vino** wine

el **violín** violin

visitar to visit, 8.2

la **víspera de Año Nuevo** New Year's Eve

la **vista** view; sight

la **viuda** widow

vivir to live, 4.1

vivo(a) lively

los **vivos** the living

la **vocal** vowel

el **volante** steering wheel, **9.2**

volar (ue) to fly

el **volcán** volcano

volcar to flip over

el **voleibol** volleyball, 7.1

    la cancha de voleibol volleyball court, 7.1

volver (ue) to return, 5.1

    volver a casa to go back (return) home, 8.1

vosotros(as) you *(pl.)*

la **voz** voice

el **vuelo** flight, 10.1; **1.1**

    el número del vuelo flight number, 10.1; **1.1**

vuelta: un boleto (billete) de ida y vuelta round-trip ticket, **3.1**

la **vuelta** lap, **11.1**

Vuestra Merced Your Highness

Y
---

y and, LP

    y cuarto a quarter past (the hour), LP

    y media half past (the hour), LP

ya already

    ¡Ya voy! I'm coming!, 11.2; **2.2**

el **yeso** cast, **11.2**

yo I; me

el **yoga** yoga, **11.1**

Z
---

la **zanahoria** carrot, 9.2; **10**

las **zapatillas** (sports) shoes, sneakers, 5.1

los **zapatos** shoes, 9.1

la **zona** area, zone

el **zoológico** zoo, **8.1**

el **zumo** juice *(Spain)*

English-Spanish Dictionary

*This English-Spanish Dictionary contains all productive and some receptive vocabulary from Levels 1 and 2. The numbers following each productive entry indicate the chapter and vocabulary section in which the word is introduced. For example, **3.2** in dark print means thtat the word was first taught in **Capítulo 3, Vocabulario 2**. A light print number means that the word was introduced in ¡Así se dice!, Level 1. LP refers to the Lecciones preliminares in Level 1. If there is no number following an entry, this means that the word or expression is there for receptive purposes only.*

A

@ la arroba, **6.1**

a, an un(a), 1.1

able: to be able poder (ue), 5.1

aboard a bordo (de), 10.2; **1.2**

about sobre; *(time)* a eso de

above por encima de, 5.2

  above all sobre todo

abroad al extranjero

accident el accidente, **11.2**

accompanied by acompañado(a) de, **3.2**

according to según

ache el dolor, 6.2

to **ache** doler, 6.2; **11.2**

  My . . . ache(s). Me duele(n)... , 6.2

activity la actividad

to **add** añadir, **10**

addition: in addition to además de

address la dirección, **6.1**

  address book la libreta de direcciones, **6.1**

  e-mail address la dirección de correo electrónico (e-mail), **6.1**

addressee el/la destinatario(a), **6.1**

adorable cariñoso(a), 2.1; adorable

advanced avanzado(a), 7.2

advantage la ventaja

afraid: to be afraid tener miedo, 7.2

after después (de), 3.1; *(time)* y

  It's ten after one. Es la una y diez., LP

afternoon la tarde

  Good afternoon. Buenas tardes., LP

  this afternoon esta tarde, 7.1

  yesterday afternoon ayer por la tarde, 7.1

again de nuevo

against contra

age la edad

agent el/la agente, 10.1; **1.1**

agricultural agrícola

air el aire

  open-air (outdoor) café (market) el café (mercado) al aire libre

air conditioning el aire acondicionado, **7**

airline la línea aérea, 10.1; **1.1**

airplane el avión, 10.1; **1.1**

airport el aeropuerto, 10.1; **1.1**

aisle el pasillo, 10.2; **1.2**

album el álbum

algebra el álgebra

all todo(a), 6.2; todos(as), 8.1

  above all sobre todo

to **allow** dejar

almost casi, 8.2; **4**

alone solo(a); a solas

already ya

also también, 1.2

although aunque

always siempre, 8.2

A.M. de la mañana

ambulance la ambulancia, **11.2**

American americano(a)

among entre

to **amuse** divertir (ie, i), 10.2; **1.2**

amusement park el parque de atracciones, 8.1

  amusement park ride la atracción, 8.1

amusing divertido(a)

ancient antiguo(a), 8.1

and y, LP

Andean andino(a)

angry enfadado(a), enojado(a), 6.1

  to make angry enfadar, 6.1

animal el animal

ankle el tobillo, **11.1**

to **annoy** molestar, enojar, 6.1

another otro(a)

answer la respuesta

to **answer** contestar, 3.1

any cualquier

  any other cualquier otro(a)

anybody alguien, 8.2

anything algo, 9.2

  Anything else? ¿Algo más?, 9.2

apartment el apartamento, el apartamiento, el departamento, 2.2; el piso

  apartment building la casa de apartamentos, 2.2

appearance la apariencia

to **applaud** aplaudir, 5.1

  to be applauded recibir aplausos, 5.1

applause el aplauso, 5.1

apple la manzana, 9.2

appreciated apreciado(a)

to **approach** acercarse a

April abril, LP

archaeology la arqueología

area la zona

area code la clave de área, **6.2**

Argentine argentino(a)

arithmetic la aritmética

arm el brazo, 11.1; **2.1**

around alrededor de, 2.2; *(time)* a eso de

arrival la llegada, **3.1**

to **arrive** llegar, 4.1

arriving from procedente de, 10.2; **1.2**

art el arte, 1.2

  art show (exhibition) la exposición de arte, 8.2

artichoke (sautéed) la alcachofa salteada

artist el/la artista; el/la pintor(a), 8.2

as como

  as . . . as tan... como

  as many . . . as tantos(as)... como

  as much . . . as tanto(a)... como

to **ask (a question)** preguntar

to **ask for** pedir (i, i), **4**

assign asignar, **6.2**

assistance la ayuda

at a, en

  at (@) sign la arroba, **6.1**

  at around (time) a eso de

  at home en casa, 2.2

  at night por la noche; de noche

  at one o'clock (two o'clock, three o'clock . . .) a la una (a las dos, a las tres…), LP

  at times a veces, 6.1; **1.2**

  at what time? ¿a qué hora?, LP

athlete el/la atleta

attached file el documento adjunto, **6.1**

to attend asistir a, 8.1

attention: to pay attention prestar atención, 3.1

attractive guapo(a), 1.1

August agosto, LP

aunt la tía, 2.1

aunt and uncle los tíos, 2.1

author el/la autor(a)

automatic automático(a), 10.2; **1.2**

  automatic dispenser el distribuidor automático, **3.1**

autumn el otoño, LP

available disponible

avenue la avenida, **8.1**

average regular

avocado el aguacate, 10; la palta

Awesome! ¡Bárbaro!, 5.2

B

back la espalda, 11.1; **2.1**

back (adj.) trasero(a)

  back button (key) el botón regresar (retroceder), **6.1**

  back door la puerta trasera, **8.1**

back: in back of detrás de, 2.2

background la ascendencia

backpack la mochila, 3.1

backpacker el/la mochilero(a), 11.2; **2.2**

backwards hacia atrás

bacon el tocino, el bacón, 4.1; **7;** el lacón, **7**

bad malo(a), 1.2; mal, LP

  The weather is bad. Hace mal tiempo., LP

  to be in a bad mood estar de mal humor, 6.1

  to get bad grades sacar notas malas, 3.1

baggage el equipaje, 10.1; **1.1**

  carry-on baggage el equipaje de mano, 10.1; **1.1**

bakery la panadería

balcony el balcón

ball (soccer, basketball) el balón, 5.1; (volleyball) el balón, 7.1; (baseball, tennis) la pelota, 5.2

  to hit the ball batear, 5.2; golpear, 5.2

  to kick (throw) the ball lanzar el balón, 5.1

ballpoint pen el bolígrafo, 3.1; el lapicero, la pluma

banana el plátano, 9.2

  fried sweet bananas los maduros

band (music) la banda, 8.1; **5.2;** el conjunto, 8.1

  city band la banda municipal, **5.2**

bandage la venda, **11.2**

bar: bar of soap la barra de jabón, 11.2; **2.2;** la pastilla de jabón

to bargain regatear, 9.2

barn el granero, **8.2**

base (baseball) la base, 5.2

baseball el béisbol, 5.2

  baseball field el campo de béisbol, 5.2

  baseball game el juego (partido) de béisbol, 5.2

  baseball player el/la jugador(a) de béisbol, el/la beisbolista, 5.2

basket (basketball) el cesto, la canasta, 5.2

  to make a basket encestar, meter el balón en la cesta, 5.2

basketball el básquetbol, el baloncesto, 5.2

  basketball court la cancha de básquetbol, 5.2

bat el bate, 5.2

to bat batear, 5.2

bath el baño, 2.2; **7**

bathing suit el bañador, el traje de baño, 7.1

bathroom el cuarto de baño, 2.2; **7**

bathtub la bañera, **7**

batter el/la bateador(a), 5.2

to be ser, 1.1; estar, 3.1

  to be able (to) poder (ue), 5.1

  to be afraid tener miedo, 7.2

  to be applauded recibir aplausos, 8.1

to be born nacer

to be called (named) llamarse, 11.1; **2.1**

to be careful tener cuidado, **9.1**

to be cold (hot) tener frío (calor), 11.1; **2.1**

to be cut off cortar la línea (a alguien), **6.2**

to be familiar with conocer, 9.1

to be fine (well) estar bien, 6.2

to be going to (do something) ir a (+ infinitive), 4.2

to be happy estar contento(a), alegre, 6.1

to be hungry tener hambre, 4.1

to be in a good (bad) mood estar de buen (mal) humor, 6.1

to be pleasing (to someone) gustar, 5.1

to be sad estar triste, deprimido(a), 6.1

to be sick estar enfermo(a), 6.2

to be sorry sentir (ie, i)

to be successful tener éxito, 6.1

to be thirsty tener sed, 4.1

to be tired estar cansado(a), 6.1

to be . . . years old tener… años, 2.1

beach la playa, 7.1

beach resort el balneario, 7.1

beans los frijoles, 4.1

  green beans (string beans) las judías verdes, 9.2

beautiful bello(a), hermoso(a)

because porque, 3.2

bed la cama, 2.2; **7**

  to go to bed acostarse (ue), 11.1; **2.1**

  to make the bed hacer la cama, **7**

  to stay in bed guardar cama, 6.2; quedarse en la cama, 11.1; **2.1**

bedroom el cuarto de dormir, la recámara, 2.2; la habitación, **7;** el dormitorio, la alcoba, la pieza

beef la carne de res, **4;** el bife

before antes de, 3.2

beforehand antes, 10.1; **1.1**

to begin empezar (ie), 5.1; comenzar (ie)

English-Spanish Dictionary

beginner el/la principiante, 7.2
behaved: to be well-behaved tener buena conducta, 6.1
behavior la conducta, el comportamiento, 6.1
behind detrás de, 2.2
to **believe** creer
bell pepper el pimiento, 9.2
bell tower la campana
bellhop el mozo, 7
to **belong** pertenecer
below debajo de, 10.2; **1.2**
beside al lado de, 2.2
besides además
best el/la mejor
better mejor
between entre
beverage la bebida, el refresco, 4.1
bicycle la bicicleta, 2.2
   to ride a bicycle andar en bicicleta, **11.1**
big gran, grande, 1.2
bike ride: to go for a bike ride dar un paseo en bicicleta
bike riding: to go bike riding andar en bicicleta, **11.1**
bill la factura
biologist el/la biólogo(a)
biology la biología
bird el pájaro
birthday el cumpleaños, 8.1
black negro(a), 2.1
blanket la manta, la frazada, **7**
block (city) la cuadra, la manzana, **9.1**
to **block** bloquear, 5.1
blond(e) rubio(a), 1.1
   to have blond hair tener el pelo rubio, 2.1
blood pressure la tensión arterial, 6.2
blouse la blusa, 3.1
to **blow (wind)** soplar
blue azul, 2.1
blue jeans el blue jean, 9.1
board: on board a bordo (de), 10.2; **1.2**
to **board** embarcar, abordar, 10.2; **1.2**
boarding el embarque, 10.1; **1.1**
   boarding pass la tarjeta de embarque, 10.1; **1.1**; el pasabordo, la tarjeta de abordar
   boarding pass kiosk el distribuidor automático, 10.1; **1.1**

boarding time la hora de embarque, 10.1; **1.1**
boat el barquito, 7.1
body (human) el cuerpo (humano), 11.1; **2.1**
to **boil** hervir (ie, i), **10**
   boiling la ebullición
bone el hueso, 5.1
   to set the bone reducir, acomodar el hueso, **11.2**
book el libro, 3.1
boot la bota, 7.2
border la frontera
to **bore** aburrir, 5.2
boring aburrido(a), 1.2
born: to be born nacer
to **bother** molestar, enfadar, enojar, 6.1
bottle la botella, 9.2
box office la taquilla, 8.2
boy el muchacho, 1.1; el niño, 6.2
brakes los frenos, 9.2
   to put on (apply) the brakes poner los frenos
brave valeroso(a)
Brazilian brasileño(a)
bread el pan
to **break** romper; romperse, quebrarse, **11.2**
   He (She) broke his (her) leg. Se rompió (Se quebró) la pierna., **11.2**
breakdown la avería
breakfast el desayuno, 4.1; **7**
   Continental breakfast el desayuno continental, **7**
   to have breakfast tomar el desayuno, 4.1; desayunarse
breaking: You're breaking up. (telephone) Estás cortando., **6.2**
breast (chicken) la pechuga, **10**
breathing la respiración, 11.1
breed la raza
to **bring** traer, 10.1; **1.1**
to **bring down** derrocar
broad ancho(a), **8.1**
broken roto(a); quebrado(a)
bronze (adj.) de bronce, 8.2
brother el hermano, 2.1
brown castaño(a), 2.1; de color marrón, 5.1
   to have brown eyes tener ojos castaños, 2.1
   to have brown hair tener el pelo castaño, 2.1

brunette moreno(a), 1.1
brush el cepillo, 11.2; **2.2**
   toothbrush el cepillo de dientes, 11.2; **2.2**
to **brush** cepillar, 11.1; **2.1**
   to brush one's hair cepillarse, 11.1; **2.1**
   to brush one's teeth cepillarse (lavarse) los dientes, 11.1; **2.1**
building el edificio, 2.2
bunk la litera
buried enterrado(a), 5.1
to **burn** quemarse, **10**
burrito el burrito
to **bury** enterrar (ie)
bus el autobús, el camión, la guagua, **8.1**; el bus
   bus stop la parada de autobús (de camiones, de guaguas), **8.1**
   school bus el bus escolar, 3.2
   to miss the bus perder el autobús, 8.1
but pero
butcher shop la carnicería
butter la mantequilla, 4.1; **7**
button el botón, **6.1**
   back button el botón regresar (retroceder), **6.1**
   delete button el botón borrador, **6.1**
to **buy** comprar, 3.2
by por; en
   by plane (car, bus) en avión (carro, autobús)
   by tens de diez en diez
   By the way! ¡A propósito!, 8.2
Bye! ¡Chao!, LP

café el café, 3.1
   outdoor café el café al aire libre
cafeteria la cafetería, 4.1
cake la torta, 4.1; el bizcocho, **5.1**; el pastel, la tarta, 8.1
calculator la calculadora, 3.1
call (phone) la llamada, **6.2**
   dropped call la llamada perdida (caída), **6.2**
to **call** llamar, 11.2; **2.2**
   Who's calling, please? ¿De parte de quién, por favor?, **6.2**
calm calmo(a), tranquilo(a), 6.1

English-Spanish Dictionary

camel el camello, **5.2**

camera la cámara, 7.1; **6.2**

  digital camera la cámara digital, 7.1; **6.2**

camping el camping, 11.2; **2.2**

  to go camping ir de camping, 11.2; **2.2**

can el bote, la lata, 9.2

Canadian canadiense

candle la vela, 8.1; **5.2**

canned enlatado(a)

canyon el cañón, 3.2

cap el gorro, 7.2

capital la capital

car el carro, 2.2; **9.2;** el coche, **9.2;** *(train)* el coche, el vagón, 3.1

  dining car el coche comedor (cafetería), la bufetería, **3.1**

  sports car el coche deportivo, **9.2**

carbonated drink la gaseosa, 4.1

card la tarjeta, 3.1; **6.2;** el carnet, 10.2; **1.2**

  credit card la tarjeta de crédito, 3.1

  ID card el carnet de identidad, 10.2; **1.2**

  phone card la tarjeta telefónica, **6.2**

careful: to be careful tener cuidado, **9.1**

carefully con cuidado

Caribbean Sea el mar Caribe

carrot la zanahoria, 9.2; **10**

to **carry** llevar, 3.1; traer, 10.1; **1.1**

  carry-on luggage el equipaje de mano, 10.2; **1.2**

cart el carrito, 9.2; **3.1**

case: in case en caso de; por si acaso

cash register la caja, 3.2

cashier el/la cajero(a)

cast el yeso, **11.2**

castle el castillo

cat el/la gato(a), 2.1

to **catch** atrapar, 5.2

catcher el/la cátcher, el/la receptor(a), 5.2

Catholic católico(a)

cattle el ganado, 8.2

to **cause** causar

to **celebrate** celebrar, 5.2

celebration la celebración

cell phone el móvil, el celular, 3.2; **6.1**

cemetery el cementerio, el camposanto, **5.1**

century el siglo

ceramics las cerámicas, 9.2

cereal el cereal, 4.1

certain cierto(a), **6.1**

chair la silla, 2.2

chairlift el telesilla, el telesquí, 7.2

to **change** cambiar, 3.2

  to change trains (transfer) transbordar, 3.2

chapter el capítulo

character el personaje

charitable purpose el propósito benévolo

cheap barato(a), 9.1

  It's all a lot cheaper. Todo te sale más barato., 9.1

check *(restaurant)* la cuenta, 4.2; **4**

to **check *(ticket)*** revisar, **3.2;** *(facts)* verificar

to **check luggage** facturar el equipaje, 10.1; **1.1**

to **check out** *(hotel room)* abandonar el cuarto, 7

cheese el queso, 4.1

  ham and cheese sandwich el sándwich de jamón y queso, 4.1

chemistry la química

chest el pecho, **11.1**

chicken el pollo, 4.1; **10**

  chicken breast la pechuga de pollo, 10

  chicken thigh el muslo de pollo, 10

  chicken wings las alitas de pollo, 10

child el/la niño(a), 6.2

children los hijos, 2.1

Chilean chileno(a)

chili pepper el ají

chocolate el chocolate, 4.1

  hot chocolate el chocolate caliente, 4.1

to **choose** escoger; seleccionar, **3.1**

chop: pork chop la chuleta de cerdo, **10**

to **chop** picar, **10**

Christian cristiano(a)

Christmas la Navidad, las Navidades, **5.2**

  Christmas Eve la Nochebuena, **5.2**

  Christmas gift el aguinaldo, **5.2**

  Christmas tree el árbol de Navidad, **5.2**

  Merry Christmas! ¡Feliz Navidad!

church la iglesia

city la ciudad, 2.2; **8.1**

civilization la civilización

clams las almejas, **4**

to **clap** aplaudir, 5.1

clarinet el clarinete

class *(school)* la clase; el curso, 1.2; *(ticket)* la clase, **3.1**

  first- (second-) class en primera (segunda) clase, **3.1**

classroom la sala de clase, 3.1

clean limpio(a), **7**

to **clean** limpiar, **7**

to **clear the table** levantar la mesa, quitar la mesa, **4**

clerk el/la empleado(a), 3.1; el/la dependiente(a)

to **click** *(computer)* hacer clic, **6.1**

cliff el risco, 3.2

climate el clima

close (to) cerca (de)

to **close** cerrar (ie), 11.2; **2.2**

closet el armario, **7**

clothes la ropa, 9.1

clothes hanger la percha, el colgador, **7**

clothing la ropa, 9.1

  clothing store la tienda de ropa, 9.1

cloud la nube, 7.1

cloudy nublado(a), 7.1

clove (of garlic) el diente

coach el/la entrenador(a)

coast la costa

code: area code la clave de área, **6.2**

  country code el prefijo del país, **6.2**

co-ed mixto(a)

coffee el café, 4.1; **7**

cognate la palabra afine

coin la moneda, **9.1**

cola la cola, 4.1

cold el frío; frío(a), 4.2; *(illness)* el catarro, 6.2

  It's cold (weather). Hace frío., LP

  to be cold tener frío, 11.1; **2.1**

  to have a cold tener catarro, 6.2

Colombian colombiano(a)

color el color, 5.1

comb el peine, 11.2; **2.2**

to **comb one's hair** peinarse, 11.1; **2.1**

to **come** venir (ie)

  I'm coming! ¡Ya voy!, 11.2; **2.2**

to **come out onto** desembocar

comical cómico(a), gracioso(a), 1.1

English-Spanish Dictionary

English-Spanish Dictionary

coming from procedente de, 10.2; **1.2**

companion el/la compañero(a)

to **complete** completar

completely totalmente

composition la composición

computer la computadora, el ordenador, 3.2; **6.1**

concert el concierto, 8.1

concourse *(train station)* el hall, **3.1**

condiment el condimento, **10**

condo(minium) el condominio

conduct la conducta, el comportamiento, 6.1

conductor *(train)* el revisor, **3.2**

connected conectado(a)

connection la conexión

consonant la consonante

to **consult** consultar

to **contain** contener (ie)

continent el continente

Continental breakfast el desayuno continental, **7**

to **continue** continuar; seguir, **9.1**

contrary: on the contrary al contrario

conversation la conversación

convertible el descapotable, el convertible, **9.2**

to **convince** convencer

cook el/la cocinero(a), **10**

to **cook** cocinar, cocer (ue), **10**

cooking la cocción

cool fresco(a), LP

   It's cool (weather). Hace fresco., LP

copy la copia, **6.1**

   hard copy la copia dura, **6.1**

corn el maíz, 9.2; el elote, el choclo

corner la esquina, **8.1**

corral el corral, **8.2**

to **cost** costar (ue), 9.1

   How much does it cost? ¿Cuánto cuesta?, 3.2

Costa Rican costarricense

costume el disfraz, **5.1**

cough la tos, 6.2

   to have a cough tener tos, 6.2

to **cough** toser, 6.2

counter *(airline)* el mostrador, 10.1; **1.1**

country el país; el campo, **8.2**

country code el prefijo del país, 6.2

country house la casa de campo, **8.2**

Spanish-speaking countries los países hispanohablantes

countryside el campo, **8.2**

course el curso, 1.2

court la cancha, 5.2

   basketball (tennis) court la cancha de básquetbol (tenis), 5.2

   volleyball court la cancha de voleibol, 7.1

courtesy la cortesía, LP

cousin el/la primo(a), 2.1

to **cover** cubrir, tapar

cow la vaca, **8.2**

crackers las galletas, 8.1

crafts la artesanía, 9.2

crazy loco(a)

credit card la tarjeta de crédito, **3.1**

to **cross** cruzar, **9.1**

cross-country *(skiing)* el esquí nórdico, 7.2; *(race)* la carrera a campo traviesa, **11.1**

crosswalk el cruce, **8.1**

crutches las muletas, **11.2**

   to walk on crutches andar con muletas, **11.2**

Cuban cubano(a)

Cuban American cubanoamericano(a)

cucumber el pepino, **10**

cuisine la cocina

culture la cultura

cup la taza, 4.1; **4**

custard el flan, 4.1

custom la costumbre

customer el/la cliente(a), 4.2; **7**

to **cut** cortar, **10**

   to cut (up) in small pieces cortar en pedacitos, **10**

   cut off: We've been cut off. *(telephone)* Se nos cortó la línea., 6.2

to **cut oneself** cortarse, **11.2**

cutlet: veal cutlet el escalope de ternera, **10**

D

daily diario(a)

   daily routine la rutina diaria, 11.1; **2.1**

dairy products los productos lácteos

to **dance** bailar, 5.2

danger el peligro

dangerous peligroso(a)

dark-haired moreno(a), 1.1

data los datos

date la fecha, LP

   What's today's date? ¿Cuál es la fecha de hoy?, LP

daughter la hija, 2.1

day el día, LP; la fiesta, 5.1

   the Day of the Dead el Día de los Muertos, **5.1**

   patron saint's day la fiesta patronal, **5.1**

   What day is it (today)? ¿Qué día es hoy?, LP

dead muerto(a), difunto(a), **5.1**

dead person, deceased person el/la muerto(a), el/la disfunto(a), **5.1**

dear querido(a)

death la muerte

deboned deshuesado(a)

December diciembre, LP

to **decide** decidir

to **decorate** decorar, **5.2**

deep profundo(a)

definition la definición

delay el retraso, la demora, 10.2; **1.2**

to **delete** borrar, **6.1**

delete key *(computer)* el botón borrador, **6.1**

delicious delicioso(a); rico(a)

to **demand** exigir

departure la salida, 10.1; **1.1**

   departure gate la puerta de salida, 10.2; **1.2**

   departure time la hora de salida, 10.1; **1.1**

to **depend** depender (ie) (de)

to **deplane** desembarcar

to **describe** describir

description la descripción

desert el desierto

desk el pupitre, 3.1

desolate inhóspito(a)

dessert el postre, 4.1

destination el destino, **3.1**

to **develop** desarrollarse

device el aparato

diagnosis el diagnóstico

to **dial** marcar el número, **6.2**

dial tone el tono, **6.2**

to **dice** cortar en pedacitos, **10**

dictation el dictado

to **die** morir (ue, u), **4**

diet la dieta

difference la diferencia

different diferente, 9.2

difficult difícil; duro(a), 1.2; avanzado(a), 7.2

difficulty la dificultad

digital camera la cámara digital, 7.1; **6.2**

diner el/la comensal

dining car el coche comedor (cafetería), la bufetería, **3.2**

dining room el comedor, 2.2

dinner la cena, 4.1

to have dinner cenar, 4.1

direction (road) sentido, **9.1**

in each direction en cada sentido, **9.1**

directions las direcciones

dirty sucio(a), 7

disadvantage la desventaja

disagreeable desagradable

to **disappear** desaparecer

to **discover** descubrir

to **disembark** desembarcar, **1.2**

disguise el disfraz, **5.1**

dish el plato, 4

dishwasher el lavaplatos, **10**

dispenser: automatic boarding pass dispenser el distribuidor automático, 10.1; **1.1**

distance: long distance de larga distancia

district el casco, el barrio, **8.1**

to **dive** bucear, 7.1

divine divino(a)

to **do** hacer, 10.2; **1.2**

to do homework hacer las tareas

to do push-ups hacer planchas, **11.1**

to do yoga practicar yoga, **11.1**

doctor el/la médico(a), 6.2

doctor's office el consultorio, la consulta, 6.2

document el documento

attached document el documento adjunto, **6.1**

dog el/la perro(a), 2.1

dollar el dólar

Dominican dominicano(a)

Dominican Republic la República Dominicana

door la puerta, **9.2**

front (back) door la puerta delantera (trasera)

dot (Internet) el punto, **6.1**

double (room) el cuarto doble, 7

doubles (tennis) dobles, 5.2

doubt la duda

to **doubt** dudar

doughnut (type of) el churro

down: to go down bajar, 7.2

downhill skiing el esquí alpino, 7.2

to **download** bajar, descargar, **6.2**

downtown el centro, **8.1**

dozen la docena

drawing el dibujo

dream el sueño

dress el vestido, 9.1

to **dress** vestirse (i, i), **4**

to **dribble** driblar (con el balón), 5.2

drink (beverage) el refresco, 4.2; la bebida, 4.1

to **drink** beber, 4.1

to **drive** conducir, manejar, **9.2**

driver el/la conductor(a), **9.2**

driver's license el permiso de conducir, la licencia, el carnet, **9.2**

dropped call la llamada caída (perdida), **6.2**

drugstore la farmacia, 6.2

dry seco(a)

during durante, 3.2

DVD el DVD, 3.2

dynamic dinámico(a), 6.1

E

e-mail el correo electrónico, 3.2; **6.1;** el e-mail

e-mail address la dirección de correo electrónico (e-mail), **6.1**

e-mail inbox la bandeja de entradas, **6.1**

e-ticket el boleto (billete) electrónico, 10.1; **1.1**

each cada, 2.2

early temprano, 11.1; **2.1**

early riser el/la madrugador(a), 11.1; **2.1**

to **earn** ganar

easily sin dificultad, 7.2

east el este

easy fácil, 1.2

to **eat** comer, 4.1

to eat breakfast (lunch) tomar el desayuno (el almuerzo), 4.1

to eat dinner cenar, 4.1

Ecuadoran ecuatoriano(a), 1.1

education la educación

physical education la educación física, 1.2

egg el huevo, 4.1; **7**

scrambled eggs los huevos revueltos, **7**

eight ocho, LP

eight hundred ochocientos(as)

eighteen dieciocho, LP

eighty ochenta, LP

either tampoco (after negation)

elbow el codo, 11.1; **2.1**

electronic electrónico(a), 10.1; **1.1**

elementary school la escuela primaria

elevator el ascensor, 7

eleven once, LP

else: Anything else? ¿Algo más?, 9.2

Nothing else. Nada más., 9.2

emergency room la sala de emergencia, **11.2**

employee el/la empleado(a), 3.2; el/la dependiente(a)

empty vacío(a), **9.2**

enchilada la enchilada

end el fin

at the end (of) al final (de); a fines de

to **end** terminar

energetic energético(a), 6.1

energy la energía, 6.1

engine el motor

English (language) el inglés, 1.2

to **enjoy** disfrutar; gozar

to **enjoy oneself** divertirse (ie, i), 11.2; **2.2**

enormous enorme

enough bastante; suficiente

to **enter** entrar, 5.1

enthusiasm el entusiasmo, 6.1

enthusiastic lleno(a) de entusiasmo, 6.1; entusiasmado(a)

entire entero(a)

entrance la entrada; (subway) la boca del metro, **8.1**

Epiphany el Día de los Reyes, **5.2**

equal igual

English-Spanish Dictionary

escalator la escalera mecánica, **8.1**

especially especialmente; sobre todo

ethnic étnico(a)

euro el euro

European europeo(a)

even aun; hasta

even *(numeric)* par

evening la noche

  Good evening. Buenas noches., LP

  in the evening por la noche

  yesterday evening anoche, 7.1

every cada, 2.2; todos(as)

  every day (year) todos los días (años)

everybody todo el mundo, todos(as), 8.1

everyone todo el mundo, **5.1** todos(as), 8.1

everything todo, 6.2

everywhere en todas partes

exactly exactamente

exam el examen, la prueba, 3.1

  physical exam el examen físico, 6.2

  to take an exam tomar un examen, 3.1

to **examine** examinar, 6.2

example: for example por ejemplo

to **exceed** exceder

excellent excelente

exception la excepción

Excuse me. Con permiso., 10.1; **1.1**

exercise los ejercicios, **11.1**

to **exercise** hacer ejercicios, **11.1**

exhibition la exposición (de arte), 8.2

to **exist** existir

exit la salida, **9.1**

exotic exótico(a)

expensive caro(a), 9.1

  less expensive más barato, 9.1

expert el/la experto(a), 7.2

to **explain** explicar

expressway la autopista, la autovía, **9.1**

extraordinary extraordinario(a)

eye el ojo, 2.1

  to have blue (green, brown) eyes tener ojos azules (verdes, castaños), 2.1

F

fabrics los tejidos, 9.2

fabulous fabuloso(a)

face la cara, 6.1

fact el hecho

fair la feria, **5.1**

fall el otoño, LP

to **fall** caerse, **11.2**

to **fall asleep** dormirse (ue, u), 11.1; **2.1**

false falso(a)

family la familia, 2.1

family *(related to)* familiar

famous famoso(a)

fan el/la aficionado(a), 5.1

fantastic fantástico(a)

far lejos (de), 3.2

fare la tarifa, **3.1**

farm la finca, la granja, la chacra, 8.2

farmer el/la campesino(a), el peón, **8.2**

farmhand el peón, **8.2**

to **fascinate** fascinar

fast rápido(a)

fastened abrochado(a), 10.2; **1.2**

fat gordo(a)

father el padre, 2.1

favor el favor

favorite favorito(a)

fear el miedo

feature la característica

February febrero, LP

to **feel** sentirse (ie, i)

to **feel like (doing something)** tener ganas de (+ *infinitive*)

Ferris wheel la noria, 8.1

fertilizer el abono

festival la feria, **5.1**

  festival of lights (Hanukkah) la fiesta de las luces, **5.2**

fever la fiebre, 6.2

  to have a fever tener fiebre, 6.2

few poco(a), pocos(as), 2.2

  a few unos(as)

fewer menos

field el campo, 5.1; **8.2**

  baseball field el campo de béisbol, 5.2

  soccer field el campo de fútbol, 5.1

fifteen quince, LP

  fifteen-year-old girl la quinceañera

fifty cincuenta, LP

to **fight** luchar

file el archivo, **6.1;** el documento

  attached file el documento adjunto, 6.1

to **fill up** *(gas tank)* llenar el tanque, 9.2

film el filme, la película, 8.2; el film

finally por fin

to **find** encontrar (ue)

fine la multa, **9.1**

fine *(adj.)* bien, LP

  to be fine estar bien, 6.2

finger el dedo, 11.1; **2.1**

to **finish** terminar

fire el fuego, **10**

fireplace la chimenea, **5.2**

fireworks los fuegos artificiales, **5.2**

first primero(a), LP

  first-class primera clase, **3.1**

  first of January el primero de enero, LP

fish el pescado, 4.1

fish market la pescadería

to **fit** quedar, 9.1

  This jacket doesn't fit you. Esta chaqueta no te queda bien., 9.1

five cinco, LP

five hundred quinientos(as)

flame el fuego, **10**

  on a low flame (heat) a fuego lento, **10**

flan el flan, 4.1

flat *(tire)* el pinchazo, **9.2**

flavor el sabor, **10**

flight el vuelo, 10.1; **1.1**

  flight attendant el/la asistente(a) de vuelo, 10.2; **1.2**

  flight number el número del vuelo, 10.1; **1.1**

to **flip over** volcar

floor el piso, 2.2

flower la flor, 2.2

flute la flauta

to **fly** volar (ue)

folder la carpeta, 3.2; **6.1**

to **follow** seguir (i, i), **4**

following siguiente

food la comida, 4.1; los comestibles, **4;** el alimento

    frozen food los productos congelados, 9.2

foot el pie, 5.1; **2.1**

    on foot a pie, 3.2

football el fútbol americano

for por, para; con destino a, 10.2; **1.2**

    for example por ejemplo

forbidden prohibido(a), **9.1**

forehead la frente, **11.1**

foreign extranjero(a)

to   **forget** olvidar

fork el tenedor, **4**

form la forma, 10.2; **1.2**

former antiguo(a)

forty cuarenta, LP

fountain pen la pluma, 5.1

four cuatro, LP

four hundred cuatrocientos(as)

fourteen catorce, LP

fracture la fractura

free libre, 4.2; **3.2**

to   **free** liberar, **11.1**

freezer el congelador, **10**

French el francés, 1.2; *(adj.)* francés(esa), **4**

french fries las papas (patatas) fritas, 4.1

frequently con frecuencia, frecuentemente

fresh fresco(a)

Friday el viernes, LP

fried frito(a)

friend el/la amigo(a), 1.1; el/la compañero(a)

friendly agradable, 6.1

from de, LP; desde

    from time to time de vez en cuando

    from where? ¿de dónde?, 1.1

front *(adj.)* delantero(a), **8.1**

    in front of delante de, 2.2

front desk *(hotel)* la recepción, **7**

front door *(car, bus)* la puerta delantera, **8.1**

frozen congelado(a), 9.2

    frozen food los productos congelados, 9.2

fruit la fruta, 9.2

fruit stand la frutería, el puesto de frutas, 9.2

to   **fry** freír (i, i), **4**

frying pan el/la sartén, **10**

full completo(a), **3.2**

    full of lleno(a) de, 6.1

fun: to have fun divertirse (ie, i), pasarlo bien, 11.2; **2.2**

funny cómico(a); gracioso(a), 1.1; divertido(a)

furious furioso(a)

furniture los muebles, 2.2

future el futuro

G

game el juego; *(match)* el partido, 5.1

garage el garaje, 2.2

garden el jardín, 2.2

garlic el ajo, **10**

gasoline la gasolina, la nafta, la benzina

gas station la estación de servicio, la gasolinera, 9.2

gas tank el tanque, 9.2

gate *(airport)* la puerta de salida, 10.2; **1.2**

general general

    generally, in general en general, por lo general

generous generoso(a)

gentle manso(a)

gentleman el señor, LP

geography la geografía

geometry la geometría

German alemán(ana)

to   **get** sacar, 3.1

    to get good (bad) grades sacar notas buenas (malas), 3.1

to   **get dressed** ponerse la ropa, 11.1; **2.1;** vestirse (i, i), **4**

to   **get off** *(train, bus)* bajar(se), **3.2**

to   **get on** *(train, bus)* subir, 3.1; *(plane)* abordar, 10.2; **1.2**

to   **get together** reunirse

to   **get up** levantarse, 11.1; **2.1**

gift el regalo, 8.1; **Christmas gift** el aguinaldo, **5.2**

girl la muchacha, 1.1; la niña, 6.2

to   **give** dar, 3.1

    to give an exam dar un examen (una prueba), 3.1

    to give back devolver (ue)

    to give (someone) stitches poner unos puntos (unas suturas) (a alguien)

    to give (throw) a party dar una fiesta, 8.1

    to give up renunciar

glass (drinking) el vaso, 4.1; **4**

glove el guante, 5.2

glove compartment la guantera, 9.2

to **go** ir, 3.2; pasar, 5.2; andar, **3.2**

    Let's go! ¡Vamos!

    to be going (to do something) ir a (+ *infinitive*), 4.2

    to go back regresar, 3.2; volver (ue), 5.1

    to go bike riding andar en bicicleta, **11.1**

    to go camping ir de camping, 11.2; **2.2**

    to go down bajar, 7.2

    to go for a hike dar una caminata, 11.2; **2.2**

    to go home regresar a casa, ir a casa, 3.2; volver (ue) a casa, 8.1

    to go horseback riding andar a caballo, **3.2;** montar a caballo, 8.2

    to go ice-skating patinar sobre el hielo, 7.2

    to go jogging hacer jogging, **11.1**

    to go on a trip hacer un viaje

    to go online entrar en línea, **6.1**

    to go out salir, 8.1

    to go over the net pasar por encima de la red, 5.2

    to go rollerblading (inline skating) patinar en línea, **11.1**

    to go scuba diving bucear

    to go shopping ir de compras, 9.1

    to go skiing esquiar, 7.2

    to go snorkeling bucear, 7.1

    to go surfing practicar la tabla hawaiana, 7.1

    to go swimming nadar, 7.1

    to go to bed acostarse (ue), 11.1; **2.1**

    to go to the movies ir al cine, 8.2

    to go through pasar por, 10.2; **1.2**

    to go up subir, 7.2

    to go waterskiing esquiar en el agua, 7.1

    to go windsurfing practicar la plancha de vela, 7.1

goal el gol, 5.1

    to score a goal meter un gol, 5.1

goal (box) la portería, 5.1

goalie el/la portero(a), 5.1

English-Spanish Dictionary

going to con destino a, 10.2; **1.2**
gold el oro
good buen, LP; bueno(a), 1.1
  to be in a good mood
    estar de buen humor, 6.1
  to get good grades sacar
    notas buenas, 3.1
  Good afternoon. Buenas
    tardes., LP
  Good evening. Buenas
    noches., LP
  Good morning. Buenos
    días., LP
  Good-bye! ¡Adiós!; ¡Chao!,
    LP
good-looking guapo(a),
  bonito(a), 1.1
government el gobierno
grade la nota, 3.1
  high grade la nota alta, 3.1
  low grade la nota baja, 3.1
  to get good (bad) grades
    sacar notas buenas
    (malas), 3.1
grandchildren los nietos, 2.1
granddaughter la nieta, 2.1
grandfather el abuelo, 2.1
grandmother la abuela, 2.1
grandparents los abuelos, 2.1
grandson el nieto, 2.1
grape la uva, 9.2
grass la hierba, **8.2**
grave la tumba, **5.1**
gravy la salsa, **10**
gray gris, 5.1
to **graze** pacer, **8.2**
great gran, grande
Great! ¡Bárbaro!, 5.2
greater (greatest) part (la)
  mayor parte
green verde, 2.1
green beans las judías
  verdes, 9.2
green pepper el pimiento,
  9.2; **10**
greengrocer (vegetable) store
  la verdulería, 9.2
greeting el saludo, LP
grill la parrilla, **10**
to **grill** asar, **10**
ground el suelo
group *(musical)* el grupo,
  el conjunto, 8.1
to **grow** *(agriculture)* cultivar, **8.2**
to **guard** guardar, 5.1
Guatemalan guatemalteco(a)
to **guess** adivinar

guest el/la invitado(a),
  (hotel) el/la cliente(a),
  el/la huésped(a), **7**
guitar la guitarra, 8.1
guy el tipo, 6.1
gymnasium el gimnasio, **11.1**

H

hair el pelo, 2.1
  to brush one's hair
    cepillarse, 11.1; **2.1**
  to comb one's hair
    peinarse, 11.1; **2.1**
  to have blond (brown,
    black) hair tener el pelo
    rubio (castaño, negro), 2.1
half *(soccer)* el tiempo, 5.1
  second half *(soccer)*
    el segundo tiempo, 5.1
half past *(hour)* y media, LP
ham el jamón, 4.1
  ham and cheese sandwich
    el sándwich de jamón y
    queso, 4.1
hamburger la hamburguesa,
  4.1
hand la mano, 3.1
  to raise one's hand
    levantar la mano, 3.1
handsome guapo(a), 1.1
hanger la percha, el colgador, **7**
Hanukkah el Hanuka, **5.2**
to **happen** pasar; ocurrir
  What's happening?
    ¿Qué pasa?
happiness la alegría, la
  felicidad
happy alegre, contento(a),
  6.1; feliz, **5.2**
  Happy Hanukkah! ¡Feliz
    Hanuka!, **5.2**
hard difícil, duro(a), 1.2
hard copy la copia dura, **6.1**
hard-working ambicioso(a), 1.2
harvest la cosecha, **8.2**
to **harvest** cosechar, **8.2**
hat el sombrero;
  (ski) el gorro, 7.2
to **have** tener (ie), 2.1; haber *(in
  compound tenses)*
  to have a cold tener
    catarro, 6.2
  to have a cough tener tos, 6.2
  to have a fever tener
    fiebre, 6.2
  to have fun pasarlo bien,
    divertirse (ie, i), 11.2; **2.2**

  to have a good time
    pasarlo bien, divertirse
    (ie, i), 11.2; **2.2**
  to have a headache tener
    dolor de cabeza, 6.2
  to have a party dar una
    fiesta, 8.1
  to have a snack tomar una
    merienda, 4.2
  to have a sore throat tener
    dolor de garganta, 6.2
  to have a stomachache
    tener dolor de estómago,
    6.2
  to have blond (brown,
    black) hair tener el pelo
    rubio (castaño, negro), 2.1
  to have blue (brown, green)
    eyes tener ojos azules
    (castaños, verdes), 2.1
  to have breakfast (lunch)
    tomar el desayuno
    (el almuerzo); 4.1
  to have dinner cenar, 4.1
  to have fun pasarlo bien,
    divertirse (ie, i), 11.2; **2.2**
  to have just (done
    something) acabar de *(+
    infinitive)*, 4.2
  to have to (do something)
    tener que, 4.2
hay el heno, **8.2**
he él, 1.1
head la cabeza, 6.2; **2.1**
headache: to have a headache
  tener dolor de cabeza, 6.2
headlights las luces, **9.2**
health la salud, 6.1
to **hear** oír, 8.1
  ¿Can you hear me?
    (telephone)
    ¿Me escuchas?, **6.2**
heart el corazón
heat el calor; el fuego, **10**
  on low heat a fuego lento, **10**
to **heat** poner en el fuego, **10**
heavy pesado(a)
height la altura
Hello! ¡Hola!, LP; **6.2;** *(on the
  phone)* ¡Diga!, ¡Dígame!,
  ¡Aló!, ¡Bueno!
helmet el casco, 7.2; **11.1**
help la ayuda
to **help** ayudar, 10.1; **1.1**
hen la gallina, **8.2**
her *(pron.)* la
  to her *(pron.)* le
her su(s)

here aquí, 9.1; acá, 11.2; **2.2**
 Here it (they) is (are).
   Aquí lo (la, los, etc.) tienes.
hero el héroe
heroine la heroína
Hi! ¡Hola!, LP
high alto(a), 3.1
high school la escuela
   secundaria, 1.2; el colegio
highway la autopista, la
   autovía, la carretera, **9.1**
hike: to take (go for) a hike
   dar una caminata, 11.2; **2.2**
hiker el/la mochilero(a),
   11.2; **2.2**
him *(pron.)* lo
 to him *(pron.)* le
his su(s)
Hispanic hispano(a)
history la historia, 1.2
to **hit** *(baseball)* batear; *(tennis,*
   volleyball) golpear, 5.2
 to hit a home run batear
   un jonrón, 5.2
holiday la fiesta, **5.1**
home la casa, 2.2; a casa; 3.2
 at home en casa
 to go home regresar a
   casa, 3.2; volver (ue) a
   casa, 8.1
home page la página de
   inicio (inicial, frontal), **6.1**
home plate el plato, 5.2
home run el jonrón, 5.2
 to hit a home run batear
   un jonrón, 5.2
homework las tareas
honest honesto(a)
hood *(car)* el capó, **9.2**
to **hope** esperar
 I hope . . . Ojalá… , **11.2**
horse el caballo, 3.2
horseback riding la
   equitación, **8.2**
 to go horseback riding
   andar a caballo, **3.2;**
   montar a caballo, **8.2**
hospital el hospital
hostel: youth hostel el
   albergue juvenil, el hostal, 7
hot: to be hot tener calor,
   11.1; **2.1**
 It's (very) hot *(weather).*
   Hace (mucho) calor., LP
hot caliente, 4.1
hotel el hotel, 7
 small (inexpensive) hotel
   el hostal, 7
hotel clerk el/la recepcionista,
   7
hour la hora
house la casa, 2.2

apartment house la casa
   de apartamentos, 2.2
private house la casa
   privada, 2.2
housekeeper la camarera, 7
how? ¿cómo?, 1.1; ¿qué?, LP
 How are things going?
   ¿Qué tal?, LP
 How are you? ¿Qué tal?,
   LP; ¿Cómo estás?
 How much does it cost?
   ¿Cuánto cuesta?, 3.2
 How much is (are) . . . ?
   ¿A cuánto está(n)… ?, 9.2
 How much is it? ¿Cuánto
   es?, LP
 How old is he (she)?
   ¿Cuántos años tiene?, 2.1
how many? ¿cuántos(as)?, 2.1
how much? ¿cuánto?, 3.1
human humano(a), 11.1; **2.1**
human being el ser humano
humble humilde
humor: to have a good sense
   of humor tener un buen
   sentido de humor, 6.1
hundred cien(to), LP
hunger el hambre *(f.)*
hungry: to be hungry tener
   hambre, 4.1
to **hurt** doler, 6.2; **11.2**
 It hurts him (me, etc.) a lot.
   Le (Me, etc.) duele mucho.,
   11.2
 My head (stomach, etc.)
   hurts. Me duele la cabeza
   (el estómago, etc.), **11.2**
to **hurt (oneself)** hacerse daño,
   11.2
husband el esposo, el
   marido, 2.1

I yo
ice el hielo, 7.2
ice cream el helado, 4.1
ice skate el patín, 7.2
to **ice-skate** patinar sobre el
   hielo, 7.2
ice-skater el/la patinador(a),
   7.2
ice-skating el patinaje sobre
   (el) hielo, 7.2
 ice-skating rink la pista
   de patinaje, 7.2
icon el icono, **6.1**
ID card el carnet
   de identidad, 10.2; **1.2**
idea la idea
idealist el/la idealista

identification
   la identidad, 10.2; **1.2**
 piece of identification
   la forma de identidad,
   10.2; **1.2**
to **identify** identificar
if si
ill enfermo(a), 6.2
ill-mannered
   mal educado(a), 6.1
illness la enfermedad
to **imagine** imaginar
immediately enseguida, 4.2;
   inmediatamente
immense inmenso
impatient impaciente, 6.1
important importante
impossible imposible
in en
 in back of detrás de, 2.2
 in front of delante de, 2.2
 in general por lo general
inbox *(e-mail)* la bandeja
   de entradas, **6.1**
incline la pendiente
to **include** incluir
 Is the tip included?
   ¿Está incluido el
   servicio?, 4.2
to **increase** aumentar
incredible increíble
to **indicate** indicar
indigenous indígena, 9.2
individual: individual sport
   el deporte individual
inexpensive barato(a), 9.1
influence la influencia
to **inform** informar
information la información,
   3.2
ingredient el ingrediente
inhabitant el/la habitante
inhospitable inhóspito(a)
injured herido(a)
injury la herida, **11.2**
inline skating el patinaje en
   línea, **11.1**
 to go inline skating
   patinar en línea, **11.1**
inn el parador
to **insert** insertar, **3.1;** introducir,
   6.2
instead of en vez de
instrument el instrumento
intelligent inteligente, 1.2
interest el interés
to **interest** interesar, 5.1
interesting interesante, 1.2
international internacional,
   10.1; **1.1**

English-Spanish Dictionary

Internet el Internet, 3.2; **6.1**
  to surf the Net navegar el Internet, 3.2; **6.1**
to interrupt interrumpir
to intersect cruzarse
intersection la bocacalle, el cruce, **9.1**
interview la entrevista
to interview entrevistar
interviewer el/la entrevistador(a)
to invite invitar
Irish irlandés(esa)
Is . . . there, please? ¿Está… , por favor?, **6.2**
island la isla
it lo, la
Italian italiano(a)

jack (car) el/la gato(a), **9.2**
jacket la chaqueta, 9.1
  ski jacket la chaqueta de esquí, el anorak, 7.2
jam la mermelada, 7
January enero, LP
Japonese japonés(esa)
jar el frasco, 9.2
jeans el blue jean, 9.1
Jewish judío(a), hebreo(a), **5.2**
jogging: to go jogging hacer jogging, **11.1**
juice el jugo, el zumo, 4.1
  orange juice el jugo de naranja, 4.1; 7
July julio, LP
June junio, LP
just: to have just (done something) acabar de (+ infinitive), 4.2
just as (like) igual que

kebabs los pinchitos, 4.2
to keep guardar, **6.1**
key la llave, 7; (computer) el botón, **6.1**
  back key el botón regresar (retroceder), **6.1**
  delete key el botón borrador, **6.1**
  magnetic key la llave magnética, 7

keyboard el teclado, **6.1**
to kick lanzar, 5.1
kilogram el kilo, 9.2
kilometer el kilómetro
king el rey
  the Three Kings (Wise Men) los Reyes Magos, **5.2**
kiosk (newsstand) el quiosco, **3.1**; (ticket dispenser) el distribuidor automático, **3.1**
kitchen la cocina, 2.2, **10**
knapsack la mochila, 3.1
knee la rodilla, 11.1, **2.1**
kneepad la rodillera, **11.1**
knife el cuchillo, 4
to know saber; conocer, 9.1
  to know how (to do something) saber, 9.1

to lack faltar, **6.1**
  He/She lacks . . . Le falta… , **6.1**
lamb el cordero, 4
lamp la lámpara, 2.2
land la tierra, 8.2
to land aterrizar, 10.2; **1.2**
landing el aterrizaje, 10.2; **1.2**
landowner el/la terrateniente
landscape el paisaje
lane (highway) el carril, **9.1**; la pista, la vía, la banda, el canal
language la lengua
lap (track) la vuelta, **11.1**
laptop computer la computadora portátil
large gran, grande, 1.2
last pasado(a) 7.1; último(a)
  last night anoche, 7.1
  last week la semana pasada, 7.1
  last year el año pasado, 7.1
to last durar
late tarde; con retraso (una demora), 10.2; **1.2**
later luego, LP; más tarde; después
  See you later! ¡Hasta luego!, LP
Latin America Latinoamérica
Latin American latinoamericano(a)
Latino latino(a)
to laugh reír
lazy perezoso(a), 1.2

to lead (from one street into another) desembocar
league la liga
to learn aprender, 4.2
least: at least a lo menos
to leave salir, 8.1
to leave (something) dejar, 4
  to leave a message dejar un mensaje, **6.2**
  to leave a tip dejar una propina, 4
left izquierdo(a), 11.1; **2.1**
  to the left a la izquierda, **9.1**
leftovers las sobras
leg la pierna, 11.1; **2.1**
lemon el limón
lemonade la limonada
less menos, 9.1
lesson la lección
to let dejar; permitir
letter la carta
letter (of alphabet) la letra
lettuce la lechuga, 4.1
lid la tapa, **10**
life la vida
to lift levantar
  to lift weights levantar pesas, **11.1**
light la luz, 5.2
  red light la luz roja, **9.1**
  traffic light el semáforo, **8.1**
to light encender, **5.2**
to light up iluminar, **5.2**
lightly ligeramente
lights las luces, 5.2; (headlights) las luces, 9.2
  festival of lights (Hanukkah) la fiesta de las luces, **5.2**
like como
to like gustar, 5.1; encantar, **6.2**
  What would you like (to eat)? ¿Qué desean tomar?, 4.2
line (of people) la cola, 10.2; **1.2**; la fila
  to wait in line hacer cola, 10.2; **1.2**; estar en fila
line la línea, **6.2**
  solid line (road) la línea continua, **9.1**
to line up hacer cola, 10.2; **1.2**
lion el león
lip el labio
to listen to escuchar, 3.2
  Listen! ¡Oye!, 1.2
literature la literatura, las letras

little pequeño(a), 1.2
  a little poco(a), 2.2
to live vivir, 4.1
livestock el ganado, 8.2
living room la sala, 2.2
lobster la langosta, 4
logical lógico(a)
long largo(a), 5.1
long-distance *(race)* de larga distancia, 11.1
long-sleeved de manga larga, 9.1
Look! ¡Mira!, 3.1
to look at mirar, 3.2
to look at oneself mirarse, 11.1; 2.1
to look for buscar, 3.2
to lose perder (ie), 5.1
lot: a lot mucho(a), LP; muchos(as), 2.1
lotion: suntan lotion la crema solar, la loción bronceadora, 7.1
love el amor
  in love with enamorado(a) de
  loved one el/la amado(a)
to love encantar, 6.2; querer (ie)
  Le encanta la música. She loves the music.
low bajo(a), 3.1
  low (heat), a fuego lento, 10
to lower *(price)* rebajar, 9.1
luck: How lucky I am! ¡Qué suerte tengo!, 9.1
luggage el equipaje, 10.1; 1.1
  carry-on luggage el equipaje de mano, 10.1; 1.1
  luggage cart el carrito, 3.1
  to check luggage facturar el equipaje, 10.1; 1.1
lunch el almuerzo, 4.1
  to have lunch tomar el almuerzo, 4.1
luxurious lujoso(a)

mad enojado(a), enfadado(a), 6.1
madam (la) señora, LP
made hecho(a)
magazine la revista, 3.1
magnetic magnético(a), 7
magnificent magnífico(a)
maid la camarera, 7
mail el correo
  e-mail el correo electrónico, 6.1

main principal
majority la mayoría; *(adj.)* mayoritario(a)
to make hacer, 10.2; 1.2; confeccionar, elaborar, 5.1
  to make a basket *(basketball)* encestar, 5.2
  to make the bed hacer la cama, 7
mall el centro comercial, 9.1
man el hombre
manners los modales, 6.1
  to have good (bad) manners tener buenos (malos) modales, 6.1
many muchos(as), 2.2
  as many . . .
  as tantos(as)… como
  how many? ¿cuántos(as)?, 2.1
map el plano, 9.1; el mapa
marathon el maratón, 11.1
March marzo, LP
mark la nota, 3.1
  bad (low) mark la nota mala (baja), 3.1
  good (high) mark la nota buena (alta), 3.1
  to get good (bad) marks sacar notas buenas (malas), 3.1
market el mercado, 9.2
  native market el mercado indígena, 9.2
market stall el puesto, el tenderete, 9.2
marmalade la mermelada, 7
mask la máscara, 5.1
to match parear
mathematics las matemáticas, 1.2
mausoleum el mausoleo, 5.1
maximum máximo(a)
May mayo, LP
maybe quizá, quizás, tal vez, 7.2
mayonnaise la mayonesa, 9.2
me *(pron.)* me
  to (for) me a (para) mí
meal la comida, 4.1
to mean significar
means of transport el medio de transporte, 8.1
meat la carne, 4.1; 4
meatball la albóndiga, 4.2
meat pie la empanada, 4.2
medicine el medicamento, la medicina, 6.2
medium *(meat)* a término medio, 4
medium-sized mediano(a)

to meet encontrarse (ue); conocer
member el miembro, 2.1; el/la socio(a)
menorah la menora, 5.2
menu el menú, 4.2; 4
merchant el/la vendedor(a), 9.2
Merry Christmas! ¡Feliz Navidad!
merry-go-round el tiovivo, 8.1
message el mensaje, 6.2
meter el metro
Mexican mexicano(a)
Mexican American mexicanoamericano(a), 1.2
microwave oven el horno de microondas, 10
Middle Ages la Edad Media
midnight la medianoche
mile la milla
milk la leche, 4.1
million el millón
  a million dollars un millón de dólares
mime el mimo, 8.1
to mince picar, 10
mind el espíritu, 11.1
mineral water el agua mineral, 4.2
mirror el espejo, 11.1; 2.1
Miss (la) señorita, LP
to miss the bus perder (ie) el autobús, 8.1
mobile phone el móvil, 3.2; el celular, 6.2
modern moderno(a)
mom mamá
moment el momento
monastery el monasterio
Monday el lunes, LP
money el dinero, 3.2
monitor *(computer)* la pantalla de escritorio, 6.1
month el mes, LP
monument el monumento
mood el humor, 6.1
  to be in a good (bad) mood estar de buen (mal) humor, 6.1
moon la luna
more más, 9.1
morning la mañana
  Good morning. Buenos días., LP
  in the morning por la mañana; de la mañana
mother la madre, 2.1
motive el motivo

English-Spanish Dictionary

mountain la montaña, 7.2
mountaintop el pico, 7.2
mouse el ratón, **6.1**
mousepad la alfombrilla, **6.1**
mouth la boca, 6.2
to **move** mover (ue)
movement el movimiento, **11.1**
movie la película, el filme, 8.2; el film
movie theater el cine, 8.2
movies: to go to the movies ir al cine, 8.2
MP3 player el MP3, **6.2**
Mr. (el) señor, LP
Mr. and Mrs. (los) señores
Mrs. (la) señora, LP
Ms. (la) señorita, (la) señora, LP
much mucho(a), LP
 as much . . . as tan… como, **11.2**
 How much is it (does it cost)? ¿Cuánto es?, LP; ¿Cuánto cuesta?, 3.2
mud el lodo
museum el museo, 8.2
music la música, 1.2
musician el/la músico(a), 8.1
mussels los mejillones, 4
my mi
mysterious misterioso(a)

name el nombre, 2.1
 My name is . . . Me llamo… , 11.1; **2.1**
 What is your name? ¿Cómo te llamas?, 11.1; **2.1**; ¿Cuál es su nombre? *(formal)*
napkin la servilleta, 4
narrow angosto(a), estrecho(a), 8.1
national nacional
nationality la nacionalidad, 1.1
 what nationality? ¿de qué nacionalidad?, 1.1
native indígena, 9.2
native person el/la indígena
nature la naturaleza
near cerca de, 3.2
necessary necesario(a)
 It's necessary. Es necesario., **11.2**
 it's necesssary to (do something) hay que, 10.2; **1.2**

neck el cuello, **11.1**
necktie la corbata, 9.1
to **need** necesitar, 3.2
negative negativo(a)
neighbor el/la vecino(a)
neighborhood el casco, el barrio, **8.1**
neither tampoco
nephew el sobrino, 2.1
nervous nervioso(a), 6.1
net *(World Wide Web)* la red, 3.2; **6.1**; *(tennis)*, 5.2
 to surf the Net navegar el Internet, 3.2; **6.1**
never nunca, 8.2; jamás
new nuevo(a), 1.1
 New Year el Año Nuevo
 New Year's Eve la Nochevieja, la víspera del Año Nuevo
news la(s) noticia(s)
newspaper el periódico, 3.1
newsstand el quiosco, 3.1
next próximo(a), **3.2;** que viene, **8.2**
 next stop la próxima parada, **3.2**
 next summer (year, etc.) el verano (año, etc.) que viene, **8.2**
next to al lado de, 2.2
Nicaraguan nicaragüense
nice simpático(a), 1.1; *(weather)* buen (tiempo)
 Nice to meet you. Mucho gusto., 1.2
 The weather is nice. Hace buen tiempo., LP
niece la sobrina, 2.1
night la noche
 at night por la noche
 Good night. Buenas noches., LP
 last night anoche, 7.1
nine nueve, LP
nine hundred novecientos(as), 9.2
nineteen diecinueve, LP
ninety noventa, LP
no no, LP; ninguno(a)
 by no means de ninguna manera
no one nadie, 8.2
nobody nadie, 8.2
none ninguno(a)
noon el mediodía

normal normal, 6.2
north el norte
North American norteamericano(a), 1
no-smoking sign la señal de no fumar, 10.2; **1.2**
not no, 1.2
notebook el cuaderno, 3.1
nothing nada, 8.2
 Nothing else. Nada más., 9.2
novel la novela
November noviembre, LP
now ahora
nowadays hoy en día
number el número, 10.1; **1.1**
 flight number el número del vuelo, 10.1; **1.1**
 seat number el número del asiento, 10.1; **1.1**
 telephone number el número de teléfono, 6.2
nurse el/la enfermero(a), 6.2; **11.2**

object el objeto
objective el objetivo
obligatory obligatorio(a)
to **observe** observar
obstinate obstinado(a), 6.1
occasionally de vez en cuando
occupied ocupado(a), 4.2; **3.2**
ocean el océano
o'clock: It's two o'clock. Son las dos., LP
October octubre, LP
odd *(numeric)* impar
of de LP
 Of course! ¡Cómo no!; ¡Claro!
 of the del, de la
to **offer** ofrecer
offering la ofrenda, **5.1**
office la oficina, 8.1
 doctor's office la consulta del médico, 6.2
often con frecuencia, a menudo
oil el aceite, 4
 olive oil el aceite de oliva
OK de acuerdo
old viejo(a), 2.2; antiguo(a), 8.1
 How old is he (she)? ¿Cuántos años tiene?, 2.1
 old city el casco (barrio) antiguo, 8.1

older mayor

oldest el/la mayor

olive la aceituna, 4.2

on sobre; en

> **on board** a bordo, 10.2; **1.2**
>
> **on foot** a pie, 3.2
>
> **on the edge of** al borde mismo de
>
> **on time** a tiempo, 10.2; **1.2**
>
> **on top of** sobre

one uno; un(a), LP

one hundred cien(to), LP

one thousand mil

one-way (ticket) el boleto (billete) sencillo, **3.1**; **(street)** la calle de sentido único, **9.1**

onion la cebolla, 9.2; **10**

online: to go online entrar en línea, **6.1**

only único(a), 2.1; solo; solamente

to **open** abrir, 4.2

open-air al aire libre, 7.2

open-minded flexible, 6.1

opinion la opinión

opponents el equipo contrario, 5.2

opposite el contrario

or o, u *(used instead of o in front of words beginning with o or ho)*

orange *(color)* anaranjado(a), 5.1

orange *(fruit)* la naranja, 4.1

> **orange juice** el jugo (zumo) de naranja, 4.1; **7**

orchard la huerta, 8.2

order *(restaurant)* la orden, 4.2

to **order *(restaurant)*** pedir (i, i)

to **organize** organizar

origin el origen

orthopedic surgeon el/la cirujano(a) ortopédico(a), **11.2**

other otro(a)

> **any other** cualquier otro(a)

our nuestro(a), nuestros(as)

outdoor al aire libre

outfielder el/la jardinero(a), 5.2

outskirts los alrededores, las afueras

oven el horno, **10**

over por encima de, 5.2

overhead bin el compartimiento superior, 10.2; **1.2**

overpopulation la sobrepoblación

own: propio(a), 5.1

oxygen mask la máscara de oxígeno, 10.2; **1.2**

to **pack** hacer la maleta, 10.1; **1.1**

package el paquete, 9.2

page la página

> **home page** la página de inicio (inicial, frontal), **6.1**

pain el dolor, 6.2

to **paint** pintar

painter el/la pintor(a), 8.2

painting el cuadro, 8.2; la pintura

pair el par, 9.1

> **pair of shoes** el par de zapatos, 9.1

pants el pantalón, 3.1

> **long pants** el pantalón largo, 9.1

paper el papel, 3.1

> **sheet of paper** la hoja de papel, 3.1
>
> **toilet paper** el papel higiénico, 11.2; **2.2**

paperback (book) el libro de bolsillo, **3.1**

parade el desfile, 5.2

> **to walk in a parade** desfilar, **5.1**

paramedic el/la socorrista, **11.2**

parents los padres, 2.1

park el parque, 11.2; **2.2**

to **park** aparcar, **8.1**; estacionar, parquear

parka el anorak, 7.2

parking lot el parking, el parqueo, **8.1**

parking meter el parquímetro, **9.1**

part la parte

> **la mayor parte** the greatest part, the majority

party la fiesta, 8.1

> **to (have) throw a party** dar una fiesta, 8.1

to **pass** pasar, 5.2; *(car)* adelantar(se), rebasar, pasar, **9.1**

passenger el/la pasajero(a), 10.1; **1.1**

passport el pasaporte, 10.2; **1.2**

past el pasado

pastry el pan dulce, **7**

path la senda, 3.2

patience la paciencia, 6.1

patient el/la paciente, 6.2

patient *(adj.)* paciente, 6.1

patron saint el/la santo(a) patrón(ona), **5.1**

> **patron saint's day** la fiesta patronal, **5.1**

pavement el pavimento

to **pay** pagar, 3.2

> **to pay attention** prestar atención, 3.1; hacer caso

pay phone el teléfono público, **6.2**

pea el guisante, 9.2

peaceful tranquilo(a), 6.1

peak el pico, 7.2

peanut el cacahuate, el maní, 8.1; el cacahuete

peasant el campesino, el peón, 8.2

pedestrian el/la peatón(ona), **8.1**

> **pedestrian crossing** el cruce peatonal, **8.1**

to **peel** pelar, **10**

pen el bolígrafo, 3.1; el lapicero, la pluma

pencil el lápiz, 3.1

people la gente, 9.1

pepper *(spice)* la pimienta, **4**; *(bell pepper)* el pimiento, 9.2; **10**; el pimentón; el ají; el chipotle; el morrón

perhaps quizá, quizás, tal vez, 7.2

to **permit** permitir

person la persona

personality la personalidad, 6.1

Peruvian el/la peruano(a)

peso el peso

pet la mascota, 2.1

pharmacist el/la farmacéutico(a)

pharmacy la farmacia, 6.2

phone el teléfono

> **cell phone** el móvil, 3.2; el (teléfono) celular, **6.1**
>
> **pay phone** el teléfono público, **6.2**
>
> **phone book** la guía telefónica, **6.2**
>
> **phone call** la llamada telefónica, **6.2**
>
> **phone card** la tarjeta telefónica, **6.2**
>
> **phone number** el número de teléfono, **6.2**
>
> **phone receiver** el auricular, **6.2**

English-Spanish Dictionary

English-Spanish Dictionary

public phone el teléfono público, **6.2**

to pick up the phone descolgar (ue) el auricular, **6.2**

to speak on the phone hablar por teléfono

photo(graph) la foto(grafía), 7.1

    to take photos sacar (tomar) fotos, 7.1

physical *(exam)* el examen físico, 6.2

    physical education la educación física, 1.2

physics la física

piano el piano

to **pick up** *(phone)* descolgar (ue) el auricular, **6.2**

to **pick up** *(speed)* agarrar velocidad

picture la foto(grafía); la imagen

    to take pictures sacar (tomar) fotos, 7.1

picturesque pintoresco(a)

piece el pedazo, el trozo (trocito)

    little piece el pedacito, 10

pig el cerdo, **8.2;** el cochinillo, el lechón, el chancho

pillow la almohada, 7

pinch la pizca

pineapple la piña, 9.2

pink rosado(a), 5.1

pitcher *(baseball)* el/la pícher, el/la lanzador(a), 5.2

pizza la pizza, 4.1

place el lugar; el sitio

to **plan** planear

plane el avión, 10.1; **1.1**

plant la planta, 2.2

to **plant** sembrar (ie), **8.2**

plantain: slices of fried plantain los tostones, 4.2; los patacones

plate el plato, **4**

platform *(railway)* el andén, **3.1**

to **play** *(sport)* jugar (ue), 5.1; *(musical instrument)* tocar, 8.1; **5.2**

    to play soccer (baseball, etc.) jugar (al) fútbol (béisbol, etc.), 5.1

player el/la jugador(a), 5.1

    baseball player el/la jugador(a) de béisbol, el/la beisbolista, 5.2

plaza la plaza, **8.1**

pleasant agradable, placentero(a)

please por favor, LP; favor de (+ *infinitive*), 11.2; **2.2**

pleasure: It's a pleasure to meet you. Mucho gusto.

P.M. de la tarde, de la noche

poem el poema

point el tanto, 5.1; el punto

    to score a point marcar un tanto, 5.1

to **point out** señalar

polite bien educado(a), 6.1

polluted contaminado(a)

pollution la contaminación

pool la piscina, la alberca, 7.1; la pila

poor pobre

popular popular

population la población

pork chop la chuleta de cerdo, **4**

portrait el retrato

Portuguese portugués(esa)

to **possess** poseer

possibility la posibilidad

possible posible

pot la olla, la cacerola, **10**

potato la papa, la patata, 4.1

    french fried potatoes las papas (patatas) fritas, 4.1

pothole el bache

practically casi, 8.2

to **practice** practicar

to **prefer** preferir (ie, i), 5.2; **4**

to **prepare** preparar; confeccionar, **5.1**

to **prescribe** recetar, 6.2

prescription la receta, 6.2

present el regalo, 8.1

    Christmas present el aguinaldo, **5.2**

to **present** presentar

president el/la presidente(a)

to **press** *(button)* oprimir, pulsar, **6.1**

pretty bonito(a), 1.1; hermoso(a)

previous anterior, 6.1

price el precio, 9.1

primary primario(a)

to **print** imprimir, **6.1**

printer la impresora, **6.1**

private privado(a), 2.2

probable probable

problem el problema

procession la procesión, **5.1**

product el producto, 9.2

public público(a)

Puerto Rican puertorriqueño(a)

pulse el pulso, 6.2

purchase la compra, 9.2

to **push** *(button)* oprimir, pulsar, **6.1**

push-ups: to do push-ups hacer planchas, 11.1

to **put** poner, 10.2; **1.2;** meter, 5.2

to **put on** *(clothes)* ponerse, 11.1; **2.1** *(brakes)* poner los frenos

to **put up** *(tent)* armar, montar, 11.2; **2.2**

puzzle el rompecabezas

quarter *(city)* el casco, el barrio, **8.1;** *(time)* el cuarto, LP

    a quarter past (the hour) y cuarto, LP

question la pregunta, 3.1

    to ask a question preguntar, 3.1

quickly rápidamente

quiet tranquilo(a), calmo(a), 6.1

quite bastante, 1.2

race la carrera, **11.1**

    cross-country race la carrera a campo traviesa, **11.1**

    long-distance race la carrera de larga distancia, **11.1**

    relay race la carrera de relevos, **11.1**

racket la raqueta, 5.2

railroad el ferrocarril, **3.1**

    railroad platform el andén, **3.1**

    railroad station la estación de ferrocarril, **3.1**

to **rain** llover (ue)

    It's raining. Llueve., LP

raincoat impermeable

to **raise** levantar, 3.1
    to raise one's hand
      levantar la mano, 3.1
ranch la hacienda, la
    estancia, el rancho, **8.2**
rare (*meat*) casi crudo, **4**
rate la tarifa; la tasa
rather bastante, 1.2
raw crudo(a), 8.1
    raw vegetables los
      vegetales crudos, 8.1
reaction la reacción
to **read** leer, 4.2
reading la lectura
ready listo(a)
really realmente
reason la razón, el motivo
to **receive** recibir, 4.2
    receiver (*telephone*)
      el auricular, **6.2**
recipe la receta, 10
recipient el/la
    destinatario(a), **6.1**
to **recognize** reconocer
record el disco
red rojo(a), 5.1
    red light la luz roja, **9.1**
redheaded pelirrojo(a), 1.1
to **reduce** (*price*) rebajar, 9.1
to **reduce** (*speed*) reducir la
    velocidad, **9.1**
reduced reducido(a)
refrigerator el refrigerador, la
    nevera, **10**
region la región
relative el/la pariente, 2.1
relay: relay race la carrera
    de relevos, **11.1**
reliability la confiabilidad
religious religioso(a)
to **remain** quedarse, 11.1; **2.1**
to **remember** recordar (ue)
to **rent** alquilar, rentar, 7.1; **3.2**
to **repeat** (*take second helping*)
    repetir (i, i), **4**
to **represent** representar
republic la república
    Dominican Republic
      la República Dominicana
to **request** pedir (i, i), **4**
required obligatorio(a)
reservation la reservación, **7;**
    la reserva
to **reserve** reservar, 7
resort: seaside resort
    el balneario, 7.1
    ski resort la estación
      de esquí, 7.2
rest: the rest lo(s) demás
to **rest** descansar, **11.1**

restaurant el restaurante, **4**
restroom el servicio, 10.2; **1.2**
result el resultado
to **return** regresar, 3.2; volver
    (ue), 5.1
    to return (*something*)
      devolver (ue), 5.2
review el repaso
to **review** repasar
rice el arroz, 4.1
rich rico(a)
to **rid** liberar, **11.1**
ride: to go for a (bike) ride
    dar un paseo en bicicleta
to **ride** (*horse*) andar a caballo,
    3.2; montar a caballo, **8.2;**
    (*bicycle*) andar en bicicleta,
    11.1
rides (*amusement park*)
    las atracciones, **8.1**
right derecho(a), 11.1; **2.1**
    right on the edge of
      al borde mismo de
    to the right a la derecha, 9.1
right: That's right! ¡Verdad!
right away enseguida, 4.2
to **ring** sonar (ue), **6.1**
ringtone el timbre (sonoro), **6.2**
rink (*ice-skating*)
    la pista de patinaje, 7.2
river el río
roast asado(a)
    roast suckling pig
      el cochinillo asado, el
      lechón asado, el chancho
      asado
to **roast** asar, **10**
roll (*bread*) el panecillo, 4.1; **7**
roll of toilet paper el rollo
    de papel higiénico, 11.2; **2.2**
rollerblading el patinaje en
    línea, **11.1**
rollerblading: to go
    rollerblading patinar
    en línea, **11.1**
roller coaster la montaña
    rusa, **8.1**
romantic romántico(a)
room el cuarto, 2.2; **7**
    bathroom el cuarto
      de baño, 2.2; **7**
    bedroom el cuarto de
      dormir, la recámara, 2.2;
      el dormitorio, la habitación,
      la alcoba, la pieza
    classroom la sala de clase,
      3.1
    dining room el comedor, 2.2
    emergency room la sala
      de emergencia, **11.2**
    living room la sala, 2.2
    restroom el servicio, 10.2; **1.2**

single (double) room el
    cuarto sencillo (doble), **7**
waiting room la sala
    de espera, **3.1**
round-trip (ticket) el boleto
    (billete) de ida y vuelta
    (regreso), **3.1**
routine la rutina, 11.1; **2.1**
    daily routine la rutina
      diaria, 11.1; **2.1**
rude mal educado(a), 6.1
ruins las ruinas
rule la regla
to **run** correr, 5.2
running water el agua
    corriente
runway la pista, 10.2; **1.2**
rural rural

sad triste, deprimido(a), 6.1
saffron el azafrán
sailboard la plancha de vela,
    7.1
saint el/la santo(a), **5.1**
    patron saint el/la santo(a)
      patrón(ona), **5.1**
salad la ensalada, 4.1
sale el saldo, la liquidación,
    9.1
salesperson el/la empleado(a),
    3.2; el/la dependiente(a)
salt la sal, **4**
salty salado(a)
same mismo(a), 1.2
sand la arena, 7.1
sandal la sandalia, 9.2
sandwich el sándwich, el
    bocadillo, 4.1; la torta
    ham and cheese sandwich
      el sándwich de jamón
      y queso, 4.1
satisfied satisfecho(a)
to **satisfy** satisfacer
Saturday el sábado, LP
sauce la salsa, **10**
saucepan la cacerola, la olla, **10**
saucer el platillo, **4**
sausage el chorizo
to **save** guardar, **6.1**
saxophone el saxófono
to **say** decir, 3.2
scenery el paisaje
schedule (*train*) el horario, **3.1**
school la escuela, 1.2;
    el colegio; la academia
    elementary school
      la escuela primaria
    high school la escuela
      secundaria, 1.2; el colegio

English-Spanish Dictionary

school (related to) escolar
  school bus el bus escolar, 3.2
  school supplies los
    materiales escolares, 3.1
science la ciencia, 1.2
score el tanto, 5.1
  to score a goal meter un
    gol, 5.1
  to score a point marcar un
    tanto, 5.1
scrambled: scrambled eggs
  los huevos revueltos, 7
screen (computer) la pantalla
  de escritorio, 6.1
scuba diving el buceo
  to go scuba diving bucear
sculptor el/la escultor(a)
sculpture la escultura, 8.2
sea el mar, 7.1
  Caribbean Sea el mar
    Caribe
seafood los mariscos, 4
seaside resort el balneario, 7.1
search: in search of en busca
  de
to search buscar, 3.2
season la estación, LP
  ¿Qué estación es? What
    season is it?, LP
seat el asiento, 10.1; 1.1;
  la plaza, 3.2
  seat number el número
    del asiento, 10.1; 1.1
  seat belt el cinturón de
    seguridad, 10.2; 1.2
second segundo(a), 5.1
  second-class segunda
    clase, 3.1
  second half (soccer)
    el segundo tiempo, 5.1
secondary secundario(a), 1.2
security (checkpoint) el control
  de seguridad, 10.2; 1.2
  to go through security
    pasar por el control de
    seguridad, 10.2; 1.2
sedan el sedán, 9.2
  four-door sedan el sedán
    a cuatro puertas, 9.2
to see ver, 4.2
  let's see a ver
  See you later! ¡Hasta
    luego!, LP
  See you soon! ¡Hasta
    pronto!, LP
  See you tomorrow! ¡Hasta
    mañana!, LP
to seem parecer

It seems to me . . . Me
  parece…
to select seleccionar, 3.1
self-service (restaurant, gas
  station) el autoservicio
to sell vender, 6.2
to send enviar, 3.2; mandar
sense: sense of humor
  el sentido de humor, 6.1
  to have a good sense of
    humor tener un buen
    sentido de humor, 6.1
sent mailbox la bandeja
  de enviados, 6.1
sentence la frase, la oración
September septiembre, LP
serious serio(a), 1.1
to serve servir (i, i), 4
  to serve as servir (i, i) de
server el/la mesero(a), 4.2, 4;
  el/la camarero(a), 4
service el servicio, 9.2
to set (table) poner la mesa, 4;
  (bone) reducir, acomodar
  el hueso, 11.2
seven siete, LP
seven hundred
  setecientos(as)
seventeen diecisiete, LP
seventy setenta, LP
several varios(as)
shack la choza, la casucha
shake (drink) el batido, 4.2
shame: What a shame!
  ¡Qué pena!, 5.1
shampoo el champú, 11.2; 2.2
shape la forma
she ella, 1.1
sheet la sábana, 7
sheet of paper la hoja de
  papel
shellfish los mariscos, 4
shirt la camisa, 3.1
  short- (long-) sleeved shirt
    la camisa de manga corta
    (larga), 9.1
shoe size el número, 9.1
  What size shoe do you
    wear (take)? ¿Qué
    número calzas?, 9.1
shoes las zapatillas, 5.1; los
  zapatos, 9.1
to shop ir de compras, 9.1
shopping cart el carrito, 9.2
shopping center el centro
  comercial, 9.1
short (person) bajo(a), 1.1;
  (length) corto(a), 9.1

short-sleeved de manga
  corta, 9.1
shorts el pantalón corto, 5.1
should deber, 4.2
shoulder (road)
  el acotamiento, el arcén, 9.1;
  (body) el hombro, 11.1
to show mostrar (ue), 10.2; 1.2
shower la ducha, 11.1; 2.1
  to take a shower tomar
    una ducha, 11.1; 2.1
shrimp los camarones, 4.2
shy tímido(a)
sick enfermo(a), 6.2
  sick person el/la enfermo(a)
side el lado
sidewalk la acera, 8.1
sign la señal, 10.2; 1.2; (road)
  el rótulo, 9.1
  no-smoking sign la señal
    de no fumar, 10.2; 1.2
similar similar
since desde; como
sincere sincero(a); franco(a)
to sing cantar, 8.1
singer el/la cantante, 8.1
single solo(a); (room) un
  cuarto sencillo, 7
singles (tennis) individuales,
  5.2
sink el lavabo, 7
sir el señor, LP
sister la hermana, 2.1
to sit down sentarse (ie), 11.1; 2.1
site (Web site) el sitio, 6.1
six seis, LP
six hundred seiscientos(as)
sixteen dieciséis, LP
sixty sesenta, LP
size (clothing) la talla;
  (shoes) el número, 9.1
  What size (clothing) do
    you wear (take)? ¿Qué
    talla usas?, 9.1
  What size (shoe) do you
    wear (take)? ¿Qué
    número calzas?, 9.1
to skate patinar, 7.2; 11.1
  to ice-skate patinar sobre
    el hielo, 7.2
  to inline skate (rollerblade)
    patinar en línea, 11.1
skateboard el monopatín, 11.1
skeleton el esqueleto, 5.1
ski el esquí, 7.2
  ski hat el gorro, 7.2
  ski jacket la chaqueta de
    esquí, el anorak, 7.2

ski lift el telesilla, el telesquí, 7.2
ski pole el bastón, 7.2
ski resort la estación de esquí, 7.2
ski slope la pista, 7.2
to **ski** esquiar, 7.2
  to water-ski esquiar en el agua, 7.1
skier el/la esquiador(a), 7.2
skiing el esquí, 7.2
  cross-country skiing el esquí nórdico
  downhill skiing el esquí alpino, 7.2
  waterskiing el esquí acuático (náutico), 7.1
skillet el/la sartén, **10**
skirt la falda, 3.1
skull el cráneo, la calavera, **5.1**
sky el cielo, 5.2
skyscraper el rascacielos, **8.1**
to **sleep** dormir (ue, u)
sleeping bag el saco (la bolsa) de dormir, 11.2; **2.2**
sleeved: short- (long-) sleeved de manga corta (larga), 9.1
slice la tajada, 9.2; la rebanada, 10; *(ham)* la lonja, la loncha; *(lemon, cucumber)* la rodaja; *(melon)* la raja
to **slice** cortar en rebanadas, **10**
slope la pista, 7.2
slot la ranura, 6.2
slow lento(a), **11.1**
slowly despacio, 9.1
small pequeño(a), 1.2
smile la sonrisa, 6.1
smoking: no-smoking sign la señal de no fumar, 10.2; **1.2**
smoothie el batido, 4.2
snack la merienda; las tapas, los antojitos, 4.2; los bocaditos
sneakers las zapatillas, 5.1; los tenis, 5.2
to **snorkel** bucear, **7.1**
  snorkeling el buceo **7.1**
snow la nieve, 7.2
to **snow** nevar (ie), 7.2
  It's snowing. Nieva., LP
snowboarder el/la snowboarder, 7.2
so tan; **(thus)** así
soap el jabón, 11.2; **2.2**
  bar of soap la barra de jabón, 11.2; **2.2;** la pastilla de jabón
soap opera la telenovela
soccer el fútbol, 5.1

soccer field el campo de fútbol, 5.1
social studies los estudios sociales, 1.2
socks los calcetines, 5.1
soda la cola, la gaseosa, 4.1
sofa el sofá, 2.2
soft blando(a)
soft drink el refresco, 4.2
solid line *(road)* la línea continua, **9.1**
some algunos(as); unos(as)
someone alguien, 8.2
something algo, 8.2
sometimes a veces, 6.1; **1.2;** de vez en cuando
son el hijo, 2.1
soon pronto, LP; dentro de poco, 10.2; **1.2**
  See you soon! ¡Hasta pronto!, LP
sore throat: to have a sore throat tener dolor de garganta, 6.2
sorry: to be sorry sentir (ie, i)
  I'm very sorry. Lo siento mucho., 5.1
soul el alma *(f.)*
soup la sopa
south el sur
South America la América del Sur, la Sudamérica
to **sow** sembrar (ie), **8.2**
space el espacio; *(parking)* el sitio (para estacionar)
Spain España
Spanish *(language)* el español, 1.2; *(person)* el/la español(a)
Spanish *(adj.)* español(a)
Spanish speaker el/la hispanohablante
Spanish-speaking hispanohablante
spare time el tiempo libre, 8.1
spare tire la rueda (llanta) de repuesto (recambio), 9.2; la rueda de refacción
to **speak** hablar, 3.1
  to speak on the phone hablar por teléfono
special especial
specialty la especialidad
spectator el/la espectador(a)
speed la velocidad, 9.1
speed limit la velocidad máxima, 9.1; el límite de velocidad
to **spend** *(time)* pasar, 7.1; *(money)* gastar
spice la especia

spirit el espíritu, 11.1
to **splurge** botar la casa por la ventana
spoon *(tablespoon)* la cuchara, **4;** *(teaspoon)* la cucharita, **4**
sport el deporte, 5.1
  individual sport el deporte individual
  team sport el deporte de equipo
sports *(related to)* deportivo(a)
sports car el coche deportivo, **9.2**
to **sprain** torcerse, **11.2**
  He (She) sprained his (her) ankle. Se torció el tobillo., **11.2**
spring la primavera, LP
square *(town)* la plaza, **8.1**
stable el establo, 8.2
stadium el estadio
stairs la escalera, **8.1**
stall *(market)* el puesto, el tenderete, 9.2
to **stand in line** hacer cola, 10.2; **1.2;** estar en fila
standing de pie
star la estrella
starving: I'm starving. Me muero de hambre., **4**
state el estado
station *(train)* la estación de ferrocarril (tren), 3.1; *(subway)* la estación de metro, 8.1; *(gas)* la estación de servicio, la gasolinera, 9.2
statue la estatua, 8.2
stay la estadía
to **stay** quedarse, 11.1; **2.1**
  to stay in bed *(illness)* guardar cama, 6.2; *(idleness)* quedarse en la cama, 11.1; **2.1**
  to stay in a hotel hospedarse, **7**
steak el biftec, **4**
steep pendiente
steering wheel el volante, 9.2
stepbrother el hermanastro, 2.1
stepfather el padrastro, 2.1
stepmother la madrastra, 2.1
stepsister la hermanastra, 2.1
still todavía
stingy tacaño(a), 9.1
to **stir** revolver (ue), **10**
stitch el punto, la sutura, **11.2**
  to give (someone) stitches poner unos puntos (unas suturas) (a alguien), **11.2**

English-Spanish Dictionary

English-Spanish Dictionary

stomach el estómago, 6.2

to have a stomachache
tener dolor de estómago,
6.2

stone la piedra

stop la parada, **3.2**

next stop la próxima
parada, **3.1**

to **stop** parar(se), **9.1**

store la tienda, 3.2

story el cuento, la historia

stove la cocina, la estufa, **10**

straight (ahead) derecho, **9.1**

to go straight (ahead)
seguir derecho, **9.1**

straw la paja, **5.2**

street la calle, **8.1**

one-way street la calle de
sentido único, **9.1**

stress el estrés, 6.2; las
tensiones, **11.1**

stretch (distance) el trecho

to **stretch** estirarse, 11.1; **2.1**

stretcher la camilla, **11.2**

string beans las judías
verdes, 9.2

strong fuerte

stubborn obstinado(a),
terco(a), 6.1

student el/la alumno(a), 1.2;
el/la estudiante; *(adj.)*
estudiantil, escolar, **3.1**

study el estudio

stuffed up (head, cold)
resfriado, 6.2

social studies los estudios
sociales, 1.2

to **study** estudiar, 3.1

suburbs las afueras, los
suburbios, 2.2

subway el metro, **8.1**

subway entrance la boca
del metro, **8.1**

subway station la estación
de metro, **8.1**

to **succeed** tener éxito, 6.1

success el éxito, 6.1

successful: to be successful
tener éxito, 6.1

such tal

suddenly de repente

to **suffer** sufrir

sugar el azúcar

suitcase la maleta, 10.1; **1.1**

**to pack one's
suitcase** hacer la maleta,
10.1; **1.1**

summer el verano, LP

sun el sol

to **sunbathe** tomar el sol, 7.1

Sunday el domingo, LP

sunglasses los anteojos de
sol, las gafas para el sol, 7.1

sunny: It's sunny. Hace
(Hay) sol., LP

suntan lotion la crema solar,
la loción bronceadora, 7.1

supermarket
el supermercado, 9.2

supplies: school supplies
los materiales escolares, 3.1

sure seguro(a)

to **surf** practicar la tabla
hawaiana, 7.1

to **surf the Web (the Net)**
navegar la red (el Internet),
3.2; **6.1**

surfboard la tabla hawaiana, 7.1

surfing la tabla hawaiana, el
surfing, 7.1

to go surfing practicar la
tabla hawaiana, el
surfing, 7.1

surgeon: orthopedic surgeon
el/la cirujano(a)
ortopédico(a), **11.2**

surprise la sorpresa, 4.1

survey la encuesta

SUV el SUV, **9.2**

sweat suit el buzo, **11.1**

sweater el suéter, 11.1; **2.1**

sweet dulce, **5.1**

to **swim** nadar, 7.1

swimming pool la piscina, la
alberca, 7.1; la pila

swimsuit el bañador, el traje
de baño, 7.1

swollen hinchado(a), **11.2**

symptom el síntoma

T-shirt la camiseta, 5.1;
el T-shirt

table la mesa, la mesita, 2.2; **4**

to clear the table levantar
(quitar) la mesa, **4**

to set the table poner la
mesa, **4**

tablecloth el mantel, 4

tablespoon la cuchara, **4;**
(in recipe) la cucharada

taco el taco

to **take** tomar, 3.1; traer, 10.1;
1.1; sacar, 7.1

to take (size) usar, calzar,
9.1

to take a bath bañarse

to take a flight tomar un
vuelo

to take a hike dar una
caminata, 11.2; **2.2**

to take a shower tomar
una ducha, 11.1; **2.1**

to take a test tomar un
examen, 3.1

to take a trip hacer un
viaje, 10.1; **1.1**

**to take an X ray of
someone** tomar una
radiografía, **11.2**

to take pictures (photos)
sacar (tomar) fotos, 7.1

to take place tener lugar

**to take someone's blood
pressure** tomar la
tensión arterial, 6.2

to take someone's pulse
tomar el pulso, 6.2

to take the (school) bus
tomar el bus (escolar), 3.2

to **take off (airplane)** despegar,
10.2; **1.2;** *(clothes)* quitarse,
11.1; **2.1**

to **take out** sacar

taken ocupado(a), 4.2; **3.2**

takeoff el despegue, 10.2;
1.2

to **talk** hablar, 3.1

to talk on a cell phone
hablar en el móvil

to talk on the phone
hablar por teléfono

tall alto(a), 1.1

tank (car) el tanque, **9.2**

taste el gusto

tax el impuesto

taxi el taxi, 10.1; **1.1**

taxi driver el/la taxista, 10.1;
1.1

tea el té

to **teach** enseñar, 3.1

teacher el/la profesor(a), 1.2

team el equipo, 5.1

team sport el deporte de
equipo

teaspoon la cucharita, **4;** *(in
recipe)* la cucharadita

teeth los dientes, 11.1; **2.1**

  to brush one's teeth cepillarse (lavarse) los dientes, 11.1; **2.1**

telephone el teléfono

  pay telephone el teléfono público, **6.2**

  (related to) **telephone** telefónico(a), **6.2**

  telephone book la guía telefónica, **6.2**

  telephone call la llamada telefónica, **6.2**

  telephone card la tarjeta telefónica, **6.2**

  telephone line la línea, **6.2**

  telephone number el número de teléfono, **6.2**

  telephone receiver el auricular, **6.2**

  to pick up the telephone descolgar (ue) el auricular, 6.2

  to speak on the telephone hablar por teléfono

television la televisión, la tele

temperature la temperatura, 7.2

ten diez, LP

tennis el tenis

  to play tennis jugar (al) tenis, 5.2

  tennis court la cancha de tenis, 5.2

  tennis player el/la tenista, 5

  tennis racket la raqueta, 5.2

  tennis shoes los tenis, 9.1

tension la tensión, **11.1**

tent la carpa, la tienda de campaña, 11.2; **2.2**

  to put up a tent armar, montar una carpa (una tienda de campaña), 11.2; **2.2**

terrace la terraza

terrible terrible

test el examen, la prueba, 3.1

  to give a test dar un examen (una prueba), 3.1

  to take a test tomar un examen, 3.1

Texan tejano(a)

text message el mensaje de texto

Thank you. Gracias., LP

that aquel, aquella, 9.1; ese(a)

that *(one)* eso

the el, la, los, las

their su(s)

them las, los, les

  to them *(pron.)* les

then luego, 3.2

there allí, allá, 9.1

  Is . . . there? ¿Está… ?, **6.2**

there is, there are hay, 2.2

therefore por eso

these estos(as)

they ellos(as), 1.2

thigh el muslo, **10**

thin flaco(a); delgado(a)

thing la cosa, 3.1

to **think** pensar (ie), 5.1

  What do you think? ¿Qué piensas?, 5.1

thirsty: to be thirsty tener sed, 4.1

thirteen trece, LP

thirty treinta, LP

thirty-one treinta y uno, LP

this este(a), 9.1

those aquellos(as), esos(as)

thousand mil

three tres, LP

  the Three Wise Men los Reyes Magos, 5.2

three hundred trescientos(as)

throat la garganta, 6.2

  to have a sore throat tener dolor de garganta, 6.2

to **throw** tirar, 5.2

  to throw (give) a party dar una fiesta, 8.1

Thursday el jueves, LP

thus así

ticket el boleto, el ticket, 7.2; **3.1;** la entrada, 8.1; el billete, 10.1; **1.1;** el tiquet(e); *(car)* la multa, **9.1**

  e-ticket el boleto (billete) electrónico, 10.1; **1.1**

  one-way ticket el boleto (billete) sencillo, **3.1**

  round-trip ticket el boleto (billete) de ida y vuelta (regreso), **3.1**

  to give (someone) a ticket clavar una multa, **9.1**

ticket counter *(airport)* el mostrador, 10.1; **1.1**

ticket dispenser el distribuidor automático, **3.1**

ticket window la ventanilla, la boletería, 7.2, **3.1;** la taquilla, 8.2

tie la corbata, 9.1

tiger el tigre

time la hora, LP; 10.1; **1.1;** el tiempo, 8.1; la vez

  at times (sometimes) a veces, 6.1; **1.2**

  at what time? ¿a qué hora?, LP

boarding time la hora de embarque, 10.1; **1.1**

departure time la hora de salida, 10.1; **1.1**

from time to time de vez en cuando, 10.2, **1.2**

full-time a tiempo completo

on time a tiempo, 10.2; **1.2**

part-time a tiempo parcial

spare time el tiempo libre, 8.1

  What time is it? ¿Qué hora es?, LP

timetable el horario, **3.1**

timid tímido(a)

tip el servicio, 4.2; la propina, 4

  Is the tip included? ¿Está incluido el servicio?, 4.2

tire la llanta, la goma, el neumático, la rueda, **9.2;** el caucho

  flat tire el pinchazo, 9.2

  spare tire la rueda (llanta) de repuesto (recambio), 9.2

tired cansado(a), 6.1

to a

toast las tostadas, el pan tostado, 4.1; **7**

today hoy, LP

  What day is it today? ¿Qué día es hoy?, LP

  What is today's date? ¿Cuál es la fecha de hoy?, LP

toe el dedo del pie, **11.1**

together juntos(as)

toilet el inodoro, el váter, 7

toilet paper el papel higiénico, 11.2; **2.2**

  roll of toilet paper el rollo de papel higiénico, 11.2; **2.2**

toll el peaje, **9.1;** la cuota

tollbooth la cabina (garita) de peaje, 9.1

tomato el tomate, 4.1

tomb la tumba, 5.1

tomorrow mañana, LP

  See you tomorrow! ¡Hasta mañana!, LP

tonight esta noche, 4.1

too también, 1.2

toolbar la barra de herramientas, **6.1**

toothbrush el cepillo de dientes, 11.2; **2.2**

toothpaste la crema dental, 11.2; **2.2;** la pasta dentífrica

  tube of toothpaste el tubo de crema dental, 11.2; **2.2**

English-Spanish Dictionary

to **touch** tocar, 5.1
tourist el/la turista
toward hacia
towel la toalla, 7.1; **7**
town el pueblo
town square la plaza, **8.1**
toy el juguete
track (train) la vía, 3.1
traffic el tráfico, **8.1;**
el tránsito
traffic jam el tapón
traffic light el semáforo, **8.1;**
la luz roja, **9.1**
track la vía, 3.1
trail el camino; la senda, **3.2**
train el tren, **3.1**
train car el coche, el vagón, **3.1**
train conductor el/la
revisor(a), **3.2**
train station la estación de
ferrocarril (tren), **3.1**
to **transfer (train)** transbordar,
3.2
**transportation: means of
transportation** los medios
de transporte, **8.2**
to **travel** viajar
tree el árbol, 2.2
trip el viaje, 10.1; **1.1**
to take a trip hacer un
viaje, 10.1; **1.1**
trombone el trombono
truck el camión, **9.2**
true *(adj.)* verdadero(a);
cierto(a), **6.1**
That's true. Es verdad., **9.1**
trunk (car) el baúl, la
maletera, 10.1; **1.1**
truth la verdad
to **try** tratar de
tube el tubo, 11.2; **2.2**
Tuesday el martes, LP
tuna el atún, 9.2
to **turn** doblar, **9.1**
to **turn around** dar la vuelta, 9.1
to **turn off** apagar, **6.1**
to **turn on** prender, **6.1**
to **turn ... years old** cumplir...
años
turn signals las
direccionales, las
intermitentes, **9.2**
TV la tele
twelve doce, LP
twenty veinte, LP
twenty-eight veintiocho, LP
twenty-five veinticinco, LP

twenty-four veinticuatro, LP
twenty-nine veintinueve, LP
twenty-one veintiuno, LP
twenty-seven veintisiete, LP
twenty-six veintiséis, LP
twenty-three veintitrés, LP
twenty-two veintidós, LP
twin el/la gemelo(a), 2.1
to **twist** torcerse, **11.2**
two dos, LP
two hundred doscientos(as)
type el tipo, 6.1
typical típico(a)

ugly feo(a), 1.1
unattractive feo(a), 1.1
uncle el tío, 2.1
under debajo de, 10.2; **1.2**
underneath debajo de, 10.2;
1.2
to **understand** comprender, 4.2;
entender (ie), 8.2
unfortunately
desgraciadamente
to **unhook (*telephone receiver*)**
descolgar el auricular, **6.2**
uniform el uniforme, 3.1
United States Estados
Unidos
from the United States
estadounidense
university la universidad
unless a menos que
unoccupied libre, 4.2; **3.2**
unpleasant antipático(a), 1.1;
desagradable
until hasta, LP
up: to go up subir, 7.2
upper superior
urban urbano(a), **8.1**
us *(pron.)* nos
to **use** usar, 3.2

vacation las vacaciones, 7.1
vanilla *(adj.)* de vainilla
various varios(as)
veal la ternera, 10
veal cutlet el escalope
de ternera, **10**
vegetable la legumbre, la
verdura, el vegetal, 4.1

vegetable store (greengrocer)
la verdulería, 9.2
vegetarian vegetariano(a), 4.1
Venezuelan venezolano(a)
very muy, LP; mucho, LP
It's very hot (cold). Hace
mucho calor (frío)., LP
Very well. Muy bien, LP
view la vista
vinegar el vinagre, 4
violin el violín
to **visit** visitar, 8.2
volcano el volcán
volleyball el voleibol, 7.1
volleyball court la cancha
de voleibol, 7.1
vowel la vocal

to **wait (for)** esperar, 10.2; **1.2**
to wait in line hacer cola,
10.2; **1.2;** estar en fila
waiter (waitress) el/la
mesero(a), 4.2; **4;** el/la
camarero(a), **4**
waiting room la sala de
espera, **3.1**
to **wake up** despertarse (ie),
11.1; **2.1**
to **walk** caminar, 5.1; andar
to walk in a procession
desfilar, 5.1
to **want** querer (ie), 5.1; desear,
4.2
war la guerra
warm-ups (*clothing*) el buzo,
11.1
to **warn** advertir (ie)
warning la advertencia
to **wash** lavar, 11.2; **2.2**
to **wash oneself** lavarse, 11.1; **2.1**
**to wash one's hair (face,
hands)** lavarse el pelo (la
cara, las manos), 11.1; **2.1**
washbasin el lavabo, 7
to **watch** mirar, 3.2; ver, 4.2
water el agua *(f.)*, 4.1
(sparkling) mineral water
el agua mineral (con gas),
4.2
running water el agua
corriente
waterskiing el esquí acuático
(náutico), 7.1
to water-ski esquiar en el
agua, 7.1

wave la ola, 7.1
way la manera
  to lose one's way perder el camino
we nosotros(as)
to **wear** llevar, 3.1; *(shoe size)* calzar, 9.1; *(clothing size)* usar, 9.1
weather el tiempo, LP
  It's cold *(weather).* Hace frío., LP
  It's cool *(weather).* Hace fresco., LP
  The weather is bad. Hace mal tiempo., LP
  The weather is nice. Hace buen tiempo., LP
  What's the weather like? ¿Qué tiempo hace?, LP
Web la red, 3.2; **6.1**
  to surf the Web navegar la red, 3.2; **6.1**
Web site el sitio Web, **6.1**
Wednesday el miércoles, LP
week la semana, LP
  last week la semana pasada, 7.1
weekend el fin de semana, 7.1
weight el peso
weights: to lift weights levantar pesas, **11.1**
welcome: You're welcome. De nada., Por nada., No hay de qué., LP
well bien, LP; pues
  Very well. Muy bien., LP
well-done *(meat)* bien hecho(a), 4
well-known renombrado(a)
well-mannered bien educado(a), 6.1
west el oeste
what ¿qué?; ¿cuál?, LP; ¿cuáles? ¿cómo?, 1.1
  at what time? ¿a qué hora?, LP
  What a shame! ¡Qué pena!, 5.1
  What day is it (today)? ¿Qué día es hoy?, LP
  What does he (she, it) look like? ¿Cómo es?, 1.1
  What's happening? What's going on? ¿Qué pasa?, 3.1
  What is he (she, it) like? ¿Cómo es?, 1.1
  What is today's date? ¿Cuál es la fecha de hoy?, LP
  what nationality? ¿de qué nacionalidad?, 1.1
  What's new (up)? ¿Qué hay?

What size shoe do you wear (take)? ¿Qué número calzas?, 9.1
What would you like (to eat)? ¿Qué desean tomar?, 4.2
What time is it? ¿Qué hora es?, LP
wheat el trigo, **8.2**
wheelchair la silla de ruedas, **11.2**
when cuando, 3.1
when? ¿cuándo?, 3.2
where donde
where? ¿dónde?, 1.1; **(to) where?** ¿adónde?, 3.2
  from where? ¿de dónde?, 1.1
which? ¿cuál?, LP; ¿cuáles?
while mientras, 5.2
white blanco(a), 5.1
who? ¿quién?, 1.1; ¿quiénes?, 1.2
  Who's calling, please? ¿De parte de quién, por favor?, **6.2**
whole entero(a)
whose cuyos(as)
why? ¿por qué?, 3.2
wide ancho(a), **8.1**
wife la esposa, la mujer, 2.1
to **win** ganar, 5.1
wind el viento, LP
window *(store)* el escaparate, 9.1; *(plane)* la ventanilla, 10.2; **1.2**
windshield el parabrisas, 9.1
windsurfing la plancha de vela, 7.1
  to go windsurfing practicar la plancha de vela, 7.1
windy: It's windy. Hace viento., LP
wings las alitas, **10**
winter el invierno, LP, 7.2
wise: the Three Wise Men los Reyes Magos, **5.2**
to **wish** desear, 4.2
with con
within dentro de
without sin, 7.2
woman la dama
wooden de madera
word la palabra
work el trabajo; *(art)* la obra
to **work** trabajar, 3.2; *(land)* cultivar, labrar, **8.2**
world el mundo
  World Cup la Copa Mundial
worldwide mundial

worse peor
worst el/la peor
to **be worth: It's not worth it.** No vale., 7.1
Would that . . . Ojalá que... , **11.2**
wound la herida, **11.2**
wreath la corona, **5.1**
wrist la muñeca, **11.1**
to **write** escribir, 4.2
written escrito(a)
wrong erróneo(a)

X ray la radiografía, **11.2**
  They're taking an X ray (of him or her). Le toman (hacen) una radiografía., **11.2**

year el año, LP
  last year el año pasado, 7.1
  to be turning . . . years old cumplir... años, 2.1
  to be . . . years old tener... años, 2.1
yellow amarillo(a), 5.1
yes sí, LP
yesterday ayer, 7.1
  yesterday afternoon ayer por la tarde, 7.1
  yesterday evening anoche, 7.1
yet aún; todavía
yoga el yoga, **11.1**
  to do yoga practicar yoga, **11.1**
you tú; *(sing. form.)* usted; *(pl. form.)* ustedes; *(pl. fam.)* vosotros(as); *(fam. pron.)* ti; te; *(form. pron.)* le
  You're welcome. De (Por) nada., No hay de qué., LP
young person el/la joven, 1.1
younger menor
youngest el/la menor
your *(fam.)* tu(s); *(form.)* su(s)
  It's your turn! ¡Te toca a ti!
youth hostel el albergue juvenil, el hostal, 7

zero cero, LP
zone la zona
zoo el zoológico, **8.1**

English-Spanish Dictionary

Culture Index

A

amigos R1, R7, R34, 42, 73, 111, 112, 153, 170, 196

Andes 22, 58, 59, 68–69, 88–89

Año Nuevo 143

Argentina en general, 216, 326; Bariloche, R52, 11; Buenos Aires, 17, 19, 37, 96, 100, 113, 119, 122, 132, 149, 161, 171, 174, 191, 231, 234, 240, 244, 264, 283, 286, 327, 345; la Casa Rosada (Buenos Aires), 17; las pampas argentinas, 228–229; Puerto Madryn, R42; Rawson, 166; Trelew, 327

arte Gaudí, Antoni, 168–169

artesanía en general, 209, 227; tejidos, 82

avión El avión en la América del Sur, 22–23

B

baile 137, 143, 148, 164

bienestar 48, 324–325, 326, 327, 332, 335, 339, 344; el hospital, 327, 334, 343; *Médicos Sin Fronteras*, 346–347; **Vida activa y buena salud,** 344–345

C

cafés y restaurantes R13, R17, 12, 102–103, 104–105, 106, 108, 109, 110, 111, 112, 113, 115, 119, 120–122, 123, 124, 125, 129, 133, 210, 299, 318, 336;

Restaurantes de España y Latinoamérica, 120–123, 299; **Sé lo que pedí,** 124–125

Camino de Santiago 218–219

camping
El camping, 58–59;
Los mochileros, 56–57

campo, la vida en el en general, 228–229, 230–231, 236–237, 246, 250; Cozumel, México, 251; isla Taquile (lago Titicaca, Perú), 256, 260; Puerto Montt, Chile, 254; Sabandía, Perú, 250; Argentina, 231; Santo Domingo, Venezuela, 230

Carnaval Puerto Plata, República Dominicana, 134–135

casas R2, R10, R11, 4, 295

Cervantes Saavedra, Miguel de 359

Ceuta (Africa) R16

Chile en general, 44, 59, 164, 326; Arica, 37, 58, 70, 94, 226; el desierto de Atacama, 23, 94, 148; **La Panamericana** (un viaje en carro por la carretera Panamericana), 282–284; la Patagonia chilena, 57; Poconchile, 71, 136; Portillo, R49; Puerto Montt, 254; Punta Arenas, 57; Saltos del Petrohué, 55; Viña del Mar, 344; Vicuña, 105

ciudad en general, 230–231, 232–233, 267, 286; Avenida 9 de Julio (Buenos Aires, Argentina), 231, 240; barrio de Panecillo (Quito, Ecuador), 241; barrio de San Telmo (Buenos Aires, Argentina), 244; Bosque de Chapultepec (Ciudad de México), 249, 258; **La ciudad y el campo,** 248–251; Caracas, Venezuela, 286;

el Casco Viejo (Ciudad de Panamá), 255; Ciudad de México, 231, 258, 274; Ciudad de Panamá, 243, 290; el Jirón de la Unión (Lima, Perú), 230; Miami, Florida, 252–253; parque de Máximo Gómez (Miami, Florida), 252; Quito, Ecuador, 247, 248; **Tráfico y más tráfico,** 286–287

Colombia en general, 66; Barranquilla, R13; Guasca, 278; Santa Marta, R20–R21, 62

comida R13, R15, R35, 102–103, 104–105, 114, 119, 121, 128, 133, 139, 140, 158, 253, 296–297, 298, 299, 303, 305, 306, 308, 312, 314, 322, 336, 338; el comer, 296–297, 298, 310; Cocina hispana, 298–299; las naranjas de Andalucía (España), 230; la paella, 299; **Una receta hispana** (arroz con pollo), 312–313; la sopa de pollo, 301; **Una receta para «la ropa vieja»,** 314–315

compras R36–R37, R43, 311; mercados indígenas, 82, 209, 227

Costa Rica en general, 35, 105, 298; Alajuela, 231; la Catarata La Paz, 64; San José, 10

Cuba en general, 70, 298; La Habana, 137; **Una receta para «la ropa vieja»,** 314–315

D

deportes en general, R28–R29, R52; 147, 326, 327, 329, 351; el béisbol, R28–R29; el ciclismo, 326, 344; el esquí, R49, R52; el fútbol, R33, 147; el jogging, 324–325, 326, 329, 344,

345, 352; el monopatín, 327, 345; el patinaje en línea, 345; el snowboard, R49, R52; **Vida activa y buena salud,** 344–345; el voleibol, 341

Día de los Muertos 137, 139, 140, 141, 154–155

Día de los Reyes 156

Don Quijote 182, 358–363

La Nochevieja en España, 158–159; Palma de Mallorca, R8, 14; San Sebastián de los Reyes, 183; Segovia, 102–103; Tenerife (islas Canarias), 281, 324–325, 326, 336; Torrelavega, 137; Valencia, R17, R36–R37, R39, R43, 45, 105, 110, 311, 347

las islas Galápagos 6

geografía de la América del Sur, 22

Guatemala en general, 123, 146, 210, 298; Antigua, 125, 150, 180, 327; Chichicastenango, 306; Ciudad de Guatemala, 2, 11, 15, 104; lago Atitlán, 201; Tikal, 298

Ecuador en general, 242, 250, 265; Baños, R53, 104; Cotacachi, 136, 144, 162, 211, 283; Galápagos, 6; Manta, 108, 202, 224; Otavalo, 209; **La Panamericana** (un viaje en carro por la carretera Panamericana), 282–284; Quito, R3, R17, 13, 241, 247, 248, 268, 283; Riobamba, 230; San Pablo, R18

escuela R7, R12, R17, R27, 28, 49, 150, 166

España en general, 71; Andalucía, 230; Asturias, R33, R46–R47, 36, 61, 194, 215; Barcelona, R33, 13, 50, 133, 150, 168–169, 265, 334, 352; Baztán, 137; Bilbao, 33; Burgos, 219; Cádiz, 112, 120, 181; Cantabria, 137; Córdoba, 87, 238; el encierro, 183; Estepona, 265; **Unas fiestas hispanas,** 154–156; Huelva, 203; Lanzarote (islas Canarias), 170; Madrid, R25, R35, 2, 75, 98, 156, 159, 207, 231, 262–263, 278, 299; Málaga, 74; Mallorca, 14; La Mancha, 264; la Mezquita (Córdoba), 87; Navarra, 137, 218; Nerja, 51;

familia R2, R8, R9, R12, 295, 347

ferias y fiestas en general, 47, 134–135, 136–137, 138, 139, 143, 144, 145, 152, 154–157, 158; el Año Nuevo, 143, 159; el Baztandarren Biltzarra, 137; Carnaval, 134–135, 136; el Cuatro de Julio (Estados Unidos), 322; el Día de la Independencia (México), 149; el Día de los Muertos, 137, 139, 140, 141, 154–155; el Día de San Juan (Puerto Rico), 152–153; los Diablos Danzantes del Yare (Venezuela), 136; el festival cubano (la Pequeña Habana, Miami, Florida), 299; la Guelaguetza (México), 136; **Unas fiestas hispanas,** 154–157; Hanuka, 143, 156; la Navidad, 136, 141, 142, 156, 162; la Nochebuena, 142; la Nochevieja, 158, 159; La Nochevieja en España, 158; la piñata, 144

Florida Una ciudad interesante (Miami), 252–253

Francia la Torre Eiffel, 114

Hanuka 143, 156, 157

hoteles y hostales 57, 200–201, 202–203, 204, 205, 207, 211, 212, 215, 216, 217, 220, 221, 224, 331; **Un hostal y un parador,** 216–217

lenguaje en general, 109, 138, 333; comparaciones con el inglés, R44, 46, 210, 240, 340; En otras partes, 5, 8, 42, 73, 76, 106, 142, 172, 177, 205, 232, 237, 266; refranes, 19, 53, 85, 117, 151, 185, 212, 245, 279, 309, 341

literatura *El Quijote,* 358–363; *Versos sencillos,* 364–367; *Marianela,* 368–381

Culture Index

Marianela 368–381

Médicos Sin Fronteras 346–347

mercados R38, 82, 116, 227, 323

México en general, 36, 77, 227, 298; la Barranca del Cobre, 89–90; Ciudad de México, R5, R51, 21, 47, 71, 171, 231, 249, 258, 273, 274, 276, 286, 287, 295; Cozumel, 251; Unas fiestas hispanas, 154–156; Guadalajara, 104, 109, 115, 208; Michoacán, 154; Oaxaca, R15, 36, 97, 136, 308, 327, 341; Puebla, 296–297, 318; Puerto Vallarta, R49; San Cristóbal de las Casas, 200–201; la Sierra Madre, 89–90; los tarahumara, 90; Tepoztlán, R19, 116, 203, 277, 298, 323; **Viajes ferroviarios fabulosos** (el ferrocarril Pacífico–Chihuahua), 88–91; Zihuatanejo, 10

Miami 253; **Una ciudad interesante,** 252

monumentos estatua de José Martí (La Habana, Cuba), 364; monumento a la Revolución (Ciudad de México), 287; monumento de la Independencia (Ciudad de México), 276; Pirámide de Mayo (Buenos Aires, Argentina), 17

museos Museo de Artes y Ciencias (Valencia, España), 324–325

música R10–R11, 149

Navidad 136, 141, 142, 144, 156, 162

Nazca (las líneas de) 24, 25

Nicaragua en general, R12; Catarina, 227; Granada, 203; lago de Nicaragua, R45; León, 171, 363; Managua, 256; Montelimar, 331

Nochebuena 142

Nochevieja 158

Nueva York 158

Nuevo México Santa Fe, 49

paella 299, 310–311

paisajes urbanos Buenos Aires, Argentina, 231; Caracas, Venezuela, R26, 264; Córdoba, España, 87; Cuzco, Perú, 91; Montevideo, Uruguay, 84; San Juan, Puerto Rico, 21

Panamá en general, 70, 170; el canal de Panamá, 93; Ciudad de Panamá, 92, 243, 255, 286, 290, 303; Colón, 92; isla de Barro Colorado, 92

papel picado 141

Paraguay Asunción, R1

Perón, Eva 161

Perú en general, 36, 82, 250, 299; Aguas Calientes, 95; Arequipa, 3; Cuzco, 88–89; Huanchaco, 61, 202, 212; Iquitos, 27; isla Taquile (lago Titicaca), 256, 260; Lima, 3, 36, 105, 230; las líneas de Nazca, 24, 25; Machu Picchu, 88–89, 91; Miraflores, 124, 179; **La Panamericana** (un viaje en carro por la carretera Panamericana), 282–284, 289; Pisco, 284; **Viajes ferroviarios fabulosos** (Cuzco y Macchu Picchu), 88–90

piñata 144

plazas Plaza de Armas (Cuzco, Perú), 88; Plaza de Armas (Lima, Perú), 248; Plaza de Armas (Quito, Ecuador), 13, 248; Plaza de Cibeles (Madrid, España), 262–263; Plaza de la Independencia (Montevideo, Uruguay), 80, 235; Plaza Mayor (Madrid, España), R25; la Puerta del Sol (Madrid, España), 158, 159

Puerto Rico en general, 152, 153; San Juan, 12, 21, 28, 355; Vieques, 32, 203

Quijote, El 358–363

refranes 19, 53, 85, 117, 151, 185, 212, 245, 279, 309, 341

República Dominicana Puerto Plata, 135; el aeropuerto La Romana, 1; Santo Domingo, R7

restaurantes y cafés → **cafés y restaurantes**

tapas 104, 107, 128, 133

tecnología 168–169, 170–171, 172, 173, 176, 181, 188; **En un mundo tecnológico,** 188–189; **La tecnología de hoy y ayer,** 190–191

tejidos 82, 227

trabajo 207

tren en general, 68–69, 70, 71, 72, 73, 76, 77, 88–90, 94, 95, 132; el AVE, 70; de Machu Picchu a Cuzco, 68–69; **De Panamá a Colón en tren,** 92–93; la estación Arica–La Paz (Chile), 70; la estación de Atocha (Madrid), 71, 75, 98; la estación de Colón (Panamá), 92; la estación General Belgrano (Buenos Aires), 100; **Viajes ferroviarios fabulosos,** 88–91

Uruguay Colonia, 129; Montevideo, 235

Venezuela en general, 22; Caracas, R26, 264, 286; Maracay, 121; Mérida, 59, 202, 326; San Juan, R9, 170; Santo Domingo, 230; San Francisco de Yare, 136; 286

Versos sencillos 364–367

viajes y vacaciones R46–R47; en avión, 1, 2, 3, 5, 9, 11, 19, 25, 33, 37, 42, 44, 54; **el camping,** 58–59, 62; la playa de Gijón (España), R46–R47; **La Panamericana** (un viaje en carro por la carretera Panamericana), 282–285; para los mochileros, 34, 35, 36, 37, 43, 45, 56; **Un viaje interesante** (las líneas de Nazca), 24–25

Grammar Index

adjectives agreement in gender and number with nouns, R7; ending in **-e** or a consonant, R7; possessive forms, R9; of nationality, 114 (4)

agreement (in gender and number) of articles and nouns, of nouns and adjectives, R7

al contraction of **a + el**, R18

andar preterite, 80 (3)

articles definite, R7

commands with **favor de** + *infinitive*, 52 (2)
tú (familiar) command: regular affirmative forms, 274 (9); irregular affirmative forms, 276 (9); negative forms, 309 (10)
formal **(usted, ustedes)** command: affirmative and negative forms, 307 (10); with object pronouns, 307 (10) (See also subjunctive mood)

comparatives and superlatives R44

comparisons of equality, 340 (11)

conditional tense regular, 277 (9); irregular, 278 (9)

conocer present, R42; **conocer** vs. **saber**, R42

dar present, R18; preterite, R51

decir present, 83 (3); preterite, 83 (3); past participle, 210 (7); future, 242 (8); affirmative **tú** command, 276 (9); conditional, 278 (9)

direct object pronouns R53; used together with indirect object pronouns, 211, 213 (7); (*See also* pronouns)

estar present, R18; **estar** vs. **ser**, R25; used with present participle to form present progressive, 15 (1); preterite, 80 (3)

future tense regular, 240 (8); irregular, 242 (8)

gustar to express likes and dislikes, R35; verbs like **gustar: aburrir, interesar,** R35

haber imperfect, 148 (5); present, 208 (7); used with past participle to form present perfect, 208 (7); future, 242 (8)

hacer present, 12 (1); preterite, 80 (3); past participle, 210 (7); future, 242 (8); affirmative **tú** command, 276 (9); conditional, 278 (9)

imperfect tense of **-ar** verbs, 146 (5); of **-er** and **-ir** verbs, 148 (5); of **haber,** 148 (5); uses of, 151 (5); with verbs that express mental activities or conditions, 180 (6) (*See also* irregular verbs; imperfect vs. preterite)

imperfect vs. preterite completed vs. repeated or habitual action, 181 (6); two past actions in the same sentence, 184 (6)

impersonal expressions with subjunctive, 336 (11)

indicative mood 304 (10)

indirect object pronouns R27; used together with direct object pronouns, 211, 213 (7) (*See also* pronouns)

infinitive with **tener que,** R8; with **ir a,** R18; commands with **favor de,** 52 (2); with object pronouns, 244 (8)

ir present, R18; **ir a** + *infinitive*, R18; preterite, R51; imperfect, 150 (5); affirmative **tú** command, 276 (9)

irregular verbs
present: **conocer,** R42; **dar,** R18; **decir,** 83 (3); **estar,** R18; **hacer,** 12 (1); **ir,** R18; **poner,** 12 (1); **saber,** R42; **salir** 12 (1); **ser,** R6; **tener,** R8, 12 (1); **traer,** 12 (1); **venir,** 12 (1)
preterite: **andar,** 80 (3); **dar,** R51; **decir,** 83 (3); **estar,** 80 (3); **hacer,** 80 (3); **ir,** R51; **poder, poner, querer, saber,** 80 (3); **ser,** R51; **tener,** 80 (3); **traer,** 83 (3); **venir,** 80 (3); **ver,** R51
imperfect: **ir, ser, ver,** 150 (5)
future: **decir, hacer, poder, poner, querer, saber, salir, tener, venir,** 242 (8)
conditional: **decir, hacer, poder, poner, querer, saber, salir, tener, venir,** 278 (9)

nouns masculine and feminine, R7; singular and plural, R7

passive voice with **se,** 116 (4)

past participle regular, 208 (7); irregular, 210 (7)

poder preterite, 80 (3); imperfect, 180 (6); future, 242 (8); conditional, 278 (9)

poner present, 12 (1); preterite, 80 (3); past participle, 210 (7); future, 242 (8); affirmative **tú** command, 276 (9); conditional, 278 (9) possessive adjectives R9

present of **ser**, R6; of **tener**, R8; of regular verbs, R15; of **ir, dar,** and **estar**, R18; of verbs with **g** in the **yo** form, 12 (1); of **decir**, 83 (3); subjunctive mood, 304 (10) (*See also* irregular verbs; stem-changing verbs; subjunctive mood)

present participle 15 (1); with object pronouns, 244 (8)

present perfect 208 (7)

present progressive 15 (1)

preterite tense of regular verbs, R51; of **ir, ser, dar, ver,** R51; of irregular verbs with **i** in stem, 80 (3); with **u** in stem, 80 (3); with **uv** in stem, 80 (3); of **decir** and **traer**, 83 (3) (*See also* irregular verbs; stem-changing verbs; preterite vs. imperfect)

preterite vs. imperfect completed vs. repeated or habitual action, 181 (6); two past actions in the same sentence, 184 (6)

pronouns indirect object pronouns, R27; reflexive pronouns, 47 (2); after a preposition, 85 (3); **se** to express passive voice, 116 (4); direct and indirect object pronouns: **me, te, nos,** R53; **le, les, lo, los, la, las,** R53; used together, 211 (7); with **se,** 213 (7); with infinitive and present participle, 244 (8); with commands, 307 (10)

querer preterite, 80 (3); imperfect, 180 (6); future, 242 (8); conditional, 278 (9)

reflexive pronouns 47 (2)

reflexive verbs 46–47 (2); with stem changes, 50 (2) (*See also* stem-changing verbs)

saber present, R42; **saber** vs. **conocer,** R42; preterite, 80 (3); imperfect, 180 (6); future, 242 (8); conditional, 278 (9)

salir present, 12 (1); future, 242 (8); affirmative **tú** command, 276 (9); conditional, 278 (9)

ser present, R6; **ser** vs. **estar,** R25; preterite, R51; imperfect, 150 (5); affirmative **tú** command, 276 (9)

stem-changing verbs
    present: (e → ie), (o → ue), and **jugar,** R33; (e → i): **freír, pedir, repetir, seguir, servir, vestirse,** 110 (4)
    preterite: (e → i): **divertirse, freír, pedir, preferir, repetir, seguir, servir, vestirse,** 112 (4); (o → u): **dormir** and **morir,** 112 (4); in subjunctive mood, 339 (11)

subjunctive mood present: regular forms, 304 (10); irregular forms, 305 (10); subjunctive form used as formal **(usted, ustedes)** command, 307 (10); used as negative familiar **(tú)** command, 309 (10); subjunctive after impersonal expressions, 336 (11); after **¡Ojalá!, ¡Quizás!,** and **¡Tal vez!,** 338 (11); stem-changing verbs, 339 (11)

superlatives and comparatives, R44

tener present, R8, 12 (1); **tener que** + *infinitive,* R8; preterite, 80 (3); future, 242 (8); affirmative **tú** command, 276 (9); conditional, 278 (9)

time expressions used with imperfect, 146 (5); used with present perfect, 208 (7)

traer present, 12 (1); present participle, 15 (1); preterite, 83 (3)

venir present, 12 (1); preterite, 80 (3); future, 242 (8); affirmative **tú** command, 276 (9); conditional, 278 (9)

ver preterite, R51; imperfect, 150 (5); past participle, 210 (7)